AMERICAN VERNACULAR
BUILDINGS *and* INTERIORS
1870–1960

John A. Wallace and Alice Wells Wallace House, Canyon, Texas. *Left to right*: Public schoolteachers Miss Parker and Miss Beasley, Bertha Wallace, Jeff Wallace, Alice Wells Wallace, Edna Wallace, and John A. Wallace.

Panhandle-Plains Historical Society, Canyon, Texas.

AMERICAN VERNACULAR BUILDINGS *and* INTERIORS 1870–1960

Herbert Gottfried and Jan Jennings

W. W. NORTON & COMPANY, INC.

New York • London

We dedicate this book to the descendants of four of our oldest German, English, Scot, and Dutch families—Youngs, Adams, Lyerly, Murph, Jennings, Vansant, Guthrie, Wallace—who settled in Pennsylvania, North Carolina, Virginia, and Texas.

Copyright © 2009, 1988, 1985 by Herbert Gottfried and Jan Jennings

Previously published titles:
AMERICAN VERNACULAR DESIGN, 1870–1940
AMERICAN VERNACULAR INTERIOR ARCHITECTURE, 1870–1940

For information about permission to reproduce selections from this book, write to Permissions, W. W. Norton & Company, Inc., 500 Fifth Avenue, New York, NY 10110

For information about special discounts for bulk purchases, please contact W. W. Norton Special Sales at specialsales@wwnorton.com or 800-233-4830

Manufacturing by Edward Brothers
Book design by Ken Gross
Production manager: Leeann Graham

Library of Congress Cataloging-in-Publication Data

Gottfried, Herbert, 1940–
    American vernacular buildings and interiors, 1870–1960 / Herbert Gottfried and Jan Jennings.
        p.   cm.
    Originally published: American vernacular design, 1870–1940. Ames : Iowa State University Press, 1988 and American vernacular interior architecture, 1870–1940. Ames : Iowa State University Press, 1993.
    Includes bibliographical references and index.
    ISBN 978-0-393-73262-7 (pbk.)
    1. Vernacular architecture—United States. 2. Architecture—United States—History—19th century. 3. Architecture—United States—History—20th century. 4. Interior architecture—United States—History—19th century. 5. Interior architecture—United States—History—20th century. 6. Building materials—United States. I. Jennings, Jan, 1946- II. Title.
    NA710.G68 2009
    720.973'09034—dc22   2009000992

ISBN: 978-0-393-73262-7 (pbk.)

W. W. Norton & Company, Inc., 500 Fifth Avenue, New York, N.Y. 10110
        www.wwnorton.com
W. W. Norton & Company Ltd., Castle House, 75/76 Wells Street, London W1T 3QT

1 2 3 4 5 6 7 8 9 0

Contents

Introduction

The history of everyday American buildings is a personal history for us. During the last 360 years members of our own families have lived in vernacular buildings in mid-Atlantic, Southeast, and Southwest regions. We can document log structures in eastern Pennsylvania, the upper reaches of the James River in Virginia, the Piedmont of North Carolina, western Arkansas, and east Texas. Typical of this kind of building is the Mathias Phifer house (*ca*.1805) in Rowan County, North Carolina. The house has a William Penn plan: a two-room main house and a kitchen extension, both with brick chimneys in Flemish bond. A layer of narrow clapboards, fastened with handmade nails, covers the logs. The house plan may have come to Rowan County with other German-speaking colonists, before Mathias and his son John built the new farmhouse. The brick mason is unknown, but the coursing pattern is unusual for log houses in the county, which suggests a source outside the immediate community. A number of building traditions influenced the appearance and use of the Phifer house. It is part of what is referred to as *folk vernacular architecture*.

Before the end of the nineteenth century, our families built houses, outbuildings, and other structures with milled lumber and machine-made nails. They got their ideas about buildings from new

I.1. Mathias Phifer House. Third Creek vicinity, Rowan County, NC. Courtesy North Carolina State Archives.

1

sources that went beyond language and kinship. Some moved to new locales. Rail lines brought manufactured building materials to those west of the Mississippi River. Railroads expanded into the South as well and so did manufacturing. As a new economy spread across the states, local people gave up living in log houses and incorporated traditions and new values into modern buildings.

PREMISES

It is our intent to contribute to the history of the making of American building materials and buildings. We suggest that patterns of assembly embedded in ninety years of construction are still part of the everyday built world, and that a number of them are still used in contemporary construction.

The book is structured on premises that are not new to the history of American architecture, but they are new to vernacular studies. A premise stands on its own merits and at the same time is integrated with the other premises. Each premise provides a theme for the narrative. The first premise is that *buildings constructed with manufactured building materials are modern buildings.* Manufactured building materials, coupled with emerging construction techniques, machines, and tools, changed the very nature of common buildings. Speed and efficiency in construction and variety in spatial configuration and appearance were the consequences of these changes.

Second, *modern vernacular buildings are planned from the inside out.* This kind of planning has a rich history, most of it allied with the concept of convenient arrangement, that advanced the cause of home improvement and the incorporation of new technology in home environs.

Third, *the production of modern vernacular buildings has a pictorial bias derived from the picturesque aesthetic.* This aesthetic has a deep hold on the American imagination. Indeed, it has shaped the perception of landscape and the relation between buildings and land and influenced the composition of buildings. The picturesque aesthetic has endured through changes in building types and styles and is alive today in the suburbs.

Fourth, *the cottage form and cottage sensibility are dominant in the production of American house types.* No other house concept has lasted so long and proved so durable. The American cottage incorporated modern space planning and building support systems.

Fifth, *the colonial revival aesthetic plays a central role in vernacular buildings.* No other aesthetic has had such continuity of application. Colonial revival building emerged with the appropriation of the English picturesque.[1] Both the colonial and the picturesque became what we might call cultural impulses that have operated in various sectors of society and at various strengths from 1850 forward. The American cottage absorbed both.

In the production of houses, the combination of modern, convenient, picturesque, cottage, and colonial values transformed American vernacular buildings from regional ethnic products to a national system of technology-driven buildings. All collateral discussions and visual materials in the book support and elaborate these topics.

APPROACH TO VERNACULAR BUILDINGS

It is appropriate to begin the discussion of our approach and its scope with several basic questions: What is this kind of building? How is it constructed? How does it work? How does it change? How is it imagined?

Our first two books, *American Vernacular Design, 1870–1940* (1985, 1988) and *American Vernacular Interior Architecture, 1870–1940* (1988, 1993) taught us the logic of vernacular and its relationship to industrialization, which influenced most aspects of nineteenth- and twentieth-century American life. The technical development of machine tools changed the scale at which natural resources could be transformed into useful materials, and the distribution of these materials created markets wherever there was any level of settlement. Manufacturers' trade catalogs, design pattern books, popular magazines, and trade publications disseminated practical information about building that influenced local values. Thus the basis upon which ordinary buildings were made was changed. Folk traditions, whether derived from ethnic practices or regional preferences, gave way to a national architecture that could still respond to differences in climate and landscape.

But the new work was also influenced by taste and what people now call *popular culture*.

Industrialization and all its economic and social aspects created a dynamic environment. The economic pressure to transform resources in the service of construction was intense. For example, rapid growth and constant shifts in populations brought increased demands for precisely dimensioned lumber. New construction techniques sped up the time it took to erect houses and community buildings associated with commerce, civil administration, or religion. The light or balloon frame evolved in the 1840s, but it was the post–Civil War period that witnessed the widespread application of that technology to construction that then took place in less time and with fewer workers.

The new building functioned differently too. It offered more rooms that could be specialized in their use and treatment, and new circulation patterns that led to new possibilities both within the rooms and in reaching the outside. Houses, in particular, took on "front" and "back" distinctions. Like traditional buildings, the new ones might be replications of others, but they offered more opportunity for variations in any part of the construction.

Such variations were encouraged by the broad distribution of information. Anyone with the required intelligence could learn about materials and building techniques. In public schools students learned to draft and to read blueprints. Whereas the traditional system relied on the cultural carryover of concepts and mental images, on word-of-mouth dissemination of plans and the organization of elevations, the new system relied greatly on the printed word and image. Pictures of machinery, products, tools, building plans and elevations, even perspective views were increasingly available.

The design of a vernacular structure built with mass-produced materials was fundamentally standardized, yet it incorporated traditional cultural impulses, especially those with deep roots. Because the system was set up to produce multiple variations of goods to address any type of construction problem, design could be diverse in outlook. More importantly, elements of design—say, a molding, a door, or an entry system—could be exchanged handily; parts of things or whole patterns were interchangeable. A crucial change we seek to understand is how American houses came to be planned from the inside out— a process that culminated in the construction of hundreds of houses at a time in developments at Levittown, New York, or in postwar Southern California. The strategy was modern in concept, but it had a rich history. Planning from the inside out reinforced the split between inside and outside architecture. Schematic plan types could be wrapped in a variety of forms. Styling became a separate skill from space planning, and market pressures drove styling options. The new system also relied on replication and variation, so the product line had broad appeal. The fact that there were variations in building from the smallest detail to the concept was not new; such experimentation had been part of American culture all along. But the volume of mass-produced materials was so great that it created many more opportunities to experiment with patterns and assemblies, and it allowed more voices to shape choices.

DRAWINGS AND PHOTOGRAPHS

All of the plan and isometric drawings reproduced in this book were done originally in one-eighth-inch scale and reduced for publication. Because the drawings were rendered in the same scale, they can be compared as to their relative size and volume. We have purposely not drawn basement and attic plans for those buildings that had them. We found both of these spaces to be of little importance to the interior organization. For the most part, these spaces remained unplanned and did not figure prominently in the rationale for form or interior aesthetic.

The drawings of ground plans in the chapters on building types have a few notations that need explanation. For example, door openings are indicated by two notations: a quarter-circle swing for primary doors, and half that for closets. The reason for this differentiation is that a number of plans had doors in positions where the operation of one door could interfere with the other. When we wanted the drawing to make a point, we used the two notations for doors to show the difference. A pair of broken lines indicates cased openings.

As indicated, the relation between form and plan is not easily discerned; most housing types have some variety in ground plan. When looking at a house from the outside, however, it is possible to estimate aspects of the plan by looking for a few clues. The placement of a large window on a façade sometimes helps to locate the living room or parlor. Similarly, a small or otherwise unusual window by itself on a side elevation may indicate a stairway. Most vernacular house types have a center hall plan (with an entrance door on the center axis of the building); a side hall plan; or entry directly into the living room. The placement of the entrance door also may indicate the general organization of the first floor.

When studying historical ground plans, much can be learned about conceptual organization from the adjacency of rooms, alignments of interior walls, location of stairs, and projections such as bay windows. Manipulation of these elements produced most interior arrangements. There is more of this kind of analysis in Chapter 1.

We also include schematic drawings of plans and interior volumes with roof plans with our building descriptions. Plan schematics have abbreviations for common rooms or spaces. These drawings were intended to document the imprint of the plan on the site and to reveal the volume. Ground plans do not show porch configurations unless the main roof covers the porch. Exceptions include houses for which we analyze the relation of porch to plan. In some cottages we also include schematic drawings of circulation patterns. The plan schematics focus on the organization of the main floor, with no drawings of upper floors. Sometimes we note the number of rooms on a second floor as part of the notes on general characteristics.

We have classified major categories of house types as single-family, two-family, or multifamily dwellings, each with numerous subtypes. Commercial buildings and churches are divided into major classes. In our original determination of building types, we examined the relation between plan and form and assumed that each type would have an equally singular interior plan. We surmised that there could be a primary configuration and an alternative. In examining the issue of building type and plan thoroughly, however, we discovered that we had underestimated the entire relation between plan and form, so much so that outside and inside variation is the rule rather than exception. Moreover, this conclusion encouraged us to reexamine whether ground

plans of houses could readily be determined by exterior form. We decided that, in most cases, they cannot.

Photographs are a significant new element in this book. Our first two books relied only on drawings. When these books were first published, we believed that clear, unrendered line drawings would help people identify basic elements of each building typology. In combining the two books and adding additional research to create this book, we relied heavily on photographs for research. We examined published preservation surveys and conducted our own field studies in places such as Cheyenne, Wyoming, Oklahoma City, and Council Bluffs, Iowa. Today historical photographs are readily accessible on the web. Indeed, complete surveys are available online. Furthermore, the Library of Congress has relevant holdings, such as the Historic American Building Survey (HABS). These helped us confirm or contradict nationwide building types and their variations. An annotated list of sources for photographic digital collections appears in the bibliography.

The photographs included in the book are from digital collections and our own collection. We turned to a twenty-first century source—eBay, the online auction site—to acquire some of the collection. In the process, we came to regard eBay as a research site and a good source for the commonplace image. Museum and library collections tend to contain the best-quality photographs and pictures of important buildings—as opposed to the typical or ordinary. A clear exception is the Digital Image Catalog, Western History and Genealogy, Denver Public Library— an outstanding photographic source for ordinary buildings.

The 1870–1960 period encompasses three types of photographs—the cabinet card, a real photograph postcard (RPPC), and the snapshot. The cabinet card, a photographic print attached to a cardboard mount, offered a new, larger type of picture than previous formats; its peak years were from 1870 to 1900. Although this type of photograph waned from 1905 to 1920, one can still find such pictures on eBay, such as the pictures of house exteriors taken in Valparaiso, Indiana in the 1920s. An RPPC, an early breed of postcard, became popular just after 1900. The image on such a postcard is an actual photograph. George Eastman developed a lightweight, hand-held box camera that greatly simplified photography and facilitated real-photo postcards. Beginning in 1902 Kodak offered a preprinted card back that allowed postcards to be made directly from negatives. Using Kodak postcard stock, itinerant professional and amateur photographers alike took an amazing array of pictures of interiors and buildings. The person who takes a snapshot, a spur-of-the-moment photograph, is motivated by the simple wish to record and perpetuate his or her life and times; buildings and interiors might be included as backdrops or as subjects. Since the first Kodak camera was introduced in 1888, it is estimated that 14 billion snapshots have been taken in the United States alone. Although most photography-based snapshots look like most other snapshots, they do not look like other kinds of photographs because they do not follow the rules of composition; they may have tilted horizons, eccentric framing, blurred subjects, and obscured view.[2] The pictures in this book are offered as evidence of authentic environments from which we extracted information about typologies as well as people's lives.

One indicator of an era's focus is book titles. Here is a chronological sample of books related to American building that used the term *modern* in the title (some are abbreviated): *Practical Economy; or, the Application of Modern Discoveries to the Purposes of Domestic Life* (1822), John Hall *A Series of Select and Original Designs for Dwelling Houses, For the Use of Carpenters and Builders* (1840, D.H. Arnot *Gothic Architecture Applied to Modern Residences* (1850), Henry Hudson Holly *Modern Dwellings in Town and Country: Adapted to American Wants and Climate* (1878), John C. Lucas *Modern House Painting Designs* (1887), Architectural Designing Co. *Plans and Designs for Bungalows, Modern Homes, Churches, Schools* (1912), Charles Edward Hooper *Reclaiming the Old House: Its Modern Problems and Their Solution* (1913), Standard Homes Company *Better Homes at Lower Cost: A Collection of Modern Homes: Homes of Distinction, Attractive in Exterior Lines and Convenient in Interior Arrangement* (1930).

Surely all of these authors did not use the term *modern* in the same sense. It is interesting to note where the term *modern* appears in each title and what it modifies. No doubt, from the first title to the last, definitions of modern were evolving. Even with this small sample, one can read the scope of the modern subject matter as a descriptor of the practical and the theoretical, of various kinds of building types, and of interior and exterior design. In short, the term *modern* comes to represent a comprehensive cultural commitment to a standard of living and a mode of building.

Modern Vernacular Building

This section has a list of primary and secondary sources that provide evidence for the historical development of modern American vernacular architecture.

1. *Manufacturers' trade catalogs.* The historic importance of trade catalogs cannot be underestimated. They contained written and graphic information about materials and design concepts, as well as glossaries and suggested applications of the products. The success of a modern vernacular architecture is based on the early and prolonged distribution of catalogs describing and pricing all types of products and elements, from millwork to plaster ornamentation to entire storefront designs. These catalogs not only made possible a nationwide distribution of vernacular architecture, but they did it in a rather timely fashion, so that builders in the remotest regions of the country got up-to-date design information and products relatively quickly.

   For example, the Sherwin Williams Company of Cleveland produced several *Home Painting* manuals containing information about the nature and proper use of paint and varnish, color harmony, how to estimate costs, individual treatment of exteriors, the treatment of floors, walls and ceilings, and cleansers and polishes. Although the information was supposed to make painting seem easy and accessible in order to encourage paint sales, the information was also well prepared and presented in a straightforward, practical manner.

2. *Serials.* This category includes three types: (a) popular magazines intended for a general au-

dience, such as *House Beautiful*, begun in 1896; (b) carpenter and builders journals, such as William A. Radford's *American Builder*, published from 1905 to 1969; and (c) specialty trade journals, such as *American Gas-Light Journal and Chemical Repertory*, begun before 1870 and devoted to the interests of illumination, heating, ventilation, sanitary improvement, and domestic economy. All three types were written to be informative and to report developments in new products or trends. Their general posture was progressive; change was assumed to be good.

Popular magazines and builder journals provided "patterns" or drawings to be replicated. In 1882 the editor of *Carpentry and Building* acknowledged the first occurrence of a magazine plan that was used for construction; he considered it a "deserved compliment" to the journal.[3] Eventually serials advertized blueprinted plans that could be purchased by the readership. In 1897–98 *The Ladies' Home Journal* sold plans (with details and specifications) of seven model houses. The *Journal* stated that the offer was not intended to compete with the work of architects but to help readers build artistic homes of moderate cost.[4] In 1897 the David Williams Company, publishers of *Carpentry and Building*, began selling a series of pattern books that contained drawings (without text) that had previously been published in the journal.[5]

Some builder magazines were more ambiguous about their potential role as suppliers of patterns. In April 1905, *American Carpenter and Builder* launched its first issue with illustrations of plans and dimensions from numbered house plans taken from Radford's plan books. By July of that year, an editor's note stated that the plans were "not for sale, but are published solely for the purpose of giving ideas and useful information to architects, carpenters, builders, and all others who may be interested in building a home."[6]

3. *Stock plan books.* These books had a narrower focus than trade catalogs because they were published by architects, builders, or lumber companies to promote a single point of view about design or to sell a company's products. There are four types of these publications: (a) architecture books written by architects or housing reformers for other architects or enlightened consumers—with a narrative and a few drawings—such as [George E.] *Woodward's Country Homes* (1865); (b) pattern books written by architects or publishing companies for builders or owner-builders—with little narrative but with sets of drawings in scale—such as A. J. Bicknell's *Specimen Book of One Hundred Architectural Designs* (1878); stock plan books written by many people for consumers—with little narrative and some illustrations of plans and perspectives—such as Portland Cement Association's *Concrete School Houses* (1928); and plan books of ready-cut buildings written by manufacturing companies for consumers—with little narrative and illustrations of at least plans and perspectives—such as Aladdin Company's *Aladdin Homes* (1927).

4. *Extension service bulletins.* These bulletins, published by land-grant universities, were different from any other kind of publication because they encouraged rural homemakers to learn the rudiments of design. From their inception in 1902, as the Cornell University Home Reading Course, these brochures explained the need to understand spatial organization and design composition in order to create more efficient and humane environments. Federal agriculture departments published bulletins about farm design, including the farmhouse and outbuildings.

5. *Articles and books of the period.* The architecture and interior design literature of 1870–1960 was driven by two approaches: the first was a professional or technical point of view; the second expressed the views of tastemakers or others who linked design with decoration or fashion. Professional or technical articles appeared in builder journals. Many of these publications were meant to be instructive. For

example, in 1922 *American Builder* ran a five-part series by A. W. Powell and H. A. Smith about improved illumination for specific rooms. Experts representing electrical contractors, dealers, jobbers, and manufacturers wrote the articles. A second example of this kind of literature is the how-to book. Manufacturers often published information about the use of their products and related topics. For example, Acme White Lead and Color Works of Detroit published manuals containing information on how to use paint and what paint to use in certain circumstances, for painters, decorators, architects, and contractors.

6. *Historic preservation surveys.* We have conducted historic preservation surveys as consultants in several states and have familiarized ourselves with surveys from many states. As much as possible we compared extant buildings with published materials. Historical and architectural survey inventories were our major sources in identifying elements used in construction. Many surveys inventoried design elements because they were fundamental to architectural descriptions on applications for National Register of Historic Places status. Surveys also proved useful in classifying building types and in plotting their dissemination across the country. We were also able to use photographs of the time period, including photographs of finished buildings in stock plan books, to identify elements and types. Lastly, we carried out on-site visits to as many vernacular environments as possible.

7. *Scholarly publications.* We have always relied on the work of others to deepen our understanding of modern vernacular. The Vernacular Architecture Forum is a scholarly group, founded in 1980, that has taken the lead in producing quality research about diverse environments. The *Perspectives in Vernacular Architecture* series, in particular, provides timely and cogent essays.

Early volumes of these scholarly publications have articles related to the historical study of common environments. Many of the subjects concern rural living and traditional building. Related fieldwork produced maps of settlements and geographies of activity and the distribution of building types. New England was the primary region of study. From the first volume it is evident that scholars are looking beyond the artifact to the context in which it was built. That interest expands over time.

In subsequent volumes there is a growing interest in material culture as a proper subject for vernacular studies. Material culture inquiries turned to physical objects, which included buildings, as primary data. Likewise there is a steady stream of articles that builds on the work of leaders in the field, such as cultural geographer Fred Kniffen and folklorist Henry Glassie. Kniffen investigated how buildings embody evidence of cultural patterns, and Glassie traced changes in patterns of thought as manifested by buildings. As the field of vernacular studies has evolved, it has become a way of looking at buildings; the "way" incorporates a number of methodologies, rooted in the social sciences and the humanities.

An overarching theme in the *Perspectives* series is the desire to use common buildings and their landscapes as a way to understand everyday history. The paths to that understanding are divided into a number of interests, including studies in methodology, building typology, and social history. *Popular culture vernacular* is an emerging category that can include the millions of common buildings constructed in the twentieth century with mass-produced materials as popular versions of traditional building types. On one level this is the architecture for the common person of the modern world who gets much of his or her information from mass media—which includes marketing and construction information about common buildings.

Both the subjects that now fall under the heading of *vernacular architecture* and the methods used to describe and interpret it keep expanding. Some inquires involve extensions of traditional methods into new subject matter, but the majority of new research initiatives entail both new methods and new subjects. For example, the editors of *Gender, Class and Shelter: Perspectives in Vernacular Architecture V*, note "what once seemed delimited areas of inquiry—others' ethnic traditions, appropriately distant time periods, remote geographical areas—came in for questioning. It soon became evident that building and landscapes of more recent times shared 'vernacular' properties. As scholars expanded the scope of their analyses beyond the pre-industrial time-scape, they embraced a much wider range of architectural and analytic issues." Topics in their volume included gender, institutions, ethnicity and race, popular culture, and rural and urban geography. Articles from the series relevant to this book have been noted throughout our general narrative.

8. *Digital library collections.* A great number of public and private institutions and organizations have digitized their historic photography collections. Selected websites are listed in the bibliography.

BOOK ORGANIZATION

American Vernacular Buildings and Interiors is, in part, a sourcebook for the period between the end of the Civil War and 1960. In our first two books we began with descriptions of elements, the materials with which buildings are constructed. We believed that it was helpful to identify products and the patterns in which they were employed. We still consider the materials used to create style in detail, but we have not developed a style guide. Elements are now the last chapter, and we take up aesthetics earlier. We want to trace some of America's cultural history through its materials and buildings.

We also consider the plan and overall massing, and how buildings have evolved from spatial and functional units into cohesive and rational designs. We discuss principles of composition in houses, commercial buildings, and churches, as well as their support systems. Lastly, we explore architectural theory and history, spatial concepts, building types, and materials.

The book is organized into seventeen chapters. The first chapter defines modern vernacular buildings, and our definition guides the overall argument. Chapter 2 introduces the notion that modern common buildings are planned and built from the inside out. Chapter 3 suggests that the making of such buildings follows a pictorial logic based on imagery from trade catalogs and popular publications. Chapter 4 considers the cottage as a unique American house type. Chapters 7–15 discuss building typologies: cottages with gable roofs and a special cottage type that we call organic; hip and mansard roof cottages; the gambrel cottage; the bungalow; ranch house; multifamily buildings; commercial buildings; churches. The last two chapters cover support systems (i.e., circuits of energy and supply; 16) and the elements (17) of which everything is composed. Typically the names for all the building types are based on historic names as recorded in the literature of the period, names listed in the trade catalogs, or names that identify prominent design element(s).

1

DEFINING MODERN
VERNACULAR BUILDINGS

Our subject is well documented; its rich history underwrites vital contemporary multidisciplinary inquiries. In the last fifty years there has been a significant surge in scholarship, a diversification of research methods, and a broadening of the overall subject matter.[1] Howard Wight Marshall's essay, "Vernacular Housing and Culture," linking vernacular housing to American culture, is a comprehensive overview of the literature.[2] Marshall covers most of the subjects addressed in essays of this type, beginning with defining vernacular, since definition can indicate research approaches. Common to most definitions are the following: *geography*, in the sense that vernacular houses can be defined by the geographical space they occupy and by the houses with which they are associated; *site*, or where people build, including landscapes, communities, and regions; *ethnicity*, in that historically people with a common culture tend to reinforce and disseminate that culture through the things they build; and *building materials and techniques*, in the sense that both may be unique to an area or a time period.

Marshall equates popular architecture with vernacular architecture, a position we also take, and he separates vernacular from high-style architecture on the basis of design—how it comes about and what it intends. One of the founding principles of vernacular

studies is the value of fieldwork, which is seen as a sound basis for documentation, analysis, interpretation, and theory. A well-developed line of inquiry called building typology, beginning with the work of cultural geographer Fred Kniffen, traces traditional building plans, roof forms, and other elements over time and within a particular geography. Identifying building types invariably addresses the issue of building style: how exterior and interior characteristics or constellations of effects relate to building form and plan. Considerations of style are necessary for full evaluations of buildings, but they are not without their difficulties. Marshall completes his essay with summaries of approaches from anthropology and ethnological studies, historical and cultural geography, art and architecture history, and folklore. He pays special tribute to material culture scholars James Deetz and Henry Glassie. Glassie, in particular, has established research themes and new methods wherein everyday houses are "studied through field research in specific community settings and then placing the forms [patterns] into broad frameworks based on geographical distribution and cultural/ethnic/religious context in time and space."[3]

Another comprehensive consideration of vernacular studies is the collection of essays *Common Places: Readings in American Vernacular Architec-*

ture, edited by Dell Upton and John Michael Vlach.[4] The anthology is organized into major research themes (building types, construction, function, social histories of life in these houses, and the process by which vernacular houses are created), and the range of research methods is diverse and engaging. This collection is the first to encourage vernacular studies to look beyond the building to the landscape. We have learned much from these essays and others like them, and we believe that they generally cover issues related to most vernacular architecture.

In addition to books that lay out the field and propose appropriate questions for research are scores of monographs and articles on all aspects of American vernacular. Many of these have been helpful when we tried to sort out the meaning of certain materials, construction systems, aesthetics, or aspects of social and cultural history. They are referenced in subsequent chapters.

Our subject matter differs from that of most people who study vernacular environments. Several characteristics of the architecture we explore in this book separate it from earlier work. In the first place, mass production generated a supply of building materials that could be applied to building needs anywhere in the country. Secondly, a national distribution system delivered these materials to any location with a spur line. Wagons and later trucks covered the remainder. A national print communica-

tion system brought technical information and models for replication, which facilitated the construction of everyday buildings.

We believe in regional variations on national trends and in the dissemination of knowledge by family members or by ethnic or social groups. The construction for vernacular building was so diverse across the country that all kinds of give-and-take with tradition and with novelty, with old knowledge and new, surely took place. Mass production lessened the role of the master craftsman on the job site, but it did not eliminate that person from the scene. Building framers and finish carpenters have been a consistent part of the vernacular building economy from 1870 to 1960.

We believe in the continuity of building types, primarily through plan. We also believe in the continuity of aesthetic systems—what we have come to think of as *cultural impulses*. We believe that it makes sense to trace aesthetic values within the culture at large rather than derive them from individual buildings or, indeed, groups of buildings. What sets our work apart from that of others is that the architecture we study is fundamentally different from traditional folk building, because it is modern in outlook and execution. It is modern by intent and by context, including the society and economy in which it operates. Its values are modern and its products are modern, even when they are linked to traditional build-

1.1 This frame farmhouse is a gable and ell type built on a stone foundation. Note that the barn was built first. There are seven workers on the crew, four adults and three boys. Authors' Collection.

ing. Our own families experienced this same development at different times and in different locations. What they learned and how they adapted to new houses mirrored what happened hundreds of thousands of times across the country.

We have discussed what to call this kind of building with many others and with each other. We have thought of it as *industrial vernacular* or *manufactured architecture* because of its roots in industrial engineering and in rational sequences of actions that created finished products with predictable dimensions and qualities. Furthermore, so much of what got produced was the product of improvements in manufacturing technology. The typical sequence of product development began with harvesting the natural resource, then moved to transforming it into a gross product that would be, in turn, reconfigured. For example, wide, rough, long boards were further transformed into discrete units suitable for very specific applications. It is in this manner that oak boards became thin strips suitable for flooring, and likewise large sheets of glass were recut for windows.

We have also thought of this kind of building as *market architecture* because it is so responsive to marketing pressure and to changes in fashion. There were new rules and yet fewer limits. The rules of composition and use of materials were open to interpretation by owner–builders, carpenters, and construction companies. To be sure, there was a sense of tradition, but the construction of a house, store, or small church was, in large measure, in the hands of the builder and the people who financed the project. Speaking of money, remember too that most of the housing stock in the country, built from 1870 to 1960, was built as a financial speculation, so a building might represent all the stakeholders in that kind of economy.

We have also thought of modern vernacular building as *practical architecture* in the sense that whatever else it is, it is useful, and the people who designed and built it intended it to be useful. This kind of thinking was pervasive in nineteenth-century America.[5] A focus on practicality, however, omits some of the theoretical and aesthetic dimensions of everyday building. These threads, if you will, weave through American cultural history, rounding out the context for building.

In terms of design, the final appearance and character of a building may be more easily influenced by the availability of local materials than by current trends. The transformation of resources, mass production, and a market economy put money and goods in motion throughout the entire nation, and the exact location and the quality and quantity of goods at any given place were not predictable. Prices, too, influenced availability. Rail shipping was expensive for a long time. The general economic climate, including the usual swings of the national and regional economies, influenced availability. So did

1.2 The owners of this clapboard cottage, sitting in their automobile, are juxtaposed against their house. The cottage is partially stripped of historical ornament, with only contrasting material in the gables and the porch wall. The overall exterior appearance is neat and precise. The house and the auto, both products of machines, are equivalent images of modern living. Authors' Collection.

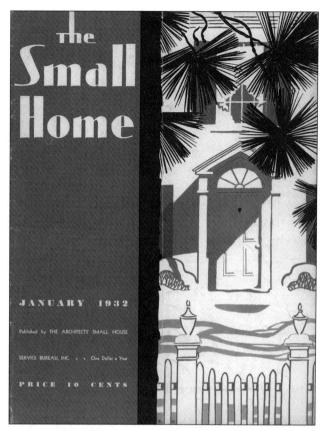

1.3. Cover. *The Small Home*, published by Architect's Small Home Service Bureau (Jan. 1932), is the kind of publication to which individuals could subscribe to keep abreast of contemporary developments.

wars. Thus from time to time it was difficult for a builder to get an ideal assembly of plan concept, exterior appearance, and interior finish at any one place. Modern vernacular building is an architecture of compromise.

What we just described is a system, a system that relied on the transmission of information by communication media. Ultimately, the shared values and trust in materials and techniques that characterized older vernacular architecture also developed in this new way of building. One invested in plan books from architectural offices; journals and magazines such as *Carpentry and Building*, *The Building Age*, *Pencil Points*, *The White Pine Series*, *House Beautiful*; services such as the Architects Small House Bureau (an architect-sponsored, Minnesota-based organization); publications telling readers "how to build your own home" and the trade catalogs of thousands of companies. All these became authorities as well as links among American social groups, diverse cultures, and different sectors of the economy.

In choosing to call the everyday buildings of the 1870–1960 period *modern*, we mean several things: that the common structures of the period were thought to be products of their own time; that their temporal frame of reference was the present and recent times; that the entire period embraced a general turn to "modern" everything, including art, architecture, literature, music, and the development of both photography and film. Then there is modern living with mass transportation and communication, widespread capitalism, and modern warfare. The production of everyday buildings is engulfed by these developments, and they change the character of the architecture. The new buildings can be distinguished from historical vernacular buildings, especially those in which handcraft and the dissemination of local knowledge were paramount.

TECHNOLOGY, THE MARKET, AND THE DISSEMINATION OF MODERN VERNACULAR BUILDINGS

In our view the production of common buildings depended on mass production technology to supply construction materials, as well as on print communications to broadcast information related to building. Print media informed the public, craftsman, builders, and construction companies. From these sources people learned about machine tools, mass production products, and innovations in construction. Moreover, the same system disseminated pictures of ideal building types and interior scenes.

Market forces developed the everyday buildings that comprise modern vernacular architecture. In the twentieth century government policies encouraged the building and purchasing of single-family houses. Being market-based, the production of everyday buildings depended on the public's general knowledge of trends and what was considered popular. The builders and the bankers who financed construction and the property owners were themselves moderns—that is, people who lived in, or belonged to, a modern political economy. As members of a modern school of thought, they viewed industrial production as a necessary basis for aesthetics, just as handcraft production had been the basis of preindustrial standards of beauty.

The history of building technology and the rise of capitalist manufacturing is well known. The treatment by architectural historian Sigfried Giedion, *Mechanization Takes Command* (1948), is an excellent summary.[6] Giedion begins with the incorporation of movement into the production of material culture and incorporation of movement, especially transportation, to all aspects of life. His next consideration is the hand, "which is to be supplanted" by mechanization: "The elimination of complicated handcraft marks the beginning of high mechanization. This transition takes place in America during the second half of the nineteenth century. . . . The system of full mechanization is the assembly line, wherein the entire factory is consolidated into a synchronous organism."[7]

Mechanization changed expectations, including the production of common buildings. New building methods and materials allowed consumers to rethink environmental experiences. Typical changes included an interest in personal comfort and the moderation of thermal environments. Cross-ventilation and natural light were major changes, as was central heating. Heating became part of the general mechanization of the household, particularly of two specific rooms: the kitchen, which took on the mechanization of nutrition through the use of ready-made foods, and the bathroom, after running water was installed. These improvements can be linked to what Giedion calls the "the creed of progress": "We perceive the world as created and existing within temporal limits; that is, that the world is determined toward a specific goal and purpose. Closely bound up with this belief that the world has a definite purpose is the outlook of rationalism . . . [which] reaches its peak in thinkers in the latter half of the eighteenth century. Rationalism goes hand in hand with the idea of progress. . . . In the nineteenth century the creed of progress was raised into a dogma, a dogma given various interpretations in the course of the century."[8]

The creed of progress became well established in America and was the basis for the culture of production that dominated everyday life after 1870. Progress was celebrated in festivals and expositions, where various kinds of mechanized processes and products were displayed. This period embraced "a rationalistic view of the world," particularly the method of breaking production into component op-erations. Such a process made products that were themselves components that required final assembly.

Beyond the technical base of modern vernacular architecture is the very real growth in population and the migration of the population. Giedion uses only two facts to illustrate the latter change: in 1850, 85 percent of the American population was rural and by 1940 less than one in four lived on farms.[9] The people who moved were realigning their lives within the creed of progress, within the culture of production, even themselves joining the assembly lines. If they did not literally work in a factory, they nevertheless benefited from the economic multiplier effect of mechanization in their communities. All these phenomena made their view of everyday buildings quite different from that of their ancestors.

THE ARRANGEMENT OF ROOMS

Modernization and mechanization produced new architectural realities in vernacular buildings. For one, the arrangement of rooms changed, and these changes are addressed in detail in subsequent chapters. For now let us begin with a convenient way of describing the theoretical arrangement of rooms in American house plans. Think of them as a conjunction of shapes wherein any two room shapes can be thought of as disjointed/separate or as aligned. In the disjointed condition, they hold no elements in common, whereas in the aligned they have between one and three elements in common.[10]

We do not find many types of house plans with a true disjointed condition, because most plans reflect adjacency; that is, rooms are physically attached to each other and need to remain so because of related functions or other design requirements. There are a few house types in the rural folk tradition that appear to have a disjointed condition, such as a house with a summer kitchen physically separated from the main building, or the dogtrot (breezeway), which has an open but covered space that divides one section of a house from another.

The most common relation among elements in American houses is the aligned condition. This is true for two- to eight-room houses in a variety of configurations and with a variety of exterior treatments. The common agent of alignment is a wall, whether load bearing or partition. Manipulating the location of aligned relationships or fragmenting the alignment so that only a portion is shared creates variety in floor plans. For our purposes, most houses rely on some interior alignment to shape the house plan.

In the simplest form, say a two-room plan, each room may share a wall completely. (1.4) The dark line in the schematic drawings indicates that kind of alignment. As the functions of rooms diversify and cultural traditions dictate arrangement and use, the ground plans become more complicated. A key element in many plan schemes is a hall because it represents an opportunity to modify a plan spatially. Halls are primarily used for circulation. The nineteenth-century reception hall is both a room and segment in a circulation pattern. A center hall passes from the front to the back of a house. Even though the hall is common to adjacent rooms, it creates the momentary impression of separation.

As openings between rooms change in location and size, any alignments may become smaller. Some house plans have fragmented alignments. Such a plan opens up the circulation and creates varieties of vistas as one moves from room to room. Other plans have rooms from one side of a house do not align with rooms on the other side, and the effect is a reduction of the need for a hall. The so-called open plan may reduce or eliminate alignments and a hall.

WHY MODERN VERNACULAR HOUSES LOOK THE WAY THEY DO

A primary convention of modern vernacular building recognizes the divorce between the interior arrangement and the exterior treatment. Regardless of plan configuration and plan dynamics, there are overarching cultural influences on a house's external appearance. From 1870 to 1960 buildings have expressed these treatments: Italianate, picturesque, colonial revival in classical or modern mode, arts and crafts, English and Spanish revival, and modern. While these names are also used to designate styles, there is more at stake here: Each type represents an attempt to define housing in terms of a nation's cultural history. At certain times in American history groups of people have thought of themselves as having a relationship to one of these cultural impulses, as manifested in construction practices, building materials, and design details. Over a lifetime a person could make an emotional and intellectual investment in more than one type. As impulses they appear and disappear and may appear again in new contexts or in association with new building types. As a product of culture, aesthetic ideas are both conservative, allowing traditional ideas to remain long after they have lost influence, and dynamic, such that new ideas and values are encouraged. Moreover, like so many things in America, an aesthetic impulse may be present as a whole entity that is, one set of values may

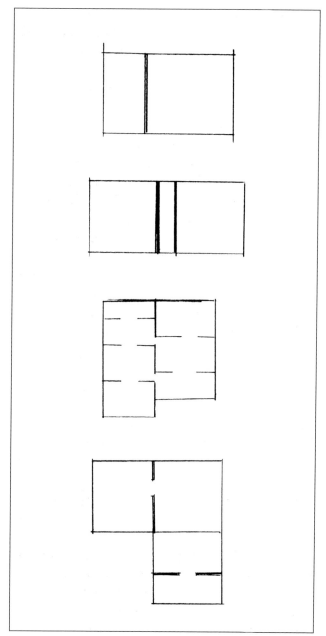

1.4. Basic plan schematics.

stand alone as a type, even a template, for replication. In another instance an aesthetic may be referenced only through a cluster of appropriated characteristics. A third option entails blending one impulse with another. The range of possibilities is broad, from novel compositions with unique effects to an overloaded eclectic. In any case, in modern vernacular architecture the treatment, both inside and out, derives from manipulations of ready-made goods, and this situation stimulates the production of both the exemplar and the derivative.

PLOTTING THE BUILDINGS

American Vernacular Buildings and Interiors represents the continuum of modern vernacular design as defined by its products and organizing principles, and those products and principles are limited to ones that seem to have been most prevalent. Thus, we do not offer an encyclopedia of all the materials ever used but, rather, a large sample of elements and types found to be popular from 1870 to 1960.[11]

Uniqueness is generally not an evaluative measure in this kind of architecture. Most buildings were meant to be somewhat ordinary, which does not mean that they were poorly built or unimaginatively designed. Likewise, the flow of building designs over time does not trail in the wake of the one big idea or of a critical invention. A pivotal or inspiring object in this vernacular might be a watercolor illustration in a trade catalog or a new building in a neighborhood.

We would add a note on the influence of technology. The General Electric Company, among others, built demonstration houses in various regions of the country. In 1935 *House and Garden* asked an ongoing question: What is the 'New American' home? "New American is not a style of architecture. It is house designed from the inside out to provide greater comfort, less labor and better health for the entire family."[12] Taken from this point of view, the significance of a vernacular building would have to include a measure of the effectiveness of the original inside-out intention. The history of this development is the subject of Chapter 2. We can also evaluate a building in terms of its functional reliability. Modern vernacular is purposeful design, just as purposeful as any other product created with the expectation of delivering

performance. Its consumers have socially and culturally determined expectations about performance that the marketplace attempts to address or shape.

A final consideration in the evaluation of the vernacular concerns the plotting of each building's total effect distributed as an event across a continuum. In this context, each building becomes an opportunity to address the demands of its period of construction. A modern vernacular building always has contextual relationships. It never operates alone as a crown jewel. It gains in demeanor and value in the presence of other structures like itself. It is always a product of its own world of mass production and market forces—and must be judged in worldly terms.

Modern vernacular design has been closely tied to the economic system and its business cycles. It registers differences in income and property values, yet has mostly been scaled to remark accessible to a range of income levels. Symbolically vernacular design has stood for more than the prospect of a capital gain. Alan Gowans sees vernacular buildings as visual metaphors in which social values and aesthetics are linked.[13] He argues that the vernacular provides continuity with our history and beliefs. To our way of thinking, the industrialization of the vernacular tradition still made it possible to express convictions and agreements about the "rightness" of forms and proportions. Rightness has at least two dimensions: a personal one in which one exercises one's preferences, and a social dimension, in which the past is appreciated and the social function—what buildings do in and for society—is realized.

Assessing change is not an easy task, but we believe that we have plotted the overall development of modern vernacular architecture reasonably well. As a hedge against extrapolating too broadly, we continually examined architectural materials and building types sold by Sears, Roebuck. Sears became a reality check. We assumed that despite the enthusiasm of manufacturers or the power of trends operating at any one time, if Sears designed the same items that appeared in other sources, the material must have had some significance. Sears consistently produced goods for middle-income people, and its design sensibility was geared to that market. Furthermore, Sears's financial success lent another layer of credibility to its catalogs. For instance, given the longevity of its house designs, the house types must have struck a positive chord with consumers. The company must have assessed market demand and responded with a range of values and design systems. It did not sell just one product line or style—there was no Sears's look. It sold value and designs that would endure.

One of the ways Sears did this was by "democratizing" its merchandise, converting the names of certain products—essentially those that represented high-style design or sounded expensive—to less culturally loaded language. For example, Sears advertised chandeliers with opal lamps in its first catalog. By the 1920s Sears was referring to these lights as "prisms of light," not as chandeliers, and soon after that they were called "fixtures," a generic name for lights of any kind.

In its strategy of democratizing the household environment, Sears also took some of the mystery out of technology. Customers could install anything Sears sold—from boilers to wallpaper. Sears debunked the expert, the highbrow, and sold anyone the tools to do the same work at home. In terms of design, Sears did not take much risk with its products: therefore at any given time Sears house types and interior elements were part of the general inventory of manufactured goods. Other companies made the same materials. For example, the entire contents of the Sears 1907 millwork catalog appears, item for item, in the 1909 *Stock List Catalogue* of the millwork company Roach Musser of Muscatine, Iowa. We assume that Roach Musser manufactured the goods for Sears. We can find no reason why this mill would copy an entire Sears catalog that was already two years old. We also know that contracting with manufacturers for goods to carry the Sears trademark was a Sears policy.

The mass production of design elements tends to push individual creativity to the background. Once building elements enter the market, the manufacturer loses control over their use. Sometimes the assemblage of elements takes on a special identity because of local customs or the presence of local workers and their concepts of good form and proper finish. But in many cases the materials are not local, and the foreignness requires some adaptation and accommodation all around.

In summary, we based our approach to this subject on a few research conventions. We sought to identify the materials with which modern vernacular buildings were created and how individual materials were assembled and spaces organized. We developed a chronology of elements and design concepts and tried to place these within the framework of American building. The latter task required the establishment of a typological order among the buildings.

2

INSIDE OUT

The vernacular environment is composed of millions of houses, apartment buildings, shops, churches, and small public buildings. Of modern vernacular buildings constructed from 1870 to 1960, houses comprise the overwhelming majority. Because of the uniformity of their plans, stores and four- and six-unit apartment buildings have less to contribute to the theory of modern vernacular building. Churches have the same limitation, because most have a simple plan inside a basic rectangular form; theology and liturgy shape their overall layout. Thus, single-family houses are the most valuable database for studying modern vernacular building.

Of the ideas and ideals that permeated domestic architecture, one of the oldest and most significant was the presentation of the exterior and the interior as parallel constructions. Such an approach implied equality—exterior and interior on a common footing, a way of thinking about a building in balance—but that is not how the model developed.[1]

ORIGINS OF THE DISTINCTION BETWEEN INTERIORS AND EXTERIORS

The exterior and interior operate as separate constructions, and the theoretical underpinning for the separation is well established. From 1870 to 1960 the issue revolved around responding to the desire for convenience on the interior, which could be at odds with the requirements for style on the exterior. The divorce of the interior from the exterior and the emergence the principle of convenience were easily absorbed into American culture. Over time the principle of convenience came to be known as *convenient arrangement*, with the term implying space planning. The theoretical construct of convenient arrangement could not have occurred without the influence of English and American domestic architects who separated the exterior from the interior as distinct zones requiring opposing values and differing treatments. The rhetoric of differentiation, between inside and outside, transpired regardless of stylistic or typological designations, urban or rural location, or clientele. The industrialization of building materials created more opportunities to exploit differentiation.

A brief chronology, beginning in the late eighteenth century, offers some examples of its development. From 1788 to 1805 English architects led the way: Sir John Soane's folio of buildings strove "to unite convenience and comfort in the interior distributions, and simplicity and uniformity in the exterior"; in *New Designs in Architecture* George Richardson conveyed plans (for villas) as convenient, utilitarian, and solid, and exterior elevations as various, elegant, and beautiful; Charles Middleton wrote that villas were elegant as well as compact and convenient; and Joseph Gandy described exteriors as possessing "particular beauty," whereas interiors embodied "accommodation and economical arrangement."[2]

Agricultural reformers in the eighteenth century urged farmers to synthesize neoclassicism with utilitarianism. A number of publications broadcast "the nature of convenience" and its relation to beauty. Many more reformers would associate an aesthetic with the theory of convenience, but beauty had already become the handmaiden of architects who

2.1 & 2.2. J. A. Oakley and Son designed a colonial revival exterior, but the aesthetic of the dining room is Arts and Crafts. The separation between inside and outside was driven by two differing theories of house design and planning. "Colonial Residence at Elizabeth, New Jersey," *Carpentry and Building* (Dec. 1904): 329–333, supplemental plates from photographs.

treated exteriors, whereas convenience became the province of all manner of reformers who moved it indoors.

Greek revival builder guides also treated the exterior and the interior separately. The guides were concerned with the details of the architectural envelope rather than with the totality of architecture itself. Heralded by its protagonists, Greek revival was architecture "applied from without," dominated by the abstract cube and its placement in space.[3]

Andrew Jackson Downing, credited for redirecting American architecture after the late 1830s, introduced the cottage as blending the English picturesque with republican simplicity. In *Cottage Residences* (1842), Downing shifted his former emphasis from style to matters of practical consideration. The "Principle of Fitness or Usefulness" concerned the ordering of interior space, not as a total volume, but as a series of rooms, each developed according to its individual function. This principle addressed a rational and utilitarian attitude toward planning, striving for maximum economy and efficiency but little concerned with aesthetic possibilities of the interior space as a whole. "Fitness or usefulness" also included Downing's advocacy of the sanitary conveniences, laborsaving gadgets, and mechanical contrivances that were "peculiarly American."[4]

Downing's "Expression of Purpose" addressed truthfulness, that is, a house should look like a house, a church like a church. Downing believed that a "blind passion for a particular style of building" tended to destroy expression of purpose. The "Principle of the Expression of Style" consisted of two elements: first, "beauty of form," and second, "sentiment associated with certain modes of building long prevalent in any age or country." Association theory was familiar to architects who wrote pattern books and to the women who published domestic guides. Many kinds of people drew upon the idea that architectural elements were signifiers of social and moral laws. In his architectural thinking Downing revealed himself as "a blend of the rationalist, or realist, and the romantic, combining utility and the picturesque.[5] A critical review of Downing's designs in 1858 stung over just this point: "Picturesque they may be at times, but often the affectation of external style puts Downing's designs into the category of Gothic follies

and Grecian villainies, in which the *outside gives the lie to the inside*" (emphasis added).[6]

William Ranlett, the first architect to design expressly for the popular *Godey's Lady's Book*, described his style as "utilitarian eclectic," reflecting his interest in a building's use as his first consideration. When he published *The Architect* in 1847, he advocated changing the prevailing taste from the "box style" to a "utilitarian style."[7] Similar phrasing occurred in agricultural literature. Lewis Allen, a land speculator and stockbreeder, described the design process of his thousand-dollar house: "comfort and convenience are the main requirements, and these obtained, if the slightest good taste is used, the house will look well." Allen's book *Rural Architecture* (1852) paid homage to Downing's ideas in that the exterior reflected prevailing styles, especially the Italianate. Conversely, the plans addressed "the everyday wants of a strictly agricultural population," emphasizing family and work spaces.[8] For rural buildings Calvert Vaux "remarked on the plan or convenient arrangement of accommodation" and the artistic design of the exteriors, and J. H. Hammond (1858) noted tasteful forms and convenient arrangements in his guide for rural economy.[9]

The differentiation between outside and inside continued into the twentieth century, when hundreds of sources demarcated the interior from the exterior in terms of treatment, and convenient arrangement became embedded in house descriptions in trade journals, popular magazines, plan books, and design competitions. In 1889 the National Architect's Union in Philadelphia recommended "a model of convenience and good arrangement" on the interior, while retaining an "irregular exterior" with "a pleasing effect upon the eye."[10] In one submittal for an inexpensive dwelling, the magazine described the design as combining "convenience, good taste, and economy," as well as a "neat dressy exterior."

Whereas distancing the exterior from the interior allowed for stylistic treatments of the outside, most agreed that the emphasis on style should remain on the inside. In an article for *Popular Science Monthly*, R. W. Edis offered that "the so-called Elizabethan, or later Renaissance" was more charming and suitable to "everyday wants and requirements than any other style," but that the "best architecture" centered on a "good common sense plan": "There is no possible excuse for a design, whether classic, Gothic or Queen Anne, which does not first of all recognize the internal necessities and conveniences, and which is not subordinate to a great extent to every-day internal requirements of a well-arranged and comfortable home."[11] Thus convenience becomes a tenet for the making of modern buildings. But there is more to the history of inside-out thinking and the making of modern common structures.

HISTORY OF "CONVENIENT ARRANGEMENT"

Thus far we have considered a modern vernacular architecture conceived from the inside out, to which we add the history of the theory of convenient arrangement. Consider thinking about the theory as bread dough. Making the dough into bread requires the right amount and kind of ingredients, the mixing of those parts, then kneading and shaping the dough into a recognizable loaf. Baking at an appropriate temperature prepares it for consumption. Now anyone can slice it and eat it. The analogy is a humble and domestic one because house design was quite different from other more highbrow kinds of architecture. The ingredients included all those precedents about building and internal arrangement passed down from Vitruvius Polli to Andrea Palladio through the Renaissance to French and English architects. It included the mixing in of English and American women's knowledge and advice about the household and its relation to the plan. The "yeast" that made convenient arrangement rise—popular—was a combination of social and cultural factors that encompassed Americans' desires to own single-family houses in the country and the suburbs. Other ingredients, such as agricultural reform and scientific facts about a healthy home, found their way into the mix. The recipe was tried over and over with variations and then disseminated widely, but no loaf was ever truly the same, because architects and women and Americans, in general, continued to experiment with the recipe or the process, sometimes modifying it and at other times changing it almost to the point of no recognition.

In the mid-seventeenth century, English agricultural writings defined beauty as a building that adhered to the principles of convenience. New Eng-land's post–Revolution agricultural reformers extended these notions, believing that the success of the republic depended on principles of economy—the conservation of time, space, and materials. They advocated small farms and a small house rather than the two-story-with-ell style favored by farmers. In 1820 New York architect Minard Lafever urged designers to plan a small farmhouse of one and a half stories with "frugality, convenience, and neatness, in a plain style."[12]

The phrase "plain style" also carried antecedents, referencing a form of preaching favored by seventeenth-century Puritans and reformers in the Anglican Church. A plain style in those contexts meant plain speaking—an unembellished use of words. A plain style became tantamount to truthfulness and authenticity; subterfuge and deception lay at its opposite end. As a metaphor for houses, interiors of convenience were meant to be simple and utilitarian, whereas exteriors tended toward more elaborate effects.

In the late eighteenth century, when frugality, simple tastes, and manners became identified with female virtues, convenience did not always translate into a spare building. However, Small's study of farmhouses in Sutton, Massachusetts argues that the two-story house with ell (the one that agricultural reformers hated) became a model of modern convenience because of women's desires for efficiency. These houses became "important tools in economizing women's labor at a time when household help was difficult to get and keep."[13]

With the principle of *la distribution*, the late-eighteenth-century French architect Jacques-François Blondel changed fundamentally how rooms would be properly distributed in a building. Rooms were to be planned according to their logical location, shape, and purpose, in relation to other rooms. The nineteenth-century theorist Viollet-le-Duc also believed that the design of a building must be the result of a rational method rather than the articulation of a preconceived image (such as Palladio's designs, in which rooms were sized and located on the basis of geometrical proportions). Like Blondel, Viollet-le-Duc insisted that buildings evolve from a careful statement of functional needs and that the arrangement of spaces in shapes and sequences fulfill those needs. Accordingly, the procedure began with a program and a plan and ended with the façade.[14]

Early-nineteenth-century English sources touted economical planning for those of moderate means and for designs that embodied "elegance, compactness, and convenience," but at mid-century, it was Robert Kerr in *The Gentleman's House; or, How to Plan English Residences*, who enumerated thirteen "principles of the plan as now established." Kerr was a self-described "working architect" who made "the Domestic Plan his specialty in business." Critics of his 1864 book lambasted his disinterest in ordinary or small houses, in preference to manor houses for the "better classes of English people." In a revised edition in 1877, Kerr stated that the fundamental principles were the same for large or small houses, differing only in scale and size, but not purpose.[15]

If Kerr intended his list of principles to be read hierarchically, then it should be noted that he positioned convenience toward the top and elegance toward the bottom, making clear once more the separate constructions of convenience and beauty. In the nineteenth century, convenience resulted from "the arrangement of the various rooms and their component parts in relation to each other in order to enable all the uses and purposes of the house to be carried on in perfect harmony with a place for everything and everything in its place—with no superfluity, no awkwardness, no doubtfulness. . . . Convenience indicated a contrivance of relationships of rooms to each other and the planning of thoroughfares."[16]

Convenient arrangement was the recommended solution for problems associated with large, costly, and poorly planned houses. *Carpentry and Building* first used the terms *internal arrangement* and *convenient arrangement* interchangeably, as if the phrases were two sides of the same coin, but after 1880, it used *convenient arrangement* almost entirely. In effect, the terms were compatible, but slight differences existed in meaning. *Internal arrangement* signified space-planning issues, such as the organization of rooms (adjacency principles and zoning of public–private spaces) and movement (circulation principles) through a house.[17] *Convenient arrangement* became a bigger concept, incorporating old ideas about internal arrangement as well as new concepts about efficiency, economy, health, science, and technology.

Central to the principle of convenient arrangement was compactness, the "concretion" of rooms to economize space. A compacted plan provided for a variety of communication methods among household members and the shortest and easiest routes. To Kerr, a house's thoroughfares (corridors and passages) constituted "the Skeleton of its Plan" upon which rooms were grouped. Staircases also merited a set of principles, including ideas regarding their safety for children, the use of broad treads and low risers for the infirm and old, and particular locations "for the ladies." For example, a décorous passage was one in which women could enter the house from the outdoors and access the stair without passing through much of the interior. The size, form, and arrangement of halls and passages "had much to do with looks and comfort."[18]

Although the theory of convenient arrangement established clear architectural and social expectations about making a dwelling comfortable in its interior, English and American architects differed on definitions. The English associated comfort with cultural characteristics that included "peculiarities" of the English climate, the "domesticated habits" of class structure, and "family reserve." If the English thought of comfort as a passive attribute, Americans viewed it as active: "American architecture will be simply carrying out, in an architectural way, the requirements of the American people in their buildings. From their homes the march of progress will be through kitchens, pantries, and dining rooms."[19]

WOMEN'S INFLUENCE ON VERNACULAR DESIGN

Blondel's and Viollet-le-Duc's notions about room adjacency, size, shape, and sequence also found their way into writing targeted at women. Among other imperatives the "housewife's" needs required efficient room arrangements, which, based on step saving, organized rooms into logical adjacent relationships to the kitchen. As "mistresses of the kitchen," women found inconvenient arrangements unsatisfactory for good housekeeping.[20]

One would expect that the best source for convenient interiors in women's terms would be found in the publications of America's "material feminists" such as Catharine Beecher. In 1869 her plans in *The American Woman's Home*, cowritten with Harriet Beecher Stowe, show careful organization of spaces and mechanical equipment for laundry and cooking for the first floor and basement. Compared with typically large kitchens in cottages, Beecher's kitchen, moved to the center of a house, becomes compact in size (nine feet square) and efficiency (a single-surface counter), a workroom with adequate sunlight and ventilation that opens into the family room.

Beecher promoted multiple-use spaces (flexibility) with the use of movable decorative screens to hide extra beds and dressing areas. Her "close packing of conveniences" relied on advanced technology and task-oriented adjacency in kitchens, but the spatial organization of her plan resembles a seventeenth-century Puritan house with hall and parlor.[21] Beecher seems to have been more interested in the details of planning than in spatial form.

The progressive farmhouse featured efficiency in the service of greater productivity. The kitchen and basement became production areas. The nature of the rural parlor was constantly debated, while the sitting room was seen as embodying country virtues of informality and family solidarity. Domestic farm planners shunned stylistic elegance, concentrating

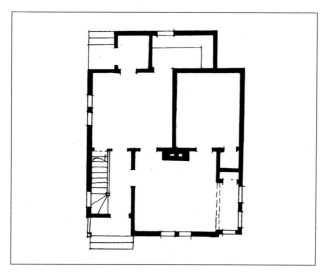

2.3. Thomas Gould's prize-winning cottage plan for *Carpentry and Building's* cheap house competition in 1879 included features of convenient arrangement: a first-floor bedroom (which could be turned into a dining room) and plentiful storage—a kitchen pantry, bedroom closets, and a trunk room. Gould also managed to create a little sewing bay. Jan Jennings, *Cheap and Tasteful Dwellings: Design Competitions and the Convenient Interior* (Knoxville, Tenn.: University of Tennessee Press, 2005), 147.

instead on internal arrangement, construction, and shape. A concern for convenience included efficiency in circulation, laborsaving principles, and room adjacencies.[22]

More often than was the case with suburban houses, convenient arrangement for farmhouse designs included multipurpose or adaptable spaces and a downstairs bedroom (sometimes noted on the plan as a "family bedroom"). Architects suggested these adaptations in notations accompanying their drawings. However, cost as well as convenience drove some of these decisions; in small houses the front "living room" also served as a dining room and parlor. Farmhouse design kept evolving through a female-oriented process of defining spatial relationships. Indeed, the National Architects Union delegated plan making to their female clients, claiming that the company's responsibilities lay elsewhere: "Arranging a floor plan is a part of house planning which you can often do for yourself better than any architect can for you; you know what you want. What you need help in is the arrangement of a tasteful exterior and roof, a proper stair plan and, before you build, clear working plans and full specifications. Here is where we help in home building."[24] In published farmhouse designs from 1900 to 1930, the exterior often looked suburban, whereas the interior offered convenient arrangements, some of which were peculiar only to farmhouses. Rural reformers of this period continued to reiterate and expand ideas about healthfulness, efficiency, and convenience.

In time the principle of convenient arrangement incorporated American scientific findings regarding the requirements for a healthy home for the city as well as the suburbs. A germ theory was first published in the United States in 1883. In the same year the Sanitary Science Club of Boston followed the advice of John Ruskin and William Morris and called for suitability and simplicity to reduce clutter and improve hygiene in the home. By the 1890s the General Federation of Women's Clubs sponsored classes on "Art and Utility in the Home," which linked the arts and crafts philosophy and aesthetic with healthful houses.[23]

Throughout the nineteenth century, instead of relying on professionals, farmers and their wives developed their own house plans. From 1830 to 1900, eleven agricultural journals published house

2.4. The National Architects Union advertised specifically to women. *Housekeeper's Weekly* 3, no. 6 (Philadelphia: April 16, 1892): 16. The Winterthur Library: Printed Book and Periodical Collection.

plans submitted by farm wives, progressive agriculturalists, and businessmen-farmers. The *Cultivator* sponsored a contest in 1830 "to improve our farm dwelling-houses, to render them convenient, economize the cost, and lessen the burden of female labor." [25] In 1895, when the *American Agriculturist* sponsored a house design contest, eleven of the thirty-one prize winners were women, most of whom were farm wives who thought house design was a legitimate exercise of their duties.

Women's direct involvement in plan making also appealed to professional home economists. In 1897 Helen Campbell, author of *Women Wage-Earners,* restated in a lecture on household economics the belief that family needs could be partially satisfied with a good floor plan and declared that "here a woman's judgment is absolutely essential. It is the woman who lives chiefly in the house and who, if common sense were brought to bear, would soon put an end to the type of thing the average builder offers her." Campbell declared that the house plan deserved scrutiny from women on the basis of function and convenience: "Why should we perpetually go up and down when going sideways is so much easier? Why should we accept stupidly planned and inadequate closets or no closets at all, and kitchens in which everything is calculated to bring the greatest unhappiness to the greatest number?" [25]

THE PRINCIPLE OF CONVENIENCE AND THE FLOOR PLAN

The theory of convenient arrangement needed grounding, and the floor plan served that need. The theory of convenient arrangement consisted of principles that had accreted around it, but it had only one mode of representation: the plan. The history of convenient arrangement is essentially a history of the plan. As the domestic interior became more important than the exterior, the plan evolved as the interior's most significant architectural drawing.

Nineteenth-century English women's advice books, reprinted in the United States, stressed economical floor plans as the method to create efficient houses. In 1845 Jane Webb Louden's *Lady's Country Companion* documented two women evaluating the merits of a house on the basis of drawings: "I have just received your letter, enclosing a plan of your house and a sketch of its present appearance; and, I confess, it appears to me that you have not complained of its gloominess without having abundant reason for doing so." [26]

American housewives in the Northeast presented themselves as a knowledgeable, if not confrontational, clientele for architects because they claimed expert knowledge in convenient arrangement. Further, they could read plan drawings to analyze cogent features of convenience. Pattern- and plan-book architects, and even style-based architects who wrote for a public audience, such as E. C. Gardner, encouraged women to sketch their own floor plans—at least, initially. Gardner, in *The House That Jill Built, after Jack's Had Proved a Failure*, explains Jill's skill in knowing how to arrange a plan, though he patronizes her ability to draw it: "Jill accordingly produced a fresh sheet of 'cross-section' paper, on whose double plaid lines the most helpless type in drawing can make a plan with mathematical accuracy provided she can count to ten, and on this began to draw the plan of the first floor, expounding as she drew."[27]

"A handy way" of compacting plans, which Kerr practiced, is to "make a complete classified list of the rooms with appropriate dimensions of each. Then cut to scale small pieces of paper, which represent the rooms. Arrange these pieces together with intervening spaces for stairs, passages and corridors. Any number of trial arrangements may be successfully effected and sketches made there from."[28]

The Beaux-Arts method, the practice of which depended on logical planning, also gave the plan a privileged status. For example, students analyzed plans of historical buildings to understand their basic outlines, their circulation systems, and the distribution of inner and outer spaces. Beaux-Arts design practice also insisted on unity and integrity in every architectural scheme. By the turn of the twentieth century, architectural schools considered planning as the foundation of design, independent of historical styles. The use of the term *planning* is significant to an understanding of domestic architecture. Louis Sullivan's description of the "theory of plan" summarizes the ethic, method, and philosophy of the Beaux-Arts system. Sullivan acknowledged the plan's status as a special visual, aesthetic, and intellectual experience.[29] The theory, however, relied on composition and plan type, rather than practical planning and convenience; it gave appearance an equal footing with practical considerations.

Conversely, for much of its existence, the theory of convenient arrangement positioned style, aesthetics, tastefulness, and appearance as adversarial elements. As it grew into a cumulative body, it became an inherited tradition, particularly for women. As a body of standards, it tended toward prescription, and therein was its fault. Anyone could learn to apply the

principles, but application did not add up to design. There was also another fundamental difference that separated the "theory of the plan," as defined by academically trained architects, from the theory of convenient arrangement. Convenience remained in the province of domestic architecture, whereas American architects, responding to the technical and practical problems presented by large and complex buildings, turned to other issues as the basis for design.

Though convenience arose more than two hundred years ago with the simplest of interior ideas, it gained momentum as other principles were introduced and became inculcated. By 1879 the theory had a head of steam. Many principles applied to circulation: reducing the number of doors in rooms, eliminating entirely the idea of passing through one room to get to another, accessing main rooms from a hall, organizing front and back stairs in the same spatial cavity. The standards for arrangement of rooms centered on the location of like spaces in close proximity (room adjacency and convenient accessibility), as well as proper retirement.

By the 1880s convenient arrangement was augmented by additional principles that had some bearing on house design: step saving as the standard for compact spaces; health and well-being for home inhabitants; ample light and appropriately distributed windows; and little or no wasted space, with every space to be useful. At the same time large spaces for a reception hall, parlor, and dining room became socially extinct, but remained functionally necessary and often multifunctional. Specialized storage emerged, including a closet for each bedroom, and the "economy of plumbing" encouraged the grouping of plumbing lines in close proximity.

THE COTTAGE AND CONVENIENT ARRANGEMENT

The picturesque cottage could not have been more inappropriate for a coupling with the theory of convenient arrangement. The cottage depended on additive effects in spaces as well as other elements that drove costs higher. Taken alone, the picturesque, the cottage, and convenient arrangement appear to contradict, yet read in a broader context of

2.5. The Dr. J. M. Black house, Canyon, Texas, is a sprawling cottage with ornamented edges, contrasting patterns, and a veranda. Panhandle-Plains Historical Society, Canyon, Texas.

design theory they were extraordinarily compatible, accommodating design from the inside out. The cottage's massing and mixture of pictorial compositions allowed the exterior walls to become malleable and irregular, a result of convenient plans.

James Gallier, architect and author, promoted the cottage as the most appropriate building type for convenient arrangement. "Under the cottage style . . . [the] interior is fashioned less with regard to the rules of architecture, than the convenient arrangement of the interior. These buildings do not depend upon architectural ornaments for their beauty, so much as upon their obvious fitness for comfort and use."[30] When the exterior form becomes the first consideration (as in classical symmetry), then the specialization of rooms, flexibility of arrangement, and convenience become subordinated.[31] In the philosophy of realistic pragmatism, convenient arrangement acted as a truth and logic endorsed and accepted in the community; its sole validation was the sanction of social approbation and custom. When the elements of convenient arrangement no longer satisfied contemporary needs, they were replaced or amended. Thus convenient arrangement can be seen as a manifesto of social custom, rules, and practices

that became "test standards for successful practice."[32] In these terms practice served as the arbiter of theory; practice monitored theory.

PROFESSIONALIZATION OF CONVENIENT ARRANGEMENT

By 1909 the theory/principle of convenient arrangement claimed three constituencies: housewives; home economists; and architects, builders, and carpenters. Each group interpreted the component principles from their distinct vantage points. In the ensuing years the professionals wrested control of convenient arrangement from the hands of amateurs as home economists and architects became its practitioners. In the first decade of the twentieth century home economists refined convenience as the basis for the scientific study of interiors. It became widespread as other reformers adapted it to new norms in home types that replaced the cottage. For example, most bungalow composition remained irregular and asymmetrical, allowing interior planning to reign. Not until the late 1920s did a house type threaten convenient arrangement's reliance on irregularity.

Colonial revival houses reverted back to classical principles such as symmetry, but by then architects and homeowners alike had accepted the canon of convenient arrangement as a truth regardless of style. With the interior organization solidified by a theory, American builders were free to respond to other ideas about exterior appearance.

There are two other aspects of convenience that need mentioning and have little to do with the historic theory of convenient arrangement and more to do with practicality. The first involves the reversed plan. The plans of most everyday houses could be reversed; flip a plan so that the original left side is now on the right. To see what a reversed plan looked like, consumers were told to hold it before a mirror. Most reversals were carried out to give a house a better fit with the building site. The second issue involves exterior treatment. Many houses were intended to have multiple exterior treatments as part of a single plan. Most were changes in cladding, for example, clapboard or brick veneer, but others included flourishes that stylized the house. Beginning in the late nineteenth century, trade journals published articles extolling the virtues of building exterior variations on the same house plan. A convenient plan lent itself to exterior variations. Professionals referred to as *practical architects* (our term) executed many of the floor plan schemes. Statements about this practice went like this: "The picture is a good illustration of the manner in which a row of houses can be rendered attractive by varying the architectural treatment of the exterior, while conforming largely to the same floor plan."[33] Plan reversal and replicating a plan among varied exteriors, elevated convenience over other house features.

2.6. Trade magazines and books are filled with examples of one plan and various exteriors. In February 1904 *Carpentry and Building* published eight photographs of colonial revival cottages designed by Jesse A. Oakley using the same floor plan. This 1946 version was dubbed the "variable exterior," "The House with Eight Faces." The overall size of each house was exactly the same, but no two houses looked alike. *House-of-the-Month Book of Small Houses*, Harold E. Group, ed. (Garden City, N.Y.: Garden City Publishing, 1946), 107.

CIRCULATION SYSTEMS

Under the wing of convenient arrangement, circulation developed into a fundamental interior planning component with explicit principles. In order to understand a modern vernacular interior, it is necessary to analyze a building's plan for the circulation system, including the passage sequence, hall configuration, and path–space relationship.

The passage sequence structures a house's organization, accommodating movement as residents and guests promenade, linger, or take in views along its path. Internal pathways help identify the social function of rooms, relations between one space and another, and may also lead to an understanding of the social interaction therein.

The form of a circulation space varies according to how its boundaries are defined; how its form relates to the form of the space it links; and how its entrances open onto it. A space functioning as a hall rarely disappears from modern vernacular house types; it perseveres in various forms because it is needed for its specialized function and also because a hall accrued meaning in American culture. From 1870 to 1960 a hall became a contested topic in interpretations of convenient arrangement. In the nineteenth century a hall grew to room size and was prized for its symbolism as the nucleus of first impression, circulation, and social interaction. In the twentieth century, when designers interpreted convenience in terms of compactness, the hall shrunk in size and value and was even designated by some as wasted space. The center hall, an old and valued circulation space that is linked with the classical, appears in all manner of house types, including the bungalow and the ranch.

In *Architecture: Form, Space and Order*, Frank Ching identifies three space–path typologies: pass-by, pass-through, and terminate in space. We add a fourth, the loop, a circulation feature of cottages. The pass-by path is located at the edge of a room, avoiding penetration of the space. In this way, the pass-by maintains the integrity of a space and social interaction without interruption.[33] The pass-through path cuts through a room, sometimes axially, sometimes interrupting social interaction.[34] A pathway terminates in a space when there is only one door opening; the way one enters a room is the way one

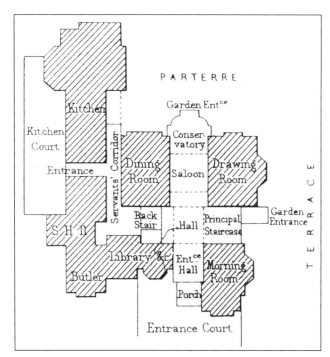

2.7. Robert Kerr's figure–ground drawing in 1877 is one of the most remarkable analyses of convenient arrangement. Naming these "Thoroughfare Plans," Kerr crosshatched all the rooms, allowing the circulation spaces (in white) to become more visible. Jennings, *Cheap and Tasteful Dwellings*, 145.

leaves a room. Ching characterizes the space in which the path terminates as a functional room or a symbolically important space.[35] In modern vernacular cottages and bungalows, internal circulation terminated in the kitchen.

A characteristic of American nineteenth-century cottage designs (small or large) was a continuous, nonaxial, and oval-shaped path that functioned like a loop by linking several rooms together. The loop opened the house's spaces to each other, implying a more communicative way of living.[36]

PRACTICAL ARCHITECTURE

As noted above, architects were part of the discussion around the pros and con of convenient arrangement. Some were sympathetic, and we think of them as practical architects; their practices concerned small architecture. As a group they can be classified as ordinary designers whose work was often replicated.

The American belief in practicality, a subject in its own right, has deep origins. Andrew Draper described the role of practicality in American education

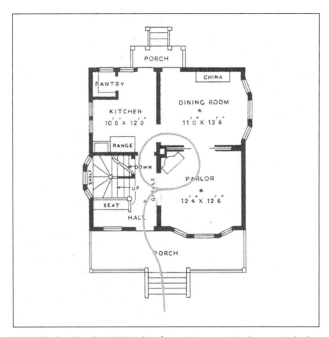

2.8. Charles Smith's 1901 plan for an inexpensive house includes a façade-width porch, a room dedicated to a reception hall with a seat and dog-leg stair, a dining room, and a kitchen with pantry. Part of the design's convenience stems from a circulation loop that begins at the front door and unites all downstairs rooms. Jennings, *Cheap and Tasteful Dwellings*, 176.

in way that applies to the production of modern vernacular architecture: "The spirit of the country is not satisfied until suggestions have been put to the practical test. If . . . initiative is needed, any number of people will supply it; if public action is necessary, nearly everybody will support it. As individuals, and even more as a people, we are bound to get all the possibilities out of the things we chance to think of. Our native energy and common optimism are ever disposed to experiment, and our free-flowing democracy and our much legislation make it easy enough to do so. . . . It all stimulates productivity. . . . Our energy and our optimism . . . lead us into some passing blunders, but they give us many enduring results."[37]

Practical architecture was promoted by period publications. From the first issue, editor David Williams intended *Carpentry and Building* to develop in the same mode as *The Iron Age*—an authoritative clearinghouse that was "eminently practical" and "useful." New York City publishers A. J. Bicknell and W. T. Comstock endorsed the publication by characterizing it as a "practical working journal." In nineteenth-century America, "practical" evoked positive cultural characteristics. Practicality had no room for

sentiment, and it derived from an attention to facts. Late-nineteenth-century and early-twentieth-century titles of articles listed in *The New York Times* confirm the popularity of the term, and its use prefaced a wide variety of subjects, including agriculture, banking, botany, chemistry, cooking, education, economics, forestry, golf, law, penmanship, philanthropy, journalism, medicine, reform, taxidermy, and theology. When Williams chose *practicality* as a philosophical cornerstone for a new building journal, he positioned his practical architects, practical construction, and practical houses in the middle of an American cultural milieu.

A practical architecture can best be explained as a pragmatic and popular approach to design that called for general solutions as distinct from specific solutions that start with particular places. In the last decade of the nineteenth century, the mobility of the population and the simultaneity with which products could be exposed to a nationwide audience diminished regionalism. Practical architecture might just as well be called *market architecture*, because it was linked to new purchasing patterns in an emerging consumerism. Participatory and interactive, it provided more information to more people and a broader range of choices than did any other system of architecture. Architects who submitted free designs to trade magazines to be copied and shared recognized a social imperative to provide cheap, architect-designed houses for ordinary Americans. Established in 1868, *The Household* (devoted to the interests of the housewife) titled its house designs "homes for the people."

Trade journals borrowed the term *practical* from the titles and prefaces of architectural pattern books, where it encompassed a number of attributes. In 1852 Lewis F. Allen stated that the plans and directions submitted in *Rural Architecture: Being a Complete Description of Farm Houses, Cottages, and Out Buildings* were intended to be of the "most practical kind: plain, substantial, and applicable," and he implied that practical architecture was familiar when he said the following: "These plans are chiefly original; that is, they are not copied from any in the books, or from any structures with which the writer is familiar. Yet they will doubtless be found to resemble buildings, both in outward appearance and interior arrangement, with which numerous readers may be acquainted."[38] *The Builder and Woodworker* in 1884 endorsed pattern-book publications as useful aids for carpenters and builders in cities, towns, and villages, as well as for mechanics, clerks, salaried men, and workingmen of every calling.

By the 1870s practical architecture had a specific set of characteristics: the designs were intended for everybody, and the buildings were erected in all sections of the country; plans should exemplify the principle of convenient arrangement, and houses should be compact; construction costs should be low or moderate; and scale drawings for an entire building should be provided without cost, often with specifications and estimates for materials and labor.

Including working drawings as a distinguishing characteristic of practical architecture implied that designs could be replicated without much regard for a specific client or a particular site. In its 1879 inaugural issue, *Carpentry and Building* acknowledged pattern books as its predecessor and borrowed the use and meaning of the term *practical* to include the publication of designs with details drawn to working scale that were useful to builders. The paper's overall stance about such things was prefigured in "builders' guides like Edward Shaw's *Modern Architect: or, Every Carpenter His Own Master* (1854), [which] portrayed a class solidarity between the practical architect, his mechanics, and clients, depicting all as middle-class men."[39]

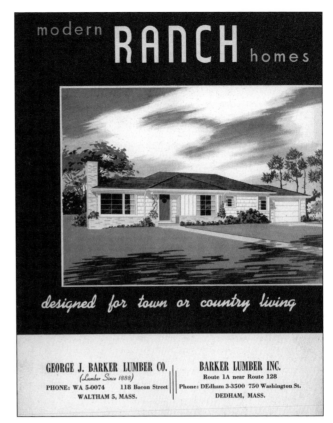

2.9. The plan book is the linchpin of practical architecture. It doesn't guarantee a successful project, but it keeps the house forms and patterns of assembly in the population's collective imagination. *Modern Ranch Homes Designed for Town or Country Living* (National Plan Service, 1951), cover; distributed by George J. Barker Lumber Co., Waltham, Massachusetts, and Barker Lumber Inc., Dedham, Massachusetts.

THE SHAPE OF MODERN VERNACULAR TIME

We have come to believe that building components and the designs they shape are just things, what art historian George Kubler refers to as "material worked by human hands under the guidance of connected ideas developed in a temporal sequence."[40] Kubler suggests that the production of artifacts, whether a work of art or a tool, can be divided into formal sequences composed of prime objects—objects that inspire imitation or change thinking—and their replications. Each made thing represents a solution to some problem, with the solutions linked in sequences.

Kubler's model suggests that there is an internal coherence in the making of common buildings. When we study a great number of them, we discover that the buildings and their key parts are composed of gradually altered replications of a trait. As a building type, the cottage is a trait; it is a unique building type with a long, rich history that includes several subtraits. The gable roof, for example, is a cottage subtrait. We can plot its pitches, coverings, structural supports, and relations to other roof types over time.

The origin of any sequence of things is thought of as a *prime object*, like a certain gable roof being used on a cottage. Once used, it is replicated until another invention or mutation forces solutions in a new direction. In general, any given time and place consists mostly of replications of known things. Replications are the heart of vernacular design; they convey a sense of order and in the long run may contribute to a sense of place. If we look inside a vernacular building, we find it is made of layers of known patterns and materials, representing scores of sequences, with each sequence consisting of linked solutions to a design problem. Following this definition, each element of a design system is, in fact, a functional class—for example, doors, windows, and stairs. But roof plans, room shapes, and spatial configurations are classes of solutions as well.

Using Kubler's theory to analyze modern vernacular building, we focus on individual characteristics of design or aggregates of elements, and then turn to the whole work. The built work represents many levels of integration. The first level may be thought of as providing solutions to problems, beginning with a fundamental problem such as framing a wall or constructing a roof. At another stage we might progress to things like joints—any location where two materials touch or abut; then there is the location and character of openings (passages for light and air) and the location of spaces for movement. Sometimes the solution to a problem may mean marking the occasion with something special, say, a particular treatment for the entrance. Our book sorts these

elements and patterns at as many levels as we could discover. The point here is "fit" or how elements and patterns work together. At a broader level, there is the issue of dealing with the overall balancing of effects. *Balancing* includes issues such as horizontal and vertical integration on the exterior, the planning of adjacent spaces on the interior, and integration of materials by type or quality anywhere in the building. The final level deals with how the building engages its physical and cultural context.

For the most part, Americans, like people everywhere, build what they already know, or they apply known elements and sequences to known construction problems. At the same time, the market economy system encourages variations in any application. Creating a cross-section through a building reveals the materials used to construct it. What we see is a collection of elements, each in a different stage of development. On the interior we might encounter an older trim system with elaborate moldings next to a

2.10. In 1908 Christian A. Wagner, an architect-builder, designed a modern interior for the Port Jervis residence of F. N. Mason. Unified by columns, the mantel and set grate have classically applied motifs; cap trim topped the mantel and the cased sliding-door opening. Jan Jennings, "The Aesthetics of Everyday Interiors," *The Interiors Handbook for Historic Buildings* (Washington, D.C.: Historic Preservation Education Foundation, 1988), 1.5–1.11.

more up-to-date wainscot or wallpaper. Whatever the stages of development the elements or patterns or a house type might indicate, clustered together they reflect design values associated with a particular aesthetic.

Vernacular building sequences are long in duration, and change is minimal. For example, some window patterns were produced continuously from 1870 to 1960, with only minor adjustments to the size of the whole window or to the window's parts—stiles, muntins, panes of glass, and molding profiles—or to the manufacturing technology. Market forces and other aspects of an economy influence sequences. A contemporary example is the way the rising cost of materials and labor modifies the design and size of elements. It has been quite a while since a wall stud has been, literally, two inches by four inches.

Most vernacular design sequences have been open-ended: that is, solutions to specific problems were actively derived throughout the whole period. It has always been possible to modify floor plans suitable for a particular building type, to modify a building type to accommodate a preferred plan, and to use identical floor plans with different exteriors.

AESTHETIC INTENTIONS

Of the all the material elements used to construct a building, millwork has proved useful in constructing design history. Historically it has played many roles and undergone many transformations. For example, in tracking the relationship of millwork to the organization of an interior wall, say, in a dining room of a house, we can create a small design history relevant to woodwork employed throughout the house, as well as to the house type, to the period in which it was built, and to an aesthetic intent.

We have determined sets of cultural rubrics for modern vernacular building. For the exterior they are clusters of interlocking solutions described as the Italianate, picturesque, colonial revival (classical and modern), arts and crafts, English and Spanish revival, and modern; for the interior they are the Italianate, ornamental, colonial revival (classical and modern), the artistic, English and Spanish revival, and modern. How each type is realized has never been a closed question, because there is no one solution, no one perfect order. The individuals responsible for assembling the elements of a house chose items from an array of possibilities, several combinations of which could reinforce a particular cultural treatment. All the treatment categories serve as indicators of values, attitudes toward time, and the social uses of buildings.

Modern vernacular buildings are based primarily on the production of unknown people—workers who operated the machinery that produced the goods, builders who constructed them, and practical architects who designed them. Operators, mill managers, and carpenters adhered to historical and current ideas about materials, patterns and profiles, and how products addressed basic construction problems. In this book we analyze modern vernacular sequences over time and attempt to calculate the time between versions of any one element, building type, or aesthetic constellation.

3

BUILDING THE PICTURE

Trading on the Imagery of Production and Design

———————◆———————

From the 1630s to the 1840s American vernacular architecture was the product of local adaptations to climate and traditional uses of construction materials and building types. After the 1840s the availability of manufactured building materials changed the very nature of architecture, and broader notions of good building form and popular aesthetics subsumed traditional regional views.[1]

Although some building materials were factory-made prior to the Civil War, it is the postwar period that is remarkable for the total industrialization of building. The 1870s were characterized by economies of scale; by expansion of the means of production, including the invention of new and more efficient machinery; and by the rapid deployment of the railroad. An integrated building industry emerged that separated the design and construction of structures into component parts. These parts, which served as both functional building materials and as design elements, were sold in wholesale and retail markets to a population that lived anywhere near the tracks of the rail companies.[2] The settlements that sprang up were linked by transportation and their reliance on building materials from common sources. One consequence was that different regions of the country began to share design ideas and values. Competition forced manufacturers to

produce like goods, and designs for buildings were drawn as models for replication. The end product was the emergence of a nationwide design system.

Economically, the developments were based on the exploitation of natural resources, one of the cornerstones of a production-centered economy. The most important resource was timber. In all its various modes, American architecture had been based on the extensive use of wood.[3] Industrial production of wood materials, however, was part of a newly oriented economy in which building materials, even whole buildings, became the equivalent of other consumer goods.

In the new economy, manufacturers generated demand for their goods through advertising and salesmen and by inculcating a new set of social values into the culture. The new economy was so successful that consumption became a cultural phenomenon.[4] In the manufacture of building materials, demand was promoted by the publication of special trade papers aimed at builders and architects and by manufacturers' catalogues, which guided retailers when stocking their lumberyards, builders when executing designs, and individual consumers when choosing products. Catalogues listed inventories of component parts and compositional patterns. Professional journals illustrated new building designs as well as new construction techniques and equipment. Augmenting these publications were plan books that described a variety of floor plans (usually accompanied by an elevation or perspective) for houses, commercial buildings, and a few churches and small schools. On the consumption side, new books, magazines, and bulletins, written by housing reformers and domestic science academics, encouraged the reorganization of interior spaces and efficient use of household goods and even broached the topics of design and home decoration. Given the high rate of production and distribution of factory-made building materials and home furnishings, new efficiencies in household work and other reforms were carried out in settings defined by industry.

The principal means by which the new information was transmitted was pictorial. The communication of ideas and values through pictures was a well-established practice; it is convenient to refer to this phenomenon as the making of a *pictorial logic*. During the nineteenth century, pictorial logic expanded to such an extent that there was a cultural dependency on pictures to create settlements, to redefine environments, to expand the economy, and to sell goods.[5] Although the development of pictorial thinking functioned as a common basis for design consumption and an agent of social change, pictures were used in different ways. Trade catalogues contained mostly pictures, and home improvement bulletins were predominantly text, but the same kinds of general information appeared in both.

Manufacturers encouraged consumers to think about the parts of a product or a design and patterns of arrangement and their effects, with an eye toward modifying the home environment. This discussion of the rise of pictorial thinking centers on the production of houses because of the value of housing in the culture, and it centers on interior design because of the role interiors played in defining progressive middle-class life.

TRADE CATALOGUES AND THE DISSEMINATION OF VERNACULAR DESIGN

The development of manufacturing trade catalogues in the 1880s and 1890s parallels the growth of American industries: catalogues portrayed the capital

3.1. Millwork catalogues disclose much about the dissemination of architectural information and manufacturers' and builders' design values. Exterior doors from Sash, Doors and Blinds (St. Louis: Joseph Hafner Manufacturing, 1891), 95. Authors' collection.

investment that firms made and the energy that they spent to capture portions of a dynamic economy. Of the various components of manufacture related to vernacular architecture, millwork is the most significant design element because of its practical uses, as noted, and its ability to accommodate aesthetics.

A study of the contents of trade catalogues published from the 1890s to the 1920s reveals the development of catalogues in general, especially the changing nature of information and methods of presentation. Throughout the period, manufacturers communicated information in various pictorial ways: elevations and sectional views of products; special illustrations of design effects, including lithographs

3.2. From a design point of view, stairs are integral to interior organization and fenestration; surface treatments—wood, walls, and floor—are components of a single system. Farley & Loetscher Manufacturing General Catalog No. 9, 2nd ed. (Dubuque, Iowa: Farley & Loetscher, 1911), 365. Authors' collection.

LAKOTA
(Craftsman Style.)
Plain Oak, waxed finish. Width 5 feet. Height 7 feet 3 inches. Tile opening 42 x 42.
Wood doors lined with plain glass, black hinges.
Mantel only, without Tile or Grate, **$38.00.**

Mantel Complete		Mantel Complete	
With **Vulcan** Grate No. 1............$56.00		With **Aldine** Grate Nos. 1 or 2.........$108.00
" " " " 2............64.50		" " " " 3, 4, 5 or 6......87.00
" " " " 3............66.00		" " " " 7............89.00
" " " " 4............71.50		" Gas Log Grate No. 107............71.00

Grate designs are illustrated on pages 403 to 410 inclusive.
Mantel Complete as shown, with Black Frame, Flue Damper, Black Andirons and Black Basket Grate, no Fire Brick, **$75.60.**

Black portable basket, as illustrated, 20 inches long, **$7.70.** For other designs, see page 441.
Black andirons, as shown, 21 inches high, **$14.00** per pair. For other designs, see page 440.
Note difference in size of Vulcan and Aldine Grates when building grate opening.
See our Price Guide.

3.3. The Lakota is marketed here as a special mantel whose design and materials distinguished it from other stock goods. Manufacturers applied the term *craftsman* to a particular cluster of traits also recognized outside the world of millwork. In trade catalogues reference to craftsman indicated artistic design—something unconventional. Farley and Loetscher Manufacturing Company General Catalog No. 9, 2nd ed. (Dubuque, Iowa: Farley & Loetscher, 1911), 423. Authors' collection.

of products and watercolors of idealized designs; and photographs of manufacturing processes or product installations. Some catalogue illustrations suggested compositions—how to integrate elements logically—whereas others appealed to consumers' emotions. Such strategies were calculated to heighten expectations about products.

A typical page from a nineteenth-century millwork catalogue might feature doors but also include other graphic cues and messages: a header that provides the name and location of the company, so when a page is torn out the customer can identify the manufacturer; a frame-like border; labels that provide product type, stock numbers, and the information that the designs shown are just two of several available; alternative views that suggest interchangeability (the heart of the industrial system); and aesthetic information about design effects.[6] The general appearance of the "front and vestibule doors" in 3.1 suggests the kind of ornamentality associated with late-nineteenth-century middle-class design. Because the products stand alone in an elevation view with no contextual references, the customer is given the choice of function.

Twenty years later millwork catalogues had changed format. Firms moved away from flat, two-dimensional presentations of goods to three-dimensional illustrations of products in place, showing goods as part of a design system, such as the relation-

ship of stairs to an interior space. (3.2) Pictures were still laced with supplemental information and implied a way of life through artifacts and their arrangement. Early-twentieth-century catalogues also featured other types of changes in presentation, such as identification of trade names or style references. (3.3) Nineteenth-century millwork catalogues had contained some style references; twentieth-century catalogues used them with increasing frequency.

Early-twentieth-century manufacturers conceived of catalogues as books and had them printed and bound accordingly. Their presentation of products

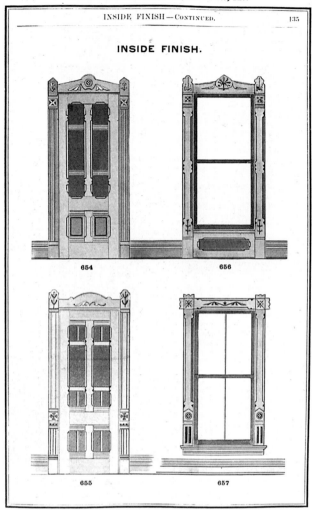

INSIDE FINISH.

654   656

655   657

3.4. The door designs are markedly different from the trim; they are part of the whole scheme but retain their own character, which is a general characteristic of nineteenth-century millwork.
Sash, Doors and Blinds (St Louis: Joseph Hafner Manufacturing Company, 1891), 135. Authors' collection.

row, the door and window finish were aligned horizontally and connected through the baseboard. In the bottom row, patterns stand alone, unconnected—a reminder that options were fundamental to this kind of architecture and kept it from becoming standardized. Early 1890s catalogues, such as Josef Hafner's, display just a few pages of inside finish but have numerous pages devoted to variants of individual elements, such as molding profiles and corner, plinth, and head blocks. The message was clear. There were opportunities for homeowners or builders to exert personal preferences. (3.4)

As product lines became more simplified in appearance in the twentieth century, the integration of primary design elements became more thorough, and manufacturers discontinued variations on individual elements in favor of controlled effects that suggested styles. Controlled effects promoted standardization that, in turn, reduced construction costs. From the manufacturer's point of view, style was less important than the effect the millwork cluster created; the firm repeated most of the elements throughout the catalogue.[8] (3.5)

From 1890 to 1925 the presentation of patterns was an important part of manufacturers' trade catalogues. Consumers enhanced their visual acuity through pattern recognition and selection. Patterns were the next level of design context beyond the single element, and firms were careful to illustrate that single element in a room for which it was suited and in a variety of patterns in which it could be arranged. Some catalogues called attention to goods that worked only as patterns, such as ceiling beams. Walls, too, could have various horizontal organizations of millwork, such as groupings of moldings integrated with wainscots and fields of wallpaper or paint. Flooring ranged from strip, parquet, and wood carpet patterns to field-and-border compositions.

By the 1910s manufacturers had most of the pictorial devices used to illustrate products firmly in place. Of these, one merits special mention: the vignette. The vignette established a context for goods, communicated social values through subject matter and presentation, and featured integrated millwork. Vignettes might be presented via drawings of ideal settings or photographs of actual settings; both had a significant impact. The appeal to the consumer's imagination accomplished by the vignette

was rhetorical. They relied on changes in typography or ink color within the descriptions to signal special design information. In addition, alternative designs were available. All these techniques helped to shape the consumer's selection. Manufacturers believed that choice, whether of a single product or a package of integrated elements, was fundamental to a demand-driven economy.

Although late-nineteenth-century catalogues relied on two-dimensional presentations of products without contextual settings, they portrayed millwork as systemically related.[7] A consumer bought a whole system, an integrated pattern, such as no. 654, with plinth block, casing, head block, and lintel. In the top

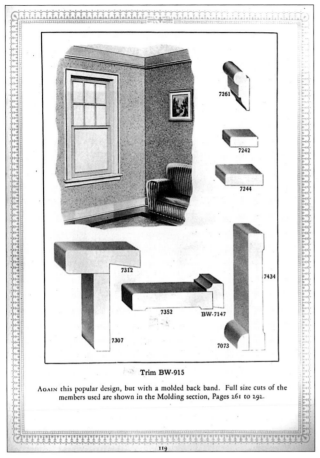

3.5. The plainness of the molding profiles and the 6:1 glazing pattern of the window suggest suitability for use in a modern colonial interior. Bilt-Well Millwork, Catalog No. 40 (Dubuque, Iowa: Carr, Ryder & Adams Company, ca. 1925), 119. Authors' collection.

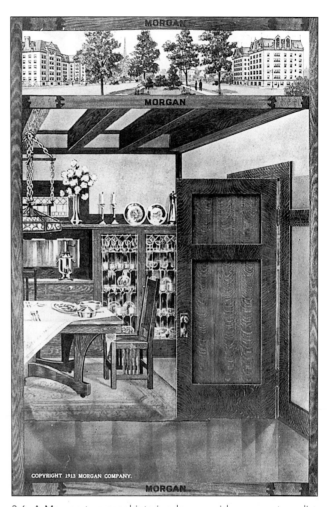

3.6. A Morgan two-panel interior door provides access to a dining room in a city apartment located along a boulevard. The Door Beautiful, 7th ed. (Oshkosh, Wis.: Morgan Company, 1916), 43. Authors' collection.

was more intense than previous visual presentations. Stock items were transformed into material wealth.

The expression of effects, whether through individual products or vignettes, was the principal visual purpose of twentieth-century trade catalogues. Catalogue pictures reflected social values such as the growing concern for hygiene and improved sanitation in houses, which was cited in reform literature of the period. Advances in disease theory had turned reformers away from the use of ornamental or irregular surfaces in moldings toward plain surfaces.[9]

THE ARTFUL PICTURE

In addition to creating general trade publications, manufacturers experimented with new methods of presentation for selected products. In 1916 Morgan Company of Oshkosh, Wisconsin published a booklet illustrating a new line of exterior and interior doors depicted in "artistic" settings. The company broke from traditional presentation methods; they used pictures that embedded their doors in the richest interior contexts used for trade catalogues of the period. For the cover of the hand-sewn, fifty-page booklet the company chose a heavy, slightly textured paper and featured calligraphic initial letters and an artful typeface. Each plate consists of two panels: a narrow horizontal section illustrating an appropriate building in which a Morgan door could be installed and a large vertical panel with a fully developed design vignette. Framing the panels are sectional drawings of Morgan door stiles and rails. Labels are minimal, but artifact-filled environments ably convey extensive information about design values. (3.6)

The trade name on the door suggests the existence of an entire furnishing style appropriate to this

Ramona C-705, a seven-room house, representative of the Western homes designed by Trowbridge and Ackerman expressly for the Curtis Companies.

3.7. In the Curtis catalogue, the manufacturer sought totality of design in which his woodwork and the architect's building form were interdependent. The Romona design. Architectural Woodwork: The Permanent Furniture of Your Home (Clinton, Iowa: Curtis Companies, 1920), 26. Authors' collection.

Views of the entrance hall, dining room and living room in the Western home, Ramona C-705, illustrated on page 26, showing Curtis Woodwork of Western character for different parts of the house.

3.8. A single product—the china closet in the dining room panel, for example—is central to a specific interior scheme, and clustered elements—French doors, a flight of stairs, and a closet door in the entrance hall—present a layered accumulation of style characteristics. Interiors for the Romona. Architectural Woodwork: The Permanent Furniture of Your Home (Clinton, Iowa: Curtis Companies, 1920), 28. Authors' collection.

setting, which represents an arts-and-crafts treatment. Design features include a dull gloss finish on heavily grained wood, rough plaster, and built-in units. The picture presents a unified aesthetic with multiple meanings: style and taste are essential for interior design, and Morgan's products engender both; the way of life depicted is obtainable for city dwellers, and architectural features are the aesthetic equal of other goods. Each page in the catalogue reflects the same socioeconomic level, the same cultural values. Although this approach is nothing more than a marketing strategy for Morgan Company, it also indicates a change in trade catalogue design and philosophy, heralding a new kind of pictorial logic for everyday architecture. In buying a door, the customer buys culture.

Four years later, Curtis Companies developed *Architectural Woodwork*, a housing and millwork catalogue aimed at middle-class buyers interested in stylistic conventions. Curtis labeled their models

"Colonial Home," "Southern House," "English Dwelling," and "Western House." The New York architectural firm of Trowbridge and Ackerman designed all of them. Curtis extended the concept of the Morgan booklet and spelled out the integration of their products in specific house styles. In earlier trade catalogues, references to specific aesthetics were uncommon; most treatments of exteriors and interiors strove for more generalized effects marketed as trade names such as those for mantels—Hilton, Kirkland, and Lakota.

Curtis introduced its presentations with a full-page painting of each house and its site to announce the style. Next came a page of narrative describing essential features of the design. The following page portrayed interior perspectives as idealized settings in which the systematized materials of Curtis Companies had been assembled in subdued and artful patterns for consumers' consideration. In this presentation Curtis integrated the graphic design of the book with the interior design of the rooms and an array of special products.

Such items were visually augmented by cultural information celebrating an ideal middle-class life: a display of furnishings and accessories that signified comfort and beauty. For the manufacturers, a way of life was easier to ascertain than a style. A china closet may have been deemed appropriate for the western house, but Curtis sales listings identified it as colonial in style. Indeed, this same item was an option for the colonial and southern houses. The company had a limited array of products that it marketed to embrace stylistic conventions of the period. The furnishings and decoration for the Western House, which are not related to the overall design of the building, indicate that the company was being opportunistic. (3.7)

In the Curtis catalogues, the totality of portrayed design is linked by millwork—bounded and integrated, wall to wall, floor to ceiling—and each design pattern reinforcing the others. Yet the millwork is subsumed into a larger image. It is the image, the illustration, that is being sold to the consumer. The products play a subtle role. The subtitle of the catalogue, *The Permanent Furniture for Your Home*, suggests that the millwork, called woodwork by the 1920s, is the design element on which consumers should rely to sustain the quality of their interior designs. (3.8)

DISSEMINATING DESIGN THROUGH PICTURES

The impact of trade catalogues on the construction of everyday buildings was enormous. Tradesmen of all kinds, general and specialized contractors, architects and their clients see studied the contents and chose details or systems for installation. But consumers learned to build the picture from a number of publications. Again there were building trade papers, such as *Carpentry and Building*, published in New York City from 1879 to 1930, which helped to disseminate design and construction information; however, such trade papers were closely tied to manufacturing.

Popular publications were directed at specific audiences. Leland Roth discusses the role of *Ladies'*

Home Journal editor Edward Bok in raising the standard for single-family houses.[10] Bok's *Journal* had wide circulation, and women across the country read it for ideas about home improvement and decorating. From 1895 to 1919 Bok published drawings of model houses commissioned from American architects, including Frank Lloyd Wright. Bok's target audience was the middle-class family; he anticipated that his readers could afford to build a house valued at three times their annual income, he assumed that they would build in the suburbs. The house models he chose to publish varied stylistically. The first was an arts and crafts type, the second a Georgian colonial revival, but he also commissioned a northern farmhouse and Elizabethan and Dutch colonial homes. Sometimes a complete set of plans was available from the model house architect.

After 1904 the magazine published articles about the California bungalow, and it is credited with popularizing the type. The journal also published "pamphlets on how to build a house as well as several plan books." There are no records about how many *Journal* model houses were built, although the company solicited photographs of such from their readers.

If *Ladies Home Journal* spoke to middle-class folks, local lumber dealers and lumber trade associations sponsored plan books that served a broad cross-section of society. Most of the publications they distributed were highly pictorial. In 1906 Wyckoff Lumber and Manufacturing of Ithaca, New York published *Cornell Portable Houses*, a catalogue of auto houses, summer cottages, playhouses, contractors' offices, and the like, that were ready-made emergency buildings "erected without nail or screw." The cottages were shipped "knocked down" and crated and could be erected or taken down in a day by two people. The primary building material was white pine, and the little buildings were constructed with "Cornell standard interchangeable sections" (sections rabbeted and held together by key-bolts and angle irons) and were "elastic as far as dimensions are concerned." The catalog has one photograph of a standard garage (an auto house) in place, and the remaining pictures are perspectives, with a facing page of information. All the drawings place the product in a context, such as trees, shrubs, and a path or driveway. Portable buildings have been part of the vernacular marketplace for a long time, and Wyckoff was merely developing a product line that fit a regional need.

More typical of lumber dealer publications are *Home and Garden*, published by J. Dyre Moyer and Thomas Lehigh Coal of Willow Grove, Pennsylvania, *Colorful Homes* put out by the Valley Lumber Corporation in Roanoke, Virginia, and *Modern Ranch Homes* offered by the Barker Lumber Company of Dedham and Waltham, Massachusetts. All three booklets are printed in color. *Home and Garden* (ca.1925) is entirely pictorial. Each page has a perspective of a house design, a plan, and two details: a drawn vignette and a photograph. The focus on the booklet is the English-type home, and the front cover home is a model called "The Lowell" that suggests New England, but "the steep roof and gables identify it as of English origin."

Colorful Homes is a large-format book with a modern colonial revival on the cover. The second page describes the National Housing Act and "the certainty of ACTUAL ownership before you," because of FHA-insured mortgages. Each page has a large perspective and a floor plan. The models are all numbered, for example, No. 778-B, and each page has a paragraph of marketing information. The index lists the houses by number of rooms—four rooms (one-story) through seven rooms (two-story)—and the National Plan Service is credited as the source for the designs. Exact copies of original working drawings are included at the back of the book, along with information about reversing plans, getting supplementary detail drawings, changes in plans, and special plans that incorporate the customer's ideas.

Barker Lumber's *Modern Ranch Houses* is a National Plan Service publication from 1951. The book features varieties of ranch houses for town or country living. An introduction lays out the advantages of the house type and is then followed by an inventory of designs, all identified by product number. Most pictures are in color, and each page has the usual perspective and plan, with one exception: plans are shown with or without a developed basement. There is also an essay on the modern kitchen, and the centerfold has a plan with four exterior treatments. On the next page the same designs are offered with an alternative plan that accommodates northern and Deep South climates and eliminates the basement.

The J. F. Anderson Lumber Company of Minnesota published a small booklet, *Anderson's "Bilt-Well" Homes*, perhaps during or just after the Great Depression. Each design scheme is offered as "a progressive program for building." Models are shown with trade names such as "The Amboy" and "The Jackson," and many have three plans: A, B, and C. Anderson suggests that house buyers build over time, as their financial situation improves. Thus plan A is a two-room house, B a four-room, and C, five or six rooms. For those who could afford to build an entire house, there were a few two-story models and a bungalow, with one exterior treatment but four different floor plans.

Local communities could put out their own plan books. A group of building contractors and merchants in Brunswick, Georgia did just that with *Homes As New as Tomorrow*. Ideal Plan Service of Gretna, Louisiana supplied the plans. The sponsors are listed on the outside and inside of the covers. Each page has a black-and-white photograph of a built house and a floor plan. Plan numbers designate the models.

In 1941 Amos D. Bridge Sons published *The Book of Bungalows* "as recommended by the F.H.A. Victory Housing, National Defense Program." Despite the control of war materials, the book encourages building. Each page has a black-and-white photograph of a built house and two plans with their own trade names. The alternative plan either increases or decreases the cubic feet of the structure.

Lumber trade associations also produced plan books for general distribution. In 1929 the National Lumber Manufacturers Association published *For Home Lovers*, an artful book with hand printing instead of set type, and pages full of photographs of built houses accompanied by plans and well-drawn sketches of scenes in the house. The Ponderosa Pine Woodwork, a trade organization of lumber producers, offered *Today's Idea House*. It is really a teaching booklet, with "New views, New pointers on increasing Home Comfort, Convenience and Beauty with Ponderosa Pine Woodwork." Single pages offer "new views" and "new pointers" on closets, doors, stock sizes, windows, and so forth, all are illustrated with photographs of wood products installed in real houses and with sketches.

Some lumber firms that specialized in designs for summer cabins and camps. Some of those firms turned to plan services for drawings, such as Adirondack Lumber Company, which produced *Summer Homes and Lodges* (1932) with the plans by National Plan Service. The Gustav Loewenthal Company, Middleton, Connecticut, produced *Our New Book of Summer Homes* (1930) with plans from the journal *Building Age*. Lastly, Exchange Sawmills Sales Company, Kansas City, Missouri, commissioned architect Harry Wagner to design the cottages. All the illustrations are hand drawn, either drafted plans or freehand sketches.

Another source for information about design and building aimed at a general audience was the materials produced as university extension bulletins and home reading courses. These were marketed throughout each state by land-grant universities and extension service specialists and were intended as guides for the improvement of farm economy and rural life. The first bulletins dealt with agricultural subjects and were directed toward men, but these were quickly followed by publications for rural women dealing with many aspects of farm life. Lessons on improving the organization and design of the farm home conveyed the viewpoint that the incorporation of design concepts into everyday living, coupled with technological advancements, could be a liberating force in the lives of rural women and their families. This progressive deterministic perspective claimed that good design provided relief from the drudgery of housework and that properly designed environments positively influenced family life.[11]

Extension bulletin authors led readers away from ornate, highly compartmentalized design schemes emphasizing eclectic picturesque effects to simpler, less cluttered schemes that emphasized respect for materials, utility, and the power of line and plane in composition. They also stressed the necessity of relating design principles to taste, which they justified by highlighting specific values. They asked women to engage in right living, to pay attention to hygiene and sanitation (for disease control), and to cultivate a new sense of beauty. The earliest such publication relating to design—the second lesson in *Cornell Reading-Course for Farmers' Wives*—emphasized the desirability of acquiring taste informed by design principles. (3.9)

In the next decade authors echoed the theme of simplicity in a multitude of bulletins. Liberty H. Bai-

CORNELL
Reading=Course for Farmers' Wives
PUBLISHED BY THE COLLEGE OF AGRICULTURE OF CORNELL UNIVERSITY, FROM NOVEMBER TO MARCH, AND ENTERED AT ITHACA AS SECOND-CLASS MATTER UNDER ACT OF CONGRESS OF JULY 16, 1894.
MARTHA VAN RENSSELAER, *Supervisor*.

| SERIES I. FARMHOUSE AND GARDEN. | ITHACA, N. Y., DECEMBER, 1902. | No. 2. DECORATION. |

DECORATION IN THE FARM HOME.

EVERY human being is responsible for making his own part of the world as beautiful as possible—to cause a flower to bloom where none had bloomed before, to rid a doorway of unsightly weeds, to paint a weather-beaten surface of the house, to hang a picture that will mean something in the life of the observer. This desire to beautify seems to be common to mankind; the one who does not find this in his inclination may have become too absorbed in arduous duties to allow it to find expression.

The farm home is the place where millions of boys and girls are bred and taught. The character of this home will impress itself on these young minds. Do you wonder that many a boy and girl, looking out into life, are attracted to the homes that they see in the city?

FIG. 10. *A simple and inexpensive decoration.*

State of New York — Department of Agriculture.— Farmers Wives' Reading-Course Bulletin No. 2.

3.9. The *Cornell Reading-Course for Farmers' Wives* conveyed the belief that any woman could learn principles in decoration if she studied nature to simplify and elevate her taste. "Decoration in the Farm Home," Cornell Reading-Course for Farmers' Wives 1, no. 2 (December 1902): cover page. Mann Library, Cornell University.

ley and Clarence A. Martin, coauthors of *Tasteful Farm Buildings* and *The Plan of the Farm House*, called for simple, direct, well-proportioned buildings: "There is no abstract canon of good taste in farm buildings except that they shall be perfectly adapted to the uses for which they were designed and shall bear no meaningless or irrelevant parts or ornament . . . Good architecture, so far as externals are concerned, consists primarily in proportions, not in trimmings, excrescences, ornaments, and oddities."[12] (3.10)

In the 1911 lesson titled "Household Decoration," Helen Binkerd Young defined design principles based on visual qualities: "Unity of effect—a

3.10. Simplicity was cited as the basis for the design of entire buildings and interiors, like this "well-aligned design" from Helen Binkerd Young, "The Farmhouse," *Cornell Reading Courses* 2, no. 39 (May 1, 1913): 175. Mann Library, Cornell University.

simple, unified effect is the first quality . . . for interiors. This is true whether the interior be one room or several connecting rooms through which vistas are seen. All parts of the home picture should harmonize so as to produce one sustained impression. . . . No single object or surface should intrude itself on our immediate notice." Young divided her discussion into major design components: walls, floors, and woodwork. Walls, for example, unite a whole interior scheme, becoming a common background for furnishings, persons, and color (tones). Nature was the source of tones, and the preferred tones were soft. Brilliant colors should be "accents or fleeting effects."[13]

To teach women how to perceive good design, Young sometimes turned to the design and arrangement of furniture, stressing that each piece should be "strong and honest, and [that] the shape of each piece should be a frank statement of its use." She elaborated: "Furniture showing an elaborate bowed or curved structure should be viewed with suspicion . . . any variation in outline, or any decoration, should follow or fit the structural shape. Gentle, unrestrained curves may be introduced to soften the outline, and angular corners may be rounded, without impairing the strength of the members. . . . The structural shape of a chair takes its cue from the human body."[14]

Other bulletin writers soon picked up the message of total design and recast it in their own terms.

Winifred Gettemy of Iowa State College of Agriculture and Mechanical Arts wrote in 1913: "Home furnishing is not a question of money, chiefly, but of knowledge. Comfort, simplicity and beauty, the essentials of a well furnished home, are within the reach of even the small income, provided the one who directs the furnishing has some understanding of line, proportion, and color, the laws that govern ornamentation." Having established her philosophy, Gettemy maintained that the ideal house "must be planned systematically, not only with respect to its construction but also with respect to climate, the character of site, the direction of winds, drainage and other factors." Like manufacturing trade catalogues of the same date, Gettemy had little interest in style and discouraged people from attempting to reproduce historic styles for inexpensive houses, arguing that "the simple straight construction line of good proportions is better adapted to the needs and moderate means of the American family."[15]

Gettemy's goal was to teach women to look for compact plans and for houses with special features: porches, formal entrances, porches counterbalanced with a chimney, and unity in balance for fenestration. She advised avoiding oval, diamond, or small-sized windows because "such irregular openings give the house a very unsystematic aspect." Gettemy redrew the image of the acceptable house in 1913. Her attack on accent windows was directed at special effects such as irregular cottage windows. She also discouraged the purchase of ready-made plans as unsuited to the needs of the family.[16]

In advising readers to rely on value in interior design, Gettemy employed pictorial imagery: "The natural divisions of a room may be likened to those in a landscape: floor—earth; walls—foreground; ceiling—sky. In a landscape these divisions are of distinct values, ranging from the earth with the darkest value, to the foreground, medium, and finally to the sky, the lightest." She encouraged housewives to think of an interior as a whole in which "connecting rooms create vistas and rooms should relate to each other and the hall."[17]

Young and Gettemy employed conventional notions of pictorial thinking to educate readers. In discussing the detailing of a house, Young asked readers to think of the house as a picture in which windows and doors appear as accents contrasting with the background of the wall. To teach figure–ground relationships, Young explained: "Windows especially are the eyes that give expression to the architectural face of the dwelling."[18] She advocated for refined proportions, simple rooflines, and interesting but not startling contrasts between roof, walls, and openings. Teaching women to read a modern house form, Young stated that building mass should be low and broad, reinforced in design from the position of the eaves and cornice lines and that the horizontal thrust of a building was mirrored by the window tops that were kept in a line but that varied the distance between floor level and sill.

Helen Scott's 1914 bulletin from Ohio State University defines the basic principles of home decoration. Scott maintained that design was a key element. A design must be purposeful, made "by combining straight lines into geometrized figures or by selecting some object from nature and adapting it to the material on which it is to be used." She reiterated a notion that things taken from nature must be changed "to harmonize with their new environment." To lend authority to her argument, Scott quoted English arts-and-crafts theorist William Morris on the necessity of simplicity, which comes from nature, and encouraged her readers to create a natural picture based on rational criteria.[19]

Scott also attacked the late-nineteenth- and early-twentieth-century predilection for collecting bric-a-brac, which, if useful, "is usually beautiful while that which has no use is a discredit to its owner." The appropriateness of bric-a-brac had been addressed in the first Cornell lesson: "To a great extent pictures take the place of bric-a-brac . . . [pictures have done more] to elevate the character and the taste of individuals than all the worked cardboard, the embroidered lambrequins, and the many fantastic objects which are collected and treasured."[20] Scott's definition of the useful as the beautiful is a resounding endorsement of industrial production and modern aesthetics. Women could find lessons for modern living in the windows of the hardware store.

By 1915 Young advises her readers that "slowly and silently an exchange of influence takes place between the individual and his environment." Because each absorbs the most conspicuous qualities of the other, frictionless environments are needed. Readers need to cultivate two qualities: a sense of

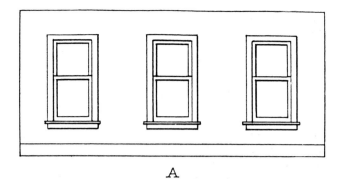

A

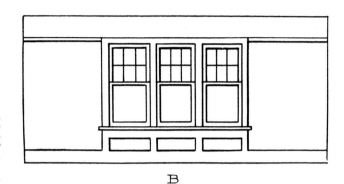

B

3.11. Young centered her argument about window arrangements on function and its correlative of beauty, and she loaded her case against separated fenestration by modifying the composition to incorporate a molding, a picture rail above, and an elaborate apron below the windows. From Helen Binkerd Young, "The Arrangement of Household Furnishings," Cornell Reading Courses 4, no. 85 (April 1, 1915): 145. Mann Library, Cornell University.

arrangement and a sense of selection. To teach principles of grouping or massing, Young turned to fenestration, pointing out that windows at wide intervals break "both the lighting and the wall areas into several insignificant parts," but if windows are grouped, the "arrangement is not only more interesting . . . but it is more sensible, since it leaves wall spaces on either hand for furniture. Furthermore, a single flood of light coming through a group of windows is more effective than three shafts of light that so cross and re-cross each other that it is almost impossible to place a piece of furniture."[21] Banding or grouping windows is a characteristic of both late-nineteenth- and early-twentieth-century architectural design, but emphasis on the benefits of concentrated light also reinforced the emerging interest in an open plan, fully realized internally when light, air, and circulation were integrated.[22] (3.11)

There was a moral imperative in home reading lessons and bulletins. Authors implied that they were making the rural home, whether old or new, a better place to live and were liberating the homemaker from housework through the enlightenment of design principles and pictorial effects. The publications advocated modernity and a new way of life.

CONCLUSION

Trade catalogues, plan books, and extension bulletins relied on pictorial logic to convey their argument for modern living. Manufacturing saturated the consumer with pictures of products and systems. Bulletin writers advised women to make a home a picture at every opportunity, inside and out; manufacturers composed their own idealized pictures of home to sell products. Although the primary motives of both groups were different, industrialization allowed their intentions to become intertwined. Historian Dolores Hayden explains that the interaction had its downside for women who struggled to overcome "the split between domestic life and public life created by industrial capitalism." The struggle was reflected in the consumption of industrial building materials and the development of the women as designers.[23]

The political assertion that the home was equal to the workplace was tied to a homemaker's capacity to arrange and define her home as a beneficial environment. In this the millwork manufacturer was an unwitting conspirator. As historian Clifford Clark put it: "By equating the benefits of the material world with moral excellence and by associating the useful and the beautiful together, plan-book writers and housing reformers elevated the single family dwelling to a new position of importance."[24] Millwork manufacturers elevated their products to the status of the house: moldings, doors, and sash represented the same moral excellence. The products themselves became the standard.

Both the reformer and the millwork manufacturer had an interest in associating the useful with the beautiful, and both had an interest in empowering men and women to make the connection. The importance of home ownership and of the single-family dwelling as the setting for culture—implied in trade catalogue pictures—was reinforced by the appeal to ethics, to the development of taste, and to the perception of beauty as tied to moral development. Nineteenth-century manufacturers were not interested in moral development, but twentieth-century producers, sensing the influence of domestic science, created home environment pictures replete with evidence of taste.[25] Their pictures invited the perception of beauty derived from the usefulness of milled products.

From 1910 on, trade catalogue vignettes were clean and fresh looking, picturing the kind of rational living that was encouraged for rural families. Outreach specialists and manufacturers shared some design values; both embraced the reform movement in housing and the new emphasis on family in American life. Their use of pictures to communicate and disseminate values is part of what made manufactured vernacular architecture a successful enterprise and made building the picture a unique cultural phenomenon.[26]

THE COTTAGE

Everyone loves a home; everyone loves trees. The mature tree ready for harvesting is not allowed to die and waste, but is converted into lumber from which homes are built. Young growing trees, stately trees, then the completed home of wood—a cycle of cooperation between man and nature—true conservation of America's only natural resource."

—Back cover, National Lumber Manufacturers Association, *For Home Lovers*, 1929.

In the nineteenth century the "natural" cycle of timber–lumber–home produced a significant inventory of house types, the leading one of which was the cottage. In terms of outward appearance and interior finish, the American cottage is largely the product of the machine technology that made the mass production of millwork possible. Beginning in the middle of the century, the cottage became a distinctive architectural object that changed the character of everyday built environments. As a representation of a cultural ideal, the cottage was the key element in a series of single-family houses that delivered the same value to different audiences—no matter the form, plan arrangement, or visual attributes—from the 1840s to the suburban house of contemporary times.

Home environments framed and finished in wood became part of everyday life. The emergence of the cottage brought specialized goods such as

MODERN PERIOD.

WITHIN the present half century domestic architecture has been running a race with the general development and prosperity of America. Countless styles from all climes, with modifications and abbreviations, have been made subservient to the convenience and tastes of a mixed population. Cottages and villas combining the beautiful with the practical and useful in design, and as variously adorned as the idiosyncrasies of the human character, dot the length and breadth of our land. Many of these are in themselves the expression of sentiment, self-respect, and artistic culture.

4.1. *The Homes of Modern America*, ed. Martha Lamb (D. Appleton & Co., 1879), 148. Authors' collection.

windows and doors, identified in trade catalogs as "cottage" style, to the marketplace. These and other wood products were shipped across North America,

4.2. Postcard, Rudman house under construction, ca. 1900. Authors' collection.

even exported to England and the European continent. Regional industrial centers developed, such as Tonawanda, New York, just north of Buffalo, that sent millions of board feet of products across the Great Lakes and to the Mississippi River towns that supplied millwork to the southern and western regions. Cottage design itself was disseminated through plan books, and thousands of homebuilders ordered inexpensive plans for local sites. Building and manufacturing papers, following the paths of the goods, disseminated design and production ideas to subscribers. Cottage neighborhoods altered the character of towns and cities, and the solitary cottage changed the landscape. Thus, nineteenth-century America developed a version of the ideal house from a culture of production that seemingly had no limits, and from houses that represented the symbolic expression of industrial power through millwork and pictorial effects. (4.2)

DEFINING THE COTTAGE

A cottage can be defined simply as an informal dwelling house, but to understand it conceptually, we need to take into account historical definitions, typical floor plans, building sites, and exterior design features. Historical definitions include the following:

- Peter Nicholson, *Dictionary of Architecture* (1854): "a name mostly applied to a small house, erected for the use and accommodation of the farm laborer, or those engaged in some other occupation, but more generally of those employed in agriculture"
- Robert Stuart, *Cyclopedia of Architecture* (1854): (from the Saxon *cot*) "A small house or habitation, the humble dwelling of the poor"
- George Garnsey, *American Glossary of Architectural Terms* (1887): "Generally applied to a small dwelling"
- Russell Sturgis, *Dictionary of Architecture and Building* (1901): "In the nineteenth century, a country house supposed to be simple as compared to the residences of the wealthy people in the neighborhood . . . a temporary home for a family which lives ordinarily in the city . . . a private dwelling house of any, even of the greatest, size and cost. . . . " And for the *cottage orne*: "In England, early in the nineteenth century, a small villa or rural residence designed in a free and semi-rustic style, far superior in finish to the common farmer's cottage, but less pretentious in architectural style than the formal villa of the time."[1]

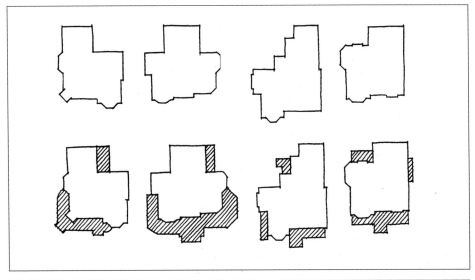

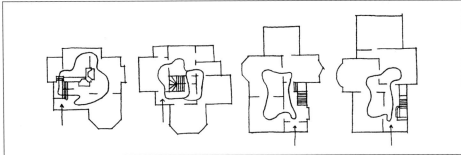

4.3 & 4.4. Typical cottage plan shapes (*top row*), plans with porches (*middle row*), and typical cottage plan circulation (*bottom row*) from Jan Jennings and Herbert Gottfried, *American Vernacular Interior Architecture, 1870–1940* (Ames: Iowa State University Press, 1988).

• John Crowley traces the invention of the modern English cottage to the middle of the eighteenth century, when the idea of comfort began to connote "self-conscious satisfaction with the relationship between one's body and its immediate physical environment."[2]

In sum, historical definitions refer to the English agricultural origins of the cottage, to informality and rusticity (nonclassical, asymmetrical forms), to freedom of expression, to variety of building materials, and to rough finish. After 1850 the rustic qualities of the American cottage came from diverse visual and tactile effects on the exterior, and, as for construction, cottages were precisely fitted, a consequence of using milled products and skilled carpenters. Geographically, the American cottage was built in rural settings (including shoreline and lakefront, hilltop, and farm site) and along suburban streets and on town lots.

The architectural character of the generic American cottage is best seen in an analysis of plan and form. A typical 1880s cottage plan reveals an irregularly shaped figure with a number of projecting elements (4.3, *top row*). If the exterior porches and verandas are added to the basic shape (the hatched spaces, *middle row*) in 4.3, then the integration of inside spaces with exterior spaces of the cottage is clarified. The full meaning of cottage spatiality becomes clear when the interior circulation is examined. Within these irregularly shaped houses, residents were free to move from room to room on a continuous path. In 4.4, a circular line circumscribes a path through the rooms; an arrow indicates the entrance to the house. Each path has a kind of organic shape that facilitates freedom of movement.

The overall three-dimensional form of a cottage is logically related to its shape or plan, and the spirit of the plan can be understood from the elevations. This is the case for a cottage by architect Thomas J. Gould, published as an "English Cottage" in *Carpentry and Building*, 1881.[3] A perspective view places the cottage in its preferred setting, a spacious lot with space for a garden. The drawing also reveals the variety in texture created by the changes in building

4.5. Front elevation (*a*), right side elevation (*b*), left side elevation (*c*), and rear elevation (*d*) of English cottage from *Carpentry and Building* III, No. 6 (June (1881): 101.

materials and the play of light and shadow across the elevations. When the elevations are linked, that is, when we see them side-by-side (as in 4.5 a–d), the degree of change from one elevation to the next is amplified: the mixture of symmetry and asymmetry; the balance of sections that project from the main body of the house with those that recede into it; the variety in geometric shapes on the walls (including the shapes and sizes of windows); and the changes in

materials—brick foundation, clapboard body, and shingled attic with brick chimneys.

The freedom of assembly that characterizes Gould's elevations reinforces the freedom of arrangement in the plans of typical cottages. The construction methods and the use of millwork are the medium of exchange in a dialogue between the interior organization and the exterior composition. Moreover, exterior and interior millwork was the character-defining material in the cottage. A historical definition of the cottage centers on the technical history of woodworking machines, the production of wood products in the second half of the nineteenth century, the conceptual basis of the cottage as a single-family house, and eighteenth- and nineteenth-century architecture and landscape design theory. The American cottage has a strong presence in the built environment that results in streetscapes of highly expressive house forms, with intricate surfaces and intimate grounds.[4]

Of all the influences on the origins of the American cottage, the visual quality of cottage design (i.e., the pictorial aspects of its composition) and the reliance on perception to link the site with the building seem most significant. A cottage not only looks like it was built from a picture but it could also be the subject of a picture. If, in Ralph Waldo Emerson's words, "Nature offers all her creatures as a picture-language," ("The Poet," 1844) the cottage and its grounds offered a "picture-language" of their own—one that offered inhabitants and spectators alike an identity of place combined with a richness of perceptual experience.

Architecture critic Marina Griswold Van Rensselaer captured such richness in *The Century Magazine* (1886), wherein she described a cottage in Massachusetts:

> The house seems a vital growth from the rocks themselves . . . Quaint irregularities of arrangement and diversities of level therefore show within, and the exterior outline is unsymmetrical and broken. The result charms by its picturesqueness [that] not only attracts but satisfies us because practical needs compelled it and each of the interior features is . . . dictated either by a material necessity or by the laudable desire to make the most of all contrasted points of outlook. . . . While it has material fitness it has also such artistic fitness that its site and its surroundings seem to have been designed for the sole sake of service.[5]

The pictorial basis of Van Rensselaer's description was prevalent in the critical writing of the period, and it was the centerpiece of the architectural interpretation of the American cottage. Behind the evocative description is her expectation that one can have an exhilarating experience in the presence of a cottage, which seems a sign of the emerging power of these houses to express values appropriate to their time. It is important to note that much of what Van Rensselaer admired about the cottage was its various profiles. The theory behind such compositions derived in large measure from the writings of Alexander Jackson Davis and Andrew Jackson Downing. Davis and Downing were versatile designers of landscapes and buildings who developed their own applications of the theory of the picturesque. Davis admired "the wilder state of nature—its qualities of irregularity, movement, variety, rough texture, and bold contrasts"—which he linked with an emphasis on irregularity, freedom, and flexibility that "brought a release from the rigidity and limitations of the traditional box shape, which was opened in all directions, both upward and outward, and it liberated the composition of masses in plan and silhouette."[6]

Downing had more influence on cottage design than Davis. Downing promoted the country house as a means to advance a progressive civilization, to elevate the national character, and to instill a sense of morality and beauty in society.[7] In a series of books written from 1842 to 1850, Downing developed an argument for the useful and the beautiful, for the absolute beauty of form and the relative beauty of expression. He suggested that domestic architecture exhibit the freedom and play of everyday life, that overall design be spirited and pleasing, the parts not balanced—a sentiment based on his interpretation of the picturesque aesthetic, especially its visual power; irregularity and asymmetry were expressions of beauty. In Downing's taxonomy of houses, the villa represented the beautiful, the cottage the true.[8] Cottage design would rely on picturesque effects, and "as picturesqueness denotes power, it necessarily follows that all architecture in which beauty of expression strongly predominates over pure material beauty, must be more or less picturesque."[9] To convey architectural truth in design, Downing called for devices that blend with the landscape: windows, doors, chimneys, piazzas, bay windows, and so forth. By 1850 most of the details he imagined for the cottage were manufactured and available as trade catalog goods.

Establishing a linkage between site and building was at the heart of Downing's approach, and his

4.6. Perspective, Design no. 12, Hubert, Pirsson & Co., *Where and How to Build*, ca. 1880 Authors' collection.

The technical development of woodworking machinery and the efficient production of goods were central to the development of the cottage. Like the cottage type, woodworking machinery evolved from British ideas. Americans patented improvements on those as well as invented specific machines that suited American needs. The context for the use of these machines was the culture of production that evolved in the last decades of the nineteenth century, a culture derived from the belief that timber resources were unlimited, which led to voracious cutting and the conviction that there would be continuous population growth, settlement, and demand for construction.[13]

The growth of machine-tool companies took place from 1850 to 1900, as indicated by the proliferation of machine-tool companies from the Northeast to the Midwest, by the increase in the number of companies advertising in trade papers, and by the range of products in their trade catalogs.[14] This growth was paralleled by a period of intense millwork production from 1870 to 1910, when national economic development stimulated an emerging machine-tool industry to create an enormous wood products industry.[15]

The architectural and cultural success of the cottage was based on the expanded industry, especially the production of finished pieces of wood, where the smoothness of the goods' surfaces came to represent the transition from nature to culture, from crude huts and cabins to cottages. At the same time, machine-made products enabled designers and builders to simulate nature's irregularity and to use contrast and texture as pictorial values. These characteristics represent conditions of compromise, a further withdrawal from nature in terms of architectural sophistication, and yet an appeal to aesthetic values derived from nature.

To understand how this development came about, it is necessary to understand the technical history of woodworking machines. Early milling machines were metalworking types that relied on slow speed. The technical knowledge learned from working metal was applied to woodworking machinery, but adapted to take into account the nature of wood, the differences among species (e.g., relative

designs for houses included planting designs for gardens, screening with trees and shrubs, and circulation pathways through the grounds. The plant materials and the formal structure of his site plans were intended to enhance visual effects and blend with the windows and piazza of the house. The cottage site was conceived as an integrated system of views: short range, mid range, and vistas (from within the grounds, from the grounds back toward the house, and from inside the house outward). Downing's house plans were too compartmentalized to sustain many interior vistas, but later in the century, such views were used to supplement exterior views.[10] The focus on viewing and pictorial effects dissolved the distinction between the house and nature, between house and garden.[11] It follows that if a garden could be a middle term between architecture and Nature, then a cottage, through the effects of its building materials and design, could be the middle term between natural and industrial power. From a historical point of view, a garden "defines itself by its fence. . . . The fence emerges as the leading constituent or theme."[12] The nineteenth-century cottage, then, became another kind of enclosure, a cultivated ground, articulated by wood products.

softness and grain character), and the actions that were appropriate for cutting with or across the grain.[16] In all cases, high speed was required because of the fibrous character of wood; slow speed tore the surface. The operations used in working wood are scission, paring, combinations of the two, and abrading.[17] Scission entails cutting the fibers across the grain. The principle scission machine is the saw, which penetrates the material, reduces it to dust, and leaves a kerf in the wood that marks the passage of the blade. Paring produces chips or shavings by acting along the fibers in the direction of their length. Machines of this type may be called planers, surfacers, matchers, molders, or routers. Combinations of scission and paring, which include lathes and boring machines, act on the wood both lengthwise and crosswise. Abrading is a finishing action; its most common tool in millwork production is the sandpapering machine.

The nineteenth-century American practice of converting timber to lumber and lumber to specialty goods took place in steps: debarking, removing the outer slabs, and resawing rough wood into boards with more precise dimensions. Most lumber sawn for millwork was thin stuff, one inch or one-and-a-quarter-inch thick, and the boards could then be cut into various widths to be planed smooth, redimensioned, and edged. Since millwork included so many products, some materials were processed for particular machines; for example, timber bolts (short logs) were cut specifically for shingle machines. Then again, period trade catalogs illustrated specialty machines for specific functions such as boring, dovetailing, shearing, and veneering. Numerous variations existed in the operation of machine types, and therein lies a good deal of the technical history of American woodworking machinery: creating specialty machines and tools for particular products, sequences of action, or multiple functions, such as the famous Woodworth planing machine (1828) that planed all four sides of a board.

From a design point of view, the history of woodworking machines centers on three points: (1) the ability of the manufacturer to increase the speed of the cutter knives—the iron and steel edges that dressed the planks; (2) the improvement of the control of the wood as it entered and exited the machine (a problem that brought about the implementation

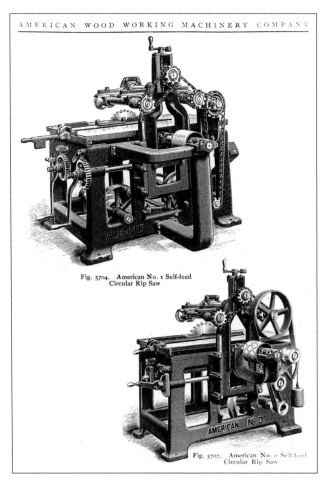

4.7. Self-feeding rip saws, *American Wood-Working Machine Company* (Chicago: the Company, ca. 1900). Authors' collection.

of power feeds to the cutters and rollers to control passage); and (3) and the development of machines that carried out multiple operations in one pass, which decreased the handling of the wood and improved overall efficiency.[18] Solving these problems in the last decades of the nineteenth century had a major impact on the production of millwork and on the physical properties of millwork, much of which featured finely finished, intricate designs, such as multiple surfaces in a molding profile. In turn, these properties influenced the appearance of any surface on the outside or inside of a cottage.

The common ingredient in the engineering considerations seems to have been control, because better control would allow for increased speeds in feeding boards to the machine and increased speed in scission and paring. With control came reliable production and the prospect of less loss of material and greater safety for the worker, though there is

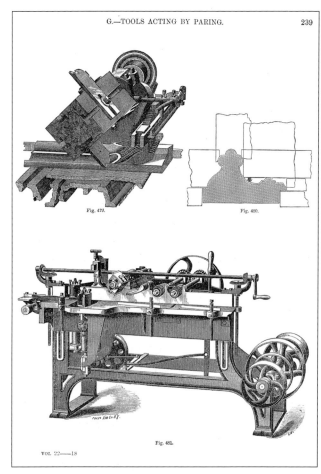

G.—TOOLS ACTING BY PARING. 239

Fig. 479.

Fig. 480.

Fig. 481.

VOL 22——18

4.8. Molding machine, cutter head and knives, with molding application. F. R. Hutton, "Report on Power and Machinery Employed in Manufacturing." *Tenth Census of the United States* (1888). Authors' collection.

little mention of safety issues the literature until the twentieth century.[19]

The history of American woodworking machinery is related to the use of timber. Although there was no national timber census until 1850, historian James Defebaugh estimated the total area of the United States in 1906 at 2.9 million square miles, of which nearly half was "original wooded area."[20] Not all the forestlands contained marketable timber, and not all species were suitable for building materials. Defebaugh notes that the history of early lumbering centers on the cutting of white pine and hardwoods, both of which were principal millwork woods. White pine forests were plentiful from Maine to eastern Minnesota, and as they were depleted, yellow pine was cut in the South and West.

By 1850 building with wood was a longstanding American tradition, and, thereafter, people every-

where in the country came to expect to build with machine-dimensioned, dried wood. The impression that timber and lumber were unlimited derived from the constant "overestimate of the supply" in the lumbering districts. Overestimates led to wasteful use and low prices, which, in turn, accommodated aggressive attitudes toward the resource, such as large-scale cutting, high production, and much investment in building.

MILLWORK AND THE COTTAGE

Cottage design is a direct outcome of the success of (1) the new framing techniques, which shifted emphasis away from a heavy timber-framing system as a prime determinant of exterior appearance, toward a lighter frame that allowed for variety in ground plan; (2) the design of elevations, especially in regard to openings for windows and doors; and (3) in surface effects, both outside and inside. Millwork was the source of the effects. The application of millwork involved the creation of pictorial arrangements in which passive walls were overlaid with active moldings and stickwork. Examples of this kind of thinking were published in period trade magazines such as *Manufacturer and Builder, Carpentry and Building, Illustrated Wood-Worker,* and plan books, so that architects, builders, and carpenters could replicate the effects.

Although much of the enthusiasm for millwork was reflected on the exterior, a cottage interior could be densely overlaid with millwork too. An early example of a full handling was published in *The American Builder* (1874). Plate 41 illustrated two interior scenes of "a model dwelling . . . its plans and general arrangement being adapted to the wants of every nine families out of ten who can afford to spend between $4,000 and $5,000 on a country dwelling."[21] "The View of Hall and Stairs" is of particular interest, as described in the text, focusing on the wood:

In design 43, plate 41, is shown a view of the hall and stairs; the beams overhead are of pine dressed and chamfered; the floor boards do not show, being covered with paper-board, then veneered with wood veneer, plain, and a molding placed in angles; a remarkable inexpensive and beautiful finish; the whole is then varnished; there is no inside painting, the woodwork being shellacked and varnished; the hall floors are narrow strips of ash and walnut; the stairs are light ash, likewise the wainscoting, and finished flat in oil, the whole effect is very fine, neat and decidedly homelike . . . [22]

It is clear from the description that the essence of the hall vignette is the quality of the woods, their finishes, and the accumulative effect of the millwork: integrated wood grains and gloss. The hall sets the tone for the cottage interior, reinforcing the visual promise of the exterior design.

Millwork was also the primary medium for the conversion of older houses into dwellings that looked contemporary. In 1878 William Woolett published *Old Homes Made New* in which he explained how a variety of building types or interior spaces could be altered to bring them into their own time, such as the conversion of a Greek Revival house into an 1870s, multigabled affair.[23]

Trade journals published examples of how millwork defined houses or how far a builder might go to realize a style based on the arrangement of milled sticks. A typical cottage is large with a complicated roof plan and big intersecting volumes, resulting in expressive forms. Contrasting textures and ornamental effects are emphasized on the exterior. The body of the house might be clad with smooth clapboards with shingles in the gables. Each elevation may be thought of as a picture with several millwork motifs, and the combined pictures constitute the aesthetic dimensions of the exterior scheme.

Garden views from each side of the house afforded the spectator a different sequence of scenic effects, some of which reflected changes in interior function; for example, the dining room might have a bay window. Variations on each elevation provided for an animated building that masked its lightly constructed, shallow walls. The irregular placement of features, especially ornament and textures, simulated the characteristics of plant materials in the garden.[24] The freedom displayed on the exterior is revealed in the floor plan. One can move uninterrupted from the sitting hall to the other rooms. Symbolically, the ground plan simulated a walk in a garden—an experience based on sequences of integrated impressions, views, and vistas.

In this period, landscape gardening for country houses had a dual purpose of providing both variety and integration of land and house: "Our efforts . . . will be at first in the way of surfaces, straight and curved, formal outlines, and strong colors; these . . . blending by means of intermediate forms and hues, with the natural undulations, so that whether one view the landscape from the window, or sallying out, surveying the house and its surroundings, the

4.9. Views before and after alteration. William M. Woolett, *Old Homes Made New* (New York: A. J. Bicknell, 1878), plate 13. Authors' collection.

4.10. Elements of the side elevation and the ornamentation serve as a stage set for an event. Real Photograph Postcard, cottage and family portrait. Authors' collection.

impression . . . will be soothing and agreeable, though in different degrees from different points."[25]

As the cottage continued to grow in cultural importance in the 1880s, the focus on individuality grew exponentially. Of consequence for suburban development was the strategy of generating individual designs from multiple treatments of the same plan. These could be styled so that the plan was obscured from exterior view, an approach popular with builders and housing contractors. The other common strategy, referenced previously, was to vary the design of the elevations and the massing (i.e., the way the big volumes and big forms intersect) as in Gould's "English Cottage." In the article on Gould's design, the *Carpentry and Building* editors describe the cottage as "an adaptation of the present fashion in dwelling house architecture to the practical wants of our people, and to the requirement of our climate and modes of living."[26] There is no indication in the drawings or text that a particular climate had been addressed in the design. Rather, "modes of living" are at stake. In the design and construction of cottages, the architectural response to the modes-of-living requirement was to build houses that displayed "variety in effect." The one was the analog of the other, what M. G. Van Rensselaer called the "true expression of varied needs and purposes."[27] So the aesthetic and social interests of the period were addressed by the production and use of building materials. Gould employs a number of devices to create this impression of variety. The intent of such manipulations demonstrates an array of visual conceits and their relation to wood products. The overall composition both inside and out, expresses "varied needs and purposes" as a way to distinguish one building from another.

Woodworking machines made design options possible because their output, in extent and diversity, offered choices in arrangement of goods. Metaphorically, such a condition constitutes another kind of "garden"—a place where we celebrate abundance, leisure, freedom, and harmony of existence.[28] *Abundance*, in our usage, relates to the freedom of choice in design effects, both exterior and interior—effects all dedicated to expressing an overall harmony.

There are thousands of alternative products and patterns of arrangement with which to create groupings: for example, the interior trim that surrounds the windows and doors, or the way in which the entrance door engages the porch on the exterior and the hall on the interior. Each choice is a detail that is part of a "mixture," a deliberate blending. The term is borrowed from Sidney Robinson's study of eighteenth-century picturesque theorists. Robinson describes *mixture* as relying on abrupt variation and novelty: "Mixture is not directed toward recovering a proper balance, but to maintaining a continuous sequence of contrast . . . the function of an element is determined by its position in a sequence, not by its intrinsic nature."[29] Mixture is a response to a pleni-

4.11. View in main hall, William DeHart house, Carthage, Illinois; George W. Payne, architect. *Carpentry and Building* (March 1892): supplemental plate in Jennings, *Cheap and Tasteful Dwellings: Design Competitions and the Convenient Interior, 1879–1909*, Knoxville: University of Tennessee Press, 2005, 169.

tude in which variety and novelty are virtues. Cottage design utilized this principle in regard to surfaces (walls, floors, ceilings) and architectural fixtures (stairs, porches, windows, doors) through the use of millwork. On a larger scale, *mixture* entailed the working out of vigorous building masses, with their complex roof plans, irregular fenestration, and intricate cladding patterns. According to Robinson, in the eighteenth century, *mixture* also had political meaning; it referenced the restraint of power. But in the cottage era, the mixing of styles was a display of industrial power invested in visually appealing architectural effects.

THE CULTURE OF PRODUCTION

The development of woodworking machinery, the production of millwork, and the evolution of the cottage were part of a general period of high productivity and technological advancement.[30] Abundant and cheap natural resources fueled much of the progress, and in the millwork industry, laborsaving machines and the ready use of natural resources conjoined to create a vigorous market for building materials.

The production of woodworking machines and millwork products paralleled timber cutting and lumber production. And the cornerstone for timber

and lumber production was the perception of the never-ending availability of timber. Defebaugh states that an overestimate of the supply led to wasteful use and low prices.[31] His data on production and the value of goods reveal steady increases in the number of mills, workers, and product value from 1850 to 1900.

These figures apply to sawmills, planing mills operated with sawmills, and timber camps. To get the total picture of production for 1900, we add the output from planing mills not connected with sawmills: another 4,200 establishments, 73,627 workers, and products valued at $168,343,003.[32] Production increased steadily from 1850, no matter the state or region that led the way, and increases in production brought estimates about remaining timber.[33] In 1906 Defebaugh projected that timber would last only 50 years. Lumber production peaked in 1909–10 with 44.5 billion feet of lumber, which was more than double the output of 1880. In the peak year, planing mill and general mill products, which included millwork, were about 34 percent of total lumber production.

Two additional aspects of the production of millwork influenced the proliferation of cottages, the waste of timber and lumber, and the dissemination of information about the woodworking industry. In 1919 Nelson Courtlandt Brown estimated that only

Table 4.1. Production and Value of Products, 1850–1900

Year	Number of Establishments	Number of Wage Earners	Value of Products
1850	17,474	51,218	$58,611,976
1870	25,832	149,997	$210,159,327
1900	33,035	382,840	$566,832,984

30–50 percent or less of wood cut in the forests was used for some product, and those figures did not take into account loss by fire, wind, insects, decay, and land clearing. Woodworking machines contributed to the waste through the size of the kerf. Loss of wood in logging and manufacturing depended on local efficiency. According to Brown, the categories of loss were bark, saw kerf, edging and trimming, slabs, inefficiency, carelessness, and loss in handling for a total of 40–57 percent. The loss in production could run as high as 55–77 percent, with little salvaged. Exhaust systems for dust and shavings were available to feed boilers by the 1870s, but this recovery accounted for only a fraction of the waste.[34]

How do we explain the industry's tolerance of such waste of timber? The only way it could have been ignored was with an assumption that the supply of timber was more than adequate for this level of consumption. Other possible explanations?: The culture of production had its own internal logic that was slow to adjust to market realities, and the consequences of production obscured the facts about large-scale woodwork production through a powerful cultural symbol—the widespread emergencies of single-family houses and the life they connoted.

A culture of production and new cottage architecture could not have developed without the dissemination of information about production and design. During the 1870s and 1880s, trade papers helped to promote the lumber, millwork, and woodworking machinery industries. All the publications relied on advertising for revenue. *Manufacturer and Builder* (1869, New York City) covered a wide range of topics in articles, illustrations, essays, and news briefs, all of which reinforced for the culture of production.

Readers could learn about production methods, new machinery, and developments in construction.

Each issue created the impression that manufacturing and housing construction were inextricably linked for the betterment of both. The articles were appreciative in point of view: manufacturing and building were part of something important, and all efforts within that framework were progressive. "New Shingle-Cutting Machine" (September 1870) is a typical machinery article, describing "Austin's Improved Shingle-Machine" with a focus on the machine's ability to reduce waste because it used a knife rather than a saw. *Manufacturer and Builder* editors stated that most of the copy for the article came from the manufacturer's literature. The journal carried advertising for machinery and building products, and often the issue in which a particular machine was featured had advertisements from the same company. Sometimes engravings that first appeared in articles were repeated in future advertisements. The same relationship existed between the articles and the manufacturers of other building materials, such as roofing goods, windows, and metal products. Building designs were included in each issue and treated the same as machines; authors assumed that every design was competent and an improvement.[35] The designers were practicing architects who intended their schemes to be replicated. Most house designs were cottages described as "picturesque in appearance" and availabletjhe in a range of prices and settings.

Illustrated Wood-Worker, begun in 1879 in New York City, became *Builder and Wood-Worker* in 1880, "A Journal of Industrial Art Devoted to Building, Wood-Working, and Decorative Interests." To distinguish it from other journals, it focused on the making of objects, such as furniture and decorative pieces, and the illustrations suggested how a design problem might be addressed. The illustrations for February 1879 were typical for the life of the journal: designs for a wall table, handrailing, mantel, and cabinet; a design for a sideboard; a Queen Anne cottage; lessons in practical carpentry and isometric projection; and a workingman's cottage. The examples were useful; they addressed skills, provided designs for copying, were diverse in subject matter, and reinforced the use of wood products. The drawings were rendered to convey aesthetic values, to look appealing.

4.12. Moving portable steam engines to the woods increased production. Here the engine powers a windlass that skids logs through the woods to a central location. Authors' collection.

The period also produced journals directed toward manufacturers, such as *Lumber World*, which began monthly publication in March 1881, in Buffalo, New York. A unique feature of *Lumber World* was a monthly report on accidents in very specific detail, including injuries and deaths that occurred on production lines. *Saw-Mill Gazette*, 1881, New York City, carried a great deal of advertising for woodworking machinery. The subtitle of the Gazette was "A Monthly Journal of Practical Information for Owners of Saw-Mills, Planing-Mills, Shingle-Mills, Sash, Blind and Door Factories, and Furniture Factories." The journal was directed at all aspects of production. An operator could find information on the latest machines or processes, and new producers could find advertisements for used machines and listings for timberlands. Reports on trade in individual states seem to have been written to inspire confidence in the business and, perhaps, encourage additional capital investment.

Trade journals were not the only means by which millwork production was acknowledged. Publications intended for architects, builders, and carpenters, such as *Carpentry and Building* (1879), published designs to be replicated and sponsored design competitions for houses. Articles about house designs included specifications for wood products. Entire books focused on specifications and on which wood species was appropriate for each function, for exam-

ple, *Specifications for Frame Houses* by Palliser, Palliser and Co. (1878).[36]

In popular writing, books such as E. C. Gardner's *Homes, and How to Make Them* (1878) were composed as a series of letters informing readers about materials and design. "Letter XIX" details the merits of wood, and each example, from framing to finish, became a rationalization for the use of machined products. For instance, Gardner encouraged the use of clapboards: "Hardly anything is better, but don't feel restricted to one mode. I send you some sketches suggesting what may be done in this department by a careful design in the use of wide boards and narrow boards, clapboards and battens; boards horizontal, vertical, and cornerwise. . . ."[37] Gardner's sketches illustrate partial, two-story elevations with the walls divided into panels, each panel filled with sticks arranged in contrasting patterns.

High production depended on vast timber resources and the belief that improvements in machinery were necessary, even natural. Innovation centered on machinery design. Patents were filed continuously during the height of productivity; the twelfth census (1900) reported 6,973 patents granted for woodworking machines. The range of patent ideas suggests the presence of technological diversity, especially in the furniture industry, where many of the same machine operations were employed. The high production of furniture and millwork during the same period increased the visible presence of wood in households.[38]

In house design, Andrew Jackson Downing suggested that the beauty of expression of the villa or cottage would derive from the character of the owner, a view generally attributed to the English theorist and critic John Ruskin.[39] During the cottage era, most houses were built on speculation rather than for clients, so the expression of beauty became identified with the expression of wooden building materials. The massive emergence of all kinds of cottages that boldly displayed millwork extended the character issue to a broader population. Downing wrote and designed for country gentlemen in the Eastern United States. Cottage designers and builders worked for any middle-class owner anywhere in the country. The whole system of mass-produced materials and replicated designs changed the ownership pattern and the geographic distribution of houses. Several historians have written about this change in the city and the suburbs, including Sam Bass Warner's study of street railway lines and urban growth in Boston; Kenneth Jackson's history of suburbanization that includes discussions of elite suburbs and affordable homes; and John Stilgoe's study of rural areas he calls "borderlands."[40] In each instance, the cottage is an agent of change.

The social movement that focused attention on the quality of home life, often referred to as the reform movement, had a cottage context. Many physical reforms, such as new arrangements of space and new interior finishes, were invented as reactions to cottages. Gwendolyn Wright studied these reforms and the model homes that replaced cottages in Chicago, in *Moralism and the Model Home*.[41] In *The American Family Home* social historian Clifford Edward Clark reconstructs the history of the ideal American middle-class home and includes discussions of how houses became individualized, how room functions changed over time, and how the cottage became the ideal suburban single-family house in the 1870s and 1880s.[42]

Early twentieth-century houses changed in overall appearance, but cottage sentiment and reliance on design effects with mass-produced millwork endured. In 1926 the Wood Homes Bureau of Cleveland, Ohio published the plan book *Better Homes at Lower Cost*. Each plate had a perspective, floor plans, and a paragraph of copy. Most houses had wood cladding, wood trim, porches, bay windows, and asymmetrical elevations.[43]

One model, "The Lynnhaven," celebrates wood construction, and millwork defines its character through a variety of products and contrasting patterns of arrangement. The nineteenth-century sense of mixture is gone in favor of a grouping of smoothly finished boards, artfully fitted around modern ideas about space and living. In the midst of the picture, one is not reminded of the industrial origins of the products but, rather, of their continuity with the English origins of the cottage, with eighteenth-century interests in utility and fitness brought to bear on the design of the common house.[44] Rhetorically, the Lynnhaven is another version of a traditional middle-class landscape—the built equivalent of a pleasant place.[45] The copy under the picture extols the natural context for this bungalow cottage. The house draws strength from its surroundings, and that makes it an "ideal suburban home."

The cottage solidified a number of different but related interests in late nineteent and early-twentieth-century America. The sense of freedom it conveyed stemmed from the wide variety of spatial configurations and exterior and interior elements it could employ. Symbolically the cottage came to represent the kind of excess Americans expected from natural resources as well as their power to transform them. The typical cottage could be airy, comfortable, and modern, while embracing the rustic (rough materials) and the smooth (manufactured finish). Composed as if the subject of a picture—strong lines, contrasting shapes and colors, augmented by the play of light and shadow both inside and out—the cottage addressed the pastoral view. It sprawled across the ground, a willing companion to a garden. Today, some of the visual qualities of cottages, especially the capacity for display, are alive in suburban house design.

5

AESTHETIC SYSTEM: EXTERIOR

Establishing inventories of construction materials and their patterns of usage and sorting structures by type are traditional approaches to investigating the origins of common everyday buildings. These methods produce quantities of facts and templates for ground plans and overall forms. Of equal importance are the various contexts in which these buildings were constructed, including how they were made and the environments to which they belong. The identification, classification and interpretation of tens of millions of structures is problematic; it means tracing the dissemination of materials and building types throughout every state and region. Thus sampling is the only way to make any headway.

Having collected a diverse sample, there are several approaches to sorting the buildings into sensible units; floor plans are a good place to start. A rich body of work derived from fieldwork in folklore and cultural geography has identified some fundamental building types based on shapes and relations between spatial units. American house plans, for example, progress from simple one- and two-room units to complex interior organizations that may include second and third stories, with spatial subdivisions on each floor or extensions from the main body of the house. In the early periods of building, reading interior organization from the

exterior was not so difficult, but over time it became more so.

A second method of sorting buildings is by considering building form, which includes the shape of a building, the volume contained by the shape, and the compositional strategies for integrating building masses on both the horizontal and vertical planes. In general all design is about how one thing relates to another as well as on what basis a relation is established and maintained. Building form is a product of relationships between the big elements: between structural units (walls and floors, walls and roof structure) and stories, between the private side of a house and its public side; between centrifugal forces spinning rooms and halls away from the center, and centripetal forces, pulling rooms and such toward the center; and between mass and void. The history of building forms is somewhat akin to the history of literary forms in that both sets of forms represent ways of thinking about the past and the present. Some forms endure because people continue to imagine their lives in association with a building type. Conversely, forms drop out of contention because people no longer imagine dwelling or working within them. In studying the modern system, there is always the issue of variation—minor deviations in the replication of previously built forms. Furthermore, market forces encourage experimentation.

The plan and the form do not address all aspects of a building. The grounds that house the building site impose relations with the body of the dwelling. The ways in which common buildings engage the land can generate a sense of locale or an affinity among groups of buildings. These landscape strategies also reveal something about how lives are led within and around the buildings proper. Cultural overlays lend both the exterior and the interior a visual and physical character. The overlays emerge from the general culture and operate as aesthetic and intellectual threads that bind periods and places together.

In all instances, reducing the millions of data to the most typical cases in each avenue of inquiry—plan, form, and aesthetic—is a reasonable first step. The point is not to restrict or limit the field of inquiry, but the sheer volume of buildings necessitates taking on obvious categories. Searches of the relevant primary and secondary literature and the reconnoitering of built environments have produced typologies for all three categories.

EXTERIOR AESTHETICS

Exterior treatments of buildings are closely allied with the dynamics of society. From 1870 to 1960, there was a considerable increase in population and major shifts in population distribution across the United States. Several developments paralleled the population changes, including changes in the econo-my and the emergence of new kinds of manufacturing and land development. Builders, architects, and developers responded in kind. The overall outcome was a new marketplace for vernacular architecture. One of the elements of the marketplace was building aesthetics, and one powerful expression of aesthetic intention was exterior appearance. The forms and, particularly, the elevations of a building were screens onto which aesthetic intentions could be projected. The primary strategy was the creation of a unified effect derived from the integration of building elements and details. A building's aesthetic treatment usually represents an ideal condition, a set of values deemed important to the time and place in which the building was constructed. The working out of the treatment or the aesthetic outcome depends on the effect of certain aspects, such as balance, unity of lines, integration of mass and void, the presence of light and shade, the use of symmetry and irregularity, and many more. Each of the aesthetic categories discussed in this chapter has a different mix of these qualities and a particular "reading" on the necessary intensity and presence of the qualities.

ITALIANATE AESTHETIC

By 1870 American building had already embraced classical design, especially the application of orders of architecture and the rules of proportion that the orders imply. Once vernacular builders moved beyond medieval English precedents and log structures, they turned to applications of classical systems. By the middle of the nineteenth century, Americans

5.1. Italianate cottage, Allen, Kansas. This small farmhouse has Italianate-style accents distributed over the form and on the surfaces, beginning with the entry system and spreading over the body of the house to the roof. Authors' collection.

were interested in adopting revival styles. Some of the new ideas, such as the Greek revival, seemed an extension of the Enlightenment cultural values that influenced government and the shaping of society at large.

Italianate design is derived from the classical tradition. It was applied to residential and commercial buildings, both in urban and rural settings. The history of Italianate building is related to two historical developments: (1) America's first foray into empire in terms of Western expansion and industrial production and (2) the adoption of aspects of French second-empire architecture (symbolized by the mansard roof). Both styles relied on the application of classical vocabulary, especially at the rooflines, the entry, and other openings. The overall approach is ornamental, meaning that enrichment, often in the form of moldings and projecting details, takes place at the junction of significant elements.

The small, square cottage in 5.1 is unusual in that the general form for Italianate houses is either a villa, sited parallel to the street, or a tall, narrow cottage built deep into a lot. But the detailing is characteristic of the style. The roof is a four-sided hip with a modest flare at the eaves and a small belvedere with a rail at the center. The façade has a porch that spans half the elevation, with six bracketed posts supporting the flat roof and a rail with balusters. The porch is a half-story above grade. The elevation has panels of wood cladding and trim, beginning with cornerboards and a frieze atop the cornerboards and a water table just above the foundation. Windows have wooden lintels. The roof establishes a profile for the house form,

5.2. This cottage is stripped of detail. The low hip roof, bay windows, and bracketed hood over the entry door indicate an Italian aesthetic intention. Authors' collection.

5.3. The Patton House, in Rapid City, South Dakota, was a small hotel. The plain form has bracketed eaves and ornamental porch posts as style details. Authors' collection.

and all the other details animate openings. The details express energy, and they counter the reserve of the Greek revival.

Italianate styling in commercial districts (figure 5.3) produced different results. It could create a bank of aligned storefronts, with their parapets and uppermost cornices in line or almost in line, and their floor divisions aligned with a stringcourse and a water table. This was especially true for brick front and cast-iron front buildings where the bonding patterns, common brick, molded structural members, and stamped metal ornament created a kind of theatrical backdrop for local commerce. An ornamental cornice gave a building an exaggerated profile that stepped down in layers toward the wall. From a distance the profiles would create an identity for an individual building or a cluster of them. Elevations were organized as bays, with symmetrical openings, and regardless of the height of the buildings' upper-story windows, transoms and display windows shared in the same horizontal band unit to unit. The whole Italianate arrangement created a rhythm, a distribution of beats and accents for as many blocks as the local economy could sustain.

PICTURESQUE AESTHETIC

When the picturesque aesthetic emerged late in the eighteenth century in England, it signaled a major change in economic and political realms, including a redistribution of centralized political power. Notably,

5.4. The full development of the cottage in the 1880s produced the F. Bajee House in New Berlin, New York. The forms and details represent the expression of industrialization. There are remnants of ornamental details, a keen interest in the picturesque shown in the variation of visual effects, and a commitment to inside and outside interaction. Authors' collection.

5.5. West side of Park Avenue, Prairie Du Sac, Wisconsin (1909). The vigor with which cottages are composed is obvious in this street scene. It is evident in irregularities in appearance, external forms, and complex roof plans. Authors' collection.

5.6. The picturesque quality of the Jesse A. and Bertha Ernsberger House, North Mill Street, Celina, Ohio is based on the placement of the roof forms and the volumes they represent in the façade. The composition is integrated and balanced despite diversity. Lewis Studio, Celina, Ohio. Authors' collection.

it developed during the onset of industrialization. By the middle of the nineteenth century aspects of the picturesque had been imported to America. Andrew Jackson Downing and others promoted English ideas and interpreted picturesque tenets through house and garden design. The popular tenets were visual; that is, the aesthetic came to rely on the visual realization of its values, such as contrast and abrupt variation. Visual contrast was realized through the juxtaposition of one element or building material against another. Moreover, the sequences in which elements and materials appeared, especially in the design of building elevations, were not predictable.

The American cottage became the testing and proving ground for the application of the picturesque. The cottage was composed of an abundant number of elements and materials, which, from any view, contributed to composition of a scene.

COLONIAL REVIVAL AESTHETIC: CLASSICAL

The colonial aesthetic appeared in two different periods and in contrasting forms. It is the national style, and the first version can be called the classical—an early twentieth century development that

5.7. A house in Woodsville, New Hampshire (1909) is an example of a restrained hip roof colonial revival. Ornamentation has given way to an expression of the house form. To be sure, plain columns on the portico and pilasters on the corners carry an architrave, frieze and cornice around the house. Of these the doorway is the most important element, and there is subtlety in their execution of details; for example, the shallow, segmental bay windows on the façade. "Kaulin Series" Eastman Photo Goods, G.H. Kendall, Fairlee, Vermont. Authors' collection.

produced houses such as those in 2.1 and 5.7.[1] The style was dominated by applications of the classical orders of architecture. While a general order could be applied to the entrance of a building, it was the details of the orders laid on other parts of the building that intensified the treatment. The picturesque aesthetic use of contrast carried through to this aesthetic in that the orders were traditionally rendered in white, which contrasted with the color of the body of the building. The classical colonial is still a cottage in its size and appeal.

The second version is the modern colonial revival. Its inspiration is the early Georgian of the colonial period. It is restrained, emphasizing the form of the building. Because of the investment in form, the elements and details of the modern colonial look resolved; things come to a state of rest. These values are, of course, classical in derivation. There is no extraneous energy working the edges of the form or at the entrance. The modern colonial continues to be built to the present day.

Both of these treatments were facilitated in their own times by the use of their aesthetics in a variety of buildings. For example, public schools, public libraries, and colleges built in both versions. Likewise, commercial buildings employed both approaches to produce buildings that looked like they belonged to a community, a region and a nation. Total American investment in colonial culture is so deep that colonial forms and effects can be found in all sectors of the built environment.

ARTS-AND-CRAFTS AESTHETIC

The bungalow cottage in 5.8 is a fine example of the application of what was called the artistic aesthetic. By the time this type of cottage was built, Americans were thoroughly invested in wood-based building, and wood materials were preferred for structure and finish. Arts-and-crafts ideas about the necessity of handcrafted products in an industrial age encouraged mill owners and house builders to create products that looked handmade. The results, like the house in Oregon, were convincing. The aesthetic did not lay out totally new ground, and the composition was highly pictorial. There are many visual effects on the exterior, especially along the edges of elements, such as the open cornice and rafter ends on the main roof and on the roof over the oriel window. The picturesque preference for rough surfaces, such as the porch piers and the chimney, is set against the smooth square, porch columns, and the clapboard cladding. This same effect reflects the picturesque preference for contrast, as in the paint scheme with the dark body and the light trim.

5.8. A bungalow cottage in Portland, Oregon (ca. 1918) executed in the Arts and Crafts aesthetic. This aesthetic centers on the display of materials and construction. The results suggest that great care was taken to build the house.
Authors' collection.

5.9. In the living room the walls and trim are reversed from the outside, with light walls and dark trim. Interior trim is relegated to a baseboard and crown molding, with a plain architrave over the windows. The rectilinear fireplace is framed by thick pieces of wood that are repeated in the mantel. The mantelshelf has short stout brackets. These details convey the impression that they are not stock inventory but are unique to this house and this aesthetic. Authors' collection.

5.10. The living room connects to the dining room through a colonnade. The contrasting light and dark color pattern remains the same for a unified effect. The dining room is dominated by millwork. The colonnade frames an interior vista with bookcases and an architrave across the ceiling. At the end of the perspective there is a wainscot capped by a plate rail, an oriel window with a built-in buffet, and cap trim over the doorway. The preference for wood suggests joinery and the meticulous assembly of architectural furniture. Authors' collection.

5.11. The kitchen is a modern, rationally organized space. The dependence on built-in work continues from the front rooms to the kitchen, with workspaces surrounded by modular storage, natural and electric light, and a contemporary gas appliance. The white enamel cabinets imply clean surfaces and the linoleum floor covering, easy maintenance and durability.

5.12. The 1911 Carter White Lead Company advertisement appeals to the logic of the modern colonial. The suggested colors, "colonial yellow" or "pure white," on the body of the house acknowledge its form. The contrasting trim includes the historical details that make it colonial: portico, chimneys, dormers, and shutters. Flower boxes are an ornamental add-on. Authors' collection.

5.13. This modern colonial imitates the ideal gable roof type. Authors' collection.

COLONIAL REVIVAL AESTHETIC: MODERN

The modern version of the colonial revival also has its picturesque qualities as evidenced by the Carter White Lead Company trade card in 5.12. The scene on the card is part of the prescriptive literature produced between 1870 and 1960 to encourage construction based on ideal types. The house, a solid upright, is fitted out with end-wall chimneys, a modest canopy entry, and shutters painted white to contrast with the yellow of the body. Each elevation is symmetrical; the only variation with the order is a screened porch to the side. If the classical version of the colonial revival could indulge some excess in its exterior features, then the modern (5.13) is all restraint. The withholding of the full power to express the colonial tradition is a picturesque value.

On the commercial side, banks and stores could be finished in modern colonial using windows, porticos, doors, and shutters from the inventory of house-related materials. Red brick and painted wood were the preferred cladding materials.

ENGLISH AND SPANISH REVIVAL AESTHETICS

Modern revivals were not limited to the American colonial tradition. Appropriating design ideas from England was itself a tradition. Twentieth-century models included cottages imitative of houses in English suburbs. The development begins in the 1920s and carries into the 1940s. As with any revival strategy, the identity comes from the successful use of details appropriate to the source of the style. That also means that the aesthetic is derived from the same details and the general execution of the house form. The exterior wall surface of half-timbered cottages is divided into panels of various shapes and sizes, separated by broad strips of wood; the spaces between the strips are covered with stucco. Their aesthetic is closely tied to picturesque effects, especially visual contrast and varieties of rough and smooth finish. The finish coat of stucco could have any kind of texture. An alternative treatment was the use of polychrome tapestry brick, which gave the exterior wall a richly textured surface. The brick

5.14. From 1920 to 1940 English revival treatments were adapted to all sizes of buildings, including this four-family apartment building. In this case historical design figures such as the exaggerated gable dormers on the façade help to define the type and the aesthetic. They also break up the elevation into visually manageable units. Authors' collection.

might be trimmed with rock-faced stone, the type of stone being tied to the region in which the house was built.

In 1935 Sears's *Modern Homes* described one of its five-room English bungalows as "Americanized English." Qualifying a house as "Americanized" was common in the 1930s. The exterior may have English roots but the inside, meaning the plan and the technology, were American. In the same year, the Architects' Small House Service Bureau offered a model with stucco walls and extensive brick trim, with the chimney adjacent to the entrance and casement windows, and two alternative plans. Trade sources characterized the English bungalow as rambling, its low profile and broad front conveying the impression that the bungalow had been there for along time. Stone, stucco, brick, timber and shingles are employed as cladding.

Spanish bungalows were duplicated in various parts of the country, particularly California, Florida, Texas, seaside resorts, and the Southeast and Southwest, but they are also found in the north and in cold climates. Trade magazines consistently portrayed the

5.15. A Spanish revival cottage in Denver. Stucco, the primary material in this example, can be decorated and adapted to any shape. The large parapet obscures a gable roof and becomes a kind of screen onto which accents may be displayed; thus the shape of the parapet and the colors of the accents establish an aesthetic treatment. The overall scheme is eclectic in that the porch is colonial, and the bay window and dormer on the side are typical cottage elements. Authors' collection.

Table 5.1. Summary of Modern Vernacular Buildings Using the Colonial Building Type

Classical 1890–1920	Modern 1920–1960
Colonial Revival—closed gable	Portico Bungalow—gable roof
Colonial Revival—hip roof	Dutch Colonial—gambrel roof
Colonial Revival—gambrel roof	Modern Colonial—gable roof
Classical Bungalow	Cape Cod—gable roof

Spanish bungalow as creating maximum appeal at a low cost. Features included a small vestibule entrance porch with an arched doorway, a small terrace on the front corner and accessible from the living room through French doors, triple windows on the front projecting room, and round-topped windows.

In 1923 a *Building Age* article codified three façade motifs for Spanish bungalows: (1) double window on the projecting room (such as a library), above which is a narrow slit of a window or ventilator meant to "relieve the blankness of a wall"; (2) an arched porch ornamented on either side with spiral fluted pilasters and turned urns; and (3) a square tower above the porch.[2] *Keith's Magazine* in January 1929 enumerated the characteristics of a Spanish bungalow as having simple lines on the exterior, and in the interior, a beam ceiling, smooth composition floors, and an elaborate hearth with a projecting chimney breast.[3]

MODERN AESTHETIC: EXTERIOR

The modern aesthetic derives from sources such as belief in the geometry of form, in contemporary technology, and in the direct expression of modern building materials. The modern is generally free of ornamentation, although a modern style of building called art deco, that utilized terra-cotta cladding, was intentionally decorative. Although buildings constructed from 1870 to 1960 included some aspect of modernity, it was a while before they reflected solely contemporary values and an aesthetic that could be called modern. The construction of modern commercial buildings increased significantly during the 1930s and 40s, and truly modern houses emerged in the 1940s and 50s. In house design, the ranch house was the primary model.

A good deal of modern commercial building entailed the remodeling of older brick-front stores. (5.16) Manufacturers sold storefront installations in glass, glass block, metal, or artificial stone. The new front would create a new identity. In the 1920s the Kawneer Company of Niles, Michigan produced metal storefronts in solid bronze or copper. The company manufactured a range of products, but it is their storefront systems that were successful. Kawneer developed a line of resilient sash bars that held plate glass in a way that protected it from excessive wind pressure and breakage. All the metalwork in a storefront system was available in an ornamental or plain style. A complete installation would exhibit a unified effect, in terms of surface treatment, from the bulkhead, sash, and corner bars—or *panel*, *soffit* and *marquise*. Over time aluminum replaced bronze and copper and plain surfaces became the standard.

Corporate oil companies erected modern gasoline stations built with a steel frame and cladding materials similar to those used on stores. The aesthetic characteristics of the commercial materials were pointedly modern—clean, smooth, and perhaps bright or lustrous. Many were produced and assembled in sheets that fit nicely on buildings with strict geometries.

Modern houses looked less industrial except for some experiments with materials, such as Lustron metal houses (prefabricated steel houses, constructed in Ohio) or poured-in-place concrete houses. Modern houses did take on simple geometric forms,

5.16. Drugstores such as Doerr's used modern design and structural pigmented glass to signal their progressiveness. Peeking up behind the new façade is a parapet from its former brick front. Authors' collection.

but they were still clad with clapboard or stucco. The ranch house was conceived of as a modern house, not only because of its commitment to modern living, but also its general design features and the aesthetic they represented. Ranch house façades were composed in abstract patterns. The plane of the front elevation was reduced to a two-dimensional design problem of arranging geometric figures in asymmetrical balance. If the plane were part of a stepped façade, then the fitting together became three-dimensional. Roof types play a role in the aesthetic, because the roof is such a large component in the composition. Flat roofs tend to reinforce the geometry of the house, but they were not popular in all climates. Most ranch houses have a gable or hip (or intersecting) roof, which places these houses closer to bungalows. The profile of the roof and house is low, so it does not have a picturesque profile. The rambler ranch house, which changes the direction of the flow of the house, takes on picturesque qualities. Rooms break away from the basic linear form, creating angles to the body of the house.

Chapter 5 concludes with tables that summarize the characteristics of various aesthetics (similar tables are included in subsequent chapters). The aesthetics tables are organized from top to bottom, beginning with the overall application—the forms of buildings and large elements (roof shapes and façade elevations)—followed by a sequence of details that identify the aesthetic at the roof edges, on the elevations at the entrances, and so forth.

Table 5.2. Characteristics of Italianate Aesthetic: Exterior

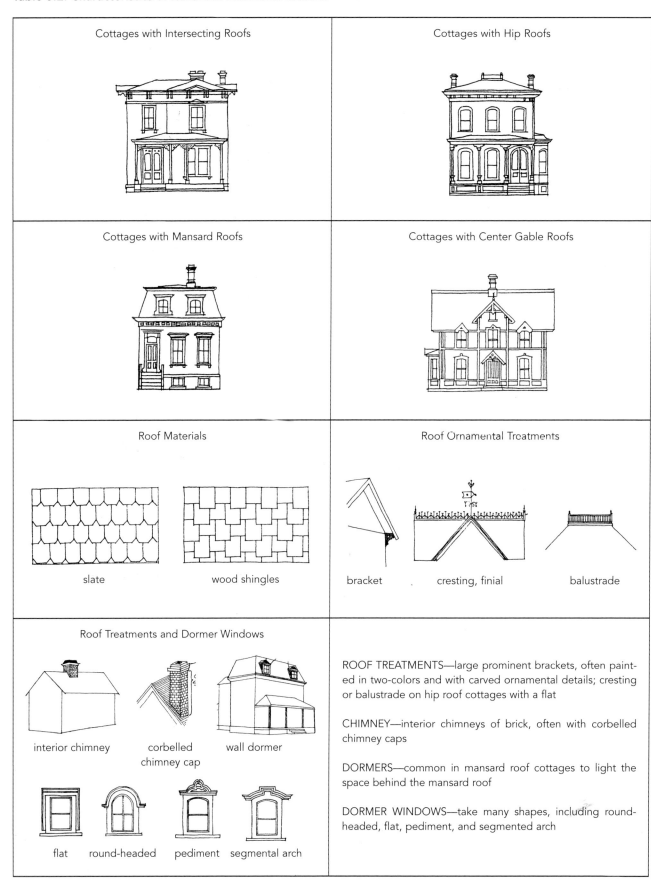

Cottages with Intersecting Roofs

Cottages with Hip Roofs

Cottages with Mansard Roofs

Cottages with Center Gable Roofs

Roof Materials

slate   wood shingles

Roof Ornamental Treatments

bracket   cresting, finial   balustrade

Roof Treatments and Dormer Windows

interior chimney   corbelled chimney cap   wall dormer

flat   round-headed   pediment   segmental arch

ROOF TREATMENTS—large prominent brackets, often painted in two-colors and with carved ornamental details; cresting or balustrade on hip roof cottages with a flat

CHIMNEY—interior chimneys of brick, often with corbelled chimney caps

DORMERS—common in mansard roof cottages to light the space behind the mansard roof

DORMER WINDOWS—take many shapes, including round-headed, flat, pediment, and segmented arch

Table 5.2. Characteristics of Italianate Aesthetic: Exterior (continued)

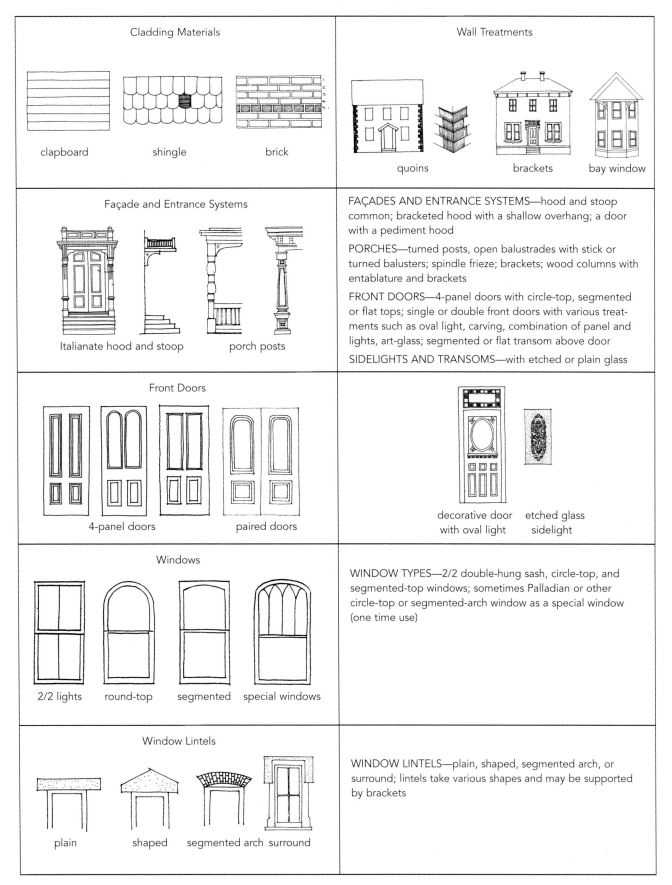

Cladding Materials			Wall Treatments		
clapboard	shingle	brick	quoins	brackets	bay window

Façade and Entrance Systems

Italianate hood and stoop   porch posts

FAÇADES AND ENTRANCE SYSTEMS—hood and stoop common; bracketed hood with a shallow overhang; a door with a pediment hood

PORCHES—turned posts, open balustrades with stick or turned balusters; spindle frieze; brackets; wood columns with entablature and brackets

FRONT DOORS—4-panel doors with circle-top, segmented or flat tops; single or double front doors with various treatments such as oval light, carving, combination of panel and lights, art-glass; segmented or flat transom above door

SIDELIGHTS AND TRANSOMS—with etched or plain glass

Front Doors

4-panel doors   paired doors

decorative door with oval light   etched glass sidelight

Windows

2/2 lights   round-top   segmented   special windows

WINDOW TYPES—2/2 double-hung sash, circle-top, and segmented-top windows; sometimes Palladian or other circle-top or segmented-arch window as a special window (one time use)

Window Lintels

plain   shaped   segmented arch   surround

WINDOW LINTELS—plain, shaped, segmented arch, or surround; lintels take various shapes and may be supported by brackets

Table 5.3. Characteristics of the Picturesque Aesthetic: Exterior

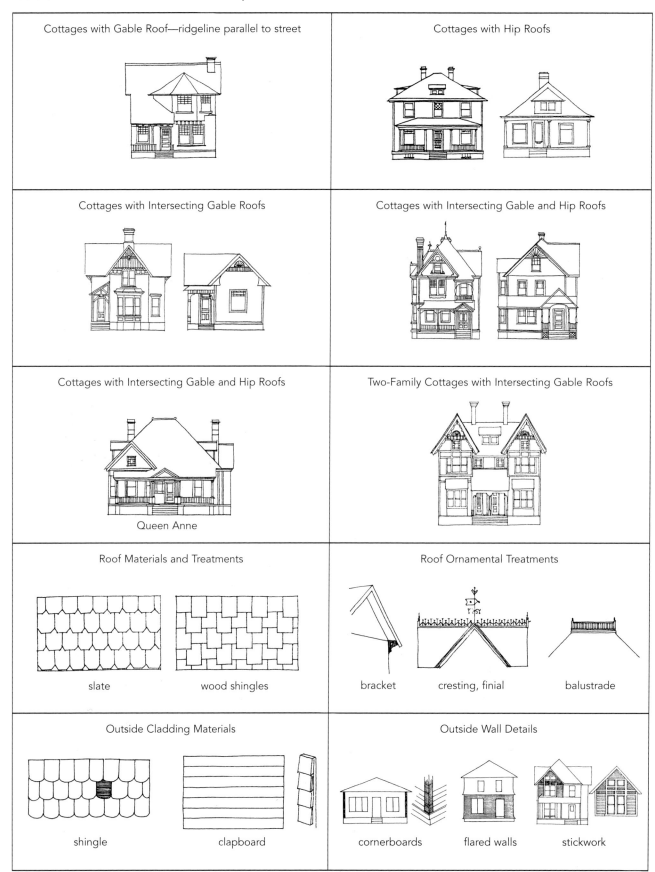

Cottages with Gable Roof—ridgeline parallel to street

Cottages with Hip Roofs

Cottages with Intersecting Gable Roofs

Cottages with Intersecting Gable and Hip Roofs

Cottages with Intersecting Gable and Hip Roofs

Queen Anne

Two-Family Cottages with Intersecting Gable Roofs

Roof Materials and Treatments

slate   wood shingles

Roof Ornamental Treatments

bracket   cresting, finial   balustrade

Outside Cladding Materials

shingle   clapboard

Outside Wall Details

cornerboards   flared walls   stickwork

Table 5.3. Characteristics of the Picturesque Aesthetic: Exterior (continued)

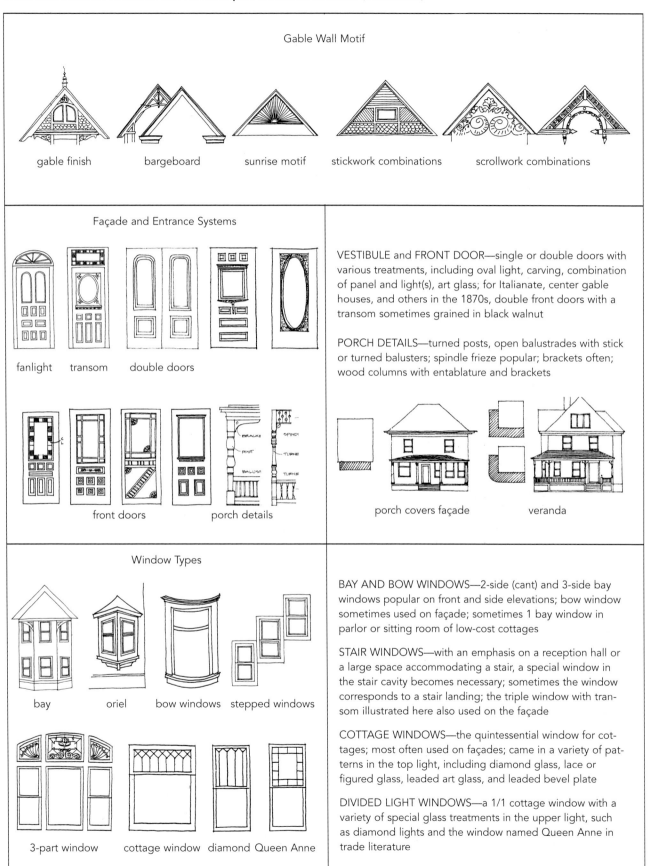

Gable Wall Motif

gable finish   bargeboard   sunrise motif   stickwork combinations   scrollwork combinations

Façade and Entrance Systems

fanlight   transom   double doors

front doors   porch details

VESTIBULE and FRONT DOOR—single or double doors with various treatments, including oval light, carving, combination of panel and light(s), art glass; for Italianate, center gable houses, and others in the 1870s, double front doors with a transom sometimes grained in black walnut

PORCH DETAILS—turned posts, open balustrades with stick or turned balusters; spindle frieze popular; brackets often; wood columns with entablature and brackets

porch covers façade   veranda

Window Types

bay   oriel   bow windows   stepped windows

3-part window   cottage window   diamond Queen Anne

BAY AND BOW WINDOWS—2-side (cant) and 3-side bay windows popular on front and side elevations; bow window sometimes used on façade; sometimes 1 bay window in parlor or sitting room of low-cost cottages

STAIR WINDOWS—with an emphasis on a reception hall or a large space accommodating a stair, a special window in the stair cavity becomes necessary; sometimes the window corresponds to a stair landing; the triple window with transom illustrated here also used on the façade

COTTAGE WINDOWS—the quintessential window for cottages; most often used on façades; came in a variety of patterns in the top light, including diamond glass, lace or figured glass, leaded art glass, and leaded bevel plate

DIVIDED LIGHT WINDOWS—a 1/1 cottage window with a variety of special glass treatments in the upper light, such as diamond lights and the window named Queen Anne in trade literature

Table 5.4. Characteristics of the Colonial Revival Aesthetic: Classical Exterior

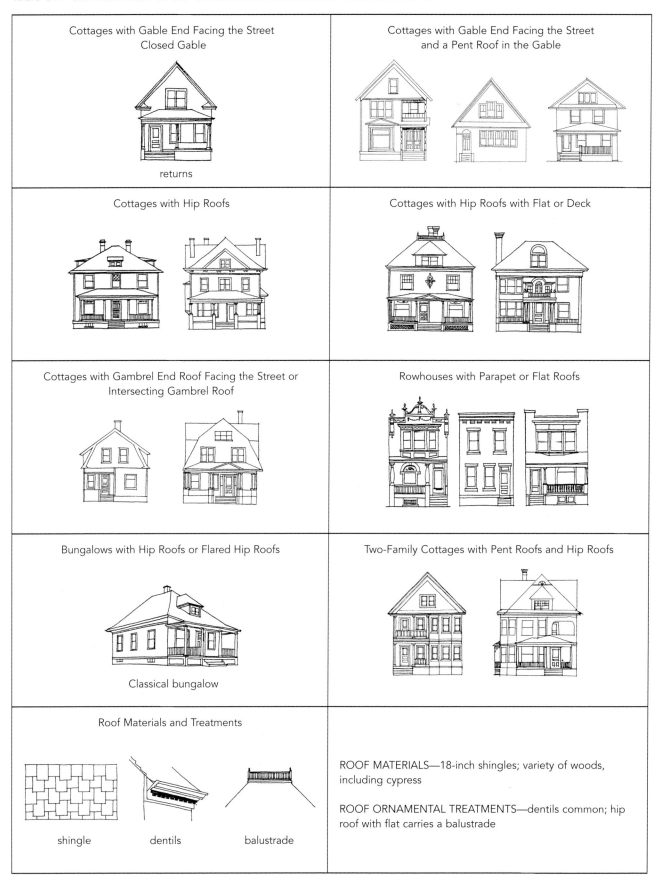

Cottages with Gable End Facing the Street
Closed Gable

returns

Cottages with Gable End Facing the Street
and a Pent Roof in the Gable

Cottages with Hip Roofs

Cottages with Hip Roofs with Flat or Deck

Cottages with Gambrel End Roof Facing the Street or
Intersecting Gambrel Roof

Rowhouses with Parapet or Flat Roofs

Bungalows with Hip Roofs or Flared Hip Roofs

Classical bungalow

Two-Family Cottages with Pent Roofs and Hip Roofs

Roof Materials and Treatments

shingle   dentils   balustrade

ROOF MATERIALS—18-inch shingles; variety of woods, including cypress

ROOF ORNAMENTAL TREATMENTS—dentils common; hip roof with flat carries a balustrade

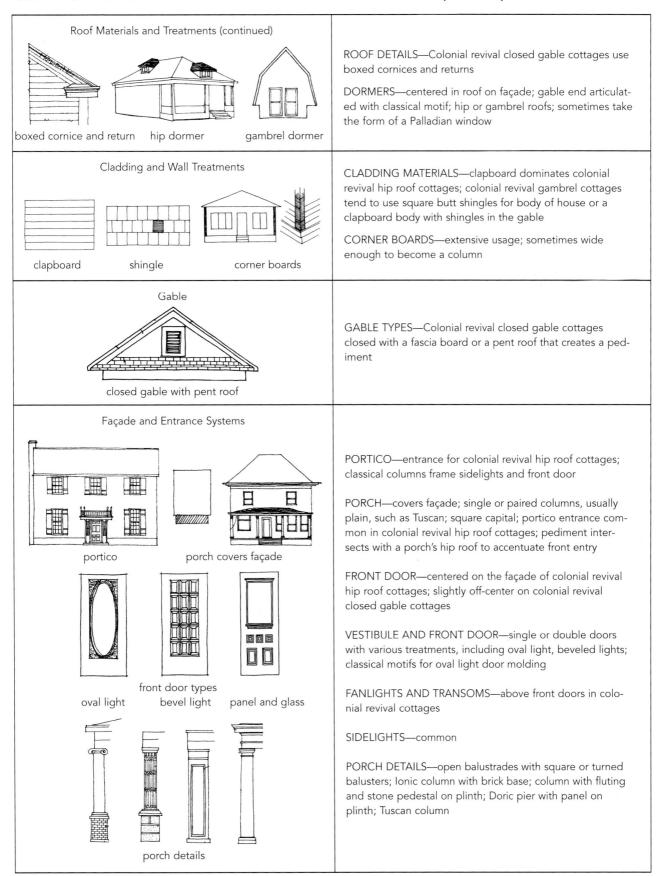

Roof Materials and Treatments (continued) boxed cornice and return hip dormer gambrel dormer	ROOF DETAILS—Colonial revival closed gable cottages use boxed cornices and returns DORMERS—centered in roof on façade; gable end articulated with classical motif; hip or gambrel roofs; sometimes take the form of a Palladian window
Cladding and Wall Treatments clapboard shingle corner boards	CLADDING MATERIALS—clapboard dominates colonial revival hip roof cottages; colonial revival gambrel cottages tend to use square butt shingles for body of house or a clapboard body with shingles in the gable CORNER BOARDS—extensive usage; sometimes wide enough to become a column
Gable closed gable with pent roof	GABLE TYPES—Colonial revival closed gable cottages closed with a fascia board or a pent roof that creates a pediment
Façade and Entrance Systems portico porch covers façade oval light front door types bevel light panel and glass porch details	PORTICO—entrance for colonial revival hip roof cottages; classical columns frame sidelights and front door PORCH—covers façade; single or paired columns, usually plain, such as Tuscan; square capital; portico entrance common in colonial revival hip roof cottages; pediment intersects with a porch's hip roof to accentuate front entry FRONT DOOR—centered on the façade of colonial revival hip roof cottages; slightly off-center on colonial revival closed gable cottages VESTIBULE AND FRONT DOOR—single or double doors with various treatments, including oval light, beveled lights; classical motifs for oval light door molding FANLIGHTS AND TRANSOMS—above front doors in colonial revival cottages SIDELIGHTS—common PORCH DETAILS—open balustrades with square or turned balusters; Ionic column with brick base; column with fluting and stone pedestal on plinth; Doric pier with panel on plinth; Tuscan column

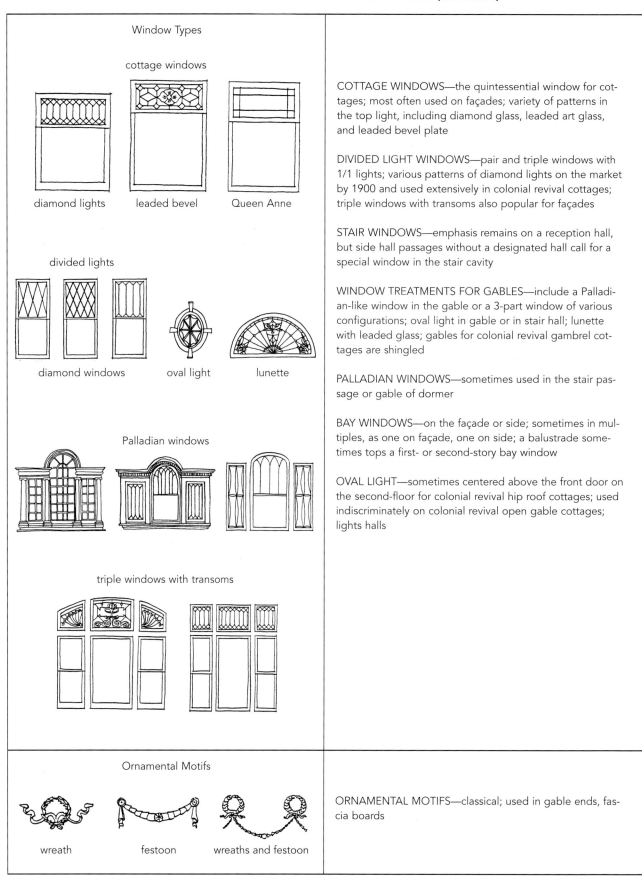

Window Types

cottage windows

diamond lights   leaded bevel   Queen Anne

divided lights

diamond windows   oval light   lunette

Palladian windows

triple windows with transoms

COTTAGE WINDOWS—the quintessential window for cottages; most often used on façades; variety of patterns in the top light, including diamond glass, leaded art glass, and leaded bevel plate

DIVIDED LIGHT WINDOWS—pair and triple windows with 1/1 lights; various patterns of diamond lights on the market by 1900 and used extensively in colonial revival cottages; triple windows with transoms also popular for façades

STAIR WINDOWS—emphasis remains on a reception hall, but side hall passages without a designated hall call for a special window in the stair cavity

WINDOW TREATMENTS FOR GABLES—include a Palladian-like window in the gable or a 3-part window of various configurations; oval light in gable or in stair hall; lunette with leaded glass; gables for colonial revival gambrel cottages are shingled

PALLADIAN WINDOWS—sometimes used in the stair passage or gable of dormer

BAY WINDOWS—on the façade or side; sometimes in multiples, as one on façade, one on side; a balustrade sometimes tops a first- or second-story bay window

OVAL LIGHT—sometimes centered above the front door on the second-floor for colonial revival hip roof cottages; used indiscriminately on colonial revival open gable cottages; lights halls

Ornamental Motifs

wreath   festoon   wreaths and festoon

ORNAMENTAL MOTIFS—classical; used in gable ends, fascia boards

Table 5.5. Characteristics of Colonial Revival Aesthetic: Modern Exterior

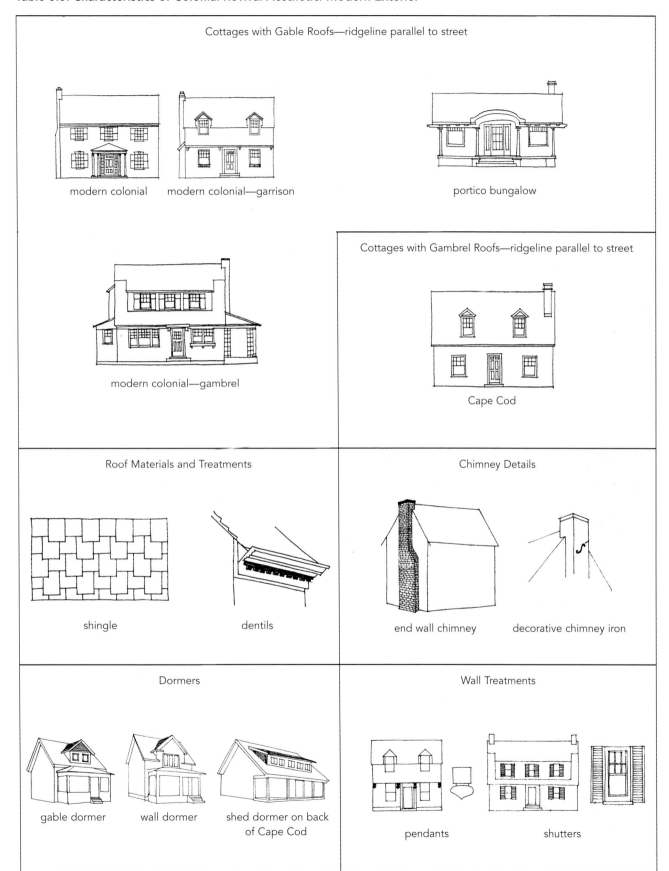

Cottages with Gable Roofs—ridgeline parallel to street

modern colonial   modern colonial—garrison

portico bungalow

modern colonial—gambrel

Cottages with Gambrel Roofs—ridgeline parallel to street

Cape Cod

Roof Materials and Treatments

shingle   dentils

Chimney Details

end wall chimney   decorative chimney iron

Dormers

gable dormer   wall dormer   shed dormer on back
of Cape Cod

Wall Treatments

pendants   shutters

Table 5.5. Characteristics of Colonial Revival Aesthetic: Modern Exterior (continued)

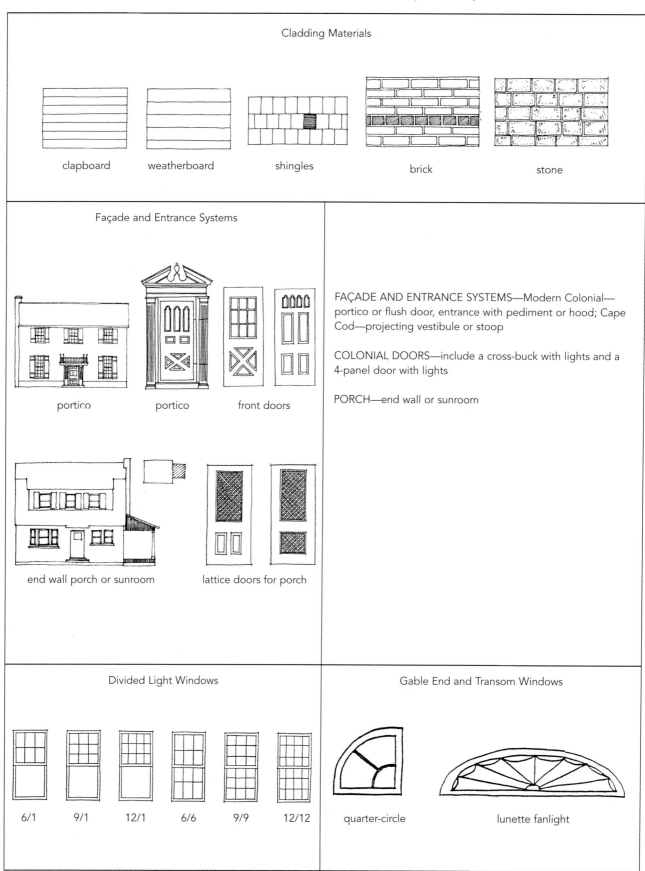

Cladding Materials

clapboard   weatherboard   shingles   brick   stone

Façade and Entrance Systems

portico   portico   front doors

end wall porch or sunroom   lattice doors for porch

FAÇADE AND ENTRANCE SYSTEMS—Modern Colonial—portico or flush door, entrance with pediment or hood; Cape Cod—projecting vestibule or stoop

COLONIAL DOORS—include a cross-buck with lights and a 4-panel door with lights

PORCH—end wall or sunroom

Divided Light Windows

6/1   9/1   12/1   6/6   9/9   12/12

Gable End and Transom Windows

quarter-circle   lunette fanlight

Table 5.6. Characteristics of the Arts-and-Crafts Aesthetic: Exterior

Bungalows with Gable Roofs—gable end facing street 	Bungalows with Intersecting Gable or Hip Roofs 
Bungalows with Hip Roofs 	Bungalows with Gable Roofs—ridgeline parallel to street  Bungalow cottage
Square Cottages with Hip Roofs 	Closed Gable Cottages—gable end facing street 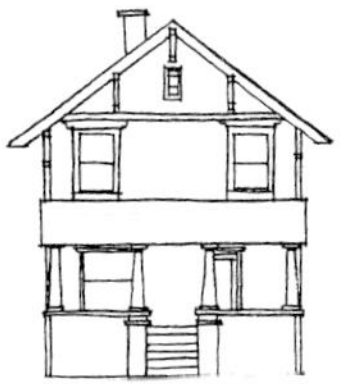
	Villas with Hip Roofs 

Roof Materials

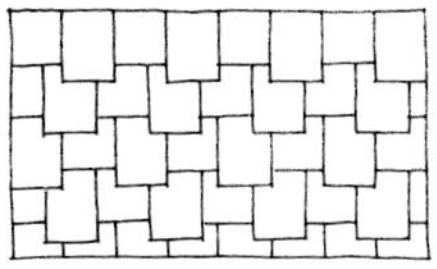

shingle   tile

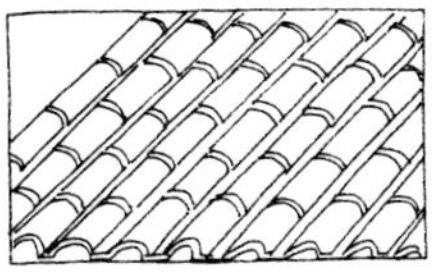

Dormers

gable   shed   dormer with balcony

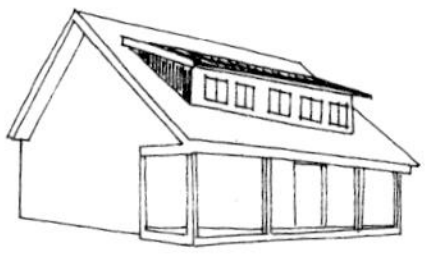

Cladding Materials

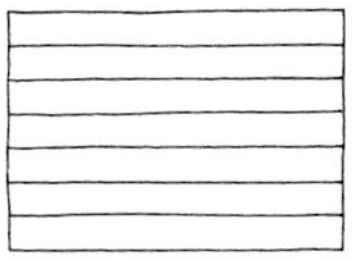

clapboard 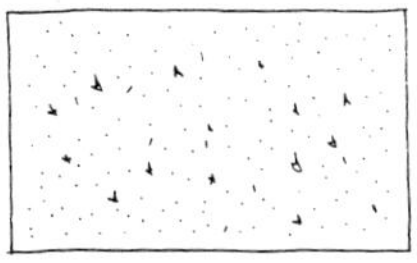   stucco or rough cast cement    brick 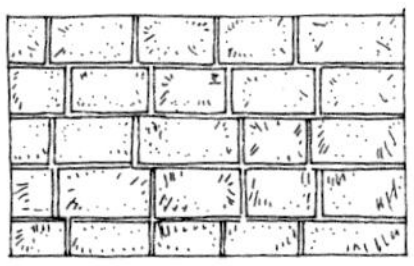   stone 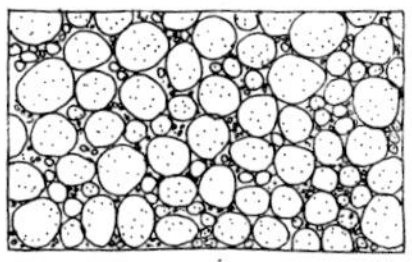   river rock

Table 5.6. Characteristics of the Arts-and-Crafts Aesthetic: Exterior (continued)

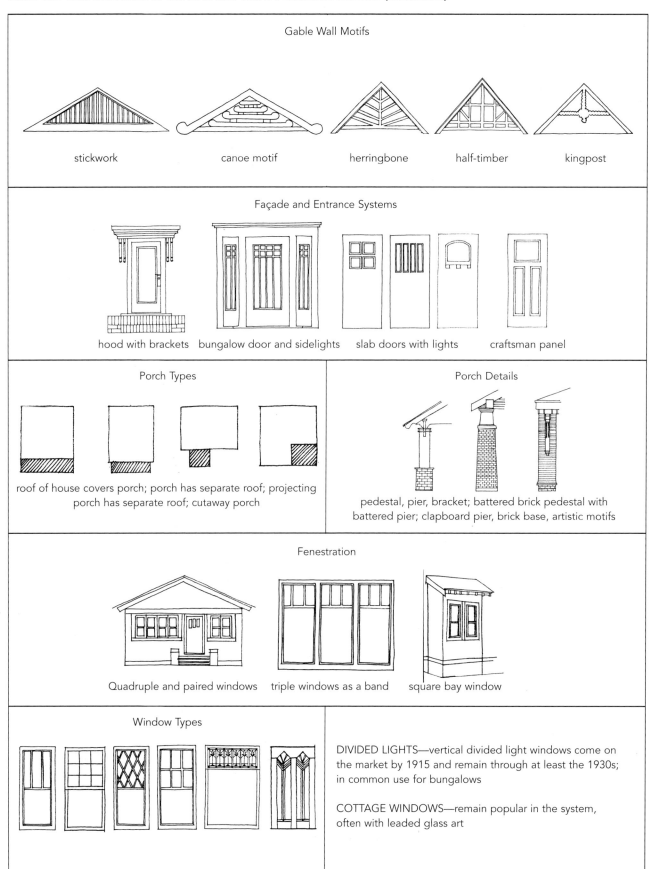

Gable Wall Motifs

stickwork   canoe motif   herringbone   half-timber   kingpost

Façade and Entrance Systems

hood with brackets   bungalow door and sidelights   slab doors with lights   craftsman panel

Porch Types

roof of house covers porch; porch has separate roof; projecting porch has separate roof; cutaway porch

Porch Details

pedestal, pier, bracket; battered brick pedestal with battered pier; clapboard pier, brick base, artistic motifs

Fenestration

Quadruple and paired windows   triple windows as a band   square bay window

Window Types

DIVIDED LIGHTS—vertical divided light windows come on the market by 1915 and remain through at least the 1930s; in common use for bungalows

COTTAGE WINDOWS—remain popular in the system, often with leaded glass art

Table 5.7. Characteristics of the English and Spanish Revival Aesthetic: Exterior

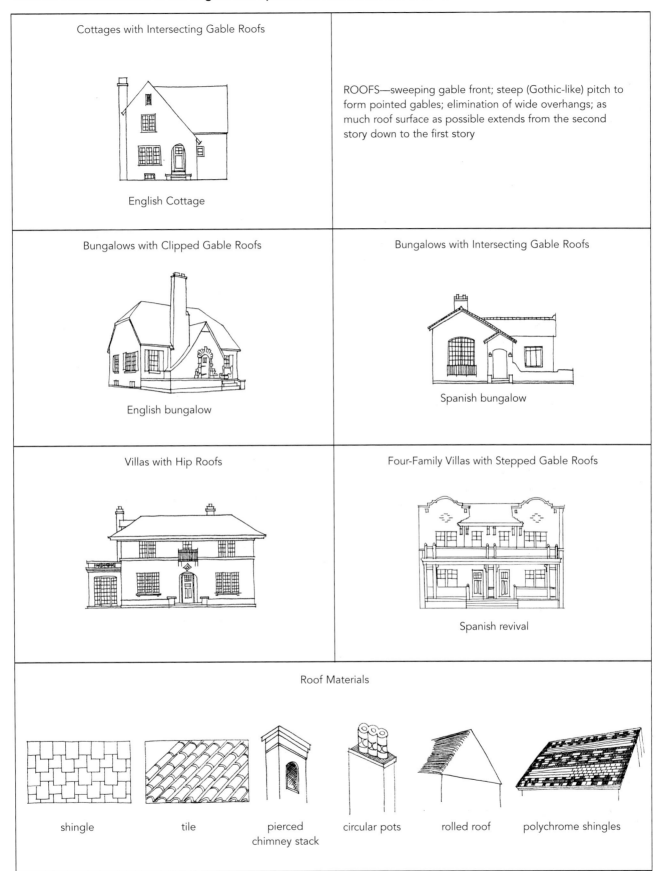

Cottages with Intersecting Gable Roofs

English Cottage

ROOFS—sweeping gable front; steep (Gothic-like) pitch to form pointed gables; elimination of wide overhangs; as much roof surface as possible extends from the second story down to the first story

Bungalows with Clipped Gable Roofs

English bungalow

Bungalows with Intersecting Gable Roofs

Spanish bungalow

Villas with Hip Roofs

Four-Family Villas with Stepped Gable Roofs

Spanish revival

Roof Materials

shingle   tile   pierced chimney stack   circular pots   rolled roof   polychrome shingles

Table 5.7. Characteristics of the English and Spanish Revival Aesthetic: Exterior (continued)

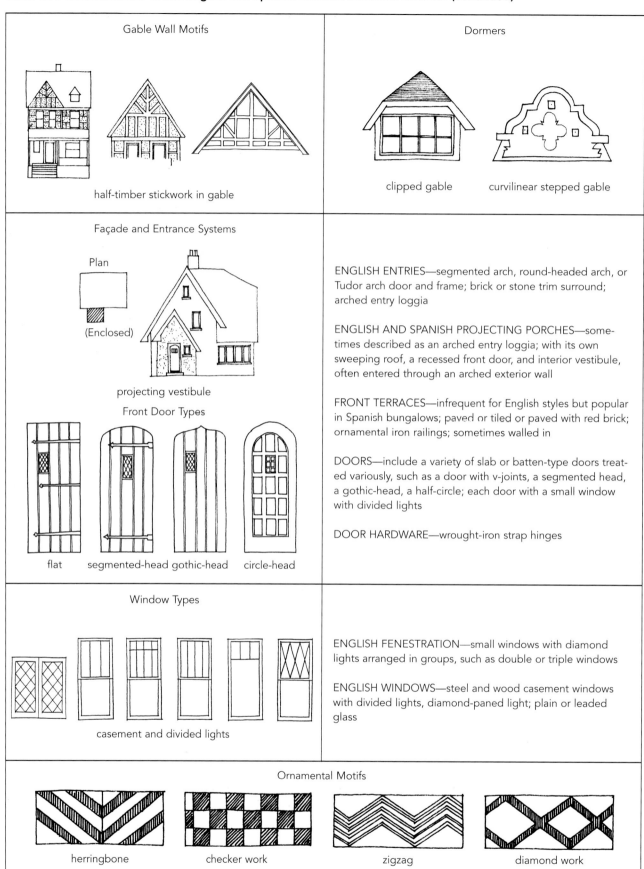

Gable Wall Motifs

half-timber stickwork in gable

Dormers

clipped gable   curvilinear stepped gable

Façade and Entrance Systems

Plan

(Enclosed)

projecting vestibule

Front Door Types

flat   segmented-head gothic-head   circle-head

ENGLISH ENTRIES—segmented arch, round-headed arch, or Tudor arch door and frame; brick or stone trim surround; arched entry loggia

ENGLISH AND SPANISH PROJECTING PORCHES—sometimes described as an arched entry loggia; with its own sweeping roof, a recessed front door, and interior vestibule, often entered through an arched exterior wall

FRONT TERRACES—infrequent for English styles but popular in Spanish bungalows; paved or tiled or paved with red brick; ornamental iron railings; sometimes walled in

DOORS—include a variety of slab or batten-type doors treated variously, such as a door with v-joints, a segmented head, a gothic-head, a half-circle; each door with a small window with divided lights

DOOR HARDWARE—wrought-iron strap hinges

Window Types

casement and divided lights

ENGLISH FENESTRATION—small windows with diamond lights arranged in groups, such as double or triple windows

ENGLISH WINDOWS—steel and wood casement windows with divided lights, diamond-paned light; plain or leaded glass

Ornamental Motifs

herringbone   checker work   zigzag   diamond work

Table 5.8. Characteristics of the Modern Aesthetic: Exterior

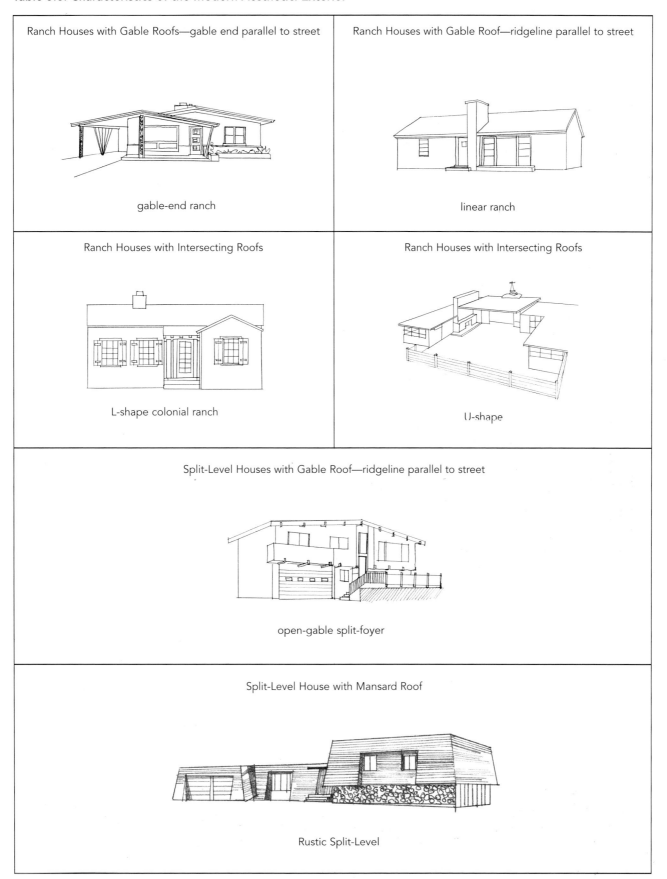

Ranch Houses with Gable Roofs—gable end parallel to street

gable-end ranch

Ranch Houses with Gable Roof—ridgeline parallel to street

linear ranch

Ranch Houses with Intersecting Roofs

L-shape colonial ranch

Ranch Houses with Intersecting Roofs

U-shape

Split-Level Houses with Gable Roof—ridgeline parallel to street

open-gable split-foyer

Split-Level House with Mansard Roof

Rustic Split-Level

Table 5.8. Characteristics of the Modern Aesthetic: Exterior (continued)

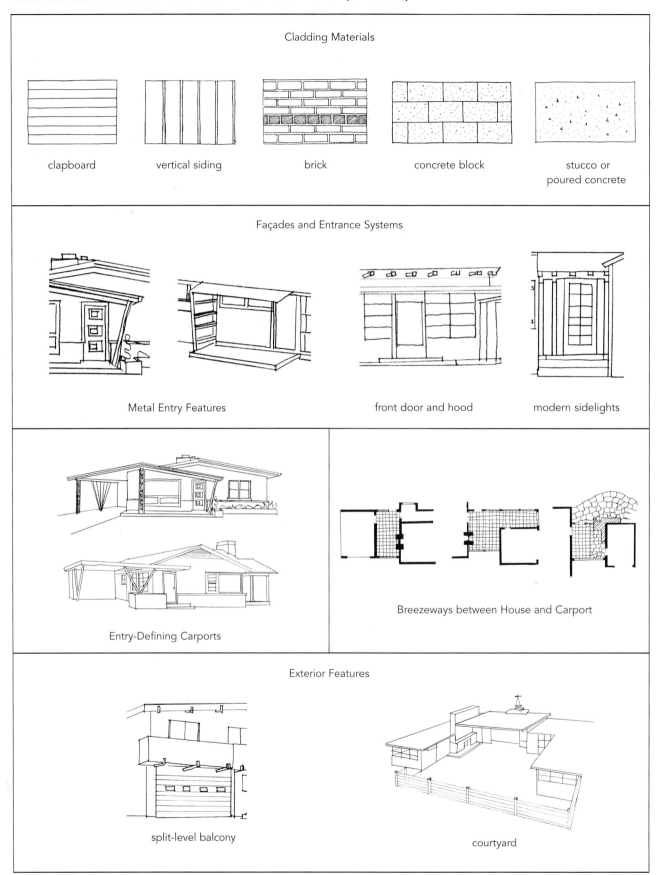

Cladding Materials

clapboard   vertical siding   brick   concrete block   stucco or poured concrete

Façades and Entrance Systems

Metal Entry Features   front door and hood   modern sidelights

Entry-Defining Carports

Breezeways between House and Carport

Exterior Features

split-level balcony   courtyard

Table 5.8. Characteristics of the Modern Aesthetic: Exterior (continued)

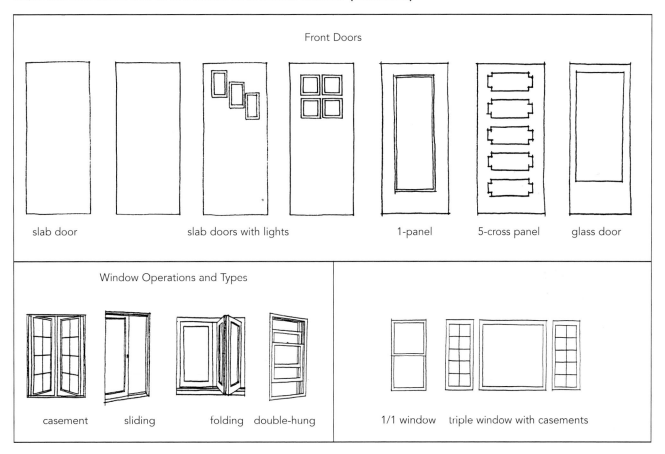

Front Doors

slab door   slab doors with lights   1-panel   5-cross panel   glass door

Window Operations and Types

casement   sliding   folding   double-hung

1/1 window   triple window with casements

6

AESTHETIC SYSTEM: INTERIOR

From both archival and field research it appears that after 1870 there were few formulas for designing interiors. Although there were different aesthetics in operation, there were few strict rules of application. Individual rooms, such as the dining room, could have a single application, and special-use rooms such as the kitchen and bath might have their own systems. Millwork is a good indicator of the presence of a specific interior aesthetic. What follows is a discussion, with summary tables, of the dominant aesthetics for the period: the *Italianate*, the *ornamental*, the *colonial*, the *artistic*, and the *modern*.

ITALIANATE AESTHETIC

The Italianate treatment was the first national revival design scheme for both exteriors and interiors. The term *Italianate* refers to design values and characteristics from Italian Renaissance architecture. In housing the principal urban building types were the palazzo and the rural villa. American vernacular building does not imitate these forms but instead applies Italian design details to what are fundamentally cottages.

The shape of the floor plan guides the interior organization, whether it is "L-shaped," "T-shaped," or a

6.1. Double doors can be found in several locations in Italianate houses, from the entry to a bedroom. These are stile and rail doors with long, narrow panels, a pattern similar to window shapes in the same style. The doors are tall to correspond to the ceiling height. The origin of the three-part wall division is classical, and here it accommodates a space for a wainscot from the baseboard to the next molding, and two fields above. A multilayered cornice caps the wall. Interior bedroom, second floor, Fountain Grove House, 1875, Santa Rosa vicinity, California; demolished 1960s. HABS CAL, 49-SANRO, 2-B-7

narrow but deep plan (say, sixteen feet by thirty-six, or one room and a hall wide), and the plan has either a center hall or side hall arrangement. In either case

87

6.2. The light through the door of an Italianate villa articulates the entire millwork system in this hallway. Each unit—door system (door, sidelights, transom), framed opening on the left (projecting moldings), and stair system (newel, balustrade and rail, and brackets)—competes for light and shadow. Warner House, 1868, Wellington, Ohio. Photograph taken 1951. Photo credit: Perry E. Borchers. HABS OHIO, 47-WEL, 2-2

6.3. Two people pose in a bedroom bay window, which suggests that the space also functions as a secondary sitting room. The Eastlake mantel, window casings, high baseboard trim, and the metal bed frame reflect the ornamental aesthetic. Authors' collection.

the hall governs the circulation sequence. People move into and out of the hall to use rooms. The appropriation of Italian classical details occurs mostly on the exterior, but there are some interior equivalents. For example, the exterior has a bold cornice that caps the vertical thrust of the building, whereas a large crown molding covers the wall and ceiling joint on the interior. Windows are treated both on the outside and inside. The interior details are of wood and include a frame and casing, a sill, and a frame and panels under the sill. Interior blinds are also common. The overall effect is to bring classical composition to the walls and ceilings of the interior.

THE ORNAMENTAL AESTHETIC

The ornamental aesthetic relates to the various revival styles of nineteenth-century architecture. Revivals gave the vernacular a predilection for decorative motifs applied in various sizes and in several mediums, for layered surfaces and for three-dimensional modeling. The ornamental was popular during the last three decades of the nineteenth century, until it gave way to the artistic/modern and the colonial.

In this system decorative motifs were applied to almost any surface. In millwork, images were carved into, or applied to, the wood surfaces as whole finished work (3.1 and 3.4). The imagery included natural and geometric figures and was usually part of something else. For example, an image would be part of a panel on a newel post rather than standing alone as an isolated figure. This integration of ornamentation had something in common with the design of furniture in the same period; both were likely to have active surfaces. A material could be made to look like another material, and there was a degree of sham—papier-mâché, veneered work, composition work, and the like—built into the system.

The ornamental system produced an interior in which the effect of the design was cumulative. In millwork, moldings and panels were built upon each other, which altered the character of each element (see 4.11). A typical ornamental wall organization consisted of a high baseboard composed of two or three pieces of wood, a dado or wainscot (the latter with a cap rail), a large portion of wall that was papered, and a wallpaper frieze at the top where the wall meets the ceiling. If wallpaper covered the entire wall—dado to frieze—the motifs in each layer would be different, and the ceiling finish, whether paper or plaster, would add a fourth motif. Adding wood or plaster moldings—as a picture molding, a cornice, or one or more ceiling moldings—often accomplished the transition from one section of wall to another.

A secondary kind of layering involved the color and natural pattern of materials. For instance, the ornamental living room and dining room housed pieces of built-in furniture, with each piece made from a different species of wood: for example, cherry, walnut, oak. The wood was left its natural color or stained to look like something else. (The same trend took place in furniture design.) Furthermore, the ornamental style permitted painted graining as a surface treatment, regardless of the grain pattern of the original wood. In a mantel the variegated pattern of the marble face and shelf were yet another layer of imagery to relate to the wood patterns and the color treatment.

A third dimension of the ornamental system was a propensity to project multiple surfaces. The cross-sectional and plan views of moldings and panels, rails and doors, reveal an internal logic only; the elements are self-referential, deriving their development only in terms of their relations to each other. Another curve or edge—usually one going in another direction or having a different shape—must "answer" a curve or an edge in one section of work.

The ornamental aesthetic is associated with the Victorian period of design, and it was no doubt related to the associative value of architecture that revival styles sought in elements and forms. For that reason, the ornamental could reference historical classicism with moldings and applied orders. Thus style is decorative. The lathe-turned baluster, for example, often relates only to things like it, or it relates to nothing else in a room. Objects of all kinds competed for attention. Symbolically, this kind of design suggested a complicated world, a world of parts for which the logic of assembly was not readily evident.

Another characteristic of the ornamental involved the way in which specific elements were clustered. For example, passage doors had raised moldings and raised panels with chamfered stiles, rails, and casings. Folding or pocket doors had similar stickwork and an added astragal to the leading edge. Architrav-

es of ornamental patterns or special work over the door were also common. The trim sets for doors and windows included pilaster casings with base, corner, and head blocks and elaborate apron panels under the windows. The windows themselves often had panes or whole sections of art glass, which added pattern, figurative imagery, and color.

Ornamental flooring included the use of different species of wood for graining and color and numerous patterns of parquet flooring. Parquet was laid in blocks or short strips with a border and a center, each with different design.

As for wall organization, we have referred previously to the division of walls by wallpaper. Wainscots provided a similar division; the wainscot was built up from the baseboard to cover about one-third of the wall with paneled sections of wood, plaster, or textile. The wainscot was finished with a cap. In walls that had no wainscot or casing, a bead was placed on the outside corners.

Ornamental plaster for walls and ceilings, done in molding patterns, was a significant element in this style. The plasterwork was done in varying widths and thicknesses, and placement was most typically as a centerpiece—a block or a rosette in the living room

6.4. In the Virginia home of Matilda Jane, the portieres look heavy when compared to the material from which her dress is made. Their physical and visual weights are part of the application. The Eastlake-inspired chairs are heavy too. The overlay of floral patterns in the portieres, floor covering, and wallpaper is typical. Authors' collection.

or over the dining-room table. Plaster molding was used also to divide a ceiling and walls into panels, an effect also achievable with wallpaper.

Openings in a wall most often were finished with pilaster casings on the face of the wall: grilles with scrollwork, beads, or spindles spanned the opening. Individual colonnades also were placed in openings and could be linked by grilles. A piece of drapery, a portiere, often completed the arrangement. Folding doors and sliding doors were popular devices for controlling the use of space in this design system. The visual effect of these elements was to add a temporary wall of wood panels to what was more than likely a partially paneled interior.

The final, permanent element of the ornamental system was the fireplace mantel. This element has been a focal point in all design systems for vernacular interiors. In the nineteenth century the fireplace was a primary source of space heating and its mantel an opportunity to celebrate the aesthetic.

In 1868 English architect and furniture designer Charles Eastlake, in his widely disseminated book *Hints on Household Taste*, promoted the use of a wooden overmantel, with a long, low strip of mirror (about eighteen inches high) and narrow shelves (six inches wide, twelve inches apart) for specimens of old china. Further, he recommended the display of plates, upright on their edges. He prevented them from slipping off by sinking a shallow groove in the thickness of each shelf—what came to be known as a plate rail. Eastlake's mantel made an overmantel a permanent element, at least for a decade or more. Mantel shelves for bric-a-brac in American homes reinforced the notion of the mantel as the site for some of the family's important possessions: "A little museum may thus be formed and remain a source of lasting pleasure to its possessors, seeing that a thing of beauty is a joy forever."[1]

American manufacturers soon offered their own interpretations of Eastlake's mantel design. In millwork catalogs from 1875 to 1900, designs are typically not labeled as Eastlake or Queen Anne, and Joseph Hafner's 1891 catalog is no exception. Hafner's catalog illustrates twenty-four stock mantels, evenly divided between those with overmantels and those with none. Of the mantels with no overmantel, the company provides no dimensions, but eight of twelve overmantel types have dimensions for those builders

6.5. Components of the American version of the Eastlake mantel underwent many design interpretations to determine which material objects were important enough to make "a little museum." In this case, portrait cabinet photographs take the place of Eastlake's preference for blue and white pottery. Authors' collection.

and clients who were looking for an Eastlake mantel. Further evidences of Eastlake's influence are Hafner's dimensions for mirrors, which did not deviate more than two inches from Eastlake's eighteen-inches high recommendation. All of Hafner's mantels are five-feet wide but vary slightly in height (measured from the floor to the highest point), the highest six feet, eight inches and the lowest six feet, five inches. Perhaps most telling are Hafner's illustrations of mantels in perspective and with bric-a-brac.[2]

In commercial interiors the ornamental aesthetic was already in use by 1870 and would remain viable through the first decade of the twentieth century. Since commercial interiors undergo much remodeling, there are few extant examples of the ornamental treatment. If the exterior displayed a fully developed ornamental, then the interior would as well, although applications were selective. For example, in a one-room office the only element might be ornate or

6.6. The ornamental aesthetic made use of large and varying patterns in wall and ceiling papers, as well as flooring. Advocates for an artistic aesthetic believed that medallions, shields, and patterns with "scrolly outline" were frivolous. Authors' collection.

striped wallpaper, the same patterns used in the home. Overlaying large numbers of calendars and magazine art on the paper was a common practice in offices. In offices with more employees, the walls were almost uniformly plain plaster with few, if any, adornments, although wainscoting was used sometimes to add a bit of formality to the room. Business buildings large enough to accommodate a president's office sometimes outfitted it with a corner fireplace, a bay window, a panel wainscot, and a branch light fixture. In stores a pressed metal ceiling might be the most ornamental element.

The ornamental design system was not carried out in the same manner throughout its period any more than the other systems. With no strict rule about elements and their application, and, since industrially based vernacular was characterized by

change, modifications were common. Changes might be made to encourage sales, to improve appearance, or to cut the costs of labor and materials. From 1875 to 1895 the ornamental system shifted away from thick, dark pieces of vigorously massed millwork to a more delicate treatment. The move corresponded with the last phase of what has been called *stickwork* cottage designs. Instead of relying on layering or the accumulation of multiples—for example, a newel post with an octagonal base, a turned shaft in a couple of shapes, and a square top—the new version reduced the size of the newel and controlled the shape more tightly. In place of ridges and turnings, ornaments in shallow relief were cut into the faces of the newel, and the balusters were made in smaller diameters and rarely numbered more than two to a tread.

Despite these refinements, the ornamental system could not survive the progressive social movements that were redefining household environments. The ornamental aesthetic relied on irregularity and flamboyant profiles, which ultimately did not fit an age that was demanding recognition for women, especially of their housekeeping role. Gwendolyn Wright, in *Moralism and the Model Home* (1980), describes how the progressive design movement changed the housekeeper's status.[3] She could now rise above the multiple design effects and control the environment from her perspective. She might have to work with manufactured elements, but she was free to determine their assemblage and their relations to each other and to herself.

The ornamental aesthetic had the capacity to overwhelm, partly because of its deep commitment to the celebration of industry. The clustering of motifs and the layering of surfaces were part of this celebration. The ornamental aesthetic represented a world demonstrating faith in the power machines that created edges, outlines, and patterns, as well as parallel, intersecting, and curvilinear lines. Yet the ornamental also recognized privacy, the opportunity to withdraw, to become part of the context.

The Wallpaper Dilemma, 1880–1910

Changes in cultural norms and in the production and marketing of consumer goods in the 1890–1910 period allowed women to assume moral guardianship of their homes. Women's magazines, mail-order catalogues, and advice books overflowed with suggestions for the decoration of the home interior. Manufacturers recognized housewives as a primary target for sales, and new marketing strategies helped to fill American middle- and working-class homes with ready-made, mass-produced objects.

In the midst of this changing "homescape," wallpaper, a seemingly benign material, became the object of friction between two groups who vied for the attention of the female consumer: manufacturers and domestic reformers. At the turn of the twentieth century, manufacturers flooded the market with ornately patterned wallpapers and resorted to various means of tempting women to purchase these products. Tastemakers and domestic advisors countered by characterizing such wallpaper as a moral problem. Their criticisms proved to be nothing new. In 1876, the editor of *Harper's Bazaar* claimed that "Indiana divorce laws may be perhaps directly traced to some frightful inharmoniousness in wall-paper."[4] This essay considers the rhetorical dimensions of these cultural and commercial forces and suggests ways in which women either succumb to sensuality or resist it. Photographs offer evidence of female reactions to dualistic messages.

SENSUOUS TEMPTATIONS: THE WALLPAPER DILEMMA, 1880–1910

Wallpaper manufacturers in the 1890–1910 period resorted to various marketing and sales techniques to tempt ordinary women to purchase their products. In one scheme manufacturers and catalogue entrepreneurs encouraged women to hang their own paper. Manufacturers followed the lead of home economists, who counseled women to take action. If the wallpaper was bad in color or pattern, they should take it off and repaper the walls. They claimed many women had done it.

A second sales device included a variety of printed materials, such as bound catalogues, idea books and trade cards, illustrating wallpaper in carefully chosen settings. The 1913 catalogue of Becker, Smith,

6.7. In 1909 the Remien and Kuhnert Company of Chicago's trade card illustrated a dining room with a trellis-pattern ceiling paper and a two-part artistic wall composition favored by arts and craft reformers. The top one-third of the wall receives a vertically oriented motif of naturalistic vine and blossom; the bottom two-thirds repeats the vertical delineation in a darker material. The ceiling's paper is a lattice pattern. Authors' collection.

and Page is a good example of the sales presentations intended to tantalize women with artfully arranged settings. The visual appeal begins with a special hand-sewn cover of heavy parchment paper delineated with an embossed, beaded border. A gold embossed seal with the company's name and catalogue date is placed slightly above center. With irregular edges, it appears as a wax impression. The cover's impression is of handmade, aged, and artful products.

Another catalogue type was the idea book, distributed by drugstores that sold wallpaper. Presented as complimentary gifts to customers, these books varied in size and number of pages but all illustrated room settings rendered as color perspectives. Vignettes of ideal rooms suggested how various patterns could be combined appropriately. The catalogues amounted to visual provocations, approximating a scene that might become real if the viewer had enough imagination and skill to build the picture. The trade card, another print device, was mailed by manufacturers' sales representatives to women's homes. The cards attempted to create a more direct relationship between buyer and salesman. Like postcards, trade cards were printed as a single color plate on one side, with the backside used for a customer's address and a message. S. A. Maxwell and Company issued trade cards with preprinted messages on the front and back of the cards. One reads: "There's No Accomplishment like good taste in dress or in your home. Attractive wallpaper often succeeds where the finest furnishings have failed. We have the latest styles in Wall Paper."[7]

The third strategy was direct sales through in-home visits and in-store settings. In an 1896 article in *Ladies' World*, Frances E. Fryatt counseled that another woman should accompany the shopper "to stand by you and counteract the persuasions of the salesman. . . . The clever salesman will tell you exactly what will suit your house. It makes no difference that he has never seen one of the rooms you are to have papered; he knows precisely what is best for them. His chief concern is to sell the paper, so he soon finds how much you are willing to pay per roll."[8] According to Fryatt, a salesman would show a shopper everything in the store until she became so bewildered as to fall back on the salesman's judgment. Fryatt advised women that prior to a store visit, one

should have "a preconceived scheme" and know what is and is not agreeable and desirable.

Sample books, in which women experienced firsthand the sensuous qualities of the material, comprised a fourth sales technique. Sears and Montgomery Ward began the production of sample books at the turn of the twentieth century. The books were smaller than they are now, and samples were cut from a full-sized strip, so a woman had difficulty understanding how the whole wall would look, especially if she combined various patterns for sidewall, border, and ceiling. To solve this problem and, no doubt, to sell more combinations of designs, manufacturers sometimes printed an elevation on the back of a sample to illustrate an entire wall.

Wallpaper selection was "one of the most arduous undertakings connected with home furnishing," because it challenged women to resist the sensuous character of the material itself, the abundance of designs in the marketplace, and the ploys of the salesman.[9] To the buying public, manufacturers succeeded in promoting wallpaper as a facile material capable of bridging two conflicting design systems: an ornamental aesthetic, with its predilection for decorative motifs, layered surfaces, and three-dimensional modeling; and an artistic aesthetic, which respected the composition of line and plane. From 1890 to 1910, sample books grew fatter with more design choices, trade cards flew through the mail, and more salesmen made their way through women's doors. The year 1890 represented the height of popularity for an aesthetic derived from the various revival styles of nineteenth-century architecture. Parlors, upholstery, and decorative art objects of this period were described by their manufacturers as rich, elaborated, well finished, elegant, and ornamental in appearance; they were praised for their detail, for their softened or softening effect, and for their contribution to the refinement of a room. This aesthetic cut across categories of culture and society, linking commercialized products with the genteel behavior prescribed by etiquette manuals.

A home economist once described the ornamental aesthetic as a "complex mingling" of materials and arrangements, overdecorated to show off bric-a-brac. These constellations of effects produced a layered interior in which the outcome of the design was cumulative.[5] As we see in the photograph of a corner of a home (6.6), the décor reveals an ornamental aesthetic: large-scale floor, ceiling, and wallpaper patterns.

By the turn of the century, the use of wallpaper to fulfill the ornamental aesthetic was commonplace. Typically, walls were organized in two ways. One arrangement consisted of a high baseboard of two or three pieces of wood, a wainscot, a large section of papered wall (the filling or field), and a wallpaper frieze. In an alternate arrangement, if wallpaper covered the entire wall (baseboard to ceiling), as it does in figure 6.6, the motifs in each layer were different, and the ceiling finish, whether paper or plaster, would add a fourth motif. The common technique of combining three different designs of various scales in a range of bright colorways for ceilings, borders, and sidewalls (sometimes with textured finishes such as embossing and even glitter), emboldened walls as backgrounds for other home furnishings.[6] Photographs of everyday rooms indicate that a large number of American middle- and working-class families perceived paper with large patterns as suitable backgrounds for a wide range of two- and three-dimensional effects.

Although wallpaper suited the requirements of the prevailing ornamental style in architecture, domestic leaders in the late nineteenth century begin to urge an alternative aesthetic. Dissatisfied with previous design values, they called on the moral position established by John Ruskin and William Morris in the English arts-and-crafts movement. Ruskin and Morris rejected industrially produced goods, supported handcrafted and appropriate use of materials, and believed in simplicity as an all-encompassing aesthetic. In the United States the movement became a new arbiter of taste and presented a rational approach to design. Catalogue and millwork companies as well as builders' journals used the term *artistic* to describe a number of individual products or ensembles inspired by the English arts-and-crafts movement, all of which used natural materials and a color palette of natural tones (6.7). The Alfred Peats wallpaper company of New York and Chicago took advantage of the popularity of women's magazines to reach "people of artistic taste," advertising their wallpapers in *Ladies' World* and *Ladies' Home Journal*. Social reformers worried about the lack of taste and fashion exhibited in women's wallpaper choices.

Tastemakers, home economists, and other progressives countered the industry's apparently successful seduction of naïve home decorators by warning women to take control of their walls. Their criticisms proved to be nothing new. In 1876, the editor of *Harper's Bazaar* claimed that "Indiana divorce laws may be perhaps directly traced to some frightful inharmoniousness in wall-paper."[4] In magazine articles and home economics tracts, they expressed concern about the sensuousness of wallpaper as a material, the problems in making proper choices amid an abundance of hundreds of tempting designs, and the lure of the salesman's pitch. In this unlikely conflict, two domains were at stake: one moral, the other economic. Before the hostilities ended, the propaganda from both sides became fierce; the market coerced, and the advisers railed.

Two waves of disputants criticized wallpaper. From 1870 to 1896, decorators wrote prescriptively about relying on taste to avoid mistakes in décor. The second wave of reformers, from 1897 to 1911, reiterated the nineteenth-century philosophy that architecture and home decoration exerted a formative effect on the family's moral character. These reformers included new female voices—home economists as well as social workers and women activists who also saw themselves as experts in wall decoration.[10] College-trained professional women and faculty in home economics programs were interested in teaching women practical and standardized housekeeping practices. Their rhetoric rested on scientific substance and reliability. They employed a new medium—the home economics manual (used as texts in high school and college courses) and sold popularly in bookstores—to reach a large population of middle-class women.

Home economists believed that in order to become intelligent consumers, women should be educated in art principles and housing design. Influenced aesthetically by the English arts-and-crafts movement, educators quoted William Morris and referenced Japanese design as models that avoided the "complex mingling" of the ornamental aesthetic. Characterizing overly decorated walls as those "clamoring for notice," they pressed the idea that modest walls were quiet and plain. The concept that beauty could be achieved by simplicity and utility suited the home economists' practical goals of easy-to-clean houses and furnishings that did not overtax the family budget. In promoting an artistic aesthetic, home economists offered it as the basis for a rational approach to design, and they disdained wallpaper as the epitome of manufactured goods that lacked taste.[11]

Wallpaper reformers identified two general categories of problems. First, the accessibility of wallpaper meant that women from a wide range of social backgrounds in diverse geographic locations could readily obtain it. Manufacturers' marketing made sure that women knew that wallpaper was less expensive than other wall finishes and furnishings and offered a variety of venues for shopping. Furthermore, women could and did do their own paperhanging. But accessibility also meant that a large number of women might make poor choices, especially if confronted by a salesman. Second, wallpaper manufacturers perpetuated the ornamental aesthetic that home economists and other progressives attempted to eradicate. Home economists, linking artistic taste to the notion of rational consumption, attacked the popular taste as unsuitably passionate and set themselves up as intermediaries between maker and consumer.

Admonitions of reform crossed class lines, from the middle class to rural women to the working-class immigrant; all women, regardless of their class status, income, or geographic location, were believed to be susceptible to the sensuous qualities of wallpaper. Like many other consumer goods, the affordability and availability of wallpaper helped to democratize the American interior and to blur the apparent boundaries of social class. The wide range in materials and prices of paperhangings, from the cheapest pulps to the Japanese leathers, were available for houses of all classes and all conditions of life. The same sense of fashion in wallpaper purchased by a merchant family could be achieved by a first-generation immigrant mill family.[12]

Advocates of the artistic movement who influenced workers' home environments used the new aesthetic to promote social improvement and cultural homogeneity. They taught both the middle-class professional woman and the working-class girl that large patterns for walls were not just unfashionable and tasteless, but anathema to the new rules of equanimity in domestic politics and the development of the new modern woman. The era's new female voluntary associations and social activists included the discussion of walls in their domestic education of working-class, immigrant, and poor women. Jane Addams, who in 1889 established the settlement-house movement in Chicago, believed in the educational potential of walls. Clients of her Hull-House could borrow reproductions of European masterpieces to hang in their rooms, a strategy designed to wean them from an insistence on garish wallpaper.[13]

Women in frontier and rural homes also changed wall surfaces with decoration. Historian Glenda Riley argues that even on the frontier, the primary focus of women's lives was domestic. Women schooled in nineteenth-century principles of domesticity were hesitant to abandon them, although the standards they sought were difficult to achieve. Women in the prairie regions of Iowa, western Indiana, northern Missouri, and parts of Illinois and Minnesota turned their humble soddies into "elegant dugouts" with the use of wallpaper, newspaper, or whitewash.[14]

To counter the market forces perpetuating ornamental paper, reformers cited the unhealthy effects of wallpaper in general and the ill effects of color in particular. As early as 1869, W. W. Hall, a New York medical doctor, proclaimed that color on walls was a health hazard. He warned women to use no paper that had a fuzzy green color because it was composed of arsenic, "capable of causing convulsions and fatal disease in a single night." The argument held validity, as bright green wallpaper contained an arsenic pigment known as Paris green.

Hall's finding was extended with the argument that the colors of wallpaper could affect the mental health of family members. The color red generated a long-lasting criticism, because red papers appeared as a popular wall color from the 1860s forward and remained consistently in sample books. Writing for *Ladies' World* in 1896, Fryatt declared: "The writer was shown yesterday a paper vivid with red color. After looking at it for an instant, she did not wonder that bulls and turkeys are maddened at the sight of this color. The red must have been of the aniline order, for to the sensitively endowed organs of sight, aniline colors, even aniline blues and greens and yellows, still more aniline reds, seem palpitatingly instinct with aggressive life. Beware of the color that has this property; it is hurtful to the eye, and fades to an ugly condition."[16] From 1890 to 1910 manufacturers ignored the advice of these writers and produced one or more red wallpaper designs in every sample book.

While unhealthy colors formed the first criticism of ornamental wallpaper, a second fault involved inappropriate patterns. This objection was nothing new. Realistic representations of natural forms in upholstery and carpet had been a subject of mid-nineteenth-century tastemakers. In *High Life in New York* (1854), Mrs. Ann S. Stephens ridiculed the fashionable dining room where the "figgers" on the parlor carpet "were so allfired gaudy." However, between 1890 and 1910, naturalistic representations of flowers, fruit, and landscapes still suited the popular taste and were commonly used in wallpaper designs. Extension course lessons used design theory to explain why contrasting patterns and naturalistic representation were inappropriate for walls: "Since a wall is a flat surface, designs should be flatly represented so as to lie tight to the wall. They should represent only two dimensions, length and breadth, not thickness. All . . . designs . . . that imitate rounded forms are false in principle. A natural rose or an actual grape vine crawling through an actual trellis is not good decoration."[17]

Conventionalized design, which was central to the artistic aesthetic, was simple in form and color and applied in an orderly arrangement. The preferred wall was a quiet wall, defined by the principles of simplicity, often interpreted as plainness. In 1881 Cook stated that quietness was not "dull or undecided in its tint. It should harmonize with the pictures and objects and diffuse the tone of the objects that hang upon it, but it should not be subordinate to them, neither over-crowding them nor making them look like isolated spots."[18]

Between 1890 and 1910, writers who assessed women's choices for paper vehemently denounced walls that did not "hold their place" and brightly colored and spottily patterned walls that "crowded" a room. The rhetoric escalated to include language that anthropomorphized walls. Wheeler complained: "It is to wallpaper that we owe most of the disturbing and mistaken decoration of our walls. Bunches of flowers seem to *start out* from every plan of surface, making it impossible to *dodge* them; or zigzag forms

6.8. Tastemakers and home economists believed that actual representation, such as appeared in Montgomery Ward's 1910 design of "green grapes perfectly colored," belongs only in pictures and statuary. Good art, in both pictures and decoration, must leave something to the imagination. From Montgomery Ward, *Wall Paper at Wholesale Prices: Newest Styles for 1910* (Chicago: The Company, 1910): sample no. 8064. Authors' collection.

writhe in platoons along the walls, until the unhappy occupant might almost as well be *struggling* with a nightmare."[19]

Advice writers equated the material with a living being—a monster. They give the monster a masculine temperament—bold, aggressive, strong, and overbearing. The most despised motifs were those associated with masculine warfare, the shields of armed combat, and the medallions of victory. In the final stages of the wallpaper conflict, criticism swells with gender-biased remarks laced with sexual innuendo. "A floral wall paper should not contain a confusion of lifelike flowers *bulging* from the wall." *Ladies' World* described a paper that "fairly *glowed* and *throbbed* with the vividness of its red coloring."[20]

6.9. When salesmen actually crossed thresholds into private homes, encounters between housewife and outsider were described like a seduction scene in a dime novel. *Ladies' World* advised, "If you have no knowledge of color or design, or the harmony of things, and put yourself unhesitatingly in the hands of the wall paper salesman, and he is clever and you are not worried about money limitations, the way is easy." Authors' collection.

Such rhetoric makes an interesting case for understanding the cultural complexities and interrelationships of popular sources in the 1890 to 1915 period. In 1892 Charlotte Perkins Gilman's descriptions in "The Yellow Wall-Paper" borrow from early critics: the "pattern is pronounced enough to constantly irritate . . . a florid arabesque, reminding one of a fungus." Gilman, like other Victorian-era disputants, believed in the emotional effect of the interior environment. She expanded the metaphor into a living creature: "The pattern *lolls* like a broken neck and two bulbous eyes *stare* at you upside down . . . up and down and sideways they *crawl*, and those absurd, unblinking eyes are everywhere. . . . This paper looks to me as if it *knew* what a vicious influence it had!"

Gilman emboldened the animation with action verbs: "It *slaps* you in the face, it *knocks* you down, and *tramples* upon you. . . . It *creeps* all over the house. I find it *hovering* in the dining-room, *skulking* in the parlor, *hiding* in the hall, *lying* in wait for me on the stairs."[21]

Animating wallpaper into a metaphorical beast intensified previous criticisms based on good taste or art principles. Now fear was counterpoised with desire, a tactic of escalating rhetoric, in which wallpaper was equated with women's purchases and with women's behavior generally. Irresponsible consumption was tantamount with inappropriate behavior; moreover, it deserved admonition. This stance intended to scare a modest woman away from any passionate decision she might make hastily, perhaps on the basis of the sensuousness of the material or the liveliness of a pattern. Logic followed: if a housewife acts irresponsibly about wallpaper, then her home—and consequently her family—would suffer for her mistake. By inference, if a woman's papered walls were respectable, then she is too. The fact that the walls of a home were such a large and visible part of the house meant that visitors could tell immediately upon entry whether the walls—and the family—were appropriate.

The solution to the wallpaper dilemma in the minds of many leaders revolved around issues of control. Women were called on to curb their desire for colorful, ornately patterned wallpaper, and to replace desire with preference. In this scenario, women were to act as rational consumers on behalf of their families' welfare rather than acting on their own desires and the enticements of the market. Self-control reaffirmed women's moral authority in the home. Applying restraint, holding emotions in check, and curbing desire constituted a virtuous life.

Gilman and domestic reformers established what amounted to a classical dialectic stance that pitted passion against reason. According to Greek thinkers, reason was a voluntary activity of the self-directed mind. Unlike emotion, reason permits the planning and controlling of actions. Emotion is considered to be an unpredictable response, incompatible with intelligent judgment. When people react with emotion, they were believed to regress to primitive, animal natures. At the turn of the century, uncontrolled and excessive sexual passion was seen as a cause of insanity, which supposedly had a higher incidence in

6.10. Good wallpaper was a metaphor for the virtues of femininity—unity, harmony, and modesty. This "quiet wall" in a Westpoint, Iowa house (ca. 1909) would have met with approval, because the patterns of paper held "flat to the wall." This restrained beauty made an appropriate backdrop for a family of musicians. Authors' collection.

females. In the delineation of gender roles, women were thought to be governed more by sentiment and emotion than men and to be more prone to emotional breakdown. Harmony ruled as the primary recommendation to temper passion, not just in social life but the realm of wall décor as well. Even Gilman, who proclaimed her independence from decoration, employed the ideals of restrained beauty. Expelling bold wallpaper symbolically diminished masculine authority in both the home and the marketplace.

Despite an overblown rhetoric about wallpaper and rational consumption, there is evidence of popular resistance to reformers' admonitions against ornamental wallpaper. First, until well after 1910, manufacturers continued successfully to produce and sell the types of designs found most objectionable by the advocates of the istic aesthetic. Second, women who hung "inappropriate" wallpaper of the 1880s and 1890s may not have replaced it with more "correct" designs in the early twentieth century. Although manufacturers and tastemakers encouraged women to change and renew wall surfaces frequently, because it was less costly than remodeling, wallpaper may have lasted on walls for many years. The photographic evidence is sketchy. When undated photographs are examined, it is difficult to determine if the wallpaper is at the height of fashion or a

ten-year-old treatment. Sequential photographs of modest houses over time also is lacking.

Disputants may have constructed a flawed strategy in posing masculine reason against feminine passion. Rationality was seen as akin to independent thought and action, but each group, depending on their motives, defined independence differently. Reformers seemingly overlooked the reality that many women possessed self-confidence about making their own consumption choices, and that self-confidence is a form of independence. Domestic leaders also ignored the power of traditional conceptions of femininity. As women papered floral motifs and layered the flowers with pictures of loved ones, they created a familiar feminine interior domain.

As we consider photographs of real women in their houses, we see walls treated as mosaics of color, pattern, and memorabilia. Despite the public debate about what women wanted and what was good for them, many women chose to retain ornamentation over simplicity on their walls. Regarded by reformers as cluttered and crammed with the furnishings and objects of manufacture, nevertheless, the ornamental aesthetic endured well into the twentieth century largely because of its capacity to fill up empty spaces.

Wallpaper was a powerful material that afforded women the opportunity to experiment with architectural and spatial perception, expanding or shrinking a room's dimensions. A woman could make her own internal landscape, and it could be as wild and colorful as she liked because she was expressing a vitality of her own spirit. The act of shopping, sifting through myriad designs, making decisions, and installing wallpaper empowered women to design the interiors of their own houses in ways that were impossible when furnishings could not be purchased or replaced easily. A woman learned that walls created an arena she could control by deciding how animated, how personal, or how modest she wanted them to be.

The wallpaper dilemma reveals more about the cultural themes of the period than it does about taste, fashion, or social class. The friction between manufacturers and reformers offers one example of the way middle-class, small-town, and rural women evaluated their circumstances, suppliers, and surroundings and how they adapted local references to the advice they read. The rhetorical arguments over wallpaper carried nineteenth-century issues of morality in the domestic interior into the twentieth century.

COLONIAL REVIVAL: CLASSICAL

The cultural lifespan of an aesthetic is not easily plotted. With so many elements in various stages of development, one may find a transitional condition complicating the effort to establish a new aesthetic. That is exactly what happened from about 1895 to 1910. We think of this occurrence as a movement toward a classical aesthetic, which had already played a significant role in American cultural history, from the original colonial styles, to the federalist and Greek and Italianate revival buildings. But the classical aesthetic was also another step toward modern interiors. The classical design system exhibited strong links to earlier generations of colonial revival. Of the four different house types that utilized this approach, three of them were intentionally colonial designs. The fourth house was the hip-roofed square type, which had a colonial-classical character because of its cubical shape, stripped-down elevations, and colonial entry porch. The other houses were the formal colonial hip-roofed cottage, the gambrel-roofed cottage, and the hip-roofed bungalow.

As for the execution of the specific aspects of this aesthetic, a center hall plan (a colonial attribute) was used more frequently than a side hall plan, and the arrangements of rooms were no different from the prevailing form in all three houses. The significant differences occurred in the choices and in the combinations of individual elements.

Once again millwork is a prime indicator of how this aesthetic was structured. A fireplace mantel was

6.11. The overall composition of this room is restrained and classical. The millwork has two appeals; the trim around the door openings is plain yet layered, while the wall piece (*on the left*), which includes the mantel and storage, has a higher degree of historic authenticity. Dining room of J. T. Kelley House; Arthur Lawrence Valk, Los Angeles architect. Authors' collection.

rectangular in shape and made with quarter-sawn oak or birch. It had a gloss finish, and the face was framed by columns extending from the hearth to the top of the overmantel. This mantel had some incised ornamentation and a few molding plants, but overall the number of ornaments had been greatly reduced. The overmantel often included a mirror (see 2.10).

The openings between rooms were spanned with grille columns, that is, with freestanding or low-pedestal colonnades that carried a deep architrave. Scrollwork and spindle work grilles could be added to the opening. The placement of large columns is of historical interest, because in the next decade (1910s) interior columns became part of colonnade furniture (see 3.2). This use of columns as an opening feature has not occurred since in vernacular interiors.

The stair plans were the same as those associated with these house types, but some of the elements of the stair were handled differently. For example, the newel post had a square base with a paneled shaft and a rather plain cap. At this time Sears sold its so-called anti-dust newel, which it identified as part of the artistic system as well as of this one. Balusters were square (a modern characteristic) or turned (colonial effect).

The interior finish also had two aesthetic options in that the baseboard had a three-part composition more or less like those in the ornamental system, but the pilaster casings around the doors and windows

6.12. The stair has a square newel with very little molding, square balusters, and a quarter-turn stair. The plainness suggests late nineteenth- and early-twentieth-century modernity. The potted plant on the newel cap is an improvement over a machine-made urn or ornamental light. The wallpaper of stylized flowers is up-to-date, but the braided rug at the foot of the stairs and the old parlor lamp indicate colonial revival interests. Authors' collection.

6.13. Most classical commercial interiors feature millwork elements such as the back bar in the Minnie Pray Store in Page, North Dakota. The large mirror, framed by Ionic columns and a full entablature, makes this section of the store a set piece. Classical framing also encourages symmetry, which is expressed here by even distribution of the lights in front of the mirror. The reflection reveals more of the store, including the ceiling light system. Photo credit: L. A. Foster Company, Kewanee, Illinois. Authors' collection.

were a reed type or a plain, round-edge. The plain casing was related to the anti-dust sensibility.

The classical aesthetic outdid all other systems in its use of cap trim over the head casing. Compositionally, a cap trim was a door cornice; most had a delicate molding—a bead or a row of small dentils—below the dust cap and the face of the casing. Wreaths and garlands sometimes were applied to the face. We have not found any cap trim in millwork catalogs before 1900, and, after 1920, such trim is referred to as colonial cap trim.

The hardware system for this aesthetic was both colonial (oval escutcheons and knobs with beaded edges) and modern (plain, beveled-edge pattern). All of the designs were less ornamental than were their predecessors.

In summary, the colonial-classical system reflected the countervailing forces of tradition and change, which were implied in the language used to describe the system. For example, an article in a trade journal (1898) referred to a hip-roofed cottage as "somewhat of the colonial character, modernized in its treatment," with "inside finish of the simplest kind." In 1908 Sears sold a hip-roofed cottage with classical attributes, the Modern House, No. 102, which had a front porch of Tuscan columns, cottage windows, plain round-edge casings with circle-pattern blocks, and a moderately curved baseboard profile.

COLONIAL REVIVAL AESTHETIC: MODERN

Every design system and its aesthetic in this ninety-year period intended to be modern. Even practitioners of the colonial, who had tradition and practice on which to fall back, insisted on being contemporary. Most studies of American cultural history agree that the 1876 Centennial Exposition in Philadelphia was important for American design. The exhibition not only exposed Americans to the materials and forms of their own past, but it also introduced Americans to the new English cottage styles. The gap between the American vernacular and the imported—between the two craft traditions—was to be bridged by technology: colonial imagery produced through manufacturing. Distribution was important, because the frontier regions of the country did not have the sense of architectural history that the Eastern states enjoyed.

Over time the concept of colonialism became generalized into a few house types, for example, the saltbox house and the garrison house, and the Georgian-inspired public building. Precisely what kind of colonial design American buildings were to display seemed at first a rhetorical question. Centennial fever had builders and manufacturers focusing on authentic detailing—mantels in the Massachusetts mode or wainscots in the manner of the Tidewater states. This archeological approach had been part of the English movements to revive historical styles. Authenticity produced a feeling of legitimacy, and it bought time.

Colonial materials, such as shingles and hand-wrought iron, and the patterns and textures they created were also of interest. Designers were well aware that texture produces effects, whether the element is a rough-cut beam or an enameled classical molding. In the end, the Georgian style, in a much-reduced state, won the day over the rustic. Georgian was dignified. Colonial vernacular was going to look rational and enlightened rather than passively medieval and locally crafted.

Common heritage and shared illusions, the turning to the English arts-and-crafts design aesthetic, the progressive spirit of the times that sought to reform housing conditions and housework environments—all this could be addressed through colonial design schemes. And indeed, as evidence for the strength of the system, colonial design has outlasted all others and proven to economical.

Colonial design was not a single-minded, all-pervasive system, but rather a series of effects to be interpreted broadly. English reformers such as William Morris, who had many followers here, preached simplicity in all things. The colonial system succeeded by clustering simple effects. Moreover, progressives in this country declared ornamented cottage design inappropriate. Frank L. Lent, pattern-book writer and practitioner, put it this way: "Whatever departure in minor details may be required in accommodation to our later mode of life or personal conveniences, the old Colonial grace, simplicity, and refinements are sure to make a favorable impression in contradistinction to foolish attempts at outward display, bedaubing with scroll-sawed brackets, freaks of the wood turner's fancy, fantastic color, lop-sided design, and cheap senseless ornaments."[21]

In his own design work, Lent relied on the gambrel roof to organize the volumes of his common-sense houses. He translated his interest in simplicity as "utility and beauty" going hand in hand. Although artistic design also promoted utility, the colonial was our most successful functional style. It delivered more modernism than the other systems, with straightforward, simple lines and forms, and at the same time it had associational value. History, John Ruskin told us, needed to be living history. With our enormous capacity to replicate anything and our hunger for a usable past, we made the colonial our national building style.

Overall, the colonial aesthetic existed in two types of design: the ornamental, from 1890 to about 1920, and the modernized colonial, between 1920 and 1960. In the first instance, colonial motifs—a Palladian window, for example—were added to cottage house forms. Cottage design was eclectic in this period, and colonial design was influenced by other styles, especially the Queen Anne, examples of which had been on display at the Philadelphia exhibition of 1876. The Queen Anne had vernacular roots, and Americans such as Henry Hudson Holly saw in it "a simple mode of honest English building, worked out

in a natural form, fitting with the sash windows and ordinary doorways which express real domestic needs."[22]

The passage suggests that Holly was attracted to the idea of effects, that windows and doorways had both functional and symbolic meaning. Holly was a New York architect and pattern-book writer who liked the direct, simple, honest forms of the colonial because architects and workmen could work readily with the structure of these vernacular styles. It was something they knew. Holly's enthusiasm for the style was romantic; that is, he saw this kind of classicism as part of the picturesque cottage tradition—buildings with "irregularities." He liked the interaction of the roofs, dormers, and chimneys. Holly imagined the colonial adapted to modern purposes, but his method for creating the modern was to express an ornamental aesthetic based on taste. He wanted refined objects, such as stained glass in the upper sash, harmonious colors relieved by Oriental rugs, a wainscot of Indian matting, and a Jacobean fireplace.

The ornamental attitude toward colonial design gave way to the modernized system in the 1920s. The shift away from surface ornamentation was tied to

6.14. *Today's Idea House* brochure promised more comfort, convenience, and beauty with Ponderosa pine woodwork. Indeed, the quintessential modern colonial living room relied on millwork—mantel surround and shelf, French doors to a sun porch, an arched niche with a shallow keystone molding. *Today's Idea House* (Chicago: Ponderosa Pine Woodwork Association, 1945), cover. Authors' collection.

the general reform of housing types in which the almost square, hip-roofed cottage replaced the Queen Anne. Colonial interior architecture became generalized into a few historical motifs that created a unified impression. Scaled down and simplified, with fewer elements for each effect, the colonial aesthetic boiled down to millwork, hardware, and some architectural furniture.

Most modernized colonial interior built between 1915 and 1935, whether in a straight gable or in a gambrel-roofed cottage, its ridgepole parallel to the street, had a central hall plan. These were two-story buildings with social and service spaces on the ground floor level and bedrooms and bathroom on the second. The stair was either a straight flight on axis with the entrance or a quarter-turned stair on axis. The floors were hardwood, at least on the ground floor level, with linoleum and tile in the kitchen and bath. The wall organization included a modest picture molding, with the rest of the area plastered or papered in a small-pattern motif. Walls were also paneled with paper, and dining rooms might have a historic scene mural. Painted walls often were stippled. The standing finish was painted—ivory was the most popular color—and the risers on the stairs received the same color as the woodwork. The treads, rail, and newel were stained a dark color, usually mahogany. Baseboard design was restrained: most had a shoe molding at the bottom, but very few added a molding to the top.

Ceilings generally were left as finished plaster, but ceiling moldings, panels, and centerpieces were common. To a lesser degree, living rooms were beamed with the same oak as in the artistic system, but in the colonial the beams were painted to match the woodwork. Stenciling died out in the 1920s and had little significance in the colonial system. According to trade catalogs, the traditional entrance door was a six-panel stile-and-rail unit with raised panels, and interior doors were the five-cross-panel type. Inventories of colonial motifs reveal many alternative choices. French doors affording access to the hall from a living room or dining room or to a sun parlor or porch became a standard element. Windows were predominantly double-hung sash types with divided lights. Window placement included singles that were wider on the façade (a leftover cottage motif), and doubles and triples especially in living and dining

rooms. Sunrooms and sleeping porches often were glazed on all three sides.

Most large interior openings were cased with pilaster finish, but uncased plastered openings and arches worked their way into the design vocabulary, just as colonnades had done in the ornamental version of the colonial. Grilles remained part of the older system. The colonial aesthetic had such a strong tie to the open fireplace that it became a requirement for colonial schemes. Most were end-wall types, with or without a chimneybreast, and featured wood mantels with pilasters or columns and an entablature as a shelf, brick facing, and a brick hearth. The molding work on the mantel, whether applied or stuck, was often the most delicately designed work in the house. Colonial architectural furniture included bookcases (more often open than closed), a buffet, corner china closets, and during the 1920s a breakfast nook.

Hardware was either machined-finished in brass, bronze, or pewter, or hand-worked in iron; most pieces had little ornamentation. There might be beading around the edge of the escutcheon plate or knob: a plate with an overall shape, such as an oval; or plates with different terminations: square, eared, round, half-round. Glass doorknobs were part of the modern and the colonial systems.

Lighting installations for the colonial seemed to require candlelights as brackets or as parts of a large dining room luminaire. Most of these designs were made to look historic and to integrate with other colonial effects. For instance, the reflectors on bracket lights looked a great deal like the hardware on the doors—a decorated edge on the plate, a ball-shaped bulb not unlike the spheroid knob on the door. And yet lighting features were always modern.

To learn more about the application of colonial design systems, we turn to examples of the style's millwork in a trade catalog. The company was Carr, Ryder and Adams of Dubuque, Iowa (hereafter noted as CRA), which had broad distribution of its product; the catalog is not dated but seems to be ca. 1927.

CRA listed elements of design systems for several styles. Elements that could be assembled for a colonial effect included doors, wainscots, stair treatments (including newel, rail, and baluster types), storage units, windows, and mantels. CRA offered thirteen

Table 6.1. Analysis of Trim Sets from Bilt Well Millwork (Dubuque, Iowa: Carr, Ryder & Adams, 1926), 112–125.

Trim	Shoe Mold	Base	Base mold	Base block	Picture mold	Head case	Head case stop	Head case mold	Casing	Back band	Stop	Stool	Apron
910	7073	7435		923	7216	7335	7186	7261	7347		7242 7244	7312	7307
912	7073	7435			7216				7352	7151	7242 7244	7312	7307
913	7073	7388			7216	7337			7356		7242 7244	7312	7307
915	7073	7434			7216				7352	7147	7242 7244	7312	7307
918	7073	7434			7216				7367	7148	7242 7244	7312	7307
921	7073	7388	7043	925	7216				7370		7236 7238	7316	7308

trim sets, and each was illustrated in a design vignette so that its application could be imagined. A set could consist of a baseboard and a quarter-round shoe molding, a casing with or without a backband, a base block, a picture molding, a choice of stops for the windows, and an integrated window stool and apron.

Of the thirteen sets, six can be identified as having a colonial context; that is, elements are shown with another CRA product and identified by the maker as "colonial" or are familiar enough to have been recognized as colonial by the trade. The term *colonial* is not used in the copy accompanying the illustrations of trim sets. The message here seems to be that if the buyer wants a colonial effect, she should choose one of the trim sets suggested as appropriate to a six-panel door, or a pilaster-framed fireplace mantel, or a divided-light window set in a 6/1, 6/6, or 8/8 configuration. In addition to the millwork products generally associated with the colonial system, each vignette has other design clues, such as wall finish. The colonial rooms have smoother plasterwork, stippled painting, and wallpaper with narrow stripes—the very finishes recommended for colonial treatments during this time.

To understand the makeup of trim sets, we have analyzed each set by its components. Table 6.1 reveals that there were many repeats in the sets; for example, the window stop, stool, and apron pieces could work in almost any context. There were virtually no choices in some series; for example, the picture molding was the same in every set.

If the shoe molding, the picture molding, and the window stool, apron, and stop remained constant, the real variables were the casing, which could be augmented by a backband molding, and the baseboard. Of these colonial sets, only one had a molding for the baseboard and only two had a base block. The modernized colonial was, therefore, a system of fewer elements than the ornamental colonial, and the elements that featured raised moldings had shallower profiles than in the ornamental. The reduction in the number of surfaces and in the depth of the cuts in the surfaces also eliminated historical references. This strategy reduced the number of dust catching edges from the older millwork elements, which no doubt pleased design reformers, and it extended the use of colonial trim into contemporary settings. Some of the casings and baseboards were so generalized that they became ubiquitous, fitting colonial, artistic, and generally modern systems.

CRA manufactured other items that could be used in a colonial setting. For example, they had five different designs for dining-room corner china cabinets, all of which included cabinet space in the base

Table 6.2. Survey of Colonial House Interiors built from 1907 to 1942 in Ames, Iowa. Survey by Mary Anne Beecher.

	Front Door	Stair Plan	Interior Door	Fireplace	Paned Door(s)	D. R. Built-ins	Newel Post	Door Hdwe	Base Board
1907									
1916									
1929									
1930									
1934									
1934							N.A.		
1934									
1936								N.A.	N.A.
1936									
1942									

and a glass door in front of the shelving; most units had two storage drawers as well. In each case, the overall size of the piece was the same—seven feet one inch by three feet, with a recess that was one foot three inches deep—but the glazing pattern on the upper doors was varied, as was the trim around the cabinet and the cabinet head. The headpiece options included a broken pediment, a keystone, and a continuous casing. Bookcases were also identified as suitable for colonial environments; the cases were open or closed (glass doors) with circle-top, flat, or segmented heads.

The breakfast nook usually was associated with bungalow design, but CRA produced a colonial nook with panels painted on the seat backs and turned legs for the benches and the table. In stair work there were five colonial newels—both starting and angle newels—of turned stock; four of the five had a square base and one ended in a spiral volute. The balusters were thin, with round or tapered shapes. CRA also illustrated two stair systems, both with a straight flight and the appropriate elements, within the context of a colonial hallway. If buyers couldn't assemble a system on their own, they could buy one intact.

The final CRA product that had bearing on the colonial system was a leaded glass door for cupboards. CRA identified the patterns as "appropriate for the Modern home" as well as for the colonial and the English. Furnished with either lead or zinc metal bars, the glazing patterns were mostly a gridiron of rectangles and diamonds.

From the array of millwork products sold during the period of 1870–1960, and from the information available from surveys of extant buildings, there seems never to have been a recognized formula for creating a colonial interior design. This conclusion holds true for the early, post-Centennial period as well as for the regenerated colonial of the 1920s. Based on what we now know of the Cape Cod house, which was first introduced as a colonial cottage, the situation remained the same for decades. The colonial, like most interior architecture systems, was created from a series of effects within a range of intensities. Just as Henry Hudson Holly referred to the Queen Anne as the "free classic," the concept of the "free colonial" seems apt for this kind of design. The phrase suggests that the system from which it springs is not rigid, and that there is an overarching quality about the work that identifies it.

Historian Mary Anne Beecher surveyed a group of colonial revival houses in Iowa to document what kinds of millwork and hardware were used to suggest a colonial aesthetic. From left to right, the table lists the construction date, entrance doorway, interior stair plan and door type, fireplace design, French door pattern, cabinets, door hardware and baseboard profile. The data reveal that there was no uniform application, and no standard way to identify the aesthetic. There were related details, however; for example, the entrance doorways have some glass either in the door or as sidelights or a transom.

ARTISTIC AESTHETIC

What is known as the arts-and-crafts movement influenced American culture as a new arbiter of taste as well as the basis for a rational approach to design. This rational approach was especially helpful for various progressive movements that sought to redefine the home environment and the role of women in it. Beyond some general principles, there was also a belief in the power of the individual to construct a meaningful environment. The concept of the housekeeper as an artist—the home artist—was the key to broadcasting design values. The point was made that any woman could succeed in these decorating and designing activities, as long as she were willing to believe in herself and in the principles the writers set forth. The imposition of self in the design scheme was critical. There were no experts in rural areas to do it for the woman, in any event. The individual had the capacity to create the appropriate composition. The authority of the treatment, its credibility, was to be found within the eye and mind of the individual housekeeper. How a particular woman accomplished this was theoretically simple. She created an environment that looked and functioned like a picture, with rooms and furnishings brought into a harmonious effect. The home economists recommended creating "a simple unified effect" so that all parts of the picture produced a sustained impression. The overall design scheme was supposed to have a concept—say, repose, freedom, or cheer—which would be reinforced by every opportunity for design in the room.

Color was a key element in these theories because the writers recognized the psychological influence of color on human perception and behavior, its power to create a warm or cold emotional atmosphere. The application of color was reduced to a matter of natural tones. The primary toning of an interior included light-colored walls and dark wood. Professional decorators went further. They recommended a generalized brown tone for everything, with some rooms getting specific natural tones: russet for halls, green for living rooms, and brown for the dining area.

Color and nature were linked further in that natural materials, such as wood, were supposed to *look* natural. Dark finishes that obscured the grain should be avoided. Moreover, there should be no artificial graining of wood, since this was considered sham design. Being truthful about surfaces and the nature of materials, and using natural light and color, would produce a home picture that had spiritual as well as material worth.

The desire to create a unified effect was linked to the bias for vistas through interior spaces. That is, the interior of a house should be connected visually and physically to the exterior, so that both the perception of space and the movement through space would be experienced as continuous. This desire for inside–outside continuity had a major impact on space planning; it was especially helpful in breaking down Vic-

torian compartmentalized spaces into the open planning we associate with modernism.

If an interior design were to present a unified picture, it had to be composed of a series of smaller pictures: a balanced arrangement of the structural parts of each room. Composition could be found by relating elements to each other, for example, doorways flank a living room fireplace, and the opposite wall has a bay window with built-in bookcases to either side. The placements unite the room and contribute to an orderly space.

The Victorian-era design system focused on the inherent value of the object itself. Modernists taught that if the design had integrity, then the furnishings, regardless of their material and perhaps of their style, could be a secondary consideration. They reasoned that an interior design with a unified effect would cause a reconsideration of the material things that filled up a home. In the new scheme, those things that were not in harmony with the total picture should be discarded. Furniture, for example, that did not follow structural lines would seem inappropriate in a room so organized.

There was more to picture making than references to vistas and analogies to artists. The reformers had a specific picture in mind—the landscape painting. The natural divisions of a room were likened to

6.15. The south end of an artistic-inspired dining room in the G. M. Worthington house in Aberdeen, South Dakota illustrates key elements that define the room: a large built-in sideboard and a plate rail, interrupted by the window casing and an electric, octagonal, leaded art glass dome above a small octagon-shaped table. Authors' collection.

those of a landscape: the floor was like the earth; the walls, the foreground of the painting; the ceiling, the sky. In terms of light values, the scheme called for a darkened floor, walls of middle value, and a light-colored ceiling. Furthermore, horizon lines fitted into this idea as a way to establish proportions within a room. For instance, a plate rail or a picture molding could serve as a horizon line. The artistic interior was therefore a picture based on principles—such as following structural lines—that could be composed by anyone who was willing to study. For the authors of university bulletins, the principles were good for anything: from the entire farm to a piece of furniture or an arrangement of pictures on a wall. Over time, the principles became institutionalized as part of public school training in home economics and part of learning programs for the general public.

The manufacturers of interior goods were not so spiritually involved with design principles, but they were interested in design effects, especially overall harmonious effects. Industry could produce the appearance of an integrated design with millwork. The home economists' point of view about quality interiors became known as the artistic view. Manufacturers were reticent to make goods in a single style, since that would limit production and work against their belief in providing for individual tastes. But manufacturers could produce a range of goods with different elements that could be labeled as "artistic," and these could be assembled in a variety of ways.

In a 1915 trade catalog, an Iowa millwork company, Gordon-Van Tine, tried to appeal to those interested in artistic compositions by highlighting mantels, inglenooks, and stairs as the features of the house that allowed "the greatest play for the talents of the architect." Gordon-Van Tine assumed that properly placed elements, such as a mantel, had a major impact on overall effect. If a mantel could be combined with other wood pieces, cut from the same species of wood and finished in the same way, then the impact of the effect could be increased significantly. To the trade interior design consisted of the control of a few effects and the linking of those effects to a few architectural details. Therefore, manufacturers could focus product design and merchandising on those issues. Engravings and photographs in advertisements and illustrated trade catalogs emphasized effects, and ancillary material in the pictures

was intended to create the illusion of a controlled effect. A Japanese flower arrangement or a piece of Southwest Indian pottery on a mantel signaled the viewer that this was indeed an artistic interior.

Sometimes the manufacturer suggested the special effect in the copy that accompanied the picture. A beamed ceiling might give a "massive" effect to a room, or a mantel might add a "rustic" quality. Portions of a space or a whole sequence of rooms might be "cheery" or "cozy." If affective appeals were not enough, there were appeals to the rational, design-principle side of things as well. Work was labeled "well proportioned" and "balanced," and the integration of parts was emphasized.

The home economists' point of view about quality interiors became known as the artistic view. The artistic view linked the desire to construct artful environments with the arts and crafts commitment to quality materials, and to the general notion of pictorial thinking. These pieces were generally rectilinear in shape and were heavy visually and physically in that they revealed solid wood construction rather than the veneers of the Victorian styles (see 5.11 and 5.12). They exploited the character of the wood, emphasizing grain and simple joinery, and created novel effects. When combined with other elements in the artistic vocabulary, such as rough plaster, burlap, art glass, and stenciling, the craftsman and mission work suggested an artistic environment.

Part of the attraction to the artistic lay in the juxtaposition and proximity of materials: smooth, dull-gloss oak panel strips on the wall set against dyed burlap and rough plaster; brass against glass; the smooth glaze of ceramics against the grain of wood. This exploitation of natural materials gave a homespun quality to the interior and vested the room with the illusion of time. Indeed, time could be purchased for the vernacular interior with the installation of historical styles, but if one rejected that as inappropriate, or if something modern were preferred, one could turn to the strength of materials and references to craft as a substitute for academic historicism.

The key to integrating natural materials and design principles was the housekeeper, the woman in charge of the home. According to Hazel Adler in *The New Interior* (1916), this modern point of view about interior design required that women see themselves

6.16. A bookcase colonnade, with short tapered columns, frames a dining room. The occupants used the casing of the colonnade as a display rail for two small landscape paintings. This dining room is articulated with a plate rail on one wall and a bay window at one end. Branched fixtures with dome shades provide electric lighting for both rooms. Authors' collection.

6.17. This picture shows a bookcase colonnade dividing a living room from a dining room. The overall treatment is eclectic and both rooms are display spaces. Authors' collection.

6.18. The treatment of the interior is shaped by the storefront space. The narrow room allows for furniture and fittings along each wall, with circulation in between. Keys to the aesthetic are the wall finish (plastered walls, a somber tone) and the store furniture. The booths have a rectilinear character—square posts, plain rails, and panels—and the display cases are plain and straightforward. The only ornamentation is hand-crafted brackets. Each wooden booth carries a craftsman (associated with artistic treatments) light fixture with a square upturned shade. The fixtures are attached to the square column of the seat back. Authors' collection.

as artists.[23] The implications of this role were sociological and political as well as stylistic. The home-artist concept implied a great deal of freedom and discipline: the willingness to eliminate the extraneous, to control the use of design details, to keep the unifying idea in perspective. The success of any interior's scheme was, therefore, a reflection of the housekeeper's personality and character.

As a final check on the artistic design system, let us return to the country's premier purveyor of middle-class design values, Sears, Roebuck and Company. Sears used the term *artistic* to describe a number of individual products or ensembles. For Sears, artistic items had a higher pictorial value than other item; the artistic was unconventional. Glass, tile, or wood products that received special surface treatments were thought to be artful. Sears was also careful not to limit the idea of the artistic to a single line of goods. The company would often combine effects in illustrations of designs. A craftsman door might be grouped with Queen Anne windows, a colonial colonnade, and a rustic fireplace (a feature in most of its designs).

Trade magazines and millwork manufacturers made the dining room an integral component of the artistic aesthetic (see 2.2) Sears's catalogs featured the application of an artistic aesthetic in dining rooms more often than living rooms, and it did so as early as 1900. Sears's *Building Supplies* catalog illustrates a modern dining room with beamed ceiling and wainscoting that is two-thirds of the wall height. By 1912 Sears manufactured or sold all the component parts of the aesthetic. Modern Home No. 230 is illustrated with a two-point perspective drawing of a dining room in harmony with the living room directly across the hall. The only separation between the two rooms is a set of French doors. Sears's drawing includes the ideal artistic aesthetic—what one could purchase to complete a fully developed aesthetic installation: beam ceiling, a built-in buffet glazed with leaded art glass doors, and skeleton paneling over two-thirds of the wall, with a plate rail. A round table is centered in the room, and above it hangs a four-light shower and chain fixture. An area rug covers most of the room, with the exception of a border of exposed strip flooring. Gordon-Van Tine, a ready-cut company, also depicted a dining room installation in which "every detail was perfect." Curtis Companies,

a high-end millwork manufacturer, used photographs of dining rooms in its 1914 catalog.

A few surviving real photograph postcards suggest that homeowners who photographed an artistic aesthetic in their dining rooms had mastered "building the picture," evidenced first by the millwork and furnishings they purchased, and second by their framing of their photographs with a colonnade or cased opening corresponding to a living room. Light fixtures offer variation, and there are differences in room size and the amount and quality of millwork elements. However, all of the photographs of artistic aesthetic applications have a common ground; they celebrate wood products, they integrate different kinds of artifacts and new technology (electric lighting) into the scheme, the rooms appear to be well used, and they have showplace appeal because there is so much to display.

ENGLISH AND SPANISH REVIVAL AESTHETIC

English revival houses entered the marketplace twice: after World War I as cottages and during the 1930s as bungalows. In both cases the interior treatments were similar. The side hall plan is popular, and the living room is the front room. Entry may be directly into the living room or into a small vestibule. The dining room occupies the middle position with a

6.19. A five-light branched fixture with ball-frosted lamps, ca. 1920, is suspended above the table in this dining room. The millwork in the room is restrained and dark. There are no vertical or horizontal wall divisions, only a ceiling molding. A segmental arch frames a small niche. Authors' collection.

kitchen behind it. The main feature of many living rooms is a stucco fireplace. Casement windows are often grouped in pairs and threes. There is a preference for curved, plastered arches for openings between the living and dining rooms in English bungalows. Trim systems are usually modern and not historical. Breakfast nooks or alcoves and small terraces were popular in both house types.

Spanish revival houses also rely on stucco as an expressive or rough finish, both outside and inside. The entry is often located in a small, enclosed terrace. Like the English type, the living room is the front room, and end-wall fireplaces are common, with tile facing. An alternative fireplace treatment is a sculptured breastwork that projects into the room. Spanish bungalows, which are more prevalent than cottages, employ plastered arches between openings and alcoves. The principal millwork accents are a plank front door and a beamed ceiling.

MODERN AESTHETIC

Interest in modern design values—that is, modern for modernism's sake—implies a deeper investment in rational schemes, machine-made effects, and efficient living. This aesthetic paralleled the emergence of the artistic development. The standard historical treatment of the first three decades of twentieth-

century-design history interprets the turn to artistic treatments as a reaction to the onset of modernism. Some of the values overlap, for example, the belief in the value of materials. But the truly modern aesthetic would exploit the mass production of building materials instead of craft production, which the artistic view required.

If the modern exterior could exploit contemporary materials, so could the interior. Both the storefront and the interior could be upgraded with new materials. Thus modern commercial interiors are a lot about finish and improvement in support systems, especially lighting. Manufacturers, particularly companies that produced aluminum bulkheads, window frames, and mullions—shaped the overall approach to remodeling. The owner exchanged one system for another; the interior was adjusted to coordinate with the merchandise. Display casework and lighting took up much of the sales floor. Changing wall and floor coverings could alter the impression of the store. The rest of construction was storage, an office, and maybe an opening for shipping and receiving.

The following tables address interior aesthetics. All were millwork-dependent, because wood materials were easily ornamented with moldings or patterns. Some exterior aesthetic details carried through to the interior, such as Italianate brackets, while some shared applications, like interior trim sets. The overall effect of any aesthetic depended a

6.20. The plain brick fireplace, a standard of modernism since the Arts and Crafts period, continues into the 1950s with a shallow mantel or none at all. This contemporary living room has a vaulted ceiling and a clerestory, as well as "early American" furnishings popularized by the Ethan Allen Company, including a hobnail milk glass and brass lamp. The large brass plate hanging above the fireplace was a common decorative object. Authors' collection.

6.21. The newspaper story that accompanied this 1955 photograph commented on the built-in storage bin that could serve as a fireside seat and as an extra service counter. The picture captures a corner of the kitchen with matching maple cabinets and forged iron cupboard hardware. A lantern pendant is positioned above the storage compartment. Authors' collection.

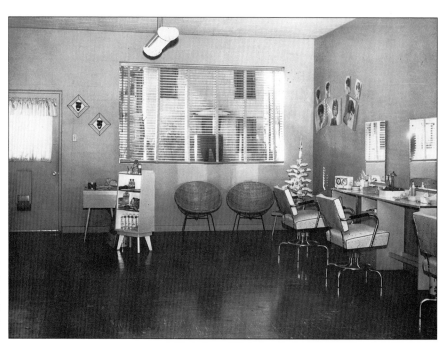

6.22. Workstations organize this small-town beauty shop. The flooring is durable and easy to maintain. Wall finishes and florescent lighting are both stock items, as are the chairs and work areas. This is a modern, practical room. Authors' collection.

great deal on the treatment of details. Some systems were additive in the way fireplaces and mantels increased in size and features in the ornamental, and others, like the colonial revival and modern, reduced the presence of details. Sometimes a new element, like a colonnade, attracted another detail like a grille, which accented the passage from one space to another.

A second aspect has to do with the how materials were treated. That changed from aesthetic to aesthetic. Likewise built-ins, or architectural furniture, were an aesthetic feature, and revival aesthetics appropriated details from another culture to distinguish an interior. Eventually interiors turned completely modern, with open, well-lighted spaces, and a bias for geometric shapes and flat surfaces.

Table 6.3. Characteristics of the Italianate Aesthetic: Interior

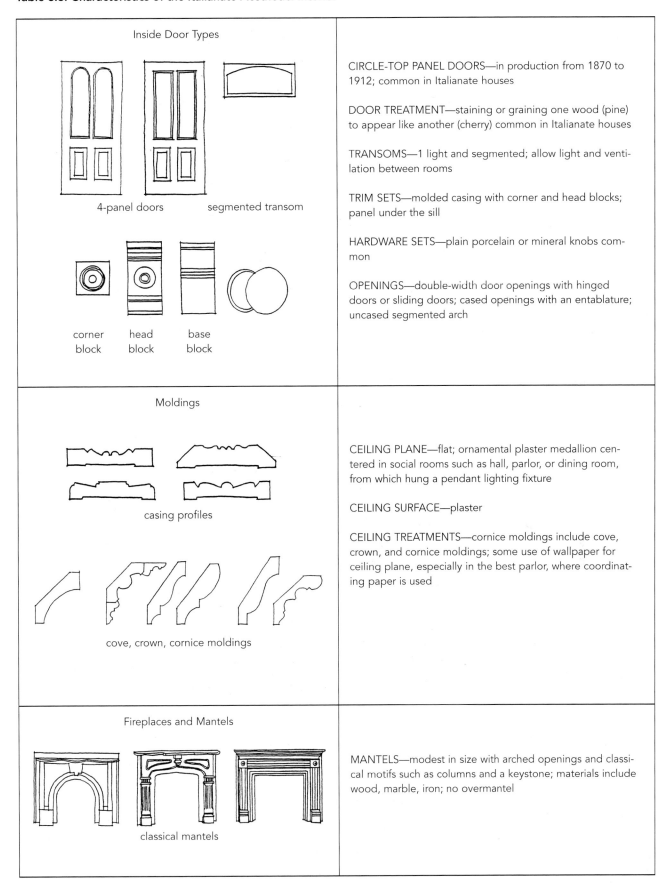

Inside Door Types

4-panel doors   segmented transom

corner block   head block   base block

CIRCLE-TOP PANEL DOORS—in production from 1870 to 1912; common in Italianate houses

DOOR TREATMENT—staining or graining one wood (pine) to appear like another (cherry) common in Italianate houses

TRANSOMS—1 light and segmented; allow light and ventilation between rooms

TRIM SETS—molded casing with corner and head blocks; panel under the sill

HARDWARE SETS—plain porcelain or mineral knobs common

OPENINGS—double-width door openings with hinged doors or sliding doors; cased openings with an entablature; uncased segmented arch

Moldings

casing profiles

cove, crown, cornice moldings

CEILING PLANE—flat; ornamental plaster medallion centered in social rooms such as hall, parlor, or dining room, from which hung a pendant lighting fixture

CEILING SURFACE—plaster

CEILING TREATMENTS—cornice moldings include cove, crown, and cornice moldings; some use of wallpaper for ceiling plane, especially in the best parlor, where coordinating paper is used

Fireplaces and Mantels

classical mantels

MANTELS—modest in size with arched openings and classical motifs such as columns and a keystone; materials include wood, marble, iron; no overmantel

Table 6.3. Characteristics of the Italianate Aesthetic: Interior (continued)

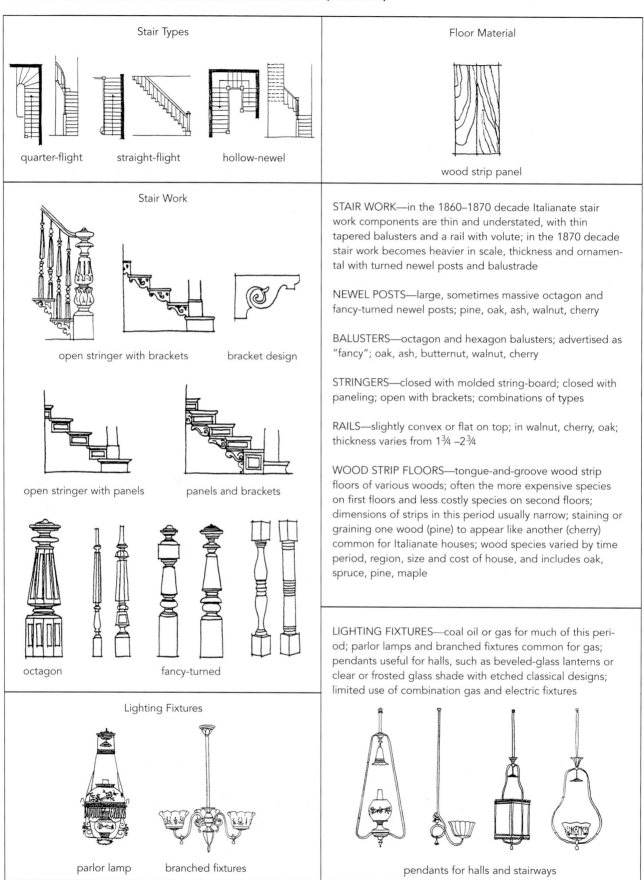

Stair Types

quarter-flight   straight-flight   hollow-newel

Floor Material

wood strip panel

Stair Work

open stringer with brackets   bracket design

open stringer with panels   panels and brackets

octagon   fancy-turned

Lighting Fixtures

parlor lamp   branched fixtures

STAIR WORK—in the 1860–1870 decade Italianate stair work components are thin and understated, with thin tapered balusters and a rail with volute; in the 1870 decade stair work becomes heavier in scale, thickness and ornamental with turned newel posts and balustrade

NEWEL POSTS—large, sometimes massive octagon and fancy-turned newel posts; pine, oak, ash, walnut, cherry

BALUSTERS—octagon and hexagon balusters; advertised as "fancy"; oak, ash, butternut, walnut, cherry

STRINGERS—closed with molded string-board; closed with paneling; open with brackets; combinations of types

RAILS—slightly convex or flat on top; in walnut, cherry, oak; thickness varies from $1\frac{3}{4}$ –$2\frac{3}{4}$

WOOD STRIP FLOORS—tongue-and-groove wood strip floors of various woods; often the more expensive species on first floors and less costly species on second floors; dimensions of strips in this period usually narrow; staining or graining one wood (pine) to appear like another (cherry) common for Italianate houses; wood species varied by time period, region, size and cost of house, and includes oak, spruce, pine, maple

LIGHTING FIXTURES—coal oil or gas for much of this period; parlor lamps and branched fixtures common for gas; pendants useful for halls, such as beveled-glass lanterns or clear or frosted glass shade with etched classical designs; limited use of combination gas and electric fixtures

pendants for halls and stairways

Table 6.4. Characteristics of Ornamental Aesthetic: Interior

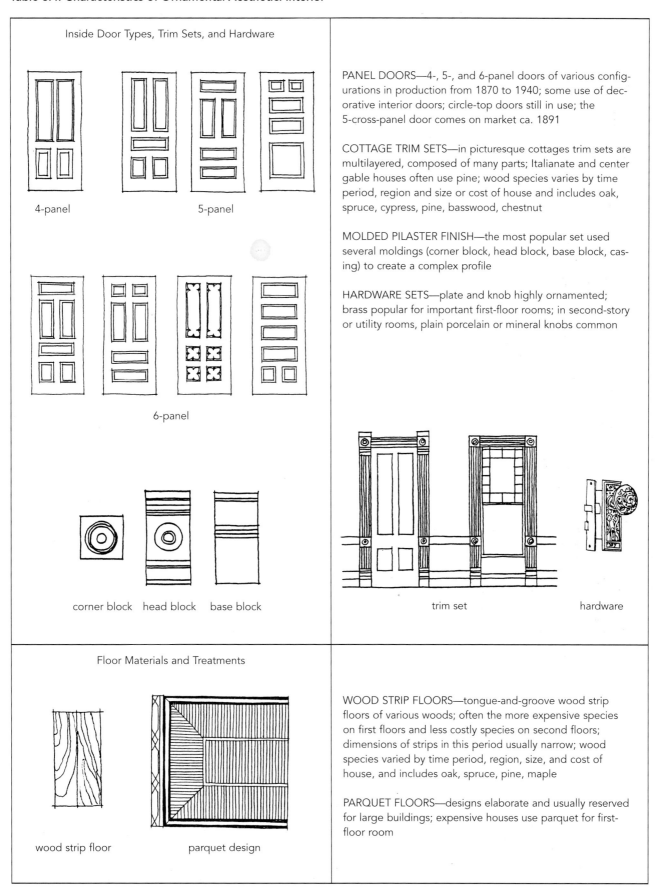

Inside Door Types, Trim Sets, and Hardware

4-panel

5-panel

6-panel

corner block   head block   base block

trim set

hardware

PANEL DOORS—4-, 5-, and 6-panel doors of various configurations in production from 1870 to 1940; some use of decorative interior doors; circle-top doors still in use; the 5-cross-panel door comes on market ca. 1891

COTTAGE TRIM SETS—in picturesque cottages trim sets are multilayered, composed of many parts; Italianate and center gable houses often use pine; wood species varies by time period, region and size or cost of house and includes oak, spruce, cypress, pine, basswood, chestnut

MOLDED PILASTER FINISH—the most popular set used several moldings (corner block, head block, base block, casing) to create a complex profile

HARDWARE SETS—plate and knob highly ornamented; brass popular for important first-floor rooms; in second-story or utility rooms, plain porcelain or mineral knobs common

Floor Materials and Treatments

wood strip floor   parquet design

WOOD STRIP FLOORS—tongue-and-groove wood strip floors of various woods; often the more expensive species on first floors and less costly species on second floors; dimensions of strips in this period usually narrow; wood species varied by time period, region, size, and cost of house, and includes oak, spruce, pine, maple

PARQUET FLOORS—designs elaborate and usually reserved for large buildings; expensive houses use parquet for first-floor room

Table 6.4. Characteristics of Ornamental Aesthetic: Interior (continued)

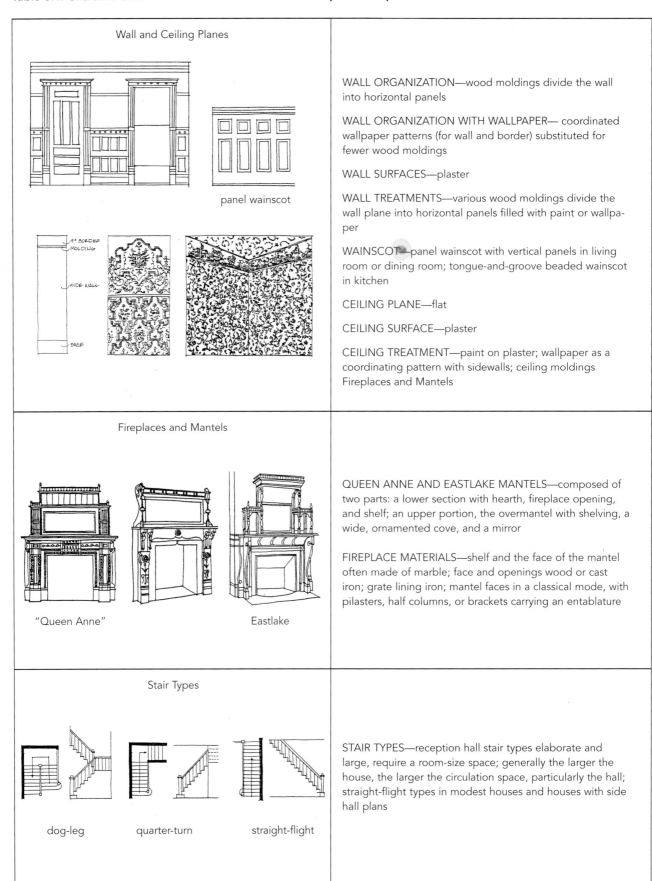

Wall and Ceiling Planes

panel wainscot

WALL ORGANIZATION—wood moldings divide the wall into horizontal panels

WALL ORGANIZATION WITH WALLPAPER— coordinated wallpaper patterns (for wall and border) substituted for fewer wood moldings

WALL SURFACES—plaster

WALL TREATMENTS—various wood moldings divide the wall plane into horizontal panels filled with paint or wallpaper

WAINSCOT—panel wainscot with vertical panels in living room or dining room; tongue-and-groove beaded wainscot in kitchen

CEILING PLANE—flat

CEILING SURFACE—plaster

CEILING TREATMENT—paint on plaster; wallpaper as a coordinating pattern with sidewalls; ceiling moldings
Fireplaces and Mantels

Fireplaces and Mantels

"Queen Anne"   Eastlake

QUEEN ANNE AND EASTLAKE MANTELS—composed of two parts: a lower section with hearth, fireplace opening, and shelf; an upper portion, the overmantel with shelving, a wide, ornamented cove, and a mirror

FIREPLACE MATERIALS—shelf and the face of the mantel often made of marble; face and openings wood or cast iron; grate lining iron; mantel faces in a classical mode, with pilasters, half columns, or brackets carrying an entablature

Stair Types

dog-leg   quarter-turn   straight-flight

STAIR TYPES—reception hall stair types elaborate and large, require a room-size space; generally the larger the house, the larger the circulation space, particularly the hall; straight-flight types in modest houses and houses with side hall plans

Table 6.4. Characteristics of Ornamental Aesthetic: Interior (continued)

Stair Work	
 newel posts	NEWEL POSTS—large, sometimes massive octagon and fancy-turned newel posts popular in Italianate houses with center halls; in expensive cottages, walnut specified for newel posts and balusters; in reception halls newel posts were ornamented and decorative, including those carved, chamfered and turned; decorative head pieces common; in large houses and commercial or public lobbies the newel post head often topped with a light fixture BALUSTERS—in reception halls, turned balusters were the norm STRINGERS—closed with molded string-board; closed with paneling; open with brackets; combinations of types
Opening and Lighting Fixtures	
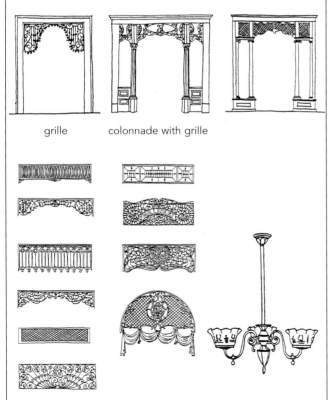 grille colonnade with grille grilles gas fixture in branch form	OPENINGS—as new heating technologies allow, doors between rooms disappear in favor of a framed opening, especially in important rooms such as the passage or reception hall, parlor, and dining room GRILLES—scrollwork, spindles, lattice, and myriad combinations of millwork readily available from manufacturers and local craftsmen COLONNADES—begin to appear in millwork catalogs, many with grilles PORTIERES—extensive use in openings, with and without grilles, and with colonnades LIGHTING FIXTURES—gas for much of this period; electricity came to rural areas as late as the 1920s; branched fixtures common for gas and electric

Table 6.5. Characteristics of Colonial Revival Aesthetic: Classical: Interior

Inside Door Types, Trim Sets, and Hardware

sliding door   5-cross-panel door   vestibule door

6-panel doors   7-panel door

cap trim

plain cap trim   egg-and-dart molding

bead edged   egg and dart   oval sets

Ceiling and Floor Plane

plaster   paneled   wood strip floor

PANEL DOORS—the 5-cross-panel door enters the market about 1890; common in hip roof cottages and other modern houses at the turn-of-the-twentieth century; 6-panel doors are also popular; the 7-panel door began production about 1890

SLIDING DOORS—double or paired sliding doors between sitting and dining rooms; single sliding doors are modern

VESTIBULE OR RECEPTION HALL DOORS—often multi-lighted with beveled, leaded, or art glass treatment

CAP TRIM—for hipped roof cottages and other colonial revival houses, stores, and churches; included a trim on top of the door resembling an abstracted entablature; molding profiles are reduced; plain and egg-and-dart molding popular; wood species varies and includes oak, fir, chestnut

HARDWARE SETS—ornamental motifs on knobs and plates, including the egg-and-dart style; Sears and others sold oval sets ca. 1900

CEILING PLANE—flat

CEILING SURFACE—plaster

CEILING TREATMENTS—moldings included classical motifs, such as egg and dart

WOOD STRIP FLOORS—tongue-and-groove wood strip floors in varying wood species; often oak on first floors and pine on second floor; dimensions of strips in this period usually narrow; sometimes parquet designs in reception hall and in social spaces of large houses

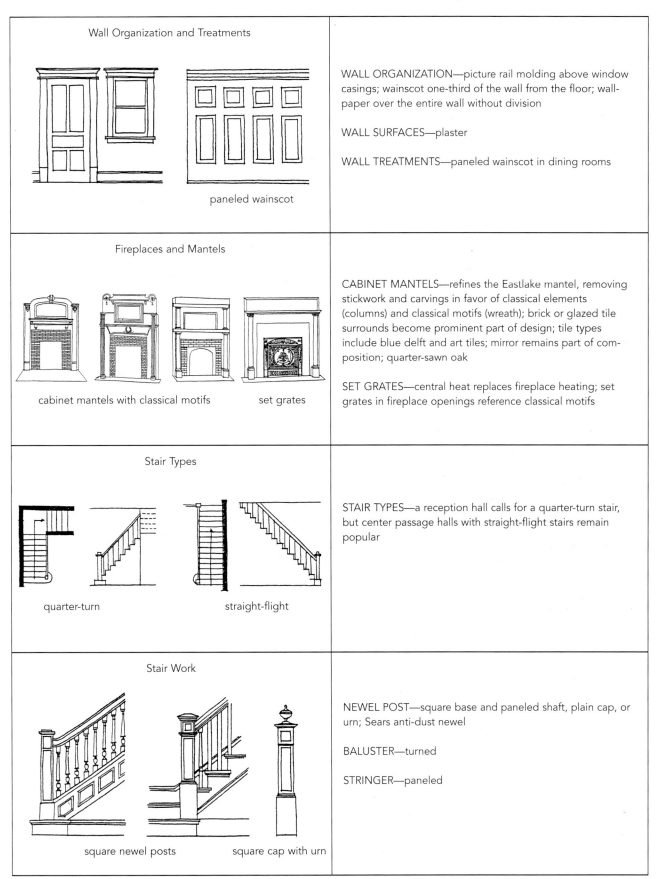

Wall Organization and Treatments	
paneled wainscot	WALL ORGANIZATION—picture rail molding above window casings; wainscot one-third of the wall from the floor; wallpaper over the entire wall without division WALL SURFACES—plaster WALL TREATMENTS—paneled wainscot in dining rooms
Fireplaces and Mantels	
cabinet mantels with classical motifs set grates	CABINET MANTELS—refines the Eastlake mantel, removing stickwork and carvings in favor of classical elements (columns) and classical motifs (wreath); brick or glazed tile surrounds become prominent part of design; tile types include blue delft and art tiles; mirror remains part of composition; quarter-sawn oak SET GRATES—central heat replaces fireplace heating; set grates in fireplace openings reference classical motifs
Stair Types	
quarter-turn straight-flight	STAIR TYPES—a reception hall calls for a quarter-turn stair, but center passage halls with straight-flight stairs remain popular
Stair Work	
square newel posts square cap with urn	NEWEL POST—square base and paneled shaft, plain cap, or urn; Sears anti-dust newel BALUSTER—turned STRINGER—paneled

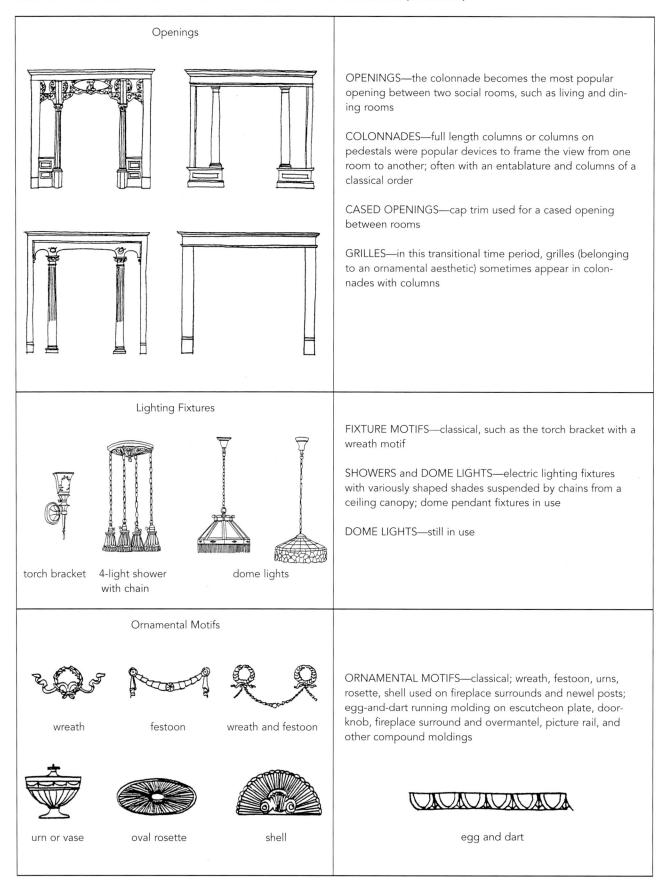

Openings

OPENINGS—the colonnade becomes the most popular opening between two social rooms, such as living and dining rooms

COLONNADES—full length columns or columns on pedestals were popular devices to frame the view from one room to another; often with an entablature and columns of a classical order

CASED OPENINGS—cap trim used for a cased opening between rooms

GRILLES—in this transitional time period, grilles (belonging to an ornamental aesthetic) sometimes appear in colonnades with columns

Lighting Fixtures

FIXTURE MOTIFS—classical, such as the torch bracket with a wreath motif

SHOWERS and DOME LIGHTS—electric lighting fixtures with variously shaped shades suspended by chains from a ceiling canopy; dome pendant fixtures in use

DOME LIGHTS—still in use

torch bracket   4-light shower   dome lights
                 with chain

Ornamental Motifs

ORNAMENTAL MOTIFS—classical; wreath, festoon, urns, rosette, shell used on fireplace surrounds and newel posts; egg-and-dart running molding on escutcheon plate, doorknob, fireplace surround and overmantel, picture rail, and other compound moldings

wreath   festoon   wreath and festoon

urn or vase   oval rosette   shell

egg and dart

Table 6.6. Characteristics of Artistic Aesthetic: Interior

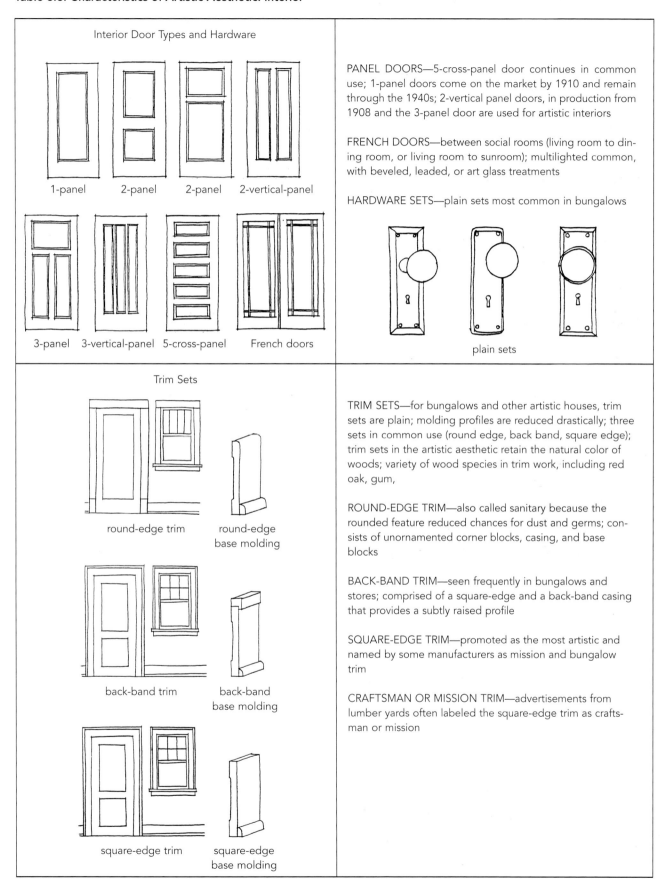

Interior Door Types and Hardware

1-panel   2-panel   2-panel   2-vertical-panel

3-panel   3-vertical-panel   5-cross-panel   French doors

plain sets

PANEL DOORS—5-cross-panel door continues in common use; 1-panel doors come on the market by 1910 and remain through the 1940s; 2-vertical panel doors, in production from 1908 and the 3-panel door are used for artistic interiors

FRENCH DOORS—between social rooms (living room to dining room, or living room to sunroom); multilighted common, with beveled, leaded, or art glass treatments

HARDWARE SETS—plain sets most common in bungalows

Trim Sets

round-edge trim   round-edge base molding

back-band trim   back-band base molding

square-edge trim   square-edge base molding

TRIM SETS—for bungalows and other artistic houses, trim sets are plain; molding profiles are reduced drastically; three sets in common use (round edge, back band, square edge); trim sets in the artistic aesthetic retain the natural color of woods; variety of wood species in trim work, including red oak, gum,

ROUND-EDGE TRIM—also called sanitary because the rounded feature reduced chances for dust and germs; consists of unornamented corner blocks, casing, and base blocks

BACK-BAND TRIM—seen frequently in bungalows and stores; comprised of a square-edge and a back-band casing that provides a subtly raised profile

SQUARE-EDGE TRIM—promoted as the most artistic and named by some manufacturers as mission and bungalow trim

CRAFTSMAN OR MISSION TRIM—advertisements from lumber yards often labeled the square-edge trim as craftsman or mission

Table 6.6. Characteristics of Artistic Aesthetic: Interior (continued)

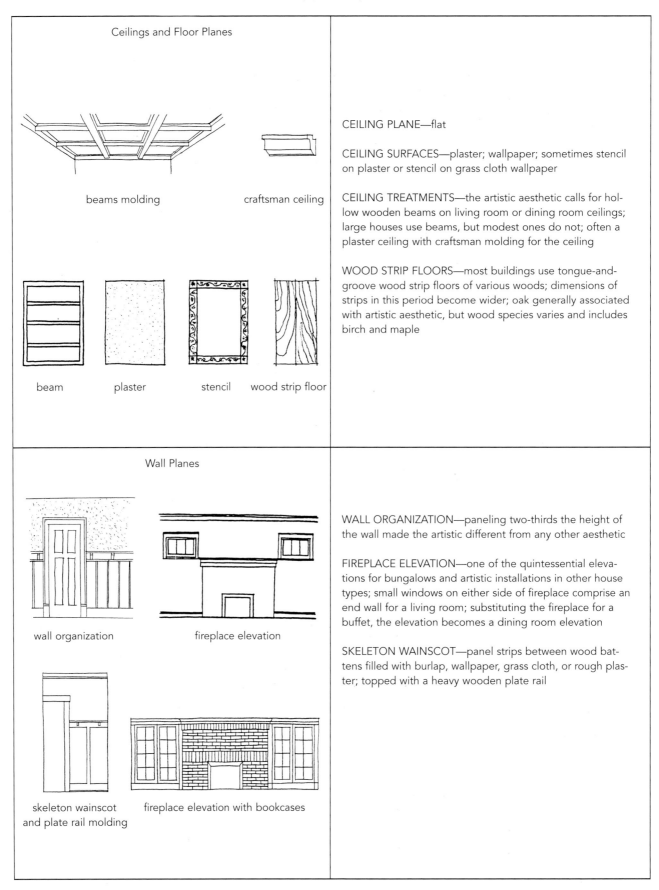

Ceilings and Floor Planes

beams molding   craftsman ceiling

beam   plaster   stencil   wood strip floor

CEILING PLANE—flat

CEILING SURFACES—plaster; wallpaper; sometimes stencil on plaster or stencil on grass cloth wallpaper

CEILING TREATMENTS—the artistic aesthetic calls for hollow wooden beams on living room or dining room ceilings; large houses use beams, but modest ones do not; often a plaster ceiling with craftsman molding for the ceiling

WOOD STRIP FLOORS—most buildings use tongue-and-groove wood strip floors of various woods; dimensions of strips in this period become wider; oak generally associated with artistic aesthetic, but wood species varies and includes birch and maple

Wall Planes

wall organization   fireplace elevation

skeleton wainscot   fireplace elevation with bookcases
and plate rail molding

WALL ORGANIZATION—paneling two-thirds the height of the wall made the artistic different from any other aesthetic

FIREPLACE ELEVATION—one of the quintessential elevations for bungalows and artistic installations in other house types; small windows on either side of fireplace comprise an end wall for a living room; substituting the fireplace for a buffet, the elevation becomes a dining room elevation

SKELETON WAINSCOT—panel strips between wood battens filled with burlap, wallpaper, grass cloth, or rough plaster; topped with a heavy wooden plate rail

Table 6.6. Characteristics of Artistic Aesthetic: Interior (continued)

Wall Treatments	WALL SURFACE—plaster
stencil Sears's Lincrusta modern Lincrusta burlap grass cloth brush stipple	WALL TREATMENTS—paint on plaster; wide use of wallpaper, as well as Lincrusta, burlap, grass cloth, stencils on plaster or grass cloth; various treatments for plaster and paint (stipple, brush, scroll, rake, score, glaze)
Fireplaces and Mantels craftsman mantel all-brick fireplace	MANTELS—the trade-named craftsman or mission models are reiterations of the Eastlake mantel, with motifs of the artistic aesthetic ALL-BRICK FIREPLACE AND BOOKCASE FIREPLACE—brick patterns provide ornamentation; thick unornamented wood shelf, sometimes with large brackets under the shelf, no overmantel
Architectural Furniture dining room buffets and sideboards fireplace nook or settle kitchen nook	ARCHITECTURAL FURNITURE—seats, bookcases, desks, china closets integrated with colonnades; built-in sideboards and buffets in dining rooms NOOKS—the fireside nook encloses the fireplace and makes it a cozy place; by 1915 a breakfast nook is a salient feature of smaller kitchens; the built-in kitchen nook allowed smaller families a less formal dining area to eat in

Table 6.6. Characteristics of Artistic Aesthetic: Interior (continued)

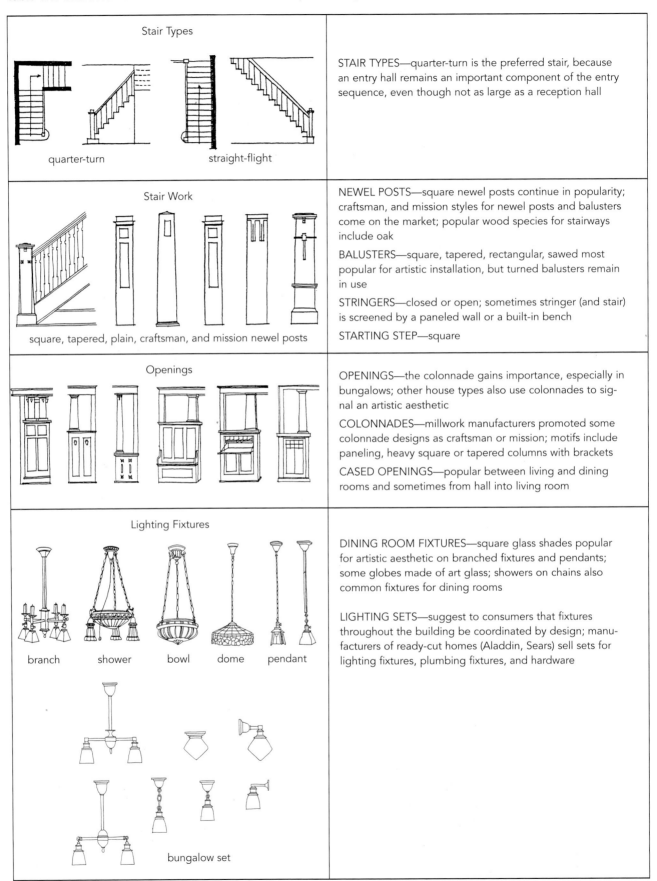

Stair Types	STAIR TYPES—quarter-turn is the preferred stair, because an entry hall remains an important component of the entry sequence, even though not as large as a reception hall

quarter-turn   straight-flight

Stair Work

NEWEL POSTS—square newel posts continue in popularity; craftsman, and mission styles for newel posts and balusters come on the market; popular wood species for stairways include oak

BALUSTERS—square, tapered, rectangular, sawed most popular for artistic installation, but turned balusters remain in use

STRINGERS—closed or open; sometimes stringer (and stair) is screened by a paneled wall or a built-in bench

STARTING STEP—square

square, tapered, plain, craftsman, and mission newel posts

Openings

OPENINGS—the colonnade gains importance, especially in bungalows; other house types also use colonnades to signal an artistic aesthetic

COLONNADES—millwork manufacturers promoted some colonnade designs as craftsman or mission; motifs include paneling, heavy square or tapered columns with brackets

CASED OPENINGS—popular between living and dining rooms and sometimes from hall into living room

Lighting Fixtures

DINING ROOM FIXTURES—square glass shades popular for artistic aesthetic on branched fixtures and pendants; some globes made of art glass; showers on chains also common fixtures for dining rooms

LIGHTING SETS—suggest to consumers that fixtures throughout the building be coordinated by design; manufacturers of ready-cut homes (Aladdin, Sears) sell sets for lighting fixtures, plumbing fixtures, and hardware

branch   shower   bowl   dome   pendant

bungalow set

Table 6.7. Characteristics of Colonial Revival Aesthetic: Modern, Interior

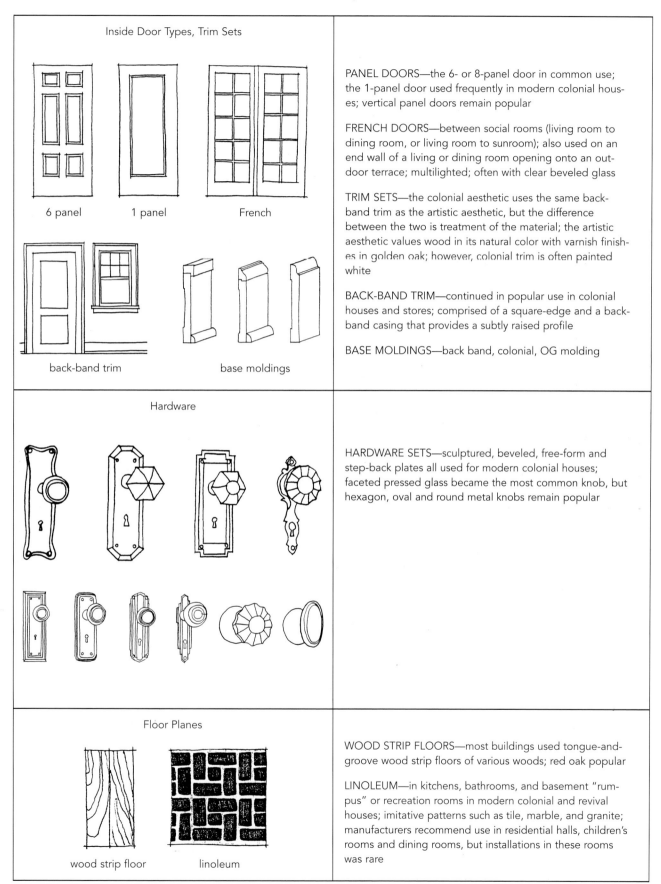

Inside Door Types, Trim Sets

6 panel   1 panel   French

back-band trim   base moldings

PANEL DOORS—the 6- or 8-panel door in common use; the 1-panel door used frequently in modern colonial houses; vertical panel doors remain popular

FRENCH DOORS—between social rooms (living room to dining room, or living room to sunroom); also used on an end wall of a living or dining room opening onto an outdoor terrace; multilighted; often with clear beveled glass

TRIM SETS—the colonial aesthetic uses the same backband trim as the artistic aesthetic, but the difference between the two is treatment of the material; the artistic aesthetic values wood in its natural color with varnish finishes in golden oak; however, colonial trim is often painted white

BACK-BAND TRIM—continued in popular use in colonial houses and stores; comprised of a square-edge and a backband casing that provides a subtly raised profile

BASE MOLDINGS—back band, colonial, OG molding

Hardware

HARDWARE SETS—sculptured, beveled, free-form and step-back plates all used for modern colonial houses; faceted pressed glass became the most common knob, but hexagon, oval and round metal knobs remain popular

Floor Planes

wood strip floor   linoleum

WOOD STRIP FLOORS—most buildings used tongue-and-groove wood strip floors of various woods; red oak popular

LINOLEUM—in kitchens, bathrooms, and basement "rumpus" or recreation rooms in modern colonial and revival houses; imitative patterns such as tile, marble, and granite; manufacturers recommend use in residential halls, children's rooms and dining rooms, but installations in these rooms was rare

AESTHETIC SYSTEM: INTERIOR

125

Wall and Ceiling Planes  wallpaper patterns 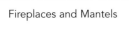 plaster molding on ceiling plane	WALL ORGANIZATION—fireplace wall symmetrical; fireplace centered with flanking windows, French doors, or door with bookcase; wall rarely divided by moldings; base molding and moldings at the ceiling line become thinner in depth and height WALL ORGANIZATION WITH WALLPAPER—wallpaper border in lieu of molding; or border and molding WALL SURFACES—plaster WALL TREATMENTS—paint on walls; paint on moldings (instead of natural color of wood); sometimes wainscot in dining room with a scenic mural above it; sometimes knotty pine for walls in dens; wallpaper patterns become smaller, delicate, pastel in color; stripes and grids organize wall CORNER CABINETS—built into two corners of a dining room to provide storage in the old colonial manner; pediments and classical motifs CEILING PLANE—flat CEILING SURFACE—plaster CEILING TREATMENT—paint on plaster; cornice moldings or plaster molding in a pattern; also cove and crown moldings; center molding medallion in center of dining room for a central lighting fixture
Fireplaces and Mantels  	MODERN COLONIAL MANTELS—most common is the one on the left, manufactured from 1917 through the 1940 decade; brick becomes a feature of the mantel in the Modern Colonial, as well as all-brick fireplaces, which last through the 1950 decade in modern colonial and ranch houses

Table 6.7. Characteristics of Colonial Revival Aesthetic: Modern, Interior (continued)

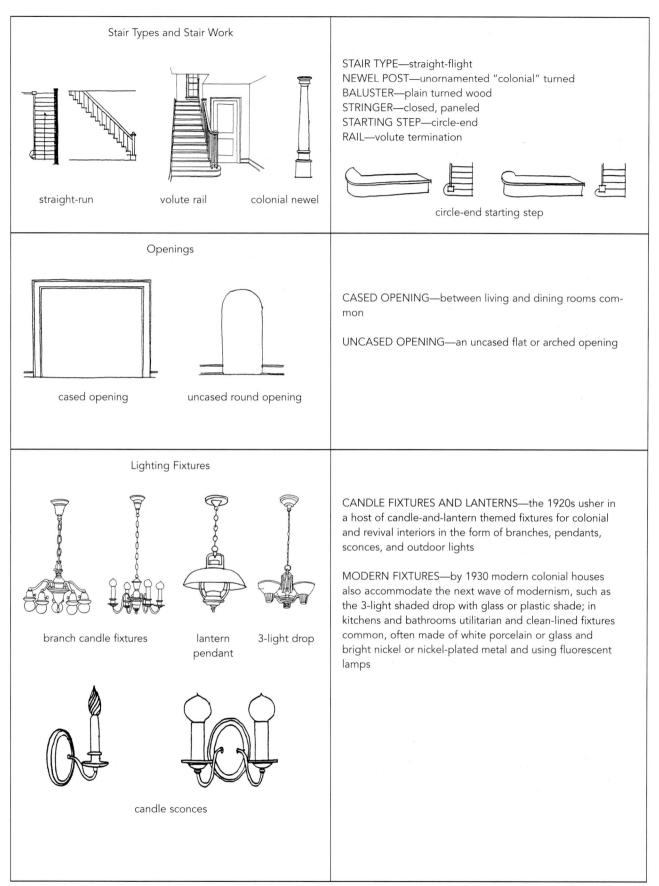

Stair Types and Stair Work

straight-run   volute rail   colonial newel

STAIR TYPE—straight-flight
NEWEL POST—unornamented "colonial" turned
BALUSTER—plain turned wood
STRINGER—closed, paneled
STARTING STEP—circle-end
RAIL—volute termination

circle-end starting step

Openings

cased opening   uncased round opening

CASED OPENING—between living and dining rooms common

UNCASED OPENING—an uncased flat or arched opening

Lighting Fixtures

branch candle fixtures   lantern pendant   3-light drop

candle sconces

CANDLE FIXTURES AND LANTERNS—the 1920s usher in a host of candle-and-lantern themed fixtures for colonial and revival interiors in the form of branches, pendants, sconces, and outdoor lights

MODERN FIXTURES—by 1930 modern colonial houses also accommodate the next wave of modernism, such as the 3-light shaded drop with glass or plastic shade; in kitchens and bathrooms utilitarian and clean-lined fixtures common, often made of white porcelain or glass and bright nickel or nickel-plated metal and using fluorescent lamps

Table 6.8. Characteristics of English and Spanish Revival Aesthetic: Interior

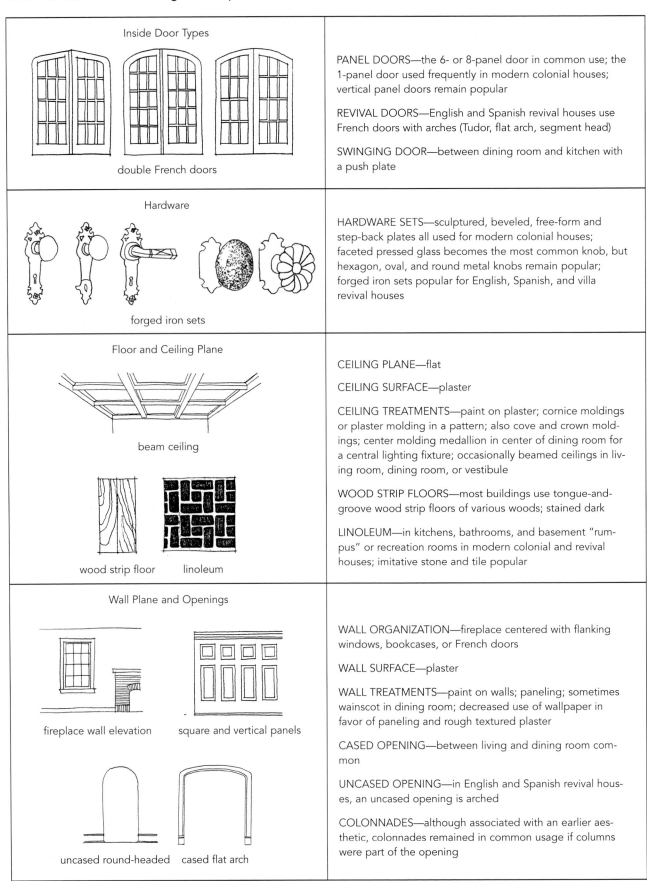

Inside Door Types

double French doors

PANEL DOORS—the 6- or 8-panel door in common use; the 1-panel door used frequently in modern colonial houses; vertical panel doors remain popular

REVIVAL DOORS—English and Spanish revival houses use French doors with arches (Tudor, flat arch, segment head)

SWINGING DOOR—between dining room and kitchen with a push plate

Hardware

forged iron sets

HARDWARE SETS—sculptured, beveled, free-form and step-back plates all used for modern colonial houses; faceted pressed glass becomes the most common knob, but hexagon, oval, and round metal knobs remain popular; forged iron sets popular for English, Spanish, and villa revival houses

Floor and Ceiling Plane

beam ceiling

wood strip floor   linoleum

CEILING PLANE—flat

CEILING SURFACE—plaster

CEILING TREATMENTS—paint on plaster; cornice moldings or plaster molding in a pattern; also cove and crown moldings; center molding medallion in center of dining room for a central lighting fixture; occasionally beamed ceilings in living room, dining room, or vestibule

WOOD STRIP FLOORS—most buildings use tongue-and-groove wood strip floors of various woods; stained dark

LINOLEUM—in kitchens, bathrooms, and basement "rumpus" or recreation rooms in modern colonial and revival houses; imitative stone and tile popular

Wall Plane and Openings

fireplace wall elevation   square and vertical panels

uncased round-headed   cased flat arch

WALL ORGANIZATION—fireplace centered with flanking windows, bookcases, or French doors

WALL SURFACE—plaster

WALL TREATMENTS—paint on walls; paneling; sometimes wainscot in dining room; decreased use of wallpaper in favor of paneling and rough textured plaster

CASED OPENING—between living and dining room common

UNCASED OPENING—in English and Spanish revival houses, an uncased opening is arched

COLONNADES—although associated with an earlier aesthetic, colonnades remained in common usage if columns were part of the opening

Table 6.8. Characteristics of English and Spanish Revival Aesthetic: Interior (continued)

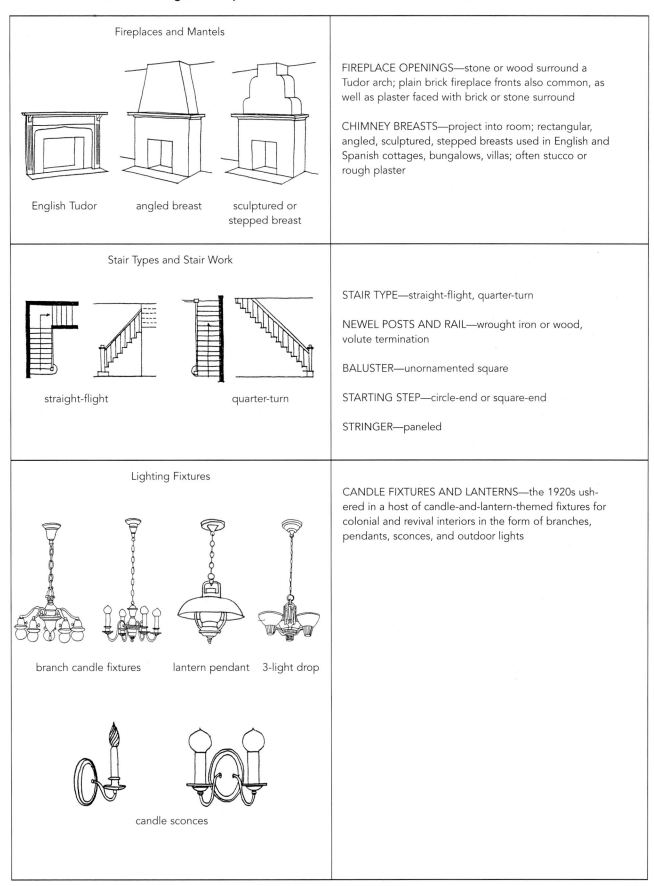

Fireplaces and Mantels

English Tudor　　angled breast　　sculptured or
　　　　　　　　　　　　　　　　　stepped breast

FIREPLACE OPENINGS—stone or wood surround a Tudor arch; plain brick fireplace fronts also common, as well as plaster faced with brick or stone surround

CHIMNEY BREASTS—project into room; rectangular, angled, sculptured, stepped breasts used in English and Spanish cottages, bungalows, villas; often stucco or rough plaster

Stair Types and Stair Work

straight-flight　　　　　　　　quarter-turn

STAIR TYPE—straight-flight, quarter-turn

NEWEL POSTS AND RAIL—wrought iron or wood, volute termination

BALUSTER—unornamented square

STARTING STEP—circle-end or square-end

STRINGER—paneled

Lighting Fixtures

branch candle fixtures　　lantern pendant　　3-light drop

candle sconces

CANDLE FIXTURES AND LANTERNS—the 1920s ushered in a host of candle-and-lantern-themed fixtures for colonial and revival interiors in the form of branches, pendants, sconces, and outdoor lights

Table 6.9. Characteristics of Modern Aesthetic: Interior

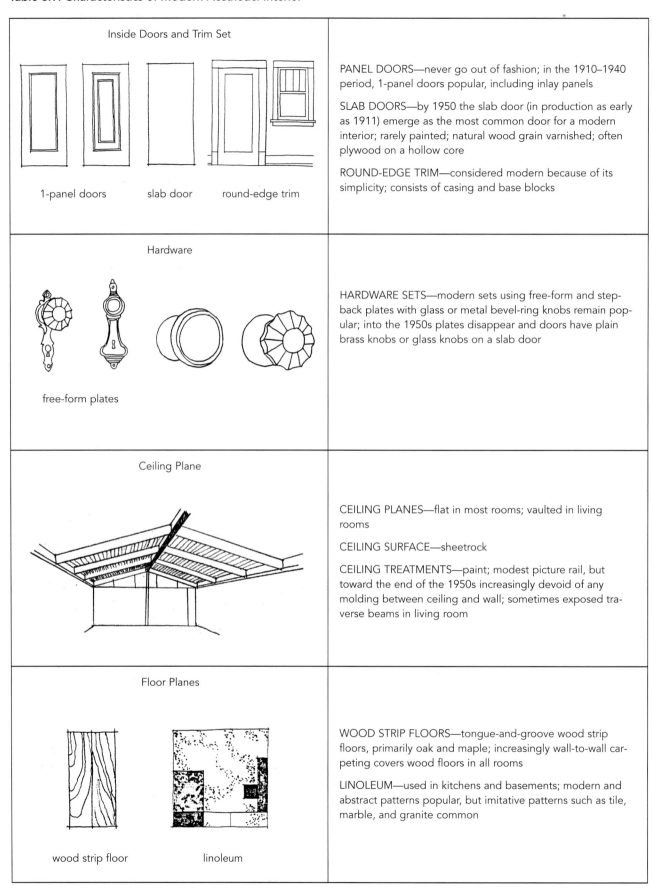

Inside Doors and Trim Set

1-panel doors   slab door   round-edge trim

PANEL DOORS—never go out of fashion; in the 1910–1940 period, 1-panel doors popular, including inlay panels

SLAB DOORS—by 1950 the slab door (in production as early as 1911) emerge as the most common door for a modern interior; rarely painted; natural wood grain varnished; often plywood on a hollow core

ROUND-EDGE TRIM—considered modern because of its simplicity; consists of casing and base blocks

Hardware

free-form plates

HARDWARE SETS—modern sets using free-form and step-back plates with glass or metal bevel-ring knobs remain popular; into the 1950s plates disappear and doors have plain brass knobs or glass knobs on a slab door

Ceiling Plane

CEILING PLANES—flat in most rooms; vaulted in living rooms

CEILING SURFACE—sheetrock

CEILING TREATMENTS—paint; modest picture rail, but toward the end of the 1950s increasingly devoid of any molding between ceiling and wall; sometimes exposed traverse beams in living room

Floor Planes

wood strip floor   linoleum

WOOD STRIP FLOORS—tongue-and-groove wood strip floors, primarily oak and maple; increasingly wall-to-wall carpeting covers wood floors in all rooms

LINOLEUM—used in kitchens and basements; modern and abstract patterns popular, but imitative patterns such as tile, marble, and granite common

Table 6.9. Characteristics of Modern Aesthetic: Interior (continued)

Wall Planes

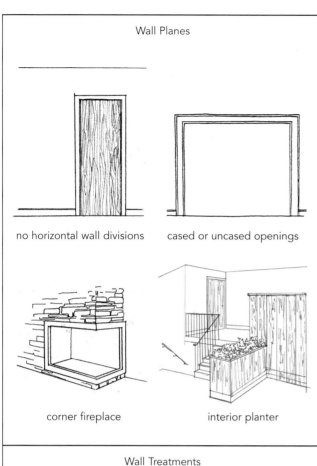

no horizontal wall divisions   cased or uncased openings

corner fireplace   interior planter

WALL ORGANIZATION—no horizontal division of wall; very few base or ceiling moldings

OPENINGS—between spatial areas become wider or disappear altogether in favor of the open plan; uncased or cased openings

BUILT-IN STORAGE—storage wall in living room or den, often used as divider between living and dining area

FIREPLACES AND MANTELS—plain mantel shelf or no shelf at all; stone or brick fireplaces; corner fireplace

INTERIOR PLANTER—common in ranch and split-level houses

Wall Treatments

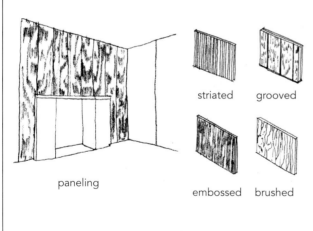

paneling

striated   grooved

embossed   brushed

wall panel patterns

vertical panels   square panels   horizontal panels

WALL SURFACE—sheetrock

WALL TREATMENTS—paint in pastel colors; wallpaper; sometimes wainscot in dining room, with a scenic mural above it

PANEL WORK—fine woods and plywood panel entire rooms; fewer base moldings on paneled walls; plywood paneling in various surface treatments; applied in vertical, square, or horizontal patterns

WALLPAPER—grass cloth; abstract modern patterns; flocked papers with large patterns and deep colors

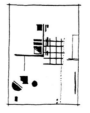

wallpaper patterns

Table 6.9. Characteristics of Modern Aesthetic: Interior (continued)

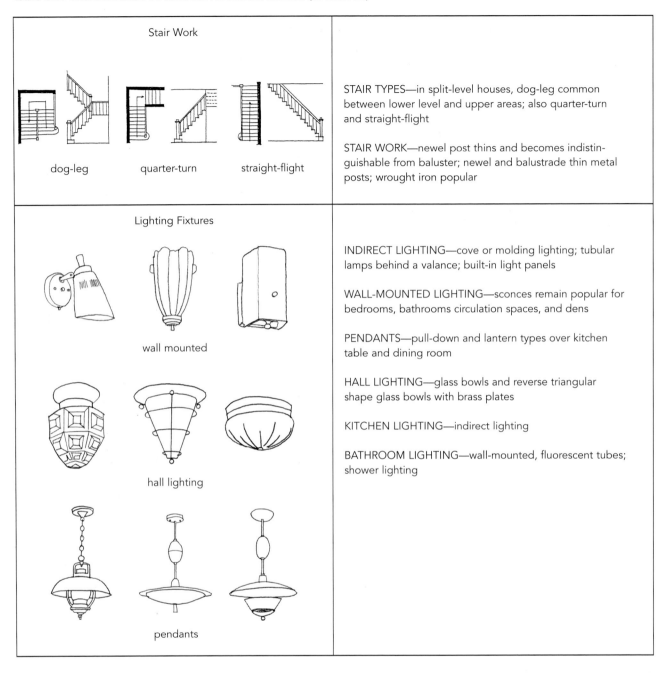

Stair Work

dog-leg　　quarter-turn　　straight-flight

STAIR TYPES—in split-level houses, dog-leg common between lower level and upper areas; also quarter-turn and straight-flight

STAIR WORK—newel post thins and becomes indistinguishable from baluster; newel and balustrade thin metal posts; wrought iron popular

Lighting Fixtures

wall mounted

hall lighting

pendants

INDIRECT LIGHTING—cove or molding lighting; tubular lamps behind a valance; built-in light panels

WALL-MOUNTED LIGHTING—sconces remain popular for bedrooms, bathrooms circulation spaces, and dens

PENDANTS—pull-down and lantern types over kitchen table and dining room

HALL LIGHTING—glass bowls and reverse triangular shape glass bowls with brass plates

KITCHEN LIGHTING—indirect lighting

BATHROOM LIGHTING—wall-mounted, fluorescent tubes; shower lighting

Table 6.10. Summary of Aesthetic Treatments in Vernacular Building Types

Exterior Aesthetic	House Type	Front Door	Porch	Window
Italianate				
Picturesque				
Colonial Revival—Classical				
Arts & Crafts				
Colonial Revival—Modern				
Modern				

Table 6.10. Summary of Aesthetic Treatments in Vernacular Building Types (continued)

Interior Aesthetic	Italianate	Ornamental	Colonial Revival—Classical	Artistic	Colonial Revival—Modern	Modern
Interior Door						
Hardware						
Wall Organization						
Mantel						

Table 6.10. Summary of Aesthetic Treatments in Vernacular Building Types (continued)

Interior Aesthetic	Italianate	Ornamental	Colonial Revival—Classical	Artistic	Colonial Revival—Modern	Modern
Stair						
Newel Post						
Opening						

BUILDING TYPE:
GABLE ROOF COTTAGE

The sections in this chapter briefly describe buildings of this type, including the vernacular form and shape, the floor plan, and the salient features. These are accompanied by schematic drawings of the general massing and plan arrangements and an isometric drawing that reveals the relationship between plan and built form. A summary table highlighting salient features accompanies each building type or variant. Where appropriate, we include a few pertinent phrases from the period to communicate something about the original intentions of the designers and manufacturers. Each building type is designated either by its principal design element or by its historical name—that is, the term used most frequently in building literature. In some cases the roof type (gable, hip, gambrel) stands for a general class of buildings.

The gable roof cottage is a prolific vernacular house type. Such cottages have been built in several formats and sited in rural areas and small towns, as well as cities. The gable roof is a traditional, vernacular organizing element, whether parallel or perpendicular to the street. By varying the roof pitch, the gable roof was easily adapted to all regions of the country. To accommodate different styling systems and interior arrangements, modifications—for example, intersecting the gable with other roof forms,

especially with another gable; clipping the apex of the gable; flaring the roof—were introduced.

CENTER GABLE COTTAGE

The center gable is an old house type, and the American version of it probably derives from an English medieval vernacular house and from Tudor pattern books. This type of house was built before 1870, but exactly when it was first built with industrial materials is not clear. One indication of its longevity is that in 1908 Sears offered it as Modern Home No. 105, and occasionally changing a few exterior elements, Sears continued to sell this house into the next decade. The center gable house was incorporated into the romantic revival houses of the mid-nineteenth century, during which time houses had multiple gables as an expression of the picturesque. The center gable as a vernacular building had two types of volumetric organization: either one room deep or two rooms deep in one and a half or two stories. Both kinds were built during the 1870s and 1880s, and both types could include a vestibule on the façade or an ell in back. Older center gable houses had a wide cornice and deep projections, but these were reduced until the façade was flat and the roof had a modest overhang.

7.1. A multigenerational family poses in front of a rural, center gable cottage. The back portion, extending past the body of the house, could be a later addition due to its location and prominent bay window. The symmetry of the composition and asymmetrical openings are part of the logic of a cottage. Authors' collection.

7.2. A portrait of a farmer near Argyle, Wisconsin, his team of horses, and the cottage farmhouse. The façade elevation is a study in how building elements and masses characterize a building: the porch projects but has little mass because it is open on three sides; the center gable extends vertically to become a dormer; the bay window projects a modest mass. Authors' collection.

On plan, both models were rectangles, wider than they were deep, with the wide side toward the street. The one-room-deep house had an ell rather than a vestibule. The house had a center hall plan with three rooms on the first floor and two rooms above. In our sample, more than half of these houses had a bay window, and, as is true for both kinds, the entrance was under the center gable. The two-room-deep house usually had a vestibule, an ell, and a bay window. In both of these configurations, the ell was not in line with either sidewall. The typical floor plan was a center hall type with a stair rising from the entrance. Despite its predilection for symmetry, one cottage in this style was described as "domestic Gothic," alluding to the four-gabled roof that might feature a "timber-trimmed gablet" (clipped gable).

Over time the front gable itself, positioned over the entrance door, lost its narrow, steeply pitched roof and widened to function more properly as a dormer. Clapboard siding covered the house frame, although shingles were later used in gable ends. The fenestration was symmetrically arranged in three bays. The house had a porch that was shallow in the older models and shallow but wide in the later ones. The porch carried its own roof, supported by posts.

Table 7.1. Characteristics of the Center Gable Cottage

Typical Façades	Exterior Characteristics
 2½ -story center gable	STORY—1–1½–2–2½ ROOF—gable roof with ridgeline parallel to street; center gable part of roof form with window in the gable CLADDING—clapboard CHIMNEY—located in the interior; brick WINDOW—double-hung sash of variable patterns; small window in center gable, such as a lunette, an oriel, small paired windows ENTRANCE—front door centered EXTERIOR WALL—cornerboards; façade has temple front
	FORM—gable and back ell MASSING—symmetrical in nineteenth-century houses; door off-center in twentieth-century houses BAYS—3 bays across façade ROOF—gable roof with ridgeline parallel to street; center gable part of roof form with window in the gable or wall dormer
 1½-story center gable with projecting center ell—Italianate Design No. 13 (1869), *Woodward's National Architect*	 1½ -story center gable wall dormer Modern Home No. 105 (1908), Sears, Roebuck & Co.
Plan—Two-Story House 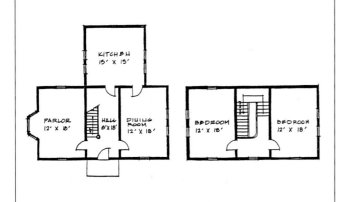	Three Rooms Downstairs PLAN—3 rooms wide (including hall); 2 rooms deep PLAN COMPOSITION—gable and ell (kitchen ell) ROOM DISTRIBUTION—4 rooms downstairs (hall, parlor, dining room, kitchen); 2 rooms upstairs (2 bedrooms) ENTRY AND HALL—center or off-center; center hall 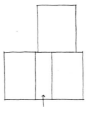

Table 7.1. Characteristics of the Center Gable Cottage (continued)

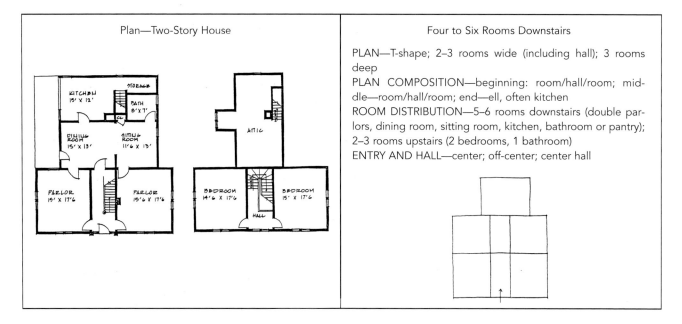

Plan—Two-Story House	Four to Six Rooms Downstairs
	PLAN—T-shape; 2–3 rooms wide (including hall); 3 rooms deep PLAN COMPOSITION—beginning: room/hall/room; middle—room/hall/room; end—ell, often kitchen ROOM DISTRIBUTION—5–6 rooms downstairs (double parlors, dining room, sitting room, kitchen, bathroom or pantry); 2–3 rooms upstairs (2 bedrooms, 1 bathroom) ENTRY AND HALL—center; off-center; center hall

As these houses continued to be built into the 1880s, the porch took on brackets and other more delicate stickwork. From 1880 to 1910 the center gable turned toward colonial revival styles, and the gable began to look like a pediment. The porch became a portico with a full order of architecture. The gable itself received a new window motif—a three-part window that echoed the Palladian—along with returns and boxed cornices. The window below the gable, whether on the full second story or a half story, became a three-part window or a bay. A few cottages had a second-story door that accessed a balcony on the porch roof. The gable was now wide enough to embrace the space between the second-floor windows or, in story-and-a-half models, to fill half the wall of the upper portion. The gable, however, remained in the same plane as the main house wall.

Like other house forms in the grand cottage age, the center gable cottage displayed cottage detailing. The entrance door moved off-center, and the fenestration patterns on the side elevations adopted cottage arrangements, including the grouping of windows into pairs and triples. The center gable, then, represents a short history of the development of the cottage. It bridged historical revival styles and, at the same time, reminded Americans of the design strength of their heritage buildings. The center gable could be adapted to suit changing family needs, yet still look like an appropriate product of its time.

GABLE AND ELL COTTAGE

The gable roof and ell cottage was popular in rural areas, where it was identified as a "village residence," but it was also built in small towns and cities throughout the United States (see fig. I.1). One of the most ubiquitous house forms ever produced, it prevailed between 1870 and 1920 and was distributed in successive territories and states as the country developed from east to west. The house has been referred to in the literature as an "upright and wing."

Styling and Plan Shapes

The distinctive feature of the two-story form was the massing of the large elements—a wing projected at a right angle to the main block. In the early years of development, the wing was narrow, but over time it widened, which paralleled the changing shape of the front room, until the wing accommodated two rooms. The organizational plan included two rooms aligned with each other in the center of the building. There was usually a porch at one corner; some variations projected from another one-story wing off the back of the main block, such as a porch, shed, or other practical space. The developmental period of the gable and ell cottage coincides with the growth of Queen Anne, Eastlake, and shingle-style cottages. The cottage assumed its overall shape from the intersection of its roof forms, one of which might be clipped or hipped, and from an ell plan.

As a one-story building it could have a projecting room off the front and two rooms side by side in the middle. The entry was nestled in the ell or on the side as part of a modestly trimmed porch of turned posts, frieze, and brackets. The cottage had three principal roof plans: a straight gable perpendicular to the street, two intersecting gables, and a hip-and-gable combination. Additional articulation included gable finish and contrasting cladding materials such as shingles in the gables. These houses were built on narrow lots, including "railroad" lots in towns. The interior organization consisted of three to five rooms arranged so that the house was deeper than it was wide. Most of the original plans for this house designated no bathroom. Machine-made stickwork trimmed the cottage, and the windows included a large cottage window in the façade, with art glass headers or borders. All the cottage's elevations celebrated the play of light on the surfaces, whether the light picked up the shingle pattern in the gable, pierced the art glass, or cast shadows from the brackets or spindle friezes on the porch or on the gable. Part of the charm of these houses resulted from the freedom with which the builder could manipulate the limited design vocabulary. In addition to using ornamentation, the designer could cant the walls or project bays to distinguish one small, low cottage from another on the same block. Historically, the house was labeled a *country cottage*, a *western cottage*, a *cheap cottage*, and a *workingman's cottage*.

The range of descriptions reveals something about the purposes the house was to serve.

The gable end and ell cottage has always been susceptible to applications of style on the elevations. The 1870s type was either a simple ell with only a single corner, which was utilized as the entrance, or a T-shape with the projecting stem toward the street and the crosspiece behind. The T-shape often provided an extra porch. The section that projected toward the street—usually a parlor room—was not centered on the crossing portion of the building. The gables of these houses and the gable end wall received systematic applications of stickwork ornament. The May 1879 issue of *Carpentry and Building* has "a study in cheap houses" in which the same gabled and ell gets an "English," "Swiss," "English" with a tower, and "French" treatment.[1] Most of the differences in these styles center on the use of stickwork and other trim boards to create effects. Fenestration in all the examples remained the same— symmetrical.

In the next decade, "cottage fever" introduced more picturesque elements, including turned posts on expanded porches, shingled gables, bay windows, and canted walls with brackets at the corners. Between 1890 and 1920, however, the gable and ell began to lose ornamentation. The exterior stickwork and porch ornament had been stripped away, and the house had become classical in its repose on farmstead sites. The house was appreciated because its lines were American—straight, simple and massive. The plan changed slightly, in that the stem of the *T* became centered on the crossing section. The edges

7.3. In T-shape cottages the projecting wing is usually on the centerline of the elevation. Variations are limited to the treatment of the end wall and the porch. The cottage has a plain gable end. The porches have different treatments, no doubt in terms of their use or what they access. W. S. Hays House, Enfield, Illinois. Authors' collection.

7.4. In L-shape cottages with a projecting front gable end and side ell, whether one-story or two, variations came down to the width of the main body and the projecting wing (that is, either one room or two), the fenestration patterns, and the inclusion of a porch with its own roof. Authors' collection.

7.5. The L-shape usually requires that one wing is longer than the other, and the length of units also indicates interior functions. The differences between figures 7.4 and 7.5 can be found in the kinds of intersections that occur and the role of porches in the junction of the wings. Authors' collection.

7.6. A tower masks the intersection of the roof forms; it may penetrate the plan at the upper story or at both upper and lower. The upper story version requires some response beneath the tower—a porch is typical. The cottage has a stick treatment on the walls, which provides contrast in pattern and materials. The house relates to the stick style house in table 7.2. R. J. Beers House, Syracuse, Nebraska. Authors' collection.

of the houses emerged, as trim boards got wider and were painted a contrasting color. The foundation wall became more prominent so that horizontal division—foundation, wall panels, gable, and roof edge—underwrote the design scheme. Fenestration remained symmetrical. The gable and ell, then, proved to be one of the hardiest of all vernacular types; it could be modified for many sites and embellished to respond to consumer demand.

Exterior Form and Footprint Schematics

The ell had one of three configurations: the ell off-center but still not in line with the main block; the ell in line with one side of the main block; and the ell centered on the main block. Overall it was a six- or eight-room house with a reception hall, either a straight-stair or an L-plan stair, a fireplace, a bay window, and a pantry. We first found one-story gable and ell cottages in towns between the Mississippi river and the west slope of the Rocky Mountains.

Interior

The interior organization was tied to the location of the porch and to the stair in the middle of the volume, at a right angle to the porch. The house was center-oriented, with spatial units clustered around the main block. The spatial organization was advertised as a square layout, which kept construction and upkeep costs low. The plan was also easily adapted for group construction.

The schematic drawings in Table 7.2 illustrate the common arrangements of rooms, which required internal alignment. Both the exterior and interior aesthetics for this type were ornamental. The one-story cottage was a modest house that communicated its practicality and domestic purpose on the exterior.

OPEN GABLE COTTAGE

The open gable cottage, built in one-, one-and-a-half-, and two-story models, had clean lines, a simple form, and no projections off the façade. The exterior form was a direct consequence of the interior organization. The façade carried the wall up into the gable, with no distinction between them until the early 1890s. The roof ridgeline was perpendicular to the street and carried short returns on the smaller houses. The roof edge projects, making the wide eaves a distinctive characteristic of this design.

7.7. The classical origin of the open gable is clear in the Hattie Wibles cottage, Ashtabula, Ohio. All the elements of the elevation align with the centerline. Everything is resolved in plain view. The scale and small pieces of ornament, at the peak of the gable and the porch posts, have a picturesque appeal. The owners have planted the site as if the house were a pavilion in a garden. Authors' collection.

7.8. The plainness of the house form is offset by the ornamental entry, which begins with the picket fence and gate and concludes with the fanciful portico and the wide cottage window to the right of the door. Photo credit: A. A. Scott, Hastings, Minnesota. Authors' collection.

Table 7.2. Characteristics of Gable and Ell Cottage

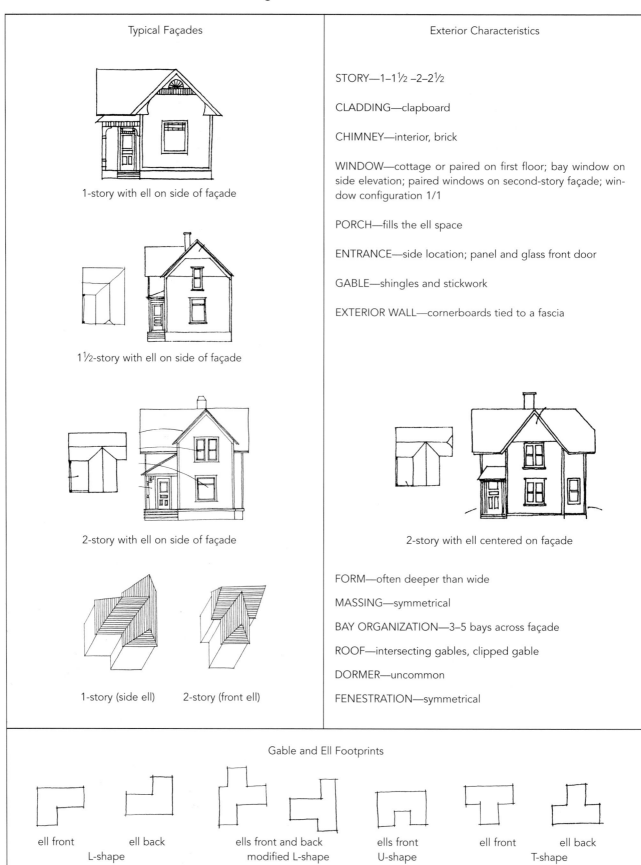

Typical Façades	Exterior Characteristics

1-story with ell on side of façade

1½-story with ell on side of façade

2-story with ell on side of façade

2-story with ell centered on façade

1-story (side ell)   2-story (front ell)

STORY—1–1½ –2–2½

CLADDING—clapboard

CHIMNEY—interior, brick

WINDOW—cottage or paired on first floor; bay window on side elevation; paired windows on second-story façade; window configuration 1/1

PORCH—fills the ell space

ENTRANCE—side location; panel and glass front door

GABLE—shingles and stickwork

EXTERIOR WALL—cornerboards tied to a fascia

FORM—often deeper than wide

MASSING—symmetrical

BAY ORGANIZATION—3–5 bays across façade

ROOF—intersecting gables, clipped gable

DORMER—uncommon

FENESTRATION—symmetrical

Gable and Ell Footprints

ell front	ell back	ells front and back	ells front	ell front	ell back
L-shape		modified L-shape	U-shape		T-shape

Table 7.2. Characteristics of Gable and Ell Cottage (continued)

Typical Façades

1½ story gable and ell with front projecting ell—stick style
Thomas Pope House (1877), Ames, Iowa

1-story gable and ell with front projecting ell
Three-room cottage, Cheyenne, Wyoming

2-story gable and ell with front and back projecting ell
"Cottage of Moderate Cost" (1894) *Carpentry and Building*;
design by F. C. Pollmar, Petoskey, Mississippi

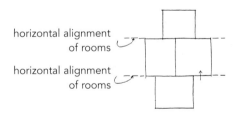

horizontal alignment of rooms

horizontal alignment of rooms

Schematic Plan for Projecting Ell Front and Back

Plan—Two-Story House, Projecting Ell Front and Back

Exterior Characteristics

2-story gable and ell with front projecting ell—Italianate
Design by T. I. Lacey (1880), Binghamton, New York

1½ story gable and ell with front projecting ell
House Design (1903), Sylva, North Carolina

side elevation, 2-story gable and ell with front and back
projecting ell; "Cottage of Moderate Cost" (1894) *Carpentry
and Building*; design by F. C. Pollmar, Petoskey, Mississippi

PLAN—2 rooms wide, 3 rooms deep

ROOM DISTRIBUTION—4–5 rooms downstairs (living room,
dining room, kitchen or hall, parlor, kitchen); 4 rooms upstairs
(3 bedrooms, 1 bathroom)

PLAN COMPOSITION
beginning—ell projects from façade
middle—2 rooms, often dining room and bedroom
end—another ell, often kitchen

ENTRY AND HALL—side entry; side hall; quarter-turn stairs

Side Entry, Four Rooms Down

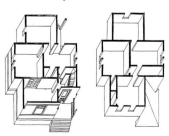

Axonometric—Projecting Ell Front and Back

The open gable cottage has a classical orientation, in that the façade is a temple front in which narrow cornerboards or pilasters carry a low, wide pediment. The introduction of cornice returns reinforces this impression. The façade is organized around a center axis running from the apex of the gable to the ground level. Gable windows are placed on or along the side axis, and when porches had three posts, the middle post was placed on the same line. What detailing appears was often derived from bungalow or craftsman design, rarely Spanish revival. The same general period used Queen Anne ornamentation on many cottage types, and the open gable style absorbed this trend through porch design and gable motifs.

One-Story Open Gable Houses: Shotgun and Industrial Houses

The shotgun house has an interesting social as well as design history. Its development has deep associations with African-Americans and the history of some Southern cities. Its migration from the Deep South was mostly limited to the Southeast and Southwest regions. The term *shotgun* refers to the unusual shape and plan of the structure. Built as inexpensive worker housing, the shotgun emerged as an object of rehabilitation in a number of cities, including New Orleans and Louisville. The house was always simple

in concept—three or four rooms aligned on a single axis. Frequently built on railroad lots, the houses were narrow and moderately deep, although some cities have double-wide shotguns. Original shotguns had no running water inside; toilets were outdoors, as were kitchens in warm climates. Later the toilet and kitchen were moved into the house. A few shotguns added an extra bedroom over the back room.

Shotguns were typically wood-frame buildings with wood cladding, although brick was used in cities. Although design concepts varied, the baseline model was a straight gable with a modest front porch. Variations included an elaborate front porch, a cutaway side porch, lintels, a modest frieze, turned posts or a corner employed to stylize the façade, gable finish of several kinds, fascia boards that girdled the building, and cottage-type porch detailing. The alternative roof for this house was the hip. Whatever the roof style, the interior organization was a jointed or segmented linear form of one room after another, with or without a connecting hall.

Shotgun cottages were often built in rows, and at first glance their design schemes seem limited to façade improvisations. While this is true, it does not represent all that was available to the builder. Other possibilities included some variety in floor plan; windowless walls on one side, so that windows would not overlap between houses; side entrances that did not

7.9. This small house in California is a variation on the shotgun type. The center entry is unusual, but the porch treatment is not. Authors' collection.

Table 7.3. Characteristics of Open Gable Cottage

Typical Façade	Exterior Characteristics
2-story (with attic)	STORY—1–1½ –2–2½ CLADDING—clapboard CHIMNEY—interior; brick WINDOW—1 or 2 centered in gable; 1/1 double-hung sash PORCH—extends across façade with steps to side; often shed roof; sometimes enclosed porch; turned or square posts ENTRANCE—side entrance common; panel and glass front door GABLE—open EXTERIOR WALL—cornerboards, façade, and side elevations flat
Typical Building Form, Massing, and Roof 	FORM—deeper than wide BAY ORGANIZATION—2–3 bays across façade ROOF—gable roof perpendicular to street DORMER—sometimes on side elevations FENESTRATION—symmetrical
Arts and Crafts 	Arts and Crafts
One-Story Shotgun or Industrial House Burbank Oil Field, Oklahoma	1½-story, off-center door 3-room house

Table 7.3. Characteristics of Open Gable Cottage (continued)

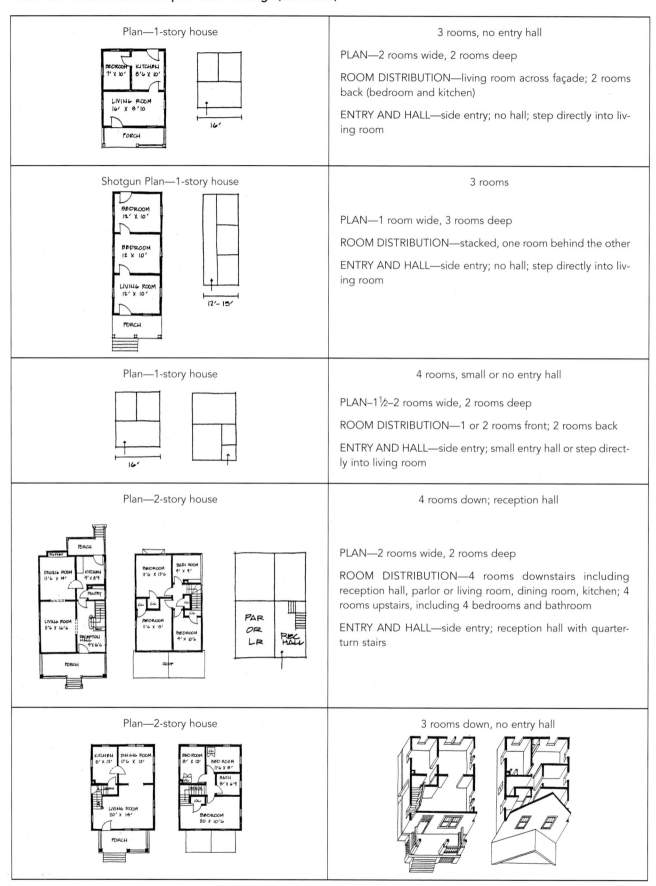

Plan—1-story house	3 rooms, no entry hall
BEDROOM 7' X 10' KITCHEN 8'6 X 10' LIVING ROOM 16' X 8'10 PORCH — 16'	PLAN—2 rooms wide, 2 rooms deep ROOM DISTRIBUTION—living room across façade; 2 rooms back (bedroom and kitchen) ENTRY AND HALL—side entry; no hall; step directly into living room
Shotgun Plan—1-story house	3 rooms
BEDROOM 12' X 10' BEDROOM 12' X 10' LIVING ROOM 12' X 10' PORCH — 12'–15'	PLAN—1 room wide, 3 rooms deep ROOM DISTRIBUTION—stacked, one room behind the other ENTRY AND HALL—side entry; no hall; step directly into living room
Plan—1-story house	4 rooms, small or no entry hall
16'	PLAN–1½–2 rooms wide, 2 rooms deep ROOM DISTRIBUTION—1 or 2 rooms front; 2 rooms back ENTRY AND HALL—side entry; small entry hall or step directly into living room
Plan—2-story house	4 rooms down; reception hall
(floor plans) PAR OR LR REC HALL	PLAN—2 rooms wide, 2 rooms deep ROOM DISTRIBUTION—4 rooms downstairs including reception hall, parlor or living room, dining room, kitchen; 4 rooms upstairs, including 4 bedrooms and bathroom ENTRY AND HALL—side entry; reception hall with quarter-turn stairs
Plan—2-story house	3 rooms down, no entry hall

abut between houses; art glass; and cornice details. By the early 1920s, the shotgun could be upgraded on the plan to include a specified living room, dining space, two bedrooms, kitchen, and bath.

Because the shotgun house was a workingman's house, thousands of these little houses were built next to, or near, industries of all kinds. The shotgun was easy to build, could be erected in a day even with modestly skilled workers, and could use local materials, which saved on cost. These houses also were built in rural areas, especially in the South, and in one-industry towns where companies built them for employees. Narrower than a plains cottage, most shotguns were twelve to fifteen feet wide and three to five rooms deep.

A housing type related to the shotgun was the industrial house, built in clusters or in rows, like the shotgun, as part of an industrial development. Most were literally "industrial houses" in that they were prefabricated. Their standard width was 16 feet, but their length varied; a typical three-room unit was twenty feet long. They were frame houses most likely clad with clapboards, and the interior was finished in pine or fir. The industrial houses had a limited design vocabulary, and there was less individualization of units than occurred with shotgun house. Their architectural effect came from a uniform appearance, a common setback from the street, and common materials (something they shared with the shotgun house).

One-and-a-Half-Story Gable End Cottages

The *Old House Journal* referred to this house as "the basic homestead house"—a designation that certainly captures the spirit of this cottage. This was a plain, straightforward house, another of the type sometimes referred to as a "worker's house" in period literature. A well-composed dwelling, it was marketed as a "conservative," simple design with straight lines. It conveyed two basic requirements of American shelter: security and clarity of purpose.

The open gable served as middle-class and working-class housing and as rural, even farmstead, housing. It had a side hall plan, with a living room across the front and two rooms behind it, or with the living room and a hall in front and a dining room and kitchen behind. The length was the greater dimen-

sion, and circulation, a pantry or breakfast nook, and a back porch absorbed any extra space. The placement and plan of the stair were variables in this house, with the quarter-circle and combination stair, with double access, as the principal arrangement. Fred Hodgson, pattern-book author and advisor to Sears, liked to turn the stairs in this type so that entry in the hall was from the side. Square plans became popular by the 1890s.

CLOSED GABLE COTTAGE

The same overall open gable house form has a closed gable version in which the triangle of the gable is transformed into a pediment by closing the foot of the triangle. Treatments used to close the gable included a fascia across the space, a change in materials in the pediment, a change in color, or a pent roof. The popular overall treatments were colonial revival and arts and crafts. In the former the treatment has more detailing than returns on the gable, and in the latter the craft response includes effects such as an exposed roof structure. Returns varied in length and detail and played various roles, which are depicted in the aesthetics tables.

7.10. A residential street (ca. 1913) with gable roof cottages in the Irving Park neighborhood of Chicago (42nd Avenue north of Bryon Street). Photo credit: M. Leonard Photo Co., Chicago, Illinois. Authors' collection.

7.11. This simple cottage has returns and a small pediment on the shed roof, which imply colonial revival values. The turned porch posts, rather than columns, suggest that the cottage lacks a clear aesthetic treatment.

7.12. The two-and-one-half-story Gladys Cain House (1918) in Akron, Ohio has a pent roof, shingles, and a reference to a Palladian-type window in the attic. The window in the gable pediment indicates a move toward the classic, whereas the rough shingles suggest the picturesque. The gable window is centered on the midline and is part of the symmetrical fenestration in the upper levels. The first-floor fenestration is asymmetrical, as are the side elevations.

COLONIAL REVIVAL

Generally, colonial revival house types fell into four subtypes of two-story or one-and-a-half-story frame buildings: a Georgian-type; the overhang, or garrison, house; the Cape Cod, which was called a colonial before it was a Cape Cod; and the gambrel cottage, or Dutch colonial. The three-gabled types were wider than they were deep, and all had a center hall plan. Many had a side porch or a sun porch on the ground floor or a sleeping porch on the second floor, and all had an end-wall chimney, although builders of Cape Cod houses sometimes included the more authentic central fireplace with multiple flues. When the entire country is taken into account, the Georgian style probably outnumbers the medieval, and the Cape, in all its variations, outnumbers all models. All the building types and aesthetic treatments remained tied to the picturesque thinking. The colonial relied on a rationally organized façade and an interior plan that was well lighted by multi-paned windows. It carried a three-bay front and utilized a bit of Georgian-style millwork to ornament the entrance. Ornamental gestures toward the vernacular tradition included using shutters for picturesque effects. The question of effects is difficult to assess because of the eclectic use of Georgian, federal style, and medieval details on different house forms.

Modern Colonial

The cottage took on colonial attributes in the last two decades of the nineteenth century. Interest in colonial culture developed early in the century and picked up momentum before 1850 and then again after the centennial celebration, where colonial buildings were displayed. As suggested earlier, Americans used some of the lessons of the English picturesque to rediscover the old colonial ways, thereby giving rise to the initial revival. Touring colonial sites was part of the rediscovery.[1] The promulgation of the style was patriotic and nationalistic. It was also part of the effort to associate American architecture with Greece and Rome, in the belief that a classical colonial appearance would convey meaning, confer status, and influence behavior in positive directions.[2]

Table 7.4. Characteristics of Closed Gable Cottage

Typical Façade	Exterior Characteristics
	STORY—1½–2–2½ CLADDING—clapboard mostly WINDOW—if colonial revival, a 3-part or Palladian window in gable; bay window on 1 or 2 elevations PORCH—extends across façade; often shed roof ENTRANCE—side entrance; off-center door GABLE—closed by a fascia board or a pediment EXTERIOR WALL—cornerboards
Typical Building Form, Massing, and Roof 	FORM—deeper than wide BAY ORGANIZATION—2–3 bays across façade ROOF—gable roof perpendicular to street DORMER—side elevations FENESTRATION—symmetrical
Plan—1-story house 3-room cottage (1908) Ouray, Colorado	**One-story Closed Gable Cottage** CLOSED GABLE—creates a pediment for this 3-room house with a cutaway porch, and there are cornerboards, but little else classical about the cottage
Aesthetic Analysis—colonial revival RETURNS—suggest colonial revival, especially if combined with a three-part gable window, columns, or other Colonial motifs	**Aesthetic Analysis—colonial revival** TRIM BOARD—makes a pediment; a 3-part window in gable and columns or other colonial motifs make a closed gable cottage a colonial revival

Table 7.4. Characteristics of Closed Gable Cottage (continued)

Aesthetic Analysis—colonial revival	Aesthetic Analysis—arts and crafts
PENT ROOF—makes a bigger gable end pediment; trim boards are wide; a 3-part window in the gable is often Palladian	TRIM BOARDS—divide gable end elevation into 1/3–2/3 sections; change in cladding from first to second floor; use of heavy brackets and tapered columns makes this closed gable an arts-and-crafts house
Plan—1-story house	4 rooms; small or no entry hall
Ready-made house #300, Montgomery Ward	PLAN–1½–2 rooms wide, 2 rooms deep ROOM DISTRIBUTION—1 or 2 rooms front; 2 rooms back ENTRY AND HALL—side entry; no hall; step directly into living room or into a small hall or vestibule
Plan—2-story	4 rooms down, reception hall
	PLAN—2 rooms wide, 2 rooms deep ROOM DISTRIBUTION—4 rooms downstairs, including reception hall, parlor or living room, dining room, kitchen; 4 rooms upstairs, including 4 bedrooms and bathroom ENTRY AND HALL—side entry; reception hall; quarter-turn stair

7.13. Mabel Sedgwick's house (ca. 1930) on Campbell Road in the Forest Park neighborhood of Valparaiso, Indiana, closely resembles the kind of modern colonial found in planned unit housing developments. The building lot allowed for excavation that, in turn, provided space for a garage, with a sun porch above. Both are modern conveniences. Authors' collection.

This first generation of late-nineteenth-century houses was eclectic in that it was associated with the imported Queen Anne and the homegrown shingle-style and hip-roofed cottages. Throughout a forty-year period, the common colonial cottage evolved from a narrow building with complex massing into a wide-bodied structure on a large lot. The house remained rectangular on plan and in shape and carried its full height throughout its development. In the 1880s the structure presented its straight gable roof to the street, with moldings that spanned the gable and converted it into a pediment. The façade carried a bay window on one or both stories, as well as on a side elevation. The entrance porch was small, with a modest but ornamented hood over the entrance. The porch had turned posts and brackets in the gable. Often there were two kinds of cladding or changes in cladding pattern.

During the 1890s the straight gable remained, as well as the bay window on the façade, but a distinctive Palladian window was placed in the closed gable, and the entire gable now overhung the main body of the house. The entrance porch widened to façade width, columns were introduced with an order of architecture, and dormers were placed on the side elevations.

By the first decade of the twentieth century, the new colonial cottage was an established suburban house in most regions (see 5.7 and 5.9). The straight, closed gable was widened, so that the classical feeling expressed on the façade organization was more emphatic. The gable overhang and the gable itself became more decorative, and the entrance became more formal, using not only the usual Tuscan order but the Ionic as well. The porch became full width. Oval windows were applied to elevations, and bay windows, which had been present throughout the development of the cottage, continued to appear on façade and side elevations. The traditional side hall plan sometimes gave way to a centered entrance with a vestibule or hall. Overall, the colonial cottage became sumptuous—a large, sometimes cubical structure that reflected colonial revival sensibility. The front Palladian window in the gable was often displayed in the dormers. Balustrades appeared on porch roofs, and secondary porches at the side or rear of the house spread the building out on the site.

Table 7.5. Characteristics of Colonial Revival: Modern

Typical Façades	Exterior Characteristics
 modern colonial (gable roof)  garrison with pendants under eaves Richard Beckman House (1936), Ames, Iowa  pediment entry Washington, D.C., 1936	STORY—1½ or 2 CLADDING—clapboard, brick, shingles, or combination CHIMNEY—end wall, brick or stone WINDOWS—double-hung sash, 6/1 window pattern common PORCH—end-wall porch or sunroom, sometimes second-story sleeping porch directly above porch ENTRANCE—center location; portico or flush door; entrance with pediment or hood; panel or panel and lights front door; sometimes sidelights GABLE—gable or gambrel end sometimes lunette on second story EXTERIOR WALL—nonfunctioning shutters; sometimes historical details, such as lunette, dentils; second floor overhang, pendants
Building Form, Massing, and Roof	Plan—2-story house
 FORM—wider than deep MASSING—symmetrical BAY ORGANIZATION—2–3 bays across the façade ROOF—gable, ridgeline parallel to street DORMER—sometimes gable dormers FENESTRATION—symmetrical	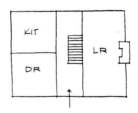 PLAN—3 rooms wide (including hall), 2 rooms deep ROOM DISTRIBUTION—4–6 rooms downstairs (hall, living room, dining room, kitchen, sometimes pantry or bathroom; sometimes an end-wall porch or sunroom); 4 rooms upstairs (4 bedrooms, 1 bathroom) ENTRY AND HALL—center entry; center hall or step directly into living room; straight-run stair

In large houses the colonial cottage maintained a central hall plan, but small models were characterized by a modern open plan. The addition of side porches, terraces, sunrooms, and the like were also concessions to modernity. The clean, relatively unadorned surfaces of these houses—despite their historical references to effects such as end-wall chimneys—and the precise alignment of elements, suggest modern as well as historical style.

The medieval type of colonial, a "garrison," was built through the 1930s and 40s and rediscovered in contemporary building. It also reflects the rational, coherent order of the general colonial design. To carry the tradition forward, certain design elements are necessary: a second-story overhang that invokes the historical New England house with a jetty and pendants. The house also carries wall dormers that curiously suggest the gables of New England vernacular houses and the dormers of the Georgian style. The medieval tradition usually included a massive interior chimney, but in time, end-wall chimneys serving fireplaces and central heating furnaces replaced it. As in the Georgian type, vertical alignment of windows, symmetrical fenestration on all elevations, cross-ventilation, and flow-through space are important design elements in the modern colonial cottage. Cladding materials also vary slightly. Clapboard covers most colonial houses, whatever the type, but brick as well as wood and asbestos cement shingles are also used.

Interior organization of the colonial always relied on a symmetrical division of rooms along a central hall. Most stair plans dictate a straight flight up from the entrance. The early-twentieth-century aesthetic for the colonial was the artistic system, which is replaced by the modern colonial. The modern opened the plan and often added a knotty pine room to the ground floor or the basement, which was evolving into a finished space.

Interior finish for these houses is less ornamented than in the earlier colonials, but molded trim sets are still appropriate for doors and windows, cased openings, and baseboards. A chair rail and a picture molding also remain part of this system. Architectural furniture for the modern colonial cottage included corner china closets, open or closed bookcases, and a pilaster and architrave mantel. French doors to a porch, a sunroom, or a hallway were a common passage effect.

Cape Cod

The Cape Cod house has been recognized as a unique vernacular type for almost 200 years, but it was not adopted by the industrial vernacular tradition until the 1920s, and even then it was referred to as a colonial cottage. Following Massachusetts's custom, the early commercial Cape was a compact house clad with shingles, featuring a small portico or pedimented entrance and a large interior central or end-wall chimney. The general form persisted, but the proportions and the elements of articulation have changed more than once. The wood-shingled exterior, which naturally weathered gray, was replaced by clapboards, bricks, or asbestos shingles. The dimensions of this house varied, but it was wider than deep, with thirty-two feet across and twenty-seven feet deep being an average size for a two-bedroom house. Many models had a low gable on the façade, twin gable dormers, or a cutaway porch. A major component of large subdivisions, the Cape Cod was often cheapened until only the basic form, with narrower gables, remained. The cladding was clapboard or brick, as well as natural or man-made shingles. The chimney disappeared and the entrance developed a projecting vestibule. The house was still sold as charming and cozy, but market forces made it a starter home.

7.14. The Cape Cod on Campbell Street Road in Valparaiso, Indiana, has simple lines, a well-proportioned shape and economy—the attic space is a useful half-story. Other than shape and form, the dormers, portico entry, end-wall chimney and shutters are colonial elements. Authors' collection.

Table 7.6. Characteristics of Cape Cod Cottage

Typical Façade	Exterior Characteristics
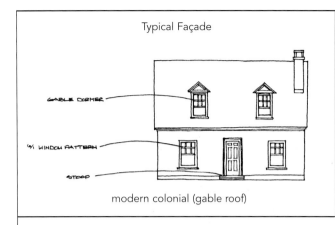 modern colonial (gable roof)	STORY—1 or 1½ CLADDING—wide clapboard or shingles CHIMNEY—interior, brick or stone WINDOW—6/6 or 6/1 window pattern PORCH—end-wall sunroom porch ENTRANCE—projecting vestibule or stoop with Colonial motifs EXTERIOR WALL—nonfunctioning shutters

Blueprint (1925), *Building Age and National Builder*

Building Form, Massing, and Roof	
 FORM—compact; slightly wider than deep MASSING—symmetrical ROOF—wide gable roof; ridgeline facing the street DORMER—gable dormers on façade; sometimes shed dormer on back	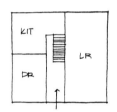 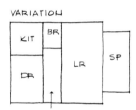 PLAN—2 rooms wide, 2 rooms deep ROOM DISTRIBUTION—3 rooms downstairs, 4–5 rooms upstairs ENTRY AND HALL—center entry; step directly into living room or into center hall stair; straight-flight stair

The Cape Cod was an especially successful modern colonial, being designed with few embellishments outside or inside. Instead of using ornamentation as a historical reference, the Cape Cod relied on the severity of its lines and on a well-proportioned form, in which a broad roof and a wide gable brought the eaves close to ground, giving it an organic quality. The concept of severe lines was carried into the interior as a straightedge casing or an uncased archway that divided the rooms. The time of the Cape Cod's greatest popularity coincided with the modern colonial aesthetic, and this was the interior system used for these houses.

The interior organization was grouped around the central hall, with a long living room on one side and the dining room and kitchen on the other, and two bedrooms, a bath, and a connecting hallway upstairs. Most stair plans were straight, rising from the entrance. Despite the presence of popular elements such as breakfast nooks, sunrooms, and sun porches, the Cape Cod expressed American traditions.

7.15. This house is a builder's cottage, modeled on English precedents. It is a free interpretation of the type, capitalizing on dramatic roof angles, stone accents in the stucco finish, and timber framing references. A short wing wall ties the front to the ground. Sign in front yard: Rellstar Bros. Builders. Authors' collection.

ENGLISH REVIVAL COTTAGE

The English revival cottage is one of the few imported, historically based house designs of the twentieth century. The primary source for this compact house was a generalized notion of English vernacular, characterized by steep roofs and contrasting roof lines; multiple cladding materials; fireplaces with tall, dramatically composed chimneys; and asymmetrical massing and fenestration.

The English cottage house was considered to have "informal charm," a tone reinforced by details—gables of stucco and half timber, brick and stone effects, round-headed doors with strap hardware, round-headed archways between rooms, entrances that were not always visible from the street, diamond-paned casements, and "quaint dormers." On plan, rooms were often clustered around a hall, and room sizes and shapes differed so as to provide new spatial experiences and opportunities for built-in furniture, a window treatment, and perhaps access to a terrace or a porch. These different interior spaces often projected from the main body of the house. Specific detailing included brick trim around openings, the use of Tudor framing in gables, some changes in materials, clipped gables, and high-contrast coloration.

Not all English cottages were the same in form or intent. Tudor models featured the application of dark wood framing that divided the walls into geometric units. The gables were broader, and the entire house had more volume than other types. The English cottage was built in suburbs in most parts of the country, but particularly in northern climates; it was constructed close to the ground, yet high enough to promote its profile.

Interior planning, like that of the exterior, was varied because of the need to create a sense of casual arrangement, as if the spatial configurations were indigenous to the culture and therefore part of local custom. Generally, each house had three or four rooms down and up, with very few houses having a full second floor. The English cottage reached the height of its popularity from 1915–1940. Its success was based in part on a multitude of effects and special spaces, including a breakfast room or nook, a fireplace, a terrace or patio in an outside corner, and a reception hall or vestibule as a projecting gable off the front. All of these effects were intended to create "a dignified, restful house of surprising convenience and no extravagance."

Table 7.7. Characteristics of English Revival Cottage

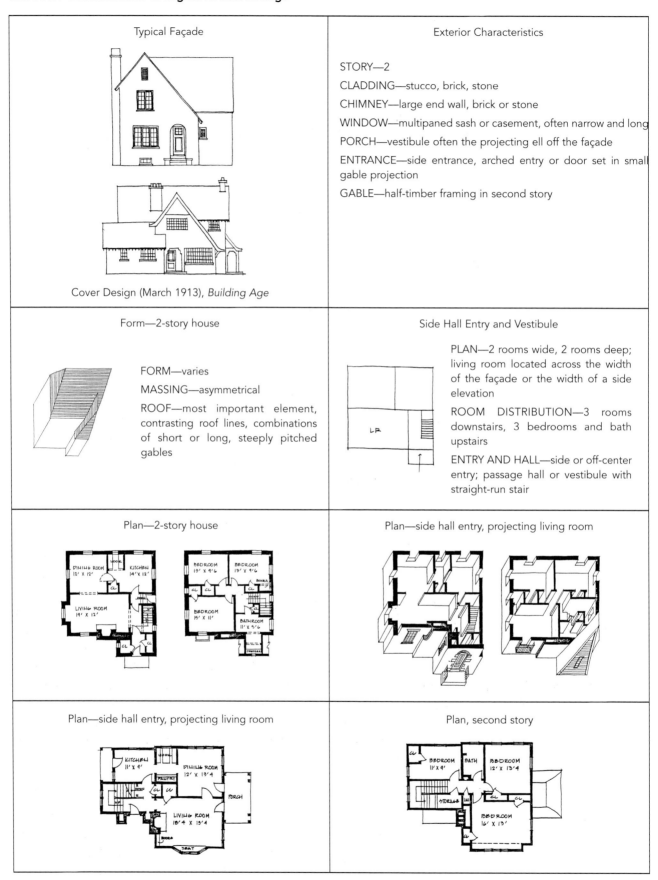

Typical Façade	Exterior Characteristics
Cover Design (March 1913), *Building Age*	STORY—2 CLADDING—stucco, brick, stone CHIMNEY—large end wall, brick or stone WINDOW—multipaned sash or casement, often narrow and long PORCH—vestibule often the projecting ell off the façade ENTRANCE—side entrance, arched entry or door set in small gable projection GABLE—half-timber framing in second story
Form—2-story house	Side Hall Entry and Vestibule
FORM—varies MASSING—asymmetrical ROOF—most important element, contrasting roof lines, combinations of short or long, steeply pitched gables	PLAN—2 rooms wide, 2 rooms deep; living room located across the width of the façade or the width of a side elevation ROOM DISTRIBUTION—3 rooms downstairs, 3 bedrooms and bath upstairs ENTRY AND HALL—side or off-center entry; passage hall or vestibule with straight-run stair
Plan—2-story house	Plan—side hall entry, projecting living room
Plan—side hall entry, projecting living room	Plan, second story

8

BUILDING TYPE: ORGANIC COTTAGE

Of all the historical American house types, the cottage embraced more stylistic and technological changes than any other dwelling. The cottage represented the integration of some English models and the rise of an American house type that would suit an emerging middle class. The cottage also helped to define the suburbs of major cities, to evolve the modern interior, and to represent a commingling of the pastoral tradition and the picturesque aesthetic that Americans had yet to inculcate into their culture (see fig. 5.5). At the heart of the development was a dramatic design concept: the organic cottage. The attribution of an organic quality to these houses stems from an open-plan arrangement of rooms and passages, organized from the inside out and expressed as an accretive massing of volumes. (Accretive refers to a kind of joining of seemingly disparate sections that once occurred in traditional building.) The combination of open circulation covered by an admixture of hip and gable roofs, with spaces emanating from the center of the plan, created a truly American house that could be distinguished from imported models (4.3, 4.4).

The examples in this chapter cover almost fifty years of design and are arranged in a general chronological order. This category of house types is broad, because it concerns a number of houses with apparently differing stylistic interests (4.5). We have sorted houses that others identify as representative of styles—stick, Queen Anne, and shingle style—under one rubric, consisting of side hall and center hall plans, with variations.

THE COTTAGE ORDER

The new house was traditional. It was easily recognized as a member of the cottage order, and it utilized traditional materials for cladding and ornamentation). It was also modern, accommodating cisterns, bathrooms, kitchens, pantries, central heating, and gas and electric lighting. But its modernity was subtle. The internal coherence of this class of houses did not come from the usual arrangement of rooms stacked across a building site. Rather, the internal coherence was spatial in nature, revealing continuities of space rather than alignments of partitions. The spatial basis for the organic cottage was expressed in the number of projections from the core of each plan type.

As for lumping so many stylistic interests into a broad category, we think of these houses as part of a number of progressive and thoughtful solutions to the problem of building a modern house. Stick,

Queen Anne, and shingle style designs were the first major break with classical schemes, although the Queen Anne and shingle retained fragments of that system. Their forms varied but all three required large, dynamic elements fused around a core of spaces. The stick type celebrated the production of lumber; the Queen Anne was the most decorative and exuberant; and the shingle eschewed the expression of details and reasserted form. These cottages incorporated modernity into their traditional skins or within their historical expectations in a fresh and original way.

The most obvious variation in the external character of the organic cottage was the height, that is, whether the cottage was a one- or two-story model. Because the organic cottage was volume-oriented, and changes in height required changes in organization. A second factor was the external treatment; organic cottages appropriated a good deal of what had become traditional details.

We have identified five schematic concepts for this house type, all of which stem from the spatial center that extends continuity to other rooms, hallways, and, in some instances, to the outside. Looking at schematic plans, some of the thrust of the core space can be read on the perimeter by the kind of projections that extend off the body of the building. Yet irregular exteriors make it difficult to predict overall floor plans from the outside.

With so much focus on the inner organization, no other term than *organic* seemed appropriate to describe the concept of the cottage. The term also suggests a biological analogy, an attention to growth and development. The buildings look and feel like they are in a stage of development. The exterior form of an organic cottage reflected the freedom with which it was assembled. Here the organic spaces of the plan were accounted for within massing elements; for example, geometric volumes clustered about the core, resulting in elevations different from each other but still interactive because of spatial interconnectedness. Circulation and interior vistas provided those connections.

An examination of the overall shapes of these houses, and of the relation of parts to the whole, suggests that interruption was a value of higher order than the continuity of principal lines or materials. For example, there is the way in which a large ele-

8.1. The Alice Davis House in Tacoma, Washington has some stickwork treatments. Stickwork dates from the 1870s and is achieved by arranging patterns of milled boards and sticks on the wall as flat panels. Authors' collection.

ment such as a turret captures a corner, breaking the plane of two walls, or the way one kind of cladding material abuts another. Other characteristics included flaring walls, imaginative fenestration patterns, complex roof plans, gable ends executed in different patterns, and masses and voids in dynamic interplay. All this articulation did not exist unconnected. Continuities held the elements within their bounds: string and belt courses, continuous sills and lintels, continuities of materials around elevations and between floors, and repeated motifs.

In a larger sense, the interpenetration of lines and volumes—especially the continuous circulation that is fundamental to these types—suggests that spatial continuity makes this house type unique. Access to all, or almost all, the ground floor rooms is possible from the entrance. We described circulation pathways, including around core space, in Chapter 2 and illustrate one in table 8.1. We imagine pathways as layers over the ground plan, with each layer generating a context within which to establish relationships between rooms. At another level, the general shape of the house and its porch overlay the principal rooms. Finally, the building site, including its gardens, overlay the house. The green space and plantings that surround the cottage are arrayed in response to the push (say from a bay window), and

8.2. The cottage in this photograph has gable elements pointing in different directions and a pyramid roof. These elements are a subtle reminder that the interior space of an organic cottage emanates from a center. Authors' collection.

8.3. The cottage is organized under large gable roofs, which offer the choices of expressing the roof and its gable as part of the wall (left side of the house) or turning the gable end into a pediment that stands alone, with its own aesthetic effects (façade pediment). This cottage is a good example of the veranda as a base from which the volume springs. G. N. Lindl House, Velva, North Dakota. Photo credit: Johnson & Olson, Alexandria, Minnesota. Authors' collection.

pull (a recess like a porch) of the massing elements, as well as aligned with views from and toward the house. Lastly, the cottage imprints itself on the neighborhood or the rural lot creating another kind of character at a new scale. It is the accumulative effect of these integrated layers that shape the originality of American cottage.

Roof plans are based on a core roof, usually a hip that spans some of the central circulation, and intersections with other roofs. In the next series of cottages gable roofs are the ancillary roofs. In terms of their influence on cottage style, the roofs appear in multiples, and each may repeat detailing or receive a treatment unique to it. Some of the design choices are whether to treat the gable as a pediment, whether to change materials, how to engage windows, and whether to treat a dormer as a unique element or one that responds to other details.

One-story organic cottages were popular in the West. What they lacked in vertical expression and overall volume, they made up with a dynamic floor plan and irregular massing. Their aesthetic appeal was driven by the picturesque. Figures 2.5 and 5.6 offer contrasts in approach. The Black house on the high plains is but a momentary interruption on an endless plain, whereas the cottage in Ohio pulls all of its energy toward the center toward town.

The inclusion of colonial details on the cottage in figure 8.4 is an indication of how all the cottages, regardless of their time period, regional location, and aesthetic intentions, could take on the colonial. For some of these building types it is not just a question of responding to deeply woven threads in the culture, but to wearing the colonial like a merit badge. You cannot be an American house type without engaging the colonial at some level.

Plan Types

As for specific spatial configurations, we have identified five individual types of cottage planning: three side hall types and two center hall types. Taken together, the plans and their accompanying external forms were developed and built from 1880 to 1910. In sorting cottages by plan typology, we find that almost every one of the plan types has a full complement of exterior style types. That is, there are several exterior treatments (what builders called *exterior finish*) included in the plan types. Finally, because these cottages were introduced into older aesthetic and spatial systems, their first-floor arrangements included parlors, sitting rooms, dining rooms, kitchens, and halls. Some of the halls were passageways and others were as large as a room and, indeed, functioned as one.

8.4. This one-and-a-half-story cottage has organic attributes. Consider the role of the conical turrets. Only the one on the porch has a clear function; it is like a pavilion. The application of colonial revival details only adds to the picturesque approach. Authors' collection.

Side hall entries are divided into two categories. The typical plan for the first category of side hall begins with a projecting parlor, adjacent to, or circumscribed by a porch, followed by a room-size reception hall and two adjoining rooms. The latter rooms were the physical center of the house, and they were both social spaces—a sitting room and a dining room. The kitchen and back porch completed the sequence. The back walls of the two central rooms were often in the same plane. In smaller houses of this type, the sitting room was dropped from the plan, and the house terminated with a pantry and a porch behind the kitchen.

A variation of the side hall plan had the following aspects. The parlor space was pulled back toward the core of the house, and the hall, whose stair was a straight flight instead of a quarter-turn, as in the first version, was narrower but longer. The center rooms—the sitting and dining rooms—had no lateral alignment, and the kitchen–pantry space was wider than the previous kitchen; in fact, their combined width was the same as that of the parlor and hall. The outside walls of the parlor and hall were continuous, and the sitting room usually had a bay window. In a smaller version of this type, the sitting room was left out of the plan, and the parlor might include a bay window or a turret, with the overall dimensions of the plan being almost cubical.

A variation of the side hall plan had a side entrance through a reception hall, a side stair located behind the hall and placed at a right angle to the flow of the house, and three social rooms on the first floor. The parlor once again projected off the core, and the center rooms were aligned sequentially from front to back. In the smaller house with this plan, the usual loss of one social room resulted in an increase in continuous walls, as the loss of volume made larger interactions of massing elements less likely.

The plan alternative for the organic cottage was the center hall type. Culturally it referenced the traditional colonial plan where the center hall ran through the house, front to back. However, in an organic cottage there was no need for the hall to continue through the house. The entry could be aligned with a short hall, but thereafter the plan gave up the linear continuity of the entire hall for multiple, even fragmented, spaces that offered much more variety of visual and spatial experience.

In summary, the new American cottage took a big step toward the modern open plan. Openness in the cottage came from "living halls" and circulation around a core space, with adjacent rooms spun away from the center. Interior vistas also started from the center. Beyond the plan, the overall design characteristics included a tall central volume (for two-stories), asymmetrical massing, patterned textures on the exterior, projecting gables and bays, and interconnected interior and exterior spaces. There was either a steep roof over the central volume or a low, spread out roof on the types that spun rooms away from the center. The roof over the core space often had a pyramidal shape. The low roof type emphasized the horizontal dimension and the ease with which people moved from room to room, and from room to outside and back again.

Table 8.1. Characteristics of the Organic Cottage

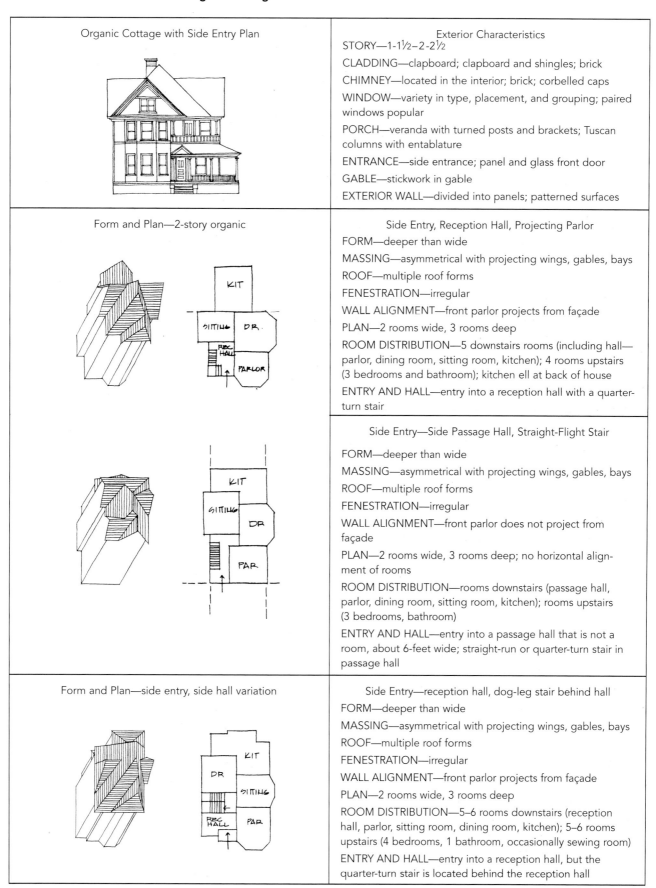

Organic Cottage with Side Entry Plan	Exterior Characteristics
	STORY—1-1½–2-2½ CLADDING—clapboard; clapboard and shingles; brick CHIMNEY—located in the interior; brick; corbelled caps WINDOW—variety in type, placement, and grouping; paired windows popular PORCH—veranda with turned posts and brackets; Tuscan columns with entablature ENTRANCE—side entrance; panel and glass front door GABLE—stickwork in gable EXTERIOR WALL—divided into panels; patterned surfaces
Form and Plan—2-story organic	**Side Entry, Reception Hall, Projecting Parlor** FORM—deeper than wide MASSING—asymmetrical with projecting wings, gables, bays ROOF—multiple roof forms FENESTRATION—irregular WALL ALIGNMENT—front parlor projects from façade PLAN—2 rooms wide, 3 rooms deep ROOM DISTRIBUTION—5 downstairs rooms (including hall—parlor, dining room, sitting room, kitchen); 4 rooms upstairs (3 bedrooms and bathroom); kitchen ell at back of house ENTRY AND HALL—entry into a reception hall with a quarter-turn stair
	Side Entry—Side Passage Hall, Straight-Flight Stair FORM—deeper than wide MASSING—asymmetrical with projecting wings, gables, bays ROOF—multiple roof forms FENESTRATION—irregular WALL ALIGNMENT—front parlor does not project from façade PLAN—2 rooms wide, 3 rooms deep; no horizontal alignment of rooms ROOM DISTRIBUTION—rooms downstairs (passage hall, parlor, dining room, sitting room, kitchen); rooms upstairs (3 bedrooms, bathroom) ENTRY AND HALL—entry into a passage hall that is not a room, about 6-feet wide; straight-run or quarter-turn stair in passage hall
Form and Plan—side entry, side hall variation	**Side Entry—reception hall, dog-leg stair behind hall** FORM—deeper than wide MASSING—asymmetrical with projecting wings, gables, bays ROOF—multiple roof forms FENESTRATION—irregular WALL ALIGNMENT—front parlor projects from façade PLAN—2 rooms wide, 3 rooms deep ROOM DISTRIBUTION—5–6 rooms downstairs (reception hall, parlor, sitting room, dining room, kitchen); 5–6 rooms upstairs (4 bedrooms, 1 bathroom, occasionally sewing room) ENTRY AND HALL—entry into a reception hall, but the quarter-turn stair is located behind the reception hall

Table 8.1. Characteristics of the Organic Cottage (continued)

Organic Cottage with Center Entry Plan 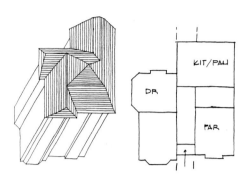	Center Hall Plan FORM—varies; deeper than wide or wider than deep MASSING—asymmetrical with projecting wings, gables, bays ROOF—multiple forms FENESTRATION—irregular WALL ALIGNMENT—front parlor projects from façade PLAN—stair located in center passage hall or turned to side behind parlor ROOM DISTRIBUTION—social spaces downstairs: parlor, dining room, library or parlor, sitting room, dining room ENTRY AND HALL—center or off-center entry; center hall punches through house on center axis
Form–1½ or 2-story organic cottage 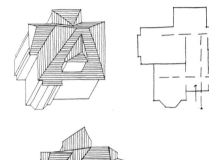	Center Hall Plan FORM—usually wider than deep MASSING—asymmetrical with projecting wings, gables, bays ROOF—multiple roof forms; steep roof pitches; central hip roof dominates DORMER—hip roof dormer and/or wall dormer FENESTRATION—irregular and varied PORCH—across façade or veranda PLAN—irregular; 3 rooms wide, 3 rooms deep ROOM DISTRIBUTION—5 rooms: parlor, dining room, and kitchen on one side of the hall; 2 bedrooms and bathroom on the other side of the hall ENTRY AND HALL—center or off-center entrance into a center hall
Stick  Tall proportions Asymmetrical massing Applied stickwork as exposed framing and bracing Roof brackets and purlins Ornate gables and projecting bays	Queen Anne  Queen Anne Strong sense of centrality Projecting wings Gables, bays, occasional turret or tower Multiple cladding materials Very ornamental in early period Less ornamental in later examples 7-room house by T. F. Schneider (1883), *Carpentry and Building*

Table 8.1. Characteristics of the Organic Cottage (continued)

Queen Anne

Central circulation core
Inside–outside continuity
Less turned and sawn ornament
Sunrise motif in gable

Cottage (1889), Boston

Queen Anne

Central hip roof with gable
projections
Less ornamentation
Multiple dormers
Entrance pediment
Side hall plan and reception
hall

Cottage (1889), Chattanooga,
Tennessee

Queen Anne

Asymmetrical composition
Tower and conical roof
Upper sash with border of
small square lights or Queen
Anne windows
Veranda

First prize design (1903), John
P. Kingston for *Carpentry and
Building*

Queen Anne

Continuous hip roofs
Bay window
Art glass window
Circular veranda
Corbelled chimney cap

John A. Wallace and Alice
Wallace House (ca. 1909),
Canyon, Texas

Shingle

Close to the ground
Horizontal flow of space
Semicircular wall or porch
Tall central hip roof
Shingle panels

Cottage (ca. 1907), Raleigh,
North Carolina

Shingle

Hidden framing
Large geometrical forms
Extended roof lines
Wide gable or gambrel roof
Partial or full shingle cladding
Sometimes flared walls

Cottage (1889), Chicago;
Frank M. Snyder, designer

Colonial Revival

Colonial Revival

Three-part window in gable
Sometimes 2-story bays on
side elevation
Symmetry upper levels, a symmetry lower level

Table 8.1. Characteristics of the Organic Cottage (continued)

Colonial Revival	Colonial Revival
 Large pediment gable and pent roof Ionic or Tuscan columns Large dormers on side Veranda or façade porch James G. Hornbeck House (1907), Port Jervis, New York	Classical gable widens Gable overhang Large pediment projects beyond house Cornerboards widen *Cement Houses and Private Garages* (1914)
Plan, first floor—side entry, reception hall with quarter-turn stair, projecting parlor 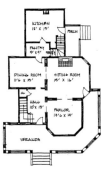	Plan, second floor—side entry, reception hall with quarter-turn stair, projecting parlor 
plan—2-story house, side entry, passage hall with straight-flight stair  	Plan—1 story, center hall 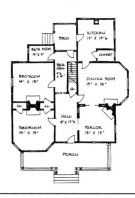
Plan—2-story center hall plan  	Axonometric—2-story center hall plan 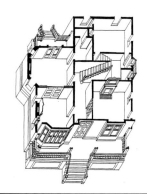 

BUILDING TYPE: HIP ROOF AND MANSARD ROOF COTTAGE

———◆———

The hip roof cottage is a fundamental house type that offers precise form with clear organization. The cottage accommodated classical detail easily, and it rarely moved toward informality or rusticity. The cottage afforded modest variations of the major design elements. A change in materials—for instance, the use of brick, stucco, or cement—might give the building a more compact quality. Other elements that lent themselves to change included the roof, which could be obscured by dormers or reduced by a flat in the center, and the porch structure, which could be enlarged or made more formal. Lesser variations included flared eaves or walls; variety in chimney placement; changes in window groupings so that double or triple windows replaced the traditional single unit; multiple dormers; and a broader display of porch details.

The square house, a subtype of the hip roof cottage, was one of those progressive house types that emerged in the nineteenth century. Its principal advocate was Massachusetts architect Eugene C. Gardner. Intellectually his ideas relate to those of Orson Squire Fowler, who pioneered the octagon house.[1] The square-type cottage, like other Gardner houses, "sprang from utility." He chose the square shape because it represented "the economy and perfection . . . was tantamount to a plan for reform." His

houses were generally three stories with similar patterns on the first and second floors, and he placed his houses so that every main room received generous sunlight. The square house was adaptable for workers' cottages, but it had its limits as to size.

SQUARE HIP ROOF COTTAGE

The square hip roof cottage is a generic house type that was built throughout most of the 1870–1960 period. It was finished in many styles, from Italianate to Western. The cottage is box-like with a large hip roof, an almost square floor plan, and compact massing that was often cubical in shape. Sold as a practical house without requiring the expense of projections, this type was referred to as a "modern square type." Implicit in that phrase is the belief that square lines are practical and permit maximum utilization of floor space.

Like all cottages, the hip cottage was conceived as a four-sided building with changes in fenestration and ornamentation possible on all elevations. This approach to styling places the hip roof cottage in the picturesque tradition. The house was built as a speculation house throughout residential areas of cities: as a distinctive suburban house, as a rural house, and

9.1. The oval windows on both floors of the Herbert Robins House in Erie, Pennsylvania, the narrow cornerboards, even a fascia board, and the porch columns are colonial accents, but the house is a modest colonial revival. Authors' collection.

9.2. This small square house has a formal application of millwork sticks that divides the elevations into panels. The window to the right of the door is a special cottage window with art glass in the upper portion. Authors' collection.

as a double house. It stood alone and was rarely built in rows on the same block. As a focal point on any block, the hip cottage might occupy a corner lot and set a tone for the remaining buildings, or it could be placed mid-block, with other cottages clustered around it.

In design, the hip roof cottage pushes a large mass straight up from ground level and caps it with a pyramidal roof. The form of the building, including its termination, is quite clear. If we stand close to the house, the eaves stop the ascent; if we are farther away from the house, the pyramid terminates the building, and our attention is drawn back to the lower levels. The horizontal lines inherent in the clapboard cladding and the low porch roof and porch proper counter the vertical thrust. Window placement can accent both directions. Vertical accents derive from the chimney, cornerboards and porch columns.

The hip roof cottage was both historical and contemporary, in that internal organization included compartmentalized spaces and some movement toward an open plan, as it came to be known, and the interior and exterior could employ historical ornamentation.

The average size for this house, which was rarely square, was about twenty-five feet wide by thirty-feet deep, with a full-width front porch. A reception room is one of the four first-floor rooms. Some interior schemes utilized the reception room plan, which placed the quarter-turn stair to the side and included a small center hall on the upper level. A bay window, on a side elevation and part of the design of the dining room, was most often on the opposite side of the house from the stairs.

Plan book companies responded to square shapes and the square–type house, because the house had little unnecessary ornamentation on the exterior, and the square shape worked well for a reception hall. Some design schemes would detail the inside stair with square balusters and newel. Variations of this type of cottage were easy to realize. A popular one also had a reception hall, but the stair was placed behind the reception partition and was entered from the side. This house also had a bay window and the same distribution of rooms as the first model, but with an increase in overall size, averaging 27 feet wide and 46 feet long. The exterior had typical square-type elevations that might include a porch or pantry off the rear of the house. This kind of house was commended for its economy of space, which suited it for a narrow lot.

ITALIANATE HIP OR MANSARD ROOF COTTAGE

The Italianate version of the square hip roof cottage is one of the oldest subtypes of the period under study. Early styles tended toward the Tuscan, which usually included a pronounced tower. The common hipped cottage is more generally Italian. In the vernacular of the period, a cottage such as this was

Table 9.1. Characteristics of Square Hip Roof Cottage

Typical Façade	Exterior Characteristics
	STORY—2–2½ CLADDING—clapboard, rarely stone or brick CHIMNEY—interior, brick WINDOW—cottage window or large window on first floor façade; 1/1 double-hung sash; bay window common on side elevation, often a dining room window PORCH—extends across entire façade; open rail with balusters; Doric or Ionic columns ENTRANCE—off-center, panel and glass door EXTERIOR WALL—cornerboards or pilasters carry a fascia or entablature; stone, brick, or cast concrete foundation

Typical Side Elevation	

Building Form, Massing, and Roof	
 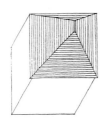	FORM—slightly deeper than wide; often pantry or enclosed porch ell in rear MASSING—asymmetrical BAY ORGANIZATION—3 bays across façade ROOF—hip with flat; pyramidal DORMER—often centered with hip roof

 Mrs. A. J. Trott House (1895), University Park, Denver, Colorado; Frank J. Grovavent, architect	 Lee H. McClung House (1909), Sapulpa, Oklahoma

Table 9.1. Characteristics of Square Hip Roof Cottage (continued)

Arts and Crafts	Outside characteristics
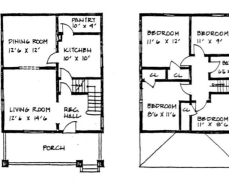 F.S. Collins House (1915), Berwyn, Illinois	STORY—2 CLADDING—clapboard, stucco, combination of materials WINDOW—3-part window on façade; vertical glazing bars in double-hung windows ROOF—overhanging eaves; exposed rafters PORCH—square posts or columns with pedestals EXTERIOR WALL—belt course; change in color or cladding between stories

Plan—side entry plan with reception hall

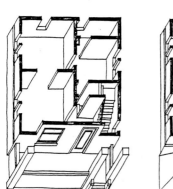

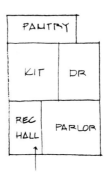

PLAN WITH SIDE ENTRY AND RECEPTION HALL—side entry, side hall stair, and a reception hall with a quarter-turn stair; 2 rooms wide, 2 rooms deep (panty or porch ell common at back)

ROOM DISTRIBUTION—4 rooms downstairs, including reception hall; 5 rooms upstairs (4 bedrooms, 1 bathroom)

ENTRY AND HALL—side hall entry; reception room; quarter-turn stair

Plan—off-center entry and reception hall

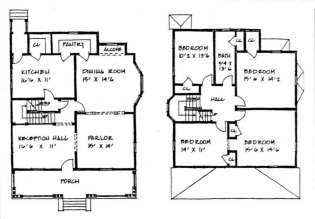

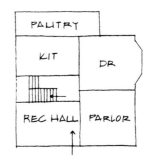

PLAN VARIATION ENTRY AND HALL—an alternative design, the entry is off-center with the stair placed behind the reception hall, locating the stair deeper into the house.

Table 9.1. Characteristics of Square Hip Roof Cottage (continued)

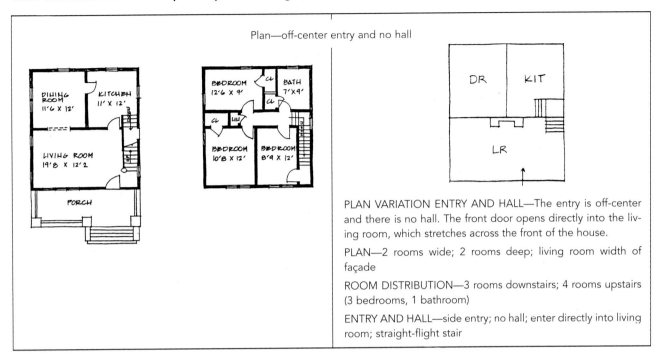

Plan—off-center entry and no hall

PLAN VARIATION ENTRY AND HALL—The entry is off-center and there is no hall. The front door opens directly into the living room, which stretches across the front of the house.

PLAN—2 rooms wide; 2 rooms deep; living room width of façade

ROOM DISTRIBUTION—3 rooms downstairs; 4 rooms upstairs (3 bedrooms, 1 bathroom)

ENTRY AND HALL—side entry; no hall; enter directly into living room; straight-flight stair

known also as a bracketed cottage, a reference to the roof projection beyond the frame of the building (sometimes twenty-four inches) and the use of heavy brackets along the cornice. The vernacular Italianate also used moldings, pronounced lintels, and sills to add texture and articulate the fenestration; and brackets, pendants, and cut or turned pieces to ornament porches and other entrances. The hip roof and the overall handling of exterior elements and interior organization were equally applicable to another cottage type, the mansard cottage or French cottage. Both houses utilized the same kinds of plans: side hall and center hall.

The one and one-and-a-half-story square hip roof cottage could receive Italianate styling (page figs. 5.1 and 9.3). For instance, the entry system in figure 9.3 has a portico that projects off the body of the house and employs ornamental porch posts, with brackets, a frieze, and cresting on the portico roof. The portico spans the space between the façade windows. The main roof has a heavier brackets, and ornamental gable finish is visible in both pediments.

A typical two-story Italianate square hip roof cottage had a strong vertical orientation centered on vertical alignment between stories, including multistory bay windows and elaborate design schemes on the axis of the entrance. The roof profile was low,

which reinforced the upward thrust of the façade, and many cottages were topped by a belvedere, which extended the building visually. In terms of composition, this type had a set of window, cornice, entry, and corner treatments that contributed to the styling effect. All of these elements were free adaptations of Renaissance motifs, reproduced in wood, tin, and iron.

9.3. This Italianate hip roof cottage frames the elevations with corner and fascia boards, and has ornamentation on the top of the walls, just beneath the eaves, and cresting on the main roof flat. Authors' collection.

9.4. This Italianate hip roof cottage with a short mansard porch roof was built in 1910 in Bolivar, New York. Double brackets, double columns, and tall cresting on the porch roof created a well-wrought porch system that set the tone for ornament—all large and aggressive. Authors' collection.

9.5. The J. L. Stover House is a common mansard roof type. The entry is Italianate but the house is plain. The second story is in the lower slope of the roof; the dormers are marked with pediments. Authors' collection.

The square plan had a "liberal arrangement" as A. J. Bicknell phrased it in his *Village Builder* (1870). The plan accommodated either a center or side hall scheme. While not exactly square, the hip roof and mansard roof cottages were just over thirty by thirty feet. George Fuller's mansard roof model of 1875 was 35 feet 8 inches wide by 32 feet deep, and S. B. Reed's house (1878) was 36 by 30.[3]

Center Hall Plan

Architects, builders, and owners saw the advantages of a big square house with two floors, a cellar, and an attic. Descriptions of their buildings included recognition of the economical construction and provisions for comfort and dignity. Reed believed that the character and quality of a house depends upon the material and manner of siding, and he recommended brick.

Italianate and French cottages with center hall plans were popular, and residential and pattern-book architects, such as Woodward (1869) and Lawrence B. Valk (1869) designed "cheap cottages with French [and hip] roofs" in the $1,000–$4,000 range. New York architect H. C. Hussey declared that no plan offered greater facilities of convenient, pleasant, and comfortable arrangement than the center-hall. He noted, however, that the house needed no less than 28 or 30 feet of frontage, and his 1876 example of a two- and two-and-a-half-story center hall cottage with a "splendid French roof" that was "fully

equipped . . . with luxurious creature comforts" in New York cost $11,000."[3] Many deemed the square Italianate design excellent for farm or village houses, and they were also built in town and suburban neighborhoods. The center hall plan and the square Italianate hip roof cottage continued in popularity in the West until the end of the nineteenth century.

Side Hall Plan

The side hall plan was the more prevalent, and houses with this spatial configuration were typically one room and a hallway wide and three rooms deep, with a second level of bedrooms and bath. This arrangement fitted into several sizes, with Italianate types being one and a half to two and a half stories high, and mansard types being one and a half, two, or three stories high. Because of its roof shape, the mansard could include a floor lighted by dormers. Within the side hall plan, the stair was either a straight-run type or a quarter-turn type, with the latter often employing winder stairs to save space. The side hall plan also included a bay window projection off one side that lit a sitting room or dining room. This arrangement was especially true for houses built in the 1870s. Later examples included a bay window on the façade, sometimes tiered so that the bay linked the floors.

The variant for the side hall plan had the same narrow, deep shape, but a new room was carved out of the center of the house just behind the stairs. The room

Table 9.2. Characteristics of Italianate Hip Roof Cottage

Façade	Exterior Characteristics
2-story square hip roof with a flat and balustrade	STORY—1–1½–2–2½ ROOF—hip with flat or mansard roof; sometimes a cupola or belvedere; large brackets (often paired), wide eaves CLADDING—clapboard, brick, stone CHIMNEY—1 or 2 end wall or interior WINDOW—tall and narrow; stone lintels or surrounds; stone sills; sometimes paired, circle-top, or bay windows PORCH—varies: stoop, façade porch; turned porch posts ENTRANCE—side entrance; single or paired panel doors; hood over door EXTERIOR WALL—high foundation; elaborate cornices; sometimes quoins, string course
Square House Plan—center entrance and center hall 	center gable and center hall FORM—almost square MASSING—symmetrical BAY ORGANIZATION—3 bays across façade FENESTRATION—symmetrical PLAN—3 rooms wide (including hall); 2 rooms deep ROOM DISTRIBUTION—4 rooms downstairs, 5 rooms upstairs; each room located in a corner of the house ENTRY AND HALL—center entry hall wide and deep; sometimes divided into a front entrance hall, a stair hall behind it, and a rear hall
Side hall plan—with projecting room and back ell 	FORM—deeper than wide PLAN—1 room plus hall wide; 3 rooms deep; parlor projects slightly from entry ROOM DISTRIBUTION—4 rooms downstairs (hall, parlor, dining room, kitchen as ell); 2–4 rooms upstairs (2–3 bedrooms and 1 bathroom) ENTRY AND HALL—side entry door recessed; narrow passage hall; straight-run or quarter-flight stair
Side Hall Plan—variation 	FORM—deeper than wide BAY ORGANIZATION—2–3 bays across façade ROOF—hip or mansard PLAN—1 room wide, 3 rooms deep; parlor projects slightly from entry ROOM DISTRIBUTION—5 rooms downstairs (hall, parlor, dining room, kitchen as ell; small sitting room or library behind stair often projected past the hall form); 2–4 rooms upstairs (2–4 bedrooms and 1 bathroom) ENTRY AND HALL—side entry door recessed; narrow passage hall; straight-run or quarter-flight stair

Table 9.2. Characteristics of Italianate Hip Roof Cottage (continued)

1½-story square (flat front) mansard roof

Cottage (1872), *Bicknell's Village Builder*

2½-story square mansard roof with

Italianate—rectangular hip roof cottage

Design No. 16 (1869), *Woodward's National Architect*

Exterior Characteristics

STORY—1–1½–2

ROOF—intersecting hip with flat or mansard roof; sometimes a cupola or belvedere; large brackets (often paired), wide eaves

CLADDING—clapboard, brick, stone

CHIMNEY—1 or 2 end wall or interior

WINDOW—tall narrow windows; stone lintels or surrounds; stone sills; sometimes paired, circle-top, or bay windows

PORCH—varies: stoop, façade porch; turned porch posts

ENTRANCE—side entrance; single or paired panel doors; hood over door

EXTERIOR WALL—high foundation; elaborate cornices; sometimes quoins, string course

Side Hall Plan—variation with a small room tucked behind the stair cavity

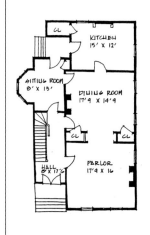

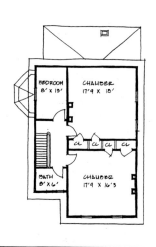

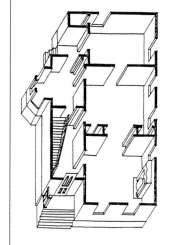

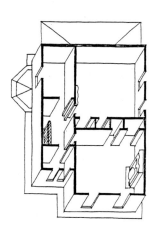

usually was small and was used as a library or den; projecting the room slightly from the side elevation, or adding a bay window, turned it into a dining room. The center hall plan had four rooms on the first floor, symmetrically arranged on each side, with a wide hall between them. Stair plans, again from the 1870s, often called for two stairs, the principal one accessible from the front door and the front rooms, and a second, hidden from view, connecting a small back hall to the upper floor. The overall shape of these houses followed from the plan type, in that the side hall house had a narrower façade than the center hall type. In both cases, however, the rooms on the first floor were aligned with each other. There were also other kinds of plans that were used less frequently. These included a stem-and-crossbar type, on the order of a T-plan, in which a section of house one room wide intersected with a two-room-wide crossbar. A second alternative had an L-shape in which two sections, each one room wide, met at right angles, with the entrance, hall, and stair included in the intersection.

COLONIAL REVIVAL HIP ROOF COTTAGE

A second type of hip roof cottage has a colonial exterior treatment with a center hall plan and a center hall stair. The arrangement was comparable to the colonial house with a gable roof. There were at least three rooms and a reception hall on the ground floor and four bedrooms and a bath upstairs. Most plans extended the living room from front to back along one side. The Potter House in Whitehall, New York (9.6) is an example of this kind of colonial revival in the grand manner. As to its shape, the house is slightly deeper than wide, which allowed for more square footage. Many of its exterior appointments were intended to imitate a late Georgian colonial, and therefore included freestanding orders of architecture and colonnades between rooms or between rooms and halls.

Colonial hip roof cottages with classical treatments were especially popular during the first few decades of the twentieth century. The overall shape and plan were closely related to the generic cottage. There is historical continuity in the use of a square plan and the cubical shape, but the real essence of this colonial revival lay in the application of colonial motifs to the basic form. The entire design became formal and, for the most part, restrained. The roof took on a flat with a balustrade and carried a central hipped dormer. The façade received slightly different treatments on each level, the first floor being a wide, plain wall pierced by large cottage windows, by a paneled door with molding plants derived from historic patterns, and occasionally by sidelights. The

9.6. The accumulation of ornament from the ground level to the enclosed flat on the roof is an essay in how to integrate such systems. The Potter House, in Whitehall, New York, relies on the traditional Ionic order as the language of the house repeated from the porch to the second-floor terrace and the third-level dormer. Columns, cornices, and modillions dominate the scheme. Authors' collection.

Table 9.3. Characteristics of Square Hip Roof Cottage: Colonial Revival

Typical Façades	Exterior Characteristics
	STORY—2–2½ CLADDING—clapboard, sometimes shingle CHIMNEY—interior, brick with ornate cap WINDOW—double-hung multipaned upper sash, 1 light in lower sash; often Palladian or oval-accent window PORCH—formal with an order of architecture, sometimes a balcony or 1–2-story portico; Ionic or Tuscan columns ENTRANCE—centered or off-center, panel and glass door EXTERIOR WALL—sometimes giant pilasters, quoins, dentils, curvilinear bays, shutters, porch lattice
 Modern House No. 102 (1908), Sears, Roebuck & Co.	
Typical Building Form, Massing, and Roof	Square Plan—center entry
 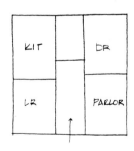	FORM—almost square; wider MASSING—symmetrical BAY ORGANIZATION—3 bays across façade ROOF—hip, often with flat and balustrade DORMER—hip or gable dormer on façade, sometimes a Palladian window FENESTRATION—symmetrical WALL ALIGNMENT—aligned PLAN—2–3 rooms deep; 2–3 rooms wide ROOM DISTRIBUTION—5 rooms downstairs (including hall); 5–7 rooms upstairs (4 bedrooms, 1–2 bathrooms) ENTRY AND HALL—center or off-center door to center hall

porch was distinctly classical: the porch posts were columns, and most often the porch treatment included an order of architecture complete with a short pediment over the porch steps. The second-floor windows may or may not align with the first. The second-floor elevation often displayed an oval window on the centerline. In some cases, a second-floor door replaced the oval window for access to a balcony. The corners of these houses usually carried a vertical board, whether corner trim or a pilaster. The boards rose uninterrupted to the cornice line, where they met a wide fascia. Other cornice details included dentils or brackets on the eaves. Side elevations were less formal and more allied with traditional cottage arrangements, so that this building never lost its cottage heritage.

Two other versions of the colonial deserve mention. One has the same shape and plan as the primary model, but expands on the colonial vocabulary by including a Palladian window on the façade and by adding a portico—frequently, a two-story structure with large columns, an entablature, and a pediment. The other version varies slightly in plan, in that it includes a circular form. The circular shape is rarely a semicircle, but it is deep enough to serve as a bay window that may extend the full height of the façade. A few designs in this mode use twin bays. An extension of this kind of plan uses circular forms in the plan of the porch while leaving the façade walls flat.

Ornamentation and other details do not vary from the prototype, except that dormers may be more common on the portico and curved-front types than on the basic colonial cottage. The curved-front cottage seems most prevalent in New England, where the building's historical antecedents are located, providing a cultural as well as aesthetic connection.

VILLA AND WESTERN HOUSE

The villa form of the hipped cottage was the most formal of all the designs in this group. It had a rectangular shape, with the long side facing the street. The villa developed from 1910 on, and early examples reflected prairie style influences on cottage design. By the 1920s the villa began to exhibit four design motifs: Italian, Spanish, French, and an eclectic type that is generally Mediterranean. By the 1930s a fifth type had appeared—an abstracted clas-

9.7. A villa is an imposing type. Here a wide porch and deep eaves spread the house across its site. The composition of this house understates the classical elements, so they mix with cottage elements. Authors' collection.

sical design featuring giant pilasters on the façade and the styling of the architect Paul Cret.

The overall form was a palazzo with a central entrance hall. The façade organization was generally symmetrical, with a sunroom or porch to one side. Style details could include a round-headed entrance and arcades and clay tiles for roofing. Ornamentation was primarily on the walls and included brackets where the wall meets the roof, quoins, balconies with iron railings, carved or cast motifs, and high-contrast paint schemes.

The Spanish or Mediterranean styles most often introduced an arcade into the façade. Common arcade placements included the entrance, with one to three arches, and the second-floor space above the entrance. Occasionally, arcades also provided a screen or side entrance to a porch or sunroom.

On the level of the everyday house, the villa had six to eight rooms; a lower level with three rooms and a quarter-turn stair, behind which was the kitchen; on the second floor were bedrooms and bath. The living room was the first room, and it spread across the entire front of the house. The plan is rectangular, and straight sides characterize the overall shape. The façades had three- or five-bay fronts covered with one or two materials, including brick veneer, stucco, clapboard, and shingles. It was a popular type because of its low cost, and it adapted well to a city or suburban lot.

The Western house, a period term, was a hip roof cottage with rectilinear qualities. In the decade

9.8. A popular version of the Western house, with its straight lines and strong rectilinear forms, had a low hip roof and bracket details. *Manitou C–165, Curtis Service*, 4, no. 5 (April 1917): n.p.

9.9. The interior of the Curtis Company Manitou model is executed in the artistic aesthetic, in which straight lines and natural materials set the tone. *Manitou C–165, Curtis Service*, 4, no. 5 (April 1917): n.p.

following 1910 it developed into an alternative to picturesque cottages. To characterize the house, the builder could eschew ornamental details, change color or materials at the upper level, use trim boards or belt courses to frame the walls into panels, and modify window placement (see figs. 3.7 and 3.8). The rectilinear was a practical design that paralleled the development of the prairie style design. The first floor of the rectilinear cottage contained social and service areas organized in an open plan, while the second floor had the usual array of bedrooms and bath.

Specific design features included a low-pitched roof with a hipped dormer on the façade side; a full-width or slightly inset porch, most commonly with a closed rail; widely and evenly spaced second-story windows; irregularly spaced first-floor windows; and polychromatic materials. Porches were plain or an understated classical style with Tuscan columns. Additional elements included a bay window in a parlor or dining room; an end-wall chimney; changes in glazing pattern, with 6/1 and 1/1 being popular; and changes in cladding. As for the latter, clapboard, shingles, brick, stucco, and cement were common, and changes in materials usually took place three-quarters of the way up the elevation, at about the windowsill line. Cast concrete block was used in foundations as well as in porch piers.

The Western hip roof cottage seems to have been both a natural outgrowth of the development of the hipped cottage, and the result of an outright borrow-ing of prairie house motifs. Like the square plan house, the prairie plan found receptive builders and owners on the prairies and plains. Indeed, some of the literature of the period referred to this preference for the unconventional stucco house as a "popular western tendency." It did have strong horizontal lines transmitted by its low roof and wide eaves. On the façade the porch roof and the banded windows reinforced the horizontal thrust of the main roof. The house often had a stucco finish that gave it a monolithic quality, which was relieved by wood strips. Other Western treatments included a type that used one kind of cladding on three-quarters of the elevations and a second cladding on the last quarter. Casement windows, were part of the vocabulary for this house, as were double-hung windows in which only the upper half of the top sash had muntins.

The house brought a change in the overall configuration of the hipped cottage. The rectilinear walls were asserted as planes. Traditional full-sized porches even became squared to the façade, so that they too described a planar system. No matter the form, this type did call attention to the idea that straight, simple lines express true beauty. Other descriptions of the period referred to the "dignity and grandeur" of the house and stated that, although the "architectural lines are strong," the resulting form is "artistic." Writers and consumers respond to the geometry of the house, which creates a strong impression yet allows for expressive details.

Table 9.4. Characteristics of Hip Roof Cottage: Villa and Western House

Typical Façades	Exterior Characteristics
	FORM—wider than deep MASSING—symmetrical BAY ORGANIZATION—3 bays across façade ROOF—low hip with flat or gable with ridgeline facing the street; clay tile roof or shingles with cresting FENESTRATION—often symmetrical STORY—2 CLADDING—stucco, brick CHIMNEY—end wall WINDOW—casement or sash, often paired or triple windows; French doors as windows PORCH—varies; front entrance hood; end-wall sunporch or second-story balconies ENTRANCE—elaborate and formal door recessed slightly from façade, surrounded by moldings, panel front door EXTERIOR WALL—relatively flat; quoins, pilasters, belt course

Mediterranean

Colonial Revival

Supplemental Plate (1915), *Building Age* · "The Magnolia" (1918), Sears, Roebuck & Co.

Wall Alignment and Plan Type	
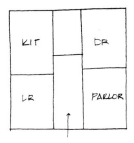	PLAN—2 rooms wide, 2 rooms deep, and a center hall ROOM DISTRIBUTION—3–4 rooms downstairs (center hall, living room, dining room, kitchen); 5 rooms upstairs (4 bedrooms, 1 bathroom); living room may comprise one side of the first floor ENTRY AND HALL—center hall with straight-run stair; stair location varies from front, middle, back of hall

Table 9.4. Characteristics of Hip Roof Cottage: Villa and Western House (continued)

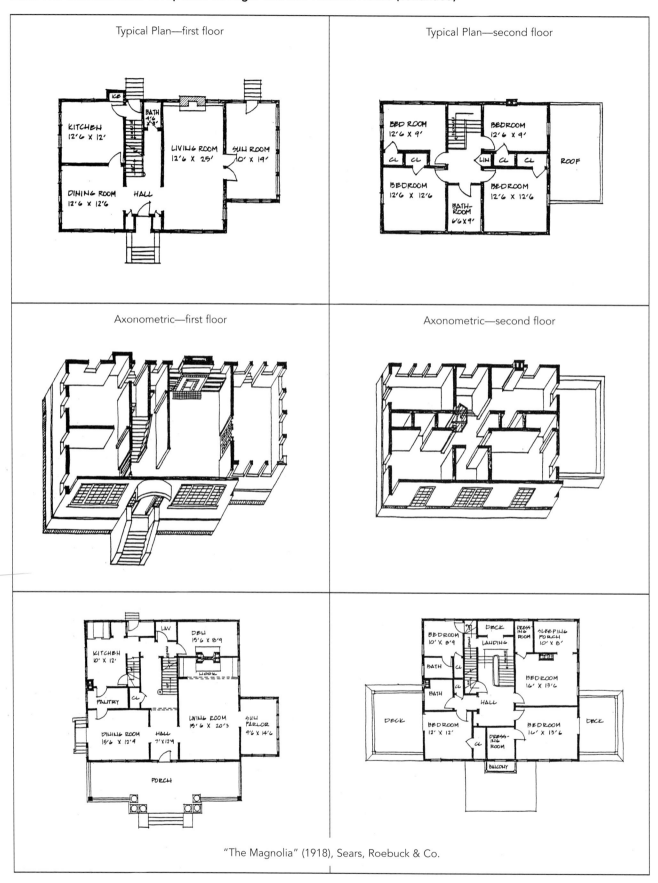

Typical Plan—first floor

Typical Plan—second floor

Axonometric—first floor

Axonometric—second floor

"The Magnolia" (1918), Sears, Roebuck & Co.

BUILDING TYPE: GAMBREL ROOF COTTAGE

There are three types of gambrel roof cottages associated with colonial revival design: gambrel end (facing the street), intersecting gambrel roofs, and a gambrel with the roof ridgeline parallel to the street. The issue of colonial authenticity centers on the use of historical sources, and the primary sources were the stone and clapboard houses of New York and New Jersey built by Dutch settlers. For a time, if a cottage had a minimal application of colonial details it might be labeled a semi-colonial. In vernacular building the house was generally referred to as "Dutch colonial" and built in various sizes.

In the gambrel end mode, the roof ran straight back or was intersected at a right angle by another gambrel. Other exterior characteristics included a projecting porch that spanned the house or a cut-away porch that created the equivalent of an outdoor room; that is, its dimensions were proportional to the interior room next to it. The long side of the house was organized into two or three bays.

The gambrel cottage with the roof parallel to the street had three or five bays and the same interior plan as the gable roof colonial cottage, including the division of space into the same social and functional spaces. The perpendicular model, which tended to have less square and cubic footage, had a side hall plan. As in most colonial designs, fireplaces were prominent.

The shape of the roof was forceful; visually it separated itself from the lower level. The largest gambrel cottages had intersecting roofs, which broke up the roof forms and expanded the square footage. The intersection also produced elevations where fenestration could be varied and changes in color and materials accommodated. The major exterior variables for this type were the size and shape of the second-floor dormers, the manner in which the roof was brought down on the walls, and the different angles made by the roof planes. Changes in color and materials helped to layer the gambrel cottage; clapboard lower stories and shingled upper stories were common.

Some houses were built with a single gambrel whose ridge was parallel to the street. In traditional façades the porch and entrance system were of two kinds: cutaway porches cut from one side or across the width of the façade, or a projecting short porch with a low-pitched roof of its own. In the first instance the void of the porch helped to balance the large volume of the gambrel end wall, while in the second the lateral flow of the porch, reinforced by an open rail or a porch roof balustrade, lightened the front of this mass-oriented structure.

Detailing on the gambrel cottage included a wide eave at the roofline which cut of the roof from the body of the house below, a bay window that provide

10.1. The composition of this façade is a lesson in balanced asymmetry. The centerline of the elevation, taken from the peak, passes between the long returns at the attic level and between the paired windows to the first floor, where it aligns with the right edge of the left window of the three-sided bay. The front steps of the cutaway porch extend beyond the entry, passing across the centerline to engage the bay window, thereby balancing the total composition. Authors' collection.

a break in a wall plane, and gable ornamentation that included special windows, stickwork to help relieve or mask the wide gable, and usually more than one dormer. The gambrel cottage was appreciated for its generally sturdy yet graceful lines. The gambrel roof was deemed economical, because so much of the upper story space was useable.

The cottage was most appropriate for suburban sites. Advantages included compact floor plans and low construction costs. The gambrel cottage became popular in the 1890s, and remained so into the 1920s, appearing in bungalow plan books. In 1910 *The Building Age* noted that "thousands upon thousands are found scattered all over the country."[1] They were built in suburban development such as Oakmont, Pennsylvania, but they were also built in small towns that had no colonial history, such as Shawnee, Oklahoma, Sterling, Kansas, and Greeley, Colorado. Plan books like Hodgson's *Practical Bungalows and Cottages for Town and Country*, Carpentry and Building's *Modern Dwellings*, and Mont-

10.2. The plain, simple form of the Vern and Jennie Chaples House (ca. 1908) illustrates the economic advantage of the gambrel type; it creates a good deal of volume without much cost. Authors' collection.

gomery Ward's *Book of Homes* included various types of singled and clapboard cottages with gambrel roofs and colonial effects.[2] Small gambrel cottages were built on frontage lots twenty-five feet wide in the nineteenth century. *Carpentry and Building* reported on such a project in Oneida, New York in 1894. The tall narrow house, designed by W. Irving Tillotson for R. M. Baker, was really a period cottage with a pair of small, intersecting gambrel roofs that enclosed the attic. *Carpentry and Building* referred to the style as "semi-colonial," no doubt because of the roof. About 1920 the house manufacturer Aladdin published *Aladdin Plan of Industrial Housing* that included "The New Eden" model designed for a lot 24 feet wide.[3] The building footprint was 20 feet by 20 feet, and the roof was single gambrel, perpendicular to the street. The house did not have a solid foundation, but was built on posts. The company boasted that textile manufacturers had selected the house, with great satisfaction to themselves and their employees. The small entry hall included a quarter-flight stair, a 12- by 10-foot living room, a 12- by 10-foot dining room, and an 8- by 10-foot kitchen. The upstairs had two bedrooms, each with a closet and a bath. In the same period, Laura Kingston designed a five-room gambrel roof cottage in Worcester, Massachusetts ssachusetts. The first floor had a miniscule entry hall with a quarter-flight stair, a sitting room, and a kitchen with a pantry; upstairs were three small bedrooms.

Table 10.1. Characteristics of Gambrel Roof Cottage

Typical Façades	Exterior Characteristics
1½ story	STORY—1½ –2–2½ CLADDING—clapboard, shingle, or combination of clapboard on first floor and shingles on second floor CHIMNEY—interior, brick WINDOW—double-hung sash; 1/1 and varieties of multiple upper lights; bay or oriel window on side elevations; sometimes paired or triple windows on second floor façade PORCH—across façade; sometimes a cutaway porch ENTRANCE—centered or off-center location; panel and glass door GABLE—returns or pent roof; changes in shingle pattern; stickwork; gable window—Palladian or 3-part window or paired or triple windows EXTERIOR WALL—high contrast color between wall and trim
2 story	2½ story

Building Form, Massing, and Roof	Plan—4-room house with reception hall
FORM—deeper than wide MASSING—asymmetrical ROOF—gambrel, gable end perpendicular to street or intersecting gables DORMER—often gable dormers on side elevations FENESTRATION—symmetrical	PLAN COMPOSITION—2 rooms wide, 2 rooms deep ROOM DISTRIBUTION—4 rooms downstairs (including hall); 4 rooms upstairs (3 bedrooms, 1 bathroom) ENTRY AND HALL—side entry, reception hall, quarter-turn stair

Typical Plan—4 rooms downstairs, reception room	Axonometric—4 rooms downstairs, reception room

10.3. Since the cottage is the dominant historical house type, it is not surprising to find a Dutch gambrel colonial being given a cottage treatment. Wood shingles can represent the colonial, but shingles can also be ornamental. In this case the porch and the dormers compromise the colonial in favor of the picturesque.

Authors' collection.

DUTCH COLONIAL COTTAGES

The so-called Dutch colonial cottage is a subtype of the generic model. The revival style presented on these pages was popular during the 1900–1940 period. The shape of the roof, which sometimes had flared eaves, dictated the shape of the building. In many models the flare was wide enough to provide some shelter over the entrance.

The roof ridge was usually parallel to the street, so that the façade was available for a full design treatment. A three-bay front was common, but five-bay units can be found. The second-floor level was outlined by either a long shed dormer that covered most of the roof or by two or three evenly spaced gable dormers. The dormers were repeated on the rear elevation. The entrance was understated, with only a hood or a pediment to mark the door and the shallow porch. Some pediments evolved into porticos with slender columns. Fenestration was, for the most part, symmetrical on all elevations.

The main house often received an extension in the form of an open or enclosed porch, a sunroom, or even a pergola, to which there was access through French doors from inside. Although the porch was formally composed, it added a bit of informality to the overall design. An end-wall chimney in brick or stone completed the design. Clapboard was the dominant cladding material, but, on the first-floor façade, brick veneer was popular.

The colonial gambrel has often included elements of the Georgian style, which accounts for the use of orders of architecture (Tuscan) on entrances and porches, and the central hall plan that many of these cottages have. The alternative to a central hall was a modern open plan in which the entrance door opened directly into the living room. The use of classical columns was one of the few instances of ornamentation on these buildings. Accents included small lights or half-lights bracketing the chimney in the gables, local stone foundations and chimneys, sidelights or a fanlight transom at the entrance door, and shutters.

The major exterior variables for this type were the size and shape of the second-floor dormer and the manner in which the roof related to the walls. All in all, the Dutch colonial was not a house that relied on small effects to carry the design. It was a large, commodious design with open space, a good relationship to its suburban site, plenty of room for family functions, and a strong, rationally, and pragmatically designed façade. Although it was not built in rows, individual units were built in a great number of subdivisions throughout the country.

Table 10.2. Characteristics of Dutch Colonial Cottage

Typical Façade	Exterior Characteristics
Dutch colonial	STORY—1½ or 2
	CLADDING—clapboard, brick, shingles, or combination
	CHIMNEY—end wall, brick or stone
	WINDOWS—double-hung sash, 6/1 window pattern common
	PORCH—end-wall porch or sunroom; sometimes second-story sleeping porch directly above porch
side elevation	ENTRANCE—center location; portico or flush door; entrance with pediment or hood; panel or panel and lights on front door; sometimes sidelights
	EXTERIOR WALL—nonfunctioning shutters; sometimes historical details, such as lunette, dentils, second-floor overhang, pendants

Building Form, Massing, and Roof	Typical Plan—center entry, center hall
FORM—wider than deep	PLAN—3 rooms wide (including hall), 2 rooms deep
MASSING—symmetrical	ROOM DISTRIBUTION—5–6 rooms downstairs (hall, living room, dining room, kitchen, sometimes pantry or bathroom; sometimes an end-wall porch or sunroom); rooms upstairs (4 bedrooms, 1 bathroom)
BAY ORGANIZATION—2–3 bays across the façade	
ROOF—gambrel, ridgeline parallel to street	
DORMER—sometimes gable dormers	
FENESTRATION—symmetrical	ENTRY AND HALL—center entry; center stair or step directly into living room; straight-run stair

KIT, DR, LR

Westchester County, New York	*Building Age, 1917*

Table 10.2. Characteristics of Dutch Colonial Cottage (continued)

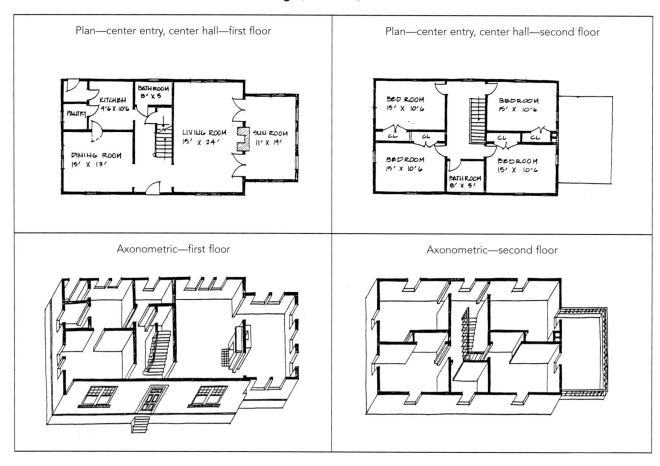

Plan—center entry, center hall—first floor

Plan—center entry, center hall—second floor

Axonometric—first floor

Axonometric—second floor

11

BUILDING TYPE: BUNGALOW

———————————

The American bungalow has international roots. Its transformation and development produced a very successful vernacular house that had national distribution. It had broad market appeal and was built in clusters, in rows, and as single houses, finished in several aesthetics, and scaled up and down both as to size and cost. To the best of our knowledge the bungalow entered the market as a "California bungalow," making its first appearance in popular literature in 1904. In January there was a notice in *Ladies' Home Journal* and a brief article in the July issue of *Carpentry and Building* describing the bungalow as "a low house, generally with a spacious interior . . . set snug and close to the ground, with overhanging eaves, and great surfaces of roof. They are only one story high, or at most one story and an attic, and are stained dark. . . . Porches are designed to be well shaded. Rough stones are used for the chimneys and visible foundations."[1] Given the nature of the design and the kind of living it suggested, it was appropriate for this form to develop on the West Coast. The rustic look—rough stones and dark stain—would not be part of the national adoption of this building. Bungalow design would engage a much wider segment of the culture.

Fred T. Hodgson, an editor and consultant to Sears, Roebuck and Company, published one of the first bungalow stock plan books that figured prominently in the development of modern vernacular architecture. In the preface of *Practical Bungalows and Cottages for Town and Country* (1906), Hodgson explained that bungalows "are the result of a popular tradition . . . a genuine expression of popular and wholesome habits of country living and . . . country building."[2] Hodgson's comment reveals that he needed to justify a new form in terms of regional folk architecture, and he suggested that there was some moral imperative behind its presence—country living represents the good life. Perhaps this point of view was left over from the romantic revivals and the development of cottages in the previous century. Whether Hodgson thought of it at this time or not, the bungalow would not turn out to be a country dwelling. It would be a subdivision house, reproduced by the hundreds in cities across the country, and a town house. The bungalow would also be characterized as progressive and modern and consciously artistic in a manner unlike country houses and country living.

One year later, in 1907, a short unsigned article in the February issue of *Carpentry and Building* extolled the "breadth, strength, and simple beauty of the plainness" in the California bungalow: "there is a pleasing absence of millwork and other ornamenta-

11.1. This freshly built bungalow would be marketed as a craftsman-style house. The wood basis of the building type and style are evident as shingles, clapboards and stick-work. Photo credit: Martin Prosser. Authors' collection.

tion."[3] The reference to millwork can be read as a reaction to picturesque cottage design, which the bungalow and the hip roof cottage would address. Moreover, the shift away from historical cottage designs was concerned not only with simplified exteriors, but also with a new feeling for interior space and organization.

These early descriptions are remarkably accurate in terms of the purposes and aesthetics of the bungalow house type. The bungalow was to have a relaxed, informal, locally derived quality about it, which could not, however, be exported immediately to all regions of the country. The early versions of the bungalow relied on rustic effects derived from West Coast living, but not all rusticity is the same. As the bungalow became more fully absorbed into the industrial production system, it lost some of its original qualities, but it gained a stronger position among house types. This prominence was due, in part, to a significant expansion of the design language associated with the type.

Historically, the bungalow did not gain popularity until the second decade. From then through the 1930s and 40s, the number of bungalows built throughout the county increased dramatically. Basic, everyday bungalows were initially built in one of three types: with a gabled roof, a hip roof, or intersecting roofs, such as intersecting gables or intersecting hip and gable. A number of plans were developed for each of these forms. Stylistically the house type had global influences, including Indian, Spanish, and Japanese, and it continued to incorporate stylistic el-

ements from other cultures and styles throughout its development. Thus the resulting American bungalow had plain models with clapboard or shingle cladding intended for vacation areas, and a Swiss chalet model for mountainous regions. It could be rustic, or clean and open in the manner of prairie houses, or clustered with patios or terraces in the Spanish colonial mode, or built up to approximate a cottage form. And it could look historical, as in the application of English cottage motifs to the basic bungalow form.

The bungalow plan reduces the distinction between outside and inside space and reflects the open, practical, outdoor living possible in warm climates. During the first part of the twentieth century, Americans became more interested in casual living, in built-in storage, in compact arrangements with plenty of air and light, and in an open plan and less complicated furnishings. The bungalow responded to those needs.

The bungalow roof is large no matter the type. Gable and hip roofs dominate the market, and they also serve as the base roof with which other roof forms intersect. Porches and their roofs provided an opportunity for some integration of roof structures. There is no standard bungalow porch, but in general such a porch covers more than half the elevation it fronts and may cover the entire width. A typical porch system includes steps with wing walls, an enclosed porch with porch piers and a rail with balusters, and, if covered by a gable roof, a gable treatment.

11.2. A bungalow with a gable roof done in the craftsman style. The house is rustic. The construction looks light and clever, as if done by hand. Authors' collection.

11.3. This house gets most of its effects from boards on, and extending from, the house. The care taken with the rooflines, the bay windows on front and the side, and the pergola suggest craftsman-like thinking—getting the most out materials and forms. Authors' collection.

The latter reflects the overall style. If the house has a craftsman touch, with exposed rafter ends, purlins, and brackets, then the porch gable may indicate that aesthetic intention.

The floor plan was spread out, necessitating a large foundation, long walls, and a large roof. If the house and porch were both gables, then the house faced the street with contiguous and receding planes. The shell of the bungalow was not always box-like. The juncture of the porch with the main body produced a break in the box, as did a bay window and a rear porch. Battering porch piers and walls, whose inclined edges broke the rectangle of the façade, was a subtle refinement. Window placements tended to pull the house out along the horizontal, as did walls

with large amounts of glass subdivided into panels of wood and glass. Broad groupings of glass contributed to the inside–outside continuity.

As for variations, changes in glazing pattern, exposed rafters, cast concrete blocks with rock faces for the foundation or porch pedestals, and sidelights for the entrance were popular. Wall treatments included flared walls on the main house and/or porch, lattice-work, cornerboards, and a water table. Some bungalows extended the porch as a separate element complete with an independent roof.

The cultural origins of the bungalow type are such that applications of craftsman aesthetics were its first important style. As stated earlier craftsman style was an American version of the international arts-and-crafts design. Its values were grounded in being true to materials and to craftsmanship, even if the latter were only an illusion—that is, the made object *looked like* it could have been made by hand, whereas in truth it was machine made. Some early versions of this aesthetic produced houses that looked like pavilions in a garden or a seasonal house. They were very much influenced by wood products—sticks, shingles, and boards. As such, they follow the cottage tradition of making wood-based single-family houses with unusual features. The next two figures are illustrations of how the craftsman style was worked out in different building configurations.

BUNGALOW PLANS

The typical bungalow that emerged from California and craftsman precedents was a one-story, two-bedroom house. It had a front porch, a fireplace, and six rooms organized into parallel rows of rooms, with a living room, dining room, and kitchen on one side, and two bedrooms and a bath, connected by a short hall, on the opposite side. Cased openings or colonnades connected adjoining rooms. The entry often was accommodated by a small vestibule or reception space that was actually part of the living room. The connection of the two front rooms created a passageway to the kitchen and the back rooms. The dining room often displayed a bay window, and many bungalows had a back porch that was a simple stoop or a cutaway porch tucked under the roof. There is enough evidence to suggest that a simple variation on this plan added a third bedroom in line with the other bedrooms, which tended to extend the entire house.

The entry hall was a fragment of the halls found in cottages. The entrance might be in the center or on one side of the elevation, but entry was most often directly into a front room, normally the living room. Some plans allowed a brief pause by a closet, but they were too small to be a hall and did little to establish circulation. The alternative to this arrangement had a small central hall, a kind of crossroads, from which one could enter any room in a suite of rooms: bedrooms, kitchen, bath, and dining room. The only true bungalow hall appeared in the private area of the house, as a small passage that connected two or three bedrooms to a bathroom, when they were aligned on the same side of the house. (See Table 11.1.)

The first alternative plan for the gabled bungalow places the living room across the front of the house, making the entire living room a reception space. Half the living room is open to the dining room and the other is partitioned; the opening is cased or colonnaded. Having the front door open directly into the living room called for some adjustments to restrict or delay visual or physical access to the inside. Bungalow builders used several devices: locating the entrance so that it opened in front of the living room back wall; setting the entryway on one side and dividing off a bit of the room for reception purposes; projecting a small vestibule onto the porch; and placing the entry in line with the dining room. In this last pattern, the sideboard built into the back wall of the dining room acted as the visual and physical terminus of the entry.

The placement of the living room across the whole width of the house aligned the interior partitions, so that successive planes of wall were bounded from front to back rooms. The back wall of the dining room and that of the front bedroom were in the same plane, and the second bedroom, bath, and kitchen completed the back row and shared a continuous wall. Specific interior elements included a fireplace as an end-wall unit-integrated storage or a fireplace and windows—located most often on the same side of the house as the dining room. Colonnades in bungalows usually included storage units. A bay window could be included, and its shape might be rectangular with multiple lights. Occasionally, the battered piers and columns of the front porch were repeated on a side porch, which was sheltered by a second gable.

A third version of the gabled bungalow plan was a combination of the first two types, in that rooms were sequentially aligned behind each other, as in the first plan, but a center hall was introduced linking the living room with the back rooms. Both sides of this plan terminated in the same wall plane, but they started at different points. The living room projected, with the front portion serving as an entrance, and the dining room occupied a recessed position. The kitchen was just behind the dining room, and the bedrooms were placed behind the living room and the kitchen, with the bath placed between the bedrooms and accessible from the hall.

Table 11.1. Characteristics of the Bungalow

Typical Façade and Elevation	Exterior Characteristics
 	STORY—1 ROOF—gable or hip CLADDING—variety of materials, shingles, stucco, brick, or combination of materials CHIMNEY—large end wall; brick common WINDOW—multipane rectangular; double-hung sash; vertical divisions in upper sash; paired or triple windows common; square bay on one elevation PORCH—large porch projected in front of house with gable, columns battered, piers also common; width of porch across the entire façade or three-quarters of the width ENTRANCE—slab door with lights; craftsman door GABLE—stickwork

Building Form, Flat Front and Roof	Axonometric
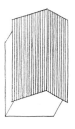 FORM—deeper than wide ROOF—gable end faces street DORMER—shed, gable, hip FENESTRATION—off-center door	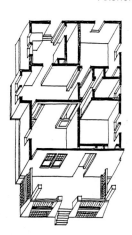 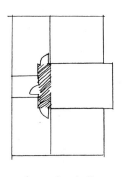 bungalow hall

Building Form and Roof-Projecting Room	
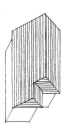 FORM—deeper than wide ROOF—gable end faces street DORMER—shed or gable FENESTRATION—off-center front door	PLAN—living room projects; small center hall ROOM DISTRIBUTION—7 rooms; 2–3 bedrooms ENTRY AND HALL—center or off-center entrance; no hall; entry opens directly into living room

Table 11.1. Characteristics of the Bungalow (continued)

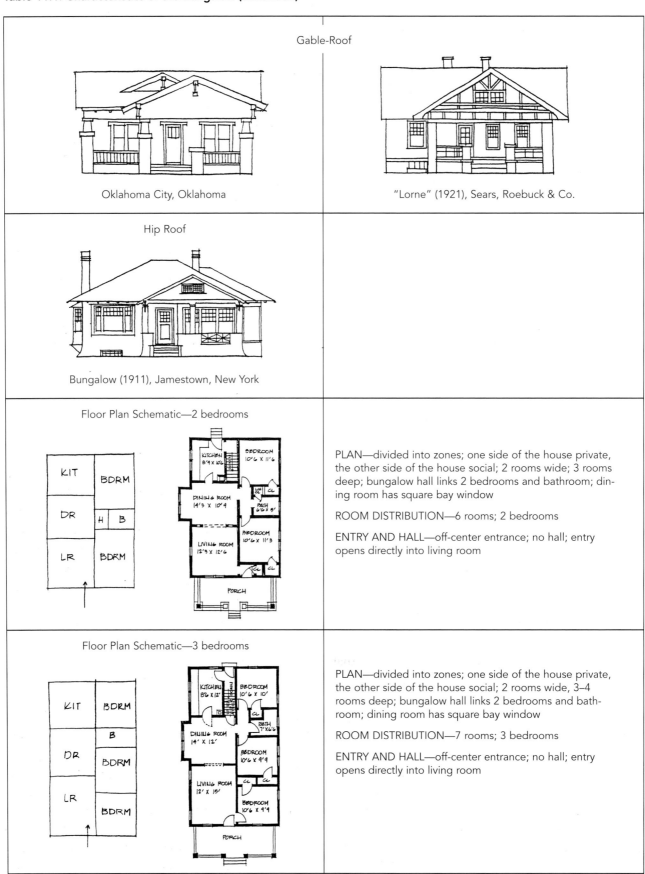

Gable-Roof

Oklahoma City, Oklahoma

"Lorne" (1921), Sears, Roebuck & Co.

Hip Roof

Bungalow (1911), Jamestown, New York

Floor Plan Schematic—2 bedrooms

KIT | BDRM
DR | H | B
LR | BDRM

KITCHEN 8'9 x 10'6
BEDROOM 10'6 x 11'6
DINING ROOM 14'3 x 10'9
BATH 6'6 x 5'
LIVING ROOM 12'3 x 12'6
BEDROOM 10'6 x 11'3
PORCH

PLAN—divided into zones; one side of the house private, the other side of the house social; 2 rooms wide; 3 rooms deep; bungalow hall links 2 bedrooms and bathroom; dining room has square bay window

ROOM DISTRIBUTION—6 rooms; 2 bedrooms

ENTRY AND HALL—off-center entrance; no hall; entry opens directly into living room

Floor Plan Schematic—3 bedrooms

KIT | BDRM
DR | B
 | BDRM
LR | BDRM

KITCHEN 8'6 x 12'
BEDROOM 10'6 x 10'
DINING ROOM 14' x 12'
BATH 7' x 6'6
BEDROOM 10'6 x 9'9
LIVING ROOM 12' x 15'
BEDROOM 10'6 x 9'9
PORCH

PLAN—divided into zones; one side of the house private, the other side of the house social; 2 rooms wide, 3–4 rooms deep; bungalow hall links 2 bedrooms and bathroom; dining room has square bay window

ROOM DISTRIBUTION—7 rooms; 3 bedrooms

ENTRY AND HALL—off-center entrance; no hall; entry opens directly into living room

Table 11.1. Characteristics of the Bungalow (continued)

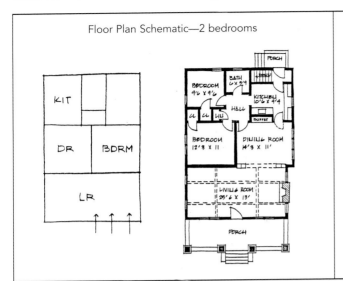

Floor Plan Schematic—2 bedrooms

PLAN— divided into 3 horizontal sections: a beginning, a middle, and an end; 2 rooms wide, 3 rooms deep

ROOM DISTRIBUTION—beginning (living room across the width of the façade); the middle (dining room, bedroom); and the end (kitchen, second bedroom, and bath); square hall (at back of house) links 5 rooms (dining room, 2 bedrooms, bathroom, kitchen)

ENTRY AND HALL—center or off-center entrance; no hall; entry opens directly into living room

In this planning system there was also an alternative of less consequence, in which the living room and dining room were placed beside each other, but the rooms were turned so that the house was wider than it was deep. The back walls of both rooms aligned, and a hallway, running parallel to the front rooms, linked the bedrooms, bath, and kitchen. The arrangement of the front rooms created the impression of a single room. The traditional arch and bookcase spanning the opening between the living room and dining room remained part of this plan, as did the built-in buffet and china closets. Some buffet closet pieces were projected off the dining room wall, in the manner of a bay window. The corner left open by the placement of the living room and dining room was filled with a porch or terrace, which became part of the entrance system.

Bungalow designers were especially adept at generating floor-plan variations and roof designs that spoke to the plans. The roofs were often tied to establishing planes. In the illustrations, the edge of each roof and the ridge (if present) of a roof all became planes. Thus reading bungalow design is, in part, a question of reading its successive elements. Windows and porch piers that help frame them reinforced the planes. Other design variations included the alternation of mass and void on the façades—a push-pull effect that helped eliminate perception of the basic rectangle present in the plane. Ornamental variations included changes in gable motifs, window

placement, and materials. This flexible vocabulary made it possible to build rows of bungalows without having to repeat forms on the same block.

THE CLASSICAL BUNGALOW

For the most part, bungalows kept the same plan variations no matter their roof type or aesthetic treatment. The classical bungalow had a low hip roof supported by three or four columns that carry a restrained entablature. A hipped dormer, an open porch rail, and pedestals for the columns relieved the temple front. The structure was low to the ground and utilized the full width of the façade for a porch. The bungalow was built with wood-frame construction, and clapboard cladding is most common. Other cladding materials included stucco, hollow tile, and cement block.

The hip roof bungalow dates from the same period as the gable fronted bungalow. One of the early sources for designs in print was Hodgson's 1906 *Practical Bungalows and Cottages*, which includes several plans, most often with a cutaway porch. Montgomery Ward offered bungalows in its 1910 *Book of Homes*. By 1913 the California bungalow was well established. The plan book by Eugene O. Murmann, *Typical California Bungalows*, summarized the value of these houses: "Its characteristic simple, horizontal lines, projecting roof, large verandas,

11.4. In this classical bungalow built in the Mesta Park district of Oklahoma City everything in the façade is resolved. The only tension is the placement of the entry door slightly off-center. The house is built on a slight rise that allowed for steps and wing walls. Photo credit: Jennings Gottfried Cheek Preservation. Authors' collection.

11.5. The Kansas home of Mrs. E. Dupyu is an example of a bungalow with a cutaway porch and a flared roof with a deep overhang. The house is low to the ground. Authors' collection.

simplicity in construction and detail, with the elimination of fancy millwork and gingerbread effects, make it the most comfortable, livable, and convenient type of home for any climate."[4]

Like all bungalows, the exterior form of this type was dominated by the large roof, which was generally pyramidal and could be pierced by dormers that lit one or two rooms in the attic. The interior organization was of two types: a plan of sequentially ordered rooms, as in the first gable plan, with the living room, dining room, and kitchen on one side, and the two bedrooms and bath on the other; and a center hall plan with one half composed of the usual living, dining, and kitchen spaces front to back, and with the bedrooms on the opposite side and the bath sandwiched between the kitchen and the corner bedroom.

The composition of this bungalow type had an air of formality not present in the rustic types. Formality was reinforced by the porch and entrance designs. Most porches were covered by the principal roof, which integrated the façade and the porch, usually in a rhythmical pattern of four equally spaced columns. This front was orderly; even if the porch had been added on and supported its own roof, the effect was classical. There was also a feeling for centrality tied to the placement of the single dormer on the center line of the porch, which was sometimes reinforced by the placement of the entrance door on the same axis.

An alternative to the open-porch model enclosed half the porch and added a bay window, triple window, or large cottage window to the wall. Since the main roof almost always covered the porch area, the porch became a cutaway type, appearing as if carved out of the main house block. The hipped bungalow has been popular in all regions of the country. In northern climates the roof was high and the porch might be cutaway or enclosed. In southern climates the roof was low, ventilators might have replaced dormers, and window placements facilitated cross-ventilation. The plans proved versatile; the most common was a six-room house and a center hall (three bedrooms), or a five-room house (two bedrooms and a bungalow hall) with entry directly into the living room.

The Worth Alston Jennings, Sr. and Eddie Vansant Jennings' house in Canyon, Texas is an example of the hip bungalow roof variation with a low profile flared roof and deep overhang. Coffee Brothers contractors constructed the house in 1914 for $1,500, excluding the lot. The Coffees constructed four other similar houses in Canyon, but after 1914. The front door was centered with two cottage-size double-hung windows on either side, one the living room, the other the front bedroom. A center hall extended from the front door and terminated three rooms deep to the bathroom door, organizing a living room, dining room, and kitchen on the left, and three

AMERICAN VERNACULAR BUILDINGS *and* INTERIORS 1870–1960

Table 11.2. Characteristics of the Classical Bungalow

Typical Façade

Exterior Characteristics

STORY—1

CLADDING—clapboard

CHIMNEY—interior brick

WINDOWS—cottage on façade; 1/1 double-hung on side elevations

PORCH—extends across façade; cutaway porch variation; 3–4 Tuscan columns; sometimes pedestals with columns

ENTRANCE—door location varies, off-center or center; panel and glass door; often oval light

EXTERIOR WALL—cornerboards, sometimes flared walls, exposed rafters; clapboard, concrete tile

Roof Variation—low pitch and wide overhang

Worth and Eddie Jennings House (1914), Canyon, Texas

Cutaway Porch Variation

Building Form, Massing, and Roof

FORM—deeper than wide

MASSING—symmetrical

BAY ORGANIZATION—3 bays across the façade

ROOF—hip; flared eaves common; roof usually covers front porch; wide overhang

DORMER—centered on façade side for attic

FENESTRATION—symmetrical cottage windows; front door slightly off-center

Plan for Center Hall

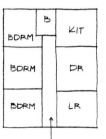

PLAN—3 rooms wide (including hall), 3 rooms deep

ROOM DISTRIBUTION—like a bungalow: divided down the middle of the house: social rooms on one side (living room, dining room, kitchen) and private rooms on the other side (2–3 bedrooms and 1 bathroom)

ENTRY AND HALL—center hall from front door to bathroom

Plan—no entry hall

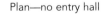

PLAN—2 rooms wide, 3 rooms deep

ROOM DISTRIBUTION—like a bungalow: divided down the middle of the house: social rooms on one side (living room, dining room, kitchen) and private rooms on the other side (2–3 bedrooms and 1 bathroom)

ENTRY AND HALL—no entry hall; front door opens directly into living room bedrooms on the right. A rear ell contained the kitchen pantry, an enclosed back porch, and a coal room. The back porch was enclosed with two-feet by two-foot glass set in quarter-inch trim; the glass was removed in the summer. This house design was always white with black trim, and there was an oval light in the front door.

It would be tempting to attribute the variation of a low-pitched roof with extra-wide eaves to an adaptation to a warm climate, but in fact, similar bungalows can be found in Cheyenne, Wyoming; Altoona, Pennsylvania; and Seattle, Washington. Plan-book architect J. W. Lindstrom built them in Minnesota, as did Frederick H. Gowing in Boston. The Oklahoma City historic preservation survey found hip roof bungalows in four different neighborhoods. They remained a popular house type for several decades; Sears' *Modern Homes* (1935) featured the Plymouth (flat façade) and the Collingwood (cutaway porch) as ready-cut houses.

BUNGALOW COTTAGE

Since the bungalow itself was thought of as a renewal in artistic form of the cottage, it is not surprising that a hybrid form, the bungalow cottage, would emerge (see 3.10 and 5.10). In the trade literature it was sometimes referenced as a semibungalow. Architect Arlington D. Isham of New York City characterized the bungalow cottage in his advertising postcard as "a unique and practicable house for a country, suburban, or summer house. The style is a modification of the famous California Bungalow. A very artistic and attractive dwelling. The rooms, stairways, halls and closets are compactly arranged; all rooms have full height ceilings."[4]

The integration of both design modes can be seen on the various elevations. The bungalow cottage as a class had striking porches and dormers. The façade—with the exception of the large central dormer—had bungalow traits. On most buildings the main roof covered the porch, which was wide and used bungalow piers; on others there was a gable entrance area attached to a pergola. In all cases the entire roofline, the porch, and first-floor wall were close to the ground. The major design change in the façade centered on two aspects: roof form, a straight

gable that ran parallel to the street; and on the domination of the roof by a large hip or gable dormer. Bungalow details at the roofline included purlins and rafters and a chimney that pierced the roof because of the wide overhang of the eaves. Cottage treatment was especially noticeable on the side elevations, where additional height allowed for cottage fenestration. The half-story provided an opportunity to change materials; shingles were popular starting at the floor line. Other side elevation features included bay windows, a water table, and an occasional decorative element in the gable.

Like other bungalows, bungalow cottages could absorb a variety of styling details, and the Toledo, Ohio house in figure 11.8 is a good example of a styling discourse in which architects and builders could engage. The house type partakes of two traditions—the American cottage and the colonial revival—in a selective manner. The Toledo house has a few colonial revival details—oval window, a balcony rail of thin balusters, Tuscan columns on the porch—and some cottage effects, such as the shingles and flared walls of the dormer, a deep balcony, a shallow bay window on the façade, and asymmetrical fenestration.

The bungalow cottage was not built in earnest until the 1910s, and by 1940 its popularity was waning. Its plan types were of two varieties. The first type balanced the rooms in an alternating format: a large living room on the one side responded to a dining room on the other; a den or parlor was answered by the kitchen. The stairs for the second level were located behind the front rooms. The second plan type extended the living space across the width of the house, with the entry opening directly into the living room with the stairway off to the side. The living room divided the house approximately in half, and the dining room and kitchen subdivided the back portion. As in all bungalow houses, fireplaces and built-in furniture were optional elements, and these were installed with regularity in bungalow cottages. Only the breakfast nook, for some unknown reason, did not seem to be a part of this development.

Overall, the bungalow cottage favored a compact form of simple and direct geometry. The house was lively, owing to the mix of motifs, yet the structure was solid, even reserved. If the house had a modest

11.6. The cobblestone foundation and chimney and the dark stained wood on this bungalow cottage illustrate the original intentions of the California bungalow. Authors' collection.

11.7. A streetscape of bungalow cottages in Rudyard, Michigan is quite like a streetscape of nineteenth-century cottages in that each stands alone, arguing vigorously for its own status. Each house offers a version of a picturesque ensemble of details. Authors' collection.

11.8. Bungalow cottages with gable dormers, such as this one from Toledo, Ohio, may have second-story balconies. Authors' collection.

Table 11.3. Characteristics of the Bungalow Cottage

Typical Façade and Side Elevation	Exterior Characteristics
	STORY—1½–2 ROOF—gable with ridgeline facing street; eaves sometimes flared CLADDING—combination of materials, often variation in materials from first to second floors CHIMNEY—end wall, brick or stone WINDOW—cottage or 3-part window on façade; bay window on first-floor side elevation; double-hung sash with colonial or vertical glazing bars PORCH—variety of bungalow treatments ENTRANCE—off-center; panel and glass or craftsman front door

Building Form, Massing, and Roof	typical plan types
ROOF—broad gable, ridgeline parallel to street; roof covers porch DORMER—shed or wide gable to provide half-story space	PLAN—2 rooms wide, 2 rooms deep plus front porch; (*left*) living room one of 4 rooms or (*right*) one of 3 rooms, stretching across the façade ROOM DISTRIBUTION—3 or 4 rooms downstairs, 2–3 bedrooms and bathroom upstairs; the fourth room downstairs often a den, bedroom, or parlor ENTRY AND HALL—off-center entry directly into living room; no hall

"Ellsworth" No. 132 (1923), Curtis Company	"Ellsworth" No. 132 (1923), Curtis Company

Table 11.3. Characteristics of the Bungalow Cottage (continued)

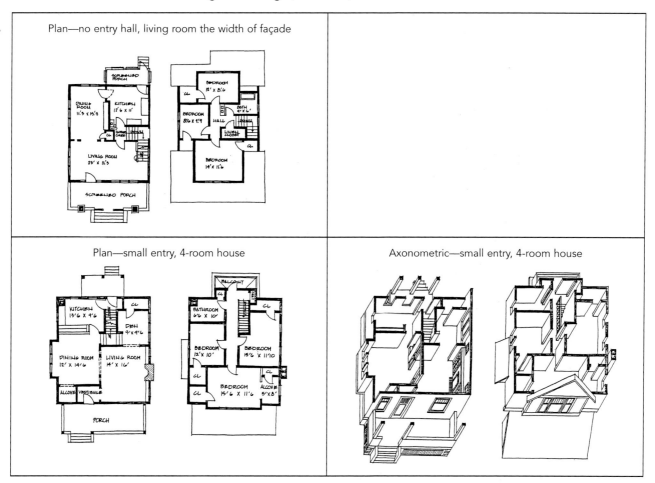

Plan—no entry hall, living room the width of façade

Plan—small entry, 4-room house

Axonometric—small entry, 4-room house

setback, the sweep of the roof and the big gable of the sides could be appreciated. A six- to eight-room house, the bungalow cottage came to be a staple of neighborhoods across the country.

AIRPLANE BUNGALOW

The so-called airplane bungalow was a minor type that emerged during the 1920s. The name *airplane* was surely applied after this style appeared on the market. The house was modest at first, extending the bungalow on the horizontal and accenting the vertical. The low gable roof forms were the key to the design. The gables were contiguous and successive, as in other structures, but the massing of roofs was quite different. Not only were roofs built so that they appeared to grow out of each other on the façade, but gables abutted the main roof on the side elevations. Smaller gables covered the second-floor

sections. This kind of house looked as if sections could have been added arbitrarily to the base structure, but that was not the case. All the roof and frame sections were integrated. Special exterior features of the airplane included thick, battered piers and porch columns, exposed purlins and rafters, and combinations of claddings and gable motifs. The proportion of window to wall area was quite high, and windows were grouped in combinations such as doubles, triples, and bands. Some windows were with wide cottage types. Porches were extensive and included multiple interior and exterior accesses to porch areas.

The airplane bungalow was a large bungalow house, having six to eight rooms on the ground level. Its broad plan was organized in two general patterns. The first type grouped the traditional social and functional spaces, adding a den, breakfast room, bedroom, back entry and porch on the first floor, and two bedrooms and a bath upstairs. The façade of this

Table 11.4. Characteristics of the Airplane Bungalow

Typical Façade	Exterior Characteristics
	STORY—1 and a partial second story CLADDING—stucco common CHIMNEY—interior WINDOW—double-hung sash; cottage, paired or triple windows common; large proportion of window to wall PORCH—large, deep porch or veranda projected in front of house; columns battered; piers also common ENTRANCE—slab door with lights, craftsman door GABLE—2 gable ends face street EXTERIOR WALL—broad horizontal alignments
Plan—entry directly into living room	Axonometric—entry directly into living room
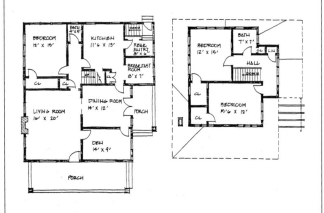	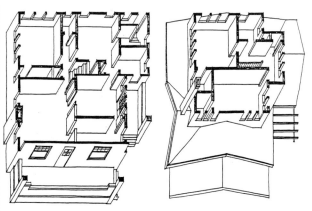
Plan—center hall	
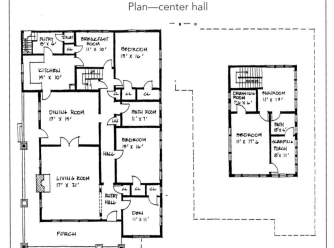	PLAN—6–8 rooms downstairs; 3–4 rooms upstairs ROOM DISTRIBUTION—specialized rooms downstairs include a den, a breakfast room; bedrooms upstairs include a bathroom, a sunroom, or sleeping porch ENTRY AND HALL—entry into a long center passage hall or directly into living room

house was straight across the front, with adjacent rooms sharing the same outside wall. The back wall of the hall was also straight; thus the entire shape was very rectilinear—an attribute expressed by the squared nature of the plan. The second plan type had a more traditional bungalow front, in that one section of the house projected toward the street, creating a corner, which was filled by a porch. The usual living room, dining room, and kitchen sequence covered one half of the plan, and the second half had a hall running through the entire house as well as an assortment of rooms, such as a den, sleeping porch, sunporch, and breakfast room. The stairs were located behind the principal rooms, just as they were in the bungalow cottage.

PORTICO BUNGALOW

Bungalow design often boiled down to a few effects with a generalized convention that could be expressed in exterior and interior details and on plan. The bungalow with a portico was an example of this kind. Given its design vocabulary, it was derivative of the classical bungalow, but at the same time it was associated with the colonial revival style. A portico with a pediment above the entrance was a special effect that was integrated into an entrance system and a floor plan to produce another bungalow prototype. The overall shape of this bungalow appeared evenly divided between models that were either wider than they were deep, or vice versa. The entrance in both cases was on center, creating direct access to the living room.

The type did not become a popular house type until the 1920s, when it gained some momentum from the success of colonial designs. Indeed, it was the colonial aspect of this house that made it unique. The design was based on simplicity and symmetry with a few historical elements, such as shutters, white clapboards, and weathered shingles on the roof.

The internal organization was comparable to other bungalows, with social spaces across the front and service areas along the back. Within this configuration were a living room (with its required fireplace) connected to a dining room, and bedrooms, bath, kitchen, and breakfast nook. French doors leading to

11.9. The portico bungalow of Oliver Freeman, in Valparaiso, Indiana, has a large pediment and returns and uses three slender columns to complete the classical feature. Authors' collection.

11.10. Bungalows could have eclectic compositions. This house is a bungalow by plan and a cottage by the manner in which the big elements have been put together. Asymmetry in massing, a clipped gable, and a bay window suggest cottage thinking, whereas the chimney and window combination on the side elevation is a standard bungalow living room motif. Authors' collection.

a terrace, a side porch, or a sleeping porch were options. But it was the entrance that characterized the portico bungalow. The pediment could be a dormer, a hood, or part of a small portico with Tuscan columns. Another frequent façade feature was a pergola; it could be part of the entrance or part of a side porch or terrace and often carried latticework.

Table 11.4. Characteristics of the Portico Bungalow

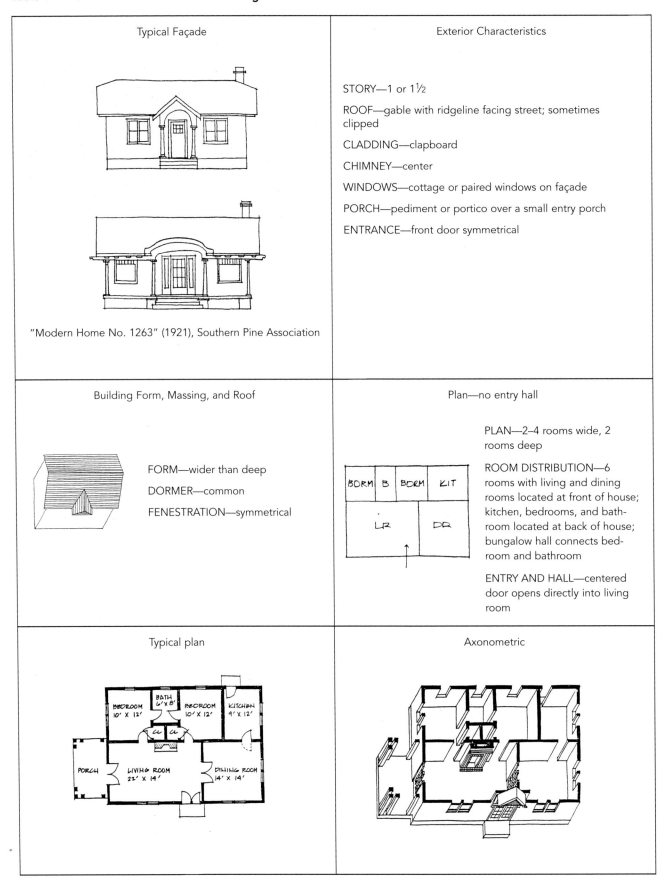

Typical Façade

"Modern Home No. 1263" (1921), Southern Pine Association

Exterior Characteristics

STORY—1 or 1½

ROOF—gable with ridgeline facing street; sometimes clipped

CLADDING—clapboard

CHIMNEY—center

WINDOWS—cottage or paired windows on façade

PORCH—pediment or portico over a small entry porch

ENTRANCE—front door symmetrical

Building Form, Massing, and Roof

FORM—wider than deep

DORMER—common

FENESTRATION—symmetrical

Plan—no entry hall

PLAN—2–4 rooms wide, 2 rooms deep

ROOM DISTRIBUTION—6 rooms with living and dining rooms located at front of house; kitchen, bedrooms, and bathroom located at back of house; bungalow hall connects bedroom and bathroom

ENTRY AND HALL—centered door opens directly into living room

Typical plan

Axonometric

ENGLISH BUNGALOW

Because of its size and efficient plan, the bungalow was especially susceptible to imported styles. A basic plan could suffice for several surface treatments. For example, the April 1933 issue of *American Builder* carried an illustration of a bungalow in the Spanish style, derived from the "Mediterranean heritage," and advertised as suitable for Florida and the Southeast. The house pictured has an L-shape of unequal parts. The section pointed toward the street has a width of one room, whereas the second portion has a double row of rooms. The detailing was Spanish. In the bottom right-hand corner there is an alternative design, labeled "Plan B"; this is a colonial design finished with brick veneer. Of course, there were

11.11. This English bungalow has a projecting gable and a side entry into a vestibule. The front door is hidden from street view. Paired 1/1 windows make this interpretation symmetrical. Authors' collection.

Table 11.5. Characteristics of the English Bungalow

Typical Façade	Exterior Characteristics
	STORY—1 CLADDING—stucco, brick CHIMNEY—often end wall WINDOWS—paired or triple windows; often steel casements PORCH—stone or tile terrace or patio provided in front, side, or rear of house; often accessed through French doors ENTRANCE—front door not visible from street or off-center on façade GABLE—gable carried to ground; pierced with rectangular or arched opening
Building Form, Massing, and Roof 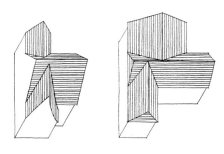 FORM—varies, sometimes wider than deep, sometimes deeper than wide; often 1 room projects from main body of house ROOF—steeply pitched intersecting gable roofs with high-pitch clipped gable or hip roof DORMER—uncommon	**Plan Types** 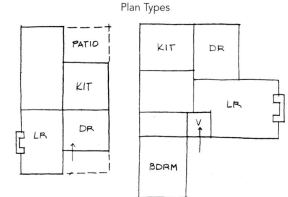 PLAN—2 rooms wide, 4 rooms deep ROOM DISTRIBUTION—living room or front bedroom projected from main body of house; divided down the middle with social rooms on one side (living, dining, kitchen, breakfast room); private rooms (bedrooms and bathroom) on the other side of the house and linked by a small private hall

Table 11.5. Characteristics of the English Bungalow (continued)

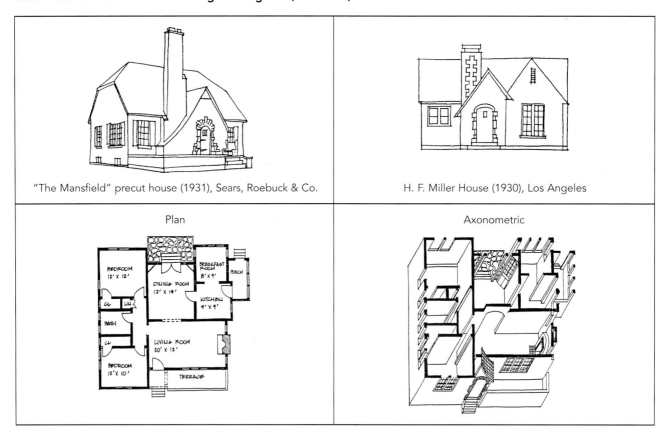

"The Mansfield" precut house (1931), Sears, Roebuck & Co. | H. F. Miller House (1930), Los Angeles

Plan | Axonometric

changes in detailing to accommodate the alternative aesthetic. So the unusual plan was intended to offer treatment alternatives.

The most popular "cultural" treatments for bungalows were the Spanish and the English. For our purposes, these aesthetics are exterior variations of the same plan, so we have combined them into a single entry. There are different series of design details, sometimes using the same material for each type.

The fundamental plan had the principal social space at a right angle to the bank of bedrooms and bath, and the dining room and kitchen form the back section. There was at least one outside space. Inside, the living room had an end-wall fireplace, and arched openings with plaster finish separated the key rooms. The kitchen area included a breakfast nook or alcove.

The English bungalow, a compact brick or stucco house with successive gables and different motifs on each gable wall, included a terrace, usually on the street side, and an end-wall fireplace chimney. Gables were steep but not broad; one raking cornice of the gable often descended far below the wall line, even to ground level. Some gables served as screens

behind which the entrance door was hidden.

Other features included varied window placement and size, combinations of cladding, a combination of roof forms (a hip on one end and clipped gable on the other), decorative louvers in the gables, arches, ornamental brickwork, and shingled roofs. All this variation produced a cozy five- or six-room house whose façade could look different from that of its neighbors.

The English bungalow also relied on a projecting vestibule on the façade, covered with a steep gable to set the tone for the design. Multiple roof forms (intersecting gables) on a low, rambling house clad with stucco or brick, perhaps a clipped gable or two, long casement windows with small panes, and a broad chimney with a pot for each flue—these were the design elements that underwrote this house. Inside, if there were any rooms projecting from the main body of the house, these were typically the living room or a bedroom. Round-headed windows and doors and rough plastered walls are traditional details. Interior finish included rough, tinted plaster and hewn rafters or a beamed ceiling.

11.12. A row of Spanish revival bungalows in Southern California illustrates how each uses a mix of details. Authors' collection.

11.13. This house has a U-shaped organization with a terrace in between. One side is wider and longer than the other. Uneven wings and flared walls are part of the bungalow system. Authors' collection.

SPANISH BUNGALOW

The Spanish bungalow developed after 1910. Geographically, it emerged in California, the Southwest, and Florida. Examples of the style can be found in other sections of the country, but they are not as numerous as in the Sunbelt climates. Throughout its development the bungalow lent itself to the imposition of fronts on a basic plan. A gable played an important role in façade design. It may be triangular or curvilinear, and the gable portion often projected in front of the main body of the house. Beyond this single gable, arches or even arcades organized other sections of the façade.

The Spanish bungalow was more rectangular than other types. Small terraces extended interior space, but generally the form was compact, and one was more aware of mass than is usual in bungalows. The walls—usually stucco, although painted cement was also popular—played a large role in design. There were two treatments with subtle differences: a Spanish colonial and a Southwestern type that imitated adobe houses. Both had plans like other bungalows. Some Spanish houses looked like a block of clay from which arches, openings for fenestration, and the like had been carved. Detailing included colonial motifs such as exposed wood (especially *viga*), wrought iron, terra-cotta ornament, decorative columns, and polychromy.

The application of Spanish motifs is usually identifiable because of the stucco exterior and red tile roof: the rooflines are low with wide gables, the corner outside space may be a patio, the entrance a covered terrace space, round-headed exterior arches and windows, some of wrought iron, and casement windows. Interior finish includes rough, tinted plaster and hewn rafters or a beamed ceiling.

Table 11.6. Characteristics of the Spanish Bungalow

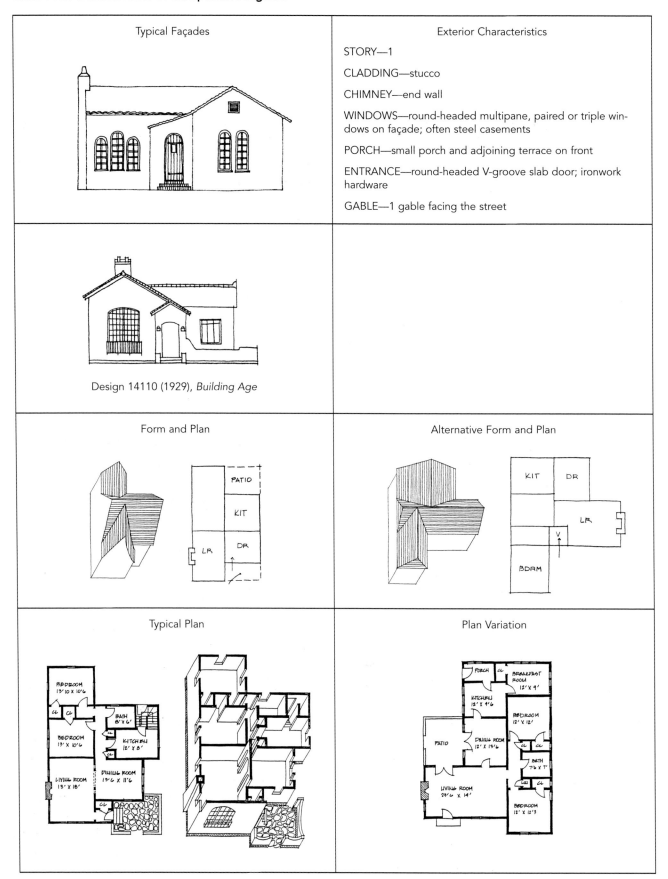

Typical Façades	Exterior Characteristics
	STORY—1
	CLADDING—stucco
	CHIMNEY—end wall
	WINDOWS—round-headed multipane, paired or triple windows on façade; often steel casements
	PORCH—small porch and adjoining terrace on front
	ENTRANCE—round-headed V-groove slab door; ironwork hardware
	GABLE—1 gable facing the street

Design 14110 (1929), *Building Age*

Form and Plan	Alternative Form and Plan
PATIO KIT LR DR	KIT DR LR V BDRM

Typical Plan	Plan Variation
BEDROOM 13'10 X 10'6, BATH 8' X 6', BEDROOM 13' X 10'6, KITCHEN 12' X 8', LIVING ROOM 13' X 18', DINING ROOM 13'6 X 11'6	PORCH, BREAKFAST ROOM 12' X 9', KITCHEN 12' X 9'6, BEDROOM 12' X 12', PATIO, DINING ROOM 12' X 13'6, BATH 7'6 X 7', LIVING ROOM 23'6 X 14', BEDROOM 12' X 12'3

12

BUILDING TYPE: RANCH AND SPLIT-LEVEL

———◆———

Whether or not California architect Cliff May designed the first modern ranch house in San Diego in 1932, he designed a large number of ranch houses and published many of them in *Sunset Magazine*. In 1946 the magazine published a plan book of May's ranch designs. While each scheme indicated informal living, each was not marked "by unmistakable style symbols." Style or styling was not the point about the ranch house. More to the point were living all aspects of house life on the ground level, moving into and out of the house freely, and having outdoor areas accessible from inside the house. Moreover, the house was flexible inside, as new family activities—playing board games, watching television, and making crafts—needed multipurpose spaces, and outside where the house could engage terrain and climate.

The following is a sample of page headings from the 1946 plan book *Western Ranch Houses*. Each serves to characterize the design below it, but these phrases also construct the rhetoric associated with the ranch house type and reveal the values embedded in the design:

- The garden is an inside room
- Built around a patio
- The garden gate is the front door
- Where there's room, let the house ramble

- The house spreads out to get a view
- Spaciousness by the division of space
- It can spread out like an oak tree
- Ranch house background may be of forest, wheat field or orange grove
- Glass, solid walls, oak trees
- Clean lines become the ranch house
- Regardless of how your lot faces, your living can face south
- There is no front or back
- Living space is the total combination of indoor–outdoor spaces[1]

The ranch house was conceived as modern and it introduced a new and modern way of living; such living relied on technology, efficiency, and new lifestyles. The ranch house did not adapt as much as it celebrated developments in society (see 2.9). As a built type, however, it evolved. For a short while the ranch house was distinctively Californian, and its emphasis on informal living owed something to the California bungalow. The bungalow was sited perpendicular to the street, with a compact plan, a fragmented hall, extensive use of wood and millwork elements, and access to the outside. Moreover, it could take a variety of exterior treatments. The ranch house had most of the same attributes, with the primary exception being its parallel orientation to the street. Right after World War II large-scale builders reduced costs to build and sell more houses. They built small square footages on a slab, reduced exterior wall breaks and hips in roofs, standardized windows and doors, and built kitchens and baths back to back to aggregate plumbing. Beyond projects driven by cost cutting and economies of scale, the ranch house became a suburban house built among other suburban types in other regions. Ultimately, the ranch is a national tract house, built two ways: in large numbers with modest changes in plan and appearance, or in smaller numbers with choices of exterior finish.

Avi Friedman's study of the typical low-cost home in the 1945–1959 period concluded that design changes reflected economics, material shortages, technological advances, and changes in consumer expectations. The typical prewar family home was a two-story structure with a pitched roof and basement. After the war, this type proved to be excessive in both size and cost. Cost-reducing features of the postwar home included the use of framing elements of standardized length and prefabricated components; multipurpose rooms; and the minimization of fixed walls, which were frequently substituted with sliding walls and movable partitions.[2] Both a redesigned Cape Cod and the new Western ranch house met the high demand for single-family housing.

As the ranch house developed out of May's early models, it remained close to the ground, with a low roof and deep eaves. Designs include planned (framed) views of the out of doors and open floor plans. Inside and outside flower boxes become architectural features. The American Plan Service's *Plans for Your Future Home* (1950) featured large "living porches" that rivaled the size of living rooms and sometimes included rooms for both outdoor living and dining.[3] The Miami-based company's adaptation of the ranch house to Florida resulted in the "lanai room" or Florida room, an enclosed sunroom facing a backyard.

Sunset advocated the use of "old materials used with simplicity" and a reliance on local materials. But the magazine also backtracked, stating, "the house seems as much at ease among the evergreens of the Pacific Northwest as it would be in the brown hills of the desert."[4] Clapboard is a popular choice, but combinations of cladding, such as brick and shakes or brick and clapboard, were also used, and vertical plywood siding was introduced in this era.

In *Designs for Convenient Living* (1946), Richard B. Pollman devoted several pages to developing a program based on good planning principles and assessing clients' needs. He also illustrated a basic plan with four different exterior treatments, such as changes in roof form and cladding. Illustrations included prefabricated plywood panels, hand-split fieldstone, block masonry units with the vertical joints left flush and the horizontal joints raked out, ledge rock and shake shingles, and cypress siding and timbers and brick in patterns.[5]

Roof forms for ranch houses also played a significant role in indicating modernism. In plan books the elevation and façade perspective sometimes disappeared in favor of a bird's-eye view in which the house is seen from above, emphasizing roof forms and the house's relation to a landscape. The California ranch had a flat roof, but as the house emerged across the country it took on the low-pitched gable and hip and the hip on gable. Plan books show few flat-roof models. Americans were accustomed to gable and hip roofs, as well as intersecting and complex roof types.

The modern ranch house accommodated cars, and the placement of the garage or carport was a key architectural element. Increasingly garages moved closer to the house, fully attached or linked by a breezeway. The breezeway further elongated a house form. The garage could be on one end, say, adjacent to the living room/dining room and kitchen units. It could be in the same plane as the rest of the elevation or set back or forward from it, or it could create an ell by extending the full length off the front or back. In the rambler model the garage was sometimes at an angle to the main body of the house.

The ordinary window became a relic as window-walls with picture windows, corner windows, and sliding glass doors assumed a heightened role. There was a definite turn away from windows with small panels. Horizontal glazing bars became popular. For viewing and ease of cleaning and insulated windows constructed of sealed panes, some with louvers for ventilation, and clear panes were preferred. In bedrooms windows also changed shape and location on the wall. *Sunset*'s designs encouraged the use of glass, particularly glass walls, around a patio or private garden as a way to let in the outdoors.

Three ranch typologies can be identified character-defining elements such as roof forms and façade treatments. The basic ranch house was a rectangular box with a gable or hip roof with the ridgeline parallel to the street, basically a large-lot house. The gable end ranch house was also box-like, slightly deeper than wide; its gable end roof faced the street, and, like its predecessor the gable end cottage, it was ideal for a narrow lot. The ranch relied on a stepped façade, stepped roofs, carport or entry structures, outdoor planters, and patios to break up the box-like façade. The stepped condition means that sections of façades had either projected forward, creating a corner, or stepped back, exposing a corner; and roofs, such as the garage roof, stepped down below the main roof, exposing a fascia board along the main roof edge or a section of exterior cladding.

By the 1950s ranch houses had intersecting gable or hip roofs, which created an L-shape, with the projecting piece from the main body of the house on the front or back. There are several L-shaped variations. There is also a T-shape in which the gable end projects forward with an ell on either side. A U-shape, which can be turned to the front or back, surrounded a patio and landscape features. The H-shaped plan was used as a model for high-style residential space planning in the 1940s and 1950s, but the H-shape was, and still is, infrequently used in ordinary subdivisions.

The *rambler*, a period term, is a variation of the L-shaped design. May's rambler designs spread out by extending sections at angles other than ninety degrees. For example, the house could be divided into four units: a double in the center and one on each end, at an angle to the main body. The rambler plan was thus sectional; it was also aggressive about taking in the landscape, and it recreated an opportunity for a California lifestyle elsewhere. Culturally, the rambler's jointed or disjointed character seems an echo of picturesque qualities.

As for the ranch plan Clifford Clark noted: "Most advocates of the ranch house concentrated their attention primarily on the interior plan. As long as the house was handsome and had relatively little decorative detail, a variety of external features were acceptable. . . . Convenience rather than style, comfort rather than some formal notion of beauty became hallmarks of the new designs."[6] Plan schemes included traditional arrangements for private, social, and work spaces, but they also dictated a reversal of the front and back of the house spaces, whereby the kitchen was brought forward, and the living room may run front to rear. Expansion was encouraged by, for example, unfinished attic space.

The Weyerhaeuser corporation's advertisement in *Small Homes Guide* (1953–1954) listed five good ideas for making a home seem larger than it was: (1) combine living and dining rooms and only partially close off the kitchen; (2) use a sliding partition for double-purpose rooms; (3) use a wall of glass in the living room; (4) make bedrooms "seem remote" by separating them from social spaces; and (5) plan for good traffic control (i.e., no room is used as a hallway).[7]

The open plan provided a modern house that could accommodate flexible living in a minimum amount of floor space. Fixed walls or partitions did not always define room boundaries. Moreover, ranch house rooms allowed multiple functions to occur. For temporary changes in room conditions, floor-to-ceiling drapes or curtains could be added provide a soft wall to separate one space from another.

Plans for ranch houses reflected modern behavior and consumption patterns. *Designs for Convenient Living* recommended dual-purpose space or the

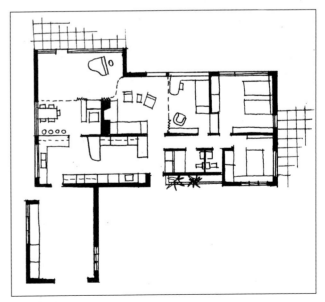

12.1. A conceptual open plan for a ranch house with an ell. The ell zone is compact, but the spaces adjacent to it are open and free, allowing movement, sight, and accommodation.

Table 12.1. Characteristics of the Linear Ranch House

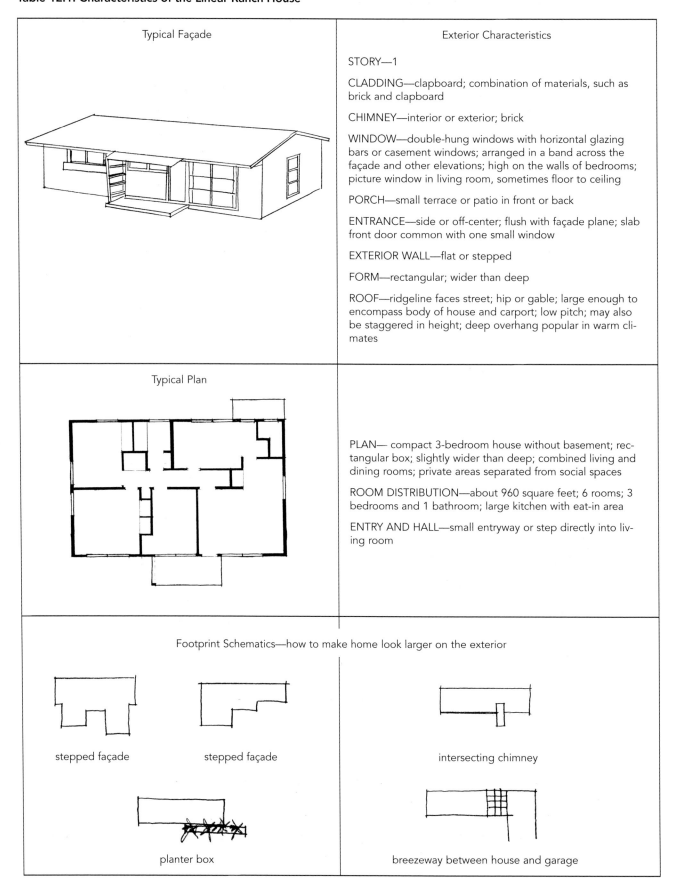

Typical Façade

Exterior Characteristics

STORY—1

CLADDING—clapboard; combination of materials, such as brick and clapboard

CHIMNEY—interior or exterior; brick

WINDOW—double-hung windows with horizontal glazing bars or casement windows; arranged in a band across the façade and other elevations; high on the walls of bedrooms; picture window in living room, sometimes floor to ceiling

PORCH—small terrace or patio in front or back

ENTRANCE—side or off-center; flush with façade plane; slab front door common with one small window

EXTERIOR WALL—flat or stepped

FORM—rectangular; wider than deep

ROOF—ridgeline faces street; hip or gable; large enough to encompass body of house and carport; low pitch; may also be staggered in height; deep overhang popular in warm climates

Typical Plan

PLAN— compact 3-bedroom house without basement; rectangular box; slightly wider than deep; combined living and dining rooms; private areas separated from social spaces

ROOM DISTRIBUTION—about 960 square feet; 6 rooms; 3 bedrooms and 1 bathroom; large kitchen with eat-in area

ENTRY AND HALL—small entryway or step directly into living room

Footprint Schematics—how to make home look larger on the exterior

stepped façade

stepped façade

intersecting chimney

planter box

breezeway between house and garage

Table 12.1. Characteristics of the Linear Ranch House (continued)

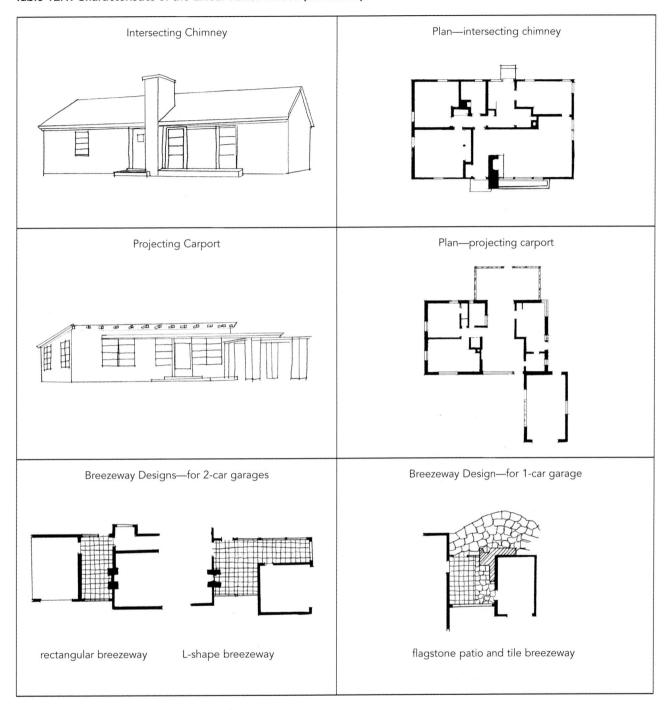

Intersecting Chimney	Plan—intersecting chimney
Projecting Carport	Plan—projecting carport
Breezeway Designs—for 2-car garages	Breezeway Design—for 1-car garage
rectangular breezeway L-shape breezeway	flagstone patio and tile breezeway

all-purpose room that, in time, would evolve into a family room. To demonstrate how television was "given every consideration in the planning," in 1951 the National Plan Service illustrated three viewing angles (living room, dining room, kitchen) with three sight lines drawn on the plan.[8] The television was placed to the side of a fireplace, breaking the symmetry of the wall elevation—in effect, shifting the symbolic significance from the family hearth to a device for modern entertainment.

12.2. Ranch house plans include a kitchen eating space or "snack space." The placement of a window above a sink is a kitchen convention. Interior view of a Holiday subdivision home, ca. 1954, in Denver. Photo credit: Guy Pourgess. Permission: Western History/Genealogy Department, Denver Public Library.

As one-floor living became the modern ideal, a stairway and a hall disappeared, except in split-level houses. A bungalow-type hall was commonly used to connect two bedrooms and a bathroom. Fixed openings between a living and dining room were removed to create a new living–dining room combination that offered flexibility.

The kitchen was a work center, regardless of its shape or location. In the postwar period the kitchen was the recipient of more improvements in household technology than any other area. But the kitchen was also a new active center that took on more roles than food preparation. The changes in function were fostered by the recognition of the kitchen as a social space. Spaces adjacent to kitchens came into play as nooks, spaces with small card tables and chairs, playrooms, and such. Over time the flexibility of the open plan encouraged the relocation of rooms from traditional locations. For example, the kitchen moved from the back of the house to the front.

12.3. The basic linear type of ranch has an entrance that is located off the centerline of the elevation. In this case it is marked by a small pediment, a leftover classical cultural accent. The rectangular chimney is perpendicular to the flow of the house, but it does not break the plane of the wall. The large picture window to the right fronts the living room, the smaller window on the far left serves a bedroom, and the next window to the right is a bedroom or a bath. Authors' collection.

LINEAR RANCH HOUSE

The linear model was the basic ranch form. It might have a gable or a hip roof, and its organization was—and still—easily read from the street. The footprint was a long, narrow box with either a flat front (i.e., everything in the same plane) or a stepped front (i.e., with some sections ahead or behind the others). Builders created variations on the basic form and plan by placing a large chimney perpendicular to the long façade wall, or by adding a patio or carport that pulled away from the body of the house.

INTERSECTING GABLE ROOF RANCH HOUSE

This type of ranch house depended on an intersecting gable or hip roof. Nationally this type was second only in production to the basic linear ranch. The roof plan and the space plan went hand in hand. The first design issue was how to distribute function the wing and in the main body.

L-Shaped Ranch House

The L-shape, with the corner of the ell on the front or back of a house, consisted of a projecting gable end or hip end. There were modifications related to the several L-shape. Joining two units of different sizes and with different purposes allowed for interpreting them differently. Moreover, it allowed for a special treatment at the junction between the forms. The "New Look" house in fig. 12.4 is a good example

12.4. "The New Look House," designed and built by R. C. Edson, relied on intersecting gable roofs to create "L-shaped simplicity." The projecting gable end is shallow compared to late-nineteenth-century gable and ell cottages. The difference is in plan type; the modern house has a compact open plan. Authors' collection.

12.5. The gable end of the stem of the T-shape is a classical composition. It is symmetrical, dividing along the centerline. Visually, the brick-faced wall, with its pilaster-like corners, supports the pediment, just as columns would in an order of architecture. Jack and Ruby Jennings House (1952), Canyon, Texas. Authors' collection.

of an attempt to define the L-shape. Both sections of the house are relatively short, which means that the spatial organization in each wing and at the intersection is compact. There are two signals about the projecting section that reference its role in the scheme: the fireplace chimney design and the window treatment at the corner. The short section, which is decidedly modern, holds the living room. The strict geometry of the chimney is a modern accent, as is the window grouping that dissolves the corner into glass and wood. The main section, parallel to the street, retreats into a traditional display of the entry and operable sash with shutters. However, all the windows have horizontal divisions of glass, another modern accent. The wood cladding changes pattern from bottom to top—clapboard, vertical panels and clapboard—that allows the gable ends in both sections to be treated as pediments.

T-Shaped Ranch House

Like the T-shaped gable and ell house, the modern ranch house also made use of a projecting *T* either as a gable end or hip roof end. The stem of the *T* was short, containing just one room. In most cases it was the living room, punctuated by a picture window or triple windows. The treatment of the gable end in the Jennings' house in figure 12.5 is traditional in that the gable is closed, with a pediment and boxed returns. The gable figure is separated from the wall below by a change in cladding materials—cedar shingles above

and a brick clad wall below. The whole section could be seen as a colonial model. The interior chimney reinforces the impression. Its shape is modern but the location suggests a Cape Cod chimney in the center of the house. Wood shingles on the body of the house also suggest Cape Cod values. But the recessed entry with a brick planter, the paired windows set high for privacy, and the garage are modern accents. The entry and garage roof are stepped below the main roof, which is a ranch house convention.

U-Shaped Ranch House

The U-shaped ranch house was very popular in warm climates, such as Florida, Texas, and California, where it embraced a patio, terrace, or landscape feature.

12.6. The shallow U-shape creates a stepped elevation; that is, end sections step forward and the center steps back. In this example the low hip roof is the dominant element, and the individual sections are understated. The carport is a big void that emphasizes the asymmetry of the scheme. Authors' collection.

Table 12.2. Characteristics of L-, T-, and U-Shaped Ranch Houses

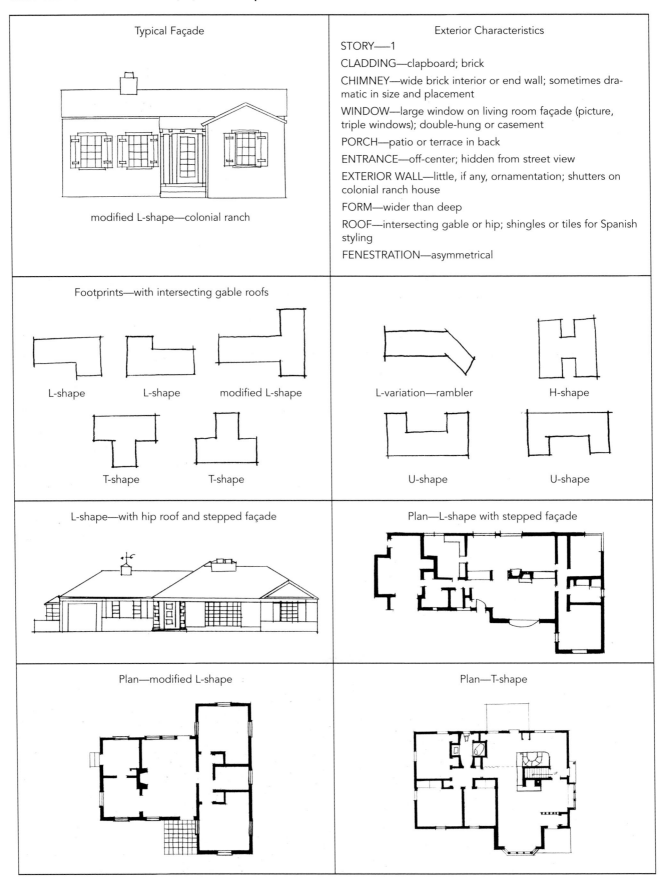

Typical Façade

modified L-shape—colonial ranch

Exterior Characteristics

STORY——1

CLADDING—clapboard; brick

CHIMNEY—wide brick interior or end wall; sometimes dramatic in size and placement

WINDOW—large window on living room façade (picture, triple windows); double-hung or casement

PORCH—patio or terrace in back

ENTRANCE—off-center; hidden from street view

EXTERIOR WALL—little, if any, ornamentation; shutters on colonial ranch house

FORM—wider than deep

ROOF—intersecting gable or hip; shingles or tiles for Spanish styling

FENESTRATION—asymmetrical

Footprints—with intersecting gable roofs

L-shape   L-shape   modified L-shape

L-variation—rambler   H-shape

T-shape   T-shape

U-shape   U-shape

L-shape—with hip roof and stepped façade

Plan—L-shape with stepped façade

Plan—modified L-shape

Plan—T-shape

U-shape	Plan—U-shape
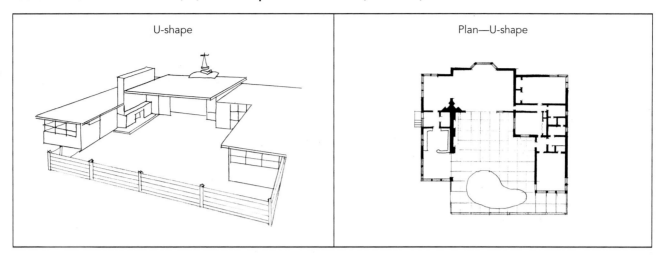	

Like the T-shaped and L-shaped houses, the U-shape could be turned toward the front or back. Like the L-shape, the depth of the wings and the length of the center section were critical dimensions. For the most part one wing was two rooms deep. A two-car garage or carport might be placed on the other side. Thus the U was shallow, and the center portion, which was the core space of the house, three or four rooms wide.

H-Shaped Ranch House

In 1943 architect Marcel Breuer developed a binuclear plan consisting of two spatial areas linked together with a narrow entry hall, roughly in an H shape. One side contained social areas, such as living room, dining room and kitchen, and the other side was comprised of private areas (bedrooms and bathrooms). Breuer experimented with the binuclear plan in various projects and discovered that the space left between the two spatial nuclei, aside from the entry area, could be used as an open porch, thereby creating a third functional space. Breuer provided each nucleus with a square silhouette in plan and elevation that could be easily read from the exterior and then accentuated the differences with a butterfly roof: a roof conformed by two sloping planes joined in opposite directions to resemble the wings of a butterfly. Since Breuer's plan consisted of two functional main nucleuses, each of the roof slopes corresponded to a different one, distinguishing among them. The plan was widely used as a model for residential space planning in the 1940s and 50s in high-end architecture, and the H-shape appeared occasionally in plan books and building trade magazines, primarily as a rambler.

12.7. This example from Arizona offers a roof plan that, in turn, provides a new organization of the massing. The gable roof over the wing on the right is balanced by the carport roof on the left, which steps down, breaking the plane of the main roof. Authors' collection.

12.8. Ranch house designs such as this one became more abstract as the cladding panels of wood and brick and the window figures were put together in two-dimensional arrangements. Geometric shapes were the basis of the Holiday subdivision houses. The designs featured exposed roof structure inside and out and a high ceiling in the living–dining room. Photo credit: Guy Pourgess. Western History/Genealogy Department, Denver Public Library.

12.9. The living room runs most of the width of the house and has natural light from two sources and exposed beams. The interior scheme has the logic of the exterior: large panels of material— wood, brick, glass—cover the walls. View of a Holiday subdivision home, ca. 1954, Denver. Photo credit: Guy Pourgess. Western History/Genealogy Department, Denver Public Library.

OPEN GABLE ROOF RANCH HOUSE

One of the late stages of ranch house design was a form in which the gable roof was flattened to look more like an airplane wing than a classical pediment (Fig. 12.8). The roof shape was compelling as it embraced the entire house. The broad gable roof type could fit on a narrow lot if it were built without the carport and small porch; with these two features the house looks spacious. The Holiday subdivision houses in Denver were just twelve hunded square feet, so their plans were compact.

SPLIT-LEVEL HOUSE

The final modern house type to be considered is the split-level. Split-level houses are multilevel: succeeding floors are staggered or separated by less than a full flight of stairs. The split-level, which emerged as a type in the 1950s, was originally designed to take advantage of sloping sites.

Although seemingly modern, the split-level revived late-nineteenth and early-twentieth-century plan conventions for a formal parlor, as well as nineteenth-century principles of convenience, such as

Table 12.3. Characteristics of the Open Gable Ranch House

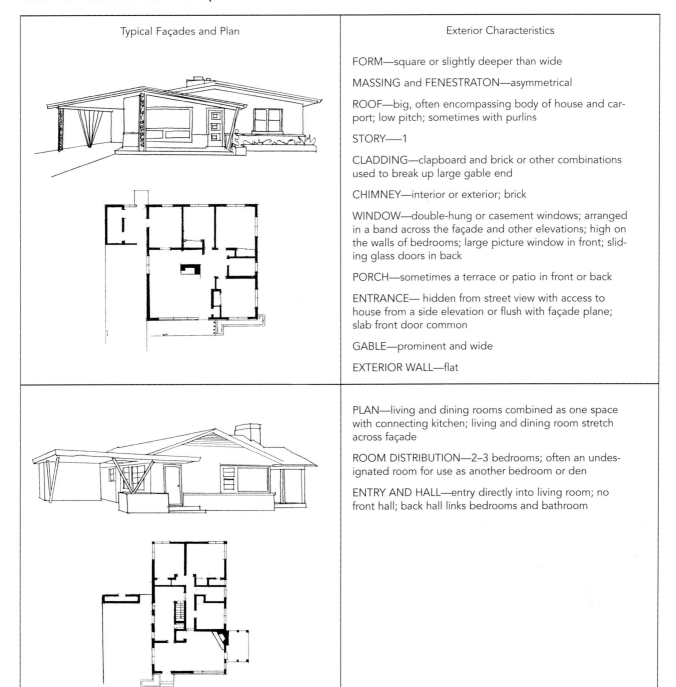

Typical Façades and Plan	Exterior Characteristics
	FORM—square or slightly deeper than wide
	MASSING and FENESTRATON—asymmetrical
	ROOF—big, often encompassing body of house and carport; low pitch; sometimes with purlins
	STORY—1
	CLADDING—clapboard and brick or other combinations used to break up large gable end
	CHIMNEY—interior or exterior; brick
	WINDOW—double-hung or casement windows; arranged in a band across the façade and other elevations; high on the walls of bedrooms; large picture window in front; sliding glass doors in back
	PORCH—sometimes a terrace or patio in front or back
	ENTRANCE— hidden from street view with access to house from a side elevation or flush with façade plane; slab front door common
	GABLE—prominent and wide
	EXTERIOR WALL—flat
	PLAN—living and dining rooms combined as one space with connecting kitchen; living and dining room stretch across façade
	ROOM DISTRIBUTION—2–3 bedrooms; often an undesignated room for use as another bedroom or den
	ENTRY AND HALL—entry directly into living room; no front hall; back hall links bedrooms and bathroom

adequate storage, step saving, the kitchen as a work center, and elimination of wasted space.

The split-level entered the market as builders continued to offer one "interchangeable plan" with varieties of exterior aesthetic treatments. It is not unusual to see designs with English revival stickwork, colonial motifs (especially shutters), or bungalow purlins used to style split-levels. The 1960s also ushered in a trend toward rusticity, an interest in natural materials, changes in textures, and brown tones both outside and inside the house. The mansard roof returned in a format that comprised all of the roof and most of the wall surface. Home Planners Inc. sold a trilevel home design as a colonial adaptation—hand-split fieldstone on the lower level and white clapboards on the upper level. During the 1950s the kitchen was still seen as a work center, and it was better integrated with other rooms in the house. However, integration encouraged styling, and the "country kitchen" became the most popular treatment for a modern house. This is an old story regarding the contradiction between function and style.

Split-level roof types, like ranch houses, were characterized by (1) a gable end that faced the street, (2) a gable or hip roof ridgeline parallel to the street, or (3) intersecting roofs. There were two schemes for roofs whose ridgelines were parallel to the street: a continuous unbroken roof covering the entire house, or separate roofs for each section of the house. In the first scheme a continuous low-sloping roof covered the entire building to tie the house together as a unit. The roof was often framed conventionally, although unified roof framing was more expensive than framing the different levels independently. For greater economy, trusses were used. The second scheme, introduced in the 1950s, had a stepped-height roof design that helped to break up a long façade; it was sometimes called a side-by-side split-level. The most common interior design arrangement was the trilevel, with three basic floors: an intermediate level slightly above grade; an upper level adjacent to the intermediate level but up a half flight of stairs; and a lower level a half flight of stairs down from the intermediate level and directly underneath the upper level. The front door opened directly into a formal living area on the midway level between two floors. The stair, usually a dogleg, was often located to the side midway into the living room. The entry level also housed the dining room and kitchen. The upper level, reached by a half flight of stairs, contained bedrooms and bathrooms. The bedroom floor was above the raised lower floor. The lower level, also accessed by a half flight of stairs, consisted of a family room, utility room, and garage. Side-by-side split-level house roofs were framed under distinct rooflines, with the pitch of the higher section running front to rear and that of the lower section running side to side.[9]

The split-foyer plan was characterized by a foyer (hall) entrance on the midway level and a split stair in which one flight of steps went up to the main level and another flight of steps went down to the lower level. Characteristically, the stair was configured with two short flights at opposite directions joined by a half landing between them. The split-foyer is a two-level (sometimes called a bilevel) house, and the lower level may be partially below ground level.

The raised ranch house came on the market in the early 1960s. It looks like a linear ranch house in which the basement has been raised off the ground by half a story, far enough to be useful for living space. Windowsills in the lower level were on grade, and entry occurred on the lower floor. The interior consisted of two floor levels, with the living area on the top floor (full-height ceilings) and accessible by a staircase close to the entry. The lower floor might have lower ceilings.

In 1960 the Small Homes Council codified basic elements of split-level design to include a living room functioning as a formal room or a reception area. Whereas the living room remained a passive element, a family room, in combination with a kitchen or recreation room, became an active family center. The family concept was introduced in the ranch house. The split-level was a large house containing a master bedroom and at least two other bedrooms. Typical sizes included twelve hundred square feet on an upper level, and eleven hundred square feet on the lower level. Bedrooms, particularly the master bedroom, were large enough to accommodate large closets and sitting space. The Small Homes Council recommended at least eight linear feet of closet space in the master bedroom and four linear feet in the remaining bedrooms. Split-level plans also emphasized one-and-a-half bathrooms or two- or two-and-a-half bathrooms, if the need existed. As in ranch design, a kitchen was open, or partially open, to an adjacent dining area or family room.

Ranch and split-level houses included ample storage, what the American Plan Service deemed "new era closets." The "all vision closet," in which one can see from floor to ceiling, was fitted with sliding wooden or mirrored doors. These closets occupied entire walls at one end of a room. Soon the walk-in closet became a popular selling point for master bedrooms. Builders promoted kitchens large enough to accommodate a storage wall, a built-in desk, and eating space. Bathroom storage also expanded. In 1950 the American Plan Service advertised its medicine chest as new, containing almost seven times the space of the normal cabinet over the lavatory and deep enough for all bottles. Available in white or eggshell enamel, this "grand cabinet" came with two sliding mirror doors. Other miscellaneous storage areas included a utility room, with a designated space for a washer and dryer. The utility level was an advantage in that it was higher than a conventional basement and received more natural light. Moreover, the distance from one level to the next was only six to eight steps. A mechanical room was another prerequisite. And finally car storage came to mean a two-car garage that was integrated into the house design.

Concepts such as livability and maximum enjoyment of outdoor living, typically used to describe ranch houses, were extended to split-level types and included the use of sundecks, balconies, patios, and terraces, accessible from a family room through sliding glass doors. Outside stairways permitted direct access to the outdoors from the utility room.

Table 12.4. Characteristics of the Split-Level House

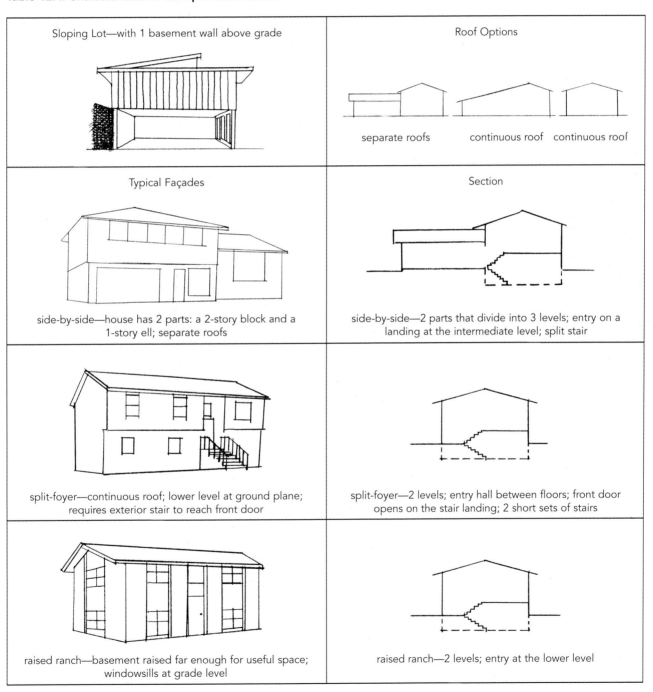

Sloping Lot—with 1 basement wall above grade

Roof Options

separate roofs   continuous roof   continuous roof

Typical Façades

side-by-side—house has 2 parts: a 2-story block and a 1-story ell; separate roofs

Section

side-by-side—2 parts that divide into 3 levels; entry on a landing at the intermediate level; split stair

split-foyer—continuous roof; lower level at ground plane; requires exterior stair to reach front door

split-foyer—2 levels; entry hall between floors; front door opens on the stair landing; 2 short sets of stairs

raised ranch—basement raised far enough for useful space; windowsills at grade level

raised ranch—2 levels; entry at the lower level

Table 12.4. Characteristics of the Split-Level House (continuted)

Split-Foyer—open-gable 	Exterior Characteristics STORY—2 CLADDING—clapboard and brick or other combinations used to break up large gable end WINDOW—picture window on façade; metal or vinyl-clad common; sliding windows in bedrooms high on the wall PORCH—balcony; patio; deck; sunroom GABLE—open; available for aesthetic motifs, such as English revival EXTERIOR WALL—often two cladding schemes FORM—slightly wider than deep ROOF—continuous
 Plan—split-foyer house	PLAN—split-foyer; center hall or slightly off-center hall ROOM DISTRIBUTION—3 bedrooms, 3 bathrooms (2 with showers); family room on lower level along with a 2-car garage and laundry area ENTRY AND HALL—entry into foyer; lit with a large window over front door
 Interior—stair and planter box	ENTRY AND HALL—separate entrance hall, often a center hall; from entryway, stairs lead to both upper and lower levels; stair-climbing reduces the number of steps required for two-story houses, particularly those with basements STAIRS—balustrade composed of thin balusters, and the newel is no longer a significant element; the look is light, often achieved with wrought iron PLANTER BOX—architectural, in that it was built in, part of the wall system, in many interiors
 Raised Ranch—colonial revival with continuous gable roof	 Split-Level—rustic with mansard roof

13

BUILDING TYPE: MULTIFAMILY

Multifamily dwellings have their own inventory of building types. Historically there were strong relations between single-family, multifamily, and commercial buildings of the same period. All three relied on the industrial system to produce building materials and finishes, and all three were built on similar town and city lots and in physical proximity to one another.

ONE-FAMILY ROWHOUSE

Rowhouses, or contiguous houses as they were called in some neighborhoods, were built by the hundreds in most of the "gritty cities" of the Eastern United States. Not all rowhouses were the same; there were a number of different types available, with variations in the use of materials and costs. Design factors included the location of the house in relation to the front building line, the square footage, the degree of elaboration in plans, and the quality of the finish goods.

The flat-front rowhouse was a less expensive type, sometimes built as philanthropic housing. The façade pattern was historical, but the industrial vernacular version had less charm. The flat-front house often was built on the building line; it was about fif-

teen feet wide and two or three rooms deep. Many featured a pressed brick front topped by a bracketed cornice; others featured a parapet and a corbeled cornice. Mansard fronts were not uncommon with dormers and wood panels that had incised ornament at the attic level.

The interior finish of this model was often pine, painted in some rooms and grained to look like oak or walnut in others. Mantels could be made of fiberboard to cut costs. The walls were papered, and stock millwork was used for doors, windows, and wainscots in the kitchen and bath.

Bay-front rowhouses, with either a two-story bay or a single on the upper level, had more articulation than the flat fronts. The façades carried references to cottage architecture with special parlor windows and front porches. As in the other types, the kitchen and bath often projected off the back of the house.

Inner-city housing in Philadelphia, Baltimore, and Trenton, New Jersey is dominated by the rowhouse. There were variations in façade design and interior layout. One type of Philadelphia rowhouse had a porch and a second-story bay window, and it was part of a large group of similar houses.

There were plans with a vestibule and reception hall that separated the parlor from the dining room. A rowhouse might have a large parlor (cottage)

221

Table 13.1. Characteristics of the Rowhouse

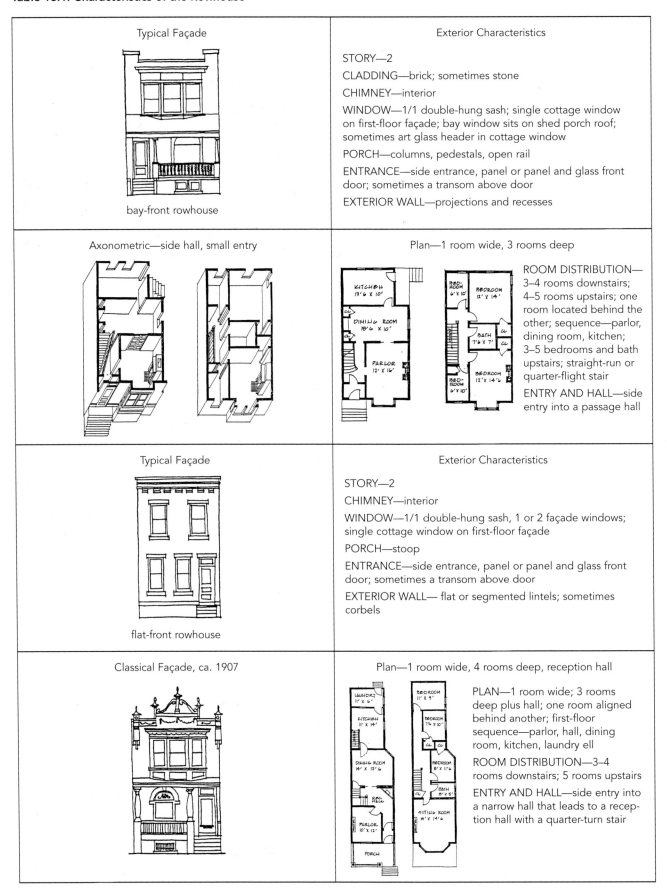

Typical Façade	Exterior Characteristics
bay-front rowhouse	STORY—2 CLADDING—brick; sometimes stone CHIMNEY—interior WINDOW—1/1 double-hung sash; single cottage window on first-floor façade; bay window sits on shed porch roof; sometimes art glass header in cottage window PORCH—columns, pedestals, open rail ENTRANCE—side entrance, panel or panel and glass front door; sometimes a transom above door EXTERIOR WALL—projections and recesses

Axonometric—side hall, small entry	Plan—1 room wide, 3 rooms deep
	ROOM DISTRIBUTION—3–4 rooms downstairs; 4–5 rooms upstairs; one room located behind the other; sequence—parlor, dining room, kitchen; 3–5 bedrooms and bath upstairs; straight-run or quarter-flight stair ENTRY AND HALL—side entry into a passage hall

Typical Façade	Exterior Characteristics
flat-front rowhouse	STORY—2 CHIMNEY—interior WINDOW—1/1 double-hung sash, 1 or 2 façade windows; single cottage window on first-floor façade PORCH—stoop ENTRANCE—side entrance, panel or panel and glass front door; sometimes a transom above door EXTERIOR WALL— flat or segmented lintels; sometimes corbels

Classical Façade, ca. 1907	Plan—1 room wide, 4 rooms deep, reception hall
	PLAN—1 room wide; 3 rooms deep plus hall; one room aligned behind another; first-floor sequence—parlor, hall, dining room, kitchen, laundry ell ROOM DISTRIBUTION—3–4 rooms downstairs; 5 rooms upstairs ENTRY AND HALL—side entry into a narrow hall that leads to a reception hall with a quarter-turn stair

window with a circle top of leaded glass. The vestibule finish in this plan has a raised panel wainscot and a ceramic tile floor. Parlor finish consisted of six-fold blinds and a colonial mantel with small columns and a marbleized slate fiberboard face.

Older houses may have had a sliding door between the dining room and hall, and a double-action door between the dining room and the kitchen. The stair had a quarter-turn plan and the balustrade was an imitation colonial. The bathroom had an overhead ventilating skylight, tiled walls, an oak parquet floor, and a low closet with a copper tank. The interior doors had six cross-panel patterns, with brass plates and wood knobs. There were gas fixtures, chandeliers, a pendant or two, and bracket lights. Eventually electric units replaced gas. Electric attachments were fitted to the parlor, dining room, and toilet lights. There was hot-water heating with open plumbing work. It was customary to paper the walls throughout the house, using Lincrusta in both the halls and the dining room.

13.1. Since the projecting units are usually the same length and volume, the entire elevation is grounded in symmetry, which implies that each side is a mirror image of the other. The center or linking portion incorporates the entry system. Authors' collection.

DOUBLE HOUSES

Double houses are houses built side by side, and residents occupy all floors, basement to the attic, or half the total building. Such a building is also called a duplex, a semidetached house, or a twin house. *Side by side* implies identical houses in form and detail. If they have side yards, a small number of these houses can fill most of a city block. They are commonly interspersed among single-family houses.

Bay-Front Double House

The bay-front double house, primarily a nineteenth-century building, was a two- or three-story structure with several roof options: a mansard roof, a gable roof with the ridge parallel to the street, or a flat roof and accompanying parapet. The primary design scheme required a full-height, usually three-sided, bay window or pavilion on each end that flanked a double entrance. The bays terminated in their own roofs. Dormers were frequently built on these units to utilize attic space, especially on those with mansard roofs.

Stylistically, the bay front was a building with a side hall and Italianate or picturesque detailing: pronounced lintels and sills, segmented arches or full-window surrounds with keystones, heavy brackets at the cornice line, an occasional wrought-iron balustrade or cresting, and a gable finish. The entrance system was often a steep stair leading to a small porch or to a wider porch with its own roof and cottage-type roof supports. A number of these buildings had high foundations with almost full-size windows, implying that the basement level was treated as a living space. Those with high foundations wrapped the building with a water table.

The bay fronts were often city buildings constructed individually or in clusters. They depended on their wide, tall bays and their rooflines for design focus. They were formidable when aligned with the same setback on both sides of a street; they walled in the street. Bay-front double houses provided a dense yet rhythmic façade.

End-to-End Double House

The end-to-end double house had a party wall that is not readily perceived. Most of these houses did not have identical floor plans and thus were less democratic and more hierarchical than twin houses. This condition was evident in the handling of entrances:

Table 13.2. Characteristics of Two-Family Houses

Double House End-to-End Double House	Two-family houses
  elevation units divided vertically plan street entrance and side entrance	ORGANIZATION—Twin or double houses—most common; units divided vertically down the middle, each unit having a first and second story ORGANIZATION—End-to-end double houses—also divided vertically down the middle, but the party wall is less evident from the street, and entrances may be on different sides of the building
Bay-Fronted Double House Double house (1885), Chicopee Falls, Massachusetts D. B. Griggs and Son, builders	**Exterior Characteristics** STORY—2 CLADDING—clapboard; brick WINDOW—1/1 double-hung sash PORCH—piazza off kitchen; turned posts and brackets ENTRANCE—side-by-side center entry GABLE—ornament, Italianate detailing EXTERIOR WALL—stickwork divides walls into panels; Italianate detailing PLAN—downstairs: parlor, sitting room, kitchen, back stair; upstairs: 3 bedrooms ENTRY AND HALL—center; passage hall six-feet wide with straight-run stair
End-to-End Double House—English revival 	**Exterior Characteristics** STORY—1–1½ –2 CLADDING—brick; clapboard WINDOW—6/6 double-hung sash, variety of lights ENTRANCE—small entry porch on street side; porch on side street DORMERS—common ROOF—intersecting gable; gambrel; low-pitched hip roof

one had primary street frontage and the other faced a side street or another building. On the other hand, end-to-end orientation produced a coherent design. The entire building had the appearance of a single-family residence that happened to have two entrances. As such, it fit well into neighborhood settings.

Most end-to-end double houses were built in the twentieth century, and most were one- or one-and-a-half-story buildings. The bungalow was the primary form employed to create this kind of house. But they were not unknown as cottages. The use of materials and ornamentation followed the same patterns as established in the detached, single-family models of these structures. Fenestration was calculated to provide as much lighting as possible so that symmetry, with variety in groupings, predominated.

13.2. Two-family houses filled blocks in cities. They added population density and maintained sound design values. In appearance they were reminders of the kind of single-family cottages that could be the next step for families. Authors' collection.

TWO- AND THREE-FAMILY FLATS

Design of the two-family house followed developments in cottages. Two-family cottages, designed as flats, had an advantage over double houses in that they provided light on all sides and cross-ventilation. The typical flat was an entire floor, front to back, forming a complete residence. The double house and the two-family flat house were often built in the close-in suburbs, and many were grouped so as to generate their own streetscape and urbanism.

Colonial Revival Flat

If a two-family house was designed as a cottage, then it could take on a variety of aesthetic treatments. The colonial revival two-family cottage employed large-scale geometric elements, such as a broad gable roof and a two-story, three-sided bay window that was answered by the formal porches. The façade divided into two "columns," the bay and the porches, topped by a pediment. Subsequent breakdowns of the large forms included five vertical bays—three in the bay window and two in the porch section—and a pair of centered windows in the gable that divided on center, making each side a mirror image of the other.

Horizontal divisions occurred at the water table, the floor line between stories, and the cornice that closed the gable. The windows were placed at the same distance from the floor and ceiling on both levels, so that they looked like a band of evenly spaced windows. The massing of elements on the façade relied on the push–pull balance between the projecting bay window and the recessed porches. The porches were detailed with columns and open rails that helped activate the surface and provided opportunity for the play of light and shadow. Although not as ornamented as the single-family colonial revival, this two-family version was not without turned and sawn materials, Palladian windows, or the columns and entablatures of classical treatments.

Hip Roof Flat

The hip roof cottage as a two-family house had some of the characteristics of the colonial revival type, in that the façade was classical and access to the second floor was through a side-hall stair. The organization of the façade also relied on the kind of classical design vocabulary used in colonial revival buildings. Both floors had an order of architecture, with the first-story columns under the second-floor pilasters. The second-floor entablature carried a fascia board around the house. The wide hip roof understated the temple front. The façade was divided into a large panel with two lights on the second story and a five-part composition on the first: entrance, three-sided bay window capped by a three-sided balustrade, and entrance. Overall, the façade had a horizontal emphasis that was echoed in the side elevations, which were long and broken only by a bay window on one side. The house was twice as long as it was wide.

13.3. This hip roof colonial revival is a rooming house. The lower floor is clapboard, but the second story has shingles; the bay windows extend interior space. Authors' collection.

The organization of the façade in Figure 13.3 is distinctive. The house was a cottage and the entrances separated from each other; there was some ambiguity as to where they went. Except for the bay window, this façade might have been used on a double house. Despite this tendency to separate elements, the design was still cohesive, and fitted within the general design scheme of neighborhood cottages.

Triple-Decker

The triple-decker, a unique multifamily structure, originated in New England mill towns and cities. It was a clapboard or shingle building that provided the most multifamily living, of all the multifamily types, in a single-family context. Triple-deckers were rarely elegant, but they were substantial, well-organized buildings that propelled the cottage design vocabulary into a less picturesque urban world.

Constructed from about 1870 to 1920, the three-family flat could absorb cottage details even though it had outgrown the cottage scale. Most were long, rectangular buildings with the narrow side toward the street. The flats provided three living spaces: one family to a floor. Most stacked one unit over the next, and ground-level motifs were repeated throughout an elevation. The main entrance, which might have had an entrance porch, was on one side of the façade. Bay windows were common on either the façade or a side elevation. Roof treatments included flat roofs with an overhanging cornice, and roofs with gable to the street and a closed gable. Regardless of the façade porch treatment, most of these buildings had rear-access porches on all three levels.

There were several basic compositions for the façades. One type turned the corner into a round or three-sided tower; another utilized a single bay window and a flat section, or two bay windows flanking a central entrance; and still another stacked façade-wide open-railing porches that culminated in a pediment gable. In general, detailing seemed to diminish in the triple-decker, yet it was not without ornament: heavy cornices; porches with columns; elevations with horizontal divisions by means of trim boards that cut walls into panels, belt courses, or continuous sills or lintels; and overhanging eaves.

FOUR-FAMILY HOUSES

The four-family house is the largest multifamily or apartment building discussed in this section. The cottage version of the four-family dwelling predated apartment buildings of the same size. The building in fig. 13.5 had light wood detailing on the porch and in the gables that helped to keep the building's size from overwhelming neighbors.

Bay-Front Four-Family Houses

The bay-front type of "flats" building was a two-story rectangular structure that combined the twin house and the two-family house, in that each side was often a mirror image of the other. However, the four-family house had two families per floor, each family having four or five rooms, a kitchen, and a bath.

Façade composition was the major statement with two kinds of organization: two bay windows, two stories in height, flanking a center section; or each

Table 13.3. Characteristics of Two- and Three-Family Flats

Flats—units divided horizontally	Two-Family Flats
  elevation two-family elevation three-family flats	ORGANIZATION—units divided horizontally; each unit is a full floor
Colonial Revival Flats 	**Exterior Characteristics** STORY—2–2½ CLADDING—clapboard, shingle CHIMNEY—none WINDOW—2-story bay window on façade PORCH—on both levels GABLE—closed gable perpendicular to street; decorative shingles in gable; windows in attic ROOF—pedimented gable
Hip Roof Cottage Flats Two-family cottage (1905), Worcester, Massachusetts; John P. Kingston, architect	**Plan—first and second floors** Two-family cottage (1905), Worcester, Massachusetts, John P. Kingston, architect
Triple-Decker 	**Exterior Characteristics** STORY—3 CLADDING—clapboard CHIMNEY—none WINDOW—one or two 3-story front bay windows; 1/1 double-hung sash PORCH—rear porches common; sometimes gable roof; open porches on front EXTERIOR WALL—horizontal division of walls ROOF—flat, sometimes gable; overhanging cornice

13.4. A multifamily cottage that divides into four flats; the entrance system acknowledges the doorway to each residence—a strategy that maintains the impression that living in a flat is independent living. Clapboards on this house are quite wide, and there are quoins instead of cornerboards. Each front door has a transom, and the lower floor flats facing the porch have square bay windows. All of these details derive from cottage design. Authors' collection.

13.5. This typical bay-front four-unit building (1910) in Winter Hill, Massachusetts engages the street with its entrance system and then pulls the body of the building back from the lot line. Authors' collection.

corner had a projecting pavilion that was one room deep and one room wide, with a setback in the middle. Bays were rounded or three-sided. The center portion could be flat with some ornament around the entrance door, or an entrance porch might bridge the entire center. Porches were usually not elaborate. The entrance generally had a decorative lintel, sidelights, or ornamental brickwork. In the projecting pavilion type the setback was often a terrace and included plantings.

Fenestration was symmetrical, with both bays and pavilions adding more windows and light than usual

to the façade. Roof composition included flat roofs with a parapet or gable, and clipped gable roofs on pavilions or bays with a flat or gable over the main body, possibly even a mansard or a large hip roof. Other details were stucco and half-timber stickwork, corbelling, roof eaves with dentils or brackets, walls with shingles or clapboard siding, and decorative sills or lintels.

These multifamily units increased population density while maintaining neighborhood scale. Each "house" often served as a starter for the incoming city population; residents enjoyed the same amenities of

13.6. A four-family colonial revival cottage in San Diego. The two-story portico entry breaks the wide front into three units, which alters the scale of the building and lessens its presence on a block. The *X*'s on the photograph must have marked a tenant's domain. Authors' collection.

neighborhood living, with access to work and services, as residents in single-family units.

Classical Portico-Front Four-Family House

Stylistically, the portico-front house was the most deliberately historical of the four-family types. The portico itself was the dominant feature, being invariably two stories in height and carrying an entablature. The orders of architecture were varied, including Doric, Tuscan, Ionic, and Corinthian. The large portico was attached to flat-front buildings or set between flanking bays or pavilions. Portico composition included four columns evenly spaced or paired, with a wide center space for the entrance; most columns sat on blocks on a shallow porch. The second-floor porch was usually railed and served as a balcony for second-floor residents. The entablature was full but usually eclectic, using moldings and ornament not true to the order. Plain architraves and friezes were popular, and the cornice line carried dentils and projected from the entablature. Some moldings and the entire cornice were often carried around the building. Some of these fronts placed a low pediment on center, in line with the entrance, as a gesture toward the full temple front. Entablatures without a pediment substituted a balustrade.

To enhance the portico on the front, more elaborate designs might place a pilaster behind each column, use quoins on the corners, place decorative lintels or sills on the façade, or employ a water table, rustication, and ornament around the entrance door. The remainder of the design was in the same mode as the bay-front building. Ironically, the portico front extended colonial and classical revival design vocabularies to buildings more in scale with classical buildings than were most cottages, creating what might be called a colonial-Roman look. In any event, this design vocabulary dressed an urban building and encouraged a particular kind of urbanity.

Four-Family Villa House

The villa style of building was the last in the hipped cottage line. It had a well-organized façade derived from the Italian and Spanish-style villa in single-family houses. The walls were greatly influenced by the symmetrical fenestration and the central entrance, which led to a long vestibule. The roof forms were either flat across the entire structure or had a gable parallel to the street with corner pediments on the front section and a flat roof on the remainder. Floor plans in the villas were similar to the other types—four- or five-room flats, side by side.

In design these structures seemed to compensate greatly for having a windowless wall: the number of windows and the variety of window size and shape increased greatly. Window types included French doors to a balcony, fixed windows of cottage size,

13.7. This four-family villa-type house in Alhambra, California (1929) is vaguely Mediterranean, with a three-bay organization centered on a projecting portico. Stucco finish with quoins, round-headed windows, iron balcony rails, and red tile roofs suggest the style. Since the villa style echoed single-family design, it also did not intrude on neighborhoods. Authors' collection.

paired and triple windows, and the odd single window used to light a special-purpose space such as the bath.

The entrance received attention: it might have an arch, a canopy, a pediment, or an elaborate hood to note its location and set a tone for the façade. Gable roofs often had brightly colored clay tiles, and flat roofs might have a parapet or cornice around the entire building. Surface treatments were usually brick or stucco on frame, hollow tile, block, or concrete walls. Some of the villas had entrance porches or terraces on the ground level.

Table 13.4. Characteristics of Four-Family Houses

Bay-Front Façade	Exterior Characteristics
	STORY—2 CLADDING—stucco, brick, shingle, clapboard WINDOW—multiple window groupings; double and triple windows common; 1/1 double-hung sash ENTRANCE—central; entrance had decorative lintel, sidelights or ornamental brickwork EXTERIOR WALL—often lateral divisions of façade wall; decorative sills and lintels
Classical Portico-Fronted Façade	STORY—2 CLADDING—brick PORCH—large 2-story projecting portico with an entablature; orders varied; second-floor balconies common; 4 columns of varied orders evenly spaced ENTRANCE—central entrance EXTERIOR WALL—sometimes quoins; decorative lintels or sills on the façade; sometimes a water table, rustication, and ornament around entrance door
Villa Façade	STORY—2 CLADDING—brick or stucco on frame, hollow tile, block or concrete walls WINDOW—multiple window groupings; French doors to a balcony or terrace; paired and triple windows; often metal casement windows PORCH—sometimes entrance porches or terraces on ground level ENTRANCE—central entrance with arch, canopy, pediment, or elaborate hood
Spanish Revival Façade	STORY—2 CLADDING—stucco, finished; dark red tile trim WINDOW—paired 4/1 double-hung PORCH—square posts and balusters with brackets ENTRANCE—central entrance

14

BUILDING TYPE:
COMMERCIAL AND BUSINESS

———•———

A historical perspective on commercial design suggests that nineteenth-century storefronts were generally uniform in appearance. Stores were built one, two, or three at a time; when built as infilling structures, they could appropriate elements and materials from the buildings around them. The first decade of this century marked the beginning of a change in commercial façade design—a consequence of the owners' desire to have their buildings express individuality. (This change had already occurred in housing design.) The logic for this change in attitude toward the function of the façade was linked to the idea of having to catch and hold the attention of the casual observer. In short, it was grounded in the desire to increase sales and profits. The enticement and engagement of passersby was related to the idea that display space ought to have aesthetic appeal. The passerby would be induced to stop and enter by some display of "artistic beauty" or "striking effect." Thus, storefront architecture became a problem to be solved with manufactured goods. The solutions expanded in several directions; the gross area allocated for display was increased; bulkhead, glass, and entry patterns were reconsidered; color became an essential element; and interior day lighting and artificial lighting became more significant in façade design. In reacting to all of this, passersby could now indulge in something known as window shopping.

The success of plate glass as the principal display material was related ultimately to solving the problems of mullion, bulkhead, and tension for large plates. When plate glass could be set in metal, display windows could be larger, more unobstructed, and easier to maintain. With the development of metalwork in steel, copper, and bronze for use in moldings, corner bars, and division bars, with heavy-gauge metal in gutters and face members, designers could control the tension between the metal members and the window glass, making large windows possible. The metal could be finished in a number of ways to match other surface treatments. In this way storefronts increased their physical presence on the street through clear, dustproof glass and metal boxes.[1]

Artistic effects generally were tied to changing a few design elements, such as styling through detailing. For example, a new storefront of brick and terra-cotta ornament could transform an entire façade aesthetically. Other changes were linked to changing the bulkhead cladding from wood to something more exotic such as marble, metal plates, or encaustic tiles, correlating materials with a new display and entrance pattern.

Stores also changed appearance to adjust to new types of business. For example, the display space for a jewelry store would not be suitable for a clothing store, nor would the raised floors of grocery store windows meet the display needs of a furniture store. Lastly, all these businesses needed special counters, tables, cases, cabinets, shelving, balconies, platforms, racks and fixtures, unobstructed floor space, ceiling and wall coverings, freight access, a ventilated toilet, a stock room, and sometimes a dumbwaiter or elevator.

SINGLE-FRONT BUILDINGS

The history of vernacular commercial building design is really the history of two phenomena. The first concerns the original installation of these buildings as part of a Main Street or courthouse square. In cities they might be located on a neighborhood corner or on streets that served as boundaries between districts. Of all the commercial buildings constructed in those places, stores were by far the most prolific type. Among stores built before 1900, the prevailing types were the common brick-fronted store and the Italianate storefront made of cast iron or of iron and brick. That we have had these storefronts for a long time brings us to the second phenomenon, which is

that the history of commercial vernacular architecture is a history of remodeling. Business buildings have been susceptible to radical alterations of their façades and major alterations of their interior space. Storefronts have always been directly associated with myths about progress and change, especially about the need to change appearance in order to stay competitive.

An article appearing in *American Builder and Building Age* (April 1935), entitled "Modernize Main Street," stated that according to Census Bureau data there were "more than 1,500,000 stores, shops, garages, offices and places of business of every kind."[2] Of that total, more than one million were food, automotive, restaurant, apparel, and general supply businesses. The majority of these businesses could have been accommodated in the kinds of stores discussed in this chapter.

False-Front

False-front commercial buildings have been associated with the settlement of the West, but false fronts were, in fact, built in upstate New York as well as in Iowa, Texas, Colorado, and Wyoming. The false front has been associated with stores, and there is no doubt that the one- and two-story storefront is the most common of extant vernacular commercial

14.1. The Bowler Restaurant, in Bowler, Wisconsin, is a false-fronted building with residential space above. Authors' collection.

buildings. This kind of building was used for services, small hotels, and as a meeting hall for social and fraternal organizations.

From a design point of view, the false front simply made the building seem larger than it was. The false portion extended the façade vertically and horizontally so that the roof over the main body—most often, a gable or flat roof—remained hidden from view. The illusion was useful in suggesting an interesting profile when one could not afford to build a large enough building, or when town developers wanted to convey an image of progress and prosperity. On one-story buildings the false portion did not extend much beyond the apex of the gable; the extra section of wall provided ornamentation, with an elaborate cornice built on the front, or it functioned as a signboard. In most cases the false front was integrated into the façade so that cornerboards, columns, or pilasters were carried up the front; panel divisions aligned with display windows below, and centered pediments aligned with the entrance. This integration was more evident on two-story fronts, whether they screened a half story or extended a second-story wall.

False-front commercial buildings did not create illusions that fooled the citizenry, but they did provide symbolic evidence of the general civilizing process. The fronts were orderly, partly because their lot sizes were similar, and because the design relationships among them were proportional. The stores helped to create enclosure and a sense of a developing center, even if the development proved transitory. The false front often got replaced by, or incorporated into, brick buildings. It maintained the scale of the original town site, so that size, shape, and materials momentarily held a community together.

Gable Front

Whereas a good number of commercial building types were designated for urban settings, the gable-front store was most often a small-town or rural building. This frame structure, usually clad in clapboard, served as a general store, hardware, grocery feed store, or small implements store. Some gable-fronted stores were used like brick fronts, with the upper level providing living space for the owner.

The gable-front was a simple design for a direct, unadorned building with an assortment of windows. It had modest display windows on the ground level, but traditional double-hung sash windows in other locations. The straight gable roof and the end-wall gable defined the form, and most elements reinforced that shape. Fenestration was symmetrical, with the entrance on center with the apex of the gable. Most elevations carried no horizontal division

14.2. The General Store in Monterey, New York is a frame, gable-fronted building, with two large display windows and a single entrance. The door on the second story indicates that goods could be hauled up for storage or lowered for sales. Authors' collection.

14.3. This single-fronted store is a later version of the gable-fronted type, because it has a closed gable pediment, with a second-story bay window in the residential part of the building. Authors' collection.

14.4. An iron-fronted store is a single-fronted type with a cast-iron frame that is rigid and structural. The parts bolt to each other and the whole composition bolts to the walls. The pilasters frame plates of glass for the clearstory, transom and display windows, and the entrance doors. The signboard is wood, but the rest is iron and glass. Authors' collection.

between floors, and corners had narrow boards. A shed roof or awning covered the entrance area. Decoration was limited to brackets in the gable, a large signboard on the façade advertising the name of the store, and other boards advertising specific products. Occasionally the gable was clipped, a gable ornament or a materials such as shingles were changed.

A business like a gable-front store was an important building in rural areas and towns; sometimes the post office was part of the store. Symbolically it represented the endpoint of the distribution of goods within the general economy. Collectively the stores were part of a network of commercial developments in outlying areas. A store's shape and scale tied it to the local economy, and its placement in town or at a crossroads marked it as a center for social activity, service, or information.

Iron Front

The iron-front store was built in all geographical areas because the technology needed to produce iron architectural materials was almost as transportable as the materials themselves. The mold makers had a predilection for classical details, so that most iron-fronted stores had at least a pair of plain pilasters at the corners or a set of stacked half columns with an entablature. Ironwork was integrated with pressed or stamped tinwork. The iron posts and beams framed the façade, and the tin pieces were used for lintels or surrounds of the windows and for the large, bracketed, molding-heavy cornice. All metal pieces were painted to prevent rust.

A catalog version of this kind of storefront would include a second story with iron pilasters dividing the façade into equal bays. The entire structure might be topped off with a series of moldings and fascia culminating in a bracketed sign band. The heavy use of ornament on the upper level and an elaborate cornice would create a distinctive profile for the store. Iron-front stores with classical motifs lost popularity in the twentieth century, but the order, occasional elegance, and rich detailing they gave to districts—especially those near the rails and rivers—can still be appreciated.

Brick-Front

The brick-front store was built as a single building or in groups with party walls up to a block in length. In vernacular design it was the most popular storefront for the longest period of time. Such buildings varied in height from one to three stories, but their plans were quite similar. Two- and three-story structures had ground-level store facilities, with storage or an apartment living space on the second or third floor. Access was from the street through a separate entrance or through the store. Single-story buildings offered no living space for store owners or renters, and they were not often built alone, but rather as a series of stores along a portion of a block tied together by cornices or other horizontal elements. The storefront had a brick façade with a deep cornice of brick laid up in decorative patterns, in panels, or as corbels. The first and second floors were tied together by the facing brick—its color, bonding pattern, and mortar joints. Except for a transom light extending across the windows and entry door, the brick-front show windows were similar to those in the Italianate store, as were the bulkheads under the windows.

The façade of a brick-front store may be likened to a grid of vertical and horizontal architectural features, beginning with the framing of the façade and continuing through the coursing of the brick, and the network of details: the base, top and corners, openings, and ornament. The logic of the placement of elements on the grid determines the coherence of the scheme. Display space was conventional, whether the entrance was centered or off-center. The large windows framed by the building's corners and the panel of brick between floors dominated the lower level. These stores were often narrow and deep, and the windows were a source of light as well as an invitation to inspect goods. The upper levels had more options, including single or double oriel windows, panels of brickwork, brick friezes and cornices featuring corbels or otherwise arranged brick, tin cornices with elaborate patterns, parapet walls of various profiles, decorative lintels or sills (especially continuous types that linked windows), and string courses or sections of belt courses that divided the wall laterally.

Despite the breadth of these choices, much of the façade's design centered on the overall framing of the shape: the structural system, post and beam, as suggested by the edges; the large lateral panels; and the cornice. The cornice functioned as a cap under which other elements were arranged and balanced.

Most design systems, therefore, were a blend of large elements and more delicate detailing. This scheme held true even when the brick front was expanded to five or six bays.

The simplest form of modern commercial building relied on a plain geometric shape to create an identity. Moreover, there was the general reduction of elements to a single effect that exploited the materiality of construction products, clean surfaces, straight lines, and contemporary technology.

Exterior Treatments

Specific style treatments of commercial buildings centered on the materials used—masonry, iron, and wood—and the manner in which the façade was organized, that is, the proportions used to divide the wall and openings into units. Most commercial buildings were façade-oriented, in that expressive details were displayed on the façade, from foundation to cornice. It was common to use inexpensive materials on party walls between structures and rear elevations.

ROMANESQUE

The Romanesque commercial style was not widespread, nor was the style easily accomplished in vernacular building. The Romanesque was picturesque in expression. At its most ambitious level, the vernacular Romanesque used coursed, rock-faced sandstone blocks, sometimes two-toned with a darker stone for trim, with round-arch windows and a low, wide, arched entrance. Surface texture and the rhythm of the arches or arcades were emphasized. Other elements could include a corner entrance marked by a single thick granite column, from which an arch sprung, and a corner tower. Romanesque buildings were also designed in stone and brick, one material serving as trim for the other, whereas other buildings were done entirely in brick. Brick changed the design somewhat, in that the rough surface was gone, so builders compensated by using elaborate corbels on brick cornices or brick arcades and arches with moldings surrounding the curved members. Both brick and stone buildings might have tin cornices. Fenestration varied by floor level: the first-floor windows might be larger than the second and be tied together by arches, or the second floor might

First National Bank,

14.5. The First National Bank in Elmer, New Jersey (ca. 1903) is based on revival architecture. The treatment is eclectic: a mansard roof, Romanesque style (rock-faced stone and an entry arch), and classical elements such as the portico, cornice, and classical ornamentation. Authors' collection.

use an alternative window such as a large-scale lunette divided by heavy mullions. Art glass or small, square panes of colored glass were a consistent detail. Romanesque was popular for banks and public buildings, but storefronts and corner business blocks—especially in brick—also received this treatment. Substantial, low, and heavy, the buildings implied security and commitment to purpose. A good number of them had corner sites, so as to anchor a business block.

CLASSICAL

Small-town or neighborhood banks started their commercial life in buildings much like stores. First- and even second-generation banks in brick-fronted stores and in the more formal temple- or classical-fronted stores were located on the same streets as all the other businesses.

Bank designs and plans sometimes were included in pattern books, just as furniture was included in millwork trade catalogs. A bank was often the most important and architecturally significant building and interior in a town, and in the nineteenth and early twentieth centuries it was often located on a corner block. Plan-book architect George W. Payne included two bank designs as corner blocks in his 1907 *Payne's Modern Homes*. In addition to providing space for regular banking a bank building could also accommodate offices, such as a loan and trust business, a lawyer's offices, or a title abstract office. A bank in a farming community might accommodate a community center and a lounge (the farmer's room), such as the one at Farmers and Merchants State Savings Bank in Manchester, Iowa.

ITALIANATE

In the Italianate storefront, popular during the 1870s and 1880s, the window treatment (which included the shape and size of the window and the lintel or sill), the cornice line, and the corners of the building offered the most opportunities for detail from the limited design possibilities. Upper windows were generally long and narrow, and lintels and sills were of metal, brick, stone, or cement. Lintels were visually heavy units, segmented or rounded. Metal pieces had ornamented surfaces. The cornice was most often metal and had an entablature organization—architrave, frieze, and cornice—with heavy brackets at the corners and lighter, perhaps paired, brackets across the cornice. Façade designs that divided the first floor from the second used an ornamented beam or surface moldings that to cap the display windows. The corners of buildings could have quoins in brick or stone, or pilasters or half columns might mark the edges and frame the lower level. It was also common to stack the upright elements on top of one another.

Italianate detailing could be accomplished through brick, iron, or wood construction; the material selected would affect the use of detail. Wood and metal offered the best opportunities for ornament. Brickwork tended to be limited to the cornice, although segmented lintels were popular. Other details included decorative anchor irons, rosettes or other floral motifs, and elaborate capitals on the pilasters. In the evolution of commercial fronts, the Italianate was one of the first successful historical style built from manufactured materials. It set a precedent and a design standard that are still evident in the great number of Italianate upper stories in business districts throughout the country.

MODERN

The simplest modern commercial building relies on abstract geometry to create an identity and a presence among other structures. Beyond form there is the general reduction of elements to a single effect, exploiting the materiality of construction products, clean surfaces, straight lines, and contemporary materials and technology.

14.6. E. A. Rankin conducted a funeral director's business on the ground floor of the Naecel Building (1892), an Italianate iron front; the family lived on the second floor. The façade is organized in horizontal stages from bottom to top: iron and glass front; three-bay apartment; bands of ornamental sheet metal; and a bracketed parapet, with a name and date plate. Authors' collection.

14.7. The size, location, remnant column, and canted entrance imply that this commercial building in Lohrville, Iowa (ca. 1910) is a remodel of an older building. Plate glass replaces the original front and the walls are brick. The effect is modern. The lone detail, a brick corbel stringcourse, ties the elevations together and creates a top or finishing piece for the walls. The corbel, a historical detail often found on commercial buildings, takes on a new role. Authors' collection.

Table 14.1. Characteristics of Single-Fronted Commercial Buildings

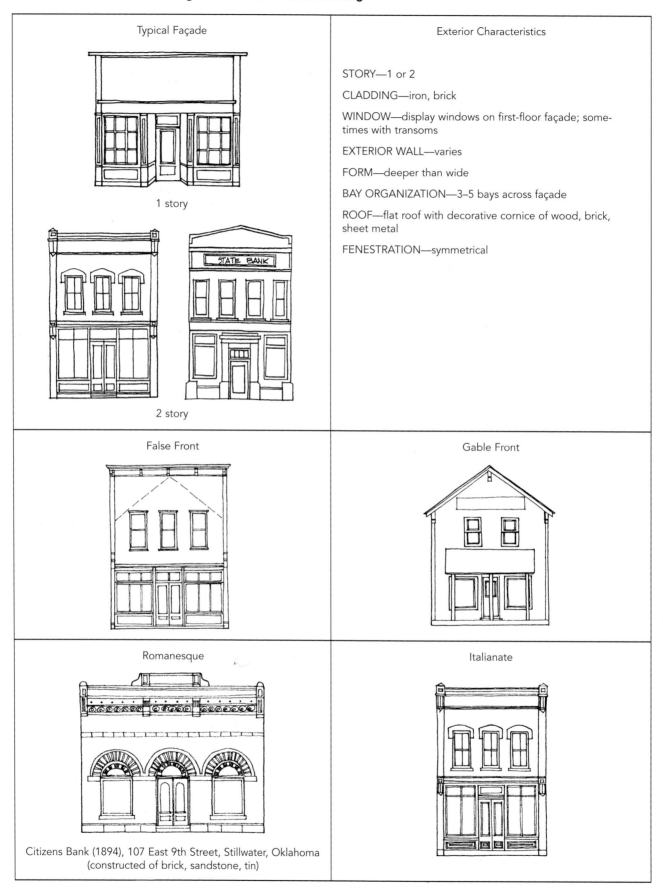

Typical Façade

1 story

2 story

Exterior Characteristics

STORY—1 or 2

CLADDING—iron, brick

WINDOW—display windows on first-floor façade; sometimes with transoms

EXTERIOR WALL—varies

FORM—deeper than wide

BAY ORGANIZATION—3–5 bays across façade

ROOF—flat roof with decorative cornice of wood, brick, sheet metal

FENESTRATION—symmetrical

False Front

Gable Front

Romanesque

Citizens Bank (1894), 107 East 9th Street, Stillwater, Oklahoma (constructed of brick, sandstone, tin)

Italianate

Classical

Classical Iron Front

Classical Brick Front

2-story brick front with corbelled cornice, second-floor windows with segmented arch, center door

Typical Pediments—for single-fronted business buildings

stepped gable

semicircular pediment

pedimented stepped gable

triangular pediment

Plan and Entry Schematics—for single-fronted business buildings

FLUSH CENTER

FLUSH SIDE

FLUSH BAY WINDOWS

RECESSED CANT

RECESSED CANT

RECESSED HALF-CANT

RECESSED SQUARE

RECESSED SQUARE

RECESSED SQUARE

RECESSED T

RECESSED STEPPED

RECESSED STEPPED

14.8. The corner business block, with a bank as the central tenant, in Winters, California (ca. 1906) has an oriel window marking the corner, and parapet walls and awnings help to distinguish one business from another. Authors' collection.

MULTIPLE-FRONTED BUILDINGS

Nineteenth-century commercial and business buildings were built in a number of configurations along a street. Successful towns added new building types, such as the double-front, to their business districts and they, in turn, changed the configurations. The single-front was simply doubled to create the new structure, with each unit maintaining its own commercial identity but sharing an architectural treatment and a firewall. The next scale up from the double-front was the business block, which could be located anywhere along an array of buildings, but was often built as a corner block in which storefronts served two streets. The block often marked the corner intersection with an architectural element such as a tower.

Corner Block

From the last quarter of the nineteenth century right down to the present, much attention has been paid to the corner commercial building, particularly one marking the edge or the heart of a business district. The arcaded block was just such a building. It was intended to be an imposing building with a strong overall shape, solid massing, and firm lines on both elevations. It was rarely uniform in size, for one elevation was often larger than the other, and one might have been designed somewhat differently from the other. As a corner property, the arcaded business block had a rich design vocabulary stemming from the history of business-block development after the

Civil War and the introduction of a new sensibility. High-style architects such as Henry Hobson Richardson and Louis Sullivan had demonstrated how an elevation could be integrated through the use of arches, round-headed elements, or arcades. The curvilinear elements were usually linked, which helped to break the wall away from domination by vertical bays. The new look presented windows in bands or clusters of light. This kind of design often gave a lighter feeling to portions of a wall and, at the same time, focused the design on the intersection of the walls. That corner typically culminated in a tower that rose from a recessed or canted ground-level entrance. Vertical accents or strict divisions of the elevations did not disappear from business-block design. Many upright elements, such as half columns or pilasters, helped to organize the walls. Some of the linking between arched units took place within these vertical bays, even to the point of stacking window groups over one another.

Stylistically, the arcaded block was an eclectic combination of classical and picturesque interests. The corner tower, tall chimneys, and occasional upper-level oriel window were also cottage motifs. Broad arches of stone blocks were part of the Romanesque revival vocabulary, whereas elaborate cornices with brackets or dentils were part of the general nineteenth-century design system.

Most arcaded blocks made distinctions between ground-level and upper-level design schemes, owing in part to the location of storefronts within the block and the use of arches or arcades in the design. For example, a corner block might employ an arch that

14.9. A corner-block type, in Vicksburg, Michigan, with a bank as the main business and single-fronted stores on each end of the block. The entry is canted to face the intersection, and a single engaged column creates the edge of the building. The bank's space is indicated by a stringcourse above the first-floor windows, and a classical cornice links the entire block. The corner of the building, above the entrance, is detailed to look like a column with a small capital. It has a visual relation with the cornice and the column below. Authors' collection.

spanned each vertical bay on ground level. The second floor might have paired windows headed by a single arch or by two arches sized to the windows. In the Romanesque style, arches meeting at the corner often met on a column of stone with an alternative material, such as granite. Other ground-level detailing included rustication and a water table of large stone blocks.

The arcaded block was one of the strongest design statements of all vernacular building types and styles. It maintained its position in business districts throughout the 1870–1960 period. It was a symbolic reminder of the importance of business in town and small-city life. Its scale also fit well with residential neighborhoods. The arcaded block was an anchor for commercial districts and evidence of the power of industrially produced design materials.

DOUBLE-FRONT BUILDINGS

Some commercial structures were designed and built as multiple stores, and many of these were also residential buildings, with the second and third floors partitioned into two- or three-bedroom flats or apartments. These doublewide or wider stores, also called double-lot stores, were related to the broad front. They were of the same general width, forty to fifty feet, and had the same overall composition, with strong piers on the corners and a large panel of brick and windows in between. Because of the size of the façade, the front had a three-part organization: show windows, commercial entry, and residential entry at the street level; upper-floor windows in rows, groups, bands, or as single units with cladding panels in between; and a cornice line that included the parapet,

14.10. Double-fronted, brick-fronted stores in Canton, New York. In the building on the left, the storefront is two bays wide, and each store has its own entry. The right grouping has three bays for the first store and two for the right in a two-story building. The door in the center would access the apartments above. Authors' collection.

Table 14.2. Characteristics of Multiple-Fronted Buildings

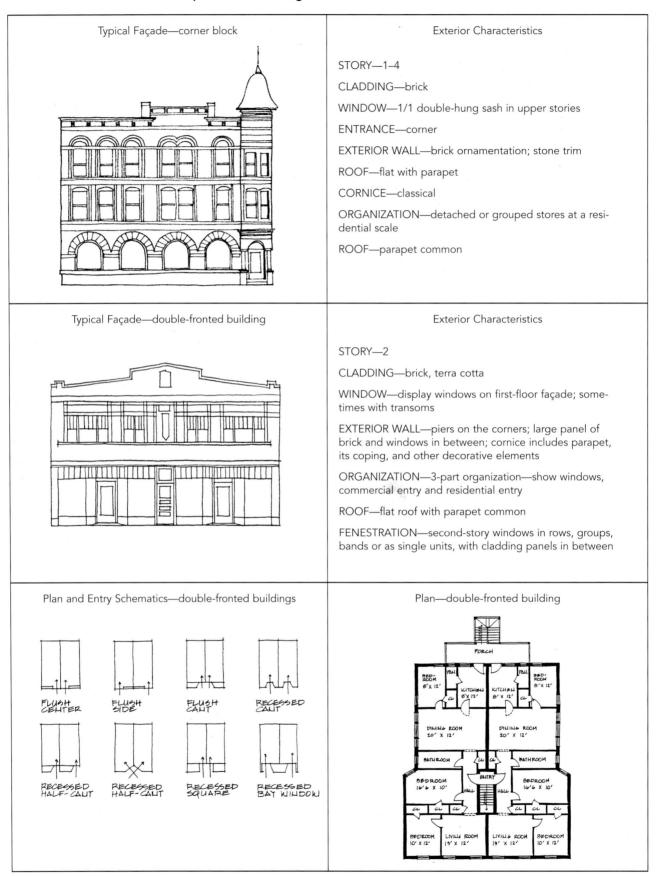

Typical Façade—corner block

Exterior Characteristics

STORY—1–4

CLADDING—brick

WINDOW—1/1 double-hung sash in upper stories

ENTRANCE—corner

EXTERIOR WALL—brick ornamentation; stone trim

ROOF—flat with parapet

CORNICE—classical

ORGANIZATION—detached or grouped stores at a residential scale

ROOF—parapet common

Typical Façade—double-fronted building

Exterior Characteristics

STORY—2

CLADDING—brick, terra cotta

WINDOW—display windows on first-floor façade; sometimes with transoms

EXTERIOR WALL—piers on the corners; large panel of brick and windows in between; cornice includes parapet, its coping, and other decorative elements

ORGANIZATION—3-part organization—show windows, commercial entry and residential entry

ROOF—flat roof with parapet common

FENESTRATION—second-story windows in rows, groups, bands or as single units, with cladding panels in between

Plan and Entry Schematics—double-fronted buildings

FLUSH CENTER

FLUSH SIDE

FLUSH CANT

RECESSED CANT

RECESSED HALF-CANT

RECESSED HALF-CANT

RECESSED SQUARE

RECESSED BAY WINDOW

Plan—double-fronted building

14.11. The Strain Building is a modern broad-fronted commercial structure in Shelby, Nebraska (ca. 1914). The span of this building type is its primary quality. Bands of horizontal ornament in the brick coursing reinforce the broad-span impression. A prism-glass transom and display windows make up half the façade elevation and bring light into the interior. A low parapet at the top of the wall corresponds to a low foundation wall of stone, and both are connected by the pilaster-like edges. Authors' collection.

its coping, and other decorative elements. The most popular materials for this building were brick and terra cotta.

BROAD-FRONT BUILDING

Commercial building prototypes did not change basic organization and design until modern materials and design encouraged the change. One modern building was the double-width storefront, which has been labeled the modern broad front. The modern broad-front store building was a special class composed of patented storefront materials. This building was both a neighborhood and a central business district building, although in the business districts it was frequently built on a side street. The broad front embraced two stores or one wide store within one span. The entry was generally recessed, and truss roof construction eliminated intermediary supporting posts, leaving the interior free of obstruction.

The broad-front building was most often a low one-story structure that could be twice as deep as it was wide. The façade design reinforced the openness of the building's face. The façade typically featured a large brick panel, symmetrically organized, with a continuous cornice, transom, and display windows. Two thick piers anchored the edges and held a brick panel that was usually subdivided. Display windows were partitioned into panels of glass with thin mul-

lions, which helped broaden the front, and they were topped by a series of continuous transom lights forming a band or clearstory. The open front might have an intermediary column on the façade that was carried that back through the building to support the roof. Very often this column was on axis with a decorative treatment on the parapet wall. Ornamentation was simple, with brickwork panels or edges or terracotta panels or copings around the edges. The broad front was a linear building that sat lightly on its site. It moved away from the dual-purpose nineteenth-century store, in that it had no living space. The broad front looked as commercially efficient as it was intended to be. Adaptable, it could house various kinds of enterprises. Though it had a few historical details as links to the past, it was originally—and today remains—a modern building.

ARTISTIC-FRONT BUILDINGS

As neighborhoods became settled and filled up with cottages, bungalows, and multifamily buildings, the increase in population and automobiles gave rise to a new kind of secondary business district. It was located within walking distance or within mass transit connections of a neighborhood or on the boundary between two neighborhoods where access by car was necessary. This kind of enterprise was a grouping of stores that offered a wide variety of goods and

Table 14.3. Characteristics of Broad-Front Commercial Buildings

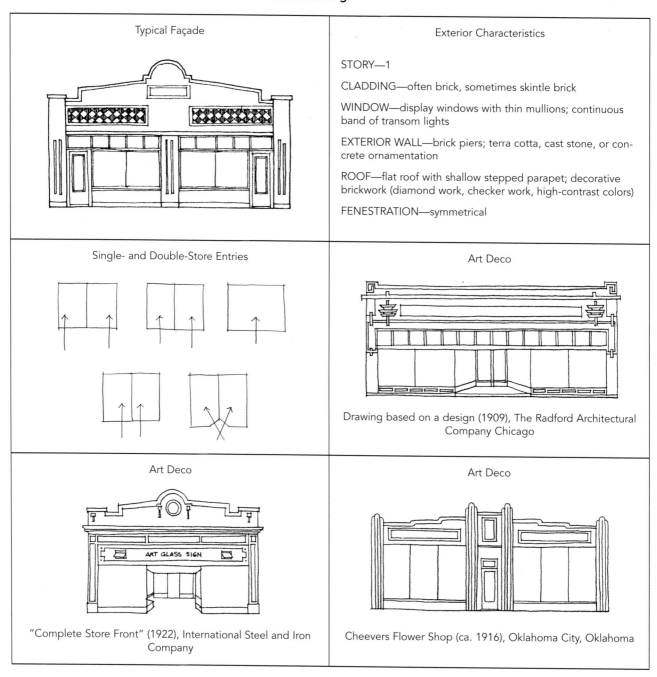

Typical Façade	Exterior Characteristics
	STORY—1
	CLADDING—often brick, sometimes skintle brick
	WINDOW—display windows with thin mullions; continuous band of transom lights
	EXTERIOR WALL—brick piers; terra cotta, cast stone, or concrete ornamentation
	ROOF—flat roof with shallow stepped parapet; decorative brickwork (diamond work, checker work, high-contrast colors)
	FENESTRATION—symmetrical

Single- and Double-Store Entries

Art Deco

Drawing based on a design (1909), The Radford Architectural Company Chicago

Art Deco

"Complete Store Front" (1922), International Steel and Iron Company

Art Deco

Cheevers Flower Shop (ca. 1916), Oklahoma City, Oklahoma

services. The stores were usually physically connected, so that utilities and façade treatments could be integrated. The major period for this development seems to have been the 1920s, although there were examples of shopping areas built before and long after that decade. They were referred to as artistic designs based on their unusual appearances, which derived from the use of architectural details as attention-getting devices. The artistic front was comprised of stores and offices that were integrated by one design concept. Sometimes the group reflected a particular quality of craftsmanship that set it apart from its neighbors, or the buildings referred to motifs, surface treatments, and patterns inspired by some style in the history of art. The phrase "artistic front" was of period usage.

The artistic front went directly to the cottage design vocabulary to create intersecting roof forms, gable fronts, stucco and Tudor-trim gables, and historical profiles all bound in clusters, so that individ-

14.12. The photograph of "Village Scene, Big Bear Lake, California" documents a stucco and timber frame artistic front that is one continuous treatment from the café on the left to the pharmacy on the right. Party walls that divide the stores come through the roof, and a dormer sits over each store. Authors' collection.

14.13. The business district of Ajo, Arizona was largely a Spanish revival artistic front. The row of stores is anchored by a two-story building on each end and an arcade with a red tile roof links the entire front. The finish is stucco and an ornamental parapet ties the center portion together. Authors' collection.

ual details could be perceived as belonging to a particular store. Thus each business separated itself from the others, yet still belonged to the group. In part, the artistic front attested to the power of the cottage-based neighborhood and to the successful use of industrially produced materials as a basis for design. Designers and builders alike had no difficulty in applying the housing vocabulary to commercial building. Occasionally these fronts were built as individual businesses (e.g., gas stations, florist shops, photography studios) and looked like cottages. Symbolically they clearly identified with the local residents and made owners appear sensitive to neighborhood design values.

Most artistic fronts had one large effect, say, a Spanish feeling, that linked several stores. In some of these arrangements, stores kept their own identity, but in others all the units were subsumed under the grand gesture. Building materials used for exterior details included stucco, brick, stone, terra cotta, marble, tiling of several kinds, and wood. Interior finish was generally not detailed, but it was not uncommon for an exterior treatment to be carried inside. Plastering, wood elements, color, and hardware all might have a broad application.

Motivating this approach to store design was the belief that exterior treatments invite favorable notice and encourage people to inspect the merchandise. Clever proportioning and correct details created the overall attractiveness of the artistic front. Much of this kind of commercial development was done at a residential scale, so that the stores seemed to fit into the community, and the shopping area looked and functioned something like a village. In other words,

Table 14.4. Characteristics of Artistic-Fronted Commercial Buildings

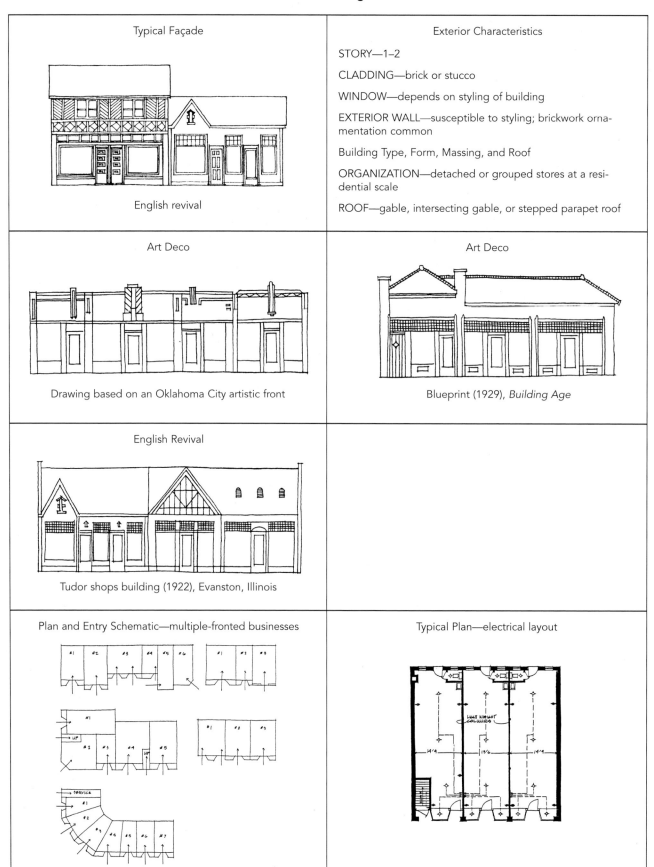

Typical Façade	Exterior Characteristics
English revival	STORY—1–2 CLADDING—brick or stucco WINDOW—depends on styling of building EXTERIOR WALL—susceptible to styling; brickwork ornamentation common Building Type, Form, Massing, and Roof ORGANIZATION—detached or grouped stores at a residential scale ROOF—gable, intersecting gable, or stepped parapet roof
Art Deco Drawing based on an Oklahoma City artistic front	**Art Deco** Blueprint (1929), *Building Age*
English Revival Tudor shops building (1922), Evanston, Illinois	
Plan and Entry Schematic—multiple-fronted businesses	**Typical Plan—electrical layout**

14.14. In 1926 the Fred Foltz Paint and Paper Store on Ohio Street in Terre Haute, Indiana was the epitome of a modern store. The rational display of the merchandise is related to the rational organization of the interior, including the modular metal ceiling and the even distribution of supporting rods and electric lights. Indiana Historical Society.

14.15. From this perspective one can see through this urban barbershop all the way to the storefront with its fixed glass-block transom. A classical metal ceiling design, pendant ceiling fixtures, and bentwood chairs make this an elegant single-fronted commercial space. Authors' collection.

the stores were disguised. Typical treatments included Spanish (stucco walls, tile roof), Tudor (stucco walls, slate roof, half timbering), art deco (glazed cladding, stylized ornament), moderne (structural glass, metal trim), and broad front (multiple fronts linked by terra-cotta trim).

PLAN TYPES FOR SINGLE-FRONT STORES

The interior organization in single-fronted stores of this time period was shaped by a building's long, narrow shell, which was enclosed by masonry load-bearing walls. The interior was created by partitions and store furniture, the design and placement of which were somewhat determined by the nature of the business. Typical plans included a display space and storage unique to the goods being sold and to the service, waiting, and security requirements. Like everything in this kind of vernacular, store furniture and other fixtures were industrially produced from a slightly different system of parts, and millwork companies produced most of these products.

Lighting was always a problem in a long, narrow store, and the introduction of transom lights helped illuminate the interiors. In time prism-glass panels of four-inch squares, glazed in sections, replaced the transom panes. Electric lighting finally solved the problem of illumination. Electric lights, however, required new reflectors for store windows and new

14.16. Merchandise is the most decorative element in many stores, such as The Fair Dry Goods Department Store (ca. 1902) in Bozeman, Montana. The metal ceiling is the only surface without goods. Authors' collection and Bozeman Historical Society.

14.17. A newsstand selling cigars could be tucked in the corner of a first-floor office building or train station, or constitute its own store in a multiple-entry building. This interior depends largely on print graphics and mosaic tile patterns for design. The benches imply that it is appropriate to sit, read, and smoke. Authors' collection.

indirect lighting for interiors. Lights were also required for cases and shelving, and so new bulbs, "daylight" or "blue bulbs," were developed to show true color indoors.

To illustrate a typical store interior for a single-front, we assembled a typical plan for a millinery and dry goods store and a newsstand and cigar store. Showcases and other millwork products are indicated on the plan or axonometric view. The millinery store is shown on the ground floor of a building; the entrance is splayed and centered between the show windows. The entry leads to the center aisle, which is fronted by counters and showcase furniture, behind which is the shelving against the wall. The back room in these stores was used for storage and toilet facilities, with larger storage and stockrooms in the basement. Special interior furniture for a specific store, as in this case, included a console, a freestanding mirrored room divider finished in veneered wood, showcases consisting of a base, glass or wood top (the latter for wrapping) and sliding doors in the back, and counters assembled from stiles, rails, and panels. Shelving was produced in units; it was common for the shelving to look like cabinetry and to be organized in bays by thin columns or pilasters to loom like cabinetry and to be organized in bays by thin columns or pilasters with an architrave and cornice across the top.

The newsstand entry is flush with the façade wall. The entry leads to the display room, with cases on both sides. Access to cases is from the front. The floor space is divided into three-quarters of the area for customers, amid the shelves of tobacco and cigars and racks of publications and one-quarter for the sales clerk and manager. The backspace, as in the dry goods store, is private space.

14.18. The Cooperstown Drug Company in North Dakota features paneled counters, marble countertops, a mosaic tile floor, art nouveau lamps, and pendant ceiling lamps. Authors' collection.

14.19. Before1920 many banks included a private space for women to conduct banking. Dubbed the "stocking room," it consisted of no more than a curtained space in one corner of the bank lobby. Authors' collection.

Millinery and Dry Goods, Newsstand and Cigar Store

Drugstore

The drugstore established planning patterns in the nineteenth century that remained intact for some time. Drugstore design followed closely the development of the pharmaceutical industry. At first druggists made prescriptions from raw materials and sold patent medicines. As the trade grew, the drugstore began to rely more on dispensing patented products and medicines that did not have to be concocted in the store. This shift changed its storage requirements. The store also started to sell items related to general health care, then added some food service—ice cream shops, candy counters, soda fountains, and the like. This last addition wrought a change in the store's interior design.

Bank

Interior space design for a bank was rather simple. There was a public space separated from the work space by a partition, with special locations along the partition for different kinds of transactions. The workspace also included a space for tellers, an office space, a bank officer's desk, and a vault. This arrangement could fit into almost any space. In banks with more interior volume a mezzanine level was introduced for additional offices, and in even larger buildings a directors' room might be included in the plan. Single- or first-floor arrangements included the banking room, a private office for the bank president or bank directors, and the vault. Eventually bank designs incorporated special facilities and spaces for women customers, largely translated in small banks as ladies' rest rooms. A *Building Age* article in 1920

Table 14.5. Characteristics of Plan Types for Single-Fronted Stores

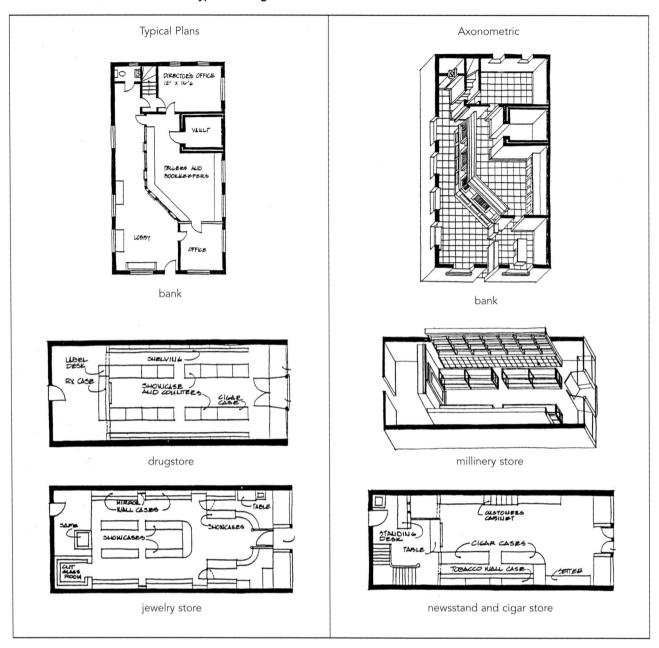

Typical Plans

bank

drugstore

jewelry store

Axonometric

bank

millinery store

newsstand and cigar store

encouraged designers to consider women before plans were drawn, because "beauty in architecture makes a conscious appeal to women. . . . The bank structure, the interior decorations and furnishings come in for a much more critical examination by the woman depositor." When the Fourth National Bank of Montgomery, Alabama was built in 1925, it included a ladies' alcove, separated from the main floor by a partition.[3]

The banking room had much in common with the development of the office regarding segregation of spaces. The bank partition separated the public lobby from the working space. Visually and physically a partition separated the bank patron from the bank clerk—the teller who handled money. The back of the banking partition included an arrangement of drawers and cupboards. Typical architectural furniture included a wood-paneled counter base and a high screen protected with metal grille work or wickets (which became known as a teller's cage) and sometimes the use of ornamental etched glass, polished plate glass, or chipped glass. More often than not, early-twentieth-century partitions were arranged in an irregular line, that is, not parallel to the wall. A canted corner was often used to emphasize the importance of a teller's window. Millwork companies also sold other bank furnishings, among these "check desks" that attached to walls or stood alone.

Bank millwork was susceptible to the aesthetic systems applied to other millwork products. Counters with ornamental panels, brackets, moldings, art glass, ornamental wickets for teller windows, railings, and other items made by assembling stiles, rails, panels, spindles, and balusters were made in the same way as goods for houses. Overall, bank interiors were somber, and their design effects and furniture had a unified appearance. As the vernacular bank became financially successful, there were changes in interior materials—substituting marble for wood—and a reworking of the façade.

14.20. The business postcard declaring "tie the bull outside" also offers insight into social conditions. The young woman and the typing table are portrayed as appendages to a manager's desk. She sits precariously between the furniture of male authority (roll-top desk and swivel chair) and an upholstered chaise lounge, a not-so-subtle reminder of the sexual nature of men and women's dissimilarities in the office. Authors' collection.

OFFICE INTERIORS

The second stories of small commercial buildings accommodated housing, often for the store owner's family or for offices. As businesses grew larger, offices constituted their own building types in single-fronted and multiple-fronted buildings. The interiors of modern vernacular workplaces, such as small banks, notary publics, abstract companies, and insurance and real estate offices, evolved and changed throughout the 1870–1960 period, as did their larger counterparts, because of technological advances such as centralized heating (radiators), plumbing, and telephones. Elevators and steel frames made skyscrapers possible.

Historian Angel Kwolek-Folland wrote persuasively about how social and cultural changes also affected office design.[4] One of the most significant of these changes was the influx of women into the workforce. The introduction of the typewriter in the 1880s brought women into offices to operate it, and from the 1890s their number grew so rapidly that by the 1910s women constituted a quarter of all clerical workers. In any occupation women had lower status than men and worked for lower wages, thus depressing the status of clerical work. Women's presence immediately raised the issue of how these sexually and socially different workers would fare in terms of

14.21. A female typist sits in very close proximity to three male workers. She works in a room whose walls are overlaid with calendar art illustrating ideal femininity. Authors' collection.

assimilation into a masculine environment. "Women's presence sexualized the office, creating several logistical and ideological management problems." Managers assumed that sexual attraction would result from the physical proximity of men and women in the workplace.

In the late nineteenth and early twentieth century the small spaces that typefied the precorporate office reinforced close relations among workers, since it was nearly impossible to remove any worker completely from other workers or from employers. An office staff of one to five people, divided from their employer only by a door or a waist-high wooden railing, was well supervised without elaborate methods.

14.22. An office without partitions or walls appears to put the three female clerks pictured on equal footing with their male colleague sitting in the corner. However, his roll-top desk, swivel chair, and vantage point of the room place him at a higher and supervisory status. Authors' collection.

14.23. With the exception of the telephone, this 1930-era scene shows few changes in small office design. The desk remains; the manager sits in a wooden swivel chair; and office railing is still in use. Authors' collection.

The work done in such offices was not officially stratified. In fact, the physical separation of workers—a mark of division of labor—would have undermined harmonious workplace relations in a small office. In these settings innumerable rules of polite behavior reinforced gender differences. Men were expected to rise when women entered a room, and male language contained two vocabularies—one for exchanges between men, and one for men and women.[5]

Women dominated the routine clerical positions that utilized machinery; women became the manual laborers of the office factory. Advertisements from the 1920s invariably show women operating most office machinery. Systematic management studies in the 1930s recommended that work spaces be divided on the basis of status and function. Spatial arrangements became a way to maximize the time workers spent at their tasks. One report emphasized that employees should be placed in front of, or around, the person having authority over them. Employee placement enabled supervisors to keep an eye on their activities.[6]

Specialized office furniture began to be introduced by the 1870s. Kwolek-Folland noted that there were no antecedents for office furniture and that early offices had been domestic spaces; therefore, the connection between public offices and domestic space lingered in household furnishings for offices. The use of domestic treatments was also present in the workplace. For example, a 1901 photograph of the America Philadelphia Incorporated insurance office in Salida, Colorado shows three seated men, one at a roll-top desk with a paper in hand, one at a flat desk with a typewriter, and another at a large flat-topped table upon which sits a vase of flowers and glass paperweights. A display case

14.24. By the 1950s a sea of wooden and metal desks, lined up one after the other, became the norm for clerks in large offices. This is the era of typing and secretarial pools. Fluorescents light the room; the linoleum pattern mimics the marching order of the desks. Metal blinds and window fans allow for some environmental adjustments. The lighting is general and not task specific. Authors' collection.

with mineral samples resides on the top shelf of the roll top. An ornamental aesthetic is present in a lively patterned wallpaper and a trim set with corner blocks. Not quite two decades later, the offices of the McCann Building in New Rochelle, New York had several walls paneled seven feet high with oak, a plate rail, and brackets in an arts-and-crafts treatment. The building's oak stair also included a square newel post.[7]

The roll-top desk became the prevailing office desk, and in historical photographs the desk provides the most architectural presence in a room. Sears, Roebuck and Company's 1902 catalog featured six serviceable "roll top curtain desks," the curtain being the high back. Sears's highest curtain model measured forty-nine inches and included six "pigeonhole filling boxes." Supporting pedestals of the desk had three drawers on the left side and, on the right side, a "book closet" (vertical partitions). In contrast to Sears's $18.45 desk is a $11.95 version, "great bargain high grade" roll-top curtain desk measuring 46 inches in curtain height. Its pedestals included a roomy cupboard on one side and four drawers on the other.[8]

The roll-top desk may be perceived now with a touch of nostalgia, as a timeless artifact of a gentler office culture. At the time, however, the desk was controversial, fraught with defenders and detractors.

The chief objection to the roll-top was that it became a receptacle for important papers, which could then be forgotten or lost. Business progressives believed that papers should be placed in files where they would be accessible to anyone. In addition, they complained that the height of a roll-top desk cut off light and air. In Adrian Forty's view scientific management had a pathological hatred for desk storage space and saw any cavity in a desk as providing an opportunity to hoard vital documents and obstruct the flow of paper through the office. Thus the typical clerk was left with a flat-top desk, with at most six drawers in it. The roll-top desk continued to be preferred by many executives on the grounds that it was useful for protecting confidential papers. In spite of the threat of disorder posed by such desks, office manuals of the 1910s accepted their use by executives. The disappearance of the roll-top, however, meant the clerk lost the ability to make the desk private. The top of the desk was expected to be in such good order that anything could be found at a moment's notice.[9]

The telephone brought new changes to the office, but contemporary photographs illustrate that office furniture types for desks and chairs, and architectural furniture for offices, such as railings, changed little in the 1920–1950 decades.

Table 14.6. Characteristics of Commercial Interiors, 1870–1900

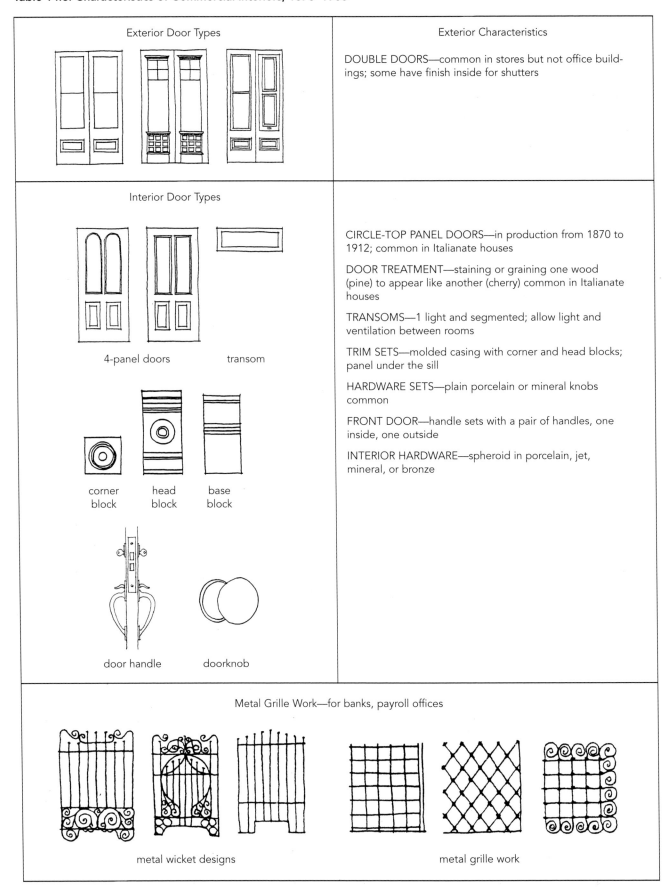

Exterior Door Types	Exterior Characteristics
	DOUBLE DOORS—common in stores but not office buildings; some have finish inside for shutters

Interior Door Types

4-panel doors   transom

corner block   head block   base block

door handle   doorknob

CIRCLE-TOP PANEL DOORS—in production from 1870 to 1912; common in Italianate houses

DOOR TREATMENT—staining or graining one wood (pine) to appear like another (cherry) common in Italianate houses

TRANSOMS—1 light and segmented; allow light and ventilation between rooms

TRIM SETS—molded casing with corner and head blocks; panel under the sill

HARDWARE SETS—plain porcelain or mineral knobs common

FRONT DOOR—handle sets with a pair of handles, one inside, one outside

INTERIOR HARDWARE—spheroid in porcelain, jet, mineral, or bronze

Metal Grille Work—for banks, payroll offices

metal wicket designs   metal grille work

Table 14.6. Characteristics of Commercial Interiors, 1870–1900 (continued)

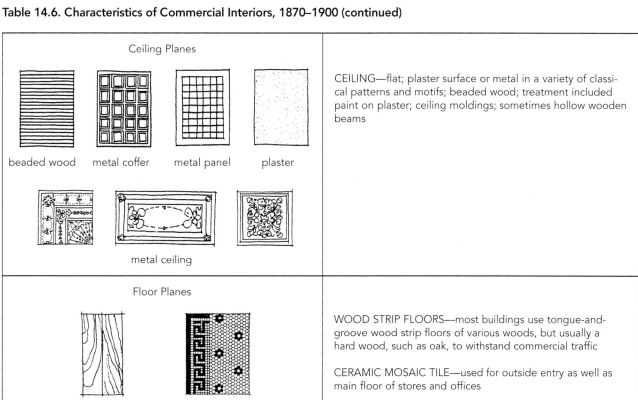

Ceiling Planes

beaded wood   metal coffer   metal panel   plaster

metal ceiling

CEILING—flat; plaster surface or metal in a variety of classical patterns and motifs; beaded wood; treatment included paint on plaster; ceiling moldings; sometimes hollow wooden beams

Floor Planes

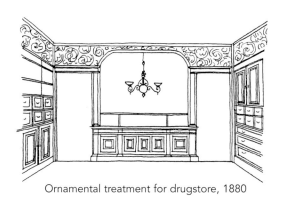

wood strip floor   ceramic mosaic tile

WOOD STRIP FLOORS—most buildings use tongue-and-groove wood strip floors of various woods, but usually a hard wood, such as oak, to withstand commercial traffic

CERAMIC MOSAIC TILE—used for outside entry as well as main floor of stores and offices

Wall Plane and Architectural Furniture for Stores

Ornamental treatment for drugstore, 1880

Ornamental drugstore counter and special glass

Architectural Furniture for Drugstores

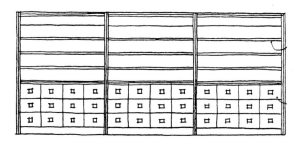

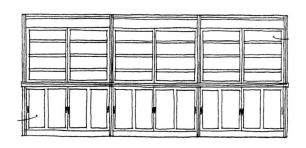

Tincture shelving with adjustable shelving and drawers

Tincture shelving with adjustable shelves and drawers

Table 14.6. Characteristics of Commercial Interiors, 1870–1900 (continued)

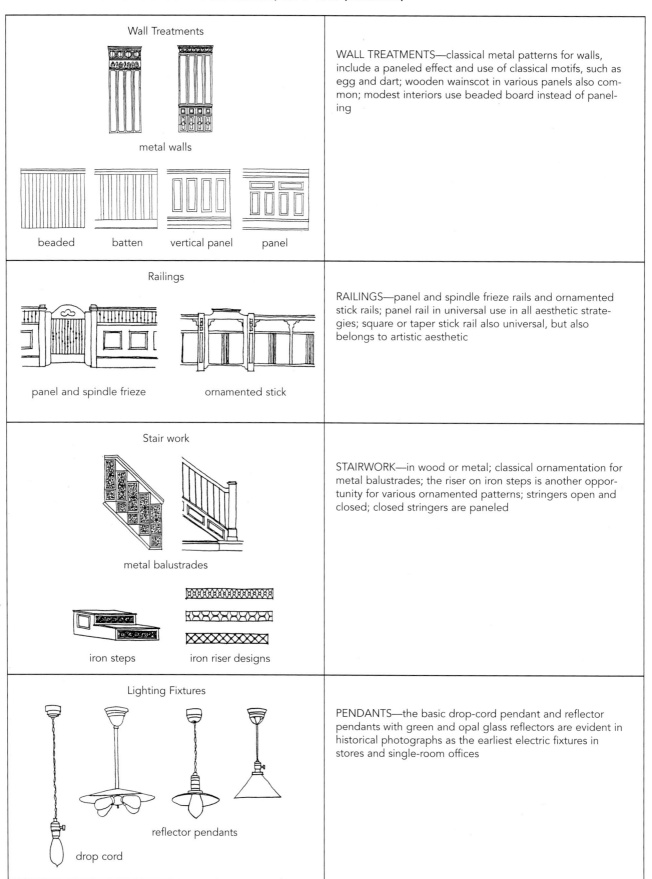

Wall Treatments	WALL TREATMENTS—classical metal patterns for walls, include a paneled effect and use of classical motifs, such as egg and dart; wooden wainscot in various panels also common; modest interiors use beaded board instead of paneling
metal walls	
beaded batten vertical panel panel	
Railings	RAILINGS—panel and spindle frieze rails and ornamented stick rails; panel rail in universal use in all aesthetic strategies; square or taper stick rail also universal, but also belongs to artistic aesthetic
panel and spindle frieze ornamented stick	
Stair work	STAIRWORK—in wood or metal; classical ornamentation for metal balustrades; the riser on iron steps is another opportunity for various ornamented patterns; stringers open and closed; closed stringers are paneled
metal balustrades	
iron steps iron riser designs	
Lighting Fixtures	PENDANTS—the basic drop-cord pendant and reflector pendants with green and opal glass reflectors are evident in historical photographs as the earliest electric fixtures in stores and single-room offices
reflector pendants	
drop cord	

Table 14.7. Characteristics of Commercial Interiors, 1901–1915

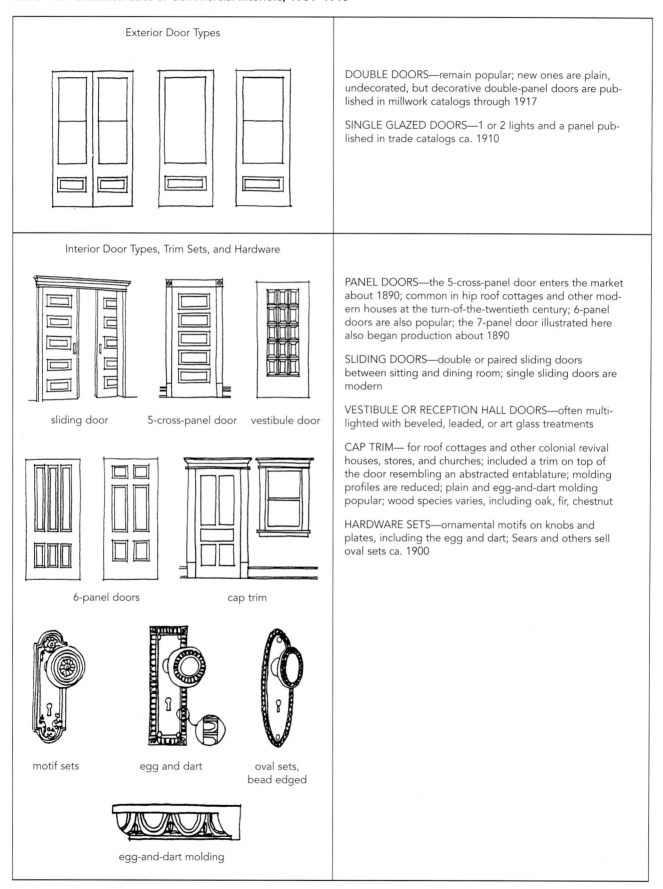

Exterior Door Types

DOUBLE DOORS—remain popular; new ones are plain, undecorated, but decorative double-panel doors are published in millwork catalogs through 1917

SINGLE GLAZED DOORS—1 or 2 lights and a panel published in trade catalogs ca. 1910

Interior Door Types, Trim Sets, and Hardware

sliding door   5-cross-panel door   vestibule door

6-panel doors   cap trim

motif sets   egg and dart   oval sets, bead edged

egg-and-dart molding

PANEL DOORS—the 5-cross-panel door enters the market about 1890; common in hip roof cottages and other modern houses at the turn-of-the-twentieth century; 6-panel doors are also popular; the 7-panel door illustrated here also began production about 1890

SLIDING DOORS—double or paired sliding doors between sitting and dining room; single sliding doors are modern

VESTIBULE OR RECEPTION HALL DOORS—often multi-lighted with beveled, leaded, or art glass treatments

CAP TRIM— for roof cottages and other colonial revival houses, stores, and churches; included a trim on top of the door resembling an abstracted entablature; molding profiles are reduced; plain and egg-and-dart molding popular; wood species varies, including oak, fir, chestnut

HARDWARE SETS—ornamental motifs on knobs and plates, including the egg and dart; Sears and others sell oval sets ca. 1900

Table 14.7. Characteristics of Commercial Interiors, 1901–1915 (continued)

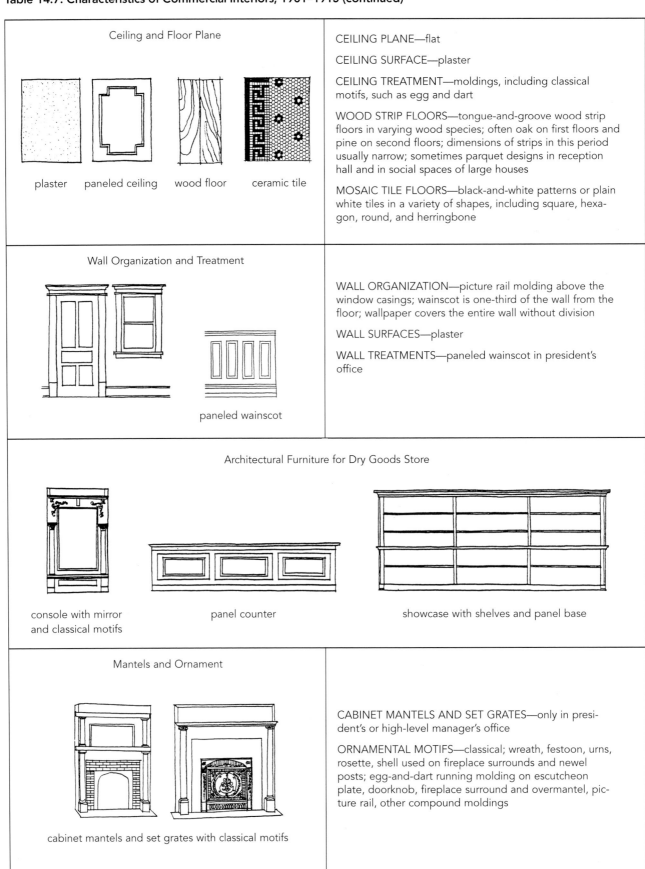

Ceiling and Floor Plane

plaster   paneled ceiling   wood floor   ceramic tile

CEILING PLANE—flat

CEILING SURFACE—plaster

CEILING TREATMENT—moldings, including classical motifs, such as egg and dart

WOOD STRIP FLOORS—tongue-and-groove wood strip floors in varying wood species; often oak on first floors and pine on second floors; dimensions of strips in this period usually narrow; sometimes parquet designs in reception hall and in social spaces of large houses

MOSAIC TILE FLOORS—black-and-white patterns or plain white tiles in a variety of shapes, including square, hexagon, round, and herringbone

Wall Organization and Treatment

paneled wainscot

WALL ORGANIZATION—picture rail molding above the window casings; wainscot is one-third of the wall from the floor; wallpaper covers the entire wall without division

WALL SURFACES—plaster

WALL TREATMENTS—paneled wainscot in president's office

Architectural Furniture for Dry Goods Store

console with mirror and classical motifs   panel counter   showcase with shelves and panel base

Mantels and Ornament

cabinet mantels and set grates with classical motifs

CABINET MANTELS AND SET GRATES—only in president's or high-level manager's office

ORNAMENTAL MOTIFS—classical; wreath, festoon, urns, rosette, shell used on fireplace surrounds and newel posts; egg-and-dart running molding on escutcheon plate, doorknob, fireplace surround and overmantel, picture rail, other compound moldings

Table 14.7. Characteristics of Commercial Interiors, 1901–1915 (continued)

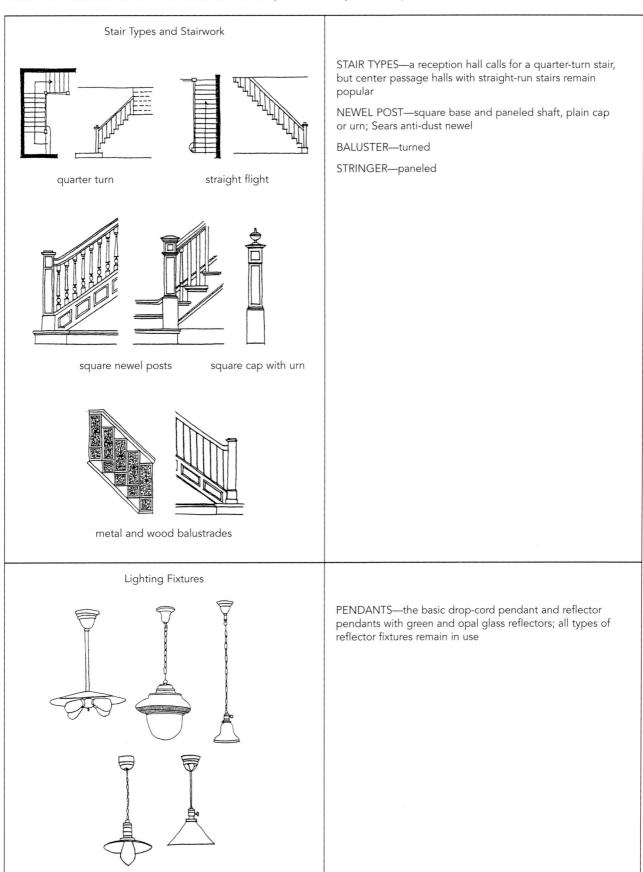

Stair Types and Stairwork

quarter turn   straight flight

square newel posts   square cap with urn

metal and wood balustrades

STAIR TYPES—a reception hall calls for a quarter-turn stair, but center passage halls with straight-run stairs remain popular

NEWEL POST—square base and paneled shaft, plain cap or urn; Sears anti-dust newel

BALUSTER—turned

STRINGER—paneled

Lighting Fixtures

PENDANTS—the basic drop-cord pendant and reflector pendants with green and opal glass reflectors; all types of reflector fixtures remain in use

Table 14.8. Characteristics of Commercial Interiors, 1910–1925

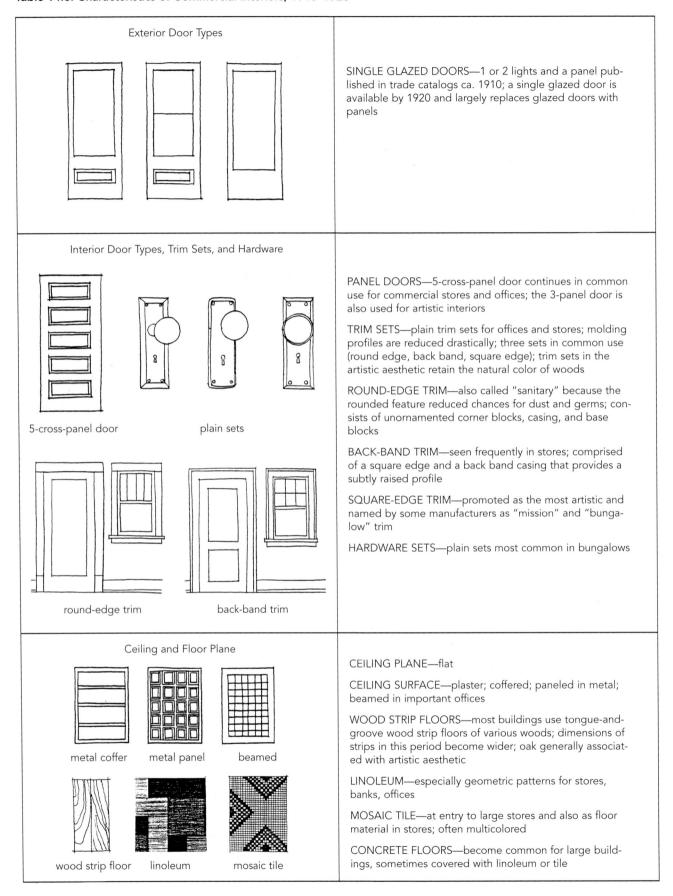

Exterior Door Types

SINGLE GLAZED DOORS—1 or 2 lights and a panel published in trade catalogs ca. 1910; a single glazed door is available by 1920 and largely replaces glazed doors with panels

Interior Door Types, Trim Sets, and Hardware

5-cross-panel door   plain sets

round-edge trim   back-band trim

PANEL DOORS—5-cross-panel door continues in common use for commercial stores and offices; the 3-panel door is also used for artistic interiors

TRIM SETS—plain trim sets for offices and stores; molding profiles are reduced drastically; three sets in common use (round edge, back band, square edge); trim sets in the artistic aesthetic retain the natural color of woods

ROUND-EDGE TRIM—also called "sanitary" because the rounded feature reduced chances for dust and germs; consists of unornamented corner blocks, casing, and base blocks

BACK-BAND TRIM—seen frequently in stores; comprised of a square edge and a back band casing that provides a subtly raised profile

SQUARE-EDGE TRIM—promoted as the most artistic and named by some manufacturers as "mission" and "bungalow" trim

HARDWARE SETS—plain sets most common in bungalows

Ceiling and Floor Plane

metal coffer   metal panel   beamed

wood strip floor   linoleum   mosaic tile

CEILING PLANE—flat

CEILING SURFACE—plaster; coffered; paneled in metal; beamed in important offices

WOOD STRIP FLOORS—most buildings use tongue-and-groove wood strip floors of various woods; dimensions of strips in this period become wider; oak generally associated with artistic aesthetic

LINOLEUM—especially geometric patterns for stores, banks, offices

MOSAIC TILE—at entry to large stores and also as floor material in stores; often multicolored

CONCRETE FLOORS—become common for large buildings, sometimes covered with linoleum or tile

Table 14.8. Characteristics of Commercial Interiors, 1910–1925 (continued)

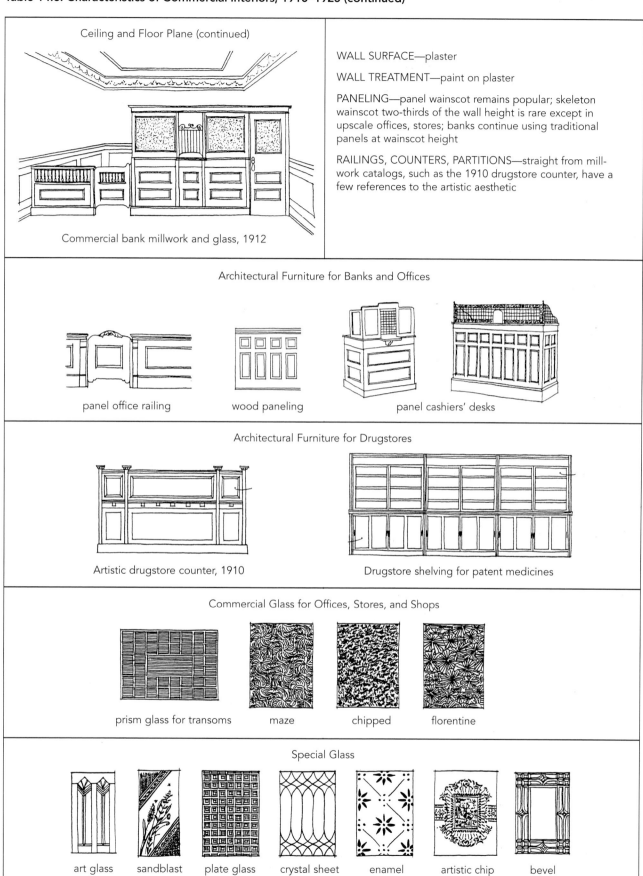

Ceiling and Floor Plane (continued)

Commercial bank millwork and glass, 1912

WALL SURFACE—plaster

WALL TREATMENT—paint on plaster

PANELING—panel wainscot remains popular; skeleton wainscot two-thirds of the wall height is rare except in upscale offices, stores; banks continue using traditional panels at wainscot height

RAILINGS, COUNTERS, PARTITIONS—straight from millwork catalogs, such as the 1910 drugstore counter, have a few references to the artistic aesthetic

Architectural Furniture for Banks and Offices

panel office railing   wood paneling   panel cashiers' desks

Architectural Furniture for Drugstores

Artistic drugstore counter, 1910   Drugstore shelving for patent medicines

Commercial Glass for Offices, Stores, and Shops

prism glass for transoms   maze   chipped   florentine

Special Glass

art glass   sandblast   plate glass   crystal sheet   enamel   artistic chip   bevel

Table 14.8. Characteristics of Commercial Interiors, 1910–1925 (continued)

Lighting Fixtures	
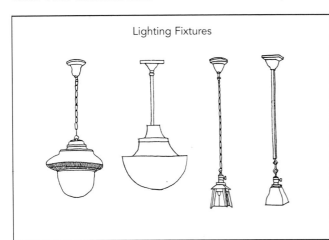	PENDANTS—with a large white glass bowl suspended from a brass stem or chain is the most used type for offices, stores, and public buildings; arranged in a grid on the ceiling plane; stems and canopies often brass; also in use are artistic shades for pendants, including art glass and square shades DOMES AND BRANCHED FIXTURES—small offices and stores use domestically scaled fixtures appropriate for residential use, such as leaded art glass shades

Table 14.9. Characteristics of Commercial Interiors, 1940–1960

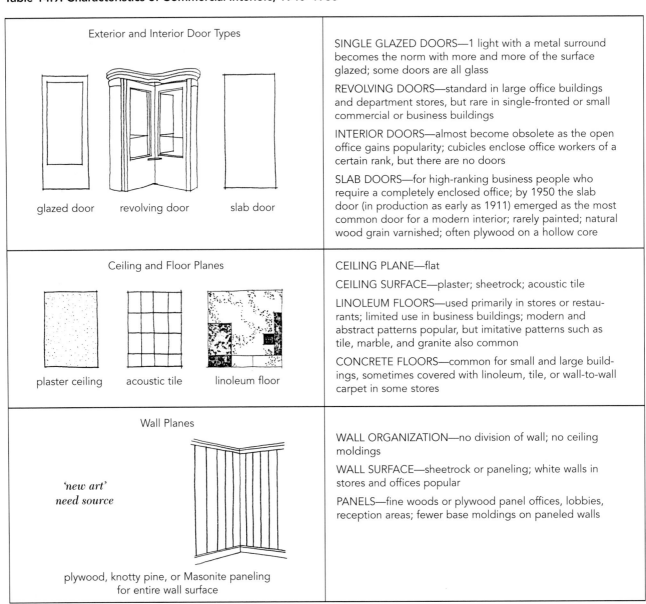

Exterior and Interior Door Types	
glazed door revolving door slab door	SINGLE GLAZED DOORS—1 light with a metal surround becomes the norm with more and more of the surface glazed; some doors are all glass REVOLVING DOORS—standard in large office buildings and department stores, but rare in single-fronted or small commercial or business buildings INTERIOR DOORS—almost become obsolete as the open office gains popularity; cubicles enclose office workers of a certain rank, but there are no doors SLAB DOORS—for high-ranking business people who require a completely enclosed office; by 1950 the slab door (in production as early as 1911) emerged as the most common door for a modern interior; rarely painted; natural wood grain varnished; often plywood on a hollow core
Ceiling and Floor Planes plaster ceiling acoustic tile linoleum floor	CEILING PLANE—flat CEILING SURFACE—plaster; sheetrock; acoustic tile LINOLEUM FLOORS—used primarily in stores or restaurants; limited use in business buildings; modern and abstract patterns popular, but imitative patterns such as tile, marble, and granite also common CONCRETE FLOORS—common for small and large buildings, sometimes covered with linoleum, tile, or wall-to-wall carpet in some stores
Wall Planes *'new art'* *need source* plywood, knotty pine, or Masonite paneling for entire wall surface	WALL ORGANIZATION—no division of wall; no ceiling moldings WALL SURFACE—sheetrock or paneling; white walls in stores and offices popular PANELS—fine woods or plywood panel offices, lobbies, reception areas; fewer base moldings on paneled walls

Table 14.9. Characteristics of Commercial Interiors, 1940–1960 (continued)

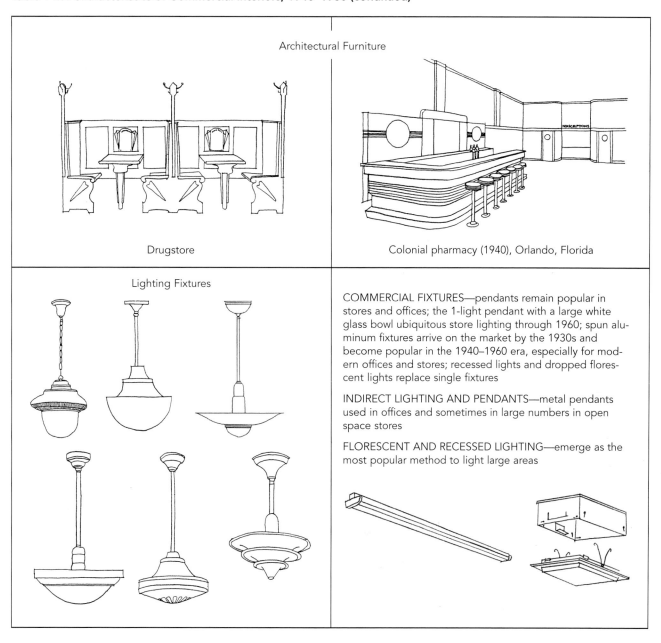

Architectural Furniture

Drugstore

Colonial pharmacy (1940), Orlando, Florida

Lighting Fixtures

COMMERCIAL FIXTURES—pendants remain popular in stores and offices; the 1-light pendant with a large white glass bowl ubiquitous store lighting through 1960; spun aluminum fixtures arrive on the market by the 1930s and become popular in the 1940–1960 era, especially for modern offices and stores; recessed lights and dropped florescent lights replace single fixtures

INDIRECT LIGHTING AND PENDANTS—metal pendants used in offices and sometimes in large numbers in open space stores

FLORESCENT AND RECESSED LIGHTING—emerge as the most popular method to light large areas

BUILDING TYPE: CHURCH

Vernacular church design focuses on the general form of the church building and the organization of its interior space. The Christian tradition of aligning churches on an east–west axis holds true for many vernacular churches, and the west-facing elevation is often the most prominent and may include the entrance. We identify six different types of church structures based on their essential design characteristics, and six different interior plans, based on the proportion of length to width, the handling of aisles, and the arrangement of seats. Generally, the shape of a church does not necessarily dictate its interior plan. Some sanctuary plans cannot be read from the outside.

The examples used to illustrate design concepts are taken from neighborhood, small-town, and rural sources. The sample is restricted to churches drawn by architects but intended for replication and churches designed and built by local people. A number of church organizations hired architects to design simple churches that could be erected in frontier, territorial, and developing community contexts. The idea of establishing generic church types as part of evangelical missions was important because the institutionalization of spiritual life in a community through the building of a church is a fundamental part of the history of vernacular architecture. Our point here is to demonstrate that the industrial system played much the same role in church construction that it played in residential, commercial, and other types of building activity. For example, the industrial housing company Aladdin included a church design as part of its "company town."

CHURCH EXTERIORS

Most vernacular churches were of wood-frame construction with wood cladding, but brick, both as load-bearing wall construction and as brick veneer over frame, was common. There were also stone vernacular churches; some were imitations of traditional models and others were simply the work of local stonemasons. Of all these materials stone is the most local, suggesting that at one time people with the skill to build in stone lived in many regions of the country.

A body of literature addresses the rationale for vernacular church design. For example, in 1853 the Central Committee of the General Congregational Convention published *A Book of Plans for Churches and Parsonages*, based on designs by leading architects: Richard Upjohn, James Renwick, and Henry Austin. The committee requested designs that could be replicated in the new towns and villages of the West. The church reissued this book in 1892 without changing anything in the original, which makes it relevant for our discussion.

Almost every aspect of church design is covered in the essay that precedes the plates, and many of the committee's concerns were related to issues in vernacular church architecture. Even the definition of what a church should be is of interest: "a place for the unified and intelligible worship of God by the whole assembled company."[1] Congregationalists, as their name implies, intended to be democratic and social.

The committee urged the church to adopt a simple architecture, with rationality being more important than emotional responses, and social values preferred over individual ones. Churches were not to be "temples of taste." The ideal church should have a commanding site and a spire (the recognized sign of religion). As for the interior, it should "correspond in style to the better class of dwellings possessed by those who occupy the church."[2] The properly built church would also be properly equipped, with a businesslike environment and a workshop complete with tools. A church should not have to double up on the use of space. There was to be a minister's room and places for the congregation to socialize. The church and its site should express a sense of time and place.

As for aesthetics, there should be no imitation of materials; things that looked like wood should be made of wood. Every church should utilize the resources of the site in construction. There was a pragmatic side to this design. Proper ventilation was important, and what we think of today as the human factor was to be taken into account in pew design. The preferred seating called for two aisles along the sides rather than a center-aisle format. Galleries were not to be hung by iron rods from the roof. Straight staircases were preferable, and the church should not have too many windows. Stained glass, in moderation, was acceptable, but interior colors should be in harmony. A stark white interior was to be avoided.

Twentieth-century essays on the subject address most of the same issues. That church design should facilitate preaching was unanimously agreed upon, but there were disagreements in other areas. Writing in 1921, Henry Tralle stated that the auditorium should be oblong and never more than twice as long as it was wide.[3] M. W. Brabham believed that the shape should be rectangular, in proportions of 3:4 or 4:6.[4] Similarly, these writers had their own ideas about aisle width, pulpit placement, acoustics, and similar topics. Most writers recommended against center-aisle plans, because preachers believed that this plan divided the congregation. On the other hand, parishioners liked the center-aisle plan for weddings and funerals. These authorities argued for separate worship and teaching rooms. They rejected the so-called Akron plan, which had four aisles and segmented rows and placed instructional rooms adjacent to the auditorium, separated by a folding partition that could be opened for additional seating during services.

The principal church roof was the gable, and for a long time the shape of a gable, which set a tone for the overall design, was a direct expression of the kind of roof truss used in construction. Scissors, arch-braced, and kingpost trusses were the most frequently used types. A scissors truss creates a sharply pitched roof, which is effective for Gothic treatments. The arch-braced truss has a wider gable, as does the kingpost.

CENTER-STEEPLE AND GABLE-END CHURCH

The center-steeple church was one of the most common types built. It was truly a national church type with plan options. Façade design relied on several center-oriented devices: the steps and porch, entry doors, window in the tower, belfry, and spire all visually aligned. The steeple dominated the façade of the church, and the entire organization built toward the steeple, including the gable roof, which helped pull the façade skyward. Designs with higher porches might align the windows and doors to broaden the elevation. The fenestration was symmetrical, and the rest of the wall was only modestly ornamented with cornerboards and fascia. In steeple design the tower was about half the height of the entire structure, which left the lantern/belfry and spire in equal proportions to the tower. The tower might be built into the wall or stand separate from it. When the tower projected from the façade, it often served as a vestibule. Despite its vertical accent, this type of

Table 15.1. Characteristics of Center-Steeple and Gable-End Churches

Center-Steeple Church	Exterior Characteristics
	STORY—1 CLADDING—clapboard WINDOW—round-headed or Gothic ENTRANCE—door on center with steeple; paired doors common; sometimes hood or roof over door ROOF—gable STEEPLE—tower; often square, pierced with window or louver, lantern-louver; most used as belfry 4-or-6-sided; terminates in cross or finial FENESTRATION—symmetrical
Gable-End Church 	STORY—1 CLADDING—clapboard WINDOW—round-headed or Gothic ENTRANCE—door on center with steeple; paired doors common; sometimes hood or roof over door GABLE—ornamented with shingles, brackets, stickwork motifs; sometimes clipped gable; sometimes boxed returns ROOF—gable STEEPLE—short or no steeple at all; lantern and spire set behind gable roof; a lantern-louver for the belfry; 4-sided spire most common FENESTRATION—symmetrical
Arch-Braced Truss with a tie-beam	**Section, kingpost trusses**
Scissor Truss for frame churches with a clerestory	**Section, Scissor Truss** with hammer-beam braces

Table 15.1. Characteristics of Center-Steeple and Gable-End Churches (continued)

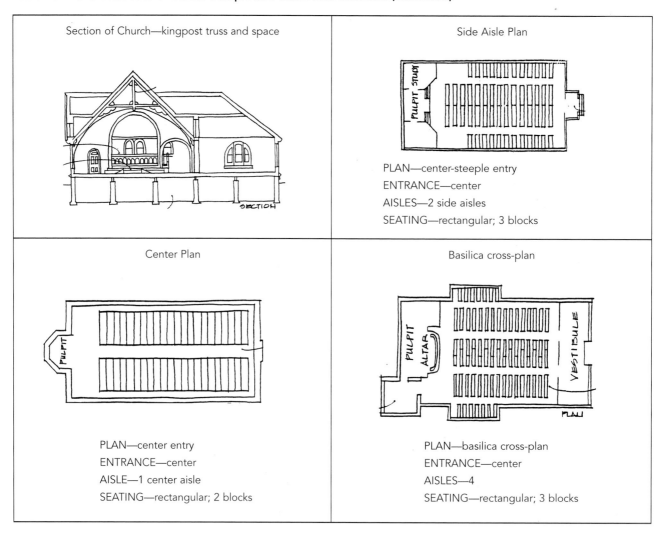

Section of Church—kingpost truss and space	Side Aisle Plan
	PLAN—center-steeple entry ENTRANCE—center AISLES—2 side aisles SEATING—rectangular; 3 blocks
Center Plan	**Basilica cross-plan**
PLAN—center entry ENTRANCE—center AISLE—1 center aisle SEATING—rectangular; 2 blocks	PLAN—basilica cross-plan ENTRANCE—center AISLES—4 SEATING—rectangular; 3 blocks

church was earthbound, directly accessible, and orderly. The center steeple interior had one of two seating plans: the center-aisle plan or the side-aisle format.

The gable-end church was a widely disseminated building style, especially in rural areas; its simple gable roof and end wall have been suitable for many denominations. It was often sited in an open area where the understated, straightforward quality of the form created a strong profile—a sensible relief against a natural background. Larger versions of this church had two-story interiors and a broad west end, which might be ornamented. Most of these frame churches were clad in clapboards, shingles, and boards with battens. They also had some gable finish in patterns borrowed from cottage design. The gable-end church was also built with brick and stone,

and the dominant plan was a center aisle with a strong axis from the entry to the chancel. As indicated by its name, the gable-end church exposes a broad gable to the street, the façade being subdivided into a few simple forms. Three-bay organization (window–entrance–window) was most common. Since the scale of these buildings was often residential, it is not surprising to find residential gable ornament on their façades. The ornamentation scheme included shingles that divided the gable visually from the rest of the wall, stickwork at the head of the gable, and brackets at the eaves. There was a two-story version of the gable-end style that might not carry any other design element. A large, broad gable rose sharply to full height, and windows, usually stained glass, pierced the wall. The entrance was built on the center axis of the façade. This kind of building might not have any

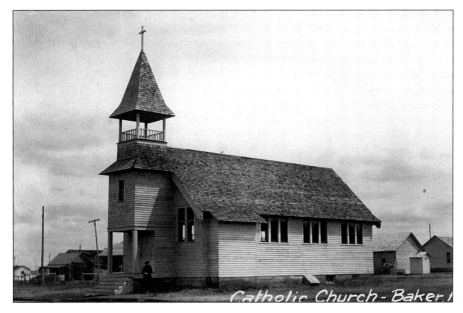

15.1. This plain Catholic church in Baker, Montana has good proportions in the relation of the steeple to the body of the church. Authors' collection.

15.2. Like a gable-end house, this Methodist Episcopal church in Richland, New York takes advantage of the broad open gable to define its purpose and organize its aesthetic. Authors' collection.

tower on the roof or any other intersecting sections. The side elevations might feature large windows to light the broad central space.

GABLE AND ELL AND SIDE-STEEPLE CHURCHES

The gable and ell design utilizes large elements and the intersection of its two broad wings to create a substantial interior space. The gables were wide, and each section could be built as high as two stories. Broad gables were opportunities for window groupings and stained glass. Overall the design consisted of large geometric pieces. Even the trim boards were cut to emphasize the geometry: many were wide boards painted a color that was complementary to the wall, so that the trim outlined and framed entire sections. At the juncture of the ell, the tower might stand attached to the main building or be built partially into the wall, so that the base of the tower was also the entrance to the church. Vertically, the tower and lantern were about the same height as the gable on the façade, with the spire about one-third the height of the tower and lantern combined.

Side-steeple churches had a west wall organization that relied on the interaction of the massing ele-

Table 15.2. Characteristics of Gable and Ell and Side-Steeple Churches

Gable and Ell Church	Exterior Characteristics
	STORY—1 CLADDING—clapboard WINDOW—peak-head or Gothic; pair or triple windows on façade ENTRANCE—small porch; tower base serves as vestibule EXTERIOR WALL—elaborate; sidewall has multiple windows and pronounced mullions ROOF—intersecting gable STEEPLE—at the ell; tower serves as entrance; lantern-exposed belfry; 4-side spire with finial FENESTRATION—symmetrical
Side-Steeple Church	**Exterior Characteristics**
	STORY—1 CLADDING—clapboard, brick or board and batten WINDOW—peak-head or pointed arch ENTRANCE—few steps; small porch; double door; many have no porch roof or hood; tower base serves as vestibule ROOF—gable STEEPLE—lantern; often open belfry; 4–6 sided spire; often shingled
Side Entry Plan	**Side Entry—Akron plan**
PLAN—side entry; tower shifts outside of main body of church ENTRANCE—tower base is entry vestibule AISLES—4; no center aisle SEATING—segmented into 3 blocks	PLAN—Akron side entry; separate room for Sunday School and classrooms ENTRANCE—side AISLES—center and 2 sides SEATING—segmented into 2 blocks

ments—the broad gable and the steeple—for effect. The steeple usually was composed in sections, building toward the spire, and the gable had a window grouping, sometimes of differently shaped windows. The placement of the steeple to the side required a bold window treatment on the façade in order to balance the design. A grouping of windows or a large window with subdivisions was quite common. Other elements that contributed to the unification of the design seemed to stem from the power of the gable to frame simple geometric shapes, many of which could be echoed in the steeple. In churches that had north–south as well as east–west gables, gable-end treatments might vary. North–south gables might also reflect modest transepts; however, transepts were not standard on vernacular churches, as most employed deep, wide naves.

Tower design was characterized by divisions of the structure; a breakdown from three to five distinct sections was common. Tower placement varied, but few were freestanding. Most towers mitigated the joining of the tower and gable, regardless of whether the tower was built into, or stood next to, the body of the building. The use of ornament on these buildings was restrained, but shingle work and stickwork were common in gables, as were cornerboards and other molding plants that divide walls into panels.

The side-steeple church was a holistically conceived building with few divisions among the constituent design elements and emphasis on containing all elements within the gable's embrace. This type of church was likely to have either an oblong or a square plan. The oblong type had three different seating configurations: a three-aisle plan, a center-aisle plan, and a two-aisle plan. The churches with these plans were all nineteenth-century buildings. The square-plan examples are twentieth-century churches, built especially from 1905 to 1925. More often than not the pew arrangement in both oblong and square churches was segmented rather than rectangular.

TWIN-TOWER AND TEMPLE-FRONTED CHURCH

The twin-tower design enhances the façade and relies on symmetrical massing for organization and aesthetic effect. Towers dominate the scheme, but towers and wall are integrated through proportional vertical and horizontal elements. For example, the width of the wall may be one and a half or two times the width of a tower, and sections of the wall and tower may align through stringcourses and cornices. These churches reflected historical treatments of façades and accordingly had special windows, moldings, and other accents. The towers and the gable end usually had some detailing that linked all three, such as water tables, stringcourses, and fascia boards.

15.3. A Seventh-Day Adventist church in Anoka, Minnesota features mirror-image symmetry and large simple forms that create a large wall or screen, through which parishioners pass. Reading from left to right, the three-part organization of tower, gable/entrance and tower is both classical and religious; the overall aesthetic is classical. Authors' collection.

Table 15.2. Characteristics of Twin-Tower and Temple-Fronted Churches

Twin-Tower Churches	Exterior Characteristics
	CLADDING—clapboard or brick WINDOW—Gothic- or round-headed; ornamented west wall window ENTRANCE—central or in towers; high steps; small porch; wing walls EXTERIOR WALL—horizontal and vertical divisions BAY ORGANIZATION—3 STEEPLE—2 twin square towers projecting from façade; lantern, square or 6-sided spires, shingled FENESTRATION—symmetrical
Temple-Fronted Church	Exterior Characteristics
	CLADDING—clapboard or brick WINDOW—rectangular sash; many lights ENTRANCE—double doors with pediment flanked by pilasters PORCH—wide and deep; low steps; portico projects from main body; 2–4 columns and full pediment ROOF—gable STEEPLE—none ENTRANCE—centered; portico or projecting vestibule FENESTRATION—symmetrical
Basilica Plan	**Basilica with Cross-Plan**
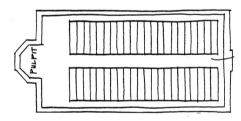 PLAN—center entry ENTRANCE—center AISLE—1 center aisle SEATING—rectangular; 2 blocks	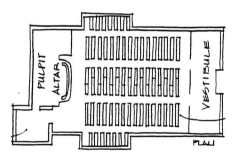 PLAN—tower shifts outside of main body of church ENTRANCE—center AISLES—3–5 SEATING—rectangular; 3 blocks

15.4. A corner location allowed this twin tower arrangement to differentiate between the towers. The tower near the corner identifies the church from a distance. This is a Gothic church with pointed and wheel windows in the gable end and the towers. The towers also have major and minor entrances, separated by a large stained-glass window. Knoxville, Pennsylvania, ca. 1906. Authors' collection.

The expressive qualities in this kind of church depended on the window treatment in the gable between the towers; on the entry, which was usually just below the window, and on the towers; which could be rendered in different shapes, profiles, and materials. As for seating plans, the format of rectilinear rows seems to have been most common.

In temple-fronted churches a large portico projected from the façade. Although the portico was derived from historical architecture, the use of orders was not extensive; Tuscan seems the most popular. The portico was almost as wide as the main body of the church, but the side aisles of the nave often projected beyond the portico. This arrangement set up an echo of pediment forms: the raking cornice of the pediment was repeated on the roof of the nave, so that the two forms established parallel planes. A great deal of wall space was given over to windows in order to admit large quantities of light. The walls exhibited little division because the fenestration was the primary organizer of the side elevations, just as the portico was the prime element of the façade. There was little ornamentation; even the entablatures were plain. Occasionally one finds an urn or a carved piece in the broken pediment over the entrance door. The temple-fronted church was the most classical of the vernacular types, because of the use of a temple-fronted portico or a façade organization based on pilasters placed at regular intervals. A composition of this kind linked the church to a colonial treatment, which allowed the fenestration to be double-hung windows, sometimes with circle-top upper lights. The seating plan for this church favored three-aisle, segmented rows, but there is evidence that the straight-row plan was also used.

CHURCH PLAN AND INTERIORS

The church plan was reduced to half a dozen popular formats, which could be installed in almost any kind of church. The basilica plan, regardless of the aisle arrangement, was the prevailing type. Vernacular churches did not use the cross plan extensively. If these churches had cross arms or transepts (if the term is appropriate for vernacular churches), they were very shallow. The seating plans, composed of straight, curved, or segmented rows, did not follow a precise logic. But the segmented rows were more popular in churches with wide (square-floor plan) auditoriums. The concept of the wide room, perhaps derived from the Germanic *Hallenkirche,* or the American meetinghouse, is a key element in vernacular churches.

The development of the chancel and choir spaces in these churches was not discussed because, although there were minor differences in the arrangements of these areas, the magnitude of the differences was not great. A number of the design concepts for churches originally were executed on the assumption that in finishing the church, adjustments would be carried out to suit a specific liturgy. While consideration was given to all the religious denominations, the majority of the churches examined were Protestant.

15.5. The exposure of roof structure in the Holy Trinity Church in Greensboro, Missouri is an old tradition in church building. Metaphorically, trusses, beams, and brackets are often thought to represent the inside of a ship. Authors' collection.

15.6. Everything in the Union Church in Orwell, New York is oriented toward the half-dome arch. The ceiling is decorated, and segmental arches mask the joints between the wall and ceiling. A chandelier focuses attention to the east. Authors' collection.

Trusses were more than supports for roofs. In many churches the trusses were left exposed so that they were part of the ceiling and the overall scheme. Truss elements could be finished to add another dimension to a design concept. Section drawings illustrate some types of interior organization, the way the volume was subdivided, and the relationship between the roof form and the interior. These drawings also provide an opportunity to illustrate the church's dependence on millwork products. (See Table 15.1 for truss types and sectional drawings.) Wood—as structure and finish, as wall and furniture—was the key material. (see Elements, Architectural Furniture: Church)

16

SUPPORT SYSTEMS

———◆———

Support systems represent the gradual but steady increase in the presence of service lines and pipes and related equipment in vernacular buildings. Most of these developments share a historical pattern in that the new service was, at first, highly visible and then began to retreat into the walls, floors, and ceilings, or in the case of equipment, into designated spaces. These changes also produced a number of large and small appliances marketed as conveniences. The control and management of buildings became technology-based.

HEATING AND VENTILATING SYSTEMS

The history of heating and ventilating in vernacular interior architecture reflects the general historical development of building technology—including new devices and new fuels—that characterizes all sectors of American architecture. During the period under study, principal heating fuels were wood, both hard and soft coal, coke, corncobs, fuel oil, kerosene, natural gas, and electricity. Heating systems included fireplaces (some with inserted hearth or mantel furnaces), stoves, hot-air furnaces, low- and high-pressure hot water, and low- and high-pressure steam. The impact of these systems on interior design centered on the presence of

grates, pipes, registers, and radiators. Many of the elements of these systems received surface ornamentation—usually a pattern—and color. The latter was applied as enamel, bronze, or gold finishes; electroplating; and leaf plating. In the case of radiators, the shape and profile of the radiator as well as its placement also had an effect on interior arrangements.

Fireplace Heating

Fireplace heating was ineffective, but it had strong emotional appeal and remains a means of heating. The simplest fireplace system heated one room by radiation, and the success of the unit depended on its drafting capability, which was often tied to the design of the fireplace throat. Most twentieth-century fireplaces were capable of heating more than one room, by drawing air from the room in which they were located as well as from outside, and passing that air behind the firebrick to a pipe that carried the heated air to a register on the next floor. Registers were designed to stop the upward flow of air so that it would enter one room only, or to take some air and allow the rest to pass to another floor or to a second register that warmed an adjacent room.

A more sophisticated fireplace system removed the fire basket and fender and inserted a set grate or mantel heater, which produced more heat than the traditional fireplace. The design of these units was generally the same, although there were variations on how to get cold air to pass around the firepot. The pots were made of iron, as were the reflective back plates. A fire clay brick lining and a series of chambers at the back and along the sides of the pot and one or two dampers, to control the fire, completed the structure. Since grates were made of cast materials, they had surface embellishments that included references to architectural ornamentation and unusual patterns for the ventilator slots. As these heaters accommodated the design values of the twentieth century, they lost ornamentation in favor of neat, plain compositions. Mantel heaters usually included a summer front or ornamental panel, first of iron and later of steel. These were inserted in the grate opening when the unit was not in use. Two inexpensive types of grates were the electric heater and the gas heater, complete with bulbs to simulate the red glow of burning coal or logs.

Warm-Air Furnaces

The most popular space-heating systems of the 1870s were warm-air furnaces and steam. Warm-air systems were cheaper. They required a centrally located heat source—usually a basement furnace, although fireplaces and room furnaces could serve the purpose. The systems relied on convection to distribute warm air and to exchange stale air for fresh. They either heated the air already present in a room or passed warmed air through the room. A typical basement warm-air furnace was constructed of three parts: a fire pot, a radiator, and a casing. The radiator was located just above the fire pot and hot gases passed through the radiator, thereby heating it, on their way to the chimney. Connected with the radiator was a drum, or plenum, consisting of thin sheets of steel or cast iron, and, if required, numerous pipes leading to various rooms in the building. Some systems also included pipes that returned air from the room to the furnace. As warm air traveled upward, it was often mixed with fresh air to effect air exchange.

Basement warm-air furnaces were of two types: the set furnace and the portable furnace. Brick walls with a door to allow tending the furnace and a covering of some material that protected the floor joists above enclosed the set furnace. The portable furnace was enclosed in a galvanized iron jacket and often set in a pit that was bricked around and bottomed with cement. Warm-air furnaces that relied exclusively on convection were inefficient, in that much heated air was lost to the outside grates and the distribution of heat was unequal. Moreover, they leaked combustion gases.

Parlor furnaces were smaller versions of the portable warm-air furnace. They were sculptural in shape and looked like furniture. They were centrally located and used their own chimney or a fireplace chimney to emit gases. As simple space heaters, parlor furnaces used convection to draw cooler air off the floor into the furnace. The overall design of these units varied, but in principal they had a three-part organization. At the bottom was a raised base on legs that contained an ash drawer and the ventilators. The fire chamber, the middle and largest portion of the heater, had a cast-iron grate. The unit was completed by what was sometimes a distinctive top. The heater was wrapped in steel—sometimes polished—and trimmed with a deflector ring, side wings, drafts for the fire, and in some models an urn on the swing top. For a while, these trim pieces were nickel-plated.

The development of warm-air furnaces was given a significant boost when a fan was introduced into the furnace to draw cold air, through a system of pipes, from the entire building for reheating. The fan helped to force the heated air up the round or oblong pipes. When placed within a partition, these ducts were called wall stacks. Cold-air returns were located near the outside walls in order to counteract cold-air currents or other infiltrations before they entered the room. Fan-assisted warm-air furnaces later were fired by oil or natural gas, which ultimately freed the basement from its fuel storage role and allowed it to assume new functions: workshop, playroom, recreation room.

Of note in regard to heating systems is that during the time period under study, heating units—as well as kitchen ranges—often did double duty in generating hot water. In most cases, coils of one kind or another were adapted to furnaces—whether within the fire chamber or just above it—in which circulating water was heated for distribution to kitchens or baths.

The basement pipeless furnace was safer than earlier models. It had increased capacity and drew cold air from the rooms in the building, from the basement, or from both. It burned hard or soft coal, wood, coke, and later oil. In operation, cold air passed around the fire pot, up through the furnace to a large register (made in various shapes) in the first floor, usually between the living room and the dining room in a house. Hallways and staircases helped to carry the warm air through the building, and ceiling registers allowed the warm air to pass into second-floor rooms.

Hot-Water and Steam-Heating Systems

The use of steam or vapor to supply heat was a direct extension of the use of steam for power. Since much of its initial use was tied to industrial developments, some time passed before steam was adapted to vernacular architecture. Steam systems were used extensively in the nineteenth century, but hot-water systems replaced them in the twentieth. The typical sophisticated steam system required a boiler, scaled down to meet the requirements of vernacular buildings (Sears, Roebuck sold easily assembled units for home use early in this century), vertical and horizontal steam supply pipes and condensation return pipes (twin pipes kept the return water from restricting the flow of the steam), and an array of radiators in appropriate locations throughout the building. Pipes often were exposed in room corners.

Radiation from the outlets was either direct, direct–indirect, or indirect. Direct radiation meant that the air in a space was heated by contact with the radiator in the room. Usually the radiator was fitted with both a steam valve and a return valve, which were opened and closed as the temperature required. In direct–indirect outfits, a fresh air supply was provided to the radiator, and the radiator often was enclosed in a screened cabinet with a register on the top. A small air duct, about three inches high, was taken through the outsidewall at or below the windowsill. Air entering through this duct was heated by convection in its passage to the top of the radiator. The indirect system was the most expensive of the three and usually was applied to larger buildings such as business or apartment buildings. Each living or working space had a separate radiator or metal coil suspended from the ceiling of the basement. An air duct was attached at the upper end of the radiator or

coil, which terminated at a register on the floor above the cellar. Higher-level floors were connected to the radiators by pipes in the walls. Many of these arrangements also had fresh air ductwork that supplied new air to the heated air as it rose in the building.

The organization of a steam system sometimes utilized an overhead arrangement in which the main supply was carried directly to the attic space, where horizontal runs (pipes) were carried to drops (vertical pipes), which were so located that they supplied the building's radiators on the way down to the cellar. There they converged into a main return line to the boiler. Condensation from the radiators dropped down into the pipes and flowed in the same direction as the steam, thereby preventing water barriers.

Hot-water units were organized in the same way as steam units. A boiler in the basement heated water that circulated through an assortment of radiators. The hot water forced the cold out of the system and returned it to the boiler. Some systems included a generator that accelerated the water and increased the efficiency of the system.

Radiators

From the point of view of interior architecture, radiators were the major factor in using steam or hot water for heating. Originally, radiators were iron pipes cut off at the right length and connected at either end to make coils. Each radiator was a stack of coils screwed to a cast-iron base. The first advance in radiator design was the development of completely cast units, which not only produced better radiator sections but also allowed for the application of ornamental motifs on the surfaces of the coils and for the production of new profiles for the coils and new special-location shapes for the radiators. Cast-iron units were replaced by pressed-steel ones, which were smaller and weighed less, thereby lightening floor loads. Most radiators were thin-edged, eight to nine inches wide and twenty to forty-five inches high. In the twentieth century radiators were made less obtrusive by the use of lightweight copper and brass heating surfaces, and even when exposed, their new tubular designs made the units more attractive.

Most radiators were placed close to sources of cold air, such as just under windows. A front-entrance radiator was placed in a wall and covered with a grille or positioned in the floor by the door for indirect radiation. Some ground-floor halls got a single unit by the stairs, and if the hall was especially large, there might be another radiator on the stair landing. In larger building installations, stepped radiators were aligned with the run of the stairs. In houses with pantries or in restaurants there were small plate-warming radiators with sections of pipe laid on the horizontal. Bathroom configurations included low types with a seat on top and indirect radiators under the floor with a register on top. Generally, radiators were adapted to suit spaces, such as window sizes and shapes and the dimensions and locations of available walls. Some design considerations were practical in another way in that bedroom units often had high legs for ease in cleaning under them, and radiators far from the riser pipes also had high legs to create the pitch needed to sustain the gravity flow of the return pipes.

Plumbing Systems and Bathrooms

Bathroom design from 1870 to 1960 centered on the development of the modern bath and parallels much of the creation of the modern kitchen. The bathroom (first written as two words) became recognized as a key ingredient for the modern building. It was, in many respects, an extension of the plumbing system. The bathroom was a special-use room in which water served the purposes of cleanliness and sanitation.

Modern plumbing consists of two series of pipes and branches. One series is for drainage—for taking sewage away from a building—and includes a line of air pipes open to the atmosphere. The second series is for supply—bringing hot and cold water to various fixtures. Early plumbing systems had several possible sources of pumping power: windmills, gravity flow, hand pumps, and pressure within public water lines.

This section discusses the overall design of bathrooms, inventorying the elements of bath design and describing the interaction between systems and elements that produced interior design.

For most vernacular buildings, running water was available even before bathrooms, and both were available before 1870 in the East. The immediate impact of plumbing on interiors was the installation of a tub, which could receive cold water directly from its supply source and hot water from a range coil or

tank in the kitchen. However, it was not long in modern bath development before the freestanding hot-water heater was connected directly to the bathroom tub.

Water heaters are a key element in this history. Typical of the early types was the instantaneous model that produced hot water on demand at the rate of about two to three gallons per minute. Some of these were gas fired and mounted on the wall between the tub and the lavatory, with a pipe to vent combustion gases rising through the bathroom ceiling to the roof. Another kind of gas heater was attached to a water tank—much like the coal or wood range and waterback in the kitchen—with a copper coil running from the bottom to the top of the boiler and gas burners heating the coil. A second type had a burner and coil in the bottom of a hot-water tank surrounded by an insulated covering. A flue took gases to the chimney, and a thermostat controlled the unit. These models also had pilot lights and relief valves and were located in the basement or the kitchen.

Gas and electricity emerged as the preferred methods of heating water by the 1930s, but there were other heating practices still functioning at that time. One was a pipe coil in the furnace that absorbed heat from the fire chamber. Another was a system whereby furnace-heated water circulating in a small tank heated another coil that led to a pipe for the bath and kitchen fixtures. Yet another system placed a coil in the chimney flue or smokestack, and the water in it took up the heat from the gases going up the stack. There were also electric heaters that relied on household current and a strainer-like attachment to a faucet; as soon as the faucet handle was turned, current flowed through a resistance coil, which heated the water flowing over it. Electric heat evolved into a freestanding, steel-jacketed tank in which water was heated by resistance coils. Finally, there were kerosene or range oil automatic water heaters designed like other jacketed insulated models, except for having an attached burner.

The acceptance of household bathing tubs and the availability of hot water were not the only factors in the creation of the modern bathroom. Installing water closets was a complicated matter and often required overcoming the fear of sewer gases. As traps and vent pipes became recognized solutions to the gas problem, the toilet completed its migration from the backyard, to the porch, to a room of its own, even to a room within a room. The plumbing stack was the key to sewer gas control. The pipe was usually four inches in diameter and led from the basement or crawl space to the roof. From the foot of the stack, a sloping pipe extended along a basement wall or under the floor, through the foundation wall, where it connected with a tile pipe extending to a sewer, septic tank, cesspool, or nearby body of water. At the top of the stack a pipe passed up through the roof, where it was open to the air. Fresh air circulated through the stack, and fixture waste pipes were connected to it. Traps, which prevented sewer gas from entering rooms, were inserted between each fixture and soil pipe. There traps were loops of pipe partially filled with water. When a fixture discharged, wastewater flowed through the loop into the soil pipe, and some water remained as a barrier.

The water closet (in England the term *closet* stood for *toilet* for a long time) was developed well before 1870, but adequate cleaning systems for the bowl were not developed until the 1890s. By design most water closets could hold water, but to be successful the bowl-and-tank combination needed to cleanse the bowl properly every time and remain an effective trap for sewer gas. There were three principal types of design: washout, washdown, and syphon. The washout was the least sanitary. Successfully emptying the closet depended upon the force of the water injected into the bowl; the water in the bowl usually was too shallow to complement the injected water effectively. The washdown unit was better because it contained a large body of water in the bowl, and its rim injection of water was an improvement, but its discharge was very noisy. In the syphon, also called the syphon jet, incoming water was divided, part entering the rim and part entering at the bottom of the bowl as a pressure jet. When the closet flushed, the entrance of a stream of water in the bottom of the bowl started the closet emptying by syphonic action (suction). The bowl's sides were washed by the rim flow, and the bowl was filled by afterwash.

Water closet design, especially bowl design, reflected the ways in which manufacturers tried to build siphoning and washing functions into the bowl shape. In profile and sectional views most bowls had an organic look, especially after they were made of molded and fired vitreous china. The bowls often revealed the tubular arrangements of the trap as well as the containment features of the bowl shape. Lastly, the top of the bowl and the base had different shapes. The overall design of the water closet also was tied to the type and placement of the water tank. At first, tanks were placed high on the wall above the bowl. Low-down models, called combinations, emerged early in the twentieth century, but the unification of the bowl and tank does not seem to have occurred until the 1930s. Turn-of-the-century toilets had a decorative dimension in that transfer prints and hand painting were used to decorate the sides of the bowl, and the tank sometimes had a decorative motif on the front. Ultimately, toilet design aesthetics centered on the integration of materials, on bowl and tank treatments, on the choice of seat design, and on the style and finish of trimmings.

Water closet materials followed the same pattern as tubs and sinks, in that wood, metal, enameled iron, and ceramic goods were used in both bowl and tank design, with ceramic becoming the preferred material. Whether made of enameled iron or china, fixtures were white until the 1920s, when colored fixtures were introduced. A short article in the *American Builder* (April 1927) announced the introduction of colored fixtures but did not mention the company producing them.

As the use of water closets increased, special units were developed, including chemical toilets and the hopper closet for cold climates. The hopper usually had the trap and supply valve deep in the ground with the valve activated by a pull chain or by the seat.

Two final features of water closet design were closet location and ventilation. Unlike English and European systems, the American water closet typically was not located in a separate room or compartment. Tenement houses and commercial and industrial buildings might have such a space, but most vernacular buildings placed the toilet in the same room with other sanitary fixtures. A minor accommodation along these lines was the inclusion of a water closet alcove in the bathroom. Ventilation often was addressed by the positioning of the toilet beneath or near an outside window. Some closet design included a local ventilator connected to a flue or a register at the back of the closet that would circulate air. Sometime during the 1930s the ceiling exhaust fan began to take over this function.

Tubs often were installed before lavatories and water closets, because their use had been well established before indoor plumbing was an option. Tubs were made of wood, sheet metal, cast iron, and ceramic materials. Historically the tub was a portable item, and late-nineteenth-century tubs reflected that heritage. They had legs and special hoses that siphoned the water out; Sears and others sold a folding tub. As the tub gained acceptance, portability was abandoned and it was recessed or fitted to a corner.

Showers were thought of first as a type of bath, and they were not popular alternatives to the tub bath. For people who were willing to engage in showering modestly, Sears sold a shower-bath yoke in 1902. This was a hose bathers placed around the neck, out of which water streamed down the body. Shower baths originally were designed like a piece of furniture—freestanding, pipe-framed, curtained, with a shallow basin for a base. The shower became integrated with the tub as well as built into its own alcove by the 1920s.

Lavatory design encompassed all of the following: the material from which the lavatory was made, the shape of the entire fixture and the shape of the basin, the thickness and shape of the slab, the profile of the back piece, the method of support, the location of the lavatory in the bathroom, the color of the fixture, and the pattern and finish of the hardware and supply and waste pipes. With design parameters that wide ranging, the selection of products was extensive. Moreover, the subtleties of lavatory design could be worked among the elements. For example, the method of support for a lavatory could make a contribution to the design scheme. Historically, supports were attached iron brackets, legs, pedestals, and "invisible" wall hangers on which the lavatory was hooked. For three of these categories, the design and finish of the support could establish a tone for the bathroom system.

In summarizing overall bathroom design, several conceptual approaches to the arrangement of fixtures and the use of space can be noted. In the late nineteenth and early twentieth centuries the bathroom was a large room containing loosely arranged fixtures, with little relationship among the diverse parts. The reform movement in housing design had an effect on baths that resulted in a smaller bathroom and the development of the room as a workshop for personal health. The third version of the modern bathroom took the workshop a step further and created a gleaming white laboratory for personal health and grooming. The final treatment reduced the bath space even more and relied on integrated, compact units, with all the practical concerns, such as sanitation, taken for granted. In this stage aesthetics entered the bathroom scene as a primary consideration.

Design parameters for relation among fixtures included height, width, and depth dimensions: the logic of placement as it related to room use (the lavatory near the door, the tub away from it), and the relation among materials. China and enameled cast-iron fixtures might be found in the same room, or a mixture of china and metal trimmings, or there might be a unified material look in which everything was either ceramic or painted enamel. Also of interest were the types of supports for fixtures—bases, pedestals, legs, brackets, hangers—and the configuration of each fixture: referential types such as a fish-shaped water closet, purely functional forms, or designed or "artistic" shapes. Likewise, the edges of fixtures and their surfaces might be treated similarly: edges were cut, rounded, or rectilinear, and surfaces were recessed and featured cups, rims, and other raised elements. Lastly, trimmings were integrated.

There was also the issue of ornamentation. Even though transfer-printed designs, most leg types, elaborate bases, and textured pedestals were dropped from the design vocabulary, other aspects of design—lines, patterns, bevels, and color, including, at first, accent color—were still important.

Similar options were available for lavatories, tubs, and shower baths. To create unified effects, plumbing manufacturers sold bathrooms as complete installations priced according to the quality of the materials, finishes, and the methods of operation. In this strategy, the manufacturers followed the unit approach that millwork manufacturers used in selling kitchen design. Once this unit, or "outfit," idea caught on, it presented a new design opportunity: coordinated design effects. For example, the forty-five-degree cut at the corners of the lavatory back could be repeated on the inside corners of the basin and on the corners of the apron. The beveled corner could also be applied to the base of the toilet, the edge of the tank cover, and the edge of the tub.

Similarly, the hardware of all the fixtures could be made of the same material and have the same style and finish. Generally, the detailing of the system was carried out in all the trimmings: toilet paper and soap holders (whether the projecting or recessed type), tumbler and toothbrush holder, towel bars, and shelf brackets. Although plumbing companies did not manufacture bathroom lights, the range of choices among lighting products made it possible to complement bath fixtures well enough to give the 1930s bathroom the ambience of total design.

KITCHEN

The history of the kitchen focuses on the elevation of a back room into a special place, with clearly established functions and special equipment. The evolution took place in the single-family home. Kitchens in non-residential buildings were adaptations of the residential model.

Prior to the development of the modern kitchen in the last quarter of the nineteenth century, the kitchen was a place to store provisions, prepare food, wash cooking utensils, wash and iron clothes, change clothes, take care of personal grooming (shaving, washing hair), eat, and pass through on the way to other rooms. Moving beyond this eclectic space to the kitchen of the 1920s and 1930s meant concentrating activities related to the use of food in the kitchen proper and relegating all other functions to other spaces. The parallel developments of the bathroom and the laundry room greatly relieved congestion. Moreover, pantry spaces—for storing dinnerware, table service, and provisions, and for serving food—were another early solution to redefining kitchen space. In response to these and other changes, and to the need to reorganize the kitchen to relieve the drudgery of housework, the kitchen was allocated less square footage and given new purpose.

By 1870 the kitchen had equipment and finish materials that would remain, in some form, part of its design for a long time. There was a refrigerator (an insulated wooden box with a space for food and another to hold blocks of ice); a range or stove that could bake, roast, and heat water; a storage unit or two; at least one shelf, a sink, a clock, a worktable and chair; and a washable floor. The organization of this kitchen was loose, with wide spaces between equipment and workstations. In one sense, the history of kitchen design is the story of how these units became physically connected to make the work area more efficient and laborsaving.

Water service was available for the nineteenth-century kitchen. In cities water was pumped under pressure through lead and galvanized iron pipes to residences and businesses. In rural areas water was brought into houses by gravity flow from springs and cisterns, by wind power, or by hand-operated force pumps connected to wells. Early water systems had exposed pipes with supply and return pipes running across ceilings and along walls. Some sections of pipe might run under a floor or through a partition, and some ran in chase. The exposure of the pipes was regarded as practical: repairs and adjustments to flow could be made easily. Each line could have stopcocks, traps, and bleeders. The presence of the pipes had another effect: they symbolically reinforced the idea that house development, especially in rooms such as the kitchen, was tied to technological advancement. The presence of pipes made the room look progressive. Most plumbing systems had access to some hot water, through either the range heater or a separate unit. The hot-water storage tank also was placed in the kitchen. Sometimes hot-water lines ran to the attic and returned from there, and air lines that prevented hammering and air bounding were also taken off the attic lines.

This kitchen was serviceable, but it still took its toll on the women who worked in it. Despite improvements, the kitchen needed a new conceptual approach, and that challenge was taken up by reformers who saw in kitchen design issues that stood for the role of women in family life and for the significance of their labor. Kitchen studies in academic domestic-science programs established standardization. Kitchen size, for example, was not to exceed one hundred and fifty square feet.

Among the reformers there was divided opinion as to the optimal shape of the kitchen—oblong, L-shaped, or the more popular square—but there was agreement about the need for windows on two sides for light and ventilation. Reformers also agreed about the need to restrict the use of the kitchen as a passageway by reducing the number of doors opening into it. Four doors was the maximum: an outside door, a pantry door, a cellar door, and one to the dining room. Reduction to two or three doors was even better, and they should be placed on adjacent walls to avoid lines of travel through the work area and to leave two sides of uninterrupted wall space. Windows should be placed three feet six inches from the floor to allow for table space beneath the sill. Counter and table heights were examined to establish appropriate working levels to reduce strain. The reorganization of the kitchen was tied to redefining the role of service functions in the house.

Kitchen design—even before the kitchen was thought of as the workshop of the home—was tied to the development of a few workstations, such as the sink and the range/stove. Sink design was the same as that for bathroom tubs and lavatories. Early wooden sinks gave way to carved soapstone, and later to models mass-produced in porcelain, enameled iron, and graniteware. Water was supplied from spigots, either in the wall or built into the sink, or from attached hand pumps. Sinks had rolled or flat rims, low or high backs of either wood or cast iron, and aprons. They might fit into corners or stand alone, with single or double basins. The sink was also a workstation and the dish-drain board, whether attached or inte-

gral, served as a food preparation area. The boards were made of wood (oak), then metal, and finally enameled or porcelain cast iron. Sink support came from integral or attached legs, brackets, wall hangers, and, finally, cabinetry.

Kitchen Storage

Storage function and storage capacity changed several times from 1870 to 1960. The 1870s kitchen had very little capacity. Foodstuffs were kept in small amounts, and fresh goods were bought more frequently. Garden produce was home-processed and stored in root or fruit cellars and pantries. Immediate kitchen storage for utensils and service items was often relegated to a "dresser," a movable piece of furniture, and to the implements shelf by the sink and the range.[1] In the 1870s, reformers already were calling for the use of storage cases and closets to help in the reorganization of the kitchen.

Like almost everything in vernacular design, a finish carpenter made the casework on the job site. Gradually, ready-made elements, at first drawers and cupboard doors, were introduced. These were augmented by casework that was fabricated completely at the mill. The rapid increase in the production of cases and competition among shops led to experimentation in case organization, so that variations in

16.1. The range advertised on this trade postcard, 1908 ("I couldn't keep house without a Quick Meal range") is one element in a modern efficient kitchen system, which reduces steps and organizes functions. Authors' Collection.

shelf and drawer size, adjustable units, special-use bins, and specially shaped closets all developed quickly.

The trend toward packaged foods led to increased storage capacity, and that led to the accumulation of more household goods. When these accumulations were tied to the desire to alleviate kitchen congestion, it prompted the design of pantries as separate spaces. Basically, a pantry was a cabinet located near the kitchen or between the kitchen and the dining room. In the latter situation, the pantry was used for serving food; it might have a variety of cabinets, a sink with hot and cold water, a pass-through door with a floor hinge for opening either way, or a small pass-through opening in the wall for serving food and collecting dishes. Casework in both kitchens and pantries often featured glass doors over the upper sections, with beveled, leaded, or art glass glazing.

Once manufactured cabinetry had taken hold in the marketplace, the development of kitchen storage was based on the linking of storage units, at first, into specific work centers and later into continuous cabinets. The ultimate success of this system all but eliminated the serving pantry from American housing. With floor-to-ceiling cabinets, organized on a gridiron principle for efficiency and ease of manufacture, the pantry's square footage could be captured for another purpose.

One final aspect of storage—built-in storage or work units—needs to be mentioned. These units appear in manufacturers' trade catalogs during the 1910s as set pieces that supplemented casework or served as workstations. Ironing boards that folded down from a wall-mounted cabinet, dumb waiters for food and goods delivery, package receivers built into outsidewalls, folding tables for temporary tasks, desks for planning and relaxation (the "quiet corner"), and breakfast nooks for informal family meals were all aspects of this development from the 1870s through the 1920s.

Kitchen Walls, Ceilings, Floors

Historical materials for kitchen walls and ceilings reflected sentiments about sanitation and efficiency. A chronological inventory of materials reads as follows: wood wainscots, one- or two-inch tongue-and-groove boards with a cap rail; the same boards, sometimes referred to as "kitchen board," for ceilings; hard plaster covered with oil-base enamel paint; oilcloth that could be washed regularly or torn off and replaced; washable wallpapers such as varnished wall tiles; glazed ceramic tile for walls, usually at wainscot height; and metal sidewall coverings in sheets or in square or oblong blocks nailed to furring strips.

The kitchen floor consisted of a subfloor covered with a hardwood such as maple. Sometimes the floor was enameled for ease of maintenance. Oilcloth, ceramic tiles (including quarry tile), linoleum (patented in the 1860s), rubber mats, and cement also were used. Over the entire period it was linoleum-type products, in a wide range of colors and patterns that carried the day. (See 5.13 for a kitchen with unit cabinets and linoleum flooring.)

Kitchen Lighting

Kitchen lighting followed the historical patterns of the period, but the kitchen was seen particularly as a place where natural lighting would alleviate eyestrain and enhance the general ambience. Artificial light sources from 1870 to 1940 included oil lamps set on metal wall brackets to light the sink and stove, gas fixtures as wall brackets and pendants hung from the center of the ceiling, and electric fixtures—as single bulbs, as clusters of bulbs in direct and indirect modes, and as bracket lights for work centers.

Beyond the concern for converting the loosely organized kitchen into a tightly grouped workshop, the kitchen was one of the primary theaters (the bathroom was the other) for the household campaign against unsanitary conditions. The desire to control disease by inhibiting the proliferation of germs had ramifications for kitchen design. The period 1900 through 1920 included a push for plain, smooth surfaces for moldings and cabinets—a rebuff to the ornamented surfaces of the last century. Ornamented edges and concave/convex surfaces collected dust, and dust was the medium for germs and bacteria. Smooth materials, especially those impervious to water, were easier to clean, and when combined with lots of sunlight and fresh air, they produced a healthful and protective environment. The design concept that produced this enthusiasm for cleanliness was the kitchen as laboratory, a gleaming white room where the results of time-and-motion and nutrition studies could be implemented. A related minor development, generated by the technological character of the modern kitchen, was the presence of a house incinerator with a chute in the kitchen. After garbage collection became common, this feature disappeared.

Once the idea of the modern kitchen was fully inculcated into house design, it was inevitable that kitchen design would return to aesthetic issues as a basis for modernity. The route to aesthetics was through a negative reaction to the harsh white interior and a positive campaign for the application of color to the room. At first color accents were confined to stencil work or accent tiles, but soon there were campaigns to tint the walls—cream, light tan, green, or gray. By the 1930s floor coverings were more dramatically colored, and kitchen equipment and utensils were manufactured tinted so that a kitchen might have one solitary tint or a two-tone effect. The increased use of color seems to have encouraged a related increase in window lighting. Some kitchen critics even called for the use of a formula that derived needed glass area from the room's square footage, with an area equal to at least one-fifth of the floor area to be devoted to glass (thirty square feet of window for a kitchen of one hundred and fifty square feet).

The call for color and other design accents was partly an appeal to the housekeeper to establish her own individuality in this work space. Now, as the manager of a standardized kitchen system—complete with measured counter heights, interchangeable cabinets, work centers arranged for the fewest steps between units, environmental controls (such as heating, cooling, lighting, cooking, exhaust), and health control—she should introduce her personal aesthetic to unify the entire system.

Kitchenettes

Once the integrated kitchen was successfully manufactured and marketed, it could be adapted to any kind of kitchen space. One especially significant effort in this vein was the miniaturization of the entire kitchen into the kitchenette—a scaled-down, tight grouping of cabinets, sink, refrigerator, and stove. The same logic transformed the pantry into the pantryette. The illustration accompanying this section was part of a 1921 advertisement by the Aladdin Company of Bay City, Michigan, makers of manufactured housing. Aladdin was selling the idea of the "Aladdinette," an apartment "that separated itself from other apartments and became a house." With proper proportioning and the adaptation of all accessories—the kind used in "expensive apartments, private railroad cars, and the like"—the single family could live in an apartment-size house. The Aladdin kitchenette, designed to keep everything in reach, included a refrigerator, sink, four-burner cook stove, worktable, and cabinets. The Aladdinette had nine hundred and twelve square feet of area that featured multiple-use rooms: living room/bedroom; dressing room/bath; dining room/bedroom; kitchen; and sunroom/bedroom. The sleeping rooms had Murphy wall beds, and eating was assigned to a dining alcove. The Aladdin products were made of wood, but steel kitchenettes could be had at this time from other manufacturers.

Breakfast Nooks

Another kitchen design specialty was the development of the breakfast space, sometimes referred to as a "Dutch breakfast room" but eventually called a breakfast nook. These rooms began appearing in the trade literature around 1915. Eight feet by ten feet was considered adequate, and it was recommended that they have lots of windows (casements were popular) and be oriented to a porch or within a projecting bay. The furnishings for breakfast rooms were informal, with easily modified arrangements of chairs and a small table. Since the breakfast room was a very expensive addition, its function was served in most houses by an alcove or a nook in the pantry or kitchen. The nook was intended to save work for housekeepers and save wear on the dining-room furniture. It was to be ventilated and lighted with natural and artificial light. The atmosphere was to be cozy and charming, with color accents and an eastern exposure to get the morning sun. Nook size was generally square, about five feet six inches to seven feet along one side. Design options for nooks were an arched or cased opening and movable or folding seats and table; folding types were called Pullman nooks. Seat and table designs were generally of two kinds, open-ended or solid, with the latter often having storage compartments under the seats. Most tables were the trestle type with straight, turned, or wide solid end pieces. Ornamentation consisted of scroll saw cuts in the table or bench supports and painted decoration.

Breakfast nooks were classified in trade catalogs as another kind of built-in furniture, and they even featured electric convenience outlets on the wall or built into the table to allow percolators and toasters to be placed within reach. The nooks were especially popular during the 1920s. While they sold for practical reasons, their success probably was related to the social transformation of the workshop–laboratory–kitchen into a family room, because family activity was associated with the nook. The table could be used for food preparation, dressmaking, ironing, children's play, letter writing, meal planning, and schoolwork.

MODULAR UNITS

There was an interest in the standardization of kitchen elements early in the twentieth century. Home economists recommended that cupboards or dressers be two feet eight inches high and from twenty to twenty-four inches wide, with a twelve- to fifteen-inch open space between lower and upper cupboards. The demand for standards had its roots in a rational, scientific approach to kitchen planning. Essentially, this approach examined kitchen uses and functions and planned space accordingly. But the scientific approach also meant measured spaces, double uses, and standardized work patterns. Georgia B. Child, in *The Efficient Kitchen* (1925), argued for the development of standard types of equipment that could be modified easily for special needs.[2]

The standardization issue was also part of the reform effort to improve the lot of housekeepers, whose work was made harder because of poorly planned and arranged equipment. The manufacturing system had been capable of responding all along, but the production of integrated cabinets in modular sizes was not well established until the 1930s. Kitchen design, by that time, utilized combinations of ready-made units, their widths based on six-inch intervals (from six to thirty inches or more) and on heights of twenty-four, twenty-eight, and thirty-five inches.

Moreover, by the 1930s cabinet design was so specialized that kitchen planners had choices of special-use cabinets to suit individual needs. With standardized units, which easily accommodated sinks, stoves, refrigerators, and dishwashers, the solution to a successful kitchen design lay in configurations that suited the house plan, the square footage available, and the housekeeper's aesthetic. It was the latter appeal that carried the kitchen into the era of conspicuous consumption, which pushed history-based design principles aside in favor of other values.

LIGHTING

Lighting design in vernacular interiors depended, in the first place, on the type of lighting power available. Power systems from private or municipal suppliers date from approximately the last decade of the nineteenth century. The first broadly based system of illumination was street lighting by natural gas, which was supplied by private companies or municipal authorities; this system soon branched into lighting for residential, public, commercial, and industrial buildings. Small gas plants were also available for lighting individual vernacular buildings. One type, the acetylene plant, had a gas generator and gas holder and used carbide crystals for fuel; it could be automatically fired by a clockwork motor. Another type, the gasoline unit, generated gas in a carburetor placed underground at some distance from the building it served; air under pressure from a compressor or pump impregnated gasoline, making gas which passed to a governor in the basement of the building. Lastly, there was the bottled (blau) gas unit: gas bottled under high pressure in steel containers.

Electric power systems were well in place by the 1920s. Offering multiple uses and improved lighting, electric systems replaced gas very quickly. Turn-of-the-century systems were not reliable, but better engineering and manufacturing soon improved them. Besides area-wide systems, there were also low-wattage house electric plants for power and lighting, which consisted of a storage battery, a small engine, a dynamo, and a switchboard. The plant was placed in the cellar or in a garage and required ventilation for safe operation. Three types of engines were used for driving the dynamo: gasoline, kerosene, and hot-air engines. Public and free enterprise utilities companies made individual plants obsolete in urban areas by the 1930s.

By the 1920s standards for wiring and for outlet, switch, and fixture locations had been established, and there was not much deviation from them over the next two decades. One circuit was required for every 500 square feet of floor space, and all rooms were served by at least two circuits to prevent interruption. In general, three essentials were recognized for electric systems: (1) a sufficient number of outlets to suit taste, but at least, one convenience outlet (for appliances) and one lighting outlet for every fifty square feet of floor space; (2) convenient control, a switch accessible to every doorway; (3) permanent installation, because wiring was strung within plaster and lath walls.

Outlets were the key to expanding electrical use in vernacular buildings. In 1931 General Electric estimated that from 1920 to 1927 the average number of outlets in a six-room house had increased from twenty-one to fifty-three. Convenience outlets, as they were called, were the single or duplex type, with one or two plugs. The duplex units often were placed on the horizontal. Baseboard and wall locations for outlets typically were eighteen to twenty-four inches above the floor. Some installations included waist-high outlets in hallways for vacuum cleaners and other cleaning equipment. In the bathroom and kitchen twin outlets were installed thirty-six to forty-eight inches from the floor. This height was also appropriate for basement outlets. Point-of-use became a significant criterion in planning systems, and over time additional standards crept into practice, such as placing a convenience outlet for every ten feet of unbroken wall space in living rooms and bedrooms. Common to most vernacular design is the development of options or specializations within a class of elements. By the 1930s there were specialty outlets: floor, radio, telephone, pilot light and switch control, heavy-duty polarity outlets, all in flush or weatherproof designs.

By 1870 vernacular buildings were lighted by oil, especially coal oil (kerosene), and natural gas. Oil lamps faded from use around this time, because of the low quality of the light and the need to keep the fixtures clean and filled. But the systematic placement of oil lamps and the general design of oil-lamp fixtures established patterns that were followed in the eras of gas and electricity. Hanging lights for general use, twenty-six to thirty inches in height, hall pendants (some adjustable) of forty-one to forty-five inches, and side lamps with reflectors for special effects or for task lighting laid a groundwork for fixture design. There were also chandeliers with a center support post and two to four fixtures branching from the post, each comprising a font, globe, and chimney. In general, gas and electric lighting fixtures were variations of these types—with the addition of a few new forms, such as the candlelight—until the stylization of fixtures and the exponential growth of electrical usage took lighting to a new dimension. This growth was accompanied by the development of specialty lights and the use of new materials for fixtures.

The majority of all light fixtures were suspended from, or attached directly to ceilings, with the remainder being attached to walls. Fixtures were suspended on metal hangers, solitary or branched stems, and chains or chords. To ensure equal radiation, lighting fixtures, regardless of the light source, were symmetrical in design. In hangers and pendants the fixture was placed on the center line of the support: in chandeliers, for example, branches with fixtures radiated from the center. Most suspended fixtures were located in the center of the room they serviced or were placed on center axis in a hallway.

Gas lights inherited the functional elements and forms of oil lamps: similar pendant frames, iron supports, tubular pieces, glass globes, chains for adjusting lights, and globe clasps or set screws. Oil fixtures usually were single units, one to a branch, and all in the same plane. Gas lighting expanded on this usage and layered the lights—large globes on the bottom and smaller ones on the top, arranged in concentric rings. In another change, the side lamp evolved into the bracket light without reflector. Since gaslights were brighter, shade design was changed to diffuse and mask the new light, and wall mounting was modified. The gaslight could be extended on its supply pipe six to twelve inches from the wall. Jointed arms, a feature of oil side lamps, were incorporated in the design vocabulary of gas brackets.

As alluded to above, natural gas lighting had advantages over oil lamp lighting. Not only was the light quality better, but also the piping of gas lines through the walls increased the number of available light sources and added permanent light location as an element in interior design. Gas lighting also encouraged fixture experimentation, including linking lights to design systems and examining the role of reflectivity in quality lighting. Gas lighting established a precedent for the development of electrical fixtures, providing light anywhere it was needed with variations in functional and atmospheric effects.

Historically, gaslight fixtures were set upright with a font at the bottom—a carryover from oil lamps—and a burner above. In the 1880s an inverted gas burner was developed, but it was not introduced until the turn of the century. The inverted burner made the gas fixture more effective for direct illumination: more light was thrown downward, and shadows were eliminated. Mantles were made shorter and double woven, and an air mixer was added to burn less gas. Other changes in fixture design included a shift away from heavy iron supports toward tubular supports with brass or bronze finishes; a modification of the fixture shade from a small-necked to a wide type; and shades that were cut, frosted, etched, ribbed, and painted. Overall, fixtures became visually and materially lighter.

As electricity gained popularity, combination gas and electric fixtures were created for pendant, chandelier, and bracket lights. Trying to compete with ranges in lamp wattage, gas units featured chains for adjusting the gas flow and the light intensity. Fixture designs that integrated the two light sources had the same shade shape, finish, and support pieces. The supports were made mostly of brass or bronze with an assortment of finishes: gilt, polished brass, old brass, nickel, green bronze, copper, ormolu, and silver. Many of the design elements were cut from sheet metal, which gave the fixtures a lighter and more linear design quality.

Electric lighting systems were assembled in much the same way as gas systems. There was a supply line diverted into circuits, with a switchboard delivering lines to rooms in the building. The turn-of-the-twentieth-century system had open or knob-and-tube wiring. Insulated copper wires needed for each circuit were stretched from point to point, supported by white porcelain knob or cleat insulators. Knobs held one wire, cleats two. Where the wires passed through framing, such as wall studs, porcelain tubes were used as insulating sleeves. Fuses for circuits were installed in porcelain blocks and mounted on the basement ceiling or the attic floor joists. Some systems had fuse cabinets in a pantry or the kitchen.

Since electric lighting was a technology-based development, and given the reform atmosphere of the time in which it was being introduced to the public, it is not surprising that the use of electric lighting was subjected to "scientific" study. Most of these studies examined the application of electric lighting to residences. The nature of illumination was of interest, and a number of publications, such as *American Carpenter and Builder* and *Keith's Magazine*, ran articles explaining the types of illumination necessary for a complete lighting system. Writers argued that electric units could provide more diversified lighting effects, and that generalized light qualities could be redefined to suit specific sites and tasks. To do that properly meant integrating the three kinds of illumination: direct, indirect, and semi-indirect.

Direct illumination, the oldest type, was limited at first by the kind of lamps that was available. Thomas Edison's carbon lamps were inefficient, and the discovery that tungsten could be utilized for light filaments improved lighting considerably. But the first filaments of this kind were pressed tungsten, which was brittle and fragile. In 1911 William Coolidge's process for making tungsten ductile, so that it could be drawn into fine wire, solved the problems of efficiency and fragility. Tungsten filament lamps made it possible to develop indirect and semi-indirect illumination.

Direct illumination fixtures sent light directly to where it was needed. Shades controlled the spread of the light. The pendant was a typical direct-illumination light. Aided by a dome-shaped shade, the pendant provided controlled light. To enhance its appearance, parchment, textiles, or art glass was used in the dome. To improve its diffusion properties, frosted lamps and quality glass were required. There was experimentation with the size of apertures, and most were reduced to just a few inches, especially for domes over dining-room tables.

Indirect illumination achieved the opposite effect, in that all the light was directed toward the ceiling, which in turn acted as a large reflector and distributed the light throughout the room. Indirect illumination provided subtle effects in light, color, distribution, and intensity. In some instances it corresponded to the lighting effect of the sky. The typical indirect light was a bowl with a silvered glass reflector concealed in an ornamented housing. Indirect lights often were concealed in some kind of architectural detail.

The third condition, semi-indirect illumination, reflected most of the light toward the ceiling but allowed some light to be transmitted down toward the floor or laterally through the fixture bowl. The density of the glass beneath the aperture of the opaque reflector controlled the amount of direct illumination. Glass of little density allowed a lot of light to pass through, whereas a very dense glass made the bottom of the fixture barely luminous. The luminous bowl combined direct and indirect effects, with the indirect effect coming from silvered reflectors; in the center a second lamp illuminated the parchment, silk, or glass and an aperture. Other semi-indirect combination lights included direct units with candlelights, shower lights with a bowl, and bowl-and-candle combinations.

Different kinds of illumination became identified with specific rooms or groups of rooms. Direct illumination was suggested for the living room, dining room, and library; indirect for the music room, den, reception room, kitchen/pantry, and sewing room; and semi-indirect for sleeping and dressing rooms, billiard and card rooms, halls, and bathrooms. Wall brackets and portable lamps complemented most of the lighting for these spaces.

In addition to illumination strategies, electric lighting was subject to studies of fixture heights and aperture openings as related to the cones of light coming through them. M. Luckiesh, in *Lighting Fixtures and Lighting Effects* (1925),[3] diagrammed the relationship between the diameter of a fixture's opening and the distance of the lamp filament above the opening as determinants for fixture height above the table. Using this formula, it was possible to light the dining table with pleasant and adequate light without direct light entering the eyes of the diners.

Luckiesh also offered recommendations for control switches and convenience outlets. A summary of his "rules" follows:

1. Place a wall switch on the knob side of a door that leads to a frequently entered room.

2. Locate baseboard outlets to accommodate furniture placement.
3. Place two duplex outlets on different sides of important rooms.
4. Activate a light in the closet by an automatic door switch in the jamb.
5. Provide hall lights with a three-way switch, allowing for off/on operation from either direction.
6. To avoid casting shadows, place no light opposite a window shade.
7. Have sidewall lights in bedrooms.
8. Have a central light in the attic.
9. Have more than one center ceiling light in a house.
10. Install a switch with a red "reminder" for the cellar light.

New light fixtures were designed to exploit the possibilities of electrical illumination. One that enjoyed great success was the shower light. It was a direct-illumination light composed of a cluster of small lamps hung by chains, with the lights attached to a plate in order to spread the light. Shower lights had two to five lamps, at first covered with bell-shaped shades: they ranged in drop length from thirty to thirty-six inches and in spread from twelve to twenty inches. The shower light and the indirect light in a bowl or urn replaced many pendants. The bowls and urns simply held more lamps and thus provided opportunities for different effects. Efficient indirect lighting and special-effect lighting required a reflective room finish. In the 1920s cream-colored paint laid on smooth plaster was the preferred scheme. On the issue of efficiency, not all lighting requirements were reduced to satisfying percentages. Any loss of light by the indirect method was considered offset by improved quality of illumination and better conditions for seeing.

By the 1920s specific kinds of lighting effects were linked to certain illuminations and fixtures. If the house was, in the language of the period, "the theater of life," then lighting could play a key role in the activities, moods, and social affairs of that theater. Lighting became decorative. The living room got one or two indirect or direct luminous bowls supplemented by wall brackets and portable lamps. Integrating the units required balancing general and local light with expressive effects. Such effects often were achieved with the use of concealed lamps in indirect fixtures. Urns, vases, corbels, capitals, cornices, moldings, plaques, decorative panels, wall boxes, window boxes, windowsills, rosettes, domes, friezes, artificial windows, niches, skylights, and finials all were used in this way.

Dining-room lighting was focused on illuminating the table. Several placements succeeded in bringing a cone of soft white light to the table. One required twenty-four inches between the top of the table and the bottom of the fixture's dome. A second dimension for a dome was fifty-four inches from the floor to the bottom of the dome. If a shower light were used, then thirty-six inches was recommended. Candlelight fixtures could be even higher: forty-five inches from the table to the bottom of the shade. Cylindrical or bud shaped shades were better at confining the light of shower lamps than were the traditional bell-shaped shades. Glass shades had been colored from the beginning of electric lighting, but more attention began to be paid to providing tinted bulbs and glass that would create special effects in the dining room. The so-called artistic styles of design modified the color of the transmitted light and used shades that harmonized with the room finish. Wall brackets with colored bulbs and shades also were used in dining rooms; they were mounted six feet from the floor and used low-wattage lamps.

Bedroom and bath spaces often received a central fixture. In bedrooms, wall brackets placed about six feet above the floor were sometimes the primary lighting. Small portable lamps on a dresser or dressing table provided local lighting. In the bathroom twin bracket lights were placed at a height of five feet above the floor, one on either side of the mirror over the lavatory.

Kitchen lighting required a centrally placed luminaire close to the ceiling with a glass reflector to distribute the light around the room. Bracket lights, notable for their smooth, easily cleaned surfaces and dense opal-glass shade, were placed above the sink, about five feet off the floor. In large kitchens, local lighting also was recommended for the range. In breakfast nooks semi-indirect light that illuminated the eating area and the storage around it was the preference.

The entrance hall, which could be either a type of reception room or merely the intermediate space between the front door and the rest of the building, usually was lighted. Generally a low-wattage lamp, close to the ceiling, sufficed for an informal hall. Reception halls called for more elaborate fixtures: urn-shaped enclosing globes with indirect lighting, candle- and torch-type wall brackets, and multiple-light drop fixtures on chains.

Special-use rooms such as laundries and utility rooms needed high-level illumination. Dome reflectors, plain porcelain sockets, ceiling lights with an all-enclosing globe, or kitchen lights if the laundry was a fully finished design were acceptable fixtures. The den or sewing room also needed high-intensity illumination, divided between a central fixture of moderate intensity and a portable lamp for close work. A ceiling light or bulb socket carried out closet illumination with a pull chain within the closet or by a wall bracket placed to direct light into the closet.

One final dimension to the standards for electric lighting was the attempt to establish wattage levels for lamps in specific rooms. In the early 1930s such recommendations were as follows: living-room and dining-room ceiling lights should be forty-watt, with wall brackets of twenty-five-watt frosted or forty-watt colored or tinted lamps; kitchen ceiling wattage should be one hundred for a frosted lamp and one hundred and fifty for a daylight lamp, with seventy-five-watt units over the sink and stove; bedroom central lights should be forty-watts, whether frosted or tinted; wall brackets should have the same wattage as those in the living and dining rooms.

The first decades of the twentieth century saw continuous developments in the efficiency of lamps and the quality of their light. Some lamps, such as the Lumiline series, stretched a filament for eighteen inches, and with the help of a long reflector, created linear light effects. These tubular lights prefigured the fluorescent units that were to make a strong impact on vernacular commercial and residential buildings.

Support systems continue to evolve due to ongoing invention and upgrading of materials, devices not previously imagined, and the evolution of construction building codes. Wood products are still used to frame and finish everyday buildings, but the dimensions of the lumber have changed, as have the kinds of wood products being used, including products that are only partially wood. Devices, especially those with electronic components, have altered the manner in which living, maintenance, and the uses of spaces are carried out. Today, synthetic materials play a major role in how a building works and what it looks like. Products derived from petroleum, chemistry, and electrical engineering continue to alter the character of vernacular structures and the systems that support them. Lastly, a computer can manage an everyday building, in part.

A REFLECTION ON VERNACULAR BUILDINGS AND INTERIORS

The industrial system that manufactured the materials from which modern vernacular buildings were built still functions today. In terms of wood products, the re-growth of forests in the Eastern time zone supports the harvest of timber in regions that were once decimated. Interior finish still includes millwork, but the millwork inventory is greatly reduced. Some historic and custom moldings are available. A building interior is finished in other kinds of manufactured goods: natural and artificial stone, chipped stone and resin and thermoplastic materials like vinyl. Building exteriors display their own assortment of materials, including engineered lumber, metal, and mixtures of wood and plastic. The manufacturing centers that originally transformed timber into wood products have closed, but new plants have sprung up in different locations. The flow of raw and finished materials is both national and international, and a vast network of truck transportation routes supplies local markets.

The demand for vernacular buildings has remained strong, especially in housing. Small-scale commercial developments, such as strip malls and convenience stores, are still built along the well-traveled streets of American towns as well. Fewer new churches are constructed in towns and rural areas, because of decreases in church-going populations. But storefront churches continue to pop up, while the recycling of old churches for adoption by new denominations or entirely new uses is ongoing.

The building communications system that evolved in the nineteenth century is still alive. Today consumers can still "build the picture," as much of the information about building is visual. House plans are readily available. Plan book schemes are published in real estate supplements which are distributed by local newspapers, and newsstands and bookstores carry plan books. Magazines devoted to building, especially for the do-it-yourself audience, are published monthly. Computers offer Web-based access for house plans. National building supply "home centers" provide information about products and videotapes and computer disks that teach building skills. Hand tools have been redesigned for homeowner use.

House planners have not lost sight of the value of the theory of convenient arrangement, although the new plan types stretch the notion of convenience, because of the preference for open plan organization. The amount of floor space devoted to open plans has increased and that, in turn, has increased the size of the roof that is required to span the core area of the plan. Alignments between rooms and hallways are greatly reduced in these configurations. The new roofs are often pyramid-shaped, and they create high vaulted interior spaces. One of the most popular spaces is the so-called great room. Other special use rooms continue to emerge, including home offices, entertainment centers, and exercise rooms.

Cross ventilation was important in late-nineteenth-century houses. Today its value has been diminished, because central heating and cooling systems, run by programmable control devices, manage the thermal environment. New technologies deliver heating and cooling in a manner that alters the experience of the interior. For example, passive solar systems using trombe walls influence the interior organization and the fenestration patterns, and zoned hot water delivered through radiant heating in floors modifies the interior experience.

The exterior characteristics of modern houses are rooted in historical practices, in that cladding materials are often mixed as to type, color, and texture. Today there is a vigorous application of historical elements and details on suburban houses and infill housing in towns and cities. These exterior accents, removed from their original contexts, appear to be used to create a mixture of visual effects. Thus, the buildings are prone to styling without the benefit of the original house type with which they were associated. Another contemporary feature is unusual distributions of windows and other openings, leaving blank walls, on the one hand, and, on the other, overloaded elevations that abut any kind of cultural or environmental amenity, such a farmland view, a valley, a body of water, a forest, or a hill.

Industrial housing has a whole new purpose. Company towns filled with a hierarchy of houses for workers and managers are no longer built. Today, industrial housing is modular housing, factory-built and portable. These houses offer an alternative to the single-family house built on speculation by a local builder. Manufactured houses display trace accents of historical details, like a center gable or a bay window.

In summary, vernacular building continues to develop, and it is still much needed to help characterize communities. The contemporary housing market is in the throes of a deep recession, but it will likely rebound to become a strong component of the economy once again. Home ownership still represents the major portion of family wealth. The study of vernacular environments needs to continue to build on the stock of historical buildings that the historic preservation movement has brought to light, and to extend research into more recent decades.

HEATING SYSTEMS: FIREPLACE HEATING

FIREPLACE CONSTRUCTION AND OPERATION

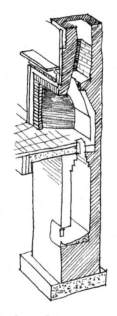

Traditional Construction

Built-in Fireplace Circulator

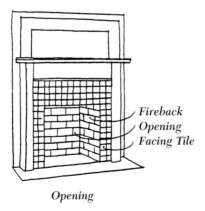

Fireback
Opening
Facing Tile

Opening

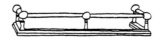

Fender or Rail

SET GRATE COMPONENTS

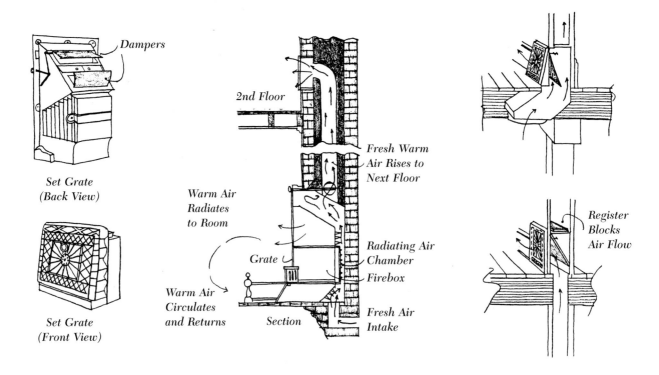

Set Grate
(Back View)

Set Grate
(Front View)

Dampers

2nd Floor

Fresh Warm
Air Rises to
Next Floor

Warm Air
Radiates
to Room

Warm Air
Circulates
and Returns

Grate

Section

Radiating Air
Chamber

Firebox

Fresh Air
Intake

Register
Blocks
Air Flow

FIREPLACE COMPONENTS

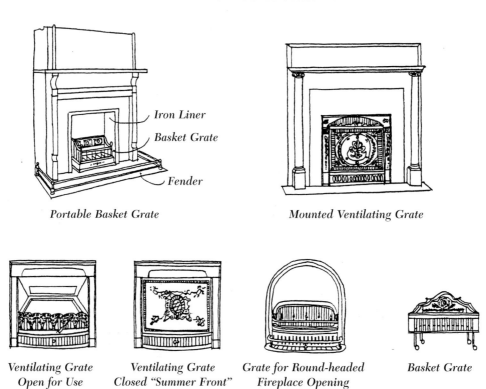

Iron Liner

Basket Grate

Fender

Portable Basket Grate

Mounted Ventilating Grate

Ventilating Grate
Open for Use

Ventilating Grate
Closed "Summer Front"

Grate for Round-headed
Fireplace Opening

Basket Grate

HEATING SYSTEMS: PIPELESS FURNACES

BURNS HARD COAL, SOFT COAL, WOOD, OR COKE

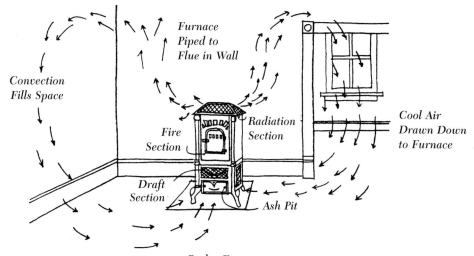

Convection Fills Space

Furnace Piped to Flue in Wall

Radiation Section

Fire Section

Draft Section

Ash Pit

Cool Air Drawn Down to Furnace

Parlor Furnace

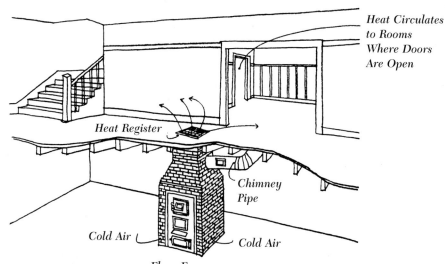

Heat Circulates to Rooms Where Doors Are Open

Heat Register

Chimney Pipe

Cold Air

Cold Air

Floor Furnace
Aladdin Co., Bay City Michigan, 1921

SUPPLY OUTLETS

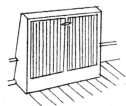

Baseboard Diffuser (for Forced Systems)

Baseboard Gravity Register

Floor Diffuser (for Forced Systems)

RETURN-AIR INTAKES

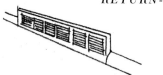

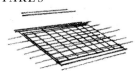

Baseboard Intake (for Forced Systems)

Floor Intake (for Gravity Systems)

HEATING SYSTEMS: HOT-WATER HEATING

OPERATION OF HOT-WATER CONVECTION HEATING

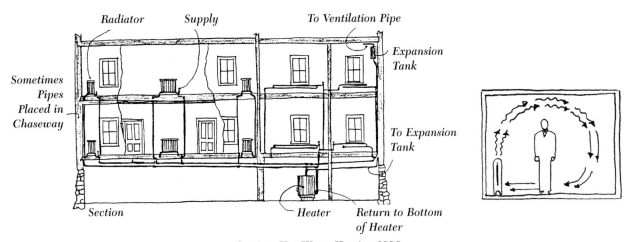

Section, Hot-Water Heating 1886
Hot Air Registers and Radiators Produce Air Currents Resulting in Uneven Room Temperatures
with Cold Floors and Hot Ceilings

RADIATORS FOR HOT-WATER CONVECTION HEATING

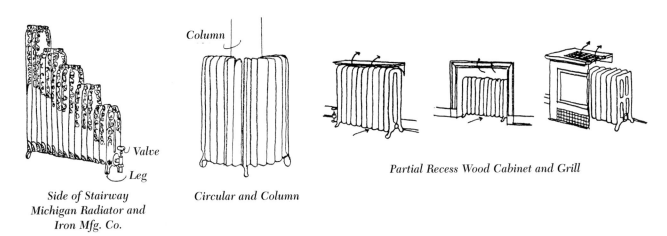

Side of Stairway
Michigan Radiator and
Iron Mfg. Co.

Circular and Column

Partial Recess Wood Cabinet and Grill

OPERATION OF HOT WATER RADIANT OR PANEL HEATING

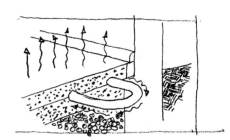

Installed in Floor, Pipes Presure-Treated
for Leakage Before Being Encased

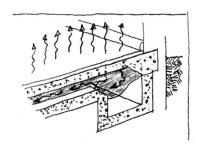

Supply Ducts Distribute Air to a Cellular
Floor Construction and Return Air Ducts
Carry Air Back to Heater for Recirculation

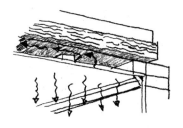

Installed in Ceiling, Permits
Use of Higher Temperatures

LIGHTING: ILLUMINATION TYPES

DIRECT LIGHTING

INDIRECT LIGHTING

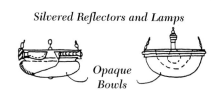

Silvered Reflectors and Lamps

Opaque Bowls

SEMI-DIRECT LIGHTING

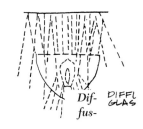

Dif-fus- DIFFU GLAS

DOWN LIGHTS

Lens and Reflector Downlight

Can Downlight

Accent Light

Wall Washer

COVE OR MOLDING LIGHT

TUBULAR LAMP BEHIND VALENCE

BUILT-IN LIGHT PANEL

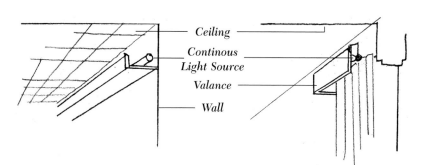

Ceiling

Continous Light Source

Valance

Wall

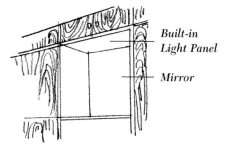

Built-in Light Panel

Mirror

For Fluorescent, Incandescent, or Cold Cathode Tubular Lamps

SUPPORT SYSTEMS

297

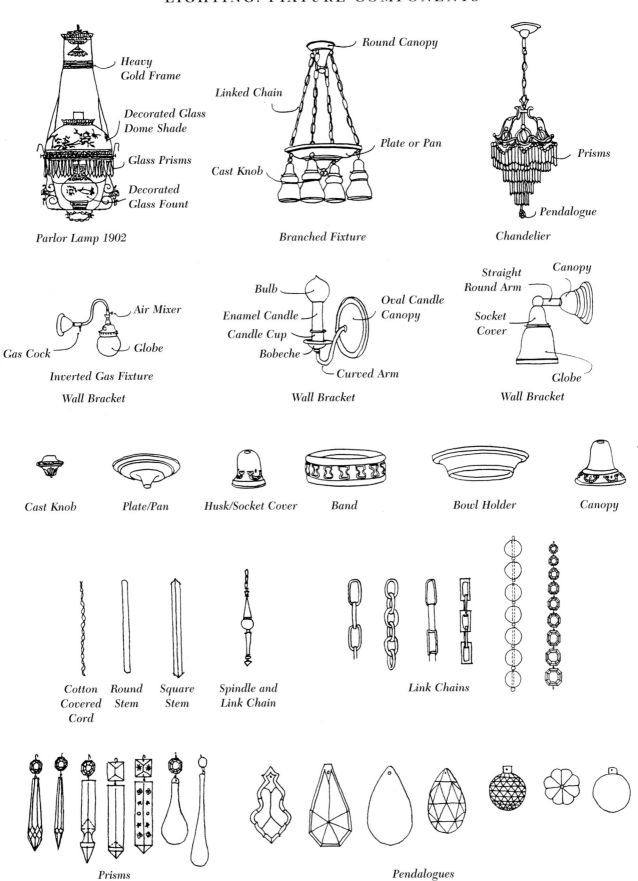

Parlor Lamp 1902

Heavy Gold Frame

Decorated Glass Dome Shade

Glass Prisms

Decorated Glass Fount

Branched Fixture

Round Canopy

Linked Chain

Cast Knob

Plate or Pan

Chandelier

Prisms

Pendalogue

Inverted Gas Fixture

Wall Bracket

Air Mixer

Gas Cock

Globe

Wall Bracket

Bulb

Enamel Candle

Candle Cup

Bobeche

Oval Candle Canopy

Curved Arm

Wall Bracket

Straight Round Arm

Canopy

Socket Cover

Globe

Cast Knob

Plate/Pan

Husk/Socket Cover

Band

Bowl Holder

Canopy

Cotton Covered Cord

Round Stem

Square Stem

Spindle and Link Chain

Link Chains

Prisms

Pendalogues

BALL

Floral Design

Open Bottomed

Crystal Stripes

Grecian Design

Pointed Bottom

Octagonal Ball

BELL

Pansy Border

Frosted

Reed and Ribbon

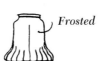

Frosted

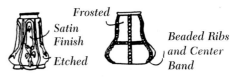

Frosted

Satin Finish

Etched

Beaded Ribs and Center Band

DOME

Leaf

Scalloped Edges

Frosted

Clear Stripes

PANELED

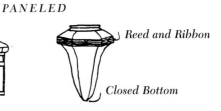

Reed and Ribbon

Closed Bottom

FANCY

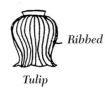

Ribbed

Tulip

Scalloped Edge

Floral Border

Prism Effect

Satin Finish

Shirred Silk Effect

SQUARE

Mission Design

Frosted

Grecian Border

STALACTITE

REFLECTOR

CHIMNEY

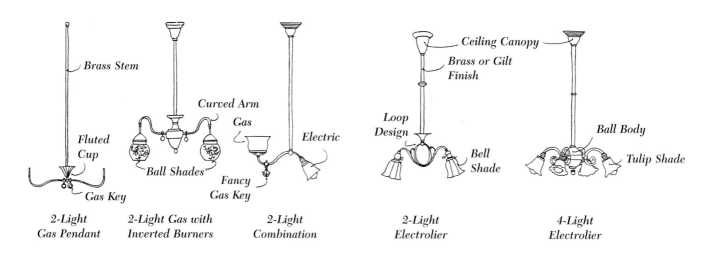

Brass Stem

Fluted
Cup

Gas Key

**2-Light
Gas Pendant**

Curved Arm

Gas

Ball Shades

Fancy
Gas Key

**2-Light Gas with
Inverted Burners**

Electric

**2-Light
Combination**

Ceiling Canopy

Brass or Gilt
Finish

Loop
Design

Bell
Shade

**2-Light
Electrolier**

Ball Body

Tulip Shade

**4-Light
Electrolier**

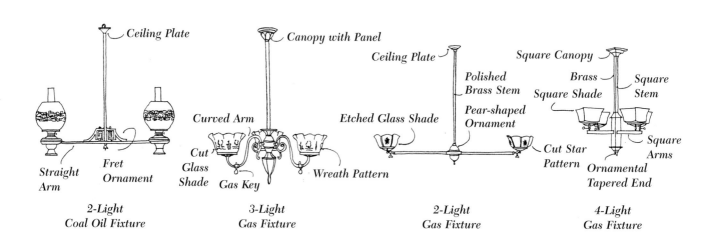

Ceiling Plate

Straight
Arm

Fret
Ornament

**2-Light
Coal Oil Fixture**

Canopy with Panel

Curved Arm

Cut
Glass
Shade

Gas Key

Wreath Pattern

**3-Light
Gas Fixture**

Ceiling Plate

Polished
Brass Stem

Pear-shaped
Ornament

Etched Glass Shade

Cut Star
Pattern

**2-Light
Gas Fixture**

Square Canopy

Brass

Square Shade

Square
Stem

Square
Arms

Ornamental
Tapered End

**4-Light
Gas Fixture**

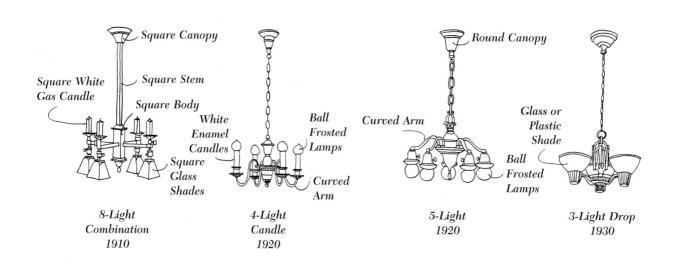

Square Canopy

Square White
Gas Candle

Square Stem

Square Body

White
Enamel
Candles

Square
Glass
Shades

**8-Light
Combination
1910**

Ball
Frosted
Lamps

Curved
Arm

**4-Light
Candle
1920**

Round Canopy

Curved Arm

Ball
Frosted
Lamps

**5-Light
1920**

Glass or
Plastic
Shade

**3-Light Drop
1930**

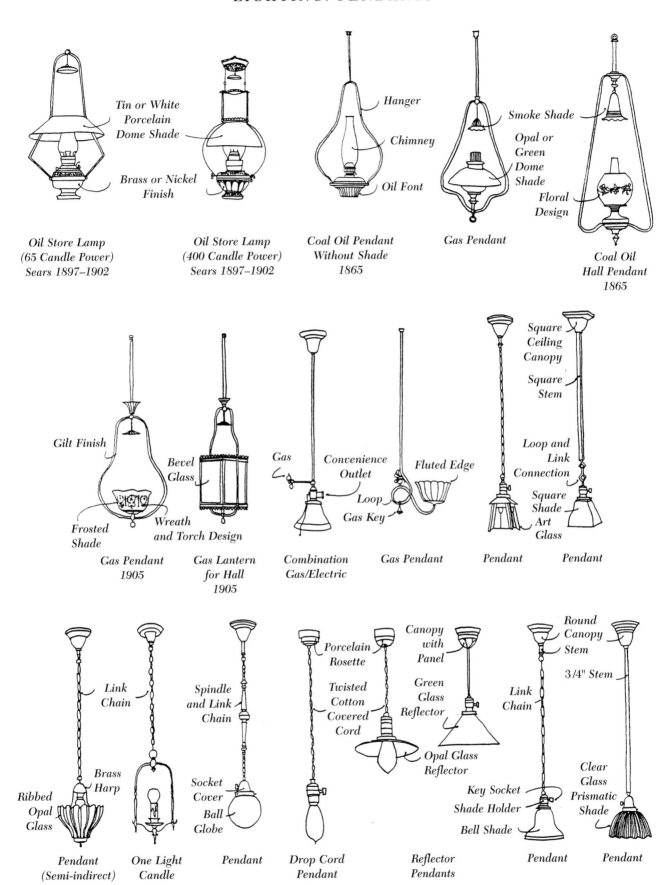

Tin or White
Porcelain
Dome Shade

Brass or Nickel
Finish

Hanger

Chimney

Oil Font

Smoke Shade

Opal or
Green
Dome
Shade

Floral
Design

Oil Store Lamp
(65 Candle Power)
Sears 1897–1902

Oil Store Lamp
(400 Candle Power)
Sears 1897–1902

Coal Oil Pendant
Without Shade
1865

Gas Pendant

Coal Oil
Hall Pendant
1865

Gilt Finish

Frosted
Shade

Bevel
Glass

Wreath
and Torch Design

Gas

Convenience
Outlet

Loop

Gas Key

Fluted Edge

Square
Ceiling
Canopy

Square
Stem

Loop and
Link
Connection

Square
Shade
Art
Glass

Gas Pendant
1905

Gas Lantern
for Hall
1905

Combination
Gas/Electric

Gas Pendant

Pendant

Pendant

Link
Chain

Spindle
and Link
Chain

Socket
Cover
Ball
Globe

Brass
Harp

Ribbed
Opal
Glass

Porcelain
Rosette

Twisted
Cotton
Covered
Cord

Canopy
with
Panel

Green
Glass
Reflector

Opal Glass
Reflector

Key Socket

Shade Holder

Bell Shade

Link
Chain

Round
Canopy
Stem

3/4" Stem

Clear
Glass
Prismatic
Shade

Pendant
(Semi-indirect)

One Light
Candle

Pendant

Drop Cord
Pendant

Reflector
Pendants

Pendant

Pendant

LIGHTING: DOMES AND SHOWERS

ART GLASS PENDANT DOMES

LANTERN PENDANT

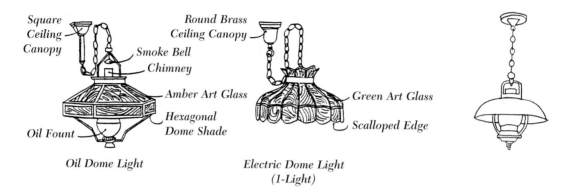

Square Ceiling Canopy

Smoke Bell Chimney

Amber Art Glass

Hexagonal Dome Shade

Oil Fount

Oil Dome Light

Round Brass Ceiling Canopy

Green Art Glass

Scalloped Edge

Electric Dome Light (1-Light)

ART GLASS PENDANT DOMES

PULL-DOWN PENDANTS

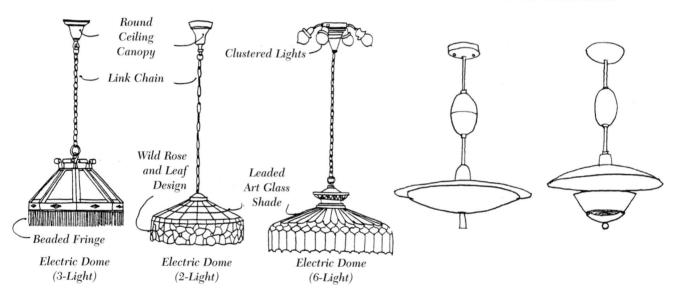

Round Ceiling Canopy

Link Chain

Beaded Fringe

Electric Dome (3-Light)

Wild Rose and Leaf Design

Electric Dome (2-Light)

Clustered Lights

Leaded Art Glass Shade

Electric Dome (6-Light)

SHOWERS

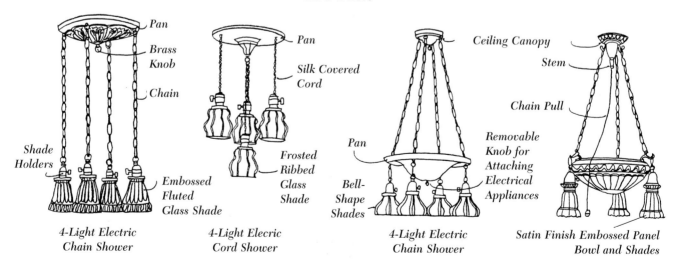

Pan

Brass Knob

Chain

Shade Holders

Embossed Fluted Glass Shade

4-Light Electric Chain Shower

Pan

Silk Covered Cord

Frosted Ribbed Glass Shade

4-Light Electric Cord Shower

Pan

Bell-Shape Shades

4-Light Electric Chain Shower

Ceiling Canopy

Stem

Chain Pull

Removable Knob for Attaching Electrical Appliances

Satin Finish Embossed Panel Bowl and Shades

FLUSH

Mirrored or
Silvered Glass
Reflector

Double-cone Reflector

Oval Plate

Embossed
Cast Metal

Ball Bulb

2-Light Ceiling Fixture

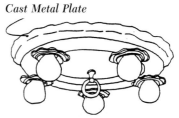

Cast Metal Plate

5-Light Ceiling Fixture

FLUSH

Frosted
Glass

2-Light Ceiling Fixture

Bowl Holder

Frosted
Glass
Bowl

Bowl Ceiling Fixture

STEM

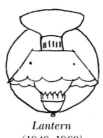

*Lantern
(1940–1960)*

Ceiling Plate

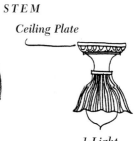

*1-Light
Ceiling Fixture*

STEM

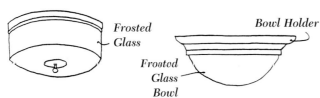

*Multi-light
Ceiling Fixture*

Enamel
Holder

Plascon
Shade

*1-light
Ceiling Fixture*

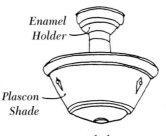

Ceiling
Canopy

Stem

Link
Chain

Socket
Cover

Frosted
Glass Bell
Shade

Ceiling Pendant

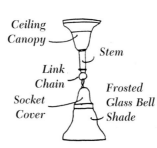

Polished
Brass

Crystal
Glass
Shade

1-light Lantern

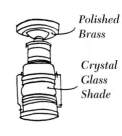

SEMI-FLUSH

CEILING BEAM LIGHTS WITHOUT SHADES (1900–1960)

*Wireless
Cluster*

*Porcelain Keyless
Socket Receptacle*

*Porcelain Pull
Socket Receptacle*

1930–1960

LIGHTING: WALL BRACKETS

WALL BRACKET ILLUMINATION TYPES

Direct Indirect Semi-indirect Cove

OIL AND GAS BRACKETS

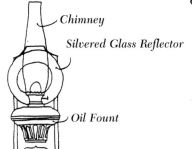

Chimney

Silvered Glass Reflector

Oil Fount

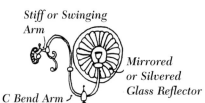

Stiff or Swinging Arm

Mirrored or Silvered Glass Reflector

C Bend Arm

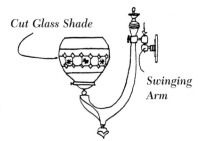

Cut Glass Shade

Swinging Arm

ELECTRIC BRACKETS

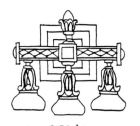

3-Light Electric Bracket

Gas

Electric

Combination Bracket

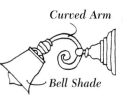

Curved Arm

Bell Shade

1-Light Electric Bracket

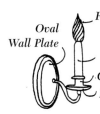

Oval Wall Plate

Flame Bulb

Enamel Candle

Candle Cup

Bobeche

1-Light Candle Bracket

Ball Frosted

2-Light Candle Bracket

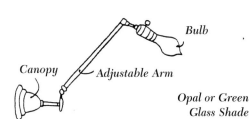

Bulb

Canopy

Adjustable Arm

Adjustable Electric Bracket

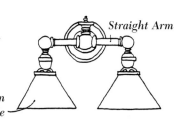

Straight Arm

Opal or Green Glass Shade

2-Light Electric Bracket

1-Light Torch Bracket

1-Light Pocket Bracket

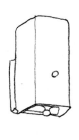

LIGHTING: SPECIAL USE FIXTURES

HALL

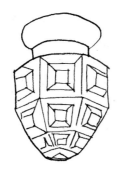 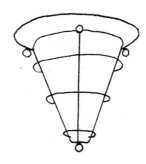 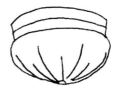

KITCHEN

BATH

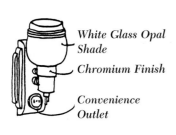  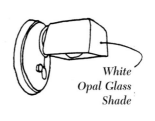 

White Glass Opal Shade

Chromium Finish

Convenience Outlet

White Opal Glass Shade

1-Light Shaded Type Bracket   *Lumiline Wall Bracket*   *Bath or Kitchen Bracket*   *Shower*

OUTDOOR LIGHTS

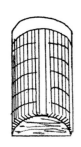   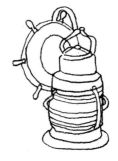

Lantern   *Lantern*   *Lantern*

PENDANTS

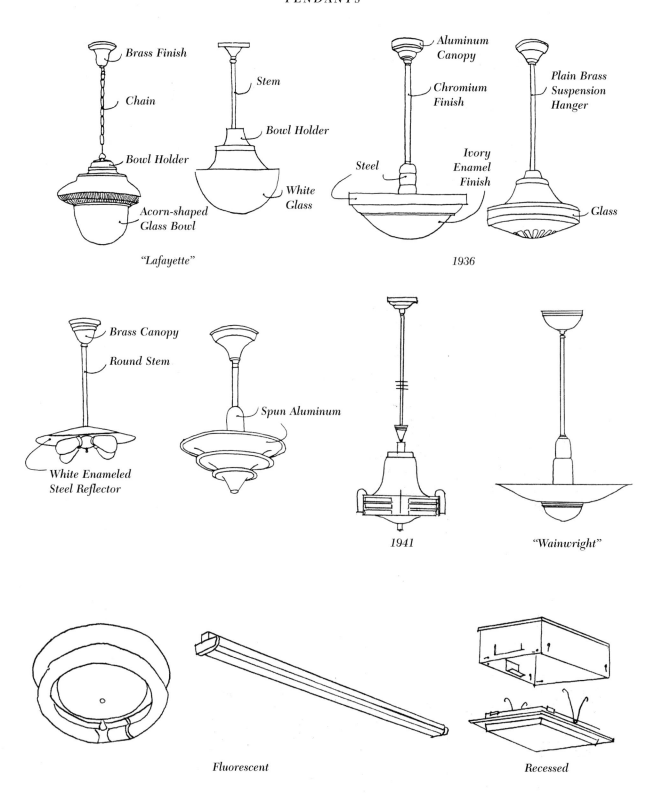

Brass Finish

Chain

Bowl Holder

Acorn-shaped
Glass Bowl

"Lafayette"

Stem

Bowl Holder

White
Glass

Aluminum
Canopy

Chromium
Finish

Steel

Ivory
Enamel
Finish

1936

Plain Brass
Suspension
Hanger

Glass

Brass Canopy

Round Stem

White Enameled
Steel Reflector

Spun Aluminum

1941

"Wainwright"

Fluorescent

Recessed

KITCHEN SYSTEM: SINKS—TIMELINE

EXPOSED PIPES FOR WATER SERVICE—1900–1935

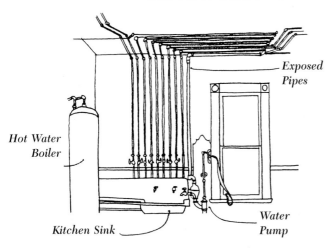

Exposed Pipes

Hot Water Boiler

Kitchen Sink

Water Pump

**Kitchen with Hot Water Boiler
Piping on Wall and Ceiling**

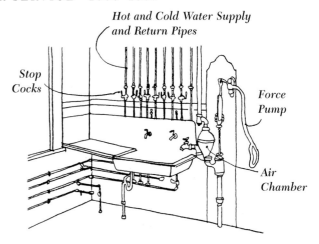

*Hot and Cold Water Supply
and Return Pipes*

Stop Cocks

Force Pump

Air Chamber

**Suburban House 1910
Piping Above and Below Sink**

SEPARATE ELEMENTS—1915–1930

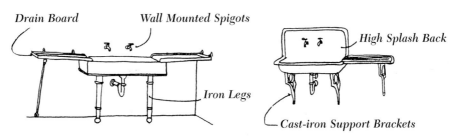

Drain Board

Wall Mounted Spigots

Iron Legs

High Splash Back

Cast-iron Support Brackets

INCREASING INTEGRATION OF ELEMENTS—1915–1940

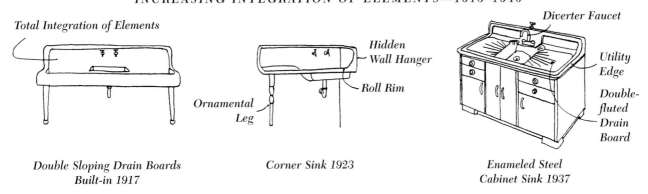

Total Integration of Elements

**Double Sloping Drain Boards
Built-in 1917**

Ornamental Leg

Hidden Wall Hanger

Roll Rim

Corner Sink 1923

Diverter Faucet

Utility Edge

Double-fluted Drain Board

**Enameled Steel
Cabinet Sink 1937**

SINK INTEGRATED INTO A WORK CENTER WITH A COUNTER TOP—1940–1960

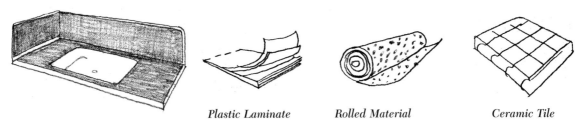

Plastic Laminate

Rolled Material

Ceramic Tile

KITCHEN SYSTEMS: CABINETS

KITCHEN CASE ORGANIZED MODULARLY ON A GRID

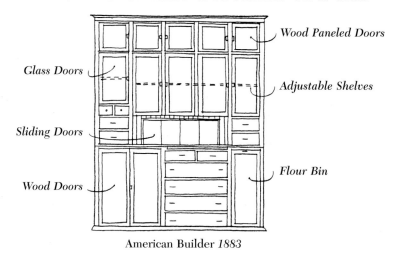

Wood Paneled Doors

Glass Doors

Adjustable Shelves

Sliding Doors

Wood Doors

Flour Bin

American Builder *1883*

KITCHEN CASE ON KITCHEN SIDE BECOMES BUFFET ON DINING ROOM SIDE

American Builder *1917*

KITCHENETTE

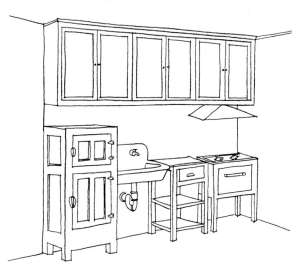

The Aladdinette Home, *Catalog No. 33, 1921*

BREAKFAST NOOK

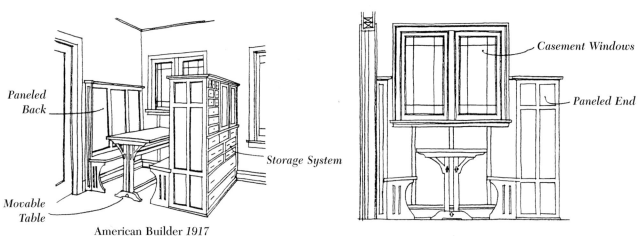

Paneled Back

Movable Table

Storage System

Casement Windows

Paneled End

American Builder *1917*

KITCHEN SYSTEM: STOCK CABINETS

WALL CABINETS

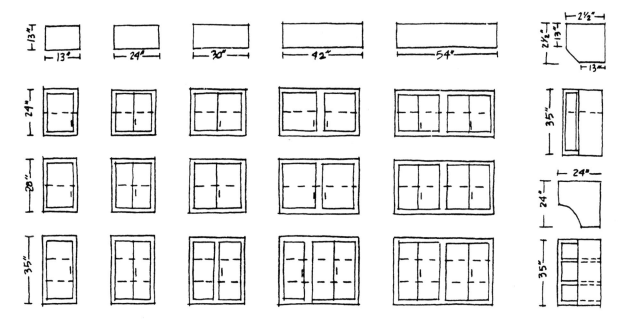

SPECIAL PURPOSE BASES

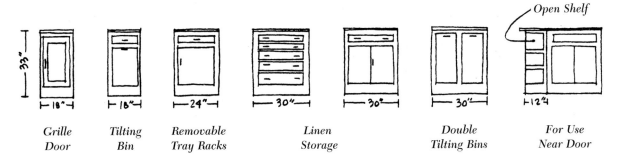

Grille Door   *Tilting Bin*   *Removable Tray Racks*   *Linen Storage*   *Double Tilting Bins*   *For Use Near Door*

KITCHEN MAID CORPORATION, 1939

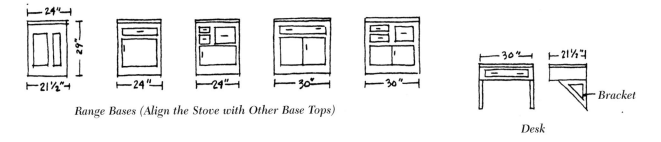

Range Bases (Align the Stove with Other Base Tops)

Desk

KITCHEN SYSTEM: PLANNING PRINCIPLES

CIRCULATION—"SYSTEM OF ROUTING WORK IN A PRACTICAL KITCHEN"
AND "STEP-SAVING"

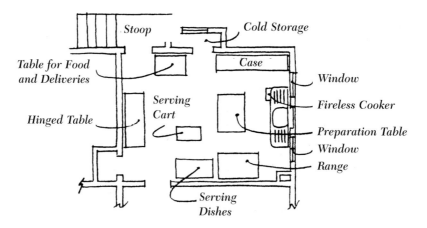

ORGANIZATION—KITCHEN AS WORKSHOP

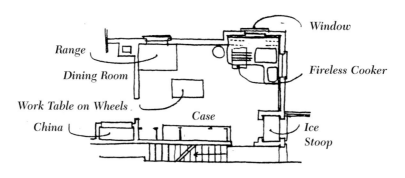

CABINETS—DIMENSIONAL STANDARDS
FOR HEIGHT AND DEPTH

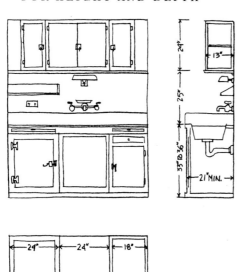

COUNTER—CONTINUOUS

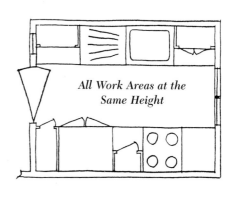

KITCHEN SYSTEM: PLANNING PRINCIPLES

STEPS SAVED BY PROPER PLANNING OF "FOCUSED" WORK CENTERS

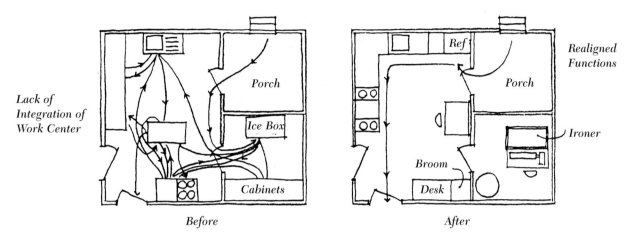

Lack of Integration of Work Center

Porch

Ice Box

Cabinets

Before

Ref

Realigned Functions

Porch

Ironer

Broom

Desk

After

3 WORK CENTERS

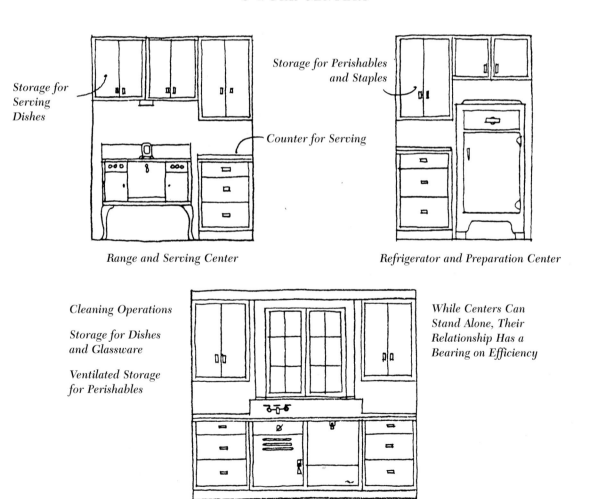

Storage for Serving Dishes

Counter for Serving

Range and Serving Center

Storage for Perishables and Staples

Refrigerator and Preparation Center

Cleaning Operations

Storage for Dishes and Glassware

Ventilated Storage for Perishables

While Centers Can Stand Alone, Their Relationship Has a Bearing on Efficiency

Sink Center
American Builder *1936*

KITCHEN SYSTEM: PLANNING PRINCIPLES

UNIT SYSTEM

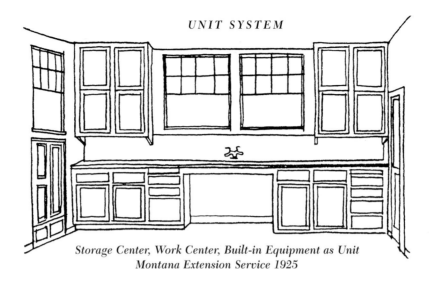

Storage Center, Work Center, Built-in Equipment as Unit
Montana Extension Service 1925

GENERAL ELECTRIC UNIT KITCHEN 1932

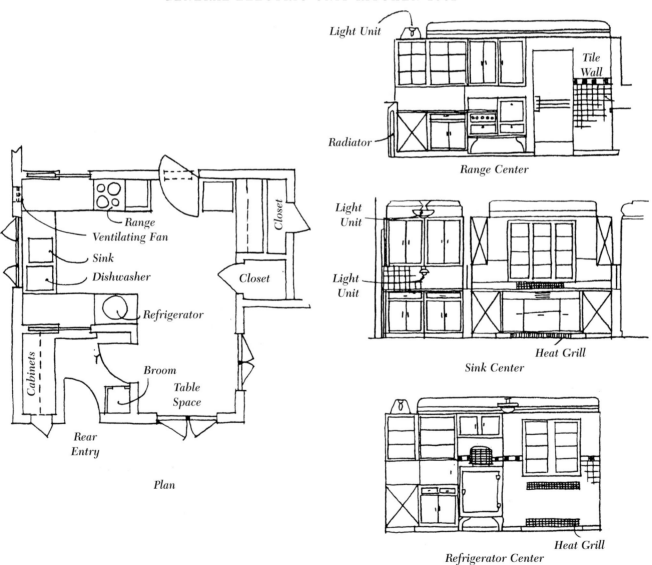

Light Unit

Tile
Wall

Radiator

Range Center

Light
Unit

Light
Unit

Heat Grill

Sink Center

Range
Ventilating Fan

Sink

Dishwasher

Refrigerator

Closet

Closet

Cabinets

Broom

Table
Space

Rear
Entry

Plan

Heat Grill

Refrigerator Center

KITCHEN SYSTEM: PLANNING PRINCIPLES

KITCHEN TRIANGLE

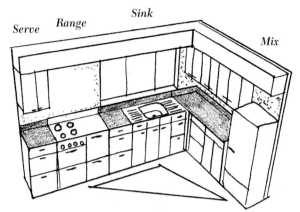

University of Illinois Extension Service 1949

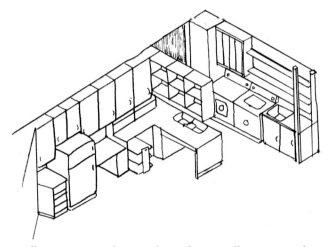

All American Inside-Outside Kitchen, Small Homes Guide, *1955*

KITCHEN SYSTEM: KITCHEN CONFIGURATIONS

PULLMAN OR PANEL TYPE OR STRAIGHT WALL TYPE (1 WALL)

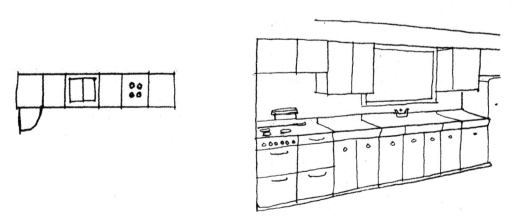

Standard Dimensions, Automobile Type Cold Rolled Steel 1945

CORRIDOR TYPE (2 WALLS)

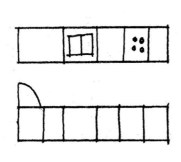
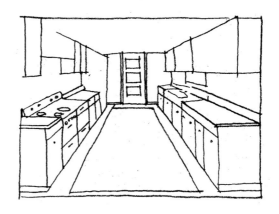

L-TYPE (2 WALLS)

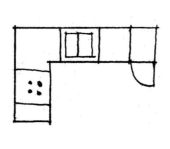

U-TYPE (3 WALLS)

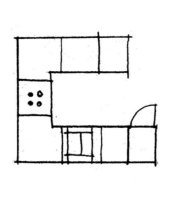

Single Unit Plan Using Metal and Plastic as Continuous and Integrated Surfaces 1936

BATHROOM SYSTEM: LAVATORY COMPONENTS

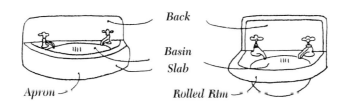

Back

Basin
Slab

Apron

Rolled Rim

LAVATORY SHAPES

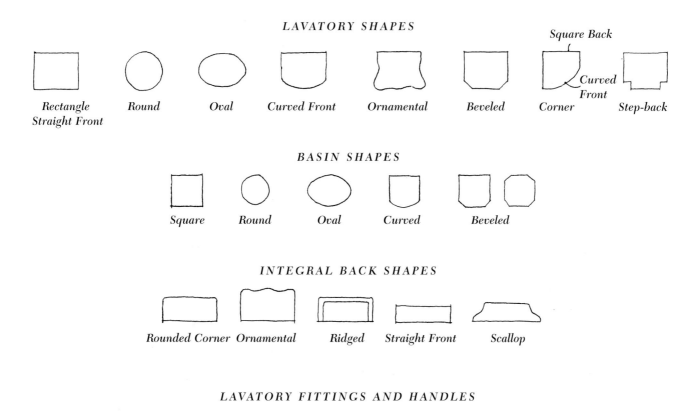

Rectangle
Straight Front

Round

Oval

Curved Front

Ornamental

Beveled

Square Back

Curved
Front

Corner

Step-back

BASIN SHAPES

Square

Round

Oval

Curved

Beveled

INTEGRAL BACK SHAPES

Rounded Corner

Ornamental

Ridged

Straight Front

Scallop

LAVATORY FITTINGS AND HANDLES

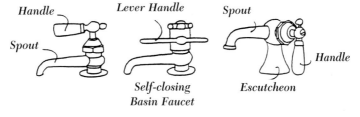

Handle

Lever Handle

Spout

Spout

Handle

Self-closing
Basin Faucet

Escutcheon

LAVATORY HANDLES

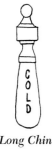

Brass
Fancy

Long China
indexed

Short China
Indexed

Brass
Plain

All China
Four-arm

China Button
Four-arm

Tee

Wheel

*Italian Marble Slab with Nickel
Plated Brackets (Sears 1902)*

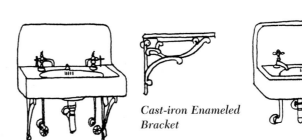

*Cast-iron Enameled
Bracket*

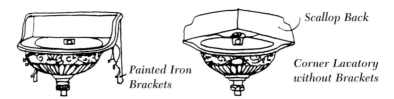

Scallop Back

*Painted Iron
Brackets*

*Corner Lavatory
without Brackets*

Roll Rim Enameled Ornamental (Sears 1902)

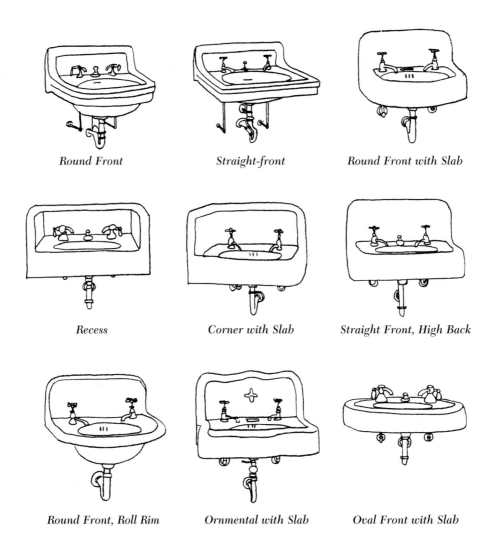

Round Front   *Straight-front*   *Round Front with Slab*

Recess   *Corner with Slab*   *Straight Front, High Back*

Round Front, Roll Rim   *Ornmental with Slab*   *Oval Front with Slab*

PEDESTALS

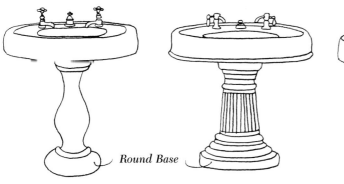

Urn-Shape, Ellipse Slab
Kohler c1890

Round Base

Fluted Pedestal, Oval Slab
Standard Sanitary 1906

Round Pedestal, Oval Slab
Kohler 1917

Square-base and Basin
Cole Supply 1928

LEGS

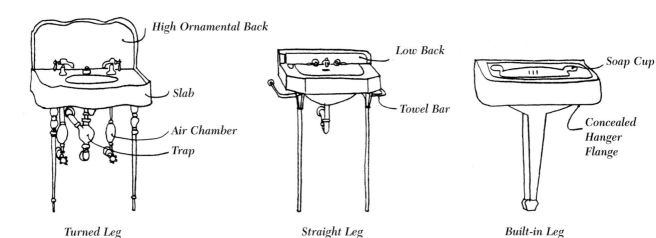

High Ornamental Back

Slab

Air Chamber

Trap

Low Back

Towel Bar

Soap Cup

*Concealed
Hanger
Flange*

Turned Leg

Straight Leg

Built-in Leg

CABINET

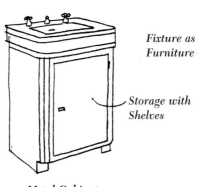

*Fixture as
Furniture*

*Storage with
Shelves*

Metal Cabinet

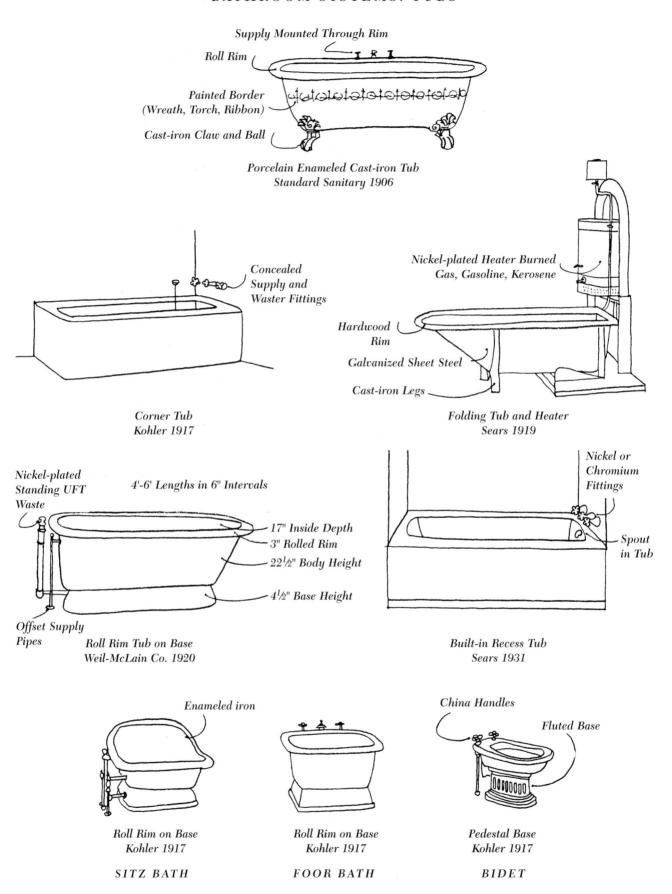

Supply Mounted Through Rim

Roll Rim

Painted Border
(Wreath, Torch, Ribbon)

Cast-iron Claw and Ball

Porcelain Enameled Cast-iron Tub
Standard Sanitary 1906

Concealed
Supply and
Waster Fittings

Corner Tub
Kohler 1917

Nickel-plated Heater Burned
Gas, Gasoline, Kerosene

Hardwood
Rim

Galvanized Sheet Steel

Cast-iron Legs

Folding Tub and Heater
Sears 1919

Nickel-plated
Standing UFT
Waste

4'-6' Lengths in 6" Intervals

17" Inside Depth
3" Rolled Rim
22½" Body Height
4½" Base Height

Offset Supply
Pipes

Roll Rim Tub on Base
Weil-McLain Co. 1920

Nickel or
Chromium
Fittings

Spout
in Tub

Built-in Recess Tub
Sears 1931

Enameled iron

Roll Rim on Base
Kohler 1917

SITZ BATH

Roll Rim on Base
Kohler 1917

FOOR BATH

China Handles

Fluted Base

Pedestal Base
Kohler 1917

BIDET

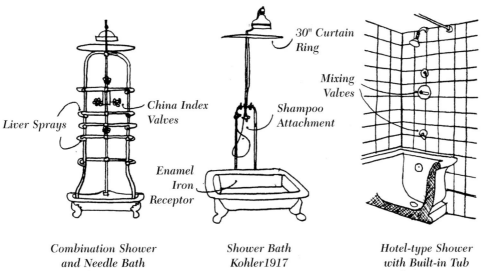

Liver Sprays

China Index Valves

Enamel Iron Receptor

**Combination Shower
and Needle Bath
Standard Sanitary 1902**

30" Curtain Ring

Shampoo Attachment

**Shower Bath
Kohler 1917**

Mixing Valves

**Hotel-type Shower
with Built-in Tub
Weil-McLain 1920**

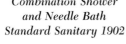

Adjustable Ball Joint Shower Head

Mixing Valve

Marble Stall

Needle Bath

**Combination Shower and
and Needle Bath Stall
Speakman 1920**

Piano Hinge

Tiled Stall

Metal Frame with Rubber Strip

Recessed Soap Dish

**Built-in Shower,
Plate Glass Door
N.O. Nelson 1928**

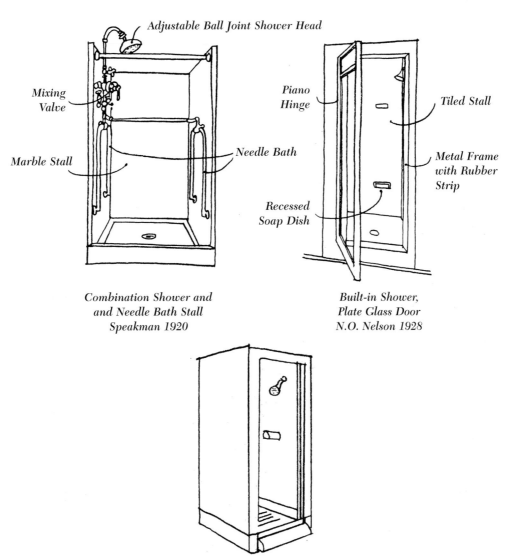

Free-Standing Shwoer Stall 1945

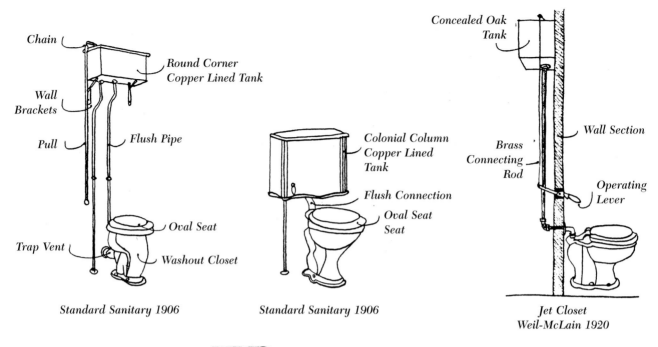

Chain

Wall Brackets

Pull

Trap Vent

Round Corner Copper Lined Tank

Flush Pipe

Oval Seat

Washout Closet

Standard Sanitary 1906

Colonial Column Copper Lined Tank

Flush Connection

Oval Seat Seat

Standard Sanitary 1906

Concealed Oak Tank

Wall Section

Brass Connecting Rod

Operating Lever

Jet Closet
Weil-McLain 1920

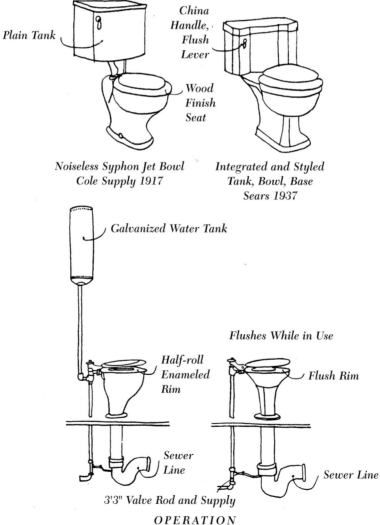

Plain Tank

China Handle, Flush Lever

Wood Finish Seat

Noiseless Syphon Jet Bowl
Cole Supply 1917

Integrated and Styled
Tank, Bowl, Base
Sears 1937

Galvanized Water Tank

Flushes While in Use

Half-roll Enameled Rim

Flush Rim

Sewer Line

Sewer Line

3'3" Valve Rod and Supply

OPERATION

BATHROOM SYSTEM: STORAGE AND TRIMMINGS

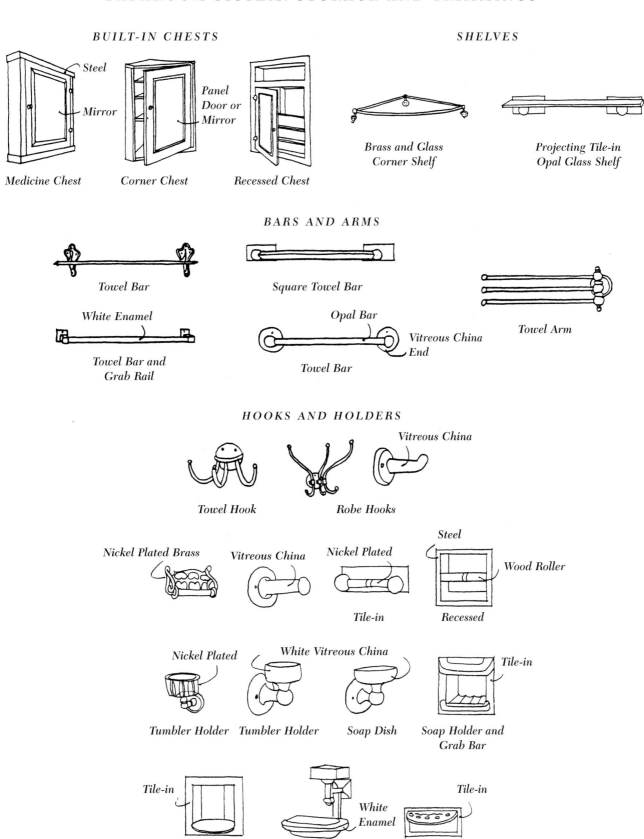

BUILT-IN CHESTS

Steel

Mirror

Panel Door or Mirror

Medicine Chest

Corner Chest

Recessed Chest

SHELVES

Brass and Glass Corner Shelf

Projecting Tile-in Opal Glass Shelf

BARS AND ARMS

Towel Bar

White Enamel

Towel Bar and Grab Rail

Square Towel Bar

Opal Bar

Towel Bar

Vitreous China End

Towel Arm

HOOKS AND HOLDERS

Vitreous China

Towel Hook

Robe Hooks

Nickel Plated Brass

Vitreous China

Nickel Plated

Steel

Wood Roller

Tile-in

Recessed

Nickel Plated

White Vitreous China

Tile-in

Tumbler Holder

Tumbler Holder

Soap Dish

Soap Holder and Grab Bar

Tile-in

White Enamel

Tile-in

Tumbler Holder

Soap and Tumbler Holder

Toothbrush Holder

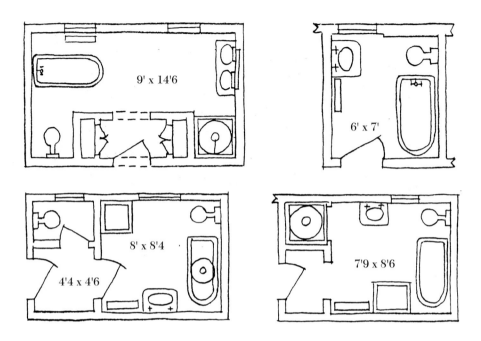

"Plans with Excellent Spacing and Good Arrangement."
William A. Wollmer, A Book of Distinctive Interiors, 1902

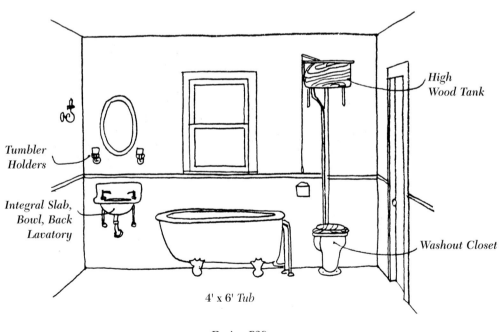

Design P38
Standard Sanitary 1906

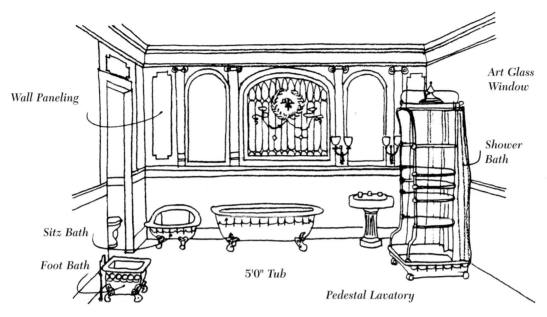

Wall Paneling

Art Glass
Window

Shower
Bath

Sitz Bath

Foot Bath

5'0" Tub

Pedestal Lavatory

Design P23
Standard Sanitary 1906

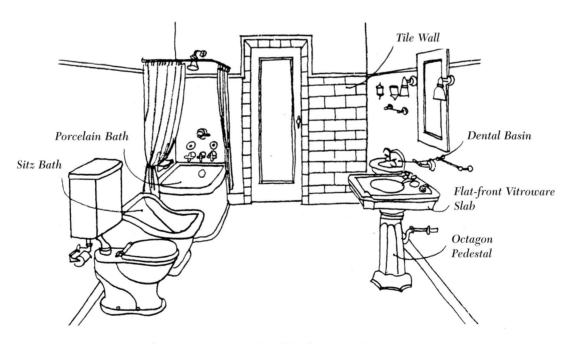

Tile Wall

Porcelain Bath

Sitz Bath

Dental Basin

Flat-front Vitroware
Slab

Octagon
Pedestal

Bathroom Design No. 1 (Parallel Alignment of Stations)
Crane 1915

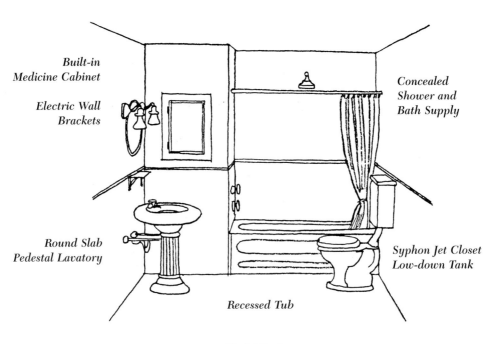

Built-in
Medicine Cabinet

Electric Wall
Brackets

Concealed
Shower and
Bath Supply

Round Slab
Pedestal Lavatory

Syphon Jet Closet
Low-down Tank

Recessed Tub

Model Bathroom
Rundle-Spence 1915

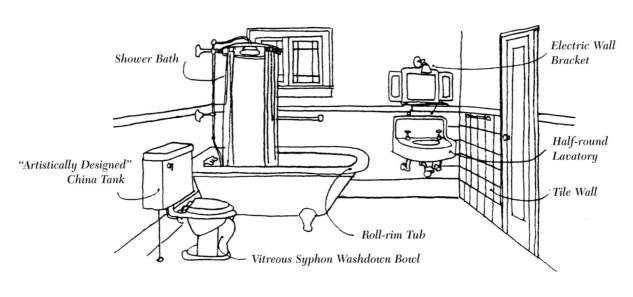

Shower Bath

Electric Wall
Bracket

"Artistically Designed"
China Tank

Half-round
Lavatory

Tile Wall

Roll-rim Tub

Vitreous Syphon Washdown Bowl

Modern Bathroom Outfit
Sears 1920

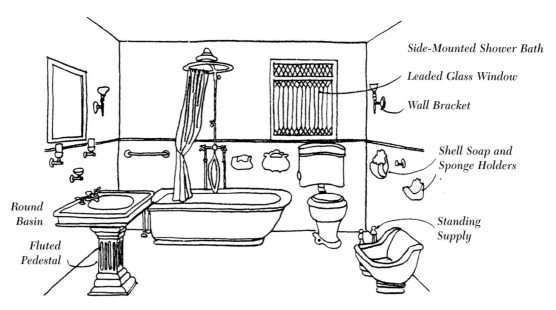

Side-Mounted Shower Bath

Leaded Glass Window

Wall Bracket

Shell Soap and Sponge Holders

Round Basin

Standing Supply

Fluted Pedestal

Modern Bathroom Outfit
Webb 1912

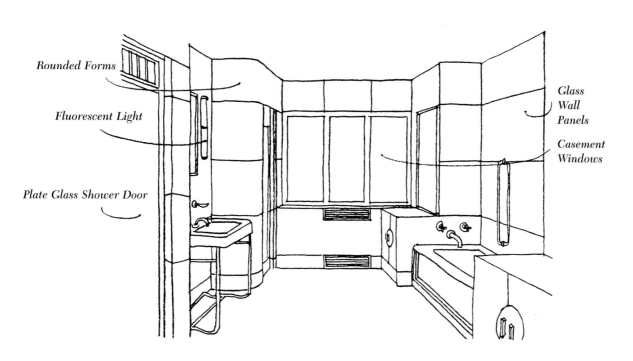

Rounded Forms

Glass Wall Panels

Fluorescent Light

Casement Windows

Plate Glass Shower Door

Vitrolite 1938

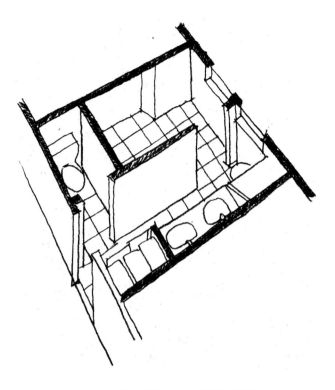

Compartmentalized Bathroom 1945–1960
Separate Spaces for Tub, Lavatory, Toilet, and Use of Double Lavatories

17

ELEMENTS

CONSTRUCTION SYSTEM: WALL FRAMING

BALLOON FRAME

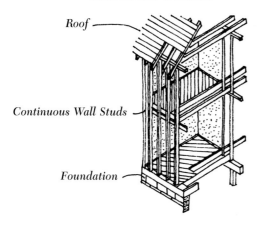

Roof

Continuous Wall Studs

Foundation

PLATFORM FRAME

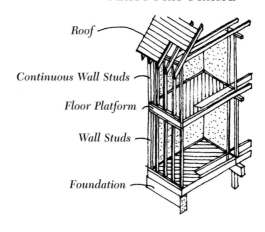

Roof

Continuous Wall Studs

Floor Platform

Wall Studs

Foundation

PANEL SYSTEM

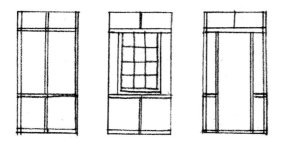

STEEL FRAME

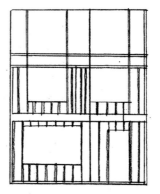

Front Elevation for a 6-Room House

CONSTRUCTION SYSTEM: MASONRY

MASONRY LOAD-BEARING

HOLLOW TILE AND CONCRETE BLOCK

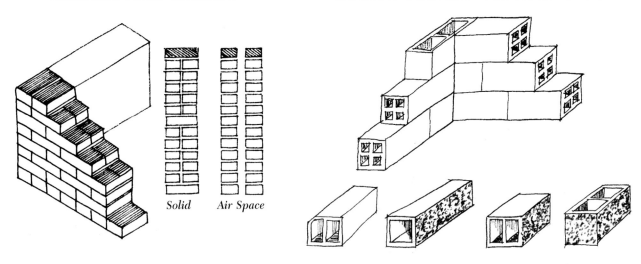

Solid   Air Space

ROOF PLANE: TYPES: GABLE AND HIP

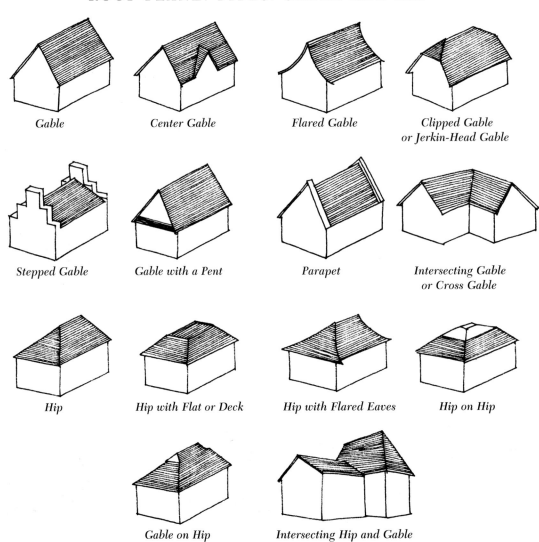

Gable

Center Gable

Flared Gable

Clipped Gable
or Jerkin-Head Gable

Stepped Gable

Gable with a Pent

Parapet

Intersecting Gable
or Cross Gable

Hip

Hip with Flat or Deck

Hip with Flared Eaves

Hip on Hip

Gable on Hip

Intersecting Hip and Gable

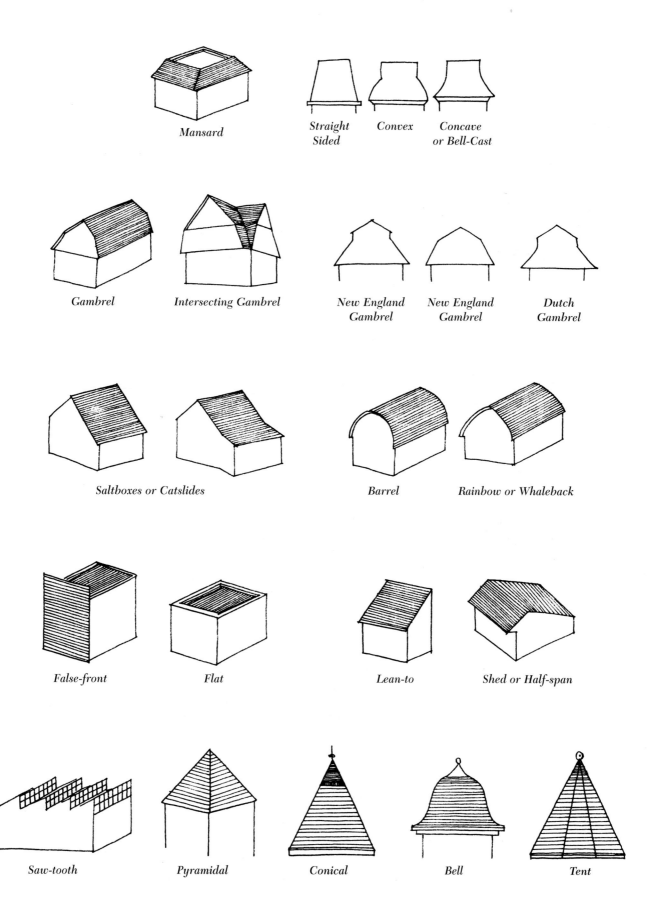

Mansard

Straight Sided

Convex

Concave or Bell-Cast

Gambrel

Intersecting Gambrel

New England Gambrel

New England Gambrel

Dutch Gambrel

Saltboxes or Catslides

Barrel

Rainbow or Whaleback

False-front

Flat

Lean-to

Shed or Half-span

Saw-tooth

Pyramidal

Conical

Bell

Tent

ROOF PLANE: MATERIALS AND ORNAMENTAL TREATMENTS

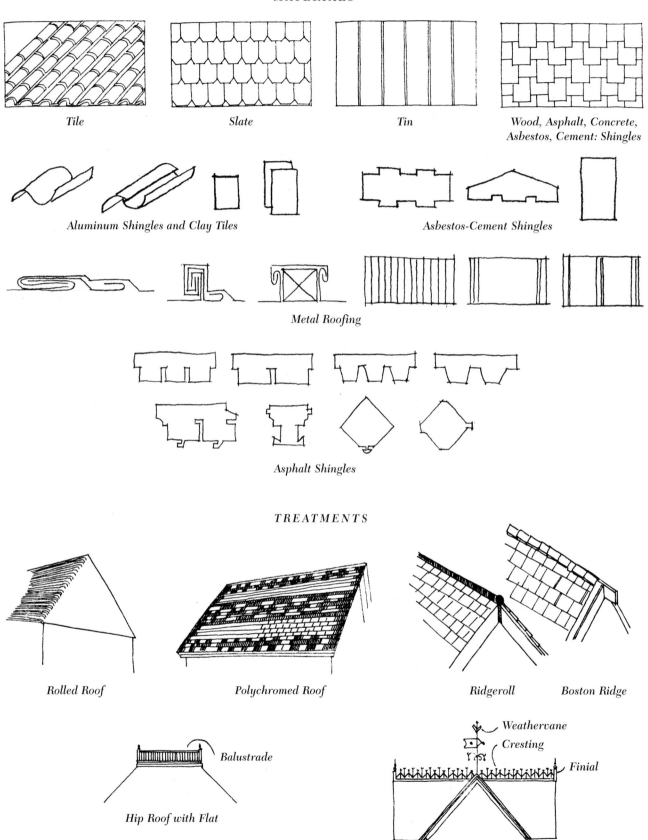

MATERIALS

Tile *Slate* *Tin* *Wood, Asphalt, Concrete, Asbestos, Cement: Shingles*

Aluminum Shingles and Clay Tiles *Asbestos-Cement Shingles*

Metal Roofing

Asphalt Shingles

TREATMENTS

Rolled Roof *Polychromed Roof* *Ridgeroll* *Boston Ridge*

Balustrade

Hip Roof with Flat

Weathervane
Cresting
Finial

ROOF PLANE: DETAILS

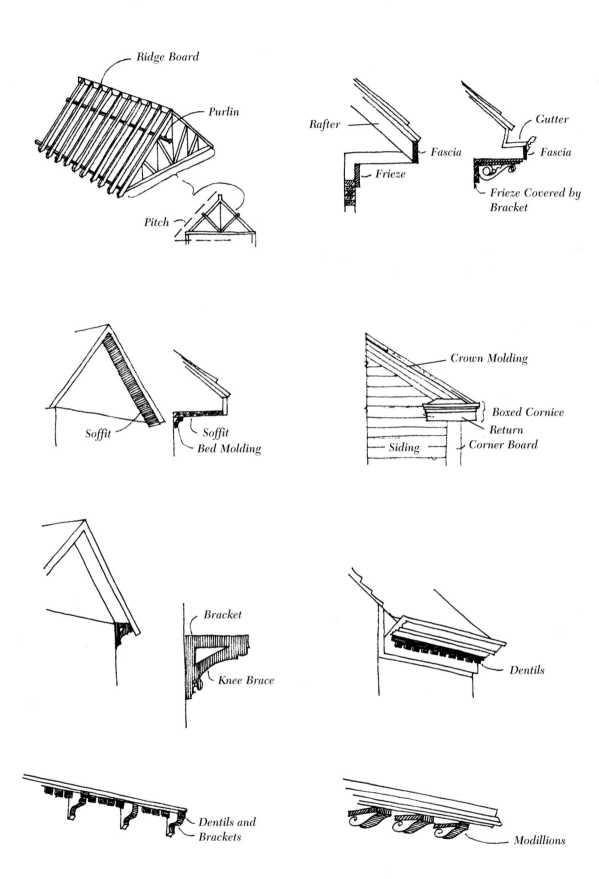

Ridge Board

Purlin

Pitch

Rafter

Fascia

Frieze

Gutter

Fascia

Frieze Covered by
Bracket

Soffit

Soffit
Bed Molding

Crown Molding

Boxed Cornice

Return

Corner Board

Siding

Bracket

Knee Brace

Dentils

Dentils and
Brackets

Modillions

ROOF PLANE: TOWERS, STEEPLES, TURRETS, AND SPECIAL STRUCTURES

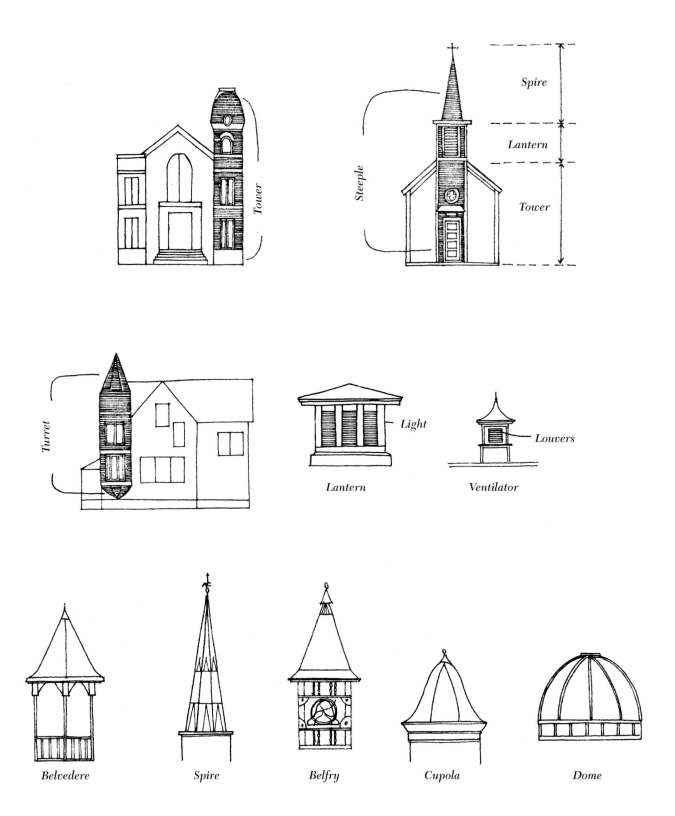

Tower

Steeple

Spire

Lantern

Tower

Turret

Lantern

Light

Ventilator

Louvers

Belvedere

Spire

Belfry

Cupola

Dome

TYPES

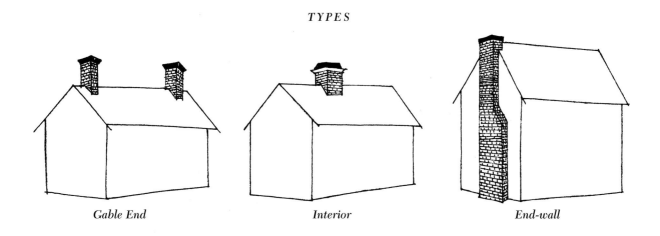

Gable End   Interior   End-wall

DETAILS

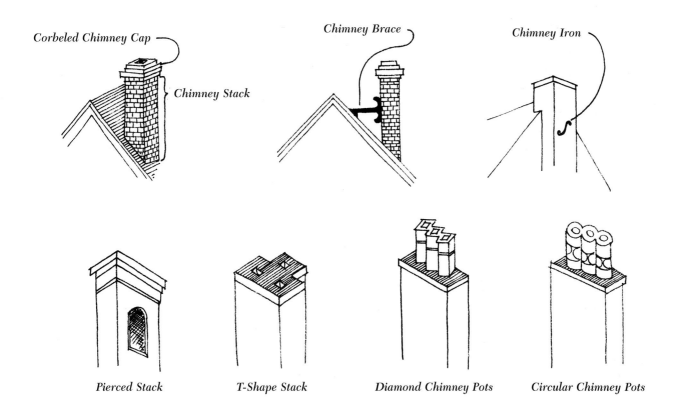

Corbeled Chimney Cap

Chimney Stack

Chimney Brace

Chimney Iron

Pierced Stack   T-Shape Stack   Diamond Chimney Pots   Circular Chimney Pots

ROOF PLANE: DORMERS

DORMER TYPES

Gable Dormer

Hipped Dormer

Shed Dormer

DORMER PLACEMENTS

Wall Dormer

Dormer with Balcony

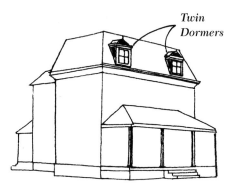

Dormers in Mansard Roof

SPECIALTY DORMERS

Flared Roof
and Walls

Gambrel

Clipped Gable

Triangular

Bay

Eyebrow

DORMER WINDOW SHAPES

Segmented

Flat

Round-headed

Pedimented

AMERICAN VERNACULAR BUILDINGS *and* INTERIORS 1870–1960

WOOD AND COMPOSITION SHINGLE PATTERNS

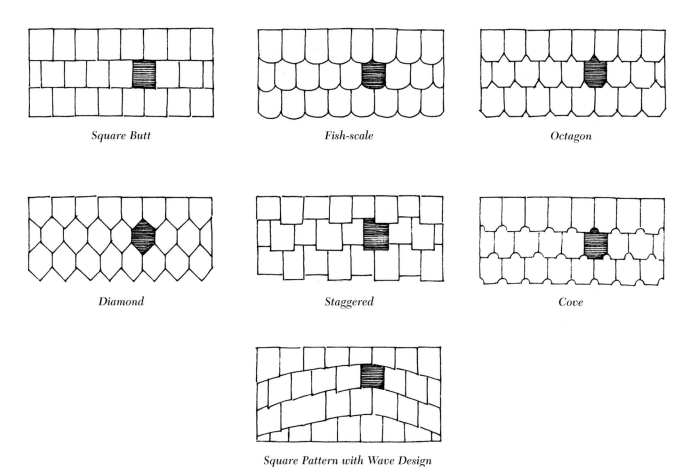

Square Butt

Fish-scale

Octagon

Diamond

Staggered

Cove

Square Pattern with Wave Design

ASBESTOS, ASPHALT, AND COMPOSITION SHINGLE PATTERNS

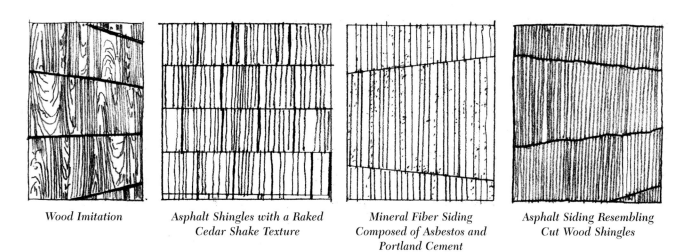

Wood Imitation

Asphalt Shingles with a Raked
Cedar Shake Texture

Mineral Fiber Siding
Composed of Asbestos and
Portland Cement

Asphalt Siding Resembling
Cut Wood Shingles

HORIZONTAL WOOD SIDING

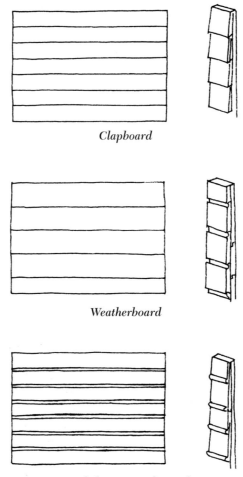

Clapboard

Weatherboard

Beaded Horizontal Board

VERTICAL WOOD SIDING

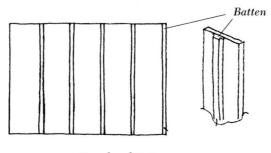

Batten

Board and Batten

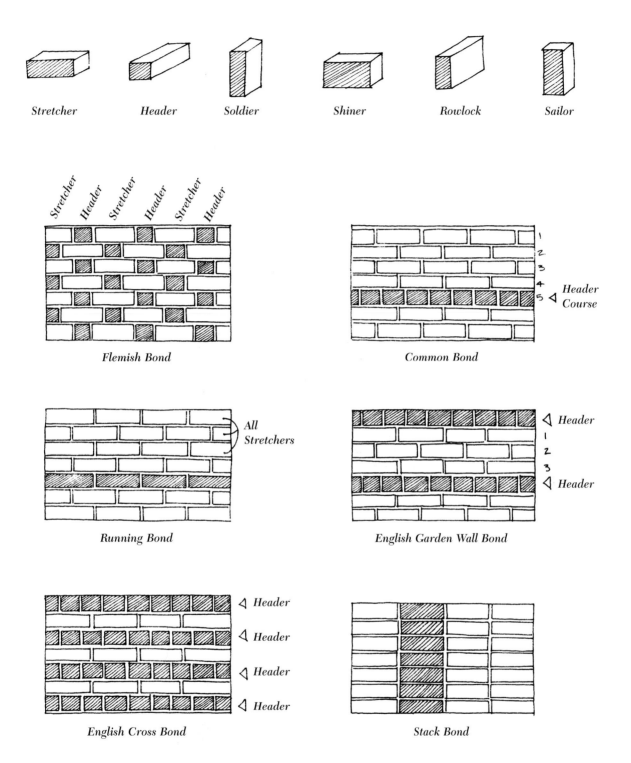

Stretcher   Header   Soldier   Shiner   Rowlock   Sailor

Stretcher Header Stretcher Header Stretcher Header

Flemish Bond

Common Bond

Header Course

Running Bond

All Stretchers

English Garden Wall Bond

Header

Header

English Cross Bond

Header

Header

Header

Header

Stack Bond

EXTERIOR WALL PLANE: CLADDING MATERIALS— STONE AND SYNTHETIC STONE

NATURAL STONE

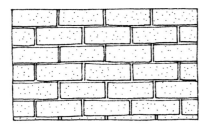

Coursed Ashlar: Smooth Faced

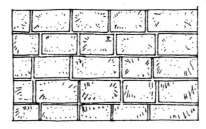

Coursed Ashlar: Rock Faced

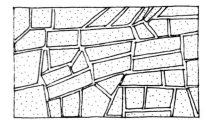

Cuncoursed Ashlar: Rough Cut

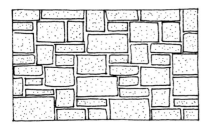

Random Ashlar

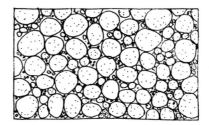

River Rock (Cobblestone)

Coursed Rubble

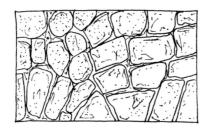

Cobweb or Puzzle Rubble

Random or Uncoursed Rubble

SYNTHETIC STONE—TUMBLED WALL

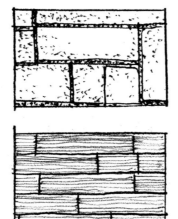

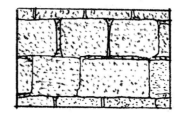

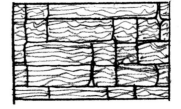

EXTERIOR WALL PLAN: CLADDING MATERIALS—MASONRY

MASONRY CLADDING MATERIAL

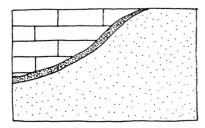

*Stucco (over Masonry)
and Hollow Tile*

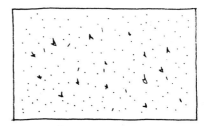

*Sprayed-on or Roughcast Cement
(with Mica Flecks)*

Terra Cotta *Profile*

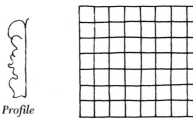

*Ceramic Tile
(Glazed or Unglazed)*

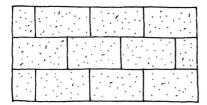

Concrete Block

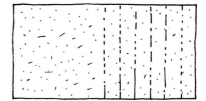

Poured Concrete

MOLDED CONCRETE BLOCKS

Horizontal Tooled Edge

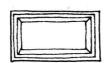

Panel Face

Cobblestone Face

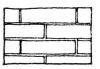

Pressed Brick Face

*Ornamental Scroll
Face*

*Ornamental Wreath
Face*

*Bushhammer Face with
Tooled Edge*

Broken Ashlar Face

EXTERIOR WALL PLANE: MASONRY ARCHES AND RUSTICATION

COMPONENTS

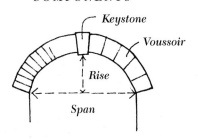

Keystone

Voussoir

Rise

Span

MASONRY ARCHES

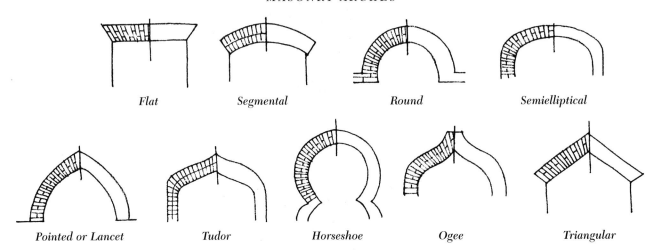

Flat   *Segmental*   *Round*   *Semielliptical*

Pointed or Lancet   *Tudor*   *Horseshoe*   *Ogee*   *Triangular*

RUSTICATION

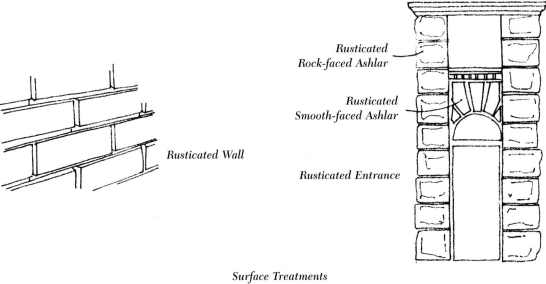

Rusticated Wall

Rusticated Rock-faced Ashlar

Rusticated Smooth-faced Ashlar

Rusticated Entrance

Surface Treatments

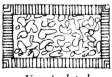

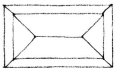

Chiseled   *Vermiculated (Tooled Margin)*   *Roughly Tooled*   *Beveled (Face and Margin)*

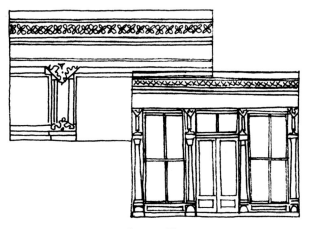

Iron or Tin

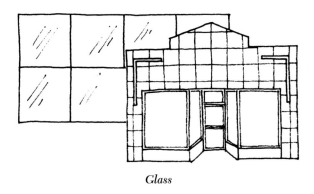

Glass

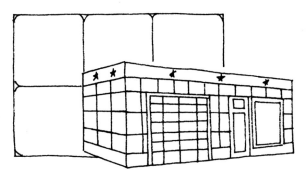

Porcelain Enamel

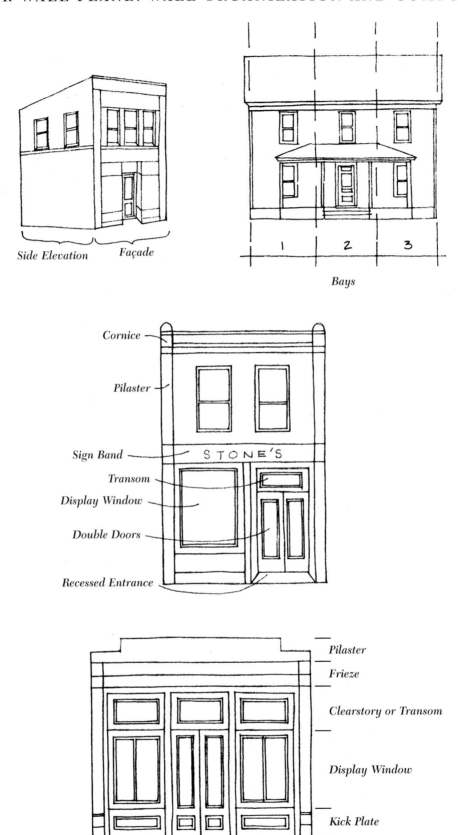

Side Elevation   *Façade*

Bays

Cornice

Pilaster

Sign Band

Transom

Display Window

Double Doors

Recessed Entrance

STONE'S

Pilaster

Frieze

Clearstory or Transom

Display Window

Kick Plate

COMPONENTS OF FACADES FOR COMMERCIAL BUILDINGS

EXTERIOR WALL PLANE: GABLE WALLS

GABLE COMPONENTS

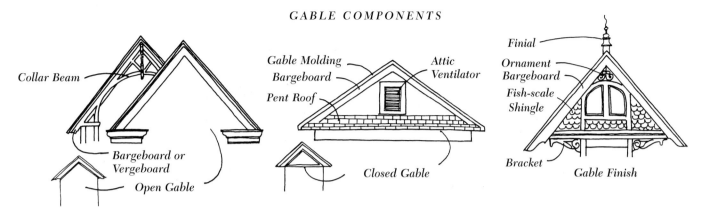

Collar Beam

Bargeboard or Vergeboard

Open Gable

Gable Molding
Bargeboard
Pent Roof

Attic Ventilator

Closed Gable

Finial
Ornament
Bargeboard
Fish-scale Shingle

Bracket

Gable Finish

GABLE SHAPES

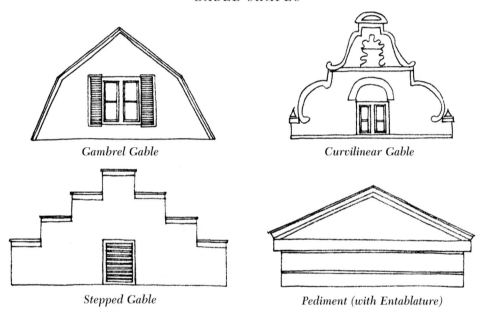

Gambrel Gable

Curvilinear Gable

Stepped Gable

Pediment (with Entablature)

GABLES FOR NON-RESIDENTIAL BUILDINGS

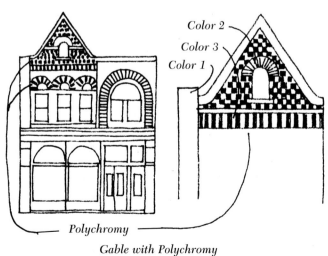

Color 2
Color 3
Color 1

Polychromy

Gable with Polychromy

GABLES FOR COTTAGES

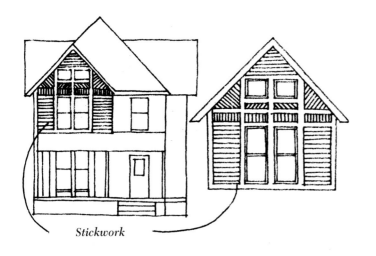

Stickwork

Sunrise or Sunburst Motif

Herringbone Motif

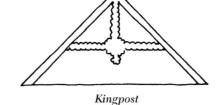

Kingpost

Scrollwork

Scrollwork

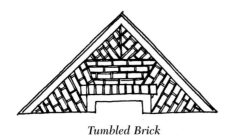

Tumbled Brick

Stickwork Combinations

GABLES FOR BUNGALOWS

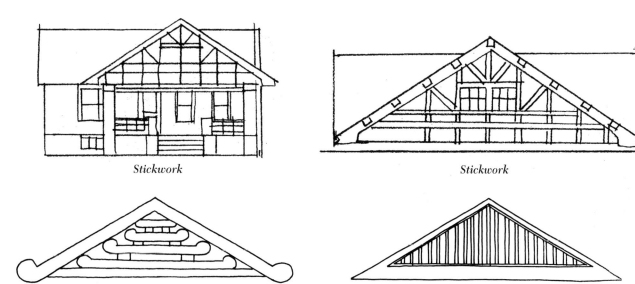

Stickwork

Stickwork

Canoe Motif

Stickwork Composed of Vertical Sticks

GABLES FOR ENGLISH COTTAGES

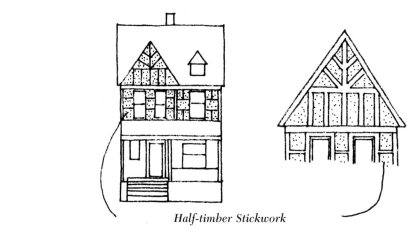

Half-timber Stickwork

Half-timber or Tudor-like Sticks

EXTERIOR WALL PLANE: WALL TREATMENTS

CANTED WALLS

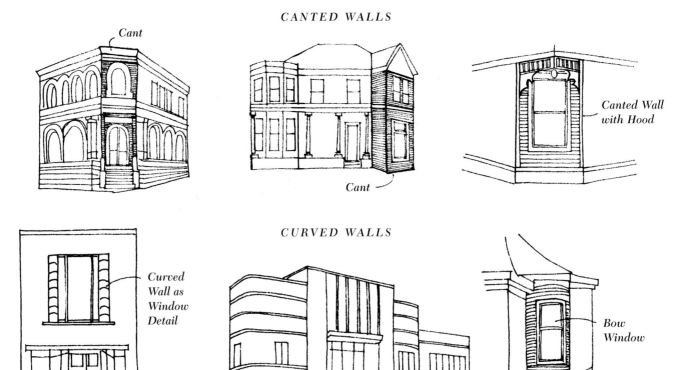

Cant

Cant

Canted Wall
with Hood

CURVED WALLS

Curved
Wall as
Window
Detail

Curved Wall Element

Curved Walls

Bow
Window

Curved Wall
at Corner of House

PILASTERS AND STEPPED GABLES

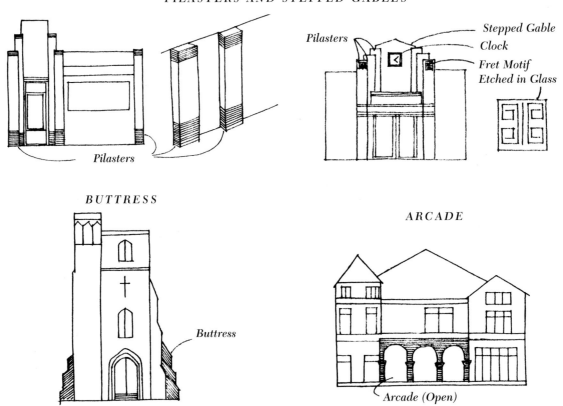

Pilasters

Pilasters

Stepped Gable

Clock

Fret Motif
Etched in Glass

BUTTRESS

Buttress

ARCADE

Arcade (Open)

AMERICAN VERNACULAR BUILDINGS *and* INTERIORS 1870–1960

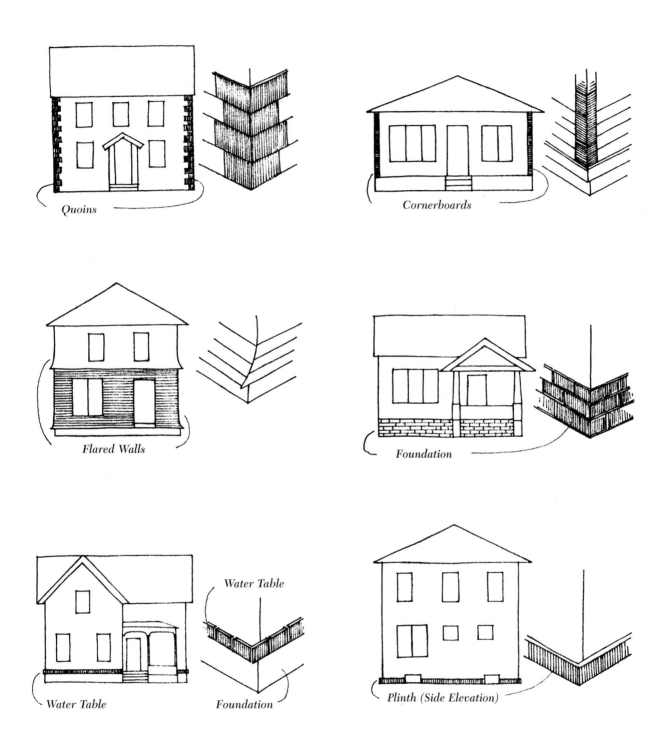

Quoins

Cornerboards

Flared Walls

Foundation

Water Table

Water Table

Foundation

Plinth (Side Elevation)

EXTERIOR WALL PLANE: WALL ORNAMENTATION

WALL ORNAMENTATION: HOUSE

Pendant

Latticework

Shutters

WALL ORNAMENTATION: COMMERCIAL

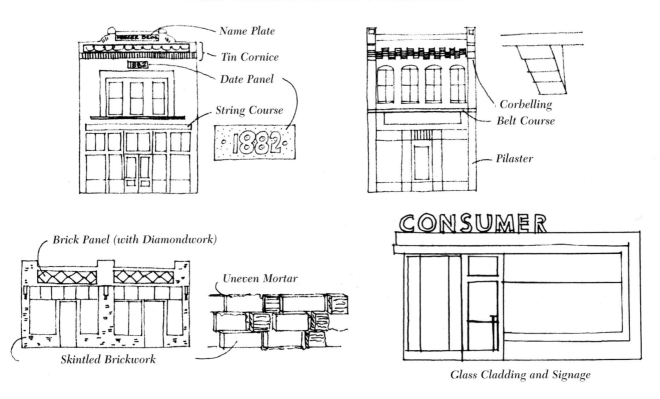

Name Plate

Tin Cornice

Date Panel

String Course

Corbelling

Belt Course

Pilaster

Brick Panel (with Diamondwork)

Uneven Mortar

Skintled Brickwork

Glass Cladding and Signage

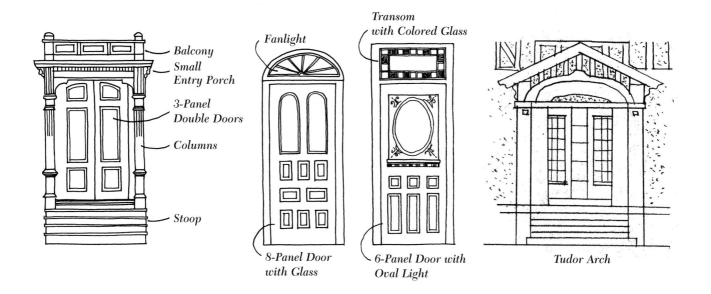

Balcony
Small Entry Porch
3-Panel Double Doors
Columns
Stoop

Fanlight
8-Panel Door with Glass

Transom with Colored Glass
6-Panel Door with Oval Light

Tudor Arch

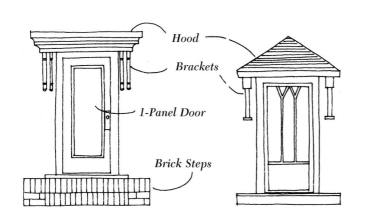

Hood
Brackets
1-Panel Door
Brick Steps

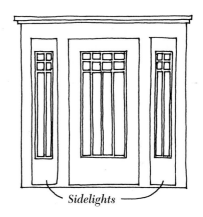

Sidelights

COLONIAL ENTRANCE SYSTEMS

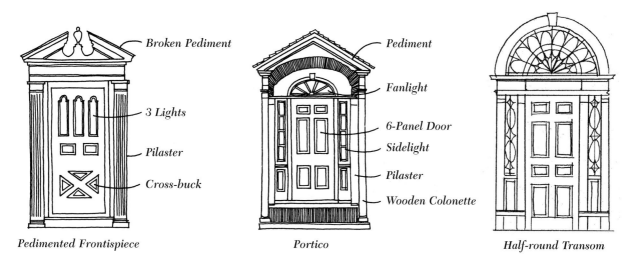

Broken Pediment
3 Lights
Pilaster
Cross-buck

Pedimented Frontispiece

Pediment
Fanlight
6-Panel Door
Sidelight
Pilaster
Wooden Colonette

Portico

Half-round Transom

FAÇADE AND ENTRANCE SYSTEM: ENTRANCES—COMMERCIAL AND PUBLIC

COMMERCIAL ENTRANCES

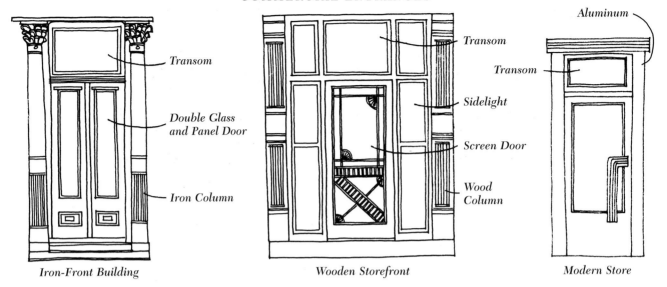

Iron-Front Building

Transom

Double Glass and Panel Door

Iron Column

Wooden Storefront

Transom

Transom

Sidelight

Screen Door

Wood Column

Modern Store

Aluminum

PUBLIC ENTRANCES

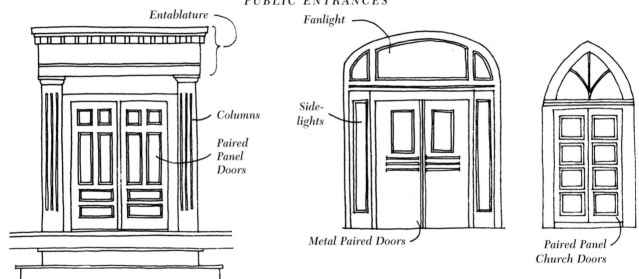

Entablature

Columns

Paired Panel Doors

Fanlight

Side-lights

Metal Paired Doors

Paired Panel Church Doors

MOVIE THEATER

Sunbeam Moving Picture Theatre [1915]
L.B. and A.L. Valk, Los Angeles

FAÇADE AND ENTRANCE SYSTEM: ENTRIES

PORTICOES

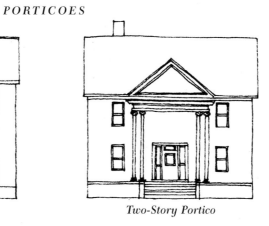

One-Story Portico   *Two-Story Portico*

PROJECTING VESTIBULES

Plan

(Enclosed)

Projecting Vestibule

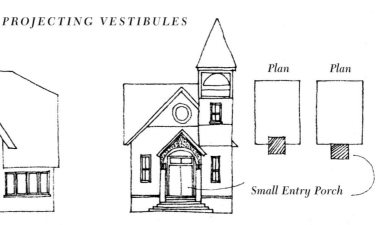

Plan   *Plan*

Small Entry Porch

HOOD AND STOOP

Balcony

Hood

Bracket

Stoop

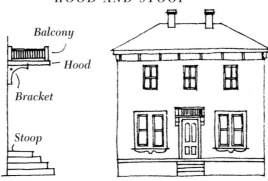

RECESSED DOORS

FAÇADE AND ENTRANCE SYSTEM: PEDIMENT AND COLUMN DETAILS

CLASSICAL PEDIMENTS

Triangular   Segmental   Broken Scroll   Entablature

Cornice
Frieze
Architrave

CLASSICAL COLUMNS

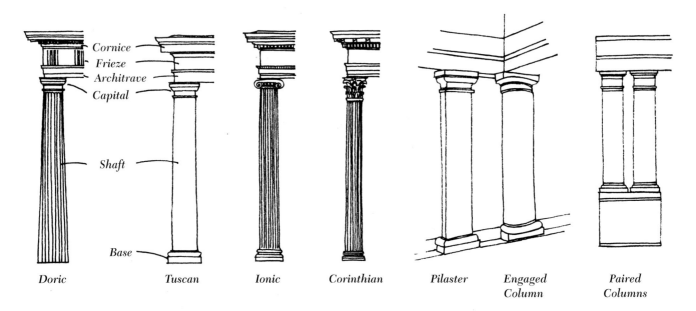

Cornice
Frieze
Architrave
Capital

Shaft

Base

Doric   Tuscan   Ionic   Corinthian   Pilaster   Engaged Column   Paired Columns

VARIATIONS OF COLUMNS

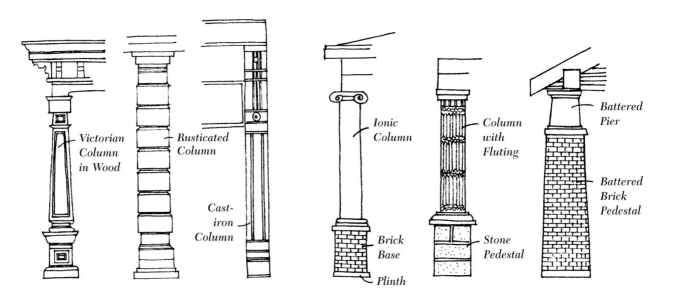

Victorian Column in Wood

Rusticated Column

Cast-iron Column

Ionic Column

Brick Base

Plinth

Column with Fluting

Stone Pedestal

Battered Pier

Battered Brick Pedestal

PORCH: PLANS AND ELEVATIONS

FAÇADE PORCHES

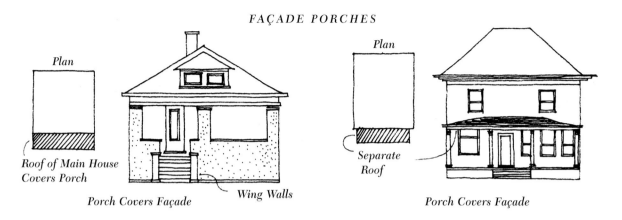

Plan

Roof of Main House
Covers Porch

Porch Covers Façade

Wing Walls

Plan

Separate
Roof

Porch Covers Façade

CUTAWAY PORCH

Plan

Cutaway Porch

END WALL PORCHES

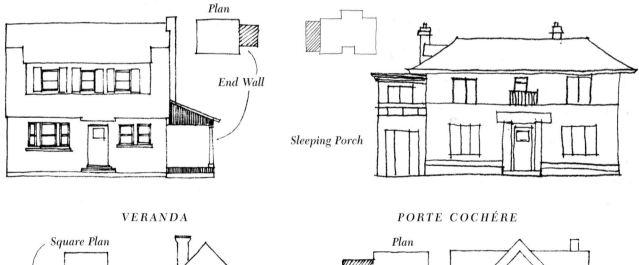

Plan

End Wall

Sleeping Porch

VERANDA

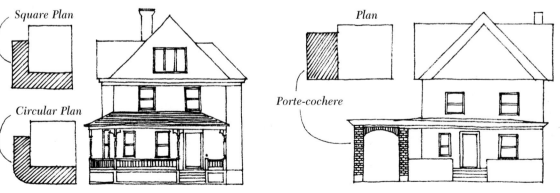

Square Plan

Circular Plan

PORTE COCHÉRE

Plan

Porte-cochere

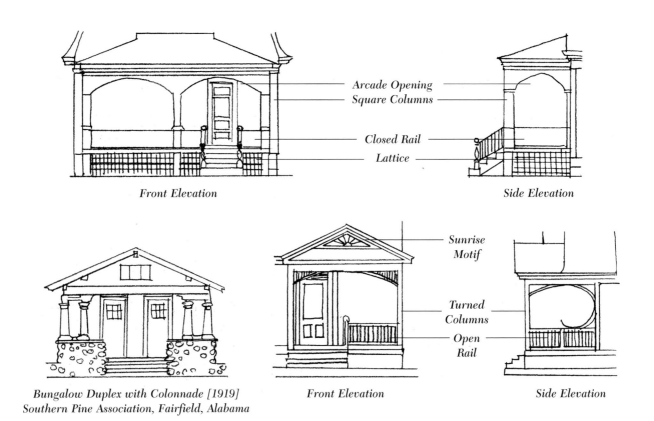

Arcade Opening
Square Columns

Closed Rail
Lattice

Front Elevation

Side Elevation

Bungalow Duplex with Colonnade [1919]
Southern Pine Association, Fairfield, Alabama

Sunrise
Motif

Turned
Columns

Open
Rail

Front Elevation

Side Elevation

PORCH DETAILS

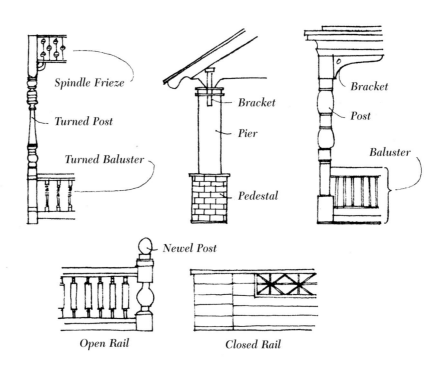

Spindle Frieze

Turned Post

Turned Baluster

Bracket

Pier

Pedestal

Bracket

Post

Baluster

Newel Post

Open Rail

Closed Rail

Asymmetrical with Single and
Paired Windows

Asymmetrical with a Band of
Windows

Symmetrical with
Paired Windows

Asymmetrical with Triple,
Paired, and Single Windows

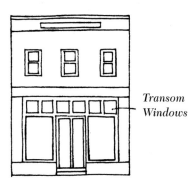

Symmetrical with Single
Windows

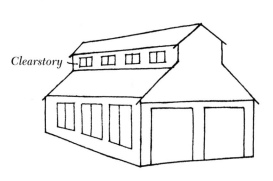

Symmetrical with Paired Windows
and Clearstory

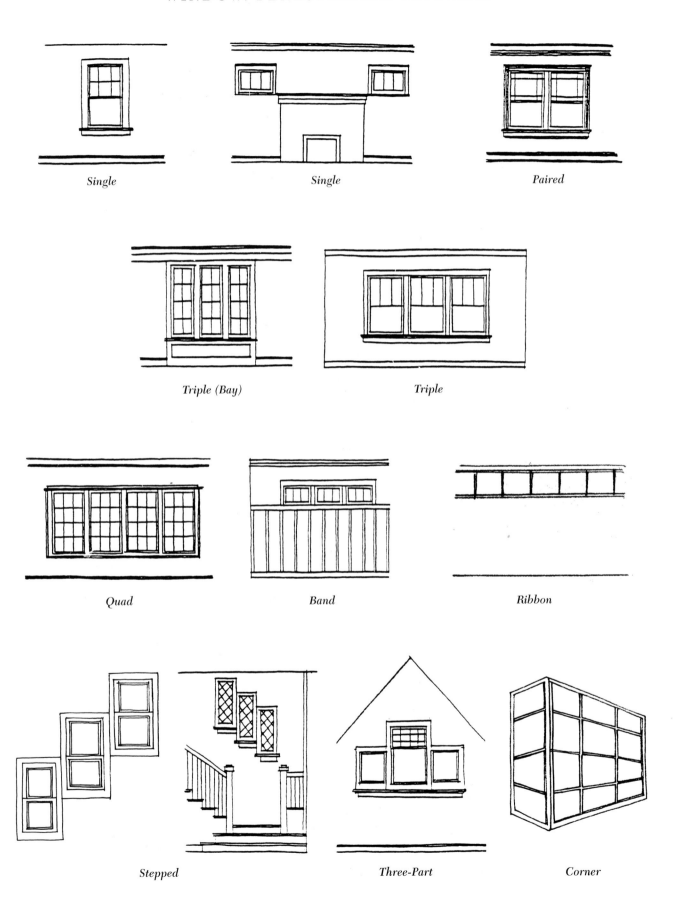

Single   Single   Paired

Triple (Bay)   Triple

Quad   Band   Ribbon

Stepped   Three-Part   Corner

WINDOW: COMPONENTS

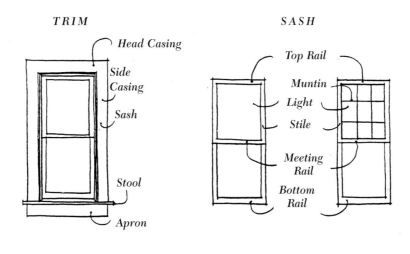

TRIM

Head Casing

Side Casing

Sash

Stool

Apron

SASH

Top Rail

Muntin

Light

Stile

Meeting Rail

Bottom Rail

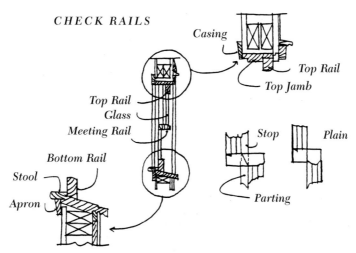

CHECK RAILS

Casing

Top Rail

Top Jamb

Top Rail

Glass

Meeting Rail

Bottom Rail

Stool

Apron

Stop

Plain

Parting

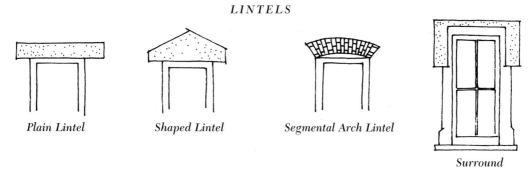

LINTELS

Plain Lintel

Shaped Lintel

Segmental Arch Lintel

Surround

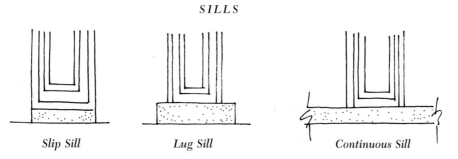

SILLS

Slip Sill

Lug Sill

Continuous Sill

WINDOW: OPERATION AND BAY WINDOWS

OPERATION

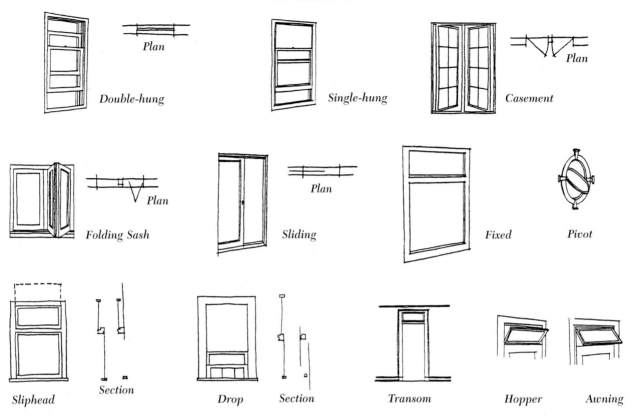

Double-hung — Plan

Single-hung

Casement — Plan

Folding Sash — Plan

Sliding — Plan

Fixed

Pivot

Sliphead — Section

Drop — Section

Transom

Hopper

Awning

BAY AND BOWED WINDOWS

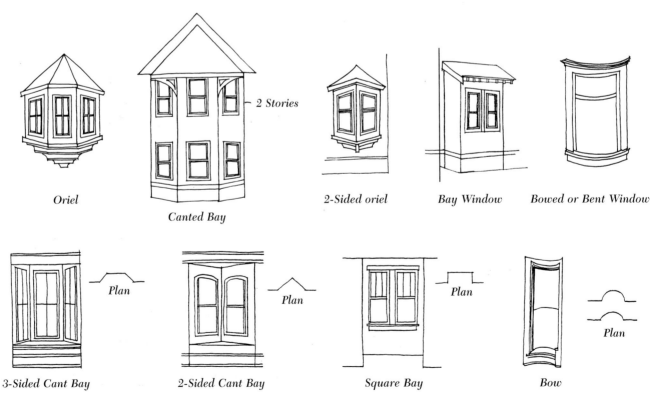

Oriel

Canted Bay — 2 Stories

2-Sided oriel

Bay Window

Bowed or Bent Window

3-Sided Cant Bay — Plan

2-Sided Cant Bay — Plan

Square Bay — Plan

Bow — Plan

COTTAGE WINDOWS

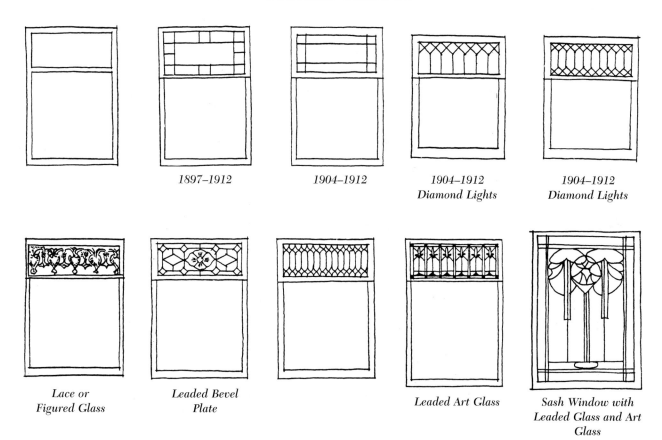

1897–1912   1904–1912   1904–1912   1904–1912
                                      Diamond Lights   Diamond Lights

Lace or   Leaded Bevel   Leaded Art Glass   Sash Window with
Figured Glass   Plate   Leaded Glass and Art
                                                                          Glass

PALLADIAN WINDOWS

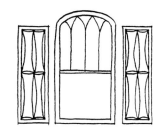

PICTURE WINDOWS (LANDSCAPE AND VIEW WINDOWS)

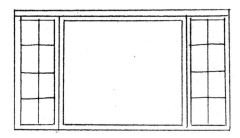
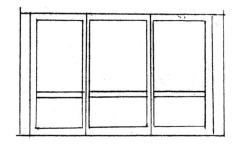

WINDOW—DIVIDED LIGHTS: TIMELINE

PATTERNS

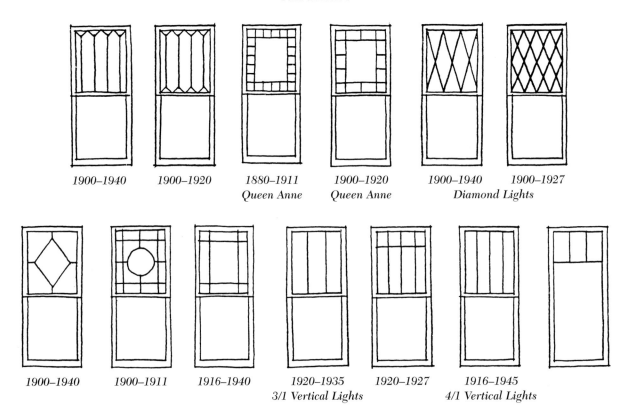

1900–1940   *1900–1920*   *1880–1911*
Queen Anne

1900–1920
Queen Anne

1900–1940
Diamond Lights

1900–1927

1900–1940   *1900–1911*   *1916–1940*   *1920–1935*
3/1 Vertical Lights

1920–1927   *1916–1945*
4/1 Vertical Lights

NUMBER OF LIGHTS

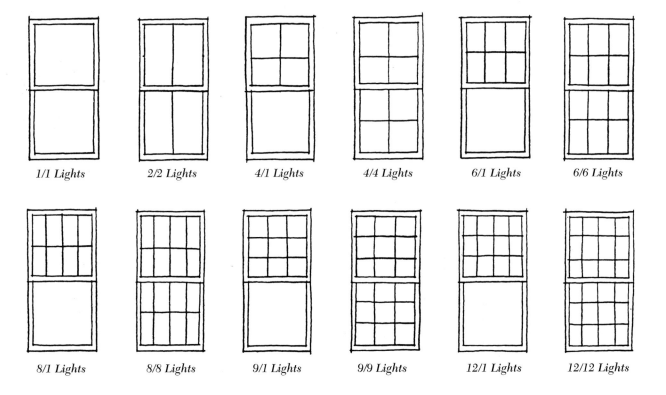

1/1 Lights   *2/2 Lights*   *4/1 Lights*   *4/4 Lights*   *6/1 Lights*   *6/6 Lights*

8/1 Lights   *8/8 Lights*   *9/1 Lights*   *9/9 Lights*   *12/1 Lights*   *12/12 Lights*

WINDOW: DIVIDED LIGHTS

CIRCLE-TOP AND PEAK-TOP WINDOWS

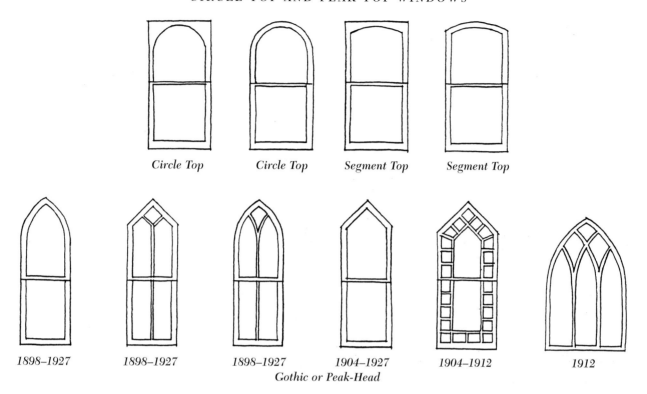

Circle Top *Circle Top* *Segment Top* *Segment Top*

1898–1927 *1898–1927* *1898–1927* *1904–1927* *1904–1912* *1912*

Gothic or Peak-Head

WAREHOUSE AND FACTORY WINDOWS

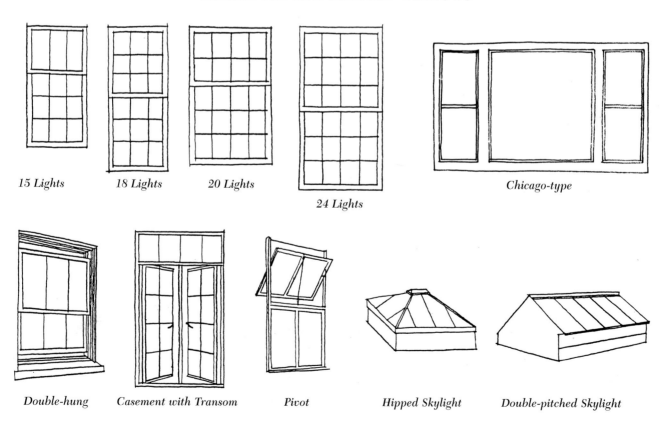

15 Lights *18 Lights* *20 Lights* *Chicago-type*

24 Lights

Double-hung *Casement with Transom* *Pivot* *Hipped Skylight* *Double-pitched Skylight*

WINDOW: DOUBLE AND TRIPLE WINDOWS AND TRANSOMS

DOUBLE AND TRIPLE WINDOWS

Triple-front with Transom

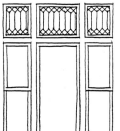

Triple with Transom

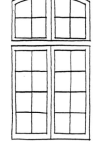

Double Casement with Transom

Double Casement Diamond Pattern

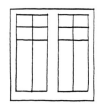

Double Casement

TRANSOMS

One Light

Two Lights

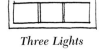

Three Lights

Segmental

Segment Top

Elliptic Head

Diamond Light

Diamond Light

Diamond Light

Circle Top

Circle Top

Circle Top

Block Corner

Block Corner

Circle Corner

Transom Heads Above Casements

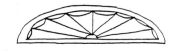

Fanlight

Gothic One Light

Gothic 3 Lights

Gothic Diamond

Gothic Diamond

WINDOW: GLASS

ORNAMENTAL GLASS

Sandblast

Lace

Artistic Chipped

Bevel

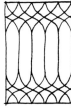

Crystal Sheet

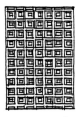

Ornamental
Plate Glass

Enamel

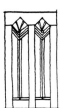

Art Glass

COMMERCIAL GLASS

Maze

Florentine

Chip

Wire

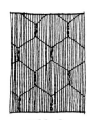

Ribbed

Prism

Section

Section   *Section*

Folding Blinds   *Sliding Blinds*   *Venetian Blinds*

BLIND PATTERNS

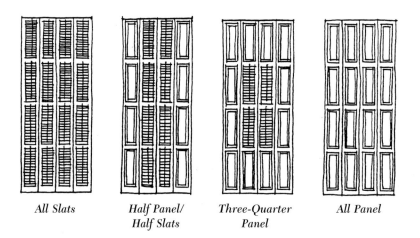

All Slats   *Half Panel/*   *Three-Quarter*   *All Panel*
                   Half Slats   *Panel*

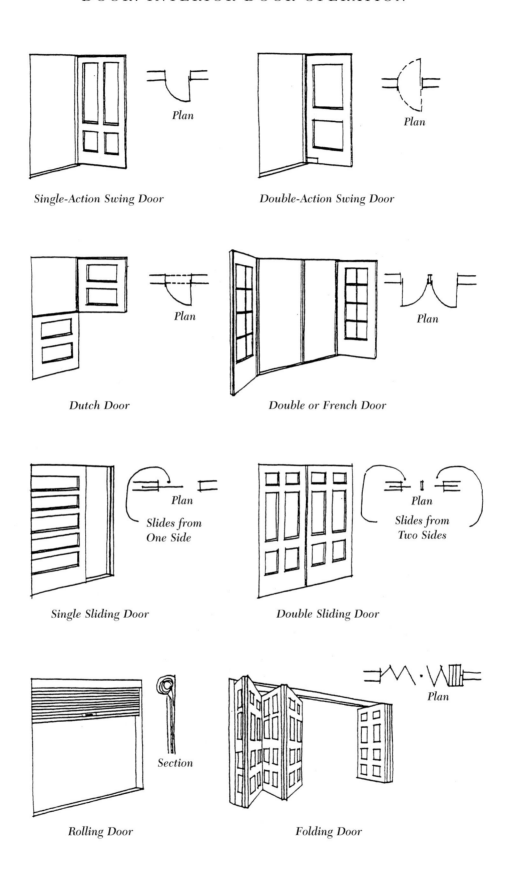

Single-Action Swing Door

Plan

Double-Action Swing Door

Plan

Dutch Door

Plan

Double or French Door

Plan

Single Sliding Door

Plan

Slides from One Side

Double Sliding Door

Plan

Slides from Two Sides

Rolling Door

Section

Folding Door

Plan

DOOR: INTERIOR COMPONENTS

DOOR FRAME CONSTRUCTION

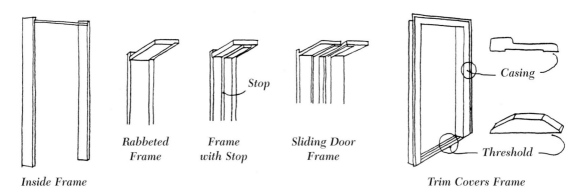

Inside Frame

Rabbeted Frame

Frame with Stop

Stop

Sliding Door Frame

Trim Covers Frame

Casing

Threshold

TRIM

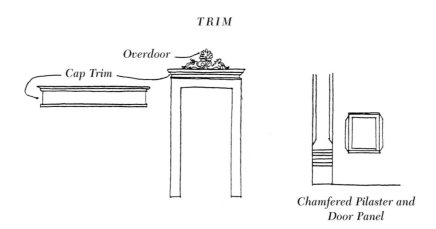

Cap Trim

Overdoor

Chamfered Pilaster and Door Panel

PANEL DOOR COMPONENTS

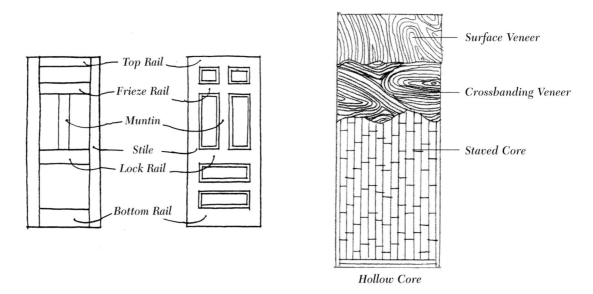

Top Rail

Frieze Rail

Muntin

Stile

Lock Rail

Bottom Rail

Surface Veneer

Crossbanding Veneer

Staved Core

Hollow Core

DOOR MOLDING PATTERNS

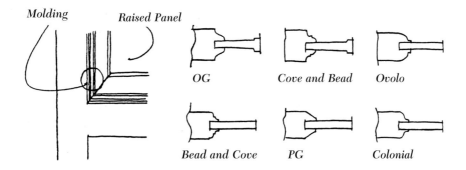

OG   Cove and Bead   Ovolo

Bead and Cove   PG   Colonial

DOOR MOLDINGS IN SECTIONAL VIEW

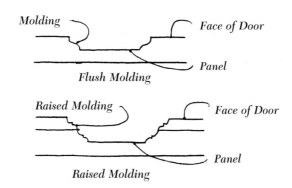

Molding   Face of Door

Panel

Flush Molding

Raised Molding   Face of Door

Panel

Raised Molding

ASTRAGAL PATTERNS FOR DOORS

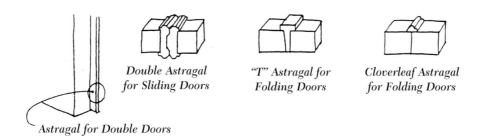

Double Astragal for Sliding Doors

"T" Astragal for Folding Doors

Cloverleaf Astragal for Folding Doors

Astragal for Double Doors

DOOR—PANEL: 1-4 PANEL DOORS—TIMELINE

1-PANEL DOORS

1911–1931
One Panel

One Panel
Planted Molding

Inner Frame

Mirror Door

1911–1940
Inlay

1912–1920
Inlay

2-PANEL DOORS

1904–1940
Two Panel

1908–1931
Vertical Two Panel

1911–1931
Two Panel

3-PANEL DOORS

Three Panel

1912–1927

1912–1926
Three Vertical Panel

3 Panel
and Light

4-PANEL DOORS

1870–1912
Circle-Top Panels

1870–1940

1912–1927

1911–1927

5-PANEL DOORS

1891–1940   1870–1926   5 Cross Panel   1900–1912
5 Cross Panel   Notched

6-PANEL DOORS

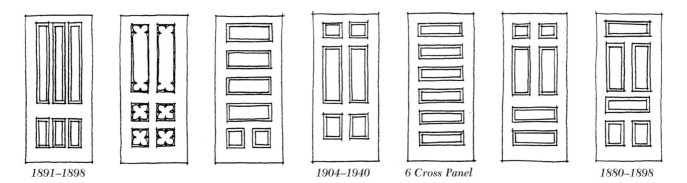

1891–1898   1904–1940   6 Cross Panel   1880–1898

8-PANEL DOORS

1891–1898   1920–1930

COTTAGE DOORS

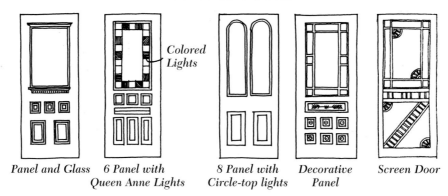

Colored Lights

Panel and Glass   6 Panel with Queen Anne Lights   8 Panel with Circle-top lights   Decorative Panel   Screen Door

BUNGALOW DOORS

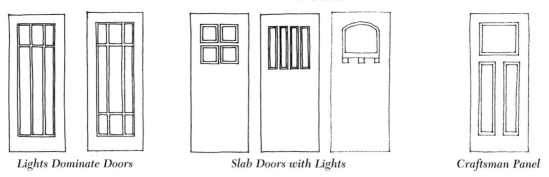

Lights Dominate Doors   Slab Doors with Lights   Craftsman Panel

COLONIAL DOORS

2 Panel   6 Panel   Cross-Buck with Lights   4 Panel with Lights   12 Lights

REVIVAL COTTAGE DOORS   RANCH HOUSE DOORS

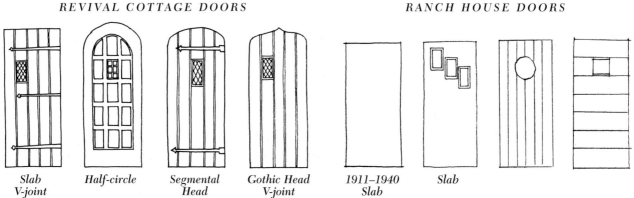

Slab V-joint   Half-circle   Segmental Head   Gothic Head V-joint   1911–1940 Slab   Slab

DOOR: USES—STORES, CHURCHES, INDUSTRIES

DOORS USED IN STORES

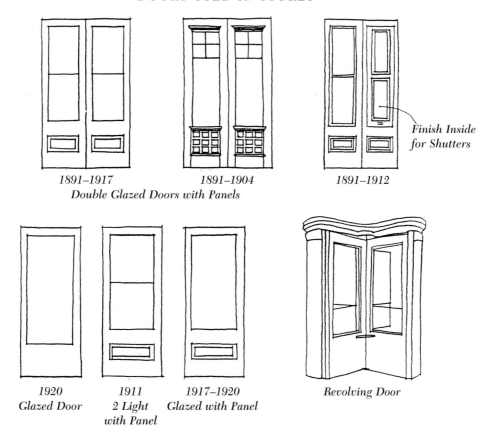

1891–1917　　　*1891–1904*　　　*1891–1912*

Finish Inside for Shutters

Double Glazed Doors with Panels

1920　　　*1911*　　　*1917–1920*　　　*Revolving Door*
Glazed Door　*2 Light*　*Glazed with Panel*
　　　with Panel

DOORS USED IN CHURCHES AND INDUSTRIES

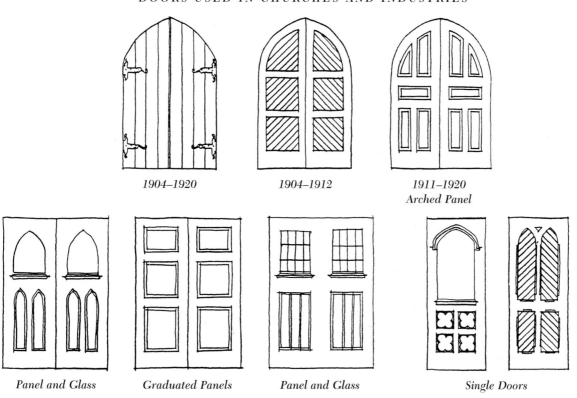

1904–1920　　　*1904–1912*　　　*1911–1920*
　　　　　　　　　　　　　　　　　Arched Panel

Panel and Glass　*Graduated Panels*　*Panel and Glass*　*Single Doors*

DOORS USED IN VESTIBULES

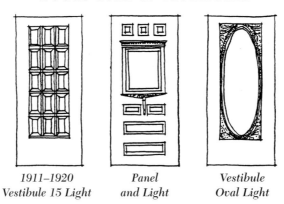

1911–1920
Vestibule 15 Light

Panel
and Light

Vestibule
Oval Light

SCREEN AND LATTICE DOORS

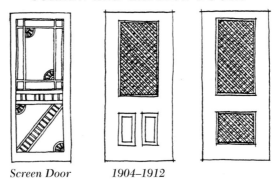

Screen Door

1904–1912

DOUBLE DOORS WITH LIGHTS (FRENCH DOORS)

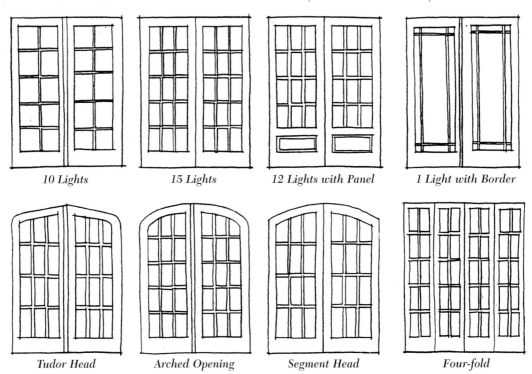

10 Lights

15 Lights

12 Lights with Panel

1 Light with Border

Tudor Head

Arched Opening

Segment Head

Four-fold

SWINGING DOORS

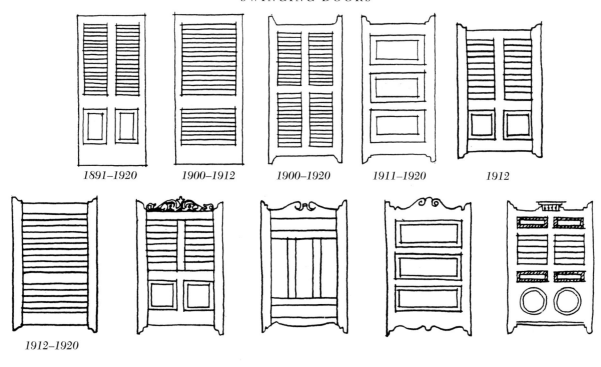

1891–1920   1900–1912   1900–1920   1911–1920   1912

1912–1920

CUPBOARD DOORS

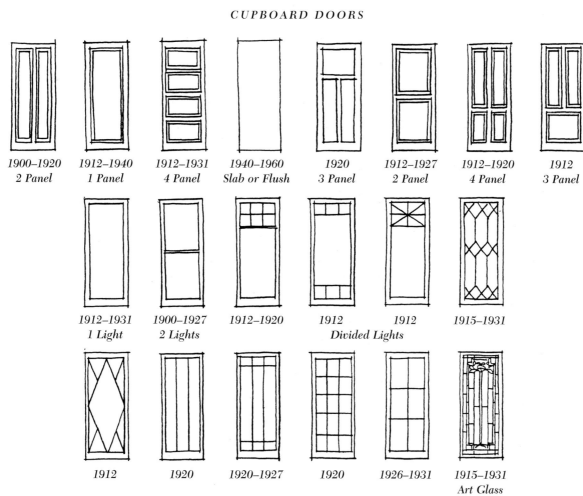

1900–1920   1912–1940   1912–1931   1940–1960   1920   1912–1927   1912–1920   1912
2 Panel   1 Panel   4 Panel   Slab or Flush 3 Panel 2 Panel   4 Panel   3 Panel

1912–1931   1900–1927   1912–1920   1912   1912   1915–1931
1 Light   2 Lights
             Divided Lights

1912   1920   1920–1927   1920   1926–1931   1915–1931
                                                  Art Glass

TRIM SETS: COMPONENTS

MOLDED PILASTER FINISH

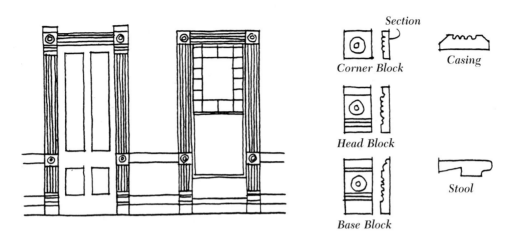

CAP TRIM

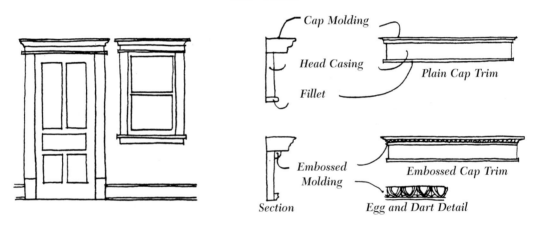

ROUND EDGE (SANITARY) FINISH

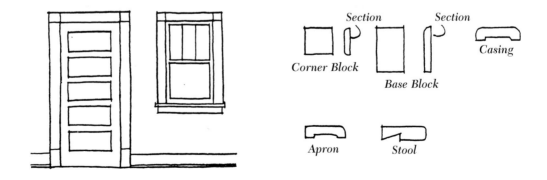

BACK BAND TRIM

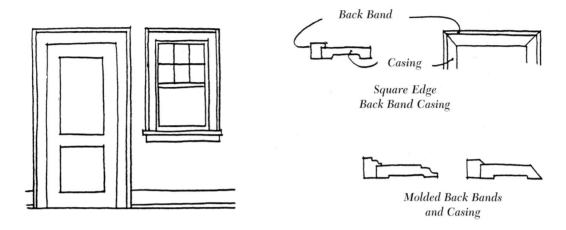

Back Band

Casing

Square Edge
Back Band Casing

Molded Back Bands
and Casing

SQUARE-EDGE TRIM

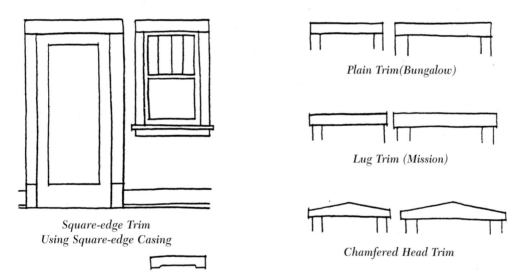

Square-edge Trim
Using Square-edge Casing

Plain Trim (Bungalow)

Lug Trim (Mission)

Chamfered Head Trim

TRIM SETS: BLOCKS AND CASINGS

CORNER BLOCKS

HEAD BLOCKS

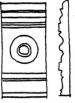 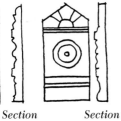 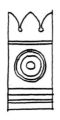     

Section   *Section*

BASE BLOCKS

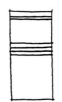  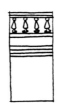 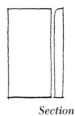

Section

CASINGS

Beads   Chamfer

1900–1912
Reeded or Beaded
Pilaster Casing

Raised Face

1904–1912
Raised Face
Pilaster Casing

Center Bead

1891–1912
Center Bead
Pilaster Casing

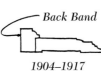

Back Band

1904–1917
Casing and
Back Band

Convex

1900–1917
Convex
Pilaster Casing

Concave

1891–1912
Concave
Pilaster Casing

Sunk Panel

1900–1920
Sunk Panel
Pilaster Casing

1891–1912
Reeded and Concave
Pilaster Casing

1891 and 1917

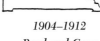

1904–1912
Bead and Cove
Molded Casing

1904–1920
OG
Molded Casing

1904–1917
Stepped Round-edge
Molded Casing

HARDWARE: DOOR LOCKSETS

LOCKSETS

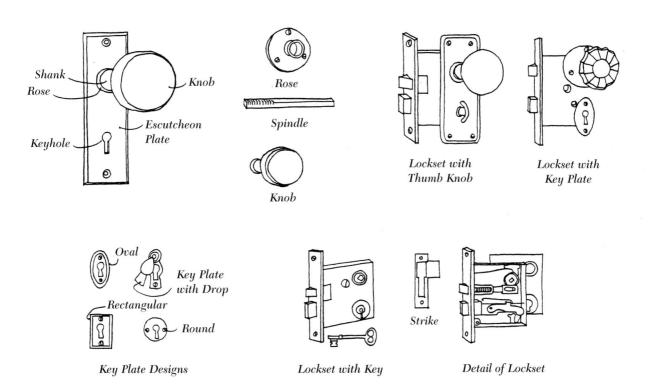

Shank
Rose
Knob
Keyhole
Escutcheon Plate

Rose
Spindle
Knob

Lockset with Thumb Knob

Lockset with Key Plate

Oval
Key Plate with Drop
Rectangular
Round

Key Plate Designs

Lockset with Key

Strike

Detail of Lockset

ENTRANCE DOOR HANDLE SETS

SLIDING DOOR SET

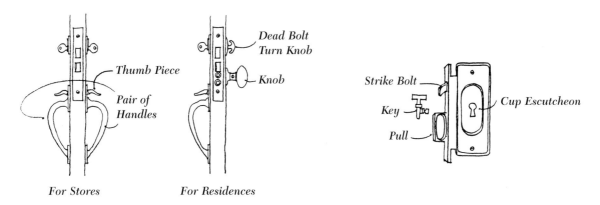

Thumb Piece
Pair of Handles

Dead Bolt Turn Knob
Knob

For Stores

For Residences

Strike Bolt
Key
Pull
Cup Escutcheon

HARDWARE: HARDWARE SETS

ORNAMENTAL OR COTTAGE SETS, 19TH CENTURY

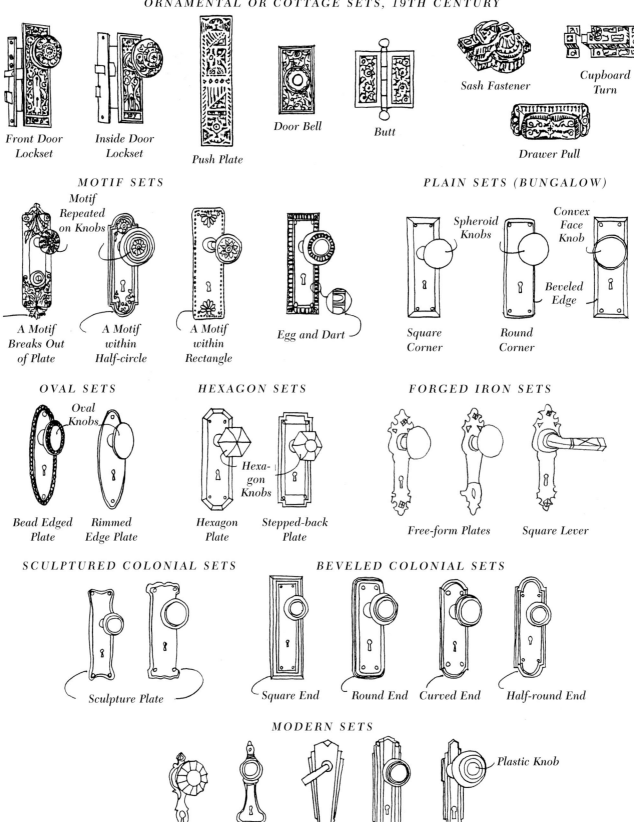

Front Door
Lockset

Inside Door
Lockset

Push Plate

Door Bell

Butt

Sash Fastener

Cupboard
Turn

Drawer Pull

MOTIF SETS

Motif
Repeated
on Knobs

A Motif
Breaks Out
of Plate

A Motif
within
Half-circle

A Motif
within
Rectangle

Egg and Dart

PLAIN SETS (BUNGALOW)

Spheroid
Knobs

Convex
Face
Knob

Beveled
Edge

Square
Corner

Round
Corner

OVAL SETS

Oval
Knobs

Bead Edged
Plate

Rimmed
Edge Plate

HEXAGON SETS

Hexa-
gon
Knobs

Hexagon
Plate

Stepped-back
Plate

FORGED IRON SETS

Free-form Plates

Square Lever

SCULPTURED COLONIAL SETS

Sculpture Plate

BEVELED COLONIAL SETS

Square End

Round End

Curved End

Half-round End

MODERN SETS

Plastic Knob

Free-form Plates

Stepped-back Plates

Spheroid
Porcelain, Jet,
Mineral, Bronze

Flat
Ornamental
Bronze

Convex Face
with a Motif

Octagon
Pressed Glass

Faceted
Pressed Glass

Octagon
Cut Glass

Convex Face

Hexagon

Square

Oval

Pointed Oval

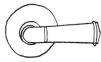

Button

Ring

Beveled Ring

Lever Handle

Iron Convex Face

Iron Rose

HARDWARE: SPECIAL USES

WINDOW SASH FASTENERS AND LIFTS

For Casement Windows   *Bar Sash Lift*   *Hook Sash Lift*   *Flush Sash Lift*

HINGES

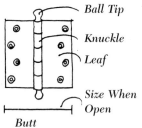

Ball Tip
Knuckle
Leaf
Size When Open

Butt

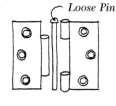

Loose Pin

Loose-pin Butt

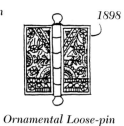

1898

Ornamental Loose-pin Butt

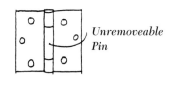

Unremoveable Pin

Fast Joint or Tight-pin Butt

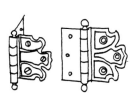

Ball-Bearing Butt

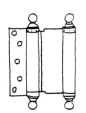

Half-mortise Butts

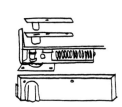

Spring Hinge

Exploded View

Horizontal Spring Pivot for Swinging Doors

CUPBOARD HARDWARE: CATCHES AND HINGES

T-Handle

Cupboard Catch

Cupboard Turn

Porcelain Knob

Cupboard Catch

Butterfly Design

Tight Pins

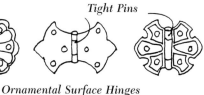

Ornamental Surface Hinges

DRAWER HARDWARE: PULLS AND KNOBS

Drawer Pull

Drop Handle

Drawer Pull

Bar

Drawer Pull

Round

Pressed Glass

Octagon

PUSH PLATES   BOLTS

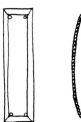

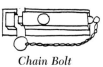
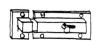

Chain Bolt   *Door Bolt*

CEILING PLANE: PROFILES, TREATMENTS, AND MATERIALS

CEILING PROFILES IN SECTIONAL VIEW

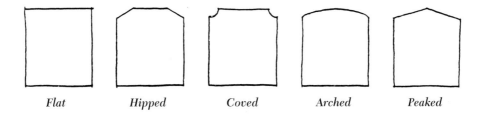

Flat   *Hipped*   *Coved*   *Arched*   *Peaked*

VARIOUS CEILING TREATMENTS WITH MATERIALS IN PLAN VIEW

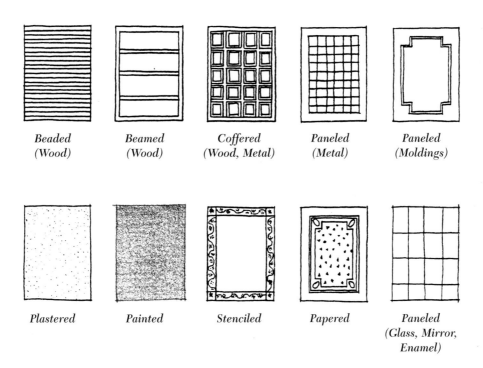

Beaded (Wood)   *Beamed (Wood)*   *Coffered (Wood, Metal)*   *Paneled (Metal)*   *Paneled (Moldings)*

Plastered   *Painted*   *Stenciled*   *Papered*   *Paneled (Glass, Mirror, Enamel)*

PLASTER CEILINGS AND MOLDINGS

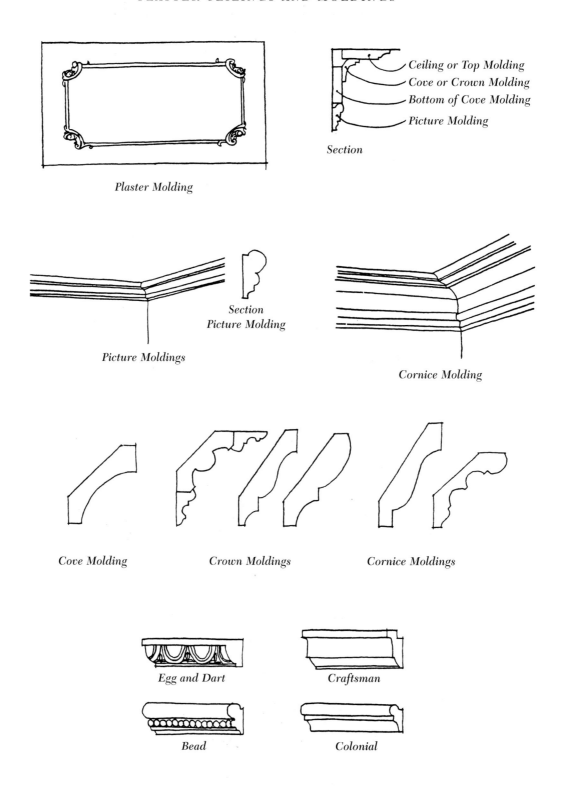

Plaster Molding

Ceiling or Top Molding
Cove or Crown Molding
Bottom of Cove Molding
Picture Molding

Section

Picture Moldings

Section
Picture Molding

Cornice Molding

Cove Molding

Crown Moldings

Cornice Moldings

Egg and Dart

Craftsman

Bead

Colonial

CEILING PLANE: BEAM CEILINGS

FINISHED BEAMS FOR A FLAT CEILING

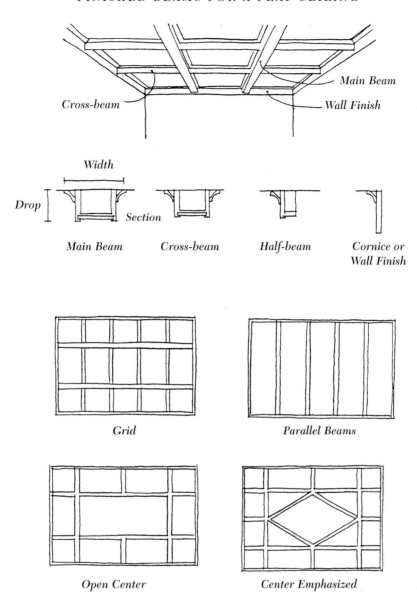

Cross-beam

Main Beam

Wall Finish

Width

Drop

Section

Main Beam   Cross-beam   Half-beam   Cornice or
                                            Wall Finish

Grid

Parallel Beams

Open Center

Center Emphasized

EXPOSED TRANSVERSE BEAMS

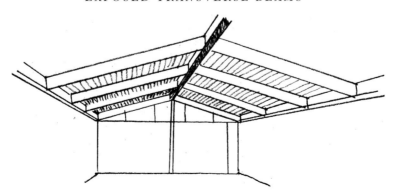

CEILING PLANE: METAL CEILINGS

COMPONENTS

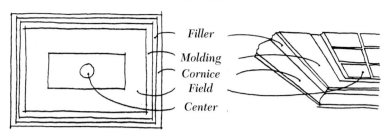

Filler
Molding
Cornice
Field
Center

Ceiling Plan

Cornice

Filler

Molding

Center

Section

PLATES

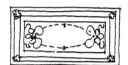

9" x 18"
12" x 24"
18" x 36"
24" x 48"

Field Plate

Field Plate

9" x 9"
12" x 12"
18 x 18"
24" x 24"

Corner Plate

Drop-block

Section

SHEETS—PATTERNS AND TEXTURES

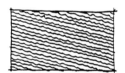

Twill Sheets

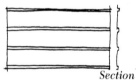

Beaad Sheet

Section

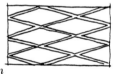

Diamond Sheet

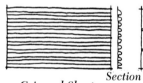

Crimped Sheet

Section

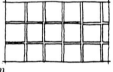

Squares Sheet

MOTIFS OF MOLDINGS AND SQUARE PLATES

Bead-and-Reel Molding

Fleur-de-lis Molding

Egg-and-dart Molding

Fret Molding

Circle

Ribbon

Square
in Square

Geometric

Guilloche

Rosette

Quatrefoil

Floral

PLAIN-SAWN AND QUARTER-SAWN BOARDS

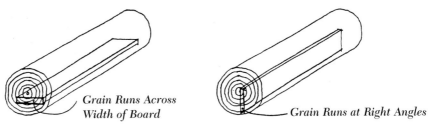

Grain Runs Across
Width of Board

Grain Runs at Right Angles

*Plain-sawn
(Flat Sawn, Flat Grain,
Slash Grain*

*Quarter-sawn
(Vertical or Edge Grain)*

FACE WIDTH

   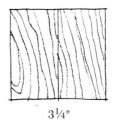

1½"   2"   2¼"   3¼"

THICKNESS

3/8"   ½"   ¾"   13/16"   7/8"   1"   1¼"

JOINT PROFILES

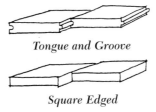

Tongue and Groove

Square Edged

FLOOR PLANE: PARQUET FLOORING AND WOOD CARPET

COMPONENTS OF A PARQUET FLOOR

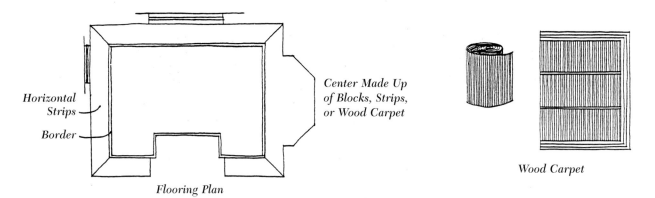

Horizontal Strips

Border

Flooring Plan

Center Made Up of Blocks, Strips, or Wood Carpet

Wood Carpet

LAYING TECHNIQUES

Parquet Individually Laid

Wood Block

DESIGNS FOR THE CENTER FIELD AND BORDER MOTIFS

      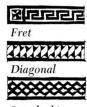

Fret

Diagonal

Interlocking Diamond

PARQUET FLOOR DESIGNS

 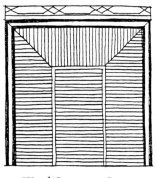  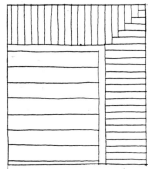

Blocks as Center

Wood Carpet as Center

Strips as Center

Pine Floor as Center (for Rug) Hardwood Border

CERAMIC MOSAICS

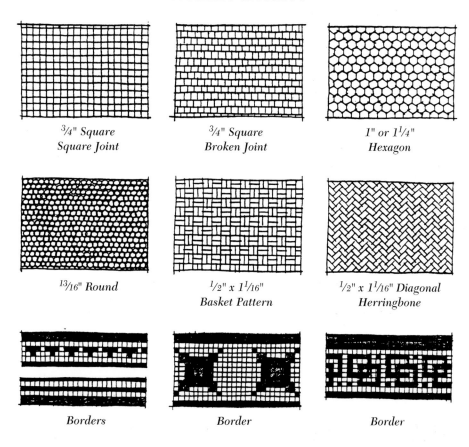

*³/₄" Square
Square Joint*

*³/₄" Square
Broken Joint*

*1" or 1¹/₄"
Hexagon*

¹³/₁₆" Round

*¹/₂" x 1¹/₁₆"
Basket Pattern*

*¹/₂" x 1¹/₁₆" Diagonal
Herringbone*

Borders

Border

Border

FLOOR DESIGNS

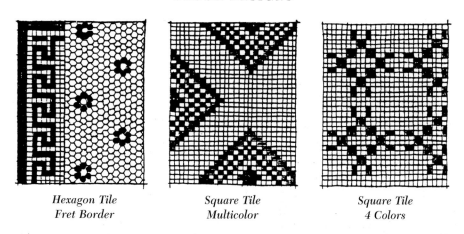

*Hexagon Tile
Fret Border*

*Square Tile
Multicolor*

*Square Tile
4 Colors*

FLOOR PLANE: LINOLEUM

TYPES OF LINOLEUM

Plain (Battleship)

Inlaid

Painted

Cork

Embossed

SIZES AND FORMS

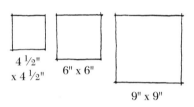

4 ¹/₂"
x 4 ¹/₂"   6" x 6"

9" x 9"

Blocks

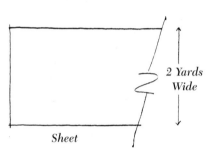

2 Yards
Wide

Sheet

INSETS AND BORDERS

Insets

PATTERNS

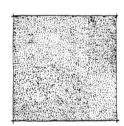

Granite

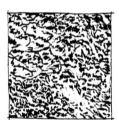

Marble

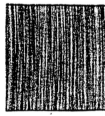

Jaspé

Geometric

Tiles

Wood

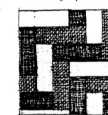

Herringbone

Checkerboard

Carpet

Jigsaw

Plaid

Modern/Abstract

WALL ORGANIZATION WITH MOLDINGS

Cornice

Frieze

Picture Molding

Filling/Field

Wainscot Cap

Wainscot/Dado

Base Trim

Various wood moldings divided the wall plan into horizontal panels to be filled with wallpaper, Lincrusta, or paint.

WALLPAPER SCHEMES FOR WALL, BORDER, AND CEILING

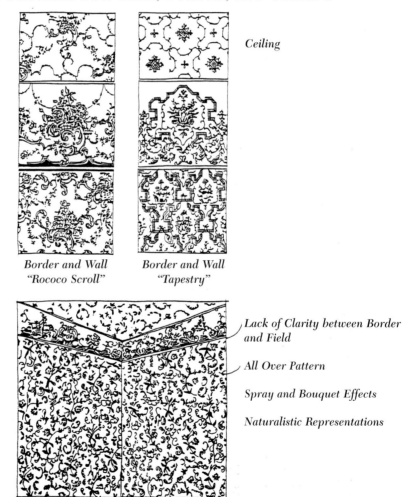

Ceiling

Border and Wall
"Rococo Scroll"

Border and Wall
"Tapestry"

Lack of Clarity between Border and Field

All Over Pattern

Spray and Bouquet Effects

Naturalistic Representations

Various patterns of wallpaper for ceiling, border, wall were used to divide the wall with few moldings.

WALL ORGANIZATION WITH MOLDINGS

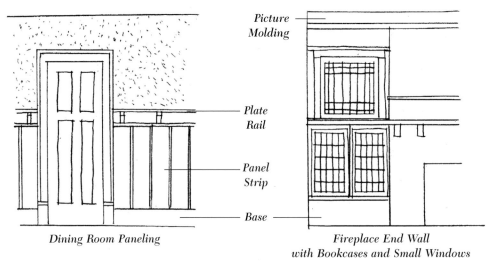

Dining Room Paneling

*Fireplace End Wall
with Bookcases and Small Windows*

*Various wood moldings divided the wall plane into horizontal panels to be filled with
plaster, burlap, grass cloth, wallpaper, or paint.*

WALLPAPER SCHEMES FOR WALL, BORDER, AND CEILING

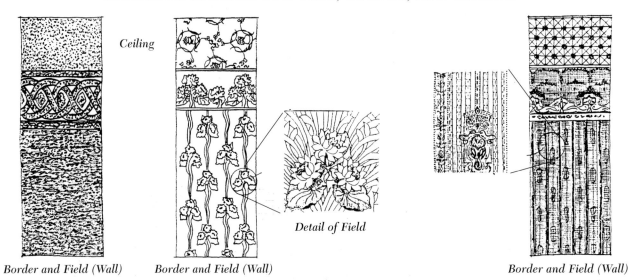

Border and Field (Wall)   *Border and Field (Wall)*   *Detail of Field*   *Border and Field (Wall)*

WALL ORGANIZATION WITH MOLDINGS AND WALLPAPER

The fireplace was placed symmetrically on the wall. The wall was rarely divided by moldings. Base molding and moldings at the ceiling line became thinner and less turned.

WALLPAPER BORDERS CONTINUED IN POPULARITY

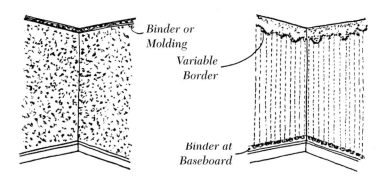

Binder or Molding

Variable Border

Binder at Baseboard

WALLPAPER PATTERNS

Dainty Flowers   Large Pastel Flowers   Graphic   Floral on Grid   Modern

INTERIOR WALL PLANE: ORGANIZATION—TIME LINE 1940-1960

WALL ORGANIZATION WITH MOLDINGS AND WALLPAPER

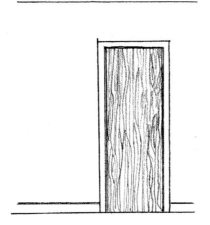

Fewer wood moldings (base, ceiling) divided the wall. Walls were painted in pastel colors or wallpapered. Doors were often plywood slabs with the wood grain revealed.

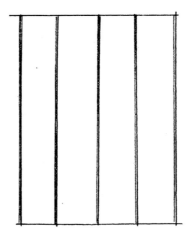

Often paneled walls had no base or ceiling moldings.

WALLPAPER PATTERNS

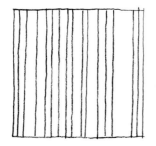

Stripes

Abstract Lines

Flowers

Two-Dimensional

Foliage

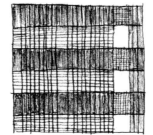

Imitative

Narrative

LINCRUSTA

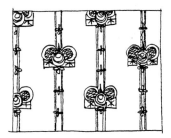

Lincrusta "Modern"
Montgomery Ward—1910

Lincrusta French Renaissance
Montgomery Ward—1910

Lincrusta
Sears, Roebuck and Co.—1915

Lincrusta
Sears, Roebuck and Co.—1915

PLASTER AND PAINT

Light Stipple

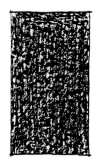

Heavy Stipple

Brush Texture

Scroll

Raked

Scored

Stippled and
Stenciled

Glazing

BURLAP   *GRASS CLOTH*   *OILCLOTH*

 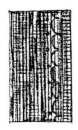   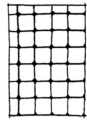

Border

Selections from Sears, Roebuck & Co., 1915

STENCILING

Conventionalized Flowers   *Scroll and Flowers*   *Scroll*   *Stylized Flowers*

Selected Stencil Patterns from Sears, Roebuck & Co., 1918

CERAMIC TILES

 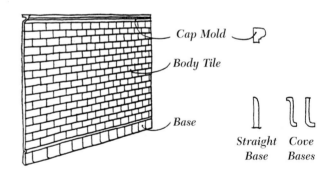

Cap Mold

Body Tile

Base

Varnished Tiles

Straight Base   *Cove Bases*

METAL

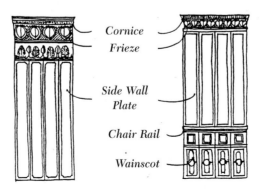

Cornice
Frieze

Side Wall Plate

Chair Rail

Wainscot

INTERIOR WALL PLANE: MATERIALS AND SURFACE TREATMENTS
(CONT'D)

WOODEN WAINSCOT

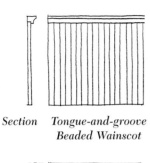

*Section   Tongue-and-groove
Beaded Wainscot*

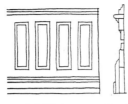

*Paneled Wainscot,   Section
Vertical panels*

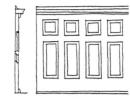

*Section   Paneled Wanscot,
Square and Vertical Panels*

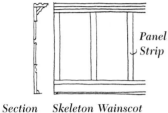

*Panel
Strip*

Section   Skeleton Wainscot

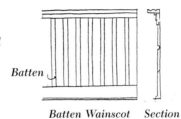

Batten

Batten Wainscot   Section

*Paneled Wainscot,   Section
Vertical and Horizontal Panels*

WOOD AND MASONITE PANEL WORK

Wood Wall Paneling

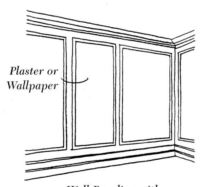

*Plaster or
Wallpaper*

*Wall Paneling with
Panel Strips or Molding*

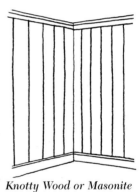

*Knotty Wood or Masonite
Paneling (Full Height)*

PLYWOOD PANEL WORK

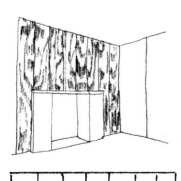

Striated

Grooved

Embossed

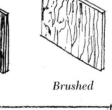

Brushed

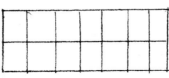

Vertical Wall Panels   *Square Wall panels*

Horizontal Wall Panels

COMPONENTS OF BASE MOLDING AND CORNER BEAD

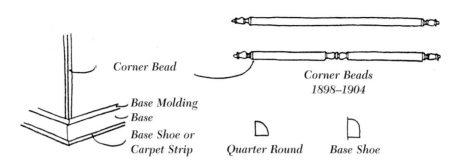

Corner Bead

Corner Beads
1898–1904

Base Molding
Base
Base Shoe or
Carpet Strip

Quarter Round   Base Shoe

BASE MOLDING PATTERNS

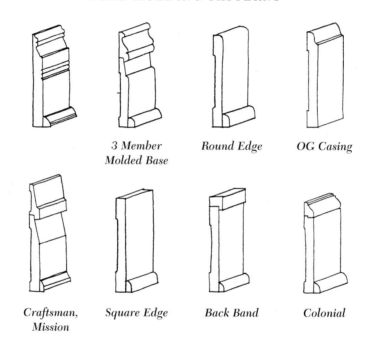

3 Member
Molded Base

Round Edge

OG Casing

Craftsman,
Mission

Square Edge

Back Band

Colonial

COMPOSITION OR PLASTER MOLDINGS

Section
V-Groove Knotty Wood
or Masonite

Panel Strips

INTERIOR WALL PLANE: MANTEL COMPONENTS AND CHIMNEY BREASTS

MANTEL COMPONENTS

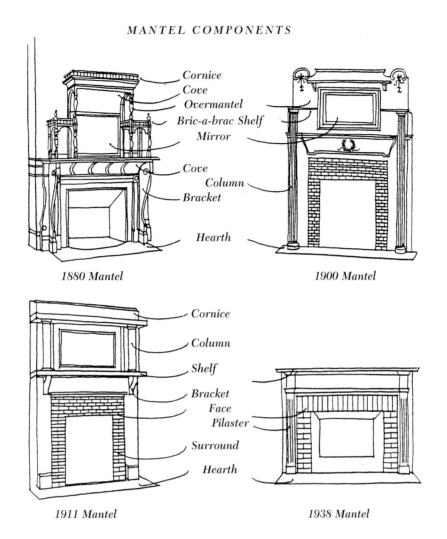

Cornice
Cove
Overmantel
Bric-a-brac Shelf
Mirror

Cove
Column
Bracket

Hearth

1880 Mantel

1900 Mantel

Cornice

Column

Shelf

Bracket
Face
Pilaster

Surround

Hearth

1911 Mantel

1938 Mantel

CHIMNEY BREASTS

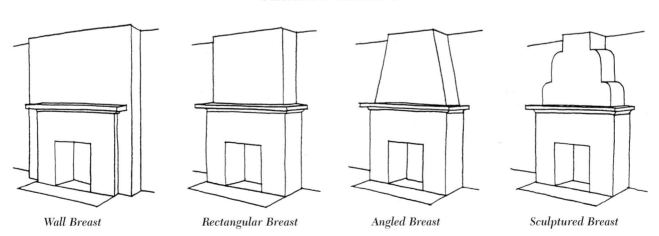

Wall Breast

Rectangular Breast

Angled Breast

Sculptured Breast

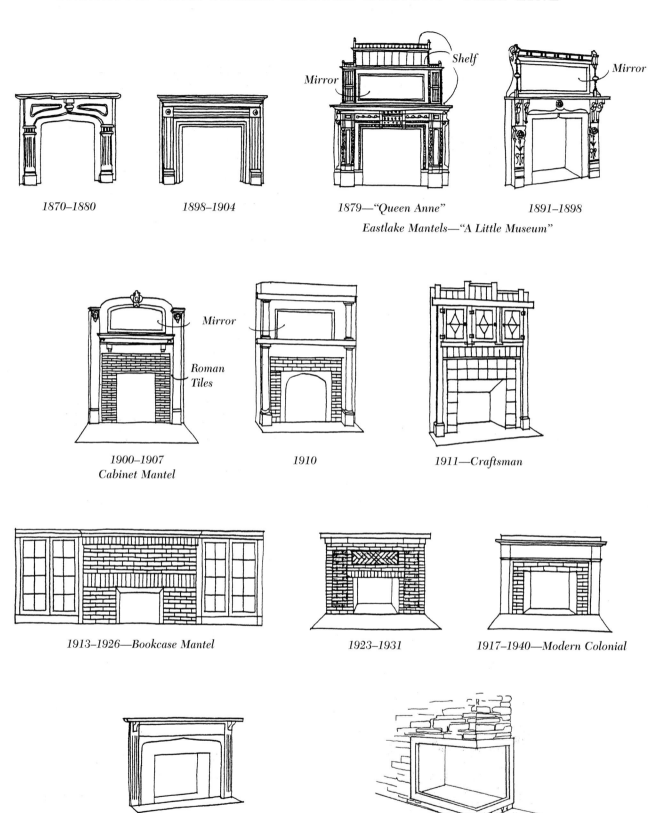

1870–1880

1898–1904

Mirror

Shelf

1879—"Queen Anne"

Mirror

1891–1898

Eastlake Mantels—"A Little Museum"

Mirror

Roman Tiles

1900–1907
Cabinet Mantel

1910

1911—*Craftsman*

1913–1926—*Bookcase Mantel*

1923–1931

1917–1940—*Modern Colonial*

1930–1940—*English Cottage*

1940–1960—*Corner Fireplace with Casing*

INTERIOR WALL PLANE: ARCHITECTURAL FURNITURE—
HOUSE AND MULTI-FAMILY HOUSES

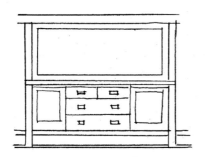

Dining Room Buffet
Radford's Portfolio *1911*

Combination Buffet and China Closet
Minneapolis Wood-working Co. *1922*

China Closet
Universal Design Book *1904*

Corner Cuboards for Dining Rooms
Angel's Standardized Woodwork *1943*

Corner Cupboard Plan

Fireplace Settle

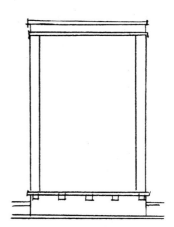

Hall Console with Beveled Plate Mirror 1911

399

ORNAMENTAL GLASS COUNTER

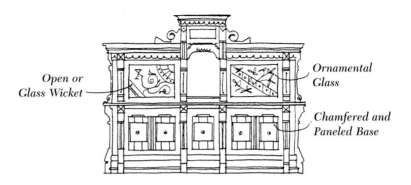

Open or
Glass Wicket

Ornamental
Glass

Chamfered and
Paneled Base

1910 PRESCRIPTION CASE

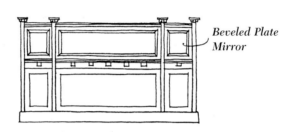

Beveled Plate
Mirror

"Neat, Artistic, Practical, Modern"

TINCTURE SHELVING

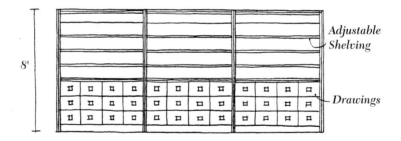

8'

Adjustable
Shelving

Drawings

PATENT MEDICINE SHELVING

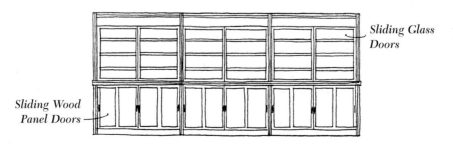

Sliding Glass
Doors

Sliding Wood
Panel Doors

ARCHITECTURAL FURNITURE: BUSINESS BUILDINGS

METAL WICKET DESIGNS

METAL GRILLE WORK

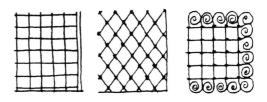

CASHIERS' DESKS WITH METAL WICKET AND GRILLE

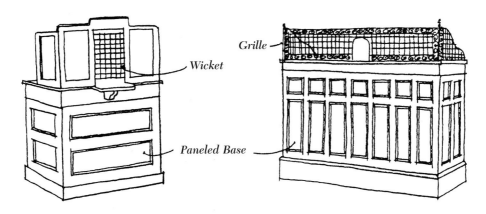

Wicket

Paneled Base

Grille

OFFICE RAILING

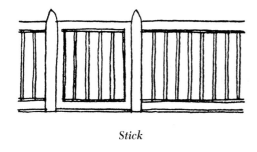

Stick

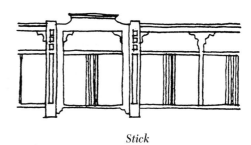

Stick

Panel and Spindle Frieze

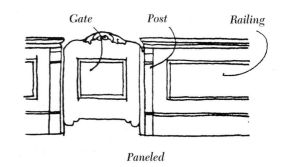

Gate *Post* *Railing*

Paneled

CONSOLE

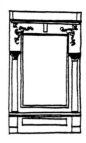

DRY GOODS SHELVING

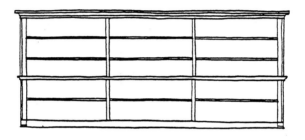

COUNTER

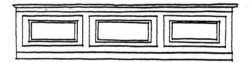

SHOWCASE

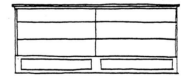

ARCHITECTURAL FURNITURE: CHURCH

PULPIT TYPES

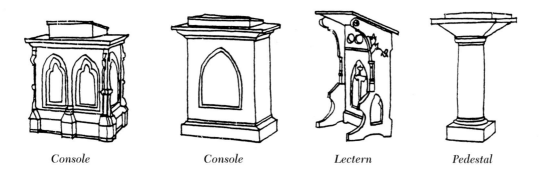

Console   Console   Lectern   Pedestal

PEW END TYPES

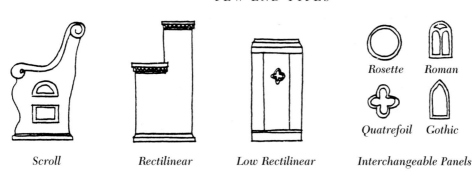

Rosette   Roman

Quatrefoil   Gothic

Scroll   Rectilinear   Low Rectilinear   Interchangeable Panels

PEW BODY TYPES

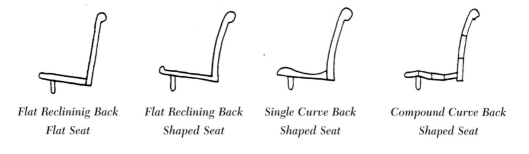

Flat Reclininig Back   Flat Reclining Back   Single Curve Back   Compound Curve Back
Flat Seat   Shaped Seat   Shaped Seat   Shaped Seat

CHOIR AND ALTAR RAILS

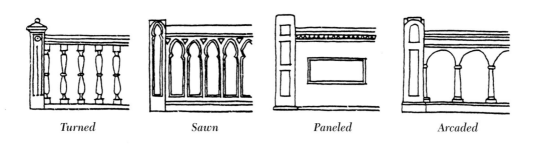

Turned   Sawn   Paneled   Arcaded

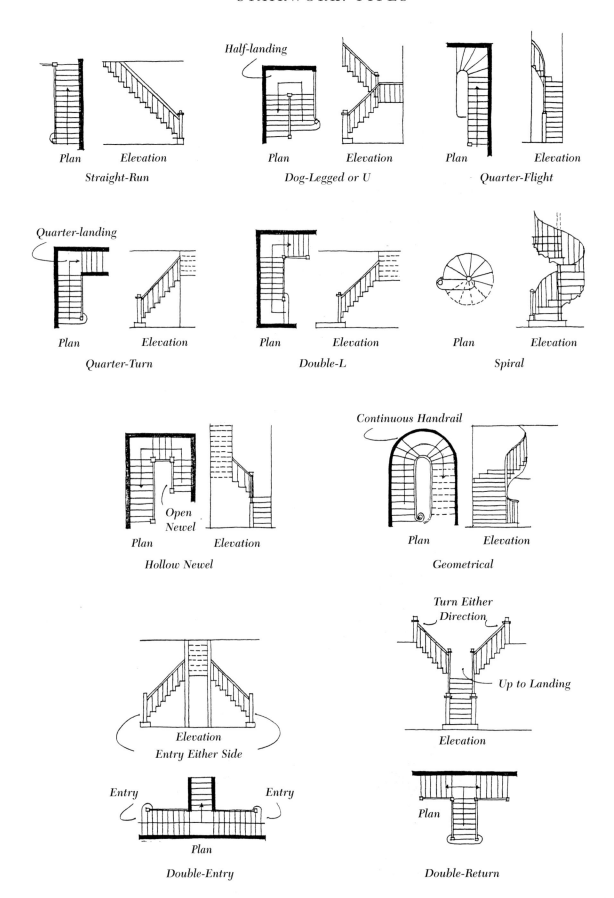

Straight-Run — Plan, Elevation

Dog-Legged or U — Half-landing, Plan, Elevation

Quarter-Flight — Plan, Elevation

Quarter-Turn — Quarter-landing, Plan, Elevation

Double-L — Plan, Elevation

Spiral — Plan, Elevation

Hollow Newel — Plan, Open Newel, Elevation

Geometrical — Continuous Handrail, Plan, Elevation

Double-Entry — Elevation, Entry Either Side, Entry, Plan, Entry

Double-Return — Turn Either Direction, Up to Landing, Elevation, Plan

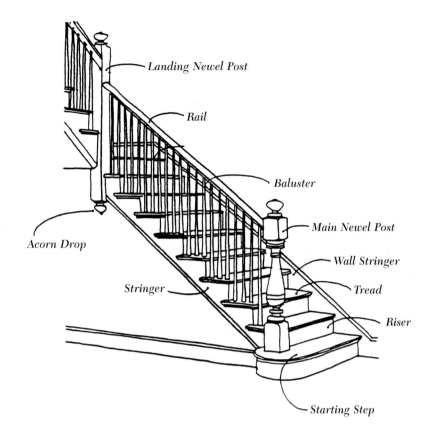

Landing Newel Post

Rail

Baluster

Main Newel Post

Wall Stringer

Tread

Riser

Stringer

Acorn Drop

Starting Step

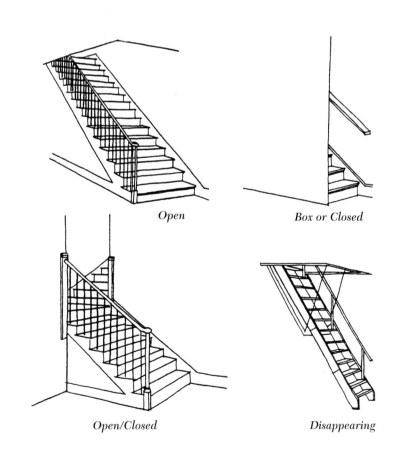

Open

Box or Closed

Open/Closed

Disappearing

STAIRWORK: STRINGERS

STRINGER TYPES

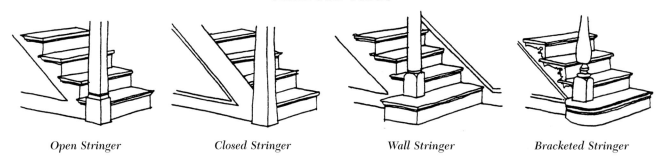

Open Stringer   Closed Stringer   Wall Stringer   Bracketed Stringer

SELECTED DESIGNS FOR STRINGERS

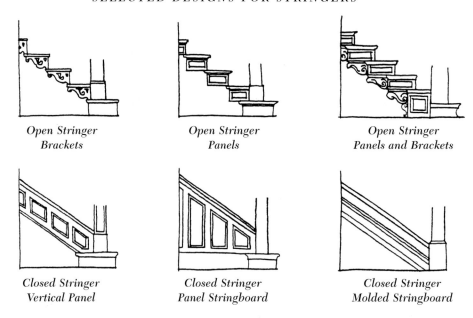

Open Stringer
Brackets

Open Stringer
Panels

Open Stringer
Panels and Brackets

Closed Stringer
Vertical Panel

Closed Stringer
Panel Stringboard

Closed Stringer
Molded Stringboard

PANEL FOR CLOSED STRINGER

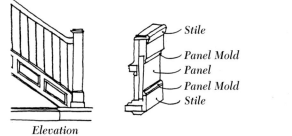

Stile
Panel Mold
Panel
Panel Mold
Stile

Elevation

BRACKETS FOR STRINGER AND RAIL

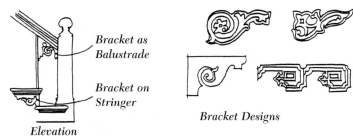

Bracket as
Balustrade

Bracket on
Stringer

Elevation

Bracket Designs

COMPONENTS

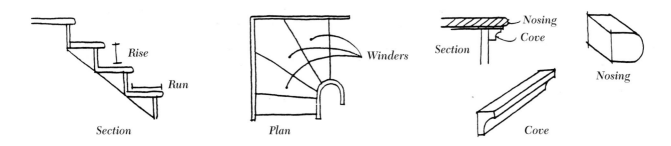

Section   Plan   Cove   Nosing

Rise   *Run*   *Winders*   *Nosing*   *Cove*   *Section*

TYPES OF STARTING STEPS

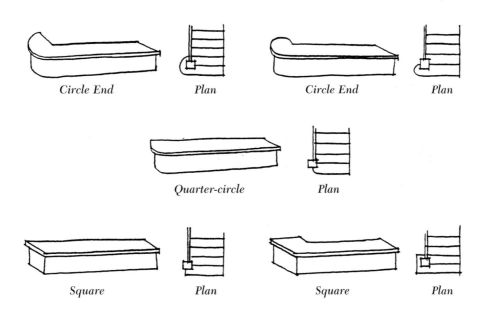

Circle End   Plan   Circle End   Plan

Quarter-circle   Plan

Square   Plan   Square   Plan

IRON STEPS AND RISERS

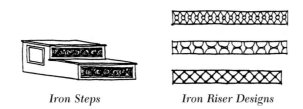

Iron Steps   Iron Riser Designs

COMPONENTS

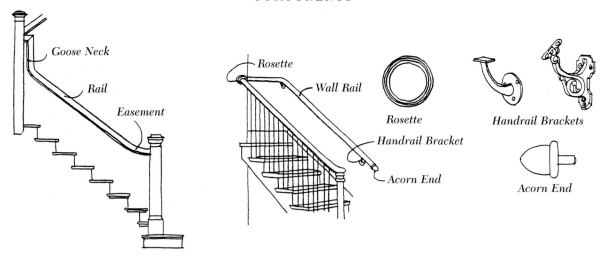

Goose Neck

Rail

Easement

Rosette

Wall Rail

Rosette

Handrail Bracket

Acorn End

Handrail Brackets

Acorn End

DESIGNS, 1871–1960

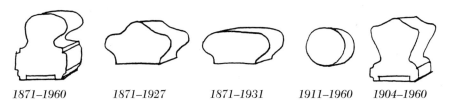

| 1871–1960 | 1871–1927 | 1871–1931 | 1911–1960 | 1904–1960 |

RAILS

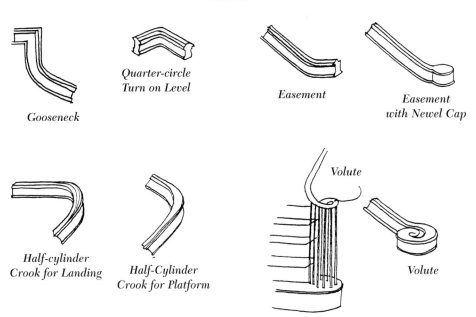

Gooseneck

Quarter-circle
Turn on Level

Easement

Easement
with Newel Cap

Half-cylinder
Crook for Landing

Half-Cylinder
Crook for Platform

Volute

Volute

BALUSTRADE DESIGNS

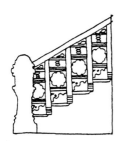

Perforated

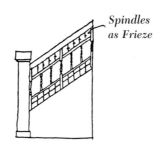

Spindles as Frieze

Frieze Spindles
and Turned Balusters

Spindles
and Panel

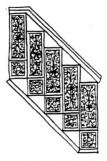

Metal Balustrade

TURNED BALUSTERS

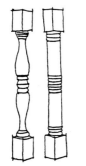

"Fancy"

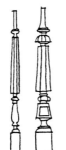

Octagon   Hexagon

Spiral

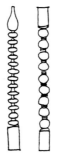

Bead-and-
Reel

Sears
1907

Colonial

SOLID BALUSTERS

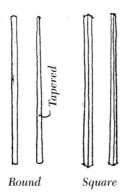

Tapered

Round

Square

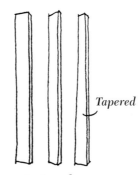

Tapered

Rectangular

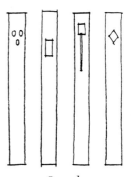

Sawed

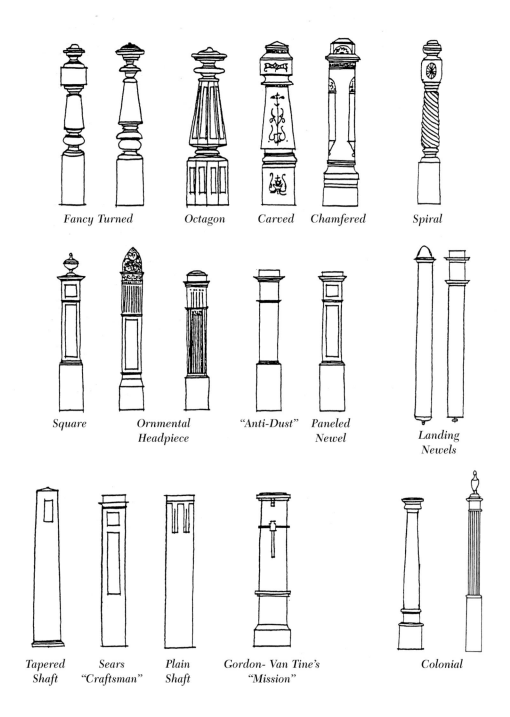

Fancy Turned   Octagon   Carved   Chamfered   Spiral

Square   Ornmental Headpiece   "Anti-Dust"   Paneled Newel   Landing Newels

Tapered Shaft   Sears "Craftsman"   Plain Shaft   Gordon- Van Tine's "Mission"   Colonial

GRILLES

Cased Opening with Grille

Lattice and Scroll Grille with Portiere

Turned Spindles and Beads

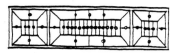

Turned Spindles

Scroll and Spindle

Commercial Scroll and Spindle

Sawn

Art Nouveau

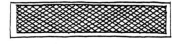

Lattice

Metal

COLONNADES WITH COLUMNS AND GRILLES

Lattice

Scroll

COLONNADES

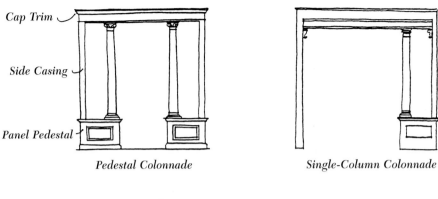

Cap Trim

Side Casing

Panel Pedestal

Pedestal Colonnade　　　　　　*Single-Column Colonnade*

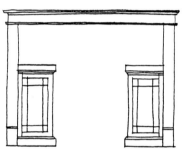

Colonnade with Full-length Columns　　*Colonnade with Architrave*　　*Colonnade with Bookcases*

COLONNADE VARIATIONS

Bookcase　　*Sears Bookcase 1916–1931*　　*Art Glass and Leaded Glass China Cabinets*　　*Lamp*

Rustic 1911　　*Craftsman 1912*　　*Craftsman 1917*　　*Mission 1912*　　*Mission 1912*　　*Bench*　　*Writing Desk*

CASED OPENINGS

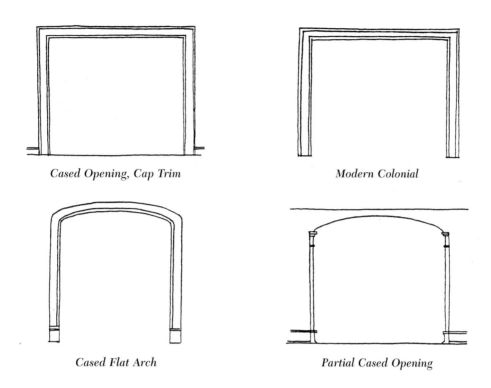

Cased Opening, Cap Trim   Modern Colonial

Cased Flat Arch   Partial Cased Opening

UNCASED OPENINGS

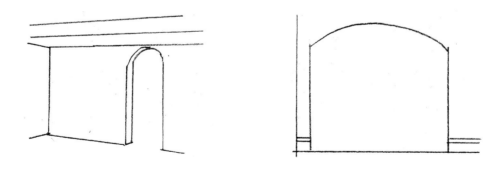

Herringbone

Checkerwork

Zigzag

Diamondwork

Dovetail

Fret

Guilloche

Running Ornament

Rinceau

Garland

Egg-and-dart

Scallops

Rope Molding

Floral and Plant Forms

Cartouche

Trefoil

Fleur-de-lis

Sunrise

Palmette

Quatrefoil

Rosettes

Patera

Animal

Allegorical

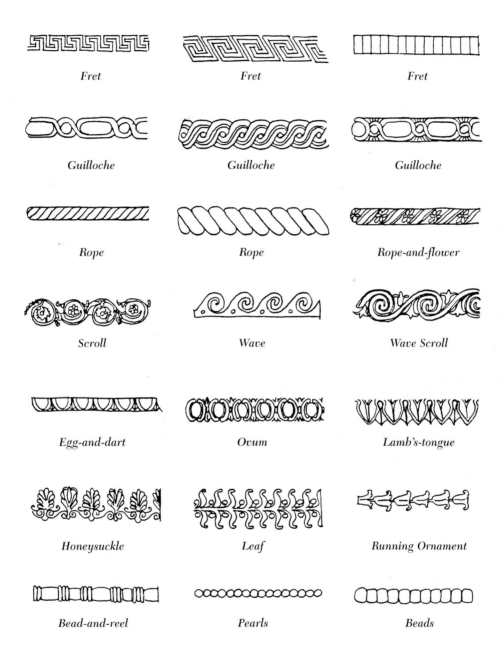

Fret   Fret   Fret

Guilloche   Guilloche   Guilloche

Rope   Rope   Rope-and-flower

Scroll   Wave   Wave Scroll

Egg-and-dart   Ovum   Lamb's-tongue

Honeysuckle   Leaf   Running Ornament

Bead-and-reel   Pearls   Beads

Round Rosettes　　Square Rosettes　　Oval Rosette　　Panel Rosette

Shields　　Vase　　Shell　　Fleur-de-lis

Drop　　Wreath　　Festoon　　Ribbon

Leaf　　Honeysuckle　　Wreaths and Festoons

Figure　　Head　　Musical Instrument　　Torch

Endnotes

Introduction

1. W. Barksdale Maynard, " 'Best, Lowliest Style,' The Early-Nineteenth-Century Rediscovery of American Colonial Architecture," *Journal of the Society of Architectural Historians* 59, no. 3 (September 2000): 338–357.

2. O. Henry Mace, *Collector's Guide to Early Photographs*, 2nd ed. (Iola, Wis.: Krause Publications, 1999), 131–133; Brian Coe and Paul Gates, *The Snapshot Photograph: The Rise of Popular Photography 1888–1939* (London: Ash & Grant, 1977), 9; James E. Paster, "The Snapshot, The Automobile, and The Americans," in *Roadside America: The Automobile in Design and Culture*, ed. Jan Jennings (Ames, Iowa: Iowa State University Press for the Society for Commercial Archeology, 1990), 55.

3. *Carpentry and Building*, 4 (March 1882): 45.

4. "The Journal's Prize Model House," *The Ladies Homes Journal*, 16 (June 1899): 23.

5. *Cottage Designs with Constructive Details*, Carpentry and Building Series, No. 1 (New York: David Williams Co., 1897).

6. "Residences," *American Carpenter and Builder*, 1, No. 4 (July 1905): 253.

Chapter 1

1. In American vernacular studies, the Vernacular Architecture Forum has assumed a leadership role in the field. See the *Perspectives in Vernacular Architecture* series.

2. Howard Wight Marshall, "Vernacular Housing and Culture," in *Popular American Housing: A Reference Guide*, Eds. Ruth Brent and Benyamin Schwartz (Westport, CT: Greenwood Press, 1995), 1–38.

3. *Popular American Housing*, 14.

4. *Common Places: Readings in American Vernacular Architecture*, Ed. Dell Upton and John Michael Vlach (Athens: University of Georgia Press, 1986).

5. Jan Jennings, *Cheap and Tasteful Dwellings: Design Competitions and the Convenient Interior, 1879–1909* (Knoxville: University of Tennessee Press, 2005), xxix–xxxiii.

6. Sigfried Giedion, *Mechanization Takes Command* (New York: Oxford University Press, 1948).

7. Giedion, *Mechanization Takes Command*, 5.

8. Ibid., 30.

9. Ibid., 41.

10. Lionel March and Philip Steadman, *The Geometry of the Environment: An Introduction to Spatial Organization in Design* (Cambridge, Mass.: MIT Press, 1974), 6, 145–56.

11. Herbert Gottfried, "A Computer Program for Recording Historic Buildings." *APT Bulletin* XVI, no. 2 (1984): 15–20.

12. Alan Gowans, *Learning to See: Historical Perspectives on Modern Popular/Commercial Arts* (Bowling Green, OH: Bowling Green State University, Popular Press, 1981), 395–456.

Chapter 2

1. Sir John Soane, *Plans, Elevations, and Sections of Buildings* (London: Messrs. Taylor, 1788), 11.

2. George Richardson, *New Designs in Architecture, Consisting of Plans, Elevations, and Sections for Varied Buildings* (London: George Richardson, 1792), 11; Charles Middleton, *Picturesque and Architectural Views for Cottages, Farm Houses, and Country Villas* (London: E. Jeffrey, 1793), 4; Joseph Gandy, *The Rural Architect* (London: John Harding, 1805), 28.

3. In Nora Pat Small, *Beauty and Convenience: Architecture*

and Order in the New Republic (Knoxville: University of Tennessee Press, 2003), 56–57.

4. Vincent J. Scully Jr., *The Shingle Style and the Stick Style: Architectural Theory and Design from Downing to the Origins of Wright*, rev. ed. (New Haven, Conn.: Yale University Press, 1971), xxvii.

5. *The Shingle Style*, xxi–xxii.

6. Ibid., xxxvi.

7. Richard C. Muhlberger, "William H. Ranlett: 19th Century Architect and Publisher," *Historic Preservation* 22, no. 1 (1970): 10–15.

8. Sally McMurray, *Families and Farmhouses in Nineteenth-Century America: Vernacular Design and Social Change* (New York: Oxford University Press, 1988), 5–6, 25, 41–45.

9. Calvert Vaux, "Hints for Country Home Builders," *Harper's Monthly Magazine* 11, No. 66 (1855): 769; J. H. Hammond, *The Farmer's and Mechanic's Practical Architect; and Guide in Rural Economy* (Boston: John Jewett, 1858), title page.

10. National Architect's Union, *Modern Rural Homes* (Philadelphia: National Architect's Union, 1889), n. p.

11. R. W. Edis in *Popular Science*, published as "The Best Architecture," *Manufacturer and Builder* 18 (March 1886): 68.

12. Minard Lafever, *The Young Builder's General Instructor* (Newark, N. J.: W. Tuttle, 1829), 157.

13. Nora Pat Small, *Beauty and Convenience*, 16–17.

14. Jacques-François Blondel, *De la Distribution des Maisons de Plaisance et de la Decoration des Edifices en general* (1737–1738), n. p.; M. F. Hearn, Ed., *The Architectural Theory of Violett-le-Duc* (Cambridge, Mass.: MIT Press, 1990), 12.

15. Robert Kerr, *The Gentleman's House; or How to Plan English Residences from the Parsonage to the Palace; with Tables of Accommodation and Cost, and a Series of Selected Plans*, 3rd ed. (London: John Murray, 1877), viii–ix. Kerr's thirteen principles were program, privacy, comfort, convenience, spaciousness, light and air, salubrity, aspect and prospect, cheerfulness, elegance, importance, ornamentation.

16. Kerr, *Gentleman's House*, 71

17. Ibid., 75.

18. Ibid., 76, 155, 176.

19. Ibid., 69.

20. "House-Building in America," *Putnam's Monthly Magazine of American Literature, Science, and Art* 10 (July 1857): 107–11.

21. Delores Hayden, *The Grand Domestic Revolution: A History of Feminist Designs for American Homes, Neighborhoods, and Cities* (Cambridge, Mass.: MIT Press, 1985), 57–59.

22. McMurray, *Families and Farmhouses*, 29–30, 67–68.

23. Mary Ann Beecher, "Building for 'Mrs. Farmer': Published Farmhouse Designs and the Role of the Rural Female Consumer, 1900–1930," *Agricultural History* 73 (Spring 1999): 252–62; Eileen Boris, *Art and Labor: Ruskin, Morris, and the Craftsman Ideal in America* (Philadelphia: Temple University Press, 1986), 53–54.

24. National Architect's Union, *Modern Rural Homes*, n. p.

25. McMurry, *Families and Farmhouses in 19th Century America*, 31.

26. Helen Campbell. *Household Economics* (New York: Putnam's, 1897), 34.

27. Jane Webb Loudon, *The Lady's Country Companion; or, How to Enjoy a Country Life Rationally* (London: Longman, Brown, Green & Longmans, 1845), 13.

28. E. C. Gardner, *The House That Jill Built, after Jack's Had Proved a Failure* (New York: Fords, Howard & Hulbert, 1882), 28–29.

29. Kerr, *Gentleman's House*, 76.

30. Hyungmin Pai, *The Portfolio and the Diagram: Architecture, Discourse, and Modernity in America* (Cambridge, Mass.: MIT Press, 2002), 64–71.

31. Review of James Gallier, "American Builder's General Price Book and Estimator," *North American Review* 43 (October 1836): 381–82.

32. Fisk Kimball, *Domestic Architecture of the American Colonies and of the Early Republic* (New York: Dover: 1922), 158.

33. Nicholas Rescher, *Realistic Pragmatism: An Introduction to Pragmatic Philosophy* (New York: State University of New York Press, 2000), 25, 60.

34. C. N. Pollock, "Nine Miles of Real Homes" (*Building Age* [August 1925]: 86–87) is a story about the builders Whitcomb and Keller in South Bend, Indiana. By 1925 they were building 250 houses a year, in four styles: New England colonial, Dutch colonial, English, and Western. Six plans were available in each period design. The company erected about five two-story homes to every cottage type, with six- and seven-room plans the most popular.

35. Francis D. K. Ching, *Architecture: Form, Space and Order*, 2nd ed. (New York: Van Nostrand Reinhold, 1996), 264.

36. Ibid.

37. Ibid.

38. Jennings, *Cheap and Tasteful Dwellings*, 174–177.

39. Andrew S. Draper, *American Education* (Boston: Houghton Mifflin, 1909), 200.

40. Lewis F. Allen, *Rural Architecture: Being a Complete Description of Farm Houses, Cottages, and Out Buildings* (New York: C. M. Saxton, 1852), xiv, xv.

41. Mary N. Woods, *From Craft to Profession: The Practice of Architecture in Nineteenth-Century America* (Berkeley: University of California Press, 1999), 149–154.

42. George Kubler, *The Shape of Time* (New Haven, Conn.: Yale University Press, 1962).

Chapter 3

1. Some scholars argue that all vernacular architecture is regional—a position that does not take into account the impact of industrialization and changes in building and transportation technology.

2. Herbert Gottfried and Jan Jennings, *American Vernacular Design 1870–1940* (1985; reprint, Ames: Iowa State University Press, 1988); Jan Jennings and Herbert Gottfried, *American Vernacular Interior Architecture 1870–1940* (1988; reprint, Ames: Iowa State University Press, 1993).

3. Fred Kniffen and Henry Glassie, "Building in Wood in the Eastern United States: A Time–Place Perspective," *Geographical Review* 56, No. 1 (1966): 40–66.

4. John N. Vogel, "Great Lakes Lumber on the Great Plains: The Laird, Norton Lumber Company in South Dakota" (Ph. D. diss., Marquette University, 1989); Grant McCracken, *Culture and Consumption: New Approaches to the Symbolic Character of Consumer Goods and Activities* (Bloomington: Indiana University Press, 1990), 3–30.

5. On pictures and the forging of a national identity: William H.

Goetzmann, *Exploration and Empire* (New York: Vintage, 1966); Barbara Novak, *Nature and Culture* (New York: Oxford University Press, 1980); William H. Truettner, Ed., *The West as America* (Washington, D. C.: Smithsonian Institution Press, 1991).

6. Joseph Hafner Manufacturing Company, *Sash, Doors, Blinds* (St. Louis, 1891), 95.

7. By 1912 Farley and Loetscher referred to "inside finish" as "interior finish."

8. James Warren, "Standardized Millwork Cuts Costs," *Building Age* 51 (April 1929): 106–7. Moldings were illustrated in full-size sectional drawings collected into the "Universal Book of Moldings." True standardization of millwork did not occur until well into the twentieth century; see William B. Lloyd, *Millwork: Principles and Practices* (Chicago: Cahners Publishing, 1966). By the 1920s the distinctiveness of individual moldings had been superseded by the grouping of moldings and other trim.

9. Gwendolyn Wright (*Moralism and the Model Home: Domestic Architecture and Cultural Conflict in Chicago, 1873–1913* [Chicago: University of Chicago Press, 1980], 232) explains the concern for sanitation. Also see Gavin Townsend, "Airborne Toxins and the American House, 1865–1895," *Winterthur Portfolio* 24, No. 1 (1989): 29–42.

10. Leland M. Roth, "Getting the Houses to the People: Edward Bok, the *Ladies' Home Journal*, and the Ideal House," in *Perspectives in Vernacular Architecture, IV*, Eds. Thomas Carter and Bernard Herman (Columbia: University of Missouri Press, 1991), 187–196, 236–238.

11. The Cornell University Reading Course for Farmers inaugurated in 1898 by the College of Agriculture.

12. L. H. Bailey, "Tasteful Farm Buildings," *Cornell Reading-Course for Farmers* 6, no. 26 (November 1905): 496, 497.

13. Helen Binkerd Young, "Household Decoration," *Cornell Reading Courses* 1, no. 5 (1911): 43–44.

14. Helen Binkerd Young, "Household Furnishing," *Cornell Reading Courses* 1, no. 7 (1912): 66.

15. Winifred S. Gettemy, "Home Furnishing," *Extension Bulletin* 17 (Ames: Agricultural Extension, Iowa State College, 1913), 3, 4.

16. Gettemy, "Home Furnishing," 7.

17. Ibid. 17, 19–20.

18. Helen Binkerd Young, "The Farmhouse," *Cornell Reading Courses* 2, no. 39 (1913): 156, 173.

19. Helen Scott, "Home Decoration," *Extension Bulletin* 9, no. 10 (Columbus: Agricultural College, Ohio State University, 1914), 6. Scott's view reflected design literature of the period, in which the natural and the rational were coequal forces.

20. Scott, "Home Decoration," 15.

21. Helen Binkerd Young, "The Arrangement of Household Furnishings," *Cornell Reading Courses* 4, no. 85 (1915): 141, 145–46. Young's "arrangement" lessons were published in a builder's journal: H. Messinger Fisher, "Short Cut Lessons on Interior Decoration for Builders," *Building Age* 46 (October 1924): 58; 47 (June 1925): 137.

22. Young, "Arrangement," 146.

23. Dolores Hayden, *The Grand Domestic Revolution* (Cambridge, Mass.: MIT Press, 1982), 4.

24. Clifford Edward Clark, Jr., *The American Family Home* (Chapel Hill: University of North Carolina Press, 1986), 4.

25. On industry and the academic world, see *Building Age* (34 [May 12, 1912]: 277) for an article on a house design, with the headline "A Five Room Bungalow: Showing How Rooms Can Be Compactly Arranged to Save Steps of the Housewife." By 1926 McDougall Company of Frankfort, Indiana was advertising domestic science built-in kitchen units manufactured by their domestic science division.

26. Young introduced interior vista as part of the discussion in "Farmhouse" (p. 159). The dissemination of the reading-course ideas about design is hard to measure. The entire information system was broader than the bulletins, and dissemination must have paralleled the distribution of information from manufacturers of building materials.

Chapter 4

1. The ornate cottage served as the American model. John Archer describes its English origins in *The Literature of British Domestic Architecture 1715–1842* (Cambridge, Mass.: MIT Press, 1985), 81. By the end of the eighteenth century, the cottage was identified as "picturesque," a characterization that set the tone for its design, so that early in the next century the cottage was seen as "free from restraint . . . homely and rustic, rejecting architectural rules," with irregular forms and rough materials, yet "a pleasing object on the landscape."

2. John E. Crowley, " 'In Happier Mansions, Warm and Dry,' The Invention of the Cottage as the Comfortable Anglo-American House," *Winterthur Portfolio* 32, no. 2/3 (1997), 169–188.

3. Thomas J. Gould, "An English Cottage," *Carpentry and Building* III, no. 6 (1881): 101–5.

4. On the history of the "stick style," Vincent L. Scully, *The Shingle Style and the Stick Style*, rev. ed. (New Haven, Conn.: Yale University Press, 1971) Vincent L. Scully, *The Architecture of the American Summer: The Flowering of the Shingle Style* (New York: Rizzoli, 1989).

5. Marina Griswold Van Rensselaer, "American Country Dwellings," *The Century Magazine* XXXII, no. 2 (June 1886): 209.

6. Jane B. Davies, "Alexander J. Davis, Creative American Architect," in *Alexander Jackson Davis: American Architect 1803–1892*, Ed. Amelia Peck (New York: Rizzoli, 1992), 14. Davis published his own pattern book, *Rural Residences*, in 1838.

7. Downing's theory is reviewed by Scully in *The Shingle Style* (see n. 6). For a brief overview, see Arthur Channing Downs, *Downing and the American House* (Newtown Square, Penn.: Downing and Vaux Society, 1988).

8. By the "true" Downing meant the cottage should express "the modesty and simplicity of cottage life . . . as its object is first utility, then beauty; the useful should never be sacrificed to the ornamental." Andrew Jackson Downing, *The Architecture of Country Houses* (New York: D. Appleton & Co., 1850; New York: Dover Publications, 1969), 44.

9. *The Architecture of Country Houses*, 29.

10. Writing after interest in the cottage declined, A. G. Robinson suggested that cottage settings involved plant materials, around and in the cottage, and that the cottage should have a visual prospect, "a house to live in and look on." In "Snapshots of Cottages Old and New," *Architectural Record* 36 (1914): 549.

11. According to James Ackerman, Downing "saw the buildings as images, noble furnishings in the landscape . . . presented in scenic views, never elevations or sections from which a builder might actually work." James S. Ackerman, *The Villa: Form and Ideology of Country Houses* (Princeton, N.J.: Princeton University Press, 1990), 244.

12. Anne van Erp-Houtepen, "The Etymological Origin of the Garden," *Journal of Garden History* 6, no. 3: 227, 229.

13. Population growth supported these assumptions: 1830: 12,866,020; 1850 23,191,876; 1870: 38,558,371; 1890: 62,979,766. Bureau of Census, *A Century of Population Growth* (Washington, D.C.: Government Printing Office, 1909), 55.

14. The trade papers and trade catalogs in the Hagley Library (Wilmington, Del.) were the source for this observation: Joseph Wickham Roe traced the evolution of American machine tools in *English and American Tool Builders* (New Haven, Conn.: Yale University Press, 1916); Others include James Lindsay Hallock, "Woodworking Machinery in Nineteenth Century America" (master's thesis), University of Delaware, 1978; Chandler W. Jones, *Planers, Matchers and Molders in America, 1800–1950* (Seattle: Chandler W. Jones, 1980); William L. Sims, *Two Hundred Years of History and Evolution of Woodworking Machinery* (Leicestershire, U.K.: Walders Press, 1985).

15. See John M. Staudenmaier, *Technology's Storytellers* (Cambridge, Mass.: MIT Press, 1985).

16. Recounted in M. Powis Bale, *Wood-Working Machinery* (London: Crosby Lockwood & Co., 1880), 71.

17. F. R. Hutton, "Report on Power and Machinery Employed in Manufacturers," *Tenth Census of the United States* (Washington, D.C.: Government Printing Office, 1880), 178; J. Richards referred to these operations as cross-severing the fiber and splitting the fiber in *A Treatise on the Construction and Operation of Wood-Working Machines* (New York: E. and F. N. Spon, 1872).

18. Correlative concerns were the need to improve bearings, lubrication systems, and saw blades.

19. General safety principles were published in *Safety in Woodworking* (New York: National Workmen's Compensation Service Bureau, 1918).

20. James Elliott Defebaugh, *History of the Lumber Industry of America*, 2d ed. 2 v. (Chicago: American Lumberman, 1906), 1, 284; Douglas W. MacCleery, *American Forests* (Durham, N.C.: Forest History Society, 1994), 3–4: "The original forest covered about one billion acres or about half the U. S. land area (including Alaska). About three-quarters of that forest covered the eastern third of the country."

20. Defebaugh, *History*, 294 (see n. 23). In *A Forest Journey* (Cambridge, Mass.: Harvard University Press, 1991) John Perlin suggests that overestimates originated in English and European expectations, wherein America's forests were perceived as mythic in stature and extent.

21. L. B. Valk, Design No. 43, *The American Builder* 11 (November 1874): 247.

22. Design No. 43, *The American Builder*.

23. William M. Woolett, *Old Homes Made New* (New York: A. J. Bicknell, 1878), plate 13.

24. In *English Taste in Landscape in the Seventeenth Century* (Ann Arbor: University of Michigan Press, 1955, 36–38), Henry V. S. Ogden and Margaret S. Ogden outline the evolution of taste in ideal landscapes, in pictures, and through the principles of variety (diversity in natural elements) and contrast.

25. Joseph Forsyth Johnson, *Residential Sites and Environments* (New York: DeLaMare Printing and Publishing, 1898), 9.

26. Gould, "English Cottage," 101 (n. 5).

27. Marina Griswold Van Rensselaer, "American Country Dwellings," *The Century Magazine* XXXII, no. 3 (1886): 422.

28. Leo Marx, *The Machine in the Garden* (New York: Oxford University Press, 1964), 43.

30. Sidney K. Robinson, *Inquiry into the Picturesque* (Chicago: University of Chicago Press, 1991), 5. In using the term *mixture*, Robinson is generalizing Uvedale Price and Richard Payne Knight's descriptions of "mixing" styles.

31. Thomas Hughes, *American Genesis* (New York: Penguin Books, 1990), 13–52, and George Basalla, *The Evolution of Technology* (Cambridge, Mass.: Cambridge University Press, 1988), 115–9.

32. Defebaugh, *History*, I. 294 (see n. 23); J. Richards, *Treatise*, 38 (see n. 20), believed a village of 2,000 could support a planing mill and other specialty shops, but that has not been proven.

33. Nelson Courtlandt Brown, *Forest Products, Their Manufacture and Use* (New York: Wiley, 1919), 3. Before 1850 Maine was first in lumbering; in 1850 it was New York, in 1860, Pennsylvania, and from 1870 to 1904, the Great Lakes states. After 1904 southern states played a major role in lumbering because of their yellow pine forests. By 1916 yellow pine represented 37 percent of the lumber production in the country. Western states were contributing pine and fir. These species replaced white pine, which fell in production from 7. 7 million feet in 1899 to 2. 7 in 1916.

34. According to Cox, et al. (*Well-Wooded Land*, 266 [see n. 1]), the gap between cutting and consumption continued growing during each decade: 1890, 28 billion board feet cut and 22 billion used; 1900, 38 billion cut and 24 billion used; Defebaugh, *History*, 540 (see n. 23).

35. Waste provided some manufacturers with an opportunity. The precut-house industry, such as Aladdin of Bay City, Michigan, used control of waste as the basis for marketing ready-cut houses. They kept prices down by using lumber more efficiently.

36. The first volume, 1869, initiated a series of articles on "Cottage and Villa Architecture," with three designs by L. B. Valk. The first article concluded with this statement about cottages: "There is perhaps no class of building that would pay capitalists a better percentage on investments than those here described. This kind of improvement upon lots newly laid out in villages, at a reasonable distance from the city, would be sure to give an increase to population, and lend character to the place. What is wanted is neat, convenient, well-built cottages, renting at the rate of two or three hundred dollars per year, and located near the railway lines running to the city." *The Manufacturer and Builder* 1, no. 2 (April 1869): 121.

37. Palliser, Palliser & Co., *Specifications for Frame Houses* (Bridgeport, Conn.: 1878), 9–13. Quality standards for lumber were established in the nineteenth century, but standardization of dimensions took longer.

38. E. C. Gardner, *Homes, and How To Make Them* (Boston: Osgood, 1878), 130–131.

39. Michael J. Ettema, "Technological Innovation and Design Economics in Furniture Manufacture," notes that machinery-based production resulted in "proliferation, not elaboration," a point echoed in millwork production. As millwork production wore on, there was a contraction in design with less elaborate profiles in moldings. In *Winterthur Portfolio* 16, nos. 2, 3 (1981): 197–223.

40. Preface to *Shingle Style* (see n. 6).

41. Sam Bass Warner, Jr., *Streetcar Suburbs: The Process of Growth in Boston* (Cambridge, Mass.: Harvard University Press, 1962); Kenneth Jackson, *The Crabgrass Frontier* (New York: Oxford University Press, 1988); John R. Stilgoe, *Borderlands* (New Haven, Conn.: Yale University Press, 1988).

42. Gwendolyn Wright, *Moralism and the Model Home* (Chicago: University of Chicago Press, 1980), chapters 1–3; see also Gwendolyn Wright, *Building the American Dream* (New York: Pantheon Books, 1981), 73–113.

43. Clark, *The American Family Home*, 3–130.

44. *Better Homes at Lower Cost* (Cleveland: Wood Homes Bureau, 1926), 73.

45. John Archer, *The Literature of British Domestic Architecture 1715–1842* (Cambridge, Mass.: MIT Press, 1985), 82–3.

46. Kenneth John Meyers discusses a pleasant place, or *locus amoenus*, in "On the Cultural Construction of Landscape Experience," in *American Iconology*, Ed. David C. Miller (New Haven, Conn.: Yale University Press, 1993), 63.

Chapter 5

1. Richard Guy Wilson, *The Colonial Revival House* (New York: Harry N. Abrams 2004), 14.

2. "Spanish Architecture for Bungalow," *Building Age* (October 1923): 52.

3. V. L. Sherman, "Characteristics of the Spanish Type," *Keith's Magazine* (January 1929): 24–25.

Chapter 6

1. Charles L. Eastlake, *Hints on Household Taste: The Classic Handbook of Victorian Interior Decoration* (London: Longmans, Green, 1878), 136.

2. *The Jos. Hafner Mfg. Co. Combined Book of Sash, Doors, Blinds, Glazed Windows, Moldings, Etc.* (Chicago: Rand, McNally, 1891), 214–35; Jennings, *Cheap and Tasteful Dwellings*, 180.

3. Gwendolyn Wright, *Moralism and the Model Home*, 251–53.

4. An expanded version of this essay was published by Jan Jennings as "Controlling Passion: The Turn-of-the-Century Wallpaper Dilemma," *Winterthur Portfolio* 31, no. 4 (1996): 243–264. For tastemakers, see Angel Kwolek Folland, "The Useful What-not and the Ideal of 'Domestic Decoration,' " *Helicon Nine* 8 (May 1983): 78; Henry T. Williams and Mrs. C. S. Jones, *Beautiful Homes; or, Hints in House Furnishing* (New York: Henry T. Williams, 1878), 3.

5. "Selection of Wall-Paper," 71; "The Use of Paper for Ceiling Decorations," *Carpentry and Building* 3 (November 1881): 208. Katherine C. Grier defines *aesthetic* as "the set of guiding constructs for appreciating the world perceived by the senses, rather than the criticism of taste," in *Culture and Comfort: People, Parlors, and Upholstery, 1850–1930* (Rochester, N.Y.: Strong Museum, 1988), 136.

6. *Modern Wall Papers: 1915 Idea Book* (Ithaca, N.Y.: F. H. Warner, 1915) comprises fourteen vignettes of bedrooms, living and dining rooms. The Rexall Store in West Union, Iowa offered a hand-size paperback idea book, *Interiors* (Chicago: Fairthorn Co., n. d.), which contains seven color plates of interiors with text.

7. The Maxwell trade postcard, postmarked 1910, may be from Van Sciver's Furniture Store, Trenton, N.J.

8. Frances E. Fryatt, "Selecting a Wall Paper," *Ladies' World* 17, no. 5 (1896): 20.

9. Fryatt, "Selecting a Wall Paper," 20.

10. Williams and Jones, *Beautiful Homes*, 3; Candace Wheeler, "Decoration of Walls," *The Outlook* 52 (November 2, 1895): 706.

11. During the 1890s, homemaking departments appeared in major colleges and universities; see Edna Anderson, et al., *Definitive Themes in Home Economics and Their Impact on Families, 1909–1984* (Washington, D. C.: American Home Economics Association, 1984), 105–6. As late as 1956, the Wallpaper Council flatly stated that "taste declined" following the 1839 invention of the four-color machine that produced as many as 400 rolls a day (*Selling Wallpaper: A Study of the Fundamental Knowledge Required for Selling Wallpaper Successfully* [New York: Wallpaper Council, 1956], 10).

12. Although the middle class is often described as the non-manual sector (downtown businessmen, retailers, owners, and superintendents of manufacturing establishments, and clerks), this definition does not always account for class perceptions in small towns and dispersed farm communities of the Midwest and West. See Stuart M. Blumin, *The Emergence of the Middle Class: Social Experience in the American City, 1760–1900* (New York: Cambridge University Press, 1989), 310.

13. Jane Addams, "Art Work," as cited in Allen F. Davis and Mary Lynn McCree, Eds., *Eighty Years at Hull-House* (Chicago: Quadrangle Books, 1969), 50–52.

14. For decoration and warmth, log cabins, wooden shacks, and houses of the plains were often lined with newspaper, blankets, or, after the beginning of the canning industry in the 1890s, with sheets of tin made from flattened cans. Glenda Riley, *The Female Frontier: A Comparative of Women on the Prairie and the Plains* (Lawrence: University of Kansas Press, 1988), 2–4, 12, 42, 56, 70, and 87.

15. W. W. Hall, *The Guide-Board to Health, Peace, and Competence; or, The Road to Happy Old Age* (Springfield, Mass.: D. E. Fisk, 1869), 683.

16. Fryatt, "Selecting a Wall Paper," 20.

17. Stephens is cited in John A. Kouwenhoven, *Made in America: The Arts in Modern Civilization* (Garden City, N.Y.: Doubleday, 1949), 125–26. Helen Binkerd Young, "Household Decoration," *Cornell Reading Courses* 1 No. 5 (1911): 47.

18. Clarence Cook, *What Shall We Do with Our Walls?* (New York: Warren Fuller, 1881), 17, 18.

19. *Household Art*, Ed. Candace Wheeler (New York: Harper & Brothers, 1893), 706.

20. Fryatt, "Selecting a Wall Paper," 20.

21. "The Yellow Wall-Paper," published in 1892, received the widest critical acclaim of the nearly two hundred short stories

Gilman produced during her lifetime. Born into a family of reformers, Gilman was the great-niece of author and abolitionist Harriet Beecher Stowe and the great-granddaughter of the influential preacher Lyman Beecher. "The Yellow Wall-Paper" in *Selected Stories of Charlotte Perkins Gilman*, Denise D. Knight, Ed. (Newark: University of Delaware Press, 1994), 11, 16, 18, 6, 13.

22. Frank T. Lent, *Sound Sense in Suburban Architecture, Containing Hints, Suggestions, and Bits of Practical Information for the Building of Inexpensive Country Houses* (Cranford, N. J.: F. T. Lent, 1893), 5.

23. Henry Hudson Holly, *Modern Dwellings in Town and Country* (New York: Harper & Brothers, 1878), 11

24. Hazel Adler, *The New Interior* (New York: Century Co., 1916).

Chapter 7

1. "A Study in Cheap Frame Houses," *Carpentry and Building* (May 1879): 92–95. Designs furnished by B. O'Rourke, of Newark, N.J.

2. W. Barksdale Maynard, " 'Best, Lowliest Style,' " 340–343.

3. Richard Guy Wilson, *The Colonial Revival House*, 6–11.

Chapter 9

1. David Handlin, *The American Home: Architecture and Society, 1815–1915* (Boston: Little, Brown, 1979), 334–48.

2. Amos Jackson Bicknell, *Bicknell's Village Builder* (Reprint Watkins Glen, New York: The American Life and Study Institute, 1976); George Fuller, *Sketches for Dwellings* (Boston?: George Fuller, 1858–1877; Samuel Burrage Reed, *House-Plans for Everybody* (New York: Orange Judd Co. 1878).

3. H. C. Hussey, *Home Building: A Reliable Book of Facts Relative to Building, Living, Materials, Costs of about 400 Places from New York to San Francisco* (New York: Leader & Van Hoesen, 1876), plate no. 32.

4. George Everton Woodward, *Woodward's National Architect* (1869, Reprint, New York: Dover, 1988) and Lawrence B. Valk, *Architecture for the Country: Valk's Cottages and Villas* (New York, Lawrence B. Valk, 1869). H. C. Hussey, *Home Building: A Reliable Book of Facts Relative to Building, Living, Materials of about 400 Places from New York to San Francisco* (New York: Leader and Van Hoesen, 1876), plate no. 32.

Chapter 10

1. "Moderate Cost Dwelling at Oakmont, PA." *The Building Age* (June 1910): 262.

2. Fred T. Hodgson, *Practical Bungalows and Cottages for Town and Country* (Chicago: F. J. Drake, 1906), David Williams, *Modern Dwellings and Construction Details* (New York: David Williams Co, 1903, 1907), Montgomery Ward, *Book of Homes* (New York: Montgomery Co. 191?).

3. Aladdin Company, *Aladdin Plan of Industrial Housing* (Bay City, Michigan, c. 1920).

Chapter 11

1. "Building Bungalows," *Carpentry and Building* (July 1904): 222; Leland M Roth, "Getting the Houses to the People: Edward Bok, the Ladies' Home Journal, and the Ideal Home," in *Perspectives in Vernacular Architecture, IV*, Eds. Thomas Carter and Bernard L. Herman (Columbia: University of Missouri Press, 1991), 194.

2. Hodgson, *Practical Bungalows and Cottages for Town and Country*, 8.

3. "Some Characteristics of the California Bungalow," *Carpentry and Building*, February 1907: 53

4. Trade postcard, plan no. 1206. Arlington D. Isham, architect, 115 Broadway, New York City. Authors' collection.

Chapter 12

1. *Sunset Western Ranch Houses*, editors of *Sunset Magazine*, in collaboration with Cliff May (San Francisco: Lane Publishing, 1950).

2. Avi Friedman, "The Evolution of Design Characteristics During the Post-Second World War Housing Boom: The U. S. Experience," *Journal of Design History* 8, no. 2 (1995): 131–146.

3. American Plan Service, *Plans for Your Future Home: Practical Designs for the Home Builder* (Miami, Florida: American Plan Service, 1950).

4. *Sunset Western Ranch Houses*, 78.

5. Richard B. Pollman, *Designs for Convenient Living* (Detroit: Home Planners, 1946), 63.

6. Clark, *The American Family Home 1800–1960*, 211, 216.

7. *Small Homes Guide*, no. 31 (1953–1954): 122.

8. *Modern Ranch Homes Designed for Town or Country Living* (Chicago: National Plan Service, 1951), 8.

9. For the side-by-side split, see Nelson L. Burbank and Oscar Shaftel, *House Construction Details*, 5th ed. (New York: Simmons-Boardman, 1959), 7.

Chapter 14

1. Pittsburgh Plate Glass Company, *Glass Paints, Varnishes, and Brushes—Their History, Manufacture, and Use* (Pittsburgh, Pennsylvania: Pittsburgh Plate Glass Co, 1923).

2. "Modernize Main Street," *American Builder* (April, 1935): 84–85.

3. Stocking room in "Planning the Modern Bank Building," *Building Age* (December 1920): 22; ladies' alcove in "Classic Lines Grace This Alabama Bank," *Building Age and National Builder* (January 1925): 136.

4. Angel Kwolek-Folland, *Engendering Business: Men and Women in the Corporate Office, 1870–1930* (Baltimore: Johns Hopkins University Press, 1994), 94–128.

5. Kwolek-Folland, *Engendering Business*, 113.

6. Ibid., 110–111.

7. "A Business Building of Attractive Architecture," *Building Age* (May 1918): 248–51; 1901 glass plate from Western History/Genealogy Department, Denver Public Library.

8. *1902 Edition of the Sears, Roebuck and Company Catalog* (New York: Crown, 1969), 756.

9. Adrian Forty, *Objects of Desire* (New York: Pantheon Books, 1986), 129.

Chapter 15

1. General Congregational Convention, *A Book of Plans for Churches and Parsonages* (New York: D. Burgess, 1853, 1892), 6.
2. Ibid., 11.
3. Henry Edward Tralle, *Planning Church Buildings* (Philadelphia: Judson Press, 1921), 35.
4. Mouzon William Brabham, *Planning Modern Church Buildings* (Nashville, Tenn.: Cokesbury Press, 1928), 54.

Chapter 16

1. Regarding the Hoosier Company and its products and manufactured cabinetry, see Mary Anne Beecher, "Promoting the 'Unit Idea': Manufactured Kitchen Cabinets" (1900–1950), *APT Bulletin* 32: No. 2/3 (2001): 27–37.
2. Georgia B. Child, *The Efficient Kitchen* (New York: Robert McBride, 1925).
3. Mathew Luckiesh, *Lighting Fixtures and Lighting Effects* (New York: McGraw Hill Book Co., 1925).

Historical Glossary of Building Terms

Part of the history of America's common buildings rests in the language used to construct them. The history of eighteenth and nineteenth century publishing was rife with fraud because there was little or no copyright protection. Of the sources used in compiling this glossary, there are numerous examples of authors publishing the same text under different titles and of authors appropriating someone else's work as their own. Even the history of a single book is complicated as in the case of Robert G. Hatfield, who published *American House Carpenter* in 1844 (New York and London: Wiley and Putnam), and then a series of books with the same title (1844, 45, 50, 52, all with Wiley) in which the main subjects were cornices, moldings and

principles of geometry. He published a second series focused on the strength of materials (1857, 68, 71). He died in 1879 and editions published after that added material on the construction of floors and girders (1880), and finally iron construction systems (1889).

The glossary entries are organized chronologically, beginning, if appropriate, with an eighteenth century entry. In editing the entries, preference has been given for any changes in meaning or changes in the explanation. For example, some glossaries prefer to describe how a thing is used while others turn to the theoretical use of it. Secondly, if an old definition carries through over time, then the original is left as a source.

abacus. The upper member of the capital of a column, serving as a kind of crowning, both to the capital and the whole column (1734 *Builder's Dictionary*); the upper number of the capital of a column whereon the architrave rests. The original object in its use was doubtless to give breadth to the top of the column, and prepare a large level bed for the reception of the entablature (1851 Shaw); the upper member of the capital of a column . . . sometimes square and sometimes curved (1882 Hodgson); the upper corbels overtopping a column, next under the architrave (1917 Shearer).

abattoir. A building built for the purpose of slaughter of animals to be used for food (1887 Garnsey).

abbey. A building appropriated for the habitation of a religious community, under the government of an abbot or an abbess (1854 Stuart).

abutment. A pier upon which the extremity of an arch rests (1825 Partington); the solid part of a pier from which an arch springs (1851 Shaw); that which receives the end of, and

gives support to anything having a tendency to spread or thrust outward; or it may be defined as the resisting surface of a body, on which another body presses in an oblique direction to the horizon, or in a different direction to the height or length of the body pressed upon (1854 Nicholson); the extremity of a bridge; the last or boundary pier of the high water-way; the land-stool; land-pier; sometimes the revetment, or facing of masonry of this pier (1854 Stuart); that part of a pier from which the arch springs (1857 Hatfield); the junction or meeting of two pieces of timber, of which the fibers of the one extend perpendicular to the joint, and those of the other parallel to it (1874 Gould); that on which a thing rests, or by which it is supported, as the abutment of an arch (1883 Sylvester); that construction of building material which is intended to receive the end thrust or lateral pressure of a vault, arch or roof (1887 Garnsey); a surface or structure on which another structure rests (1924 *House Beautiful*).

accompaniment. An ornament added to some other ornament for the greater beauty of the work (1736 Neve); buildings or ornaments having a necessary connection or dependence, and which serve to make a design more or less complete (1882 Hodgson).

acroteria. The small pedestals placed in the extremities and apex of a pediment, originally intended as a base for sculpture (1857 Hatfield); any angle of a pediment or gable, usually the upper or pitch angle. An ornament or statue placed at the point of a pediment angle. The ornamental prow or stern of a classical galley(1917 Shearer); a pedestal placed on the lower corners and apex of a gable, or pediment, of Greek and Roman temple (1924 *House Beautiful*).

aedicule. A small temple, but sometimes denoting the inner part of the temple, in which the altar and statue of the deity were placed; at other times, a niche in the wall, for receiving a statue (1854 Nicholson).

aisle. Aisles, passages in theaters, houses, rooms and the space between the walls and the columns (1833 Haviland); passage to and from the pews of a church. In Gothic architecture, the lean-to wings on the sides of the nave (1857 Hatfield); the wings, inward side porticos of a church, the inward lateral corridors which enclose the choir, the presbytery, and the body of the church along its sides (1882 Hodgson).

altar. A place sacred to divine worship in churches (1736 Neve); in modern churches, the area within the railing in front of the pulpit (1857 Hatfield); a pedestal or pillar used by the ancients for sacrifices and offerings, and by Christians for the celebration of the sacrament (1887 Garnsey).

amphiprostyle. A kind of temple which had four columns in the front, and the same number in the face behind (1734 *Builder's Dictionary*); a Grecian temple which has a columned portico on both ends (1882 Hodgson); a temple having columns surmounted by gables or pediments at each end, or front and rear (1887 Garnsey); having columns at each end, but not at the sides (1917 Shearer).

anchor. An ornament in form of an anchor, or arrow's head, employed in the echinus, or ovolo, between the borders which surround the eggs (1854 Nicholson); an ornamental metal decoration; also, the term is applied to ties and fastenings in constructive architecture (1887 Garnsey); a metal rod connecting and strengthening the juncture of two walls at right angles to each other (1924 *House Beautiful*).

ancon. The corners or coins of walls, cross-beams, or rafters (1734 *Builder's Dictionary*); the consoles, a sort of brackets and shouldering pieces (1736 Neve). the carved key-stones of arches (1825 Partington); the trusses or consoles sometimes employed in the dressings of apertures, as an apparent support to the cornice, upon the flanks of the architrave (1854 Nicholson); a consol or bracket to a cornice (1887 Garnsey); a bracket supporting the structure over the opening of a door or window (1924 *House Beautiful*).

angle bar. In joinery, an upright bar at the angles of polygonal windows, a mullion (1882 Hodgson); a horizontal bar or muntin to a window sash or frame (1887 Garnsey).

angle brace. A piece framed across the angle of a piece of framing. It is also termed an angle-tie, or diagonal-tie, and is nearly synonymous with brace (1858 Silloway); a piece of timber fixed on two sides of a quadrangular frame, forming the area of the frame into an octagonal opening (1882 Hodgson); a brace or angle framing in constructive architecture (1887 Garnsey); a tie or strut placed in the corner of a framing to prevent alteration of shape (1908 Ellis).

annulet. A narrow flat molding which is common to divers places of the columns, as in the bases, capitals, etc. (1736 Neve): a small square molding commonly used to connect the others (1825 Partington); a small square molding, used to separate others; the fillet which separates the flutings of a column is sometimes known by this term (1856 Smeaton); a small square molding, which crowns or accompanies a larger. Also that fillet which separate the flutings of a column. It is sometimes called a list or listella (1880 Vogdes); a ring molding often worked on a corner block used to join door casings and window casings (1917 Shearer).

anta. A kind of shaft of a pilaster, without base or capital, and even without any molding (1734 Builder's Dictionary); a pillar adjoining to the wall (1734 Salmon); a small projection from the wall to receive the entablature from the columns of a portico, and having bases and capitals different from columns (1825 Partington). [plural] the jambs of doors, or square posts supporting the lintel; pillars forming the entrances of edifices in general (1854 Stuart); a pilaster attached to the wall not usually diminished from bottom to top (1897 Edwards); a pilaster with capital and base, usually formed by thickening the wall (1917 Shearer).

antechamber. An apartment preceded by a vestibule, and from which is approached another room called the inner chamber or cabinet; the chamber that leads to the chief apartment (1854 Stuart); [ante-room] a small room giving access to a larger room (1906 Ellis).

antefix. An upright ornament . . . placed along the eaves to embellish the terminations of the convex tiles which cover the junctions of the flat roofing tiles (1924 *House Beautiful*).

apophyge. That part of a column which connects the upper fillet of the base and the under one of the capital with the cylindrical part of the shaft (1856 Smeaton); the curvature at the top and bottom of a classic column, where it expands to meet the moldings of the base and capital (1887 Garnsey).

apron. The horizontal piece in wooden stairs supporting the carriages at their landings (1858 Silloway); the piece of woodwork immediately below the stool of a window (1887 Garnsey).

arabesque. An Eastern style of ornament, consisting of a fantastic mixture of foliage, flowers, fruits, etc. made use of both in painting and sculpture (1854 Nicholson); an enriching and ornamentation of flat surfaces, panels, pilasters, etc., with scroll-work, vines, flowers, etc (1887 Garnsey); decorative scroll work (1924 *House Beautiful*).

arcade. The covered walk along the side or middle of a building, where columns support the arches (1870 Todd); a series of arches, supported on columns or pilasters (1887 Garnsey); a series of arches together with the columns or piers which support them, open, or with openings on one or both sides and with an open clear passage running lengthwise (1917 Shearer): a series of two or more arches and their columns (1924 *House Beautiful*).

arch. An inward support to the superstructure and is either circular, elliptical or straight (1736 Neve); an artful arrangement of bricks, stones, or other materials, in a curvilinear form, which by their mutual pressure and support perform the office of a lintel, and carry superincumbent weights, the whole resting at its extremities upon piers or abutments

(1851 Shaw); such an arrangement, in a concave form, of building materials, as enables them, supported by piers or abutments, to carry weights and resist strain (1856 Smeaton); an arrangement of stones or other material in a curvilinear form, so as to perform the office of a lintel and carry superincumbent weights (1857 Hatfield); a curved, self-sustaining structure of wood, stone, or other material, with the ends supported on pillars, or abutments (1870 Todd); a scientific arrangement of bricks, stones, or other materials in a curvilinear form, which by their mutual pressure and support, perform the office of a lintel, and carry superincumbent weights, the whole resting at its extremities upon the piers or abutments (1880 Vogdes); a mechanical arrangement of building materials arranged in the form of a curve, which preserve a given form when resisting pressure, and enables them, supported by piers or abutments, to carry weights and resist pressure (1882 Hodgson).

architrave. The lower of the primary divisions of the entablature. It is placed immediately upon the abacus of the capital (1851 Shaw); that part of the entablature which rests upon the capital of a column, and is beneath the frieze. It is supposed to represent the principal beam of a timber building (1856 Smeaton); the casing and moldings about a door or window (1857 Hatfield); a block of stone or beam of timber carried from one column or support to another (1924 *House Beautiful*).

archivolt. The inner court of an arch, or a frame set off with moldings, running over the faces of the arch-stones, and bearing upon the imposts (1736 Neve); the ceiling of a vault: the under surface of an arch (1857 Hatfield); the collection of moldings projecting from and running round the face of an arch (1887 Garnsey); an architrave curved into an arch to span a semicircular, instead of a rectangular, opening; or, an ornamental molding following the contour of an arch (1924 *House Beautiful*).

area. The extent of a floor, etc. (1734 *Builder's Dictionary*); this term is applied to superficies, whether of timber, stone, or other material, and is the superficial measurement, that is, the length multiplied into the breadth. The word sometimes signifies an open space (1856 Smeaton); the superficial contents of any figure—an open space or court within a building (1882 Hodgson); a space, a court-yard, a sunken court (1887 Garnsey); when a cellar is deep and the windows reach down below the surface of the ground, the earth is removed and the space is boxed around with brick or concrete. The opening is called an area (1917 Shearer).

areostyle. A sort of building where the pillars stand at the greatest distance from each other that can be (1736 Neve); a manner of proportioning the intervals between columns ranged in pairs (1854 Stuart); that style of building in which the columns are distant from one another from four to five diameters (1856 Smeaton).

arris. The intersection or line on which two surfaces of a body, forming an exterior angle, meet each other (1854 Nicholson).

arris-filet. A triangular section of timber used in raising slates against shafts of chimneys, and similar work (1882 Hodgson).

ascendant. [ascendants] the perpendicular frame of a door or window (1887 Garnsey).

ashlar. Common or free stones, as they come out of the quarry, of different lengths and thicknesses (1736 Neve); cut or hewn stone used in the face of a wall, generally with vertical and horizontal square joints (1887 Garnsey); a squared and finished building stone distinguished from stone of irregular shape, or such stone used as a veneer on the face of a wall made of some inferior material (1924 *House Beautiful*).

ashlering. Quartering (to tack to) in garrets about 2½, or 3 foot high, perpendicular to the floor, up to the under side of the rafters (1736 Neve); the short studs of a building between the plate and girt of the attic-floor. Buildings are framed in this manner where the attic is designed for occupation, the short studs cutting off the acute angle that the rafters would make, were they permitted to come to the floor (1858 Silloway); perpendicular studding between the sloping roof and the floor of an attic chamber for fixing the plaster to (1908 Ellis).

astragal. A little round member, in the form of a ring or bracelet, serving as an ornament at the tops and bottoms of columns (1734 *Builder's Dictionary*); a small molding, semicircular in profile (1825 Partington); a small round molding with two annulets (1833 Haviland); a small molding consisting of a half-round with a fillet on each side (1857 Hatfield); a small semicircular molding, sometimes plain and sometimes ornamented (1882 Hodgson); a strip of molding the length of the door of any desired pattern to be applied to one of a pair of folding doors so as to form a rabbet. Single, for folding doors—a strip the length of the doors with a cross-section usually similar to a letter "T"—used to form a rabbet. Double, for sliding doors—a pair of strips the length of the doors-rabbeted to receive the doors on the back and molded or grooved reciprocally on the face to make a tight joint. Joint, for sliding doors—a molding or groove worked reciprocally on the meeting edges of each of a pair of doors to make a tight joint.

attic. A low story erected over an order of architecture, to finish the upper part of the building, being chiefly used to conceal the roof, and give greater dignity to the design (1851 Shaw); the garret of a dwelling-house, or the upper story, immediately beneath the roof. When a house has a flat roof, so that the walls overhead in the upper rooms are not inclined, the upper story is not properly called the attic, but the upper or third story (1870 Todd); a sub-story rising above a cornice or contained in the roof (1887 Garnsey).

attic order. A sort of little order raised upon a larger one, by way of crowning, or to finish the building (1734 *Builder's Dictionary*); an order of low pilasters, generally placed over some other order of columns (1851 Shaw); a term improperly used to denote the pilasters which are frequently employed in the decoration of an attic (1854 Nicholson); the order of architecture used in the construction of an attic (1887 Garnsey).

back flap. Additional breadths hinged to the front shutters for covering the aperture completely, when required to be shut (1874 Gould); the center portion of a set of inside blinds (1887 Garnsey).

back lining. That parallel to the pulley-piece, and next to the jamb, on either side, is called the back lining (1854 Nicholson).

baguette. In carpentry, a kind of astragal or hip-molding, on the hips or corners of a roof . . . in architecture, it is a small round molding, less than an astragal (1736 Neve); a small astragal molding, sometimes carved and enriched with pearls, laurels, etc. (1854 Nicholson).

badigeon. A mixture of plaster and free-stone, well sifted, and ground together: it is used by statuaries to fill up the small holes, and repair the defects in stones of which their work is made. The term is used by joiners, for a composition of sawdust and strong glue, with which the chasms of their work are filled (1854 Nicholson).

balcony. A projection from the surface of a wall, supported by consoles or pillars, and surrounded by a balustrade (1851 Shaw); a projecting platform, cage, or short gallery, resting on brackets or consoles enclosed by a parapet (1917 Shearer).

baldachin. A piece of architecture, built in fashion of a canopy, or crown, supported by several pillars, to serve for a covering to an altar; a shell over the front door of a house(1736 Neve).

balk. (balks) Large pieces of timber brought from abroad in floats (1854 Nicholson); small sticks of roughly hewn timber, being the trunks of small trees partially squared (1858 Silloway).

ballon. The round globe of the top of a pier, or pillar (1736 Neve).

baluster. Little pillars joined by a rail, at a convenient height, for the elbows to rest upon (1734 *Builder's Dictionary*); small columns or pilasters, of different sizes . . . adorned with moldings . . . placed with rails on stairs, in the fronts of galleries, in churches, etc. round altar-pieces in churches, on terrace walks, and in balconies, and platforms, etc.(1736 Neve); a small pillar supporting a rail; commonly used as a parapet (1825 Partington); a small column, or pillar, of wood, stone, etc. used on terraces or tops of buildings for ornament, and to support railing, and, when continued, form a balustrade (1833 Haviland); the upright portions of a railing or balustrade. These pieces are sometimes turned round, and sometimes are four-square, or of an octagonal form (1870 Todd).

balustrade. A number of balusters connected by the rail (1825 Partington); a connected range of a number of balusters on balconies, terraces round altars (1851 Shaw); the railing made of the hand rail, the banisters, the "newel post" and corner posts, along a flight of stair (1870 Todd); a row of balusters set in a line with cap and base, serving as a railing or fence for altars, balconies, etc.(1897 Edwards).

band. A term used to express what is generally called a face, or fascia. It more properly means a flat low square profiled member, without respect to its place (1851 Shaw); a flat member, or molding, smaller than the fascia(1854 Stuart); a square member (1856 Smeaton).

bandelet. A little fillet, or band, encompassing a pillar quite about like a ring . . . the three parts that compose an architrave (1736 Neve); any flat molding, or fillet. *See* band (1854 Nicholson).

banister. An improper name for baluster (1833 Haviland); a vulgar term for a baluster (1854 Stuart); an obsolete term for baluster (1887 Garnsey).

bar. A piece of iron or wood for the security of doors, windows, and for several other uses(1736 Neve); used in a court of justice to denote an enclosure made with a strong partition or timber . . . where the counsel are placed to plead causes . . . the benches where the lawyers or advocates are seated. a piece of wood or iron used for fastening doors, windows, shutters, etc.(1854 Stuart).

barbican. An outwork in a building, or a kind of watchtower. Among the moderns barbican is a kind of opening left in a wall for the passage of water . . . or as a drain to a terrace(1736 Neve); a watch tower attached to a fortress; an aperture in a wall for drainage (1887 Garnsey).

bargeboards. Two boards attached to the gable ends of a roof, fixed near the extremity of the barge-course, and following the inclination of the roof, used for the purpose of protecting the under side of the barge course from the weather(1854 Nicholson); or verge-boards, are the finishing boards on the gable end of a building, the upper edge of which is even with top of the roofing boards (1870 Todd); boards nailed against the outer face of a wall, along the slopes of a gable end of a house to hide the rafter, etc. and to make a neat finish (1882 Hodgson); a board used as a finish to a gable, covering the ends of the rafters and frequently cut into ornamental forms (1887 Garnsey); ornamental boards covering the ends of the roof timbers projecting over gable ends of buildings (Ellis 1908); a board placed just under the roof of a gable, covering the rafters or taking their place (1924 *House Beautiful*).

barge-course. Projecting bricks forming a continuous projection capping a gable wall (1917 Shearer).

base. Any body which bears up another; but particularly applied to the bottoms of columns and pedestals (1736 Neve); the lower part of a column, molded or plain, on which the shaft is placed. The word also signifies any support (1851 Shaw); the lowest part of a wall, column, etc. (1857 Hatfield); the lower projecting part of a room, consisting of the plinth and its moldings. The part of a column between the top of the pedestal and the bottom of the shaft (1883 Sylvester); the lower part of a column on which the shaft is placed; also the skirting board fastened to the wall just above the floor all round the room (1897 Edwards).

basement, basement story. The lower part or story of a building, on which an order is placed, with a base or plinth, die and cornice (1851 Shaw); that which is immediately under the principal story, and included within the foundation of the building (1857 Hatfield); the first story of a building (1887 Garnsey) that part of a building below the ground line (1908 Ellis).

basilica. a kind of public hall or court of justice—when applied to a church it conveys an idea of great magnificence (1882 Hodgson).

basso-relievo. The representation of figures projecting from a back ground, without being detached from it (1851 Shaw); in sculpture, the representation of figures projecting from a back ground so as to give it relief (1854 Nicholson).

baston. A round molding in the base of a column; also called torus (1883 Sylvester).

bat. A part of a brick (1854 Nicholson).

batten. A strip of board, either thick or thin, narrow or wide, secured to the surface of smooth work. Narrow strips, called battens, are nailed over the cracks of boards that are put on buildings vertically (1870 Todd); a scantling of stuff from two inches to seven inches in breadth, and from half an inch to one inch and a half in thickness (1874 Gould); a narrow strip of board used to cover seams or joints in boarding. Any narrow strip of board (1883 Sylvester); a name given to a piece of board, from 2 to 4 or more inches wide, and about an inch thick, used to nail over joints in wider boards; also the cross pieces in a common door to which all the others are fastened and which holds the door together (1897 Edwards); a market form of converted timber less than 3 in. thick and 9 in. wide (1906 Ellis).

batten doors. A ledged door, or a barred door (1882 Hodgson).

batter, battering. A wall, piece of timber, or other material which does not stand upright, but inclines away from you when you stand before it; but, when on the contrary, it leans towards you, they say of its inclination that it overhangs (1880 Vogdes); a term used to designate the slant of a wall, where it is built narrow at the top and wide at the bottom (1887 Garnsey).

battlements. Indentations on the top of a parapet, or wall, first used in ancient fortifications; and afterward applied to churches and other buildings (1851 Shaw).

bay. An opening between piers, beams, or mullions (1825 Partington); the space intervening between two given portions of the wall or floors of a building (1858 Silloway).

bay window. Such a one as is composed of an arch of a circle standing without the stress of the building; by which means spectators may the better see what is acted in the street (1736 Neve); a projecting window of a polygonal plan, and rising from the ground or the basement of the building (1854 Nicholson); consists of an exterior projection of a house provided with circular, or angular windows, resting on a foundation that extends below the surface of the ground (1870 Todd); a projecting wall of an angular or circular shape, forming a recess in an apartment, generally pierced with windows (1887 Garnsey).

bead. In joinery, a molding of a circular section, stuck on the edge of a piece of stuff, by a plane of the same name (1854 Nicholson); a molding of a circular section, frequently set on the edge of each fascia of an architrave, also used as the moldings of doors, shutters, skirtings, imposts and cornices (1854 Stuart); a circular molding, which lies level with the surface of the material in which it is formed (1856 Smeaton); a molding whose vertical section is semi-circular (1880 Vogdes).

bead and butt. A piece of framing in which the panels are flush, having beads stuck or run upon the two edges with the grain of the wood in their directions (1851 Shaw); a panel molded with a bead. The term is used to designate the butting joint (1887 Garnsey); [bead and butt shutters] shutters with panels flush with the stiles and rails on one side and with beads lengthwise of the panels, at or near the stiles on one side only (1911 Carr & Adams).

bead and flush. A piece of panel work, with a bead run on each edge of the included panel (1851 Shaw); same as bead and butt (1887 Garnsey).

bead and quirk. A bead stuck on the edge of a piece of stuff, flush with the surface, with one quirk only, or without being returned on the other surface (1854 Nicholson); same as bead and butt, excepting that between the joint of the bead and surface is a sunk square recess (1887 Garnsey).

bead, butt and square. A piece of framing, having bead and flush on one side, and nothing but square work on the other; chiefly used indoors (1854 Nicholson); a piece of framing in which the panels are flush, having beads stuck or run upon the two edges, having the grain of the wood in their direction (1854 Stuart).

beak. A little fillet on the edge of the eaves of a house, which forms a canal, and makes a kind of pendant (1736 Neve); a small fillet in the under edge of a projecting cornice, intend-ed to prevent the rain from passing between the cornice and fascia (1856 Smeaton).

beam. A piece of timber, which always lies cross the building, into which the feet of the principal rafters are framed (1736 Neve); a piece of timber in a building laid horizontally, and intended to support a weight, or to resist a strain (1856 Smeaton); a piece of timber or metal of a rectangular section, used in buildings for sustaining a weight, or resisting some strain, either in a longitudinal or transverse direction (1854 Stuart); a large and long piece of squared timber, used in horizontal positions for supporting a superincumbent weight, or for counteracting two opposite forces, tending either to stretch or to compress it in the direction of its length. Employed as a lintel, or for the support of the ends of joists in a floor, it simply sustains a weight; if employed as a tie-beam to the truss of a roof, it resists the strain or thrust exerted by the truss-rafters; or, if as a collar-beam between the heads of truss-rafters, it resists the strain they exert, and is compressed (1858 Silloway); a stick of timber of considerable size (1917 Shearer).

collar beam. Timbers placed across a roof from the middle of one rafter to another (1830 Haviland); a beam in the construction of a roof, above the lower ends of the rafters, or base of the roof (1854 Nicholson).

hammer-beam. A short timber often used in ancient timber-roofs at the foot of the principal rafters. They extend a short distance out from the wall on the inside of the building, and are supported by a brace from the underside (1858 Silloway).

bearer. A prop, or anything that supports a body in any place; as a wall, post, strut, etc. (1854 Nicholson).

bearing of a timber. That part of a piece of timber which is unsupported, or is between two or more props or supports (1854 Stuart); [bearing] the length between bearers, or walls: thus, if a beam rests on walls twenty feet apart, the bearing is said to be twenty feet (1856 Smeaton); the distance in which a beam or rafter is suspended in the clear: thus, if a piece of timber rests upon two opposite walls, the span of the void is called the bearing, and not the whole length of the timber (1874 Gould); that portion of a timber resting on a wall (1887 Garnsey).

bed. With masons, is a course or range of stones (1736 Neve); the horizontal surfaces on which the stones or bricks of a wall lie in courses (1880 Vogdes); in architecture, the bottom side of a stone (1887 Garnsey).

bed-molding. Moldings which project around the panels of a framing (1854 Stuart); ornamental moldings on the lower face of a projecting cornice (1882 Hodgson).

belfry. The part or section of a steeple in which the bell is suspended. The term was formerly used to denote more particularly the framing to which the bell was hung (1858 Silloway).

bell cot. A bell turret generally placed at the apex of a gable or roof (1887 Garnsey).

bell gable. A term applied to a gable having a niche for the reception of a bell (1887 Garnsey).

belt. A course of stones projecting from a brick or stone wall, generally placed in a line with the sills of the first floor windows; it is either molded, fluted, plane, or enriched with pateras at regular intervals (1854 Stuart).

belvedere. A turret, or some part of an edifice raised above the roof, for the purpose of affording a view of surrounding scenery. The term is also applied to single edifices or temples, sometimes erected in gardens and pleasure-grounds (1854 Nicholson).

bigg, bigger. [bigg] To build. [bigger] A builder (1887 Garnsey).

binder. A term used for brick or stone placed with their greatest length transverse the wall (1887 Garnsey).

binding joists. Those beams in a floor, which support transversely the bridging above, and the ceiling-joists below (1854 Nicholson).

binding rafter. The same as a purlin (1854 Nicholson).

birds mouth. The interior angle or notch cut on the extremity of a piece of timber, so that it may be received on the edge of another piece, as a rafter (1880 Vogdes); a v-shaped opening in the end of a piece of timber. Sometimes it is made ornamental (1917 Shearer).

blades. Principal rafters of a roof framing (1887 Garnsey).

blank door. A doorway that has been blocked up to prevent entrance: also a false door placed in an apartment opposite to the real door, or in a correspondent recess to that in which the real door is, for the sake of uniformity (1854 Stuart).

blank window. That which is made to appear a real window, but is only formed in the recess of a wall (1854 Nicholson); used similarly as a blank-door (1882 Hodgson).

blind. Screens forming an appendage to a window, for the purpose either of excluding light, or of preventing persons outside from seeing into the interior of an apartment (1854 Nicholson); a light frame or screen to a door or window (1887 Garnsey); there are both inside and outside window blinds, both made of wood. Inside blinds fold back into recesses in the box window frame. Outside blinds usually are made in pairs and swing out and back against the side of the building (1917 Shearer).

board. A plank, or table, or any piece of wood for flooring and other uses (1736 Neve); a piece of timber of any length or width and from 1/2 in. to 2 in. in thickness (1858 Silloway); a substance of wood contained between two parallel planes: as when the baulk is divided into several pieces by the pit-saw, the pieces are called boards (1874 Gould); an American term for a piece of timber 1 inch thick, 4 to 24 inches wide, any length. Generally applied to fir and pine cut up into lumber one inch in thickness (1887 Garnsey).

boarding. [of walls] . . . the nailing up of boards against a wall (1736 Neve).

boarding joists. Those joists in naked flooring to which the boards are fixed (1854 Nicholson); the same as floor-joists (1858 Silloway); the act of covering joists with boards (1887 Garnsey).

boast. The paring of a stone with a broad chisel and mallet (1854 Stuart); [boasting] the rough cutting of a stone to form the outline of a design preparatory to the more finished carving (1887 Garnsey).

bolster. [bolsters] Pieces of timber used in the construction of centers for arches. The connection between the volutes on the sides of an Ionic capital. (1887 Garnsey).

bond. Fasten the two or more pieces of timber well together, either with tenanting or mortising, or dove-tailing, etc. (1736 Neve); any thing that connects and retains two or more bodies in a particular position (1858 Silloway); that connection between bricks and stones formed by lapping them upon one another in carrying up the work, so as to form an inseparable

mass of building, by preventing the vertical points falling over each other (1880 Vogdes).

bond stones. Stones used in un-coursed rubble-walling, having their length placed in the thickness of the wall. These stones are placed at regular intervals, both horizontally and vertically, so that every stone of one row falls of the vertical joint that is in the course below (1854 Stuart); stones running through the thickness of the wall at right angles to its face, in order to bind it together (1880 Vogdes).

booth. A stall or standing in a fair or market; the term is also applied to any temporary structure, designed for shade and shelter (1854 Stuart).

boss. (in Gothic architecture) A sculptured protuberance at the inter-junction of the ribs in a vaulted roof (1825 Partington); a projection in shape of a segment of a sphere, or somewhat so whether for use or ornament, often carved or cast (1882 Hodgson).

bow. A part of some buildings projecting forward from the face of the wall, and raised from a plan generally on the arc of a circle, so as to form the segment of a cylinder (1854 Nicholson); any projecting part of a building in the form of an arc of a circle. A bow, however, is sometimes, polygonal (1882 Hodgson).

brace. A piece of timber placed in an inclined position, and used in partitions or roofs, to strengthen the framing (1856 Smeaton); a piece of timber fixed across the internal angle of the larger timbers of a frame; by which arrangement the whole of the work is stiffened, and the building is prevented from swerving either way (1858 Silloway); a prop to prevent two timbers from coming together. In modern plank frame construction a brace may also be a tie (1917 Shearer).

bracket. A cramping iron, a kind of stay in timber-work. Also a piece of wood to support shelves, etc. is so called (1736 Neve); a small support fixed against a wall to sustain anything (1854 Nicholson); a support for shelves, stairs, balconies, but now more commonly for projecting roofs (1870 Todd); a brace or support fixed against a vertical surface, supporting a weight (1887 Garnsey); a projecting piece of board, frequently triangular; the vertical side attached to the wall, and the horizontal side supporting a shelf; often made in ornamental shapes (1897 Edwards).

branches. Are those arches in Gothic vaults, which traverse from one angle to another, diagonal-wise, and form a cross between the other arches, which make the sides of the square, of which the arches are diagonals (1736 Neve); the diagonal ribs of a Gothic vault, rising upwards from the tops of the pillars to the apex, and seeming to support the ceiling or vault (1854 Nicholson).

break. Any projection from the general surface of a building (1880 Vogdes); that portion of a facade which changes its style or ground plan (1887 Garnsey).

brest-summer. A lintel-beam in the exterior walls, supported by wooden or iron posts, or by brick or stone pillars, for sustaining the superincumbent part of the wall (1854 Nicholson); a lintel beam in the exterior wall of a building, principally used over shop-windows, to sustain the superincumbent part of the wall (1854 Stuart).

brick nogging, brick and stud. A wall constructed with a row of posts or quarters, disposed at three feet apart, and with brickwork, so as to fill up the intervals (1854 Nicholson); brickwork between quartering (1856 Smeaton); brick work laid between wooden studs or scantling, forming a wall (1887 Garnsey).

brick trimmer. A brick arch abutting against the wooden trimmer under the slab or hearth of the fireplace, to prevent the communication of fire (1880 Vogdes).

bridgeboard. A board into which the ends of wooden steps are fastened (1882 Hodgson); a stair stringer (1917 Shearer).

bridging. An American term for fixing diagonal pieces of wood between joists or studs, for the purpose of equalizing the weight placed on the floor (1887 Garnsey); short pieces of scantling with beveled ends nailed between joists to stiffen the floor. These blocks reach from the bottom edge of one joist to the top edge of the next (1917 Shearer).

broad-stone. Free-stone so called, because raised broad and thin out of the quarries, viz. not above two or three inches in thickness (1736 Neve).

building. A mass formed by the junction of materials (1854 Nicholson); a fabric or edifice of any kind, constructed for occupancy; as a house, barn, church, etc. (1858 Silloway).

bulker. A timber beam or rafter (1887 Garnsey).

bull's eye. [bullock's eye] A little skylight in the covering or roof, designed to illumine a granary or the like (1854 Stuart).

butt joint. In hand-railing, a joint at right angles to the curve of the rail (1854 Nicholson); a joint formed by the meeting of the square ends of two pieces of wood, or the joint formed by the square end of one piece meeting the side or edge of another piece. (1883 Sylvester).

butment cheek. The solid part or shoulder of a mortise (1887 Garnsey).

buttress. A kind of butment built archwise, or a mass of stone, or brick, serving to prop or support the sides of a building, wall, etc. on the outside, where it is either very high, or has any considerable load to sustain on the other side, as a bank of earth, etc. (1734 *Builder's Dictionary*); a pier or external support, designed to resist any pressure from within which may affect the wall or thing supported (1858 Silloway); a projecting support to the exterior of a wall; most commonly applied to churches in the Gothic style, but also to other buildings, and sometimes to mere walls (1883 Sylvester).

cabin. A little hut, or lodging-room, particularly on board of ship (1736 Neve); the huts and cottages of poor people, and those of savages (1854 Stuart); a small cottage or house (1887 Garnsey).

cabinet. The most retired place in a building, set apart for writing, studying, or preserving any thing that is valuable (1854 Stuart); a highly ornamented kind of buffet or chest of drawers set apart for the preservation of things of value (1882 Hodgson); a small room; a closet (1887 Garnsey).

cable. A molding of a convex circular section, rising from the back or concave surface of a flute, so that its most prominent part may be in the same surface as the fillet on each side of the flute (1854 Nicholson).

caisson. A name for sunk panels of geometric forms (1825 Partington); in water building, a large chest of strong timber, made water-tight, and used in large and rapid rivers for building the pier of a bridge. Signifies also the sunken panel in a vaulted ceiling, or in the soffit of a cornice (1854 Nicholson); the sunken panels of various geometrical forms symmetrically disposed in flat or vaulted ceilings, or in soffits; a cavity in a ceiling (1880 Vogdes).

calotte. A concavity in form of a cup or niche, lathed and plastered, to diminish the height of a chapel, cabinet, or alcove, which would otherwise be too elevated for the breadth (1854 Nicholson); a concavity in the form of a niche, serving to decrease the height of a chapel or alcove (1887 Garnsey).

camber. An arch on the top of an aperture or on the top of a beam (1856 Smeaton) to give a convexity to the upper surface of a beam (1854 Stuart); the convexity of a beam upon the upper edge, in order to prevent its becoming straight or concave by its own weight, or by the burden it may have to sustain, in course of time (1874 Gould); a slight upward curve given to a beam or truss to allow for its settlement, after it is in position (1897 Edwards).

camber-beams. Those which are cut with an obtuse angle on the upper edge, forming a declivity each way from the middle of their length (1854 Nicholson); those beams used in the flats of truncated roofs, and raised in the middle with an obtuse angle, for discharging the rain-water towards both sides of the roof (1874 Gould).

came. In glazing, small slender rods of cast lead, about 12 or 14 inches long, to be drawn through a vice, in order to make turned lead; each such bar is called a came (1854 Nicholson).

camp ceiling. The ceiling of an attic when all the walls are inclined equally (1908 Ellis).

canal. Is also used for a flute. (of the Ionic volute), the spiral channel or sinking on the face; (of the larmier), the channel recessed upwards on the soffit, for preventing the rain-water from reaching the bed or lower part of the cornice (1854 Nicholson).

cancelli. Latticed windows, or such as are made with cross bars of wood or iron; also the balusters or rails which compass a court of justice, communion table, or the like (1854 Stuart).

canopy. (in Gothic architecture) The ornamented dripstone of an arch. It is usually of the ogee form (1851 Shaw); a magnificent covering for an altar, throne, tribunal, pulpit, chair, or the like. *See* baldachin. Also the label or projecting molding that surrounds the arches and heads of Gothic niches (1854 Stuart); an ornamental projection in the Gothic style over doors and windows (1883 Sylvester).

cant. An external angle, or corner, of a building (1854 Stuart); a term amongst carpenters to turn over a beam of timber (1882 Hodgson); any part of a surface that breaks out at other than a right angle (1908 Ellis).

cantilever(s). Pieces of wood framed into the front or other sides of a house to sustain the moldings and eves over it (1734 *Builder's Dictionary*); a projecting beam supported at one end only (1908 Ellis).

cant molding. A molding with a beveled surface (1854 Stuart).

cap. The moldings which form the head of a pier or pilaster. In joinery, the uppermost part of an assemblage of principal or subordinate parts. The term is applied to the capital of a column, the cornice of a door, the capping or uppermost member of the surbase of a room, the hand-rail of a stair, when supported by an iron strap, etc. (1854 Nicholson); the head of a pier column or newel post (1908 Ellis).

capital. The uppermost part of a column or pilaster, serving as the head or crowning thereof, placed immediately over the shaft, and under the entablature (1734 *Builder's Dictionary*); in architecture, the head or uppermost part of a column or pilaster, usually molded, foliated or voluted, and constitutes the most distinguishing part of an order; it is indispensable aesthetically, but not a positive necessity, yet it forms an agreeable transition from the shaft to the architrave (1887 Garnsey).

caracol. a stair-case in a helix or spiral form (1736 Neve).

carcass. The timber-work (as it were the skeleton) of a house, before it is lathed and plastered (1736 Neve).

casement. Applies to a sash or pair of sash made to be hung on hinges to swing (1911 Carr & Adams).

castellated. A style of building where embattlements are used at the termination of walls and parapets . . . A building made to imitate an ancient castle (1887 Garnsey).

causeway. A raised or paved way (1854 Stuart).

cavetto. The classic "hollow" molding (1908 Ellis).

ceiling. The inside of a roof; the top of an apartment opposite to the floor; it may have a horizontal or curved surface; a name given to boards planed and matched (1887 Garnsey).

ceiling joists. Small scantlings fixed to the under side of the floor joists to carry the plaster ceiling (1908 Ellis).

cellar. The lower story of a building; sometimes built entirely under ground; generally used for a storeroom (1887 Garnsey).

centering. The temporary wood work over which the masonry of an arch is formed (1897 Edwards).

chamber. All those rooms are called chambers that are situated between the cellars and garrets (1736 Neve); an upper apartment in a building, often applied to a sleeping room (1887 Garnsey).

chambranle. The border of stone, or the wooden frame, surrounding the three sides of a door, window, or chimney (1854 Nicholson); the frame-work surrounding a door or window opening. It is often ornamented in fret and carved work (1887 Garnsey).

chamfer. An arris, taken off a right-angle corner, at an angle of forty-five degrees, the terminations being molded or beveled (1887 Garnsey).

chancel. A part of the choir of a church, between the altar, and the communion-table, and the balustrade or rails that enclose it (1734 *Builder's Dictionary*).

channel. A canal, or long gutter, sunk within the surface of a body (1854 Nicholson).

chaplet. A molding carved into beads, olives, etc. (1857 Hatfield).

cheek. The two solid parts upon the sides of the mortise (1854 Nicholson).

chevron. An ornament turning this and that way like a zigzag or letter Z (1882 Hodgson).

chimney. That part of a room, chamber, or apartment, wherein the fire is made (1734 Builder's Dictionary); the passage through which the smoke ascends from the fire, in a dwelling house (1854 Stuart).

chimney jambs. [chimney jamb and breast] That portion of a chimney on which is placed the mantel (1887 Garnsey).

chimney piece. Certain, moldings of wood, or stone, standing on the fore-side of the jambs, and coming over the mantle-tree (1736 Neve).

choir. That part of a church, cathedral, etc. where the priests, choristers, and singers sit (1734 *Builder's Dictionary*).

cincture. A ring, or lift, at the top and bottom of a column, dividing the shaft at one end from the base, and at the other from the capital (1736 Neve).

cinque foil. A five-leafed ornament, in circular and other divisions of the windows of ancient churches, and also on panels. It is a rosette of five equal leaves (1854 Stuart); an ornament

much used in the pointed style of architecture, consisting of five cusps or points, arranged at stated intervals (1887 Garnsey).

clapboard. A thin board, used as a covering to walls of frame buildings (1887 Garnsey); pieces of cleft wood used to cover the sides and roof of buildings in a similar manner to tiles (1908 Ellis).

clearstory, clerestory. The upper story of a church rising clear above the adjoining parts of the edifice, and containing a range of windows (1854 Nicholson); [clear story windows] such as have no transom intersection (1854 Stuart); the upper part of the nave of a church above the roofs of the aisles (1857 Hatfield).

clinkers. Bricks impregnated with niter, and more thoroughly burnt, by being placed next to the fire in the kiln (1854 Stuart).

cloister. A covered range of building attached to a monastic or collegiate establishment, forming a passage of communication between the various buildings, more especially between the church and chapter-house (1854 Nicholson).

closet. Small apartment, frequently made to communicate with a bed-chamber, and used as a dressing-room. Sometimes a closet is made for the reception of stores, and then it is called a store-closet (1854 Nicholson).

cob wall. Wall built of straw, lime, and earth (1854 Nicholson).

coffer. A recess used anciently in level soffits and in the intrados of cylindrical vaults. They recede like inverted steps around the panel, each internal angle being filled with moldings (1854 Stuart); the sunk panels which are placed in vaults and domes, often ornamented with flowers in their centers (1880 Vogdes).

collar beam. A beam framed cross betwixt two principal rafters (1736 Neve); a beam above the lower ends of the rafters of a roof. They are formed into queen-posts in trussed roofs, but in common roofs, into the rafters themselves (1854 Stuart); a horizontal beam framed between two principal rafters above the tie-beam (1857 Hatfield); a beam used to prevent the bending or sagging of the rafters in a common roof (1858 Silloway); a beam used in the construction of roofs, extending from one rafter horizontally to another, acting as a tie (1887 Garnsey).

colonnade. A range of pillars, quite surrounding a building, and standing within the walls of it; a circular portico of pillars (1736 Neve); a series or continuation of columns (1830 Haviland); a range of attached or insulated columns, supporting an entablature (1854 Nicholson).

column. A round pillar made to support or adorn a building (1734 *Builder's Dictionary*).

compartition. A graceful and useful distribution of the whole ground-plot of an edifice, into rooms of office, and of reception or entertainment (1736 Neve); the distribution of the ground-plot of an edifice into apartments and passages (1854 Nicholson); one portion or division of an edifice (1887 Garnsey).

compass headed. Circular-headed, as a window (1887 Garnsey).

composite order. The last of the five orders of columns, so called, because its capital is composed out of those of the other columns (1734 *Builder's Dictionary*); an order of architecture made up of the Ionic order grafted on the Corinthian; also called the Roman or Italic order (1883 Sylvester).

conduits. Canals or pipes for the conveyance of water or other fluid matter (1734 *Builder's Dictionary*); a long narrow passage between two walls, or underground, for secret communication between different apartments. Also a canal or pipe for the conveyance of water (1854 Stuart).

conservatory. A building used for the preservation of any special object, as a conservatory for flowers (1887 Garnsey).

console. See ancon (1836 Shaw); a bracket, or projecting body, formed like a curve of contrary flexure, scrolled at the ends, used for supporting a cornice, bust, or vase (1854 Nicholson); a bracket twice the height of its width, used to support a cornice or other projection (1917 Shearer).

coping. The top, or cover of [a wall] made sloping to carry off the wet (1736 Neve).

corbel. A block of stone or other material projecting from the face of a wall, and used to support a superincumbent weight, such as the beams of a roof, ribs of vaulting, columns, and such like (1854 Nicholson); a bracket, or piece of timber projecting from a wall (1856 Smeaton).

corbel table. A series of corbels disposed at regular intervals projecting from a wall, to support a parapet or other continuous projection, and frequently seen under the eaves of a roof (1854 Nicholson).

Corinthian order. The third of the orders of classical architecture, and the first of the foliated (1854 Nicholson).

cornice. The uppermost member of the entablature of a column, or that which crowns the order (1734 *Builder's Dictionary*); a projecting member which constitutes the upper finishing of a wall or entablature (1825 Partington); the projecting finish beneath the eaves and at the gable ends of a roof (1870 Todd); the ornamental projection at the top and eaves of a building or other construction, consisting of flat horizontal and perpendicular surfaces with moldings (1897 Edwards).

corona, crown. A large flat strong member of the cornice, so called, because it crowns not only the cornice, but the entablement and the whole order (1734 *Builder's Dictionary*); that part of a cornice which is between the crown-molding and the bed-moldings (1857 Hatfield); the broad, vertical member of a classical cornice (1887 Garnsey).

corridor. A long gallery round a structure, which leads to several different apartments (1736 Neve); a kind of gallery or passage way, either on the inside or the outside of a building, which furnishes easy communication with various apartments of the edifice (1870 Todd).

cot. Saxon. A little house, cottage or hut, inhabited chiefly by country folks of low degree (1736 Neve).

cottage. A name mostly applied to a small house, erected for the use and accommodation either of the farm laborer, or those engaged in some other occupation, but more generally of those employed in agriculture (1854 Nicholson).

couple close. A pair of rafters (1887 Garnsey).

course. A continued range of bricks, or stones, of the same height throughout the length of the work (1736 Neve).

court. An open area before or behind a house, or in the center, between the body of the building and the wings (1854 Stuart).

coussinet. The first stone whence a vault or arch commences (1736 Neve); the stone that surmounts a pier and upon which rests the first springer of an arch (1887 Garnsey).

cove bracketing. The term cove bracketing is generally applied to that of the quadrantal cove (1854 Stuart); the frame or furring work of a cove ceiling (1887 Garnsey).

coved ceiling. The ceiling of a room formed after the cove (1887 Garnsey).

cresting. Carved work on the top of a building. The ridges of roofs, the copes of battlements and the tops of gables were called crests (1882 Hodgson).

cross beam. A large beam going from wall to wall; or a girder that holds the sides of the house together (1854 Stuart).

cross springer. In a groined ceiling, the ribs springing from the diagonals of the piers or pillars on which an arch rests (1858 Silloway).

crown post. A crown post, called also king post, or joggle post, is the truss post that sustains the immediate bearing of the principal rafters of a roof (1854 Stuart).

crypt. A subterraneous vault generally beneath churches. In late years used for burial (1882 Hodgson).

cul de sac. A kind of court, open at one end only (1887 Garnsey).

cupboard. A recess in a wall, fitted up with shelves, to contain articles when not in use (1854 Nicholson).

cupola. A round roof or dome, in the form of an inverted cup (1830 Haviland); a spherical roof; the interior surface of a dome (1908 Ellis); a small dome-shaped roof. An ornament on the top of a tower in lantern style (1917 Shearer).

curb roof. Sometimes mansard-roof, but more commonly in the United States, gambrel-roof, a roof with the lower half inclined at a steeper angle (1870 Todd).

cusp. The pendants in the gothic style. Assembled, they form trefoils, quatrefoils, etc. (1854 Stuart).

cyma. A molding which is hollow in its upper part and swelling below (1836 Shaw); a molding, whose section is a curve of a contrary flexure; it is commonly denoted by workmen an ogee (1854 Nicholson); an undulating molding, which is generally the upper one of a cornice (1854 Stuart).

dado. The dye, or that part in the middle of the pedestal of a column which is between its base and cornice. It is of a cubic form, and thence takes the name of dye (1734 *Builder's Dictionary*); that part of a room comprehended between the base and surbase (1854 Nicholson); a plane used to cut grooves in boards at right angles to the grain of the wood; the groove itself is also called a dado; much used in neat shelving (1897 Edwards).

dentil. An ornament in cornices, bearing some resemblance to teeth (1734 *Builder's Dictionary*); small square blocks or projections used in the bed moldings of the cornice (1851 Shaw); square blocks introduced as ornaments into cornices, chiefly of the Ionic and Corinthian orders, in the form of indentations or teeth; a small circular piece is sometimes cut out, and at other times they are fluted (1882 Hodgson); a row of blocks or solids placed in a cornice at equal distances (1887 Garnsey).

ears. Same as ancones (1887 Garnsey).

earth table. The course of masonry or other work level with the ground (1854 Nicholson).

eaves. The margin or edge of the roof of an house; being the lowest tiles, slates, or the like, that hang over the walls, to throw off water to a distance from the walls (1734 *Builder's Dictionary*).

echinus. A convex molding, generally ornamented with spheroids or eggs . . . only used in the entablature or capital (1854 Stuart).

engaged column. [under columns, engaged] Seem to penetrate a wall from between one-fourth to one-half of their diameter (1854 Nicholson).

English bond. In bricklaying, a disposition of bricks, wherein a course of headers succeeds a course of stretchers alternately (1854 Nicholson).

entablature. That part of a classical building resting immediately on the columns, and forming the lower part of the cornice, as the architrave and frieze. Same as coping (1887 Garnsey).

entry. A door, gate, passage, etc. through which we arrive at any place (1734 *Builder's Dictionary*).

extrados. The outside of an arch of a bridge, vault, etc. (1854 Stuart); the exterior or convex curve forming the upper line of the arch stones (1880 Vogdes).

eyebrow. A list or fillet (1736 Neve).

eye of a dome. An opening at the top of a dome, etc. (1736 Neve); the aperture at its summit (1880 Vogdes).

eye of a volute. The middle of an Ionic Volute, or scroll, cut in the form of a rose (1734 Salmon); the middle of the Ionic volute, from which the different centers for drawing it are found (1854 Stuart).

façade. The front of a building, or the side on which the chief entrance is. Also it is sometimes used for the side that it presents to a street, garden, court, etc., and sometimes for any side opposite to the eye (1734 *Builder's Dictionary*).

fanlight. A transom light (1887 Garnsey).

fascia. A flat member, having a considerable breadth, and but a small projection; as the bands of an architrave (1734 *Builder's Dictionary*); a band or fillet. This term is usually employed to denote the flat members into which the architrave is divided (1825 Partington); the broad flat surface between the sash and the cornice in a shop front; any wide flat band in a cornice (1908 Ellis); in American house building the part of the finish under the roof projection that lies flat against the side of the building is called the fascia (1917 Shearer).

feather-edged. [feather-edged boards] Narrow boards made thin on one edge. They are used for facings or boarding of wooden walls (1851 Shaw); [feather-edged boards] boards, thicker at one edge than the other, and commonly used in the facing of wooden walls, and for the covering of inclined roofs, etc. (1874 Gould); *See* weather-boards (1908 Ellis).

fenestration. The arrangement of windows in a building (1854 Nicholson); the space between the windows of a classic building (1887 Garnsey).

festoon. An ornament or garland of flowers, fruits, and leaves, intermixed or twisted together (1734 *Builder's Dictionary*); a carved ornament resembling a wreath, attached to both ends and falling in the middle (1825 Partington); an ornament of carved work in the form of a wreath of flowers, fruits, and leaves, represented as depending or hanging in an arch (1883 Sylvester).

fillet. A little square member, or ornament, or molding, used in divers places, and upon divers occasions; but generally as a corona or crowning over a greater molding (1734 *Builder's Dictionary*); See annulet (1825 Partington); a small square molding of slight projection (1856 Smeaton).

finial. In the gothic style of architecture, the figure of a lily, trefoil, endive, acorn, or other flower, foliage, or fruit, made to terminate canopies, pinnacles, high-pointed pediments, and other parts of buildings (1854 Stuart); an ornament at the apex of a gable or spire (1908 Ellis).

flashing. A term given to any metal, as tin, copper or lead, used around gutters, chimneys, windows, etc., for the purpose of making them water tight (1887 Garnsey); pieces of tin or other metal let into joints to lap over gutters, &c., as about chimneys; the broad pieces of tin laid in the valleys of a slate or shingle roof are flashings (1897 Edwards).

Flemish bond. That method of laying bricks in which headers and stretchers appear alternately in the length of each course (1854 Nicholson).

flight. The stairs from one landing-place to another (1736 Neve).

floor. The underside of the room, or that part whereon we walk (1734 *Builder's Dictionary*); by the word floor, understand as well the framed work of timber, as the boarding over it (1736 Neve).

floor joist. Such joists as support the boarding in a single floor (1854 Nicholson); the scantling and timbers on which a floor is laid (1887 Garnsey).

floor plan. The plan or diagram of the apartments of a building (1887 Garnsey).

flutes. The vertical channels on the shafts of columns, which are usually rounded at the top and bottom (1851 Shaw).

flyers. A series of steps whose treads are all parallel (1854 Nicholson); stairs which rise without winding (1854, Smeaton).

folding doors. Made to meet each other from opposite jambs, on which they are hung; and when they are rebated together, their edges meet, folding over each other, with a bead at the joint, to give the appearance of one entire door (1854 Stuart).

footing. The spreading courses at the base or foundation of a wall (1880 Vogdes).

fornicated. An arched vault (1880 Vogdes).

foundation. The lowest part of a building (generally laid underground) upon which the walls of the superstructure are raised (1736 Neve).

frame. The name given to the woodwork of windows, enclosing glass; the outward work of doors or window-shutters, enclosing panels; and in carpentry, to the timber works supporting floors, roofs, ceilings; or to the intersecting pieces of timber forming partitions (1854 Stuart).

fret. A decoration for enriching and filling-up flat empty spaces, every turn of which must be at right angles (1736 Neve); an ornament laid on plain narrow surfaces, formed by one or more fillets running along in a zigzag direction; generally in right angles, and keeping a space between each fillet equal in width to the fillet itself (1830 Haviland); a kind of continued knot or ornament consisting of one or more small fillets running vertically and horizontally, and at equal distances in both directions (1880 Vogdes).

frieze. A large flat member, which separates the architrave from the cornice (1736 Neve); that part of the entablature of a column which is between the architrave and cornice. It is a flat member or face, often enriched with figures of animals or other ornaments of sculpture, whence its name (1883 Sylvester).

frontispiece. Sometimes signifies the whole face or aspect of a building; but is more properly applied to the decorated entrance of a house (1830 Haviland).

furring. Flat pieces of timber, plank, or board, used by carpenters to bring dislocated work to a regular surface (1851 Shaw); means studs, or pieces of plank spiked to a brick or concrete wall, on the inside, for holding the lath. Also, thin strips of boards or lath to narrow joists, to make the edges even with the wide ones, for receiving the lath (1870 Todd).

gable. The triangularly-headed wall which covers the end of a roof (1825 Partington); the upright triangular end of a building, in classical architecture called a pediment (1851 Shaw); the vertical triangular piece of wall at the end of a building, bounded by a horizontal line level with the eaves, together with the two inclined lines of the roof (1858 Silloway).

gable roof. A building having a pitched roof (1887 Garnsey).

gablet. An architectural construction in the form of a gable; a small gable (1887 Garnsey).

gable window. A window in the gable end of a building (1854 Nicholson).

gain. The beveled shoulder of a binding joist (1854 Stuart).

gallery. An apartment; a passage; an arcade; an elevated portion of a room or building; a balcony (1887 Garnsey); A long, narrow floor with a low balustrade along the front side.

garland. An artistic creation or arrangement of fruits, leaves and flowers (1887 Garnsey).

garret. The uppermost floor of a house (1736 Neve).

girder. [girders] Some of the largest pieces of timber on a floor, the ends of them are for the most part framed into the summers or breast-summers, and the joints are framed in at one end to the girders (1734 Neve); the principal beam in a floor for supporting the binding and other joists, whereby the bearing or length is lessened (1857 Hatfield).

gorge. A concave molding (1887 Garnsey).

grange. An ancient term for a barn, wherein to lay up and thrash corn. The word is sometimes also used in a more extensive sense for the whole farm, with all the appendages, as barns, stables, stalls, and other necessary places for husbandry (1734 *Builder's Dictionary*).

grillage. A frame work of beams laid longitudinally and crossed by similar beams notched upon them, used to sustain walls to prevent irregular settling (1882 Hodgson).

groin. The diagonal line formed by the intersection of two vaults in a roof (1825 Partington).

ground plan. The plan of the story of a house on the same level with the surface of the ground, or elevated only a few steps before the door (1854 Nicholson); the horizontal section of that part of a building lying next above the surface of the ground (1858 Silloway).

ground plate. The lowest pieces of timber in a timber building, on which the whole superstructure is erected (1734 *Builder's Dictionary*); same as sill (1887 Garnsey).

grout. A thin semi-liquid mortar, composed of quick-lime with a portion of fine sand, which is prepared and poured into the internal joints of masonry (1854 Nicholson).

guilloche. Ornaments made by circular fillets crossing and re-crossing each other, generally encompassing a patera or flower (1830 Haviland); an ornament composed of fillets in curvilinear directions, which form a continued series by their repetition (1880 Vogdes).

guttae. Ornaments of a conic form, on the cornice of the Doric order; they are supposed to represent drops (1854 Stuart).

gutter. Kind of valleys in the roofs of buildings, serving to receive and drain off the rain waters (1734 *Builder's Dictionary*); a channel at the eaves of a roof to carry off the rain (1883 Sylvester).

half round. A semi-circular molding, which may be either a bead or torus (1854 Nicholson).

half-timbered house. One in which the walls are constructed of a framework of timber filled in with brickwork or plaster (1908 Ellis).

hall. The entrance apartment; a passage (1887 Garnsey).

hammer beam. A short timber often used in ancient timber-roofs at the foot of the principal rafters. They extend a short distance out from the wall on the inside of the building and are supported by a brace from the underside (1858 Silloway); a horizontal piece of timber introduced towards the lower part of a rafter acting as a tie (1880 Vogdes).

hand rail. The rail of a stairway (1887 Garnsey).

hatch. The cover of an opening in a roof or floor (1908 Ellis).

hatchway. An aperture through the ceiling, to afford a passage to the roof (1854 Nicholson); an opening in a floor or ceiling (1887 Garnsey).

hearth. The brick or stone bottom to a fire-place (1887 Garnsey).

heel of a rafter. The end or foot that rests upon the wall plate (1851 Shaw).

herringbone. A term applied to a particular kind of masonry, in which the stones are laid aslant, inclining alternately right and left (1854 Nicholson).

hip roof. A roof of a building formed by equally inclined planes rising from each side (1854 Stuart); a roof with sloping ends, or that slants on every side of the building and terminates in a point or nearly so, at the summit (1870 Todd); a roof the ends of which rise immediately from the wall-plate, with the same inclination to the horizon, and its other two sides (1874 Gould).

hood molding. See drip (1825 Partington); a projecting molding over the head of an arch (1883 Sylvester).

house. A habitation or dwelling, wherein men preserve themselves and their goods from the injuries of the weather, and other inconveniences (1736 Neve); a habitation erected for man's shelter, comfort, and protection (1887 Garnsey).

hut. A small cottage, built of wood and earth (1854 Stuart).

ichnography. A description or draught of the plat-form or ground-work of a house or other building. Or it is the geometrical place or plat-form of an edifice or ground-work of a house or building delineated upon paper, describing the form of the several apartments, rooms, windows, chimneys, etc. (1734 *Builder's Dictionary*); the transverse section of a building, which represents the circumference of the whole edifice; the different rooms and apartments, with the thickness of the walls; the dimensions and situation of the doors, windows, chimneys; the projection of columns, and every thing that could be seen in such a section, if really made in a building (1851 Shaw).

imbrication. [imbricated tracery] A pattern similar to the tiles of a roof (1887 Garnsey).

impost. Any combination of moldings serving as the capital or cornice of a pier, upon which either extremity of an arch rests (1825 Partington); the capital of a pilaster supporting an arch (1880 Vogdes).

incrustation. An adherent covering. This term is frequently applied to plaster, or other tenacious materials employed in building (1854 Nicholson).

inlaid floors. In joinery, the method of joining together on a general ground a number of pieces so as to form one general design or figure (1887 Garnsey).

intercolumniation. The space between two columns (1736 Neve).

interties. Horizontal pieces of timber, placed between upright posts, to tie or bind them together (1854 Nicholson); short pieces of joist or timber used in floors and partitions to bind the work together. The word is synonymous with bridging (1858 Silloway).

intrados. The under curved surface or soffit of an arch (1854 Stuart); the interior or concave curve of the arch stones (1880 Vogdes).

inverted arch (inflected arch). An arch constructed the reverse of upright, or, where the concavity is below the center (1887 Garnsey).

ionic order. An order whose distinguishing feature is the volute of its capital. The column is more slender than the Doric and Tuscan, but less slender and less ornamented than the Corinthian and Composite (1883 Sylvester).

jamb. Door-posts, also the upright posts at the ends of window-frames, are so called. Also, bricklayers wall the upright sides of chimneys, from the hearth to the mantle-tree, by this name (1736 Neve); the side pieces of any opening in a wall which bear the piece that discharges the superincumbent weight of such wall (1880 Vogdes).

jerkin head. A roof the end of which is constructed in a shape intermediate between a gable and a hip; the gable being continued, as usual, up to the line of the top of the collar-beam: and, from this level, the roof is hipped, or inclined backwards (1858 Silloway); the peak of a hip roof; a half gable and half hip roof (1887 Garnsey).

jetty. A part of a building overhanging or projecting (1887 Garnsey).

joggle piece. A truss post, with shoulders and sockets for receiving the lower ends of the struts (1880 Vogdes).

joinery. The art of working in wood, or of fitting and assembling various parts or members together (1734 *Builder's Dictionary*); the art of framing wood for the finishing of houses (1880 Vogdes).

joint. A place where one member, whether of stone or wood, is added to another (1736 Neve); the abutting surfaces of two prepared pieces of wood (1908 Ellis).

joist(s). One or more horizontal rows of parallel equidistant timbers in a floor, on which the flooring is laid (1854 Nicholson); the timbers to which the boards of a floor or the laths of a ceiling are nailed (1857 Hatfield); the timbers of a floor, which extend from beam to beam, or from stud to stud, as in a balloon frame (1870 Todd).

jut window. A projecting or oriel window (1887 Garnsey).

kerf. The sawn away slit in a piece of timber or board (1736 Neve); the way which a saw makes in dividing a piece of wood into two parts (1874 Gould); to saw a notch in wood, to make it flexible or easily bent (1883 Sylvester).

keystone. The middle stone of an arch, which binds the sweeps of the arch together (1736 Neve); the highest stone of an arch, to which a projection is usually given, and which is sometimes cut in ornaments (1830 Haviland); of an arch or vault, the last stone placed on the top thereof, which being wider and fuller at the top than at the bottom, wedges, as it were, and binds in all the rest (1854 Nicholson); the last and central stone placed in an arch; a wedge-shaped stone placed in the center of an arch to counteract the crushing pressure (1887 Garnsey).

king post. A piece of timber standing upright in the middle between two rafters. The same as crown post (1734 Neve); the

center-posts in a trussed roof. This post is also known as curb-post and prick-post (1858 Silloway); the middle post of a trussed roof, for supporting the tie-beam at the middle and the lower ends of the struts (1874 Gould).

knee. A piece of timber cut crooked with an angle, is called a knee-piece, or knee-rafter (1736 Neve); a piece of timber bent to receive some weight, or to relieve a strain (1856 Smeaton); a convex bend in the back of a hand-rail. *See* ramp (1857 Hatfield).

knot. Same as boss (1887 Garnsey).

label. A name for the drip or hood-molding of an arch when it is returned square (1825 Partington); a drip or small molding extending around and over the head of a Gothic opening, door or window (1887 Garnsey).

labyrinth fret. A fret-work with many angles (1887 Garnsey).

lacunar. Panels or coffers in ceilings, or in the soffits of cornices; the flat roof of a room (1854 Stuart); same as coffer (1887 Garnsey).

landing. That part of a floor at the termination of a flight of stairs, either at the bottom or top (1858 Silloway).

lantern. An erection on the top of a roof or dome, having an aperture for the admission of light. Its plan may be either circular, elliptical, square, or polygonal (1858 Silloway); a sky-light with lights in the sides (1908 Ellis).

lean-to. A small building, with a shed-roof, attached to a larger one (1854 Nicholson); a building against another, in which the rafters of the former lean against the latter (1880 Vogdes).

ledge. A projection from a plane, as the slips on the sides of window-frames to keep them steady in their places, or those against the door-frame, against which the door shuts (1854 Stuart).

lierne rib. A cross rib, in vaulting (1887 Garnsey).

lintel. The pieces of timber that lie horizontally over the tops of doors and windows (1736 Neve); a horizontal piece of timber or stone, over a door, window, or other opening, to support a superincumbent weight (1858 Silloway); a beam timber or girder of wood or metal used over an opening in a wall to support weight (1887 Garnsey).

list. A little square molding, serving to crown or accompany a larger; or on occasion to separate the flutings of a column (1734 *Builder's Dictionary*).

lobby. An anti-chamber (1734 Salmon); an enclosed space, or passage, communicating with the principal room or rooms of a house (1857 Hatfield); a hall, rotunda, entrance or waiting room (1887 Garnsey).

lock rail. The center rail of a standard four-panel door (1911 Carr & Adams).

loft. A raised balcony, gallery or attic room (1887 Garnsey).

loggia. A passage, entrance or gallery, open on one side, and supported by a colonnade or arches (1887 Garnsey); an enclosed veranda. More part of a house than a porch. Usually not the entrance way. An outdoor room opening into a parlor or living room (1917 Shearer).

louver boards. Boards nailed on the sides of buildings or lanterns, or across apertures, so as to admit air but exclude rain (1882 Hodgson).

lozenge. A quadrilateral figure or pattern (1887 Garnsey).

lucarne. A dormer or attic window (1887 Garnsey).

lunette. Opening in a cylindrical or spherical ceiling to admit light (1887 Garnsey).

lying panel. Those which are cut out with the grain of the wood, not, as is usual, with the grain in a vertical, but horizontal direction (1854 Stuart).

m roof. A roof formed of two common roofs by placing their eaves against and parallel to each other, like the letter W inverted (M) (1858 Silloway); a double-gabled roof (1887 Garnsey).

machicolation. (in Gothic architecture) Small openings in an embattled parapet, for the discharge of missile weapons upon the assailants. Frequently these openings are underneath the parapet in which case the whole is brought forward and supported by corbels (1825 Partington).

magazine. A building used for the storage of gunpowder (1887 Garnsey).

mansard roof. See curb roof (1854 Nicholson).

mantle. The lower part of the chimney, or that part laid across the jambs, and which sustains the compartment of the chimney piece (1734 *Builder's Dictionary*); the work over a fireplace in front of a chimney, especially a narrow shelf above the fireplace; called also mantle-piece (1883 Sylvester).

margin. The flat part of the stiles and rails of framed work (1874 Gould).

marquetry. Inlaid work; a curious kind of work composed of pieces of hard fine wood, of different colors, fastened in thin slices on a ground, and sometimes enriched with other matters, as tortoise-shell, ivory, tin, and brass (1854 Nicholson).

match boards. Boards grooved and tongued on the edges, the tongues being formed in the solid (1908 Ellis).

meander. A fret ornament (1887 Garnsey).

medallion. A circular tablet, on which are embossed figures or other ornaments (1854 Nicholson).

meeting rails. The rails of a window which meet when the window is hung and closed (1911 Carr & Adams.).

member. The different parts of a building; the different parts of an entablature; the different moldings of a cornice, etc. (1851 Shaw).

merlon. The solid portions of a battlement alternating with the open spaces or embrasures (1887 Garnsey).

metope. The intervals or square space between the triglyphs of the frieze of the Doric (1734 *Builder's Dictionary*).

mezzanine. Same as entresol. (1734 *Builder's Dictionary*); a low story between two floors (1825 Partington).

modillion. A sort of cantilevers, little inverted consoles, under the soffit, or bottom of the drip (1736 Neve); a projection under the corona of the richer orders resembling a bracket (1825 Partington).

module. Is a certain measure or bigness taken at pleasure, for regulating the proportions of columns, and the symmetry or distribution of the whole building (1734 *Builder's Dictionary*); the semi-diameter of a column, and is divided into thirty minutes. It is the measure by which the architect determines the proportions between the parts of an order (1854 Smeaton).

mortar. A sort of plaster, commonly made of lime, sand, and water, used by masons and bricklayers, in building of walls of stone and brick (1736 Neve); the calcareous cement used in building, compounded of burnt limestone and sand (1854 Stuart).

mortise. The hole made in one piece of wood, to receive the tenon of another (1736 Neve).

mortise lock. A lock made to fit into a mortise cut in the style and rail to receive it (1854 Nicholson).

mosaic. A curious piece of work, or an assemblage of marble, precious stones, pebbles, pieces of glass, etc. also cockles and shells of various colors, cut square, and cemented on a ground of stuck, etc. in imitation of the natural color and gradation of painting (1734 *Builder's Dictionary*); a term applied to pavements, and other work, when formed of various materials of different shapes and colors, laid in a kind of stucco, so as to present some pattern or device (1856 Smeaton).

molding. Under this name are comprehended all those jettings or projectures beyond the naked of a wall, column, etc. which only serve for ornament (1736 Neve); [moldings] architectural details, generally of a concave, convex, prismatic or combined form or surface (1887 Garnsey).

mullion. The short upright posts that divide the several lights in a window-frame (1736 Neve); the frame-work of a window (1825 Partington); a large vertical bar of a window-frame, separating two casements, or glass-frames, from each other (1874 Gould); an upright or vertical bar, usually wider than the ordinary bar, dividing the glass in a sash, or a wide upright bar dividing two sash in a frame. Applied also to single blinds made to represent pairs (1911 Carr & Adams).

muntin. The vertical pieces of the frame of a door between the stiles (1874 Gould) applies to any short or light bars—either vertical or horizontal—in a sash or in a door between panels not extending the full width or length of the article (1911 Carr & Adams).

naked. The surface or plane in a wall or member from whence the projectures arise (1736 Neve); a plain surface, or that which is unfinished; as the naked walls, the naked flooring—that is, uncovered. The word is sometimes applied to flat surfaces before the moldings and other ornaments have been fixed.

narthex. An enclosed space in a church. The vestibule of a church (1887 Garnsey); the outer court or atrium in church architecture (1917 Shearer).

nave. The body of the church, or the place where the people are disposed (1734 *Builder's Dictionary*); the middle or body of a church, extending from the choir or chancel to the principal entrance; also the part between the wings or aisles (1883 Sylvester).

neck. [neck of a capital] The space between the astragal above the shaft and the annulet there over (1880 Vogdes).

net masonry. Stone-work in a diamond pattern (1887 Garnsey).

newel. The upright post, about which a pair of winding-stairs are turned (1736 Neve); in a circular staircase, the center round which the steps ascend (1825 Partington); a post at the starting or landing of a flight of stairs (1857 Hatfield); [newel post] the post, plain or ornamental, placed at the first or lowest step, to receive or start the hand rail upon (1897 Edwards).

niche. The hollow places in a wall, wherein statues or images are set (1736 Neve); a square or cylindrical cavity in a wall or other solid (1851 Shaw).

nogging. A species of brickwork carried up in panels between quarters (1854 Nicholson); brick-work filled in or built between studding (1887 Garnsey).

nose. [nosings] The rounded and projecting edges of the treads of a stair (1882 Hodgson).

notching. A hollow cut from one of the faces of a piece of timber, generally of a rectangular form (1854 Stuart); a joint formed by cutting a piece out of one timber equal to the thickness of the piece crossing it (1908 Ellis).

octostyle. A building with eight columns in front (1857 Hatfield).

ogee. A sort of molding in architecture, consisting of two members, the one concave the other convex (1736 Neve); *see* cyma reversa (1825 Partington); a molding consisting of a portion of two circles turned in contrary directions, so that it is partly concave and partly convex, and somewhat resembles the letter S (1854 Smeaton); a molding, the transverse section of which consists of two curves of contrary flexure (1874 Gould); [O.G.] a solid mold which is a combination of a cove and a quarter round with no fillet between. The standard sticking for doors, sash and blinds (1911 Carr & Adams).

orb. Same as boss; a blank window or panel (1887 Garnsey).

orders. A system of the several members, ornaments and proportions of columns and pilasters; or it is a regular arrangement of the projecting parts of a building, especially those of a column; so as to form one beautiful whole (1734 *Builder's Dictionary*); an assemblage of parts, consisting of a base, shaft, capital, architrave, frieze and cornice, whose several services requiring some distinction in strength, have been contrived or designed in five several species (1851 Shaw); the perfect arrangement and composition of any architectural work; but the term is more especially used to designate the various methods of arrangement employed in Grecian or Classical architecture, and is definitely applied to such a portion of a building as may comprehend the whole design by a continuity and repetition of its parts (1854 Nicholson); a term used to designate a certain classification or arrangement of the several details and parts of a distinct period of architecture (1887 Garnsey).

oriel. [oriel window] A large bay or recessed window in a hall, chapel, or other apartment (1857 Hatfield); a projecting window, supported on a corbel or other projection (1870 Todd).

orlo. A fillet under the quarter round of a capital (1734 *Builder's Dictionary*); the same as the plinth or square under the base of a column, or of its pedestal (1736 Neve).

ornament. Used to signify all the sculpture or carved work wherewith a piece of architecture is enriched (1734 *Builder's Dictionary*).

orthostyle. The arrangement of columns in a straight line (1887 Garnsey).

out-bond. [out-and-in-bond] Quoins used alternately on corners (1887 Garnsey).

out of wind. [out of winding] Perfectly smooth and even, or forming a true plane (1854 Stuart).

ovolo. A round molding, whose profile or sweep in the ionic and composite capitals, is usually a quadrant of a circle; whence it is also popularly called the quarter round (1734 *Builder's Dictionary*); same as echinus (1734 Salmon); a solid mold which is a quarter round with a small fillet on each side (1912 Farley & Loetscher).

pale(s). Boards set up for partitions of gardens and enclosures (1736 Neve).

palisade. A fence of pales or stakes driven into the ground (1857 Hatfield).

pane. A square of glass (1736 Neve); a surface figure, as a square, octagon, rectangle, etc., as a pane of glass (1887 Garnsey).

panel. A compartment enclosed by moldings (1825 Partington); a thin board having all its edges inserted in the groove of a surrounding frame (1851 Shaw); a sunken space, most commonly applied to the portion of a door between the upright pieces called stiles, and the horizontal pieces called rails (1870 Todd); any surface sunk into its surroundings, particularly a thin wide piece between the members of a framing (1908 Ellis).

pantry. A room to set victuals in; a store-room (1736 Neve).

parapet. A little wall, or sometimes a rail, serving either as a rest for the arm, or as an enclosure about a key, bridge, terrace, etc. (1736 Neve); a low wall round the roof of a building (1825 Partington).

pargeting, plastering. The plastering of walls; [parget] sometimes for the plaster itself (1854 Nicholson); a rough plastering, commonly adopted for the interior surface of chimneys (1856 Smeaton).

parlor. A speaking-place; a place for conversation; a fair lower room designed principally for the reception, and entertainment of company (1736 Neve); the sitting-room or living room of a family, or for the common intercourse of a family; but at present more commonly restricted to a room for visitors (1870 Todd); a term given to the principal apartment of a modern house (1887 Garnsey).

parquet. A kind of inlaid floor composed of small pieces of wood either square or triangular which are capable of forming, by their disposition, various combinations of figures (1882 Hodgson).

parsonage. The residence of a minister of the church (1887 Garnsey).

parterre. A level division of ground, facing for the most part, the south and best front of a house, and generally furnished with greens, flowers, etc. (1736 Neve).

parting. [parting bead, parting strip] A small bead or strip grooved into the pulley stile of a window frame, separating the sash (1887 Garnsey).

partition. A wall dividing one room from another (1858 Silloway).

party wall. In building, partitions of brick made between buildings in separate occupations, for preventing the spread of fire (1854 Nicholson); the brick or stone division between buildings in separate occupations (1880 Vogdes); a wall generally erected between two separate buildings and centered upon the dividing line of two lots of ground (1887 Garnsey).

parvis. Formerly a room over the church porch, where schools used to be held (1854 Stuart); the main entrance to a church, a porch or portico (1887 Garnsey).

passage. An entry, or narrow room, serving for a thorough-fare, or entrance into other rooms (1736 Neve); a communication or hall between rooms (1887 Garnsey).

patera. A goblet or vessel . . . is an ornament in architecture, frequently introduced in friezes, fascias, and imposts. (1854 Nicholson).

patio. A Spanish word meaning a court in the rear and in connection with a building. The buildings form three sides of the enclosure, there may be a building or a high fence across the near end (1917 Shearer).

pavillion. A kind of turret, or building usually insulated, and contained under a single roof; sometimes square, and sometimes in the form of a dome; and thus called from the resemblance of its roof to a tent. Pavilions are sometimes also projecting parts, in the front of a building, marking their middle (1854 Nicholson); the projecting apartment at the flanks of a building. Now frequently applied to a summer or garden house (1880 Vogdes); a temporary movable building or tent (1883 Sylvester).

pedestal. A square body, with a base and cornice, serving as a foot for the columns to stand upon (1736 Neve); a low basement under a column or wall; that arrangement on which columns are sometimes placed: it is divided into three parts, the cornice, the die, and the base (1856 Smeaton).

pediment. The triangular crowning ornament of the front of a building, door, etc. (1825 Partington); a low triangular crowning ornament in the front of a building, and over doors and windows. Pediments are sometimes made in the form of a segment of a circle (1856 Smeaton); the triangular part of a portico, or roof, which is terminated by the sloping lines of the roof (1858 Silloway).

pendentive. The whole body of a vault, suspended out of the perpendicular of the walls (1854 Stuart); [pendentive vault, pendentive bracketing, pendentive cradling] terms used to express various forms of constructive processes employed in building vaulted ceilings (1887 Garnsey).

pendant. A hanging ornament, used in roofs, ceilings, etc., much used in Gothic architecture (1883 Sylvester); an ornamental, carved or turned drop (1887 Garnsey).

penthouse. A shelter from the weather placed over a door or window (1736 Neve).

pent roof. A roof with a slope on one side only; a lean-to (1887 Garnsey).

perbend. A header in masonry (1887 Garnsey).

peristyle. A place encompassed with pillars standing round about on the inside; in ancient Roman and Greek architecture an open court surrounded by a colonnade (1887 Garnsey); a complete set of columns with entablature in circular or elliptical form, usually placed around a court to connect two parts of a building or two separate buildings (1917 Shearer).

perron. A staircase lying open, or outside the building; properly, the steps before the front of the building, leading into the first story, when raised a little above the ground (1854 Nicholson).

pew. A wooden seat or bench used in churches, of sufficient length to contain several persons. The term has, of late years, been particularly applied to the closed boxes provided with doors, but is equally applicable to the open seats of a previous age, which are now again happily superseding the closed pews (1854 Nicholson).

piazza. Signifies a broad open place or square; whence it became applied to walks or portico's around them (1734 *Builder's Dictionary*); usually a covered walk on one or more sides of a building, supported on one side by pillars. It is used nearly synonymous with veranda, although the latter generally means a portion of a building that has a lean-to roof (1870 Todd).

pier. A kind of pilaster or buttress, to support, strengthen, or ornament. The pier of a bridge, is the foot or support of the arch. The wall between windows or doors. Also, square pillars of stone or brick, to which gates are hung (1830 Haviland); *see* caisson (1854 Stuart); usually of stone, concrete or brick, built solid with footings firmly imbedded in the ground (1917 Shearer).

pier arch. An arch springing from a pier (1887 Garnsey).

pilaster. A square column, sometimes insulated; but more frequently let within a wall, and only showing a fourth or fifth part of its thickness (1734 *Builder's Dictionary*); a pillar of a rectangular plan (1825 Partington); square pillar insulated, or engaged to the wall, and is usually enriched with a capital and base (1856 Smeaton); a pier projecting from a wall about one-third of its width, having capital, shaft and base to correspond with columns (1917 Shearer).

pile(s). Great stakes rammed into the earth to make a foundation to build upon in marshy ground (1734 *Builder's Dictionary*); large timbers, usually shod with pointed iron caps, driven into the ground for the purpose of making a secure foundation (1856 Smeaton); a term given to buttresses built against the walls of a house (1882 Hodgson).

pillar. A kind of round column, disengaged from any wall, and made without any proportion; being always either too massive, or to slender (1734 Salmon); an irregular, and rude column . . . the form and dimensions of pillars are guided by no rules (1854 Stuart); a pier or support of irregular form, the proportions of which are not subject to the rules of classic architecture; hence the distinction between a pillar and a column (1897 Edwards); may be either pier or column. A symbol of strength (1917 Shearer).

pin. A piece of wood, commonly of chestnut or oak, sharpened at one end, and used to confine timbers together (1858 Silloway); a mechanical invention or device for securing framing timbers (1887 Garnsey).

pinnacle. The top or roof of a house, which terminates in a point (1734 *Builder's Dictionary*); a small spire (1825 Partington); a slender turret, or part of a building elevated above the main building (1883 Sylvester); a point, the crowning apex of any architectural creation (1887 Garnsey).

pise. A very useful and economical kind of building . . . the manner of operation is merely by compressing earth in moulds or cases, that we may arrive at building houses of any size or height (1854 Stuart); a certain kind of wall built of earth or clay (1887 Garnsey).

pitching piece. A horizontal timber, with one of its ends wedged into the wall, at the top of a flight of steps, to support the upper end of the rough strings (1854 Stuart).

placard. The decorations of a chamber door (1854 Stuart); the interior finish or head casing of a door (1887 Garnsey).

plan. The draught of a building, taken on the ground floor, showing the distribution, form, and extent, of its several rooms, passages, etc. (1854 Stuart); the representation of the horizontal section of a building, showing the disposition of the rooms by the arrangement of the partitions, etc. The word plan is quite extensive in its signification, and, as commonly used, denotes the general idea; hence, the design of the several parts of a building, whether as regards finish, arrangement of rooms, or the composition as a whole, may with propriety be termed its plan; but, among architects, the term more properly denotes a drawing exhibiting the form, arrangement, and size of the rooms on the several floors (1858 Silloway).

plancher. A plank or board (1736 Neve); the underside of a cornice projection. The ceiling that is nailed to the under edges of the rafters outside of the building (1917 Shearer).

plank. A general name for all timber, excepting fir, which is from one inch and a half to four inches thick (1854 Nicholson); all boards above one inch thick (1874 Gould); a name generally applied to timber from 2 to 4 inches thick and from 4 to 12 inches wide (1887 Garnsey); cut stuff, thicker than 1¾ in. and wider than 10 in. (1908 Ellis).

platband. Any square molding with little projection; the fascia of an architrave; the list between the flutings, etc . . . of a door or window (1882 Hodgson); any flat band or molding as a fascia or fillet (1887 Garnsey).

plate. Horizontal timbers bedded in brick, or other walls, for the purpose of sustaining other timbers, etc. (1854 Nicholson); the horizontal piece of timber that lies immediately on the top of the posts of a frame, or on the top of the walls of a brick or stone building (1858 Silloway); a horizontal piece of timber in a wall, generally flush with the inside, for resting the ends of beams, joists, or rafters, upon; and, therefore, denominated floor or roof plates (1874 Gould).

platform. A row of beams, which support the timber work of a roof, lying at the top of the wall; a terrace, or open walk at the top of a building (1854 Stuart); the raised portion of a floor (1887 Garnsey).

plinth. A square, flat, piece or table, under the moldings or the bases of columns and pedestals (1736 Neve); a square, projecting, vertically faced member, forming the lowest division of the base of a column. The plain, projecting face at the bottom of a wall, immediately above the ground (1883 Sylvester).

pocket. A recess or box forming part of a window frame or sliding door (1887 Garnsey).

podium. A continued pedestal; a projection from a wall, forming a kind of gallery (1882 Hodgson); a sort of continuous base or pedestal or railing (1887 Garnsey).

pole plate. A horizontal timber resting on the ends of the beams of roofs, and for supporting the feet of the common jack rafters (1882 Hodgson); a purlin secured at the lower ends of a set of roof trusses to carry the foot of rafters (1887 Garnsey).

pommel. A boss or knob terminating a conical or dome-shaped roof (1854 Nicholson); a pinnacle (1887 Garnsey).

porch. The entrance of a house, church, etc. (1736 Neve); an arched vestibule at the entrance of a church, or other building (1851 Shaw); a kind of vestibule, supported by columns (1854 Nicholson); much the same meaning as portico, which see; a shelter to a doorway (1908 Ellis).

portico. A kind of gallery raised upon arches, where people walk under shelter (1736 Neve); a long covered space, composed either of vaults supported by arcades, or of flat roofs supported by pillars, the sides being quite open (1854 Stuart); a covered ambulatory of colonnade form usually at the entrance of a building and usually in classical style (1917 Shearer).

postern. A back door or gate (1736 Neve).

post. A piece of timber set erect in the earth. Perpendicular timbers on the wooden frame of a building (1851 Shaw); all upright or vertical pieces of timber (1874 Gould).

presbytery. The part of the church appropriated to officiating priests, comprising the choir, and other eastern portions of the edifice (1854 Stuart).

principal brace. A brace under the principal rafters (1882 Hodgson).

principal rafter. The main rafter forming the upper part of a roof truss (1887 Garnsey).

pronaos. The front porch of an ancient temple (1854 Stuart).

prostyle. A row of columns in front of a temple, etc. (1736 Neve).

pseudoperipteral. An ancient temple having engaged columns on each side (1887 Garnsey).

pulpit. An elevated place for public speeches; the place in a church whence the sermon is announced (1854 Stuart).

puncheon. A piece of timber placed upright between two posts, whose bearing is too great, serving together with them to sustain some great weight. The puncheon is usually lower and slighter than the posts, and is joined by a brace or the like of iron. Puncheon is also a piece of timber raised upright, under the ridge of a building, wherein the little forces are jointed (1734 *Builder's Dictionary*); nearly synonymous with post. It also denotes the short studs in a partition over a door (1858 Silloway); a post or strut, a brace (1887 Garnsey).

purlin. Those pieces of timber that lie a-cross the rafters, on the inside, to keep them from sinking in the middle of their length (1736 Neve); the horizontal timbers in the sides of a roof, for supporting the spars or small rafters (1874 Gould); a horizontal piece of timber resting upon and reaching from one truss rafter to another for the purpose of carrying the common rafters (1887 Garnsey); used in pairs in roof construction. Purlins extend horizontally across the building and support the rafters between the plate and the peak (1917 Shearer).

putlog. Pieces of timber about seven feet long, used in building scaffolds (1854 Stuart); horizontal pieces for supporting the floor of a scaffold, one end being inserted into put-log holes, left for that purpose in the masonry (1882 Hodgson).

quarrel. A lozenge-shaped pane of glass: also a tile or other material of the same form; same as quarry (1854 Nicholson); a diamond shaped tile, slate or light of glass (1887 Garnsey).

quarter. Slight upright timber-posts framed together and employed instead of walls for the separation of apartments; they are lathed over in the same manner as ceilings, to receive plastering, but when used for external work they are boarded (1854 Nicholson); pieces of timbers used in an upright position for partitions (1856 Smeaton); [quarters] scantlings of studs from two to four inches thick (1887 Garnsey).

quarter cut, quarter grain, quarter sawed. [quarter sawed or rift sawed] A method of sawing timber transversely to the circular rings or plates, or cutting the medullary rays at right angles with the circles of growth (1887 Garnsey).

quatrefoil. An ornament much used in gothic architecture, formed by a molding disposed in four segments of circles, forming four cusps or points at their intersection (1854 Nicholson); a Gothic form, the outline of which is derived by the intersection of four circles, the points of meeting being termed cusps (1887 Garnsey).

quay. A bank of masonry, on the side of the sea, or of a river for the purpose of unlading goods conveniently (1854 Stuart).

queen post. A timber post employed in roofs, for the purpose of suspending the tie-beam. It performs the same office as a king-post, but the term is applied to such suspenders only when there is more than one in a single truss; when there is only one, it is termed a king-post (1854 Nicholson); used in pair in roof construction. Instead of one center king post two queen posts are placed, extending from the tie beam up to the purlins (1917 Shearer).

quirk. A piece taken out of any regular ground-plot, or floor (1736 Neve); a piece of ground taken out of a plot. The term is also applied to a particular form of molding, one that has a sudden convexity (1856 Smeaton); a groove or recess. a narrow groove or sinking on the side of a bead (1908 Ellis).

quirk molding. A convex molding (1887 Garnsey); a corner molding with a square inside corner and a bead worked on the outside corner. Used to protect the outside exposed corner of a wall (1917 Shearer).

quoin. The corners of brick or stone-walls. Also the stones in the corners of brick buildings (1736 Neve); stones or other materials put in the corners of buildings, to strengthen them (1854 Stuart).

rabbet. A channel or kind of semi-groove, cut at the edge of boards, door-cases, etc. for letting other boards or doors, etc. into them (1736 Neve); a channel or groove sunk into a piece of framing lumber; a square recess or sink (1887 Garnsey).

rafter(s). Pieces of timber, which, standing by pairs on the reason-piece or raising-piece, meet in an angle at the top, and form the roof of a building (1854 Nicholson); the inclined timbers of a roof, which support the covering (1858 Silloway); scantling or small timber reaching from the eaves to or towards the peak or top of the roof (1917 Shearer).

rag work. A rough kind of stone-work (1887 Garnsey).

rail(s). Pieces of timber which lie horizontally between the panels of wainscot, and over and under them. The word is also applied to those pieces of timber which lie over and under balusters in balconies, staircases, etc. Also, to the pieces of timber that lie horizontally from post to post in fences (1854 Nicholson); the horizontal pieces which contain the tenons in a piece of framing, in which the upper and lower edges of the panels are inserted (1874 Gould); a term used to designate certain parts of a structure, as hand rail, top rail, bottom rail, lock rail, etc.(1887 Garnsey); the cross or horizontal pieces of the framework of a sash, door or blind (1911 Carr & Adams).

railing. A sort of fence constructed with posts and rails (1854 Nicholson).

raising piece. Pieces that lie under the beams, and over the posts or puncheons (1854 Nicholson).

raising plate. The plates on which the roof is raised (1874 Gould).

raking molding. [raking work] That which (for instance, in molding) is to be joined by mitering exactly, to prevent the work tuning off, as workmen call it, after it's put together (1736 Neve); a term applied to moldings whose arrises are inclined to the horizon (1851 Shaw).

random jointed ashlar work, random range work. A term applied to stone-work where the courses are not all of an even thickness (1887 Garnsey).

range work. Stone-work where the courses are all in the same line (1887 Garnsey).

recess. Same as alcove; a cavity (1887 Garnsey).

recessed vault or arch. One vault recessed within another (1887 Garnsey).

reduct. In carpentry, a little place taken out of a larger, for uniformity sake; also for convenience, as for cabinets, alcoves, etc. (1736 Neve).

reeding. A molding formed like a bundle of beads or reeds (1887 Garnsey).

reglet. A little, flat, narrow, molding, used chiefly in compartments and panels, to separate the parts or members from one another, and to form knots, frets, and other ornaments (1736 Neve); see annulet (1825 Partington); the same as listel (1836 Shaw); a flat, narrow molding principally to divide panels (1887 Garnsey).

regula. A fillet under the ovolo or quarter round of a capital (1734 *Builder's Dictionary*); the same as the plinth or square under the base of a column, or of its pedestal (1735 Neve); see annulet (1825 Partington); the same as listel (1836 Shaw); a band below the taenia in the Doric architrave (1854 Nicholson).

reins of a vault. The sides or walls which sustain the arch (1854 Nicholson).

relief. The projecture of any ornament (1736 Neve); a term applied to a figure which projects from the ground, or plane, on which it is formed, whether it be cut with the chisel, molded, or cast (1854 Nicholson).

relish. A term denoting the piece cut out between two tenons existing on the same piece of wood; also a piece cut from the edge of a tenon when it would be too wide if its whole width were left (1858 Silloway); the projection of the shoulders of a tenon (1887 Garnsey).

reredos. A screen or division wall, placed behind an altar, rood-loft, in old churches (1854 Stuart).

reservoir. A place where water is collected and reserved to be conveyed occasionally through pipes or to be sprouted up (1734 *Builder's Dictionary*); a basin, cistern or tank for the supply of water (1887 Garnsey).

respond. A half pillar or pier attached to or abutting against a wall (1854 Nicholson).

reticulated work. A kind of wall in which the stones are square, and placed lozenge-wise (1825 Partington); that in which the courses are arranged in a net-like form. The stones are square, and placed lozenge-wise (1855 Shaw).

return. The continuation of a molding, projection, etc. in an opposite direction; a side or part which falls away from the front of a straight work (1854 Stuart); in any body with two surfaces, joining each other at an angle, one of the surfaces is said to return in respect to the other; or, if standing before one surface, so that the eye may be in a straight line with the other, or nearly so (1874 Gould); the act of extending a molding or any part in an opposite direction or on another angle.

return bead. A bead which appears on the face and edge of a piece of stuff in the same manner, forming a double quirk (1854 Nicholson); same as bead and quirk (1887 Garnsey).

reveal. The vertical joints or sides of an opening in a wall, from the face to the frame. the outer sides or edges of a door or window opening in an outer wall; the interior sides of the openings are called jambs (1908 Ellis).

rib. An arched piece of timber sustaining the plaster-work of a vault (1851 Shaw).

ridge. The meeting of the rafters on the top of the house (1736 Neve); the highest part of the roof, or covering of a house. The term is particularly used for a piece of wood in which the rafters meet (1854 Nicholson); the uppermost horizontal member in a roof (1908 Ellis).

ridge pole. The piece of wood against which the top ends of the rafters bear is called the ridge-piece or, ridge-pole (1858 Silloway); the highest horizontal timber in a roof, extending from top to top of the several pair of rafters of the trusses, for supporting the heads of the jack rafters (1882 Hodgson).

ridge tile. Roofing tile of a convex shape for covering a ridge (1887 Garnsey).

riser. That board in stairs set on edge under the tread or step of the stair (1856 Smeaton); generally a term used to designate that portion of a stairs between the steps or treads, secured to the front edge of one and the back edge of the other (1887 Garnsey).

roll. A large bead (1887 Garnsey); [ridge roll] a round piece of wood running attached to a ridge as a finish, and also to act as a core to the lead flashing (1908 Ellis).

roof. The covering of a house; but the word is used in carpentry, for the timber-work of the covering (1734 Salmon); the upper covering of a building, whatever may be the pitch (1870 Todd.).

rose. An ornament cut in the resemblance of a rose (1734 *Builder's Dictionary*); an ornament applied to the center of each side of the abacus of the Corinthian capital (1854 Nicholson).

rosette. A flower ornament used in the abacus of the Corinthian capital, from the use of which the rosette came into favor (1887 Garnsey).

rose window. A circular window, with compartments of mullions or tracery, branching from a center; it is sometimes also called a Catherine-wheel, or marigold window (1854 Stuart).

rotunda. A building which is round, both within and without (1830 Haviland); . . . any large circular room the ceiling of which is arched like a dome (1858 Silloway).

rough cast. An exterior finishing, much cheaper than stucco . . . composed of fine gravel, clean washed from all earthy particles, and mixed with pure lime and water, till the whole is of a semi-fluid consistency (1854 Nicholson); a kind of mastic, or a rough mortar or cement for covering the exterior walls of buildings, mixed with pebbles, or small shells (1870 Todd).

rudenture. The figure of a rope or staff, sometimes plain and sometimes carved, wherewith the flutings of columns are frequently filled up (1736 Neve).

ruderation. A kind of pavement with pebbles or little stones, with mortar compounded of lime and sand, after the ground is well beaten to prevent its cracking (1736 Neve).

rustication. [rustic work] That where the stone, instead of being smooth, is hatched or picked with the point of a hammer (1736 Neve); [frosted rustic work] has the margins of the stones reduced to a plane parallel to the plane of the wall, the intermediate parts having an irregular surface (1854 Stuart).

rustic joint. A joint in stone-work the shape of which is a V (1887 Garnsey).

rustic order. An order with rustic quoins, rustic work, etc. (1734 *Builder's Dictionary*).

rustic work. The term is applied to those stones in a building which are hatched or picked in joles, resembling a natural rough appearance (1830 Haviland); the courses of stone or brick, in which the work is jagged out in to an irregular surface, Also, work left rough without tooling (1851 Shaw); building with the faces of stone left rough, and the joining sides wrought smooth. Also ornamental wood structures, with the bark on; or rustic work may be made of roots of trees, scraped clean and put together in the form of chairs or long seats (1870 Todd).

sacristy. A strong room attached to a church, in which sacred vestments and utensils are deposited (1854 Stuart).

saddle. A thin beveled board placed at a doorway on the floor for the door to close onto; often called a threshold (1887 Garnsey).

saddleback coping. Stone coping cut with a raised or slanting top to shed water (1887 Garnsey).

sally. A projection of any kind. In carpentry, the term denotes the end of a piece of timber when cut to an acute angle, obliquely to the fibers of the wood (1858 Silloway); a term used to denote the act of notching a piece of timber; as the foot of a rafter (1887 Garnsey).

sash. The wooden frame which holds the glass in windows (1851 Shaw); a sash indicates a single piece to fill a given opening (1912 Farley & Loetscher).

sash cord. The line by which the sash is suspended to the balancing weight (1897 Edwards).

sash frame. The frame in which the sash runs up and down, or to which it is hinged. When the sash is hung, the frame is made hollow to contain the balancing weights, and is said to be a box frame (1897 Edwards).

sash pulley. A metal pulley used to carry the sash cord (1887 Garnsey).

scantling. The name of a piece of timber, as of quartering for a partition, when under five inches square, or the rafter, purlin, or pole-plate of a roof (1851 Shaw); the transverse dimensions of a piece of timber; sometimes, also the small timbers in roofing and flooring (1874 Gould); a term used to denote a piece of timber of small width and breadth but of any length, as a 2x2, 2x4, 2x6 or 2x8. The term is also used to designate the size of a stone (1887 Garnsey).

scape. A term sometimes given to the shaft of a column, more commonly to the place where it rises from the base (1854 Stuart); the shaft of a column. The quarter-round that connects the shaft with the base or capital (1887 Garnsey).

scarf, scarfing. The jointing and bolting of two pieces of timber together transversely, so that the two appear but as one (1851 Shaw); a joint used in lengthening a piece of timber in which the two ends are cut to lap over and fit each other, chiefly used in carpentry (1908 Ellis).

scheme arch. Those which are less than a semi-circle (1734 *Builder's Dictionary*); an arch whose outline is a segment of a circle (1887 Garnsey).

scotia. The name of a hollowed molding, principally used between the tori of the base of columns (1851 Shaw); a concave molding used in the base of a column, between the fillets of the tori, and in other situations. Its outline is a segment of a circle, often greater than a semicircle. The molding which is put under the nosing of steps (1883 Sylvester).

screen. A light frame of wood or metal used for several purposes (1887 Garnsey).

scroll. See volute (1854 Nicholson); a carved curvilinear ornament, somewhat resembling in profile the turnings of a ram's horn (1856 Smeaton); a convolved or spiral ornament, The volute of the Ionic and Corinthian capitals (1883 Sylvester).

setting coat. The last coat of brown mortar (1887 Garnsey).

severy. A compartment or section of a scaffolding; a room or compartment of a building; the bay or division of a vaulted ceiling (1887 Garnsey).

shaft. The body of a column; that part between the base and capital (1856 Smeaton).

shank. The space between the channels of the Doric triglyph, which is sometimes termed the leg of the triglyph (1854 Stuart).

sheathing. Roof boards. Also boards used to side up a house before applying building paper and siding (1917 Shearer).

shed. A penthouse or shelter made of boards, generally feather-edged (1736 Neve).

shingle. [shides] Small pieces of wood, or quartered oaken boards, sawed to a certain scantling; but they are more usually cleft to about an inch thick at one end, and made like wedges . . . used to cover houses with (but more commonly churches and steeples) instead of tiles, or slates (1736 Neve); thin pieces of wood used for covering, instead of tiles, etc. (1874 Gould); may be of wood, metal or asphalt. Slate shingles are called tile (1917 Shearer).

shooting. Planning the edge of a board straight, and out of winding (1851 Shaw).

shouldering pieces. A bracket (1736 Neve); thin strips of wood or cement laid under the upper edge of slate, so as to raise them as to close the laps (1887 Garnsey); [shoulder] the abutting parts of a mortise and tenon joint (1908 Ellis).

shread head. See jerkin head (1854 Nicholson).

shutters. The boards or wainscoting which shut up the aperture of a window (1851 Shaw); a light framework of wood or metal, used to close or partially close the opening of a window (1887 Garnsey); blinds with solid panels instead of slat panels (1917 Curtis).

side posts. Used in roofs as Queen-posts (1887 Garnsey).

siding. The exterior side covering of boards to a building. Sidings are often called clapboards (1870 Todd).

sill. The timber or stone at the foot of a window or door; the ground timbers of a frame which supports the posts (1851 Shaw); the timber or stone at the foot of a door, also given to the bottom pieces which support quarter and truss partitions (1854 Stuart); [ground sills] are the timbers on the ground which support the posts and superstructure of a timber building. The term is most frequently applied to those pieces of timber or stone at the bottom of doors or windows (1882 Hodgson).

single-hung. When only one sash of a window is moveable in the same vertical plane (1854 Stuart).

site. The situation of a house, etc. (1736 Neve); the position or seat of a building; the place where it stands (1897 Edwards).

skewback. The inclined stone from which an arch springs (1882 Hodgson); that part of an arch that cuts into a wall beyond the perpendicular line of the opening (1887 Garnsey).

skirting boards. The narrow boards fitted round the under side of wainscot against the floor (1736 Neve); the narrow boards round the margin of a floor, forming a plinth for the base of the dado, or simply a plinth for the room itself, should there be no dado (1854 Nicholson); baseboard; the board placed about the room against the wall, just above the floor (1897 Edwards).

skylight. A light frame of wood or iron for the purpose of holding glass. The term is generally applied to a roof window (1887 Garnsey).

sleeper. Timber placed on the ground to support the ground-joists or other woodwork (1856 Smeaton).

slit deal. A board, a thin piece of lumber (1887 Garnsey).

socle. See zocle (1854 Stuart).

soffit. Used for the under side or face of an architrave (1734 *Builder's Dictionary*); the underside of an architrave, corona, etc. The underside of the heads of doors, windows, etc. (1857 Hatfield); underside of stairways, archways, entablatures, cornices, or ceilings (1883 Sylvester).

spandrel. The angle formed by a stairway (1882 Hodgson).

span roof. A roof consisting of two simple inclined sides in contradistinction to shed-roofs (1858 Silloway); a term used to denote a gable or truss roof (1887 Garnsey).

spire. A steeple that rises tapering by degrees and ends in a point at top (1736 Neve); a body that shoots up in a conical form; a steeple (1883 Sylvester).

splay. [splay, splayed] The slanting or beveling of the sides or jambs of a window or door opening (1887 Garnsey).

springer. The base of an arch; the roof of a groined house (1870 Todd); the point where the upright support of an arch terminates and the curve begins (1897 Edwards).

springing course. The top course of stone forming the springer (1887 Garnsey).

spur. Same as bracket (1887 Garnsey).

squinch. A small arch thrown across the angles of square towers to support octagonal spires (1854 Nicholson).

stack of chimneys. A number of chimney-shafts combined in one (1870 Todd).

stair. The steps whereby we ascend and descend from one story of a house to another (1736 Neve).

staircase. The complete construction comprised in one or more successive flights of stairs (1908 Ellis).

stay. Any thing performing the office of either a tie or a brace, which prevents the swaying of the work to which it is affixed (1858 Silloway).

steeple. An appendage generally erected at the west end of churches, to contain the bells, and rising either in form of a tower or of a spire (1854 Stuart); a roof diminishing in dimensions towards the top by abrupt stages; a series of reduced towers one above the other (1908 Ellis).

step. The degrees in ascending a staircase, which are composed of two parts, the tread or horizontal part, and the riser or vertical part (1851 Shaw).

stereobat. The bases or foundation, from which a wall, column, or building rises (1854 Stuart).

stile. The upright pieces in framing or paneling (1856 Smeaton); [stiles] the upright or vertical outside pieces of a sash, door or blind (1911 Carr & Adams).

stilted arch. An arch whose springing-line is above the impost, or which is raised, as it were, upon upright stilts or props (1854 Nicholson); an arch on high posts (1917 Shearer).

stool. A term given to the inside sill of a window frame (1887 Garnsey).

stoop. A wide step in front of an entrance door, large enough to hold a seat, with steps leading to the ground. It may have a roof cover (1917 Shearer).

stop. A small molding used to stop doors against or to enclose sash (1887 Garnsey); [stops] pieces of wood nailed on the frame of a door when the frame has no rebate worked in the jambs to form the recess or rebate into which the door shuts; also pieces fastened in base boards behind doors to keep the knobs from touching and injuring the plaster when the door is opened wide (1897 Edwards).

story. That vertical division of a building occupying the space from the top of one floor to the under side of that immediately over it (1858 Silloway); a certain division of a building. A vertical section (1887 Garnsey).

straining piece. A beam placed between two opposite beams, to prevent their nearer approach, as rafters, braces, struts, etc. (1854 Stuart); a horizontal beam generally used in trusses to counteract a force or strain in the direction of its length (1887 Garnsey).

strap. An iron plate, to secure the junction of two or more timbers, into which it is secured by bolts (1851 Shaw).

stretcher(s). A term applied to bricks or stones so placed in a wall that their longest side shall be parallel to the face of the wall (1854 Nicholson); a brick or block of masonry laid lengthwise of a wall (1882 Hodgson).

striae. The fillets or rays which separate the furrows, or grooves, of fluted column (1854 Nicholson); fillets; narrow flat bands (1887 Garnsey).

string board. A board placed next to the well-hole in wooden stairs, and terminating the ends of steps (1854 Stuart); the boards or plank under and supporting stairs, sometimes cut out to receive the steps and risers; in which case they are open strings; when the steps and risers are let into the strings, they are said to be housed in the strings, and the latter are then called close strings (1897 Edwards).

string course. A narrow continuous horizontal molding or platband projecting slightly from the face of the wall (1854 Nicholson).

strut. Oblique framing pieces, joined to the king-posts, or queen-posts, and the principal rafters; they are sometimes called braces (1854 Stuart); this term is nearly synonymous with brace . . . a timber designed to keep extended those parts of the work against which its ends come. The term brace may be used as a substitute for strut, but not strut for brace. A strut, therefore, is always in a state of compression, while a brace may be either compressed or extended (1858 Silloway); pieces of timber which support the rafters, and which are supported by the truss-posts stretching piece. To hold apart. A brace placed at an angle between two parallel timbers (1917 Shearer).

stub mortise. A short mortise (1887 Garnsey).

stud. An upright piece of timber inserted in or nailed to a sill to support the plate of a building. Stud is a term usually applied to the upright scantling of a frame (1870 Todd); [studs] the timbers used in lath and plaster partitions and walls, and placed either 12 or 16 inches apart, as it is desired that a lath which is 4 feet long may have 4 or 5 nails in its length; studs may be of various sizes from 2 x 4 to 4 x 6 (1897 Edwards).

stuff. All the wood that joiners work upon (1736 Neve); wood used in joinery; in carpentry termed timber (1908 Ellis).

stylobate. A plane surface raised either upon a certain number of steps, which were contained all round or upon a podium, which afforded no approach but in front (1882 Hodgson).

summer. A large piece of timber supported by piers or posts; when it supports a wall, it is called a breast summer (1856 Smeaton); any large beam designed to cover a wide opening. A small summer is called a lintel (1858 Silloway); a large beam in a building, either disposed in an outside wall, or in the middle of an apartment, parallel to such wall (1874 Gould).

superstructure. The upper portion of a building raised upon the foundations (1854 Nicholson).

surmounted arch. Those which are higher than a semicircle (1854 Stuart); same as stilted arch (1887 Garnsey).

symmetry. The relation or equality in the height, length and breadth of the parts necessary to compose a beautiful whole (1734 *Builder's Dictionary*); the conveniency that runs between the parts of a building and the whole (1734 Salmon); the harmony, proportion, or uniformity, that runs between the parts of a building and the whole (1736 Neve).

systyle. An intercolumniation of two diameters (1825 Partington); that kind of intercolumniation which had two diameters between the columns (1854 Stuart).

tabernacle. In Catholic churches, the name of tabernacle is given to a small edifice in form of a temple, constructed of marble, precious stones, or metal, and placed upon the altar, for the purpose of containing the consecrated vessels, etc. (1854 Stuart).

table. A flat surface, generally rectangular, charged with an ornamental figure. A table which, projects from the naked of the wall is termed a raised or projecting table (1854 Stuart).

taenia. The term for the fillet separating the frieze from architrave in the Doric order (1825 Partington).

tail trimmer. A trimmer next to the wall, into which the ends of joists are fastened, in order to avoid the flues (1854 Nicholson); a beam or double joist framed across openings or in front of a chimney to carry tail-joist (1887 Garnsey).

talon. A French term for the same molding which we call the ogee (1854 Stuart).

templet. A short piece of timber laid under the end of a beam or girder in the walls of a brick or stone building (1858 Silloway).

tension bar, tension rod. A rod usually of wrought iron, employed to tie together any two parts of a structure which have a tendency to separate or be thrust asunder (1854 Nicholson).

terrace. An area raised before a house, or other building, above the level of the ground, for walking upon. The word is sometimes used for balcony, or gallery (1854 Nicholson); a raised portion; an embankment; a balcony or gallery (1887 Garnsey).

terra cotta. Baked earth (1854 Nicholson).

tesselated pavement. A collection of minerals, woods, etc., inlaid so as to form geometrical or other designs in gradation of colors (1887 Garnsey).

tetrastyle. A building or portico with four columns in front or four pilasters on the side (1887 Garnsey).

threshold. The door-sill; the plank, stone, or piece of timber or board, that lies at the bottom or under a door of a house or other building (1883 Sylvester).

tie beam. [tie] A timber, rod, chain, etc. binding two bodies together, which have a tendency to separate or diverge from each other. The tie-beam connects the bottom of a pair of principal rafters, and prevents them from bursting out the wall (1882 Hodgson); a beam generally employed in a roof framing for the purpose of overcoming strains (1887 Garnsey).

tie rod. An iron rod used in the same sense as a tie-beam (1887 Garnsey).

tile. An artificial stone, or broad thin brick, made of dried earth, and burnt in a kiln, used in covering buildings (1854 Nicholson).

tongue. A projecting part on the edge of a board, to be inserted in a groove ploughed in the edge of another (1854 Nicholson); a small fillet or square, cut on the edge of flooring, or a piece of thin lumber (1887 Garnsey).

torus. A thick, round molding, used in the bases of columns: it is the bigness that distinguishes the torus from the astragal (1734 *Builder's Dictionary*); a large molding, semi-circular in profile, used in bases (1825 Partington); a molding that has a convex semicircular or semi-elliptical profile (1856 Smeaton).

tower. A lofty building, much higher than it is broad, either standing along or forming a part of another edifice of a church, castle, etc. (1883 Sylvester).

tracery. In Gothic architecture, the intersection in various forms of the mullions in the head of a window or screen (1854 Stuart); in Gothic art the small, radiating and curvilinear branches or subdivisions of windows, panels, groins, etc. (1887 Garnsey).

transept. That portion of a cruciform church which extends across the main body of the building, and usually separates the nave and choir (1854 Nicholson); the transverse portion of a cruciform church (1857 Hatfield).

transom. A piece placed over a door, when there is to be an opening for light immediately over the door. When the opening over is circular, it is generally called an impost (1830 Haviland); a beam across a double-lighted window: if the window have no transom, it is named a clear-story window (1851 Shaw).

tread. The horizontal part of the step of a stair (1854 Stuart); that part of a step which is included between the face of its riser and that of the riser above (1857 Hatfield).

trefoil. An ornament, consisting of three cusps in a circle (1825 Partington).

trellis. An open framing, pieces crossing each other so as to form diamond or lozenge-shaped openings (1856 Smeaton); a reticulated framing made of thin bars of wood for screens, windows, etc. (1857 Hatfield).

treenail. A wooden pin, used in heavy framings (1887 Garnsey).

tribune. A platform for a speaker (1887 Garnsey).

triglyph. The ornament in the Doric frieze, supposed to represent the end of beams (1825 Partington); the tablets in the Doric frieze, chamfered on the two vertical edges, and with two channels in the middle, called glyphs or carvings (1854 Nicholson); a projecting block or tablet on the frieze of the Doric order (1887 Garnsey).

trim. A term used to denote the act of fitting or joining. The finishing or wood trimming of a building (1887 Garnsey); to construct a framed opening in a roof or floor (1908 Ellis).

trimmer. A small beam, into which the ends of several joists are framed (1854 Nicholson); [trimins] pieces of timber framed at right angles to the joists for chimneys, and the well holes for stairs, when several joists are framed into one beam it is called a trimmer and the joists trimming joists (1882 Hodgson); the joist carrying the intermediate joists forming a landing, or the ends of the joists cut to form the stairway (1908 Ellis).

triumphal arch. An architectural structure erected to commemorate a victory (1887 Garnsey).

trunk. See shaft (1851 Shaw); a term used to designate the shaft of a pilaster (1887 Garnsey).

truss. Pieces of timber used in framing, to support the middle of any great span (1830 Haviland); an arrangement of timbers for increasing the resistance to cross-strains, consisting of a tie, two struts and a suspending piece (1857 Hatfield); a horizontal timber supported by bracings above, so as to form a long span without posts below (1870 Todd); a frame constructed of several pieces of timber, and divided into two or more triangles by oblique pieces, in order to prevent the possibility of its revolving round any of the angles of the frame (1874 Gould); a scientific arrangement or combination of timber so framed as to be self-supporting (1887 Garnsey); an arrangement of timber and iron so combined as to make an unyielding frame; so named because it is trussed or tied together (1897 Edwards).

turret. A small tower, often crowning the angle of a wall (1854 Stuart); a little tower or spire attached to a building, and rising above it (1883 Sylvester).

Tuscan order. The simplest order of architecture, formed in Italy in the fifteenth century (1870 Todd); the order admits of no ornaments; the columns are never fluted (1882 Hodgson); the most ancient and simple of the orders of architecture. The capital is plain, unornamented, and much like that of the Doric order (1883 Sylvester).

tympanum. The space within a pediment: it is sometimes adorned with sculpture (1825 Partington); the naked face of a pediment, included between the level and the raking moldings (1857 Hatfield); the plain triangular space of a pediment; the die of a pedestal; the panels of a door (1887 Garnsey); the space between a smaller arch and a larger arch placed over it, or the space in the upper part of an arch above a lintel. The face of a pediment recessed, in an arch or gable (1917 Shearer).

undercroft. A crypt, or subterranean apartment (1854 Nicholson).

upright. A representation or draught of the front of a building. The same as elevation (1736 Neve); an old term signifying the elevation or facade of a building (1887 Garnsey).

urn. An architectural decoration or ornament generally used to finish a balustrade (1887 Garnsey).

vagina. the part of a terminus, resembling a sheath, in which the lower part of the statue is inserted (1854 Nicholson); the base of a pillar or pedestal with a niche for a bust (1887 Garnsey).

valley. The internal angle of two sides of a roof (1851 Shaw). the junction of two roofs connected at right angles to each other (1917 Shearer).

valley rafter. The rafter which supports the valley (1836 Shaw); the rafters of a roof framed at the valley (1887 Garnsey); the rafter in the re-entrant angle of a roof (1897 Edwards).

vault. An arched roof (1825 Partington); an arched roof, the stones or materials of which are so placed as to support each other (1830 Haviland); underground buildings with arched ceilings, whether circular or elliptical (1856 Smeaton).

vaulting shaft. The shaft which supports the ribs of a groined vault (1854 Nicholson); a small column or shaft projecting from a wall and supporting the vaulting ribs of a groining (1887 Garnsey).

veneer. A very thin leaf of wood, of a superior quality, for covering doors, or articles of furniture made of an inferior wood (1854 Nicholson); a thin sawing or leaf from selected woods, used in decorative art (1887 Garnsey).

Venetian door. A door which is lighted on each side (1836 Shaw); a door having panes of glass on each side for lighting the entrance hall (1870 Todd).

Venetian window. A window in three separate apertures, divided by slender piers, and having the center aperture larger than the side ones (1854 Nicholson).

veranda. A kind of open portico, formed by extending a sloping roof beyond the main building (1883 Sylvester); an open portico or light external gallery, with sloping roof, supported on slender pillars (1897 Edwards).

verge. A term used to denote an edge or eave (1887 Garnsey).

verge board. An edgewise perpendicular border board suspended from the end of the roof on the gable end of a building (1917 Shearer).

vermiculated work. Stones, etc. worked so as to have the appearance of having been eaten by worms (1854 Stuart); a peculiar kind of stone-work in imitation of worm-eaten wood (1887 Garnsey).

vestibule. A large open space before the door, or at the entry of a house (1736 Neve); an ante-hall, lobby, or porch (1851 Shaw); an apartment which serves as the medium of communication to another room or series of rooms (1857 Hatfield); an enclosure at the entrance to a building, and within the building, in which it differs from a porch, the latter being exterior to the building (1908 Ellis).

vestry. A room adjoining to a church, etc. where the priests vestments, and sacred utensils are kept; and where the heads of the parish assemble for transacting the business of the parish (1736 Neve); a room adjoining a church, where the vestments of the minister are kept and parish meetings held (1882 Hodgson).

viaduct. A term applied to a roadway supported on a succession of arches (1854 Nicholson); a bridge; a trestle-work; a structure spanning a valley or river (1887 Garnsey).

villa. A country house, for the retreat of the rich (1854 Stuart); a country or suburban residence, a large dwelling (1887 Garnsey).

volute. A sort of scroll or spiral contortion used in the Ionic and Composite capitals (1734 *Builder's Dictionary*); one of the principal ornaments in the Ionic capital, composed of two or more spirals of the same species, having one common eye and center, variously channeled, or hollowed out in the form of moldings (1854 Nicholson); a peculiar scroll-like vine used as the principal feature of the capital of the Greek and Roman orders of architecture (1887 Garnsey).

voussoir. A vault stone, or stone proper to form the sweep of an arch (1736 Neve); the wedge-shaped stones forming the curvature or intrados of an arch (1854 Nicholson).

wainscot. The paneled work round, or against the walls of a room (1736 Neve); the wood work lining the sides of the room, generally from 2 to 6 feet high, with molded capping; often paneled (1897 Edwards).

wall. The enclosures of whole houses, or particular rooms; as also gardens, orchards, etc. if made of brick or stone. Walls are either entire and continual, or intermitted and the intermissions are either pillars or pilasters (1736 Neve); a body of masonry, of a certain thickness, formed of stones or bricks (1836 Shaw); those masses of materials which generally have their faces in vertical or plumb-lines; or, at least are so disposed, that a plumb-line from any point in either surface will fall entirely within the surface, or within the thickness of the wall (1854 Nicholson); a term for the enclosing structure of a building (1887 Garnsey).

wallplate. A piece of timber laid on the top of a wall, in which are laid the joists and framing of the roof (1830 Haviland); a piece of timber placed horizontally on the top of a wall. The term plate denotes the same thing (1858 Silloway).

water closet. An apartment so generally known as to render any definition of it unnecessary (1854 Nicholson).

weatherboard. The nailing up of boards against a wall; sometimes it is used to signify the boards themselves, when nailed up (1734 Salmon); a board on the gable from the ridge to the eaves: the outer boards of a building nailed so as to overlap and throw off rain (1870 Todd).

weather moldings. A molding carried over a door or window, for the purpose of diverting rain-water from the parts beneath; otherwise termed drip-stone or label (1854 Nicholson).

well hole. The hole left in the floor for the stairs to come up through (1736 Neve); the space occupied by a flight of stairs: the space left in the middle, beyond the ends of the steps, is called the well-hole (1851 Shaw); the whole apartment in which the stairs are placed ought to be called the well; and the void formed by the ends of the steps the well-hole (1854 Nicholson); the space enclosed by the walls of a circular staircase (1870 Todd).

wicket. A little door within a gate, or a hole in a door, through which to view what passes without (1734 *Builder's Dictionary*).

winders. Those stairs by which, in a continuous flight, the direction of ascent is changed, the risers being disposed as radii of a circle, and the treads in consequence being narrower at one end than the other; the width of the treads at the center should be the same as that of the flyers (1854 Nicholson); in stairs, steps not parallel to each other (1857 Hatfield); the triangular steps of a circular stairway (1887 Garnsey).

window. An aperture or open place in the sides of an house to let in air and light (1734 *Builder's Dictionary*); a window indicates two pieces—one upper, one lower—to fill an opening arranged to slide vertically (1911 Carr & Adams).

window shutter. The wooden doors by which the windows are occasionally closed, or secured (1854 Nicholson); [window blind, window jamb, window shutter, window stool] terms used in building to designate parts of a window (1887 Garnsey).

wing. The outlying and returning ends of a building (1854 Nicholson); a small part or building attached to the side of the main edifice (1897 Edwards).

wreath. The twisted work (1736 Neve).

wreathed column. Columns twisted in the form of a screw (1854 Stuart); twisted columns; one entwined with wreaths (1887 Garnsey).

yard. An enclosed court or area (1854 Nicholson).

zocle. A small kind of standing pedestal; being a low square piece or member serving to support a bust, statue, or the like . . . to support a column or other part of a building (1734 *Builders Dictionary*); a low square member, which serves to elevate a statue, vase, etc. also, when a range of columns is erected on one continued high plinth, it is called a zocle. It differs from a pedestal, being without base or cornice (1830 Haviland); a molding of a square section (1887 Garnsey).

Glossary Bibliography

The Builder's Dictionary, or Gentleman and Architect's Companion. Washington: Association for Preservation Technology, 1981, reprint of 1734 ed., London: A. Bettesworth and C. Hitch.

Curtis Catalog, General Millwork. Clinton, Iowa: Curtis Brothers and Co., 1914.

Edwards 1897

Ellis. George. *Modern Practical Joinery, a Treatise on the Practice of Joiner's Work . . .* , Fresno, CA: Linden Publishing, 1987, reprint of 3rd edition, London: Batsford and New York: Scribner's, 1908.

Farley and Loetscher Mfg. Co., *General Catalog No. 9. 2nd ed.* Dubuque, Iowa: Farley and Loetscher Mfg. Co. 1912.

Garnsey, George O. *The American Glossary of Architectural Terms*, Chicago: Clark and Longley, 1887

Gould, Lucius D. *The Carpenter's and Builder's Assistant and Wood Worker's Guide*, New York: A. J. Bicknell, 1874

Haviland, John. *The Practical Builder's Assistant*, Baltimore: Fielding Lucas Jr., 1830

Hatfield, Robert Griffith. *The American House Carpenter*, New York: Wiley & Halsted 1857

Hodgson, Fred T. *Stair Building Made Easy*, New York: Palliser Palliser & Co., 1882

House Beautiful (vol. 34) 1924

Illustrated Catalog, 1911-12 Carr and Adams Co. Des Moines, Iowa: Carr and Adams, 1912.

National Builder, "Our Dictionary of Trade Terms" Vol. 38: March 80, April 111, May 60-61, June 72-73 (1916)

Neve, Richard. *The City and Country Purchaser's and Builder's Dictionary, or The Complete Builder's Guide*, 3rd. ed. London: B. Sprint, D. Browne, J. Osborn, S. Birt, H. Lintot, and A. Wilde, 1736

Nicholson, Peter. *Nicholson's Dictionary of the Science of Architecture, Building, etc.*, London and New York: London Print and Publishing Co. 1854

Partington, Charles Frederick. *The Builder's Compete Guide . . .*, London: Sherwood, Gilbert & Piper, 1825

Salmon, William. *Palladio Londinensis, or, The London Way of Building*, Part III, The Builder's Dictionary, London: Ward and Wickstead, 1734

Shaw, Edward. *The Modern Architect or Every Carpenter His Own Master . . .*, Boston: Dayton & Wentworth 1854 [1836, 1855]

Shearer, Herbert Abram. *Farm Buildings, With Plans and Descriptions*, Chicago: F. J. Drake c.1917

Silloway, Thomas William, *Text-book of Modern Carpentry*, Boston: Crosby, Nichols, and Co. 1858

Smeaton, A.C. *The Builder's Pocket Companion*, Philadelphia: Carey, 1856

Stuart, Robert. (pseud.) Meikleham, Robert. *Cyclopedia of Architecture, Historical, Descriptive, Topographical, Decorative, Theoretical, Mechanical . . .* New York, 1854

Sylvester, W. A. *The Modern House-Carpenter's Companion and Builder's Guide . . .*, Boston: Damrell & Upham, 1883

Todd, Sereno Edwards. *Todd's Country Homes*, Hartford, CT: Hartford Pub. Co., 1870

Vogdes, Frank W. *The Architect's and Builder's Pocket Companion*, Philadelphia: Henry Carey Baird 1871

Bibliography

Selected Trade Catalogs

Allen Mfg. Co. *Sales Plan, Allen's Parlor Furnace.* Nashville, Tenn.: Allen Mfg. Co., n.d.

American Face Brick Assoc. *A Manual of Face Brick Construction.* Chicago: American Face Brick Assoc., 1920.

American Kerament Corp. *Kerament Store Front Details.* A.I.A. File No. 239. New York: Amer Kerament Corp., n.d.

Angel Novelty Co. *Angel's New Line of Standardized Woodwork for the Home.* Fitchburg, Mass.: Angel Novelty Co., 1942.

The American Life Foundation and Study Institute. *Late Victorian Architectural Details. Combined Book of Sash, Doors, Blinds, Moldings, Etc.* 1898; Reprint. Watkins Glen, N.Y.: American Life Foundation, 1978.

Armstrong Cork Co., and Agnes Foster Wright. *Floors, Furniture and Color.* Lancaster, Penn.: Armstrong Cork Co., Linoleum Division, 1924.

Armstrong Cork Products. *Pattern Book, 1936, Armstrong's Linoleum. (Armstrong's Linoleum Quaker Rugs Floor Covering, 1936.)* Lancaster, Penn.: Armstrong Cork Products Co., Floor Division, 1936.

Associated Tile Manufacturers. *Ceramic Mosaic.* Publication No. K-500. Beaver Falls, Penn.: Associated Tile Manufacturers, 1922.

Badger, Daniel D. *Illustrations of Iron Architecture.* 1865; Reprint of *Badger's Illustrated Catalogue of Cast-Iron Architecture.* New York: Dover, 1981.

Bardwell-Robinson. *Catalogue of Bardwell-Robinson Co., Wholesale Manufacturers—Windows, Doors, Blinds.* Minneapolis, Minn.: Bardwell-Robinson Co., 1904.

M. H. Birge and Sons. *The Birge Special Designs Paper Hangings and Birge Velours for Season of 1889 and '90. (Illustrations, Special Designs of the Birge Paper Hangings and Velours for the Season 1889 and 90.)* Buffalo, N.Y.: M. H. Birge and Sons, 1889.

———. *A Book of Illustrations of New Patterns of Paper Hangings for the Season of 1916.* Buffalo, N.Y.: M. H. Birge and Sons Co., 1916.

Builders Wood-Working Co. *Built-In Furniture.* Minneapolis, Minn.: Builders Wood-Working Co., 1922.

Burlingame and Darbys Co. *New Perfection Oil Cook Stoves.* North Adams, Mass.: Burlingame and Darbys Co., 1916.

Canton Art Metal Co. *Catalog "F": Canton Line Stamped Steel Ceilings. (Canton Line Steel Ceilings.)* Canton, Ohio: Canton Art Metal Co., n.d.

Carr and Adams. *Illustrated Catalog, 1911–12 Carr and Adams Co.* Des Moines, Iowa: Carr and Adams Co., 1912.

Bilt Well Millwork, for Every Home of Comfort. Dubuque, Iowa: Carr, Ryder and Adams Co., 1921.

Carr, Ryder and Adams Co. *"Bilt-Well" Millwork, Catalog No. 40.* Minneapolis, Minn.: Carr, Ryder and Adams Co., n.d.

Carter White Lead Co. *The Paint Beautiful.* Chicago: Carter White Lead Co., n.d.

Chantrell Hardware and Tool Co. *From Bungalow to Skyscraper. Manufactured by Chantrell Hardware and Tool Co.* Reading, PA: Chantrell Hardware and Tool Co. 1927.

Gardner Hardware Co. *Gardner Hardware Co., Wholesale and Retail, Builders' Hardware and Contractor's Supplies.* Minneapolis, Minn.: Gardner Hardware Co., (ca. 1910).

Charles K. Spaulding Logging Co. *Pacific Universal Catalog of Sash, Doors, Millwork, Art Glass, and Odd Work.* 1923.

Chicago Millwork Supply Co. *Millwork and Building Material of Guaranteed Quality, Catalog No. 355.* Chicago: Chicago Millwork Supply Co., 1924.

Chicago Wrecking House Co. *Catalog No. 160 A, 1909–1910.* Chicago: Chicago Wrecking House Co., 1909.

Cochran-Sargent Co. *Cochran-Sargent Company General Catalogue "C."* St. Paul, Minn.: Cochran-Sargent Co., 1921.

George H. Cole Supply Co. *Catalogue C—Geo. H. Cole Supply*

Co. *Plumbing and Heating Supplies.* Troy, N.Y.: George H. Cole Supply Co., 1917.

Congoleum. *Congoleum Nairn 1942.* N.p.: Congoleum, 1942.

P. and F. Corbin. *Catalog.* New Britain, Conn.: P. and F. Corbin, 1871.

Crane Co. *Crane Plumbing Catalog B.* Minneapolis, Minn.: Crane Company, 1915.

Curtis Brothers. *Book of Designs, 1899.* Clinton, Iowa: Curtis Brothers and Co., 1899.

————. *Curtis Catalog, General Millwork.* Clinton, Iowa: Curtis Brothers and Co., 1914.

Cutting and DeLaney. *Price List of the Cutting and DeLaney Decorative Lattice Work.* (*Decorative Lattice; Our Doors and Windows; How to Decorate.*) Buffalo, N.Y.: Cutting and DeLaney, (ca. 1889).

Decorators Supply Co. *Illustrated Catalogue of Composition Capitals and Brackets.* Chicago: Decorators Supply Co., June 1909.

DeKosenko Mfg. Co. *Catalogue No. I. The DeKosenko Manufacturing Co. Electric, Gas, and Combination Fixtures.* Philadelphia: DeKosenko Mfg. Co., n.d.

Detroit Steel Products Co. *Fenestra Fencraft Casements.* Detroit: Detroit Steel Products Co., 1930.

Edwards Manufacturing. *Edwards Metal Roofing, Siding, Ceiling.* Cincinnati: Edwards Manufacturing, 1913.

Faithorn Co. *Interiors.* West Union, Iowa. Chicago: Faithorn Co., n.d.

Farley and Loetscher Mfg. Co. *Farley and Loetscher Mfg. Co., General Catalog No. 9.* 2nd ed. (*Design Book No. 9, Farley and Loetscher Mfg. Co., Makers of Everything in Millwork.*) Dubuque, Iowa: Farley and Loetscher Mfg. Co., 1912.

Garry Iron and Steel Roofing Co. *Catalogue of Garry Iron and Steel Roofing Company.* Cleveland: Garry Iron and Steel Roofing Co., 1892.

General Electric Co. *Home Lighting Fundamentals.* Cleveland: General Electric Co., Nela Park Engineering Dept., May 1931.

George W. Blabon Co. *Blabon Art Linoleums, Styles for 1921.* Philadelphia: George W. Blabon Co., 1921.

Gernet Brothers. *Gernet Bros. Lumber Co.* Louisville, Ken.: Gernet Bros. Lumber Co., 1898.

Gordon-Van Tine Co. *Gordon-Van Tine Co.* Davenport, Iowa: Gordon-Van Tine Co., (ca. 1920).

————. *Grand Millwork, Catalog for Home Builders.* Davenport, Iowa: Gordon-Van Tine Co., spring 1911.

Robert Graves and Co. *The Robert-Graves-Co., Manufacturers of Fine Wall Papers and Decorations, Season of 1889.* New York: Robert Graves Co., 1888.

Harris Brothers Co. *Harris Brothers Co.* Chicago: Harris Brothers Co., 1926.

Harrison Bros & Co. *Harrison's "Town and Country" Ready Mixed Paints.* Philadelphia, 1877.

Hart, Bliven and Mead Manufacturing Co. *1876 Centennial Appendix to the Hart, Bliven and Mead Manufacturing Co.'s Catalogue of 1873.* New York: Hart, Bliven and Mead Manufacturing Co., 1876.

Home Builders Catalog Co. *Home Builders Catalog.* New York: Home Builders Catalog Co., 1925.

Huttig Brothers Mfg. Co. *Catalogue of Huttig Bros. Mfg. Co. Wholesale Manufacturers of Doors, Glazed Sash, Blinds . . . and Everything in the Line of Millwork in any Wood, Foreign or Domestic.* Muscatine, Iowa: Huttig Brothers Mfg. Co., 1900.

Joseph Hafner Mfg. Co. *The Jos. Hafner Mfg. Co. Combined Book of Sash, Doors, Blinds.* St. Louis: Joseph Hafner Mfg. Co., 1891.

Iron City Sanitary Manufacturing Co. *Iron City Enameled Plumbing Fixtures.* Pittsburgh: Iron City Sanitary Mfg. Co., 1924.

Kalamazoo Stove Co. *Stoves, Ranges and Furnaces.* Kalamazoo, MI: Kalamazoo Stove Co. 1933.

The Kawneer Company, *Kawneer Store Fronts*, Catalog M, A.I.A. File No. 26–b–1. Niles, Michigan, 1928.

Kimball Brothers Co. *Kimball Elevators.* Council Bluffs, Iowa: Kimball Brothers Co., (ca. 1921).

J. M. Kohler Sons Co. *Catalog, J. M. Kohler Sons Co.* Catalogue edition 7105. Sheboygan, Wisc: J. M. Kohler Sons Co., n.d.

Late Victorian Architectural Details. Combined Book of Sash, Doors, Blinds, Moldings, Chicago, 1898; reprint, Watkins Glen, N.Y.: American Life Foundation and Study Institute, 1978.

Louisiana Steam Sash, Blind and Door Factory. *Roberts and Co. Illustrated Catalogue of Moldings, Architectural and Ornamental Woodwork, Door, and Window Frames, Sash, Doors and Blinds.* New Orleans: Louisiana Steam Sash, Blind and Door Factory, 1891.

M. A. Disbrow and Co. *Book of Designs.* Lyons, Iowa: M. A. Disbrow and Co., 1891.

Macbeth-Evans Glass Co. *Fifty Years of Glass Making, 1869–1919.* Pittsburgh: Macbeth-Evans Glass Co., 1920.

Michigan Radiator and Iron Mfg. Co. *Michigan Radiator and Iron Mfg. Co.* Detroit: Michigan Radiator and Iron Mfg. Co., n.d.

Millwork Catalog No. 121. Fond Du Lac, Wis.: Moore and Galloway Lumber Co., 1900.

Millwork Supply Corp., *Millwork-Flooring.* Seattle: Millwork Supply Corp., ca.1930.

Montgomery Ward. *Wallpaper at Wholesale Prices—Newest Styles for 1910.* Chicago: Montgomery Ward and Co., 1910.

————. *Ward's Fine Non-Fading Wallpaper—Wallpaper Style Book for 1934.* Chicago: Montgomery Ward and Co., 1934.

Montgomery Ward and Co. *Coverall Paint, 1918.* Chicago: Montgomery Ward and Co., 1918.

Morgan Co. *The Door Beautiful.* 7th ed. Oshkosh, Wisc: Morgan Co., 1916.

Moran and Hastings Mfg. Co. *Moran and Hastings Mfg. Co., Catalogue No. 23, Gas Fixtures.* Chicago: Moran and Hastings Mfg. Co., n.d.

Morse and Co. *Catalogue for Carpenters and Builders.* Bangor, Maine: Morse and Co., n.d.

H. Mueller Manufacturing Co. *Mueller Water, Plumbing and Gas Brass Goods.* Catalog E. Decatur, Ill.: H. Mueller Mfg. Co., 1918.

National Lead Co. *Nuggets of Wisdom from an Old House Painter.* New York: National Lead Co., 1899.

National Lumber Manufacturers Assoc. *Modern Home Interiors.* Washington, D.C.: National Lumber Manufacturers Assoc., 1929.

N. O. Nelson Manufacturing Co. *"Nonco" Plumbing Fixtures.* 5th ed. St. Louis: N. O. Nelson Mfg. Co., 1928.

Niagara Blue Ribbon. *Gregory and Gregory.* Westfield, N.Y.: Niagara Blue Ribbon, (ca. 1925).

Perfection Stove Co. *Superflex Oil Burning Heaters.* Cleveland, Ohio: Perfection Stove Co., n.d.

Pittsburgh Plate Glass Co. *Easyset Store Fronts.* Pittsburgh: Pittsburgh Plate Glass Co., 1930.

———. *Glass, Paints, Varnishes and Brushes—Their History, Manufacture, and Use.* Pittsburgh: Pittsburgh Plate Glass Co., 1923.

———. *Vitrolite Fixtures. Furniture for Restaurants and Drug Stores.* Chicago: Vitrolite Co., 1927.

Reading Hardware Co. *Reading Hardware Company's Illustrated Catalog of Locks and Hardware.* Reading, Penn.: Reading Hardware Co., 1897.

Roach and Musser Sash and Door Co. *Stock-List Catalogue.* Muscatine, Iowa: Roach and Musser Sash and Door Co., 1908.

Roberts-Hamilton Co. *Rohaco Dealers Catalog and Simplified Price Book, Manufacturers of Plumbing, Heating and Electrical Supplies.* Minneapolis, Minn.: Roberts-Hamilton Co., April 1921.

Rundle-Spence Manufacturing Co. *Catalogue H—Rundle-Spence Mfg. Co., Producers of Supplies for Plumbers and Steam Fitters.* Milwaukee, Wisc: Rundle-Spence Mfg. Co., 1915.

Russell and Erwin Mfg. Co. *Illustrated Catalogue of American Hardware of the Russell and Erwin Manufacturing Company.* New Britain, Conn., 1865; reprint, (N.p.): Assoc. for Preservation Technology, 1980.

———. *"Russwin" Hardware for Doors, Garages and Windows.* New Britain, CT: 1927.

Yale and Towne Mfg. Co. *"Yale Products." Catalog No. 26.* Stamford, Conn.: Yale and Towne Mfg. Co., 1929.

St. Paul Roofing, Cornice and Ornament Co. *Section "O"—Steel Ceilings, Paneled and Continuous.* St. Paul, Minn.: St. Paul Roofing, Cornice and Ornament Co., 1904.

Sears, Roebuck and Co. *1897 Sears Roebuck Catalogue.* General Catalog. Chicago, 1897; reprint, New York: Chelsea House Publishers, 1968.

———. *A Book of Wall Paper Samples from Sears Roebuck & Co.* Chicago: Sears, Roebuck and Co., (ca. 1906).

———. *Builder's Supplies.* Chicago: Sears, Roebuck and Co., 1900.

———. *Building Material and Millwork.* Chicago: Sears, Roebuck and Co., (ca. 1918).

———. *Building Material and Millwork.* Chicago: Sears, Roebuck and Co., 1925.

———. *High Grade Wallpapers.* Chicago: Sears, Roebuck and Co., (ca. 1902).

———. *High Grade Wall Papers, Season 1915.* Chicago: Sears, Roebuck and Co., 1915.

———. *Honor Built Building Materials.* Chicago: Sears, Roebuck and Co., 1931.

———. *Master-Art Wall Papers—Wall Paper Samples, Season 1928.* Philadelphia: Sears, Roebuck and Co., 1928.

———. *Sears Building Materials.* Philadelphia: Sears, Roebuck and Co., 1936.

———. *The Sears, Roebuck Catalogue.* General Catalog. Chicago, 1902; reprint, New York: Crown Publishers, 1969.

———. *Sears, Roebuck and Co. Catalogue, No. 140.* General Catalog. Chicago: Sears, Roebuck and Co., Spring 1920.

———. *Wallpaper, Certified Fadeproof, New Styles for 1932.* Chicago: Sears, Roebuck and Co., 1932.

———. *Washable, Fadeproof Wallpaper.* Chicago: Sears, Roebuck and Co., 1935.

Sherwin-Williams Co. *The Home Painting Manual.* Cleveland: Sherwin-Williams Co., 1922.

Smith and Wyman. *Price List, Smith and Wyman, Sash, Doors, Blinds.* Minneapolis, Minn.: Smith and Wyman, January 21, 1884.

Southern Hardwood Producers. *Southern Hardwood Interiors.* Southern Hardwood Information Series, No. 3. Memphis, Tenn.: Southern Hardwood Producers, 1937.

Standard Sanitary Manufacturing Co. *Color and Style in Bathroom Furnishing and Decoration.* Pittsburgh: Standard Sanitary Mfg. Co., 1929.

———. *"Standard" Plumbing Fixtures for the Home.* Pittsburgh: Standard Sanitary Mfg Co. 1925.

"Sweet's" Indexed Catalogue of Building Construction. New York: Architectural Record Co., 1906.

Richard E. Thibaut. *Thibaut's Art Wallpapers.* New York: Richard E. Thibaut, 1900.

Toch Brothers. *The "R.I.W." Book.* Long Island City, N.Y.: Toch Brothers, 1908.

Henry R. Towne. *Locks and Builders Hardware.* New York: John Wiley and Sons, 1904.

Tyler Co. *Elevator Cars.* Chicago: W. S. Tyler Co., 1932.

Waite, Diana S., ed. *Architectural Elements, The Technological Review.* The American Historical Catalog Collection. Princeton, N.J.: Pyne Press, 1972.

Weil-McLain Co. *Weil Plumbing Fixtures, Catalogue C.* Chicago: Weil-McLain Co., 1920.

M. Winter Lumber Co. *Winter's Catalogue No. 87, Commercial Furniture.* Sheboygan, Wisc.: M. Winter Lumber Co., 1910.

Wholesale Sash, Door and Blind Manufacturer's Assoc. of the Northwest and the General Sash and Door Assoc. *Universal Millwork Design Book No. 20.* Dubuque, Iowa: Universal Catalogue Bureau, 1920.

———. *The Victorian Design Book. Universal Design Book,* Oct. 15, 1903; reprint, Ottawa, Ontario: Lee Valley Tools, 1984.

W. O. Dresser. *Artistic Wallpapers.* Tonopah, Nev.: W. O. Dresser, 1922.

Serials

Aladdin's Magazine; (*Aladdin's Weekly*). Bay City, Mich.; before 1917–21?

American Builder; (*American Carpenter and Builder*). Chicago; 1905–69.

American Gas-Light Journal and Chemical Repertory. New York: before 1871?

American Homes and Gardens. New York; 1905–15.

The Architect, Builder and Decorator; (*Northwestern Builder, Decorator and Furnisher; Northwestern Builder and Decorator; Builder and Decorator*). Minneapolis, Minn.; 1882–95.

Beautiful Homes. St. Louis; 1908–10.

Beautiful Homes Magazine; (*Homebuilder; Keith's Home-Builder; Keith's Magazine on Home Building; Keith's Beautiful Homes Magazine*). Minneapolis, Minn.; 1899–1931.

Building Age; (*Carpentry and Building*). New York; 1879–1930.

Building Systems Design; (*Heating and Ventilating Magazine; Heating and Ventilating; Air Conditioning, Heating and Ventilating*). New York; 1904–79.

The Cement Age. New York; 1904–12.

Concrete; (*Concrete-Cement Age*). Detroit; 1904–12.

The Craftsman. Eastwood, N.Y.; 1901–16.

Creative Designs in Home Furnishings. (*Creative Design*). New York; 1934–39.

Curtis Service. Clinton, Iowa; 1913–15?

Edison Electric Light Company Bulletin. New York; 1882–84.

Edison Monthly. New York; 1908–28.

E.E.I. Bulletin; (*Edison Electric Institute Bulletin*). Philadelphia; 1933–74.

General Electric Company; (*Edison Lamp Works*). Harrison, N.J.; 1911–18?

Home Decoration. New York; 1886–89.

Home Improvements. Chicago; 1936–39?

House Beautiful. Chicago; 1896–current.

House and Garden. Greenwich, Conn.; 1901–current.

Ladies Home Journal; (*Ladies Home Journal and Practical Housekeeper*). Philadelphia; 1883–current.

The Millwork Magazine. Louisville, Ken: 1909–10.

Modern Home Builder. Racine, Wisc.; 1902–?

Modern Paint and Coatings. New York; 1911–74.

Rock Products. Louisville, Ken.; 1902–current.

ROHACO Price Bulletin. Minneapolis, Minn.; 1919–?

Your Home; (*Own Your Own Home*). Dunellen, N.J.; 1925–31.

Plan Books

Aladdin Co. *Aladdin Homes, Built in a Day, Catalog 31, 1919*. Bay City, Mich., 1918; reprint, Watkins Glen, N.Y.: American Life Foundation, 1985.

———. *Alladin Plan of Industrial Housing*. Bay City, Mich.: Aladdin Co., 1920.

———. *Aladdin Readi-Cut Houses*. Catalog No. 43. Bay City, Mich.: Aladdin Co., 1929.

———. *Aladdin Readi-Cut Homes*. Catalog No. 49. Bay City, Mich.: Aladdin Co., 1937.

All American Homes. Los Angeles: E. W. Stillwell and Co., 1927.

America's Best Small Houses. Ed. William J. Hennessey, New York: Viking Press, 1949.

Allen, Lewis F. *Rural Architecture*. NY: Saxton, 1960.

Architectural Designs Issued by the T. W. Harvey Lumber Co. Chicago: T. W. Harvey Lumber Co., 1889.

Better Built Homes, Volume VI. Clinton, Iowa: Curtis Companies, Inc., 1921.

Better Built Homes, Volume VII. Clinton, Iowa: Curtis Companies, Inc., 1920.

Bicknell's Village Builder and Supplement. 1872; Reprint Watkins Glen, N.Y.: The American Life Foundation and Study Institute, 1976.

Blodgett and Osgood. *Ready-Made Houses*. St. Paul, Minn.: Blodgett and Osgood, (ca. 1890).

The Book of Bungalows. St. Paul, Minnesota. Home Plan Book Company, 1941.

Book of Homes. Gordon-Van Tine Co. Davenport, Iowa: Gordon-Van Tine Co. ca.1932.

Brown-Blodgett Co. *The Book of 100 Homes, Book C*. (*Hayes-Lucas Lumber Co.*) St. Paul, Minn.: Brown-Blodgett Co., 1936.

The Building Brick Association of America. *One Hundred Bungalows*. Boston: Rogers and Manson, 1912.

Bungalowcraft: New English Bungalows. Los Angeles: The Bungalowcraft Co., 1930.

Cement Houses and Private Garages with Constructive Details. Building Age Series, No. 5. New York: David Williams Co., 1912.

Chicago and Riverdale Lumber Co. *Small House Plan Book Series #500*. Chicago: Chicago and Riverdale Lumber Co. c.1910.

Chicago House Wrecking Co. *A Book of Plans*. No. 54. Chicago: Chicago House Wrecking Co., 1909.

Child, Edward S. *Colonial Houses for Modern Homes, A Collection of Sketches, Perspectives and Plans for Modern Houses with Colonial Details*. New York: E.S. Child, 190?.

Colorful Homes. Elmhurst, Illinois: National Plan Service, n.d.

Comstock, William Phillips. *Bungalows, Camps and Mountain Houses*. New York: The William T. Comstock Co., 1908.

Contractors and Builders Book of Attractive Small Homes. Waterloo, Iowa: C.W. Hutton & Son. 1930.

Cornell Portable Houses. Ithaca, New York: Wyckoff Lumber & Manufacturing Company, 1906.

Cosy Bungalows Picturing 10 Bungalows with Floor Plans for People in That Part of the Country. Los Angeles: Trimlett and Combellick, c.1920.

Curtis Companies. *Better Built Homes, Volume 16*. 2nd ed. Clinton, Iowa: Curtis Companies, 1923.

E. F. Hodgson Co. *Hodgson Houses*. Boston: E. F. Hodgson Co., 1935.

Ellis, Mary Heard, and Raymond Everett. *The Planning of Simple Homes*. Austin: University of Texas, 1916.

Embury, Aymar II. *The Dutch Colonial House*. New York: McBride, Nast and Co., 1913.

For Home Lovers. Washington, D.C.: National Lumber Manufacturers Association, 1929.

Gibson, Louis H. *Convenient Houses with Fifty Plans for the Housekeeper*. New York: Thomas Y. Crowell and Co., 1889.

Gordon-Van Tine. *Gordon-Van Tine Co., Architectural Details, 1915*. Davenport, Iowa, 1915; reprint, Watkins Glen, N.Y.: American Life Foundation, 1985.

———. *Book of Homes*. Davenport, Iowa. Gordon Van-Tine Co. 1932.

———. *Gordon-Van Tine's Grand Book of Plans for Everybody*. Davenport, Iowa: Gordon-Van Tine Co., n.d.

Gowing, Frederick H. *Building Plans for Bungalows, Cottages and Other Medium Cost Homes*. Boston: Frederick H. Gowing, 1922.

Harris Brothers Co. *A Plan Book of Harris Homes, Edition No. 73*. Chicago: Harris Brothers Co., 1917.

Hinkle and Co. *Hinkle and Co.'s New Book on Building*. Cincinnati, Ohio: Hinkle and Co., 1869.

Holly, Henry Hudson. *Modern Dwellings in Town and Country*. New York: Harper and Brothers, 1878.

Home Plans. Madison, Wis.: Marling Lumber Co., 1925.

Homes As New As Tomorrow. Greta, Louisiana, Ideal Plan Service, c. 1940s.

Homes for Workmen. New Orleans: Southern Pine Association, 1919.

Homes of Today. Chicago: Sears, Roebuck and Co., 1931.

House Plans Design for Southern Families. Birmingham, Alabama: Oxmoor House, Progressive Farmer Co. 1973.

Keith's Plan Book Inexpensive Homes. Minneapolis: Keith Corporation, 1928.

Keith's Twenty Wonder Houses. Minneapolis: M. L. Keith, n.d.

Lent, Frank T. *Sound Sense in Suburban Architecture*. New York: W. T. Comstock, 1895.

Lindstrom, J. W. *Bungalows*. Minneapolis: J. W. Lindstrom, 1922.

———. *Cottages and Semi-Bungalows*. Minneapolis: J. W. Lindstrom, 1922.

———. *Two Story Homes*. Minneapolis: J. W. Lindstrom, 1922.

Low-Cost Houses with Constructive Details. Carpentry and Building Series, No. 2. New York: David Williams Co., 1907.

Modern Architectural Designs and Details. William T. Comstock Co. 1881.

Modern Dwellings with Constructive Details. Carpentry and Building Series, No. 3. New York: David Williams Co., 1907.

Modern Homes. New Orleans: Southern Pine Association, 1921.

Our New Book of Summer Camps and Lodges. Worcester, Mass, W.H. Sawyer Lumber Company, n.d.

Our New Book of Summer Homes. New York, New York: Building Age Publishing Company, 1930

Palliser's Model Homes. 1878; rpt. Felton, Calif.: Glenwood Publishers, 1972.

Pedersen, Jens. *Practical Homes*. St. Paul: Brown, Blodgett and Sperry Co., 1922.

Peker, Charles. *How to Read Plans*. NY: Industrial Publication Co. 1908.

Pennsylvania School Architecture. Thomas Henry Burrowes, Ed. Harrisburg: Hamilton Co. 1855.

Pollman, Richard B. *Designs for Convenient Living*. Detroit: Home Planners, Inc. 1948.

Pollman, Richard B. and Irving E. Palmquist. *Home Planners Designs for Convenient Living*, Book No. 51, Detroit: Home Planners Inc. ca. 1960.

Portland Cement Assoc. *Portland Cement Stucco*. Chicago: Portland Cement Assoc., (ca. 1925).

Radford's Stores and Flat Buildings, Illustrating the Latest and Most Improved Ideas in Small Bank Buildings, Store Buildings, Double or Twin Houses, Two, Four, Six and Nine Flat Buildings. Chicago: Radford Architectural Co. 1909.

———. *The Radford American Homes.100 House Plans*. Riverside, IL: The Radford Architectural Co. 1903.

Rural Architecture. Minneapolis, Minn.: Adams-Herr Co., 1884.

Sample Pages Taken at Random from the 98 Page Catalogue of Architectural Plans for Churches and Parsonages Furnished by the Board of Church Extension of the M.E. Church. Philadelphia: Benjamin Price & Co. 1887.

Saxton, Glen L. *The Plan Book of American Dwellings*. Minneapolis: Glen L. Saxton, 1914.

Sawyer Plan Service. W.H. Sawyer Lumber Co. Worcester: Mass. ca. 1930.

Saylor, Henry H. *Bungalows*. 2nd Ed. New York: McBride, Nast and Co., 1913.

Schumacher, W. H. *A New Book of Distinctive Houses*. Oklahoma City: Distinctive Books Publishers, 1938.

Sears, Roebuck and Co. *Book of Modern Homes and Building Plans*. 1st ed. Chicago: Sears, Roebuck and Co., (ca. 1908).

———. *Book of Modern Homes*. Chicago: Sears, Roebuck and Co., (ca. 1911).

———. *Electric, Gas and Combination Light Fixtures*. Chicago: Sears, Roebuck and Co. 1921.

———. *Honor Built Modern Homes*. Chicago: Sears, Roebuck and Co., (ca. 1921).

———. *Honor Built Modern Homes: Leading Eastern and Western Designs of Bungalows, Houses, Cottages, Flat-Buildings, Farm-Houses and Farm-Buildings*. Chicago: Sears, Roebuck and Co., (ca. 1917).

———. *Homes of Today*. Chicago: Sears, Roebuck and Co., 1931.

Shopell, Robert W. *How to Build, Furnish, and Decorate*. New York: Cooperative Building Plan Association, 1883.

Stickley, Gustav. *Craftsman Homes*. New York: The Craftsman Publishing Co., 1909.

———. *More Craftsman Homes*. New York: The Craftsman Publishing Co., 1912.

Southern Pine Assoc. *Homes for Workmen: A Presentation of Leading Examples of Industrial Community Development*. New Orleans: Southern Pine Association, 1919.

Standardized Housing Corporation. *The Manufacture of Standardized Houses. A New Industry*. NY: Standardized Housing Corp. *1917*.

Suburban Homes with Constructive Details. Building Age Series, No. 4. New York: David Williams Co., 1912.

Summer Cottages. Kansas City, Missouri: Exchange Sawmills Sales Company, n.d.

Summer Homes and Lodges. Elmhurst, Illinois. National Plan Service, 1932.

Sunset Western Ranch Houses. Editors, Sunset Magazine. San Francisco: Lane Publishing, 1950.

Two-Family and Twin Houses. New York: William T. Comstock, 1908.

Victorian Architecture. Reprint of A. J. Bicknell, *Detail, Cottage and Constructive Architecture*, 1873, and William T. Comstock, *Modern Architectural Designs and Details*, 1881. Watkins Glenn, N.Y.: The American Life Foundation and Study Institute, 1979.

Von Holst, Hermann Valentin. *Modern American Homes*. Chicago: American School of Correspondence, 1913

West Coast Lumbermen's Assoc. *Distinctive Homes of Red Cedar Shingles*. Seattle: West Coast Lumbermen's Assoc., (ca. 1910).

Today's Idea House. Chicago, IL: Ponderosa Pine Woodwork, 1945.

Whitehead, Russell F. *Good Houses: Typical Historic Architectural Styles for Modern Wood-Built Homes*. St. Paul: Weyerhouser Forest Products, 1922.

Wills, Royal Barry. *Houses for Good Living*. New York: Architectural Book Publishing Co. 1946.

Wooden and Brick Buildings with Details. New York: A. J. Bicknell and Co., 1875.

Extension Service, Government, and University Bulletins

Bailey, L. H. "Tasteful Farm Buildings." *Cornell Reading Course for Farmers*, Series VI, No. 26. Ithaca, N.Y.: College of Agriculture of Cornell University, Nov. 1905.

Bane, Geneva M., and H. P. Twitchell. *Just Kitchens*. Extension Bulletin, Vol. 20, No. 2. Columbus, Ohio: Agricultural Extension Service, Ohio State University, 1924–25.

———. *Just Kitchens*. Bulletin No. 66. Columbus, Ohio: Ohio State University Agriculture Extension Service, (Oct. 1927).

Barrows, Effie S. *Rural Kitchen Improvement*. Extension Service New Series, Circular No. 9. Logan, Utah: Extension Service, Utah Agricultural College, April 1928.

Conway, Mary Geneva. *Make the Farm Kitchen Convenient*. Publication 71. Knoxville, Tenn.: Division of Extension, College of Agriculture, University of Tennessee, Aug. 1918.

"Decoration in the Farm Home." *Cornell Reading—Course for Farmers' Wives*, Series I, No. 2. Ithaca, N.Y.: College of Agriculture of Cornell University, Dec. 1902.

Etherton, W. A. *Inexpensive Plumbing for Farm Kitchens.* Extension Bulletin No. 9. Manhattan, Kan.: Kansas State Agricultural College, Division of College Extension, April 1916.

Fenton, F. C., and H. E. Stover. *Farm Lighting.* Extension Bulletin 64. Manhattan, Kansas: Kansas State Agricultural College, Extension Service, June 1929.

———. *Wiring the Farmstead.* Extension Bulletin 63, revised. Manhattan, Kansas: Kansas State College of Agriculture and Applied Science, Extension Service, May 1938.

Frazier, F. F. *Sewage Disposal for Country Homes.* Extension Bulletin No. 6. Manhattan, Kansas: Kansas State Agricultural College, Division of College Extension, March 1916.

Gettemy, Winifred S. *Home Furnishing.* Extension Bulletin No. 17. Ames, Iowa: Iowa State College of Agriculture and the Mechanic Arts, Dec. 1913.

Goeppinger, Helen. "Walls and Wall Treatments." *Home Information,* Bulletin No. 8. Lafayette, Ind.: Better Homes in America, Purdue University, April 1936.

"Good Lighting in Houses." *Home Information,* Vol. 2, No. 30. Lafayette, Ind.: Better Homes in America, Purdue University, June 1937.

Hoffman, Gertrude. *The Kitchen.* No. 75. Bozeman, Mont.: Montana Extension Service in Agriculture and Home Economics, Montana State College, Aug. 1925.

Holman, Araminta. *Art Applied in Home Furnishing and Decorating.* Extension Bulletin 43. Manhattan, Kan.: Extension Service, Kansas State Agricultural College, June 1923.

Keller, Lillian L. *The Country Home of Good Taste.* Publication 183. Knoxville, Tenn.: Agricultural Extension Service, University of Tennessee, Feb. 1934.

———. *The Living Room that is Livable.* Publication 134. Knoxville, Tenn.: Tennessee Extension Service, University of Tennessee, Dec. 1925.

———. *The Well Planned Kitchen.* Publication 202. Knoxville, Tenn.: College of Agriculture, University of Tennessee, Feb. 1937.

———, and M. M. Johns. *Farm Home Electrification.* Publication 198. Knoxville, Tenn.: Tennessee College of Agriculture, University of Tennessee, Feb. 1937.

Long, Marian. "Interior Decoration." *College Bulletin,* No. 78. Denton, Tex.: College of Industrial Arts, June 1, 1920.

Lynn, Gertrude. *The Step Saving Kitchen.* Home Economics Bulletin No. 47. Ames, Iowa: Iowa State College of Agriculture and Mechanic Arts, Extension Service, June 1924.

Martin, Clarence A. "The Plan of the Farmhouse." *Cornell Reading—Course for Farmers,* Series VI, No. 28. Ithaca, N.Y.: College of Agriculture of Cornell University, Jan. 1906.

"A Month of Education Study." *Cornell Reading—Course for Farmers' Wives,* Series VI, No. 27. Ithaca, N.Y.: New York State College of Agriculture at Cornell University, Jan. 1908.

Osmund, I. Thornton. *The Lighting of Farm Houses.* Bulletin No. 103. College Park, Penn.: Pennsylvania State College Agricultural Experiment Station, Sept. 1910.

Planning and Equipping the Kitchen. Home Economics Bulletin No. 8. Ames, Iowa: Iowa State College of Agriculture and Mechanic Arts, Extension Service, reprint Aug. 1923.

"Planning the Electrical Installation for Greatest Use." *Home Information,* Vol. 2, No. 29. Lafayette, Ind.: Better Homes in America, Purdue University, May 1937.

Pond, Julia, and Evelyn Turner. *Household Closets and Storage Spaces.* Extension Bulletin No. 142. East Lansing, Mich.: Extension Division, Michigan State College of Agriculture and Applied Science, Dec. 1934.

Reis, Gertrude. *Color in Home Decoration.* Extension Bulletin No. 169. East Lansing, Mich.: Extension Division, Michigan State College, Nov. 1936.

Richardson, Elsie. *Artistic Windows.* Home Economics Bulletin No. 73. Ames, Iowa: Iowa State College of Agriculture and Mechanic Arts, 2nd reprint, Aug. 1927.

———. *Color and Design in the Home.* Home Furnishing Booklets. Ames, Iowa: Iowa State College Extension Service, June 1928.

———. *Floor Coverings.* Home Economics Bulletin No. 87. Ames, Iowa: Iowa State College of Agriculture and Mechanic Arts, Extension Service, Dec. 1925.

———. *Furnishing the Home.* Home Economics Bulletin No. 42. Ames, Iowa: Iowa State College of Agriculture and Mechanic Arts, Extension Service, April 1924.

Scott, Helen. *Home Decoration.* Extension Bulletin, Vol. IX, No. 10. Columbus, Ohio: Agricultural College, Ohio State University, June 1914.

Smith, L. J., Rudolph Weaver, and M. Minerva Lawrence. *Convenient Farm Homes.* Bulletin No. 91. Pullman, Wash.: Extension Service, State College of Washington, Sept. 1922.

Suggestions for Rural Housing Planning. Bulletin No. 102. Bozeman, Mont.: Extension Service, Montana State College, June 1929.

Ulmer, C. Paul. "Description and Cost Analysis of a House Built of Reinforced Concrete: House No. 3, Purdue Housing Research Project." *Home Information,* Vol. 1, No. 23 and 24. Lafayette, Ind.: Better Homes in America, Purdue University, Dec. 1936.

Walters, John Daniel. *The Water Supply of the Farmhouse.* Extension Bulletin No. 10. Manhattan, Kan.: Kansas State Agricultural College, Division of College Extension, April 1916.

Ward, Walter G. *Farm Buildings for Kansas.* Extension Bulletin No. 50. Manhattan, Kan.: Extension Service, Kansas State Agricultural College, Jan. 1925.

Wilder, Susan Z. *New Wall Finishes.* Circular 231. Brookings, S.D.: Extension Service, South Dakota State College of Agriculture and Mechanical Arts, Nov. 1925.

———. *Planning the Living Room.* Extension Circular 228. Brookings, S.D.: Extension Service, South Dakota State College of Agriculture and Mechanical Arts, Aug. 1925.

Wilson, Elmira T. *Modern Conveniences for the Farm Home.* Farmer's Bulletin No. 270. Washington, D.C.: U.S. Dept. of Agriculture, 1906.

Young, Helen Binkerd. "The Arrangement of Household Furnishings." *Cornell Reading—Courses,* Vol. IV, No. 85, Farmhouse Series No. 7. Ithaca, N.Y.: New York State College of Agriculture at Cornell University, April 1, 1915.

———. "The Farmhouse." *Cornell Reading—Courses Lesson for the Farm Home,* Vol. II, No. 39, Farmhouse Series No. 6. Ithaca, N.Y.: Cornell University, May 1, 1913.

———. "Household Decoration." *Cornell Reading—Courses Lesson for the Farm Home,* Vol. I, No. 5, Farm House Series No. 1. Ithaca, N.Y.: New York State College of Agriculture at Cornell University, Dec. 1, 1911.

———. "Household Furnishing." *Cornell Reading—Courses for the Farm Home,* Vol. I, No. 7, Farm House Series No. 2. Ithaca, N.Y.: New York State College of Agriculture at Cornell University, Jan. 1, 1912.

———. "Planning the Home Kitchen." *Cornell Reading—Courses for the Farm Home*, Farmhouse Series, Lesson 108. Ithaca, N.Y.: New York State College of Agriculture at Cornell University, July 1916.

Handbooks and Dictionaries

The Architects' and Builders' Reference Book. Chicago: Oscar M. Smith and Co., 1889.

Blackburn, Graham. *Illustrated Interior Carpentry*. Indianapolis, Ind.: Bobbs-Merrill Co., 1978.

Blumenson, John J. -G. *Identifying American Architecture*. Nashville: American Association for State and Local History, 1977.

Burbank, Nelson L. *Carpentry and Joinery Work*. New York: American Builder Publishing Corp., 1936.

Burke, Arthur E., J. Ralph Dalzell, and Gilbert Townsend. *Architectural and Building Trades Dictionary*. Chicago: American Technical Society, 1950.

Carpenter, J. H. *Hints on Building*. Hartford, Conn.: Case, Lockwood, and Brainard Co., 1883.

The Complete House Builder with Hints on Building. Chicago: Donohue, Henneberry and Co., 1890.

Corkhill, Thomas. *A Glossary of Wood*. London: Nema Press, 1948.

Ellis, George. *Modern Practical Carpentry*. 2nd ed. London: B. T. Batsford, 1915.

———. *Modern Practical Joinery*. London: B. T. Batsford, 1908.

Fleming, John, Hugh Honor, and Nikolaus Pevsner. *The Penguin Dictionary of Architecture*. Baltimore: Penguin Books, 1966.

Foley, Mary Mix. *The American House*. New York: Harper Colophon Books, 1980.

Gwilt, Joseph. *Encyclopedia of Architecture*. Aberdeen: Aberdeen University Press, 1912.

Hammett, Ralph W. *Architecture in the United States*. New York: John Wiley and Sons, 1976.

Harris, Cyril M., ed. *Dictionary of Architecture and Construction*. New York: McGraw-Hill Book Co., 1975.

———. *Historic Architecture Sourcebook*. New York: McGraw-Hill Book Co., 1977.

Hodgson, Fred T. *The Carpenter's Cyclopedia*. For Sears, Roebuck and Co. Chicago: Frederick J. Drake, 1913.

———. *Common-Sense Stair Building and Handrailing*. (*Common Sense Hand-Railing, Modern Staircases*.) Chicago: Frederick J. Drake and Co., 1903.

Jacques, Daniel Harrison. *The House: A Pocket Manual of Rural Architecture: Or, How to Build Country Houses and Outbuildings*. NY: Fowler and Wells, 1859.

Kidder, Frank E., and Harry Parker. *Kidder-Parker Architects' and Builders' Handbook*. 18th ed. New York: John Wiley and Sons, 1942.

Lloyd, William B. *Millwork: Principles and Practices*. Chicago: Cahners Publishing Co. and The National Woodwork Manufacturers Assoc., 1966.

Moss, Roger. *Century of Color, 1820–1920*. Watkins Glenn, N. Y.: The American Life Foundation and Study Institute, 1981.

Quin, Charles, W. *The Complete House Builder with Hints on Building*. Chicago: M. A. Donohue, 1904.

Radford, William A. *Practical Carpentry*. Vol. II. For Sears, Roebuck and Co. Chicago: Radford Architectural Co., 1907.

———. *The Steel Square and Its Uses*. Vols. I and II. For Sears, Roebuck and Co. Chicago: Radford Architectural Co., 1913.

Rifkind, Carole. *A Field Guide to American Architecture*. New York: New American Library, 1980.

Saylor, Henry H. *Dictionary of Architecture*. New York: John Wiley and Sons, 1952.

Scott, John S. *The Penguin Dictionary of Building*. New York: Penguin Books, 1964.

Sturgis, Russell. *A Dictionary of Architecture and Building*. New York: Macmillan Co., 1902.

Sylvester, W. A. *The Modern House-Carpenter's Companion and Builder's Guide*. Subscription ed., 7th Thousand. Boston: W. A. Sylvester, 1883.

Walker, Lester. *American Shelter*. Woodstock, N. Y.: Overlook Press, 1981.

Whiffen, Marcus. *American Architecture since 1780*. Cambridge, Mass.: M.I.T. Press, 1969.

Whiton, Sherrill. *Elements of Interior Design and Decoration*. Philadelphia: J. B. Lippincott Co., 1951.

Historic Preservation Surveys and Rehabilitation Guides

The Buildings of Biloxi: An Architectural Survey. Biloxi, Miss.: City of Biloxi, 1976.

Bunting, Bainbridge, and Robert H. Nylander. *Report Four: Old Cambridge*. Survey of Architectural History in Cambridge. Cambridge, Mass.: Cambridge Historical Commission, 1973.

The Burlington Book. By the Historic Preservation Program, Department of History, University of Vermont. Burlington, Vt.: University of Vermont Historic Preservation Program, 1980.

Charles City, Iowa: A Historic Inventory. Charles City, Iowa: City of Charles City, 1976.

Cheyenne Landmarks. Cheyenne, WY: Laramie County Chapter, Wyoming State Historical Society, 1976.

Downing, Antoinette F., Elisabeth MacDougall, and Eleanor Pearson. *Report Two: Mid-Cambridge*. Survey of Architectural History in Cambridge. Cambridge, Mass.: Cambridge Historical Commission, 1967.

Early Cheyenne Homes: 1880–1890. Cheyenne, WY: Laramie County Chapter, Wyoming State Historical Society, 1975.

Field Guide to Historic Sites Survey in South Dakota. Vermillion, S. Dak.: Historical Preservation Center, 1982.

Gebhard, David, et al. *A Guide to Architecture in San Francisco and Northern California*. 2nd ed. Santa Barbara: Peregrine Smith, Inc., 1973.

Goeldner, Paul. *Utah Catalog—Historic American Buildings Survey*. Salt Lake City: Utah Heritage Foundation, 1969.

Goins, Charles R., and John W. Morris. *Oklahoma Homes Past and Present*. Norman, Okla.: University of Oklahoma Press, 1980.

Heimsath, Clovis. *Pioneer Texas Buildings: A Geometry Lesson*. Austin: University of Texas Press, 1968.

Henderson, Arn, Frank Parman, and Dortha Henderson. *Architecture in Oklahoma: Landmark & Vernacular*. Norman, Okla.: Point Riders Press, 1978.

Heritage Preservation Associates, Inc. *Building Kenosha*. Kenosha, Wis.: City of Kenosha, Department of Community Development, 1982.

———. *Historic Janesville: An Architectural History of Janesville, Wisconsin*. Janesville, Wis.: City of Janesville, Department of Community Development, 1982.

Hoffstot, Barbara D. *Landmark Architecture of Palm Beach.* Pittsburgh: Ober Park Associates, Inc., 1980.

Howard, Cynthia. *Your House in the Streetcar Suburb.* Medford, Mass.: City of Medford Department of Community Development, 1979.

Indianapolis Architecture. Indianapolis: Indiana Architectural Foundation, 1975.

Krim, Arthur J. *Report Five: Northwest Cambridge.* Survey of Architectural History in Cambridge. Cambridge, Mass.: Cambridge Historical Commission, 1977.

Lafore, Laurence. *American Classic.* Iowa City: Iowa State Historical Department, 1975.

Legner, Linda. *City House: A Guide to Renovating Older Chicago-Area Houses.* Chicago: Commission on Chicago Historical and Architectural Landmarks, 1979.

Linley, John. *Architecture of Middle Georgia.* Athens, Ga.: University of Georgia Press, 1972.

Nineteenth Century Houses in Lawrence, Kansas. Lawrence: University of Kansas Museum of Art, 1968.

Omaha City Architecture. Omaha, Nebr.: Landmarks, Inc., and the Junior League of Omaha, Inc., 1977.

Pearson, Arnold, and Esther Pearson. *Early Churches of Washington State.* Seattle: University of Washington Press, 1980.

Peat, Wilbur D. *Indiana Houses of the Nineteenth Century.* Indianapolis: Indiana Historical Society, 1962.

Pitts, Carolyn, Michael Fish, Hugh J. McCauley, and Trina Vaux. *The Cape May Handbook.* Philadelphia: The Athanaeum of Philadelphia, 1977.

Preservation Guidelines. Trenton, N.J.: City of Trenton Department of Housing, 1979.

Preserving Waukesha's Past. Waukesha, Wis.: City of Waukesha, 1982.

Proctor, Mary, and Bill Matuszeski. *Gritty Cities.* Philadelphia: Temple University Press, 1978.

Rehab Right: How to Rehabilitate Your Oakland House without Sacrificing Architectural Assets. Oakland, Calif.: City of Oakland Planning Department, 1978.

Reiff, Daniel D. *Architecture in Fredonia, 1811–1972.* Fredonia, N. Y.: The Michael C. Rockefeller Arts Center Gallery and State University College, 1972.

Report Three: Cambridgeport. Survey of Architectural History in Cambridge. Cambridge, Mass.: Cambridge Historical Commission, 1971.

Saint Anthony Falls Rediscovered. Minneapolis: Minneapolis Riverfront Development Coordination Board, 1980.

Schwartz, Helen. *The New Jersey House.* New Brunswick, N. J.: Rutgers University Press, 1983.

Shank, Wesley I. *The Iowa Catalog: Historic American Buildings Survey.* Iowa City: University of Iowa Press, 1979.

Sherwood, Bruce T., Ed. *On the Mountain, in the Valley: Catskills Architecture, 1750–1920.* Hobart, N. Y.: The Catskill Center for Conservation and Development, Inc., 1977.

Shivers, Natalie. *Those Old Placid Rows.* Baltimore: Maclay and Associates, 1981.

The Shotgun House. Louisville: Preservation Alliance of Louisville and Jefferson County, Inc., 1980.

Sommer, Lawrence J. *The Heritage of Dubuque.* Dubuque, Iowa: The First National Bank of Dubuque, 1975.

Stoehr, C. Eric. *Bonanza Victorian.* Albuquerque: University of New Mexico Press, 1975.

Thomas, George E., and Carl Doebley. *Cape May, Queen of the Seaside Resorts.* Philadelphia: The Art Alliance Press, 1976.

Tulsa Art Deco: An Architectural Era, 1925–1942. Tulsa, Okla.: The Junior League of Tulsa, Inc., 1980.

Wilson, Richard Guy, and Sidney K. Robinson. *The Prairie School in Iowa.* Ames, Iowa: The Iowa State University Press, 1977.

Woodbridge, Sally B., and Roger Montgomery. *A Guide to Architecture in Washington State.* Seattle: University of Washington Press, 1980.

Books

Adler, Hazel H. *The New Interior.* New York: Century Co., 1916.

Architectural Interiors. Scranton, Pa.: International Textbook Co., 1931.

Bevier, Isabel. *The House: Its Plan, Decoration and Care.* Chicago: American School of Home Economics, 1907.

Borchert, James. *Alley Life In Washington: Family, Community, Religion and Folklife in the City, 1850-1970.* Urbana: University of Illinois Press, 1980.

Brabham, Moklson William. *Planning Modern Church Buildings.* Nashville: Cokesbury Press, 1928.

Bronner, Simon J., ed. *Consuming Visions: Accumulation and Display of Goods in America, 1880-1920.* New York: W.W. Norton, 1989.

Bruce, Alfred, and Harold Sandbank. *A History of Prefabrication.* Research Study 3. New York: John B. Pierce Foundation, 1944.

Brunner, Arnold W., and Thomas Tryon. *Interior Decoration.* New York: W. T. Comstock, 1887.

Burbank, Nelson L. and Oscar Shaftel. *House Construction Details.* 5th edition. New York: Simmons-Boardman Publishing Corp. 1959.

Caldwell, Frank C. *Modern Lighting.* New York: Macmillan Co., 1930.

Child, Georgie Boynton. *The Efficient Kitchen.* New York: McBride, Nast and Co., 1914.

———. *The Efficient Kitchen.* New York: Robert M. McBride, 1925.

Clute, Eugene. *The Treatment of Interiors.* New York: Pencil Points Press, 1926.

Coleman, Oliver. *Successful Houses.* Chicago: Herbert S. Stone and Co., 1899.

———. *Successful Houses.* New York: Fox Duffield and Co., 1906.

The Cost of Making A Settler's Home in the Famous Kern Delta. Bakersfield, Calif.: Kern County Land Co., n.d.

Crane, Caroline Bartlett. *Everyman's House.* Garden City, N.Y.: Doubleday, Page and Co., 1925.

Crane, Ross. *The Ross Crane Book of Home Furnishing and Decoration.* Chicago: Frederick J. Drake and Co., 1925.

Daniels, Fred Hamilton. *The Furnishing of a Modest Home.* Worcester, Mass.: Davis Press, 1908.

Eastlake, Charles L. *Hints on Household Taste.* Boston: James R. Osgood and Co., 1878. Reprint, New York: Dover Publications, 1986.

Eberlein, Harold Donaldson, Abbott McClure, and Edward Stratton Holloway. *The Practical Book of Interior Decoration.* Philadelphia: J. B. Lippincott Co., 1919.

————, and Donald G. Tarpley. *Remodeling and Adapting the Small House.* Philadelphia: J. B. Lippincott, 1933.

Ellis, Mary Heard, and Raymond Everett. *The Planning of Simple Homes.* Austin, Texas: University of Texas, 1916.

Ellis, Raymond A. *When You Build.* New York: Woman's Home Companion, 1920.

Ferro, Maximilian L., and Melissa L. Cook. *Electric Wiring and Lighting in Historic American Buildings.* New Bedford, Mass.: Preservation Partnership and AFC/A Nortek Co., 1984.

Frangiamore, Catherine Lynn. *Wallpapers in Historic Preservation.* Washington, D.C.: National Park Service, Technical Preservation Services, 1977.

Frohne, Henry W., Alice F. Jackson, and Bettina Jackson. *Color Schemes for the Homes and Model Interiors.* Grand Rapids, Mich.: Dean-Hicks Co., 1919.

Gardner, E. C. *Home Interiors.* Boston: James R. Osgood and Co., 1878.

Gardner, F. B. *Everybody's Paint Book.* New York: M. T. Richardson, 1888.

Garner, John S. *The Model Company Town.* Amherst, Mass.: University of Massachusetts Press, 1984.

Gibson, Louis H. *Convenient Houses with Fifty Plans for the Housekeeper.* New York: Thomas Y. Crowell and Co., 1889.

Godinez, F. Laurent. *The Lighting Book.* New York: McBride, Nast and Co., 1913.

Goodnow, Ruby Ross. *The Honest House.* New York: Century Co., 1914.

Gray, Greta. *House and Home: A Manual and Text-Book of Practical House Planning.* Philadelphia: J. B. Lippincott Co., 1923.

Grier, Katherine C. *Culture and Comfort: Parlor Making and Middle-class Identity, 1850-1930.* Washington: Smithsonian Institution Press, 1997.

Grow, Lawrence, ed. *Old House Plans.* New York: Universe Books, 1978.

Handlin, David P. *The American Home: Architecture and Society, 1815-1915.* Boston: Little, Brown and Company, 1979.

Hellyer, S. Stevens. *The Plumber and Sanitary Houses.* 3rd ed. London: B. T. Batsford, 1884.

Hess, Alan. *Ranch House,* New York: Harry N. Abrams, 2004.

Hirshorn, Paul, and Steven Izenour. *White Towers.* Cambridge, Mass.: MIT Press, 1979.

The Home. Supplement Given with Year's Subscription to *Woman's Weekly.* (n.p.): Magazine Circulation Co., 1922.

Home Building and Furnishing. New York: Doubleday, Page and Co., 1903.

Homes Almanac and Year-Book for 1923. Chicago: American Homes Bureau, 1922, pp. 3–14.

The House Beautiful Furnishing Annual 1926. Boston: Atlantic Monthly Co., 1925.

Hunter, Christine. *Ranches, Row Houses and Railroad Flats: American Homes; How They Shape Our Landscapes and Neighborhoods.* New York: W.W. Norton, 1999.

Illsley, Charles E. *House Planning at Home; A Practical Manual for Self-Instruction for Members of Building Associations and Others.* St. Louis: C. B. Woodward Co., 1894.

Jackson, Kenneth T. *Crabgrass Frontier: The Suburbanization of the United States.* Oxford: Oxford University Press, 1985.

Jennings, Arthur Seymour. *The Decoration and Renovation of the Home.* London: W. R. Howell and Co., 1923.

————. *Wallpapers and Wall Coverings.* New York: William T. Comstock, 1903.

Kellogg, Alice M. *Home Furnishing, Practical and Artistic.* New York: Frederick A. Stokes Co., 1905.

The Key to Your New Home: A Primer of Livable and Practical Houses. Ed. Lewis Stoors. New York: McGraw-Hill Book Co. 1938.

Luckiesh, M. *Lighting Fixtures and Lighting Effects.* New York: McGraw-Hill Book Co., 1925.

————. *Lighting the Home.* New York: Century Co., 1920.

McClelland, Nancy. *The Practical Book of Decorative Wall-Treatments.* Philadelphia: J. B. Lippincott Co., 1926.

Marling, Karal Ann. *George Washington Slept Here: Colonial Revivals and American Culture, 1876-1986.* Cambridge: Harvard University Press, 1988.

Martin, Ray C. *Glossary of Paint, Varnish, Lacquer and Allied Terms.* St. Louis: American Paint Journal Co., 1937.

Mayhew, Edgar de N., and Minor Myers, Jr. *A Documentary History of American Interiors—From the Colonial Era to 1915.* New York: Charles Scribner's Sons, 1980.

Meloy, Arthur S. *Theatres and Motion Picture Houses.* New York: Architects' Supply and Pub. Co., 1916.

Myers, Denys Peter. *Gaslighting in America: A Guide for Historic Preservation.* Washington, D.C.: U.S. Department of the Interior, 1978.

Nylander, Richard C. *Wall Papers for Historic Buildings.* Washington, D.C.: Preservation Press, National Trust for Historic Preservation, 1983.

Parsons, Frank Alvah. *The Art of Home Furnishing and Decoration.* Lancaster, Penn.: Armstrong Cork Co. Linoleum Dept., 1918.

————. *Interior Decoration.* New York: Doubleday, 1915.

Peterson, Charles E., ed. *Building Early America: Contributions toward the History of a Great Industry.* The Carpenters' Company of the City and County of Philadelphia. Radnor, Penn.: Chilton Book Co., 1976.

Popular American Housing; A Reference Guide. Ed. Ruth Brent and Benyamin Schwartz. Westport, CT: Greenwood Press. 1995.

Rapoport, Amos. *House Form and Culture.* Englewood Cliffs, N.J.: Prentice-Hall, 1969.

Representative Plans for Farm Houses. Extract from a report submitted to the President's Conference on Home Building and Home Ownership by the Committee on Farm and Village Housing. n.p.: U.S. Dept. of Agriculture, Dec. 1931.

Robinson, L. Eugene. *Domestic Architecture.* New York: Macmillan Co., 1917.

Rolfe, Amy L. *Interior Decoration for the Small Home.* New York: Macmillan Co., 1917.

————. *Interior Decoration for the Small Home.* New York: Macmillan Co., 1924.

Sabin, Alvah Horton. *House Painting.* New York: John Wiley and Sons, 1918.

————. *The Industrial and Artistic Technology of Paint and Varnish.* New York: John Wiley and Sons, 1905.

Romanoff, Victoria, and Sarah W. Adams. *New York State Storefronts.* Trumansburg, N.Y.: Tompkins Co., n.d.

Seal, Ethel Davis. *The House of Simplicity.* New York: Century Co., 1926.

Sell, Maud Ann, and Henry Blackman Sell. *Good Taste in Home Furnishing.* New York: John Lane Co., 1915.

Simpson, Pamela H. *Cheap, Quick and Easy: Imitative Architectural Materials 1870-1930*. Knoxville, TN: University of Tennessee Press, 1999.

Stansky, Peter, and Shewan, Rodney, eds. *The Aesthetic Movement and the Arts and Crafts Movement*. New York: Garland Publishing Co., 1978.

Sugden, Alan Victor, and Edmondson, John Ludlam. *A History of English Wallpaper, 1509–1915*. New York: Charles Scribner's Sons, 1925.

Sutherland, Daniel E. *The Expansion of Everyday Life, 1860-1876*. New York: Harper and Row Publishers, 1989.

Sutherland, W. G. *Modern Wall Decoration*. Manchester, England: Decorative Art Journals Co., 1893.

Throop, Lucy Abbot. *Furnishing the Home of Good Taste*. New York: McBride, Nast and Co., 1912.

Tralle, Henry Edward. *Planning Church Buildings*. Philadelphia: Judson Press, 1921.

Varney, Almon C. *Our Homes and Their Adornments: Or How to Build, Finish, Furnish, and Adorn a Home*. Detroit: J. C. Chilton and Co., 1882.

Vieyra, Daniel I. *"Fill 'er Up.": An Architectural History of America's Gas Stations*. New York: Collier Macmillan Publishers, 1979.

Vollmer, William A., ed. *A Book of Distinctive Interiors*. New York: McBride, Nast and Co., 1912.

Waite, Diana S., ed. *Architectural Elements, The Technological Review*. The American Historical Catalog Collection. Princeton, N.J.: Pyne Press, 1972.

Wangner, Ellen D. *The American Home Book of Kitchens*. Garden City, N.Y.: Doubleday, Doran and Co., 1931.

Warner, Sam B., Jr. *Streetcar Suburbs: The Process of Growth in Boston*. Cambridge, Mass.: Harvard University Press and M.I.T. Press, 1962.

Wheeler, Candace. *Principles of Home Decoration*. New York: Doubleday, Page and Co., 1903.

White, Charles E. *The Bungalow Book*. New York: Macmillan Co., 1923.

White, Charles E., Jr. *Successful Houses and How to Build Them*. New York: Macmillan Co., 1914.

Wiebe, E. Bijker. *Of Bicycles, Bakelites, and Bulbs: Toward a Theory of Sociotechnical Change*. Cambridge: MIT Press, 1995.

Wilson, Richard Guy. *The Colonial Revival House*. New York: Harry Abrams, 2004.

Winter, Robert. *The California Bungalow*. Los Angeles: Hennessey and Ingalls, Inc., 1980.

Wrenn, Tony and Elizabeth D. Muloy, *America's Forgotten Architecture*, National Trust for Historic Preservation, New York: Pantheon Books, 1976.

Wright, Richardson, ed. *House and Garden's Book of Color Schemes*. New York: Condé Nast Publications, (ca. 1929).

———. *House and Garden's Book of Houses*. New York: C. Nast and Co., 1920.

———. *House and Garden's Book of Interiors*. New York: C. Nast and Co., 1920.

———. *House and Garden's Complete Guide to Interior Decoration*. New York: Simon and Schuster, 1942.

———. *House and Garden's Second Book of Houses*. New York: Condé Nast Publications, 1925.

———. *Inside the House of Good Taste*. New York: Robert M. McBride and Co., 1922.

Your Wallpaper Tells Who You Are. New York: Wallpaper Guild of America, (ca. 1923).

Articles

Alderson, Caroline. "Re-Creating a 19th Century Paint Palette." *APT Bulletin* 16:1 (1984): 47–56.

Alto, J. E. "A Plea for Painted Walls." *American Homes*, Sept. 1900, 562–63.

Armagnac, A. S. "Heating Steps Forward." *Building Age* 51 (April 1929): 136–37.

Arthur, William. "Suggestions for Building a Modern Dwelling." *Building Age* (monthly series) (March 1910-December 1910).

"Artistic Fronts for Small Business Buildings." *Building Age* 39 (Dec. 1917): 675–77.

Baker, Henry G. "Hardware for Good Buildings." *Building Age* 51 (April 1929): 154–55.

Bigsby, J. M. "American Kitchens Glorified Too." *Building Age* 51 (April 1929): 142–43.

———. "Built-In Features and Furniture That Make Modernizing Desired." *Building Age* 51 (Jan. 1929): 68–69.

Bishir, Catherine. "Black Builders in Ante-bellum North Carolina," *North Carolina Historical Review* 61 (1984): 423–61.

Bishop, C. H. "Plumbing—Sanitation Plus." *Building Age* 51 (April 1929): 138–39.

Blackman, Leo, and Deborah Dietsch. "A New Look at Linoleum." *Old House Journal*, Jan. 1982, 9–12.

Blythe, Robert W. "Unraveling the Threads of Community Life: Work, Play, and Place in the Alabama Mill Villages of the West Point Manufacturing Company." In *Constructing Image, Identity, and Place: Perspectives in Vernacular Architecture IX*, edited by Alison K. Hoagland and Kenneth A. Breisch. Knoxville: University of Tennessee Press, 2003.

Bond, Alexander. "Floors Keep Step with Progress." *Building Age* 51 (April 1929): 116–17.

Bradbury, Bruce. "Anaglypta and Other Embossed Wallcoverings—Their History and Use Today." *Old House Journal*, Nov. 1982, 231–34.

———. "A Layman's Guide to Historic Wallpaper Reproduction." *APT Bulletin* 16:1 (1984): 57–58.

———. "Lincrusta–Walton—Can the Democratic Wallcoverings Be Revived?" *Old House Journal*, Oct. 1982, 203–7.

Brownfield, Marion. "The Cozy Kitchen Nook." *Keith's Magazine*, March 1924, 114–15.

———. "The Latest Ideas for the Kitchen." *Keith's Magazine*, Nov. 1924, 221–23.

"Builders' Reference and Checking List: Large Buildings." *American Builder*, June 1925: 195–203.

"Builders' Reference and Checking List: A Specification Guide for All Classes of Buildings." *American Builder*, June 1925, 189–94.

"Building Bungalows." *Carpentry and Building* 26 (July 1904): 222.

Butterfield, Emily H. "A Family Kitchen." *Keith's Magazine*, Nov. 1923, pp. 208–9.

Byers, Charles Alma. "Concerning Modern Bedrooms." *Keith's Magazine*, Jan. 1923, 11–15.

———. "Fireplaces That Add Beauty to the Home." *Building Age* 41 (June 1919): 186–87.

———. "Planning the Fireside Corner." *Keith's Magazine*, Dec. 1915, 375–78.

———. "Practical Sleeping Porches." *Keith's Magazine*, July 1923, 10–13.

Campbell, C. J. "Electrify All Buildings: Wiring the Home for Comfort." *American Builder* (April 1924), pp. 171, 172, 174, 176.

Candee, Richard M. and Greer Hardwicke. "Early Twentieth-Century Reform Housing by Kilham and Hopkins, Architects of Boston". *Winterthur Portfolio* 22, No. 1 (Spring 1987): 47-80.

Clausen, Arthur C. "Construction Details of the Home—Built-In Sideboards." *Keith's Magazine*, Dec. 1911, 382–85.

"Construction Details of the Home—The Bathroom." *Keith's Magazine*, Feb. 1912, 93–95.

"Construction Details of the Home—Built-In Pantries." *Keith's Magazine*, Jan. 1912, 20–23.

"Construction Details of the Home—Entrances, Front and Interior Doors, Advantages of Sidelights." *Keith's Magazine,* Sept. 1911, 160–63.

"Construction Details of the Home—Windows, Their Location and Design." *Keith's Magazine*, Nov. 1911, 230–33.

Coppes, D. W. "Lighting Your Home." *Beautiful Homes Magazine*, Sept. 1930, 6–9.

"Creating Better Store Architecture." *Building Age and the Builder's Journal*, Oct. 1922, 30.

Cromley, Elizabeth Collins. "A History of American Beds and Bedrooms." In *Perspectives in Vernacular IV*, edited by Thomas Carter and Bernard L. Herman. Columbia, Missouri: University of Missouri Press, 1991.

Crowley, John E. "'Happier Mansions, Warm and Dry': The Invention of the Cottage as the Comfortable Anglo-American House." *Winterthur Portfolio* 32: 2/3 (Summer-Autumn, 1997): 169–188.

Crowley, John E. "Houses, Gender and the Picturesque Landscape: The Designs of Catherine Beecher and Andrew Jackson Downing." In *Gender and Material Culture in Historical Perspective.*, edited by Moira Donald and Linda Hurcombe. New York: St. Martin's Press, 2000.

"Designs for Wood Ceilings." *Carpentry and Building* 1 (Feb. 1879): 21–22.

"Designs of Sash and Solid Partitions." *Building Age* 34 (June 1912): 307–8.

"Dining Room Mantel and Mirror." *Carpentry and Building* 2 (Nov. 1880): 201–3.

"Door Hardware Should be Selected for Its Permanence as Well as for Its Beauty." *Keith's Beautiful Homes Magazine*, May 1929, 204–06.

Dunlea, Nancy D. "The New Home Hardware." *Keith's Magazine*, May 1925, 230–31.

Ednie, John. "The Decoration of a City House." *House Beautiful*, Dec. 1903, 34–42.

"Electrify All Buildings: The Electrical Home Efficient." *American Builder*, May 1924, 184, 186, 190, 192.

"Fireplace Treatments." *Keith's Magazine*, Jan.–Dec. 1908, n.p.

"Foster-Munger Hard Wood Mantels." *Carpentry and Building* 22 (Jan. 1900): xii.

Fox, C. J. "Ornamental Tile Work." *Carpentry and Building* 29 (Oct. 1907): 331–32.

Friedman, Avi. "The Evolution of Design Characteristics During the Post-Second World War Housing Boom: The US Experience." *Journal of Design History*, 8, No. 2 (1995): 131–146.

"Fully Rented Before Completion." *American Builder*, Nov. 1933. 44.

"Furnishing and Decorating the Home." *Modern Homes*, June–July 1914, 9.

Garvin, James L. "Mail-Order House Plans and American Victorian Architecture." *Winterthur Portfolio* 16 (1981):309–34.

Gebhard, David. "The American Colonial Revival in the 1930s." *Winterthur Portfolio*, 22: 2/3 (Summer-Autumn, 1987): 109–148.

———. "Royal Barry Wills and the American Colonial Revival." *Winterthur Portfolio*: 27:1 (1992): 45–74.

Gerth, Ruth L. "The Dining Room." *Keith's Magazine*, Oct. 1923, 155–59.

Hale, O. H. "Outlets Outlaw Housework." *Building Age* 51 (April 1929): 140–41.

Hardwick, M. Jeff. "Homesteads and Bungalows: African-American Architecture in Langston, Oklahoma." In *Shaping Communities: Perspectives in Vernacular Architecture, VI*, edited by Carter L. Hudgins and Elizabeth Collins Cromley, Knoxville, TN: University of Tennessee Press 1997.

Hart, Arthur A. "M. A. Disbrow & Company: Catalogue Architecture." *The Palimpsest* 20, No. 4 (July–Aug. 1975): 98–119.

Harvey, L. H. "Effective Design with Wallboard." *Building Age* 41 (Aug. 1919): 266–67.

———. "How Wallboard Was Used in Remodeling an Old Home." *Building Age* 40 (Dec. 1918): 552–54.

Harvey, Thomas. "Mail-Order Architecture in the Twenties." *Landscape* 25:3 (1981):1–9.

Harwood, Buie. "Stencilling: Interior Architectural Ornamentation." *Journal of Interior Design Education and Research* 12 (Spring 1986): 31–40.

Heath, Kingston WM. "False-Front Architecture on Montana's Urban Frontier." In *Perspectives in Vernacular Architecture III*, edited by Thomas Carter and Bernard L. Herman. Columbia, Missouri: University of Missouri Press, 1989.

Higbie, H. H. "Good Lighting Adds to Comfort and Charm in the Home." *Beautiful Homes Magazine*, Dec. 1929, 167–69, 187.

Hill, Amelia Leavitt. "The Sunroom." *Keith's Magazine*, May 1924, 248–251.

Hill, W. R. "Door Hardware for the Modern Home." *Building Age* 41 (Aug. 1919): 253–54.

Hillen, R. C. "Designing a Store in a Residential District to Have Same Characteristics and General Appearance of a Home." *The Home Designer*, Sept. 1921, 69.

"Hints on Home Adornment, Number Four." *Godey's Lady's Book and Magazine* 96:574 (1878): 350–51.

Howett, Catherine M. "Reflections on the Picture Window." *Journal of American Culture* 6, no. 3 (Fall 1983): 26–37.

Hubka, Thomas C. "In the Vernacular: Classifying American Folk and Popular Architecture." *The Forum*, 7, No. 2 (Dec. 1985), n.p. Insert in *Newsletter, The Society of Architectural Historians*, 30:1 (Feb. 1986).

"The Impression of the Hall." *Keith's Magazine*, Oct. 1911, 220–25.

"Interior Decoration: Suggestions for the Hall, Dining Room, Bedrooms, Etc." *Shoppell's Homes, Decorations, Gardens*, Jan. 1907, 14–18.

"Japanese Lattice-Work." *Carpentry and Building* 8 (July 1886): 123–25.

Johnson, Louise H. "Our Bedroom." *Keith's Magazine*, April 1919, 245–48.

Kauffman, Elizabeth Macy. "Wooden Walls Again." *Your Home*, Nov. 1929, 45–47, 70.

Kingsley, K. S. "What Makes a House Colonial?" *Building Age* 51 (Aug. 1929): 66–67.

"The Kinnear Improved Steel Ceiling." *Carpentry and Building* 21 (Jan. 1899): xiv.

Kraft, Gertrude. "Looking at the Ceiling." *Beautiful Homes Magazine*, Jan. 1931, 23–26.

Kupsinel, Morgan M. "Interior Architectural Millwork Components in the Plains States (1900–1930)." Thesis, University of Nebraska, 1980.

Lancaster, Clay. "The American Bungalow." *The Art Bulletin* 40 (Sept. 1958): 239–53.

Lawall, G. R. "Bringing Light to the Kitchen." *Keith's Magazine*, March 1923, 134,136.

———. "Lighting the Dining Room." *Keith's Magazine*, June 1923, 284, 286.

———. "Luminaires for the Living Room," *Keith's Magazine*, Oct. 1923, 182–84.

Liccese-Torres and Kim A. O'Connell, "Lustron House Preservation Efforts in Arlington County, Virginia." *CRM: The Journal of Heritage Stewardship* 4:2 (Summer 2007): 69–73.

"Lincrusta-Walton." *Carpentry and Building* 5 (Feb. 1883): 30.

Little, M. Ruth, "The Other Side of the Tracks: Middle-Class Neighborhoods That Jim Crow Built in Early-Twentieth-Century North Carolina." In *Exploring Everyday Landscapes; Perspectives in Vernacular Architecture VII*, edited by Annmarie Adams and Sally McMurry. Knoxville: University of Tennessee Press, 1997.

Longstreth, Richard. "Compositional Types in American Commercial Architecture." In *Perspectives in Vernacular Architecture II*, edited by Camille Wells. Columbia, Missouri: University of Missouri Press. 1986.

Luckey, Gertrude Appleton. "Breakfast Alcoves." *Keith's Magazine*, April 1917, 242–45.

"The Lustron Home: A New Standard for Living." *The Preservationist* 11, No. 2 (Fall/Winter 2007): 12–16.

Manca, Joseph. "On the Origins of the American Porch." *Winterthur Portfolio* 40: 2–3 (Summer-Autumn, 2005): 91–132.

"Mantels, Tiles and Grates." *The National Builder*, Oct. 1887, 50–51.

Marlatt, Abby L. "Consider the Housewife First!" *American Builder and Building Age*, March 1933, pp. 16–17, 50, 52.

Marshall, Howard Wight. "Vernacular Housing and American Culture." In *Popular American Housing; A Reference Guide*, edited by Ruth Brent and Benyamin Schwartz. Westport, CT: Greenwood Press. 1995.

Martin, John Howard. "The Overmantel and Fireplace." *Keith's Magazine*, Feb. 1920, 68–70.

Maynard, W. Barkesdale. "'Best, Lowliest Style,' The Early Nineteenth Century Rediscovery of American Colonial Architecture," *Journal of the Society of Architectural Historians* 59, No. 3 (September 2000): 338–357.

"Modern Builders Hardware." *American Carpenter and Builder*, April 1911, 41.

"Modernized Store Buildings Get the Trade." *American Builder*, June 1925, 233–35.

"The Modern Kitchen—Most Important Room in the House." *American Builder and Building Age*, March 1933, 15.

"The Modern Living Room." *Modern Homes*, Feb. 1915, 5, 21.

"Mosaics." *American Homes*, Oct. 1900, 621–25.

"Mosaic Vestibule Tiling." *Carpentry and Building* 8 (Nov. 1886): 210.

Mulrooney, Margaret. "A Legacy of Coal: The Coal Company Towns of Southwestern Pennsylvania." In *Perspectives in Vernacular Architecture IV*, edited byThomas Carter and Bernard L. Herman. Columbia, Missouri: University of Missouri Press, 1991.

National Park Service. *"The Preservation of Historic Pigmented Structural Glass."* (Vitrolite and Carrara Glass). Preservation Brief 12. Washington, D.C.: Dept. of Interior, Feb. 1984.

Neumann, Dietrich. " 'The Century's Triumph in Lighting': The Luxfer Prism Companies and Their Contribution to Early Modern Architecture." JSAH 54:1 (March 1995): 24–53.

Newberry, Mary. "A Model Bath-Room." *House Beautiful*, July 1904, 21–22.

"New Factory-Finished Flooring at Low Price." *American Builder*, Dec. 1932, 37.

"1930 Trend of Style." *American Builder*, Feb. 1930, 85–92.

"1936 Building Outlook BEST in Years." *American Builder and Building Age* 58, No. 1 (Jan. 1936): 28–31, 74.

Northend, Mary H. "The Dining Room As It Should Be." *Keith's Magazine*, Feb. 1911, 76–82.

Ore, Janet. "Jud Yoho, 'The Bungalow Craftsman,' and the Development of Seattle Suburbs." In *Shaping Communities: Perspectives in Vernacular Architecture*, VI, edited by Carter L. Hudgins and Elizabeth Collins Cromley, Knoxville, TN: University of Tennessee Press, 1997.

Oren, E. M. "The Wide Range of Textured Wall Finishes." *American Builder*, June 1927, 114–15.

Otter, Paul D. "Built-In Furniture That Adds Convenience to the Home." *The Building Age* 40 (April 1918): 184.

———. "Embossing on Wood." *Carpentry and Building* 21 (June 1899): 151."Painting Floors." *Carpentry and Building* 8 (July 1886): 128.

Parsons, D. J. C. "Tiling the House." *Keith's Beautiful Homes Magazine*, Sept.1929, 80–82, 95.

Parsons, Frederick. "Modern House Decoration—Part I: Decorative Wall Coverings." *The Western Painter*, (April 1896), pp. 165–79.

Peterson, Fred W. "Anglo-American Wooden Frame Farmhouses in the Midwest, 1830-1900: Origins of Balloon Frame Construction." In *People, Power, Places: Perspectives in Vernacular Architecture VIII*, edited by Sally McMurry and Annmarie Adams. Knoxville: University of Tennessee Press, 2000.

Pickett, A. D. "Tile Floors and Tile Walls." *Building Age* 51 (April 1929): 112–13.

"Planning the Modern Kitchen." *American Builder and Building Age*, March 1933, 18–20.

———. "Improved Illumination for the Dining Room." *American Builder*, Aug. 1922, 98–100.

———. "Trend of Electric Fixture Design in Modern Home." *American Builder*, June 1922, 102–4, 150.

———. "Trend of Electric Fixture Design in Modern Home." *American Builder*, July 1922, 104–7.

Pillsbury, Richard. "Patterns in the Folk and Vernacular House Forms of the Pennsylvania Culture Region." *Pioneer America* 9:1 (July 1977):12–31.

"Queen Anne Sideboard and Mantel." *Carpentry and Building* 1 (Jan. 1879): 19.

Randall, Kate. "The Modern Kitchen." *Keith's Magazine*, Oct. 1912, 250–52.

Rapoport, Amos. "An Approach to Vernacular Design." In *Shelter: Models of Native Ingenuity*, edited by James Marston Fitch. Katonah, N.Y.: The Katonah Gallery, 1982.

Reedy, William B. "The Rooms in the House: The Bedroom." *American Builder*, April 1922, 86–87.

"Restyling Main Street for the New Deal in Beverages." *American Builder and Building Age*, April 1933, 32–33.

Roth, Leland M. "Getting the Houses to the People: Edward Bok, The Ladies Home Journal, and the Ideal House." In *Perspectives in Vernacular Architecture IV*, edited by Thomas Carter and Bernard L. Herman. Columbia, Missouri: University of Missouri Press, 1991.

Sakier, George. "Permanent Floor Coverings—A Review." *House and Garden* (Feb. 1935), pp. 37–39, 69.

Sautter House Five, Wallpapers of a German-American Farmstead. Omaha, Neb.: Papillion Area Historical Society and Douglas County Historical Society, 1983.

Scofield, Merle. "Achieving an Harmonious Interior." *The Home Designer*, Nov. 1921, 147, 157.

Sexton, R. W. "A Successfully Planned Business Center." *American Builder*, Jan. 1935, 36–37.

"Sheet-Metal Ceiling." *Carpentry and Building* 8 (Oct. 1886): 188–89.

"Sheet Metal in Interior Decoration." *Carpentry and Building* 22 (March 1900): 69, 70; (April 1900): 117–19; (July 1900): 201–2.

"The Sleeping Porch is Now Considered Indispensable." *Modern Homes*, Dec. 1914, 7.

Smith, Margaret S. and John C. Moorhouse, "Architecture and the Housing Market: Nineteenth Century Row Housing in Boston's South End," *Journal of the Society of Architectural Historians* LII (June 1993): 159-178.

"Some California Bungalows." *The Architectural Record* 18 (Sept. 1905): 217–23.

"Some Characteristics of the California Bungalow." *Carpentry and Building* 29 (Feb. 1907): 53.

Sovereign, O. E. "The Readi-Cut Structure Demands Attention of the Home Owner." *Modern Homes*, March 1915, 14–15.

Sterling, Florence J. "What Comprises a '100% Modern Kitchen'?" *American Builder and Building Age*, Jan. 1931, 94–95.

Stewart, Ross E. "Millwork and Interior Finish, The Elements that Produce Satisfactory Work." *The American Architect* 127 (June 1925): 519–20.

Stillwell, E. W. "What Is a Genuine Bungalow?" *Keith's Magazine*, April 1916, 273–91.

Stowell, Kenneth K. "Today's Home, Looking Backward—and Ahead." *Building Age* 51 (April 1929): 89–91.

"Style Review—New and Tested Products." *American Builder and Building Age*, April 1933, 14–19, 56, 58.

"Suggested Treatment of Wall Spaces in Suburban Homes." *Building Age* 34 (Aug. 1912): 413.

Swiatosz, Susan. "A Technical History of Late Nineteenth Century Windows in the United States." *APT Bulletin* 17:1 (1985): 31–37.

Taylor, John. "Interior Decoration." *Keith's Magazine*, Feb. 1908, 74–75.

Teasdale, O. R. "Wood for Fine Interiors." *Building Age* 51 (April 1929): 114–15.

"The Tendency in Home Architecture." *Carpentry and Building* 22 (June 1900): 165.

"Twenty-five Years." *American Builder*, April 1930, 87–88.

Townsend, Gavin. "Airborne Toxins and the American House, 1865-1895." *Winterthur Portfolio* 24: No. 1 (Spring 1989): 29-42.

"Wall Decorations—Paper Hangings." *Carpentry and Building* 1 (April 1879): 61–62.

"Wall Papers." *Carpentry and Building* 2 (Dec. 1880): 221–24.

"Walls and Ceilings." *Home Decoration*, June 12, 1886, 138.

Warren, James. "Standardized Millwork Cuts Costs." *Building Age* 51 (April 1929): 106–7.

"Why Build Stores that Look Like These; When for the Same Money You Can Have Artistic Designs Like These?" *Building Age and National Builder*, June 1926, 108.

Williams, E. A. "Bathrooms, Don't Neglect a Single Detail." *Building Age* 51 (Oct. 1929): 58–59, 96.

Wolfe, Tom and Leonard Garfield. "A New Standard for Living: The Lustron House, 1946-1950." in *Perspectives in Vernacular Architecture III*, edited by Thomas Carter and Bernard L. Herman. Columbia, Missouri: University of Missouri Press. 1989.

Worth, John. "Flexible Finishes, Today's Style." *Building Age* 51 (April 1929): 118–19.

Index

Page numbers in *italic* refer to captions or illustrations not otherwise referenced in text.

office interiors, 253–55
ornamental aesthetic, 90–91
storefront design, 233
wall ornamentation, *348*
see also single-front commercial buildings
Common Places: Readings in American Vernacular Architecture, 9–10
Concrete School Houses, 6
construction methods and techniques
  in evolution of American vernacular design, 2, 3
  masonry, *328*
  modern vernacular, 10
  wall framing, *327*
convenient arrangement, 17, 20–21, 22, 23–26, 292
Cornell Reading-Course for Farmers' Wives, 41
cottage form and sensibility, 2, 25
  bungalow cottages, 196–99
  circulation system, 27, 47
  colonial aesthetic, 102
  convenient arrangement and, 24–25
  definition and characteristics, 46–50
  dissemination, 45–46
  elevations, 47–48, 53
  evolution in U.S., 19
  front door design, *370*
  mansard roof, 168–75
  millwork, 48–49, 52–55, 58
  mixture of design elements, 54–55
  picturesque aesthetic, 49, 53–54, 63
  plan, 47
  significance of, 45, 159
  site considerations, 49–50
  social and historical context, 45, 58
  technological advancement and, 50, 51
  traits and subtraits, 29
  see also gable roof cottages; gambrel roof cottages; hip roof cottages; organic cottage
Cottage Residences, 19
country cottage, 141
craftsman style, 35, *189,* 189–90
Cret, Paul, 177
Crowley, John, 47
cultural context, 10
Curtis Companies, 38–39, *178*
Davis, Alexander Jackson, 49
Deetz, James, 9
Defebaugh, James, 52, 55
Designs for Convenient Living, 208, 209–11
doors, exterior. *see* entrance systems
doors, interior
  artistic aesthetic, *121, 134*
  astragal patterns, *367*
  colonial revival, *118, 125, 134*
  commercial buildings, *256, 259, 262, 264*
  components, *366*
  cupboard doors, *373*
  drawn plans, 3
  English and Spanish Revival, *128*
  frame construction, *366*
  French doors, *372*
  hardware, 377–80

Italianate aesthetic, *113, 134*
modern aesthetic, *130, 134*
moldings, *367*
operation, *365*
ornamental aesthetic, 89, *115, 134*
panel types, *368–69*
swinging doors, *373*
vestibule doors, *372*
double-front commercial buildings, 243–45
double houses, 223–24
Downing, Andrew Jackson, 19, 49–50, 58, 63
Draper, Andrew, 27–28
duplex houses, 223
Dutch colonial style, 181, 184, *185–86*
economic environment
  development of American modern vernacular, 11, 15, 33–34, 60
  ranch house design and development, 208
Edis, R. W., 19–20
Edson, R. C., *213*
education in building techniques, 3
English revival aesthetic
  bungalow design, 203–4
  commercial buildings, *248*
  evolution of American architecture, 157
  exterior characteristics, 66–67, *81, 82,* 157, *158*
  front door designs, *370*
  gable wall motifs, *345*
  interiors, 110–11, *128–29,* 157, *158*
entrance systems
  arts-and-crafts style, *80, 133*
  center gable cottages, 140
  classical colonial revival, *75, 133, 349*
  colonial, *349, 370*
  commercial buildings, *256, 259, 262, 264, 350, 371*
  components and types, 349–52
  English and Spanish revival, *82, 370*
  four-family villas, 230
  front door designs, *370–71*
  gable-end churches, 270–71
  gambrel cottages, 181
  Italianate aesthetic, *71, 133,* 171
  modern aesthetic, *84, 85, 133*
  modern colonial revival, *78, 133*
  picturesque aesthetic, *73, 133*
  portico bungalow, 201
  porticoes, *351*
  projecting vestibules, *351*
  recessed doors, *351*
  side entry churches, 272
Exchange Sawmills Sales Company, 41
extension service bulletins, 6, 41–44
exteriors
  aesthetic classification, 60
  airplane bungalow, *200*
  artistic front commercial buildings, 247–49
  arts-and-crafts, 64, 79–80, *133*
  broad-front commercial buildings, 245, *246*
  bungalow cottage, 196, *197, 198*
  bungalow design, *191, 192, 195*
  Cape Cod cottage, 155, *156*